For anyone generally interested in how networks and studios make money and put money at risk, from the TV shows and movies they produce to the novel challenges they're facing today, this book provides a unique overview and a glimpse into the future.

—Blair Westlake, Corporate Vice President Media
& Entertainment Group, Microsoft

Jeff Ulin brings his practical experience and academic understanding of today's complicated media world together to provide us with a comprehensive guide to navigating a world that changes almost daily!

—Marion Edwards, President, 20th Century Fox
International Television

It's very difficult to find a text that gives both a comprehensive overview of the history of the entertainment industry as well as informed insight into its future landscape. Nothing out there does it better.

—Judd Funk, Former Head of Legal Affairs, Universal Pictures;
Associate Professor, Lawrence and Kristina Dodge College
of Film and Media Arts, and School of Law,
Chapman University

Anyone who wants to know more about how films and TV shows are distributed and exploited can learn a huge amount from this book.

—Jim Morris, Pixar Animation Studios General Manager, EVP,
Production and Producer, *Wall•E*; Former President,
Industrial Light & Magic

Jeff Ulin's broad spectrum of expertise, spanning all aspects of motion picture and television distribution, from theatrical to home entertainment to new media and television licensing, render him uniquely qualified to illuminate the business side of the entertainment business.

—Hal Richardson, President of Paramount
Worldwide Television

The Business of
Media Distribution

Monetizing Film, TV, and Video
Content in an Online World

Second Edition

Jeffrey C. Ulin

Focal Press
Taylor & Francis Group

NEW YORK AND LONDON

First edition first published 2010
This edition first published 2014
by Focal Press
70 Blanchard Road, Suite 402, Burlington, MA 01803

And published in the UK
by Focal Press
2 Park Square, Milton Park, Abingdon, Oxon OX14 4RN

Focal Press is an imprint of the Taylor & Francis Group, an informa business

© 2014 Jeffrey C. Ulin

The right of Jeffrey C. Ulin to be identified as author of this work
has been asserted by him in accordance with sections 77 and 78
of the Copyright, Designs and Patents Act 1988.

Notices
Knowledge and best practice in this field are constantly changing.
As new research and experience broaden our understanding, changes
in research methods, professional practices, or medical treatment
may become necessary.

Practitioners and researchers must always rely on their own
experience and knowledge in evaluating and using any information,
methods, compounds, or experiments described herein. In using such
information or methods they should be mindful of their own safety
and the safety of others, including parties for whom they have a
professional responsibility.

Product or corporate names may be trademarks or registered
trademarks, and are used only for identification and explanation
without intent to infringe.

Library of Congress Cataloging-in-Publication Data
Ulin, Jeff.
    The business of media distribution: monetizing film, tv and video
    content in an online world/Jeff Ulin.—2nd ed.
    pages cm
    1. Motion pictures—Marketing. 2. Video recordings—Marketing.
    3. Television broadcasting—Marketing. 4. Digital media—Marketing.
    I. Title.
    PN1995.9.M29U45 2013
    384.06'8—dc23   2013017336

ISBN: 978-0-240-82423-9 (pbk)
ISBN: 978-0-240-82454-3 (ebk)

Typeset in Giovanni and Optima
by Florence Production Ltd, Stoodleigh, Devon, UK

Bound to Create

You are a creator.

Whatever your form of expression — photography, filmmaking, animation, games, audio, media communication, web design, or theatre — you simply want to create without limitation. Bound by nothing except your own creativity and determination.

Focal Press can help.

For over 75 years Focal has published books that support your creative goals. Our founder, Andor Kraszna-Krausz, established Focal in 1938 so you could have access to leading-edge expert knowledge, techniques, and tools that allow you to create without constraint. We strive to create exceptional, engaging, and practical content that helps you master your passion.

Focal Press and you.

Bound to create.

> We'd love to hear how we've helped
> you create. Share your experience:
> **www.focalpress.com/boundtocreate**

 Focal Press
Taylor & Francis Group

For Eve, Charlie, Teddy,
and the dogs

Contents

x

xiii

Foreword

Blair Westlake

Corporate Vice President Media &
Entertainment Group, Microsoft

The Business of Media Distribution is an important book for anyone who wants to understand how all the key pieces of the entertainment distribution ecosystem work.

The economics of the entertainment industry was already challenging enough historically to appreciate because it involved a web of separate but related ecosystems, including film, TV, video, merchandising, and a variety of other ancillaries.

Today, the complexity is exponentially greater. Changes are precipitated by the evolving digital and online technologies. Jeff has been able to cogently pull together issues relating to legal concerns, economics, technology, supply chain organization, and management that cut across creative goods, software, and distribution platforms.

I am reminded of the scene in the original *Jurassic Park*, when the characters are breathlessly trying to escape a charging *Tyrannosaurus rex*, chasing their SUV. The camera shows the *T. rex* in the side mirror and the conspicuous words "objects in mirror are closer than they appear." Paraphrasing, "the evolution of media today, from analog to digital, is far more complicated and daunting than it appears from a distance." Jeff's book is an essential read—to ensure you are not caught off guard. Jeff's book ensures you are not doing a "Shoulda, woulda, coulda" when it comes to making key decisions.

I have known and worked with Jeff for more than 20 years, both when he was at Lucasfilm and as a colleague when I was at Universal in the home entertainment division and headed Universal Television and Jeff was a senior executive at Universal's international home video joint venture (co-owned by Paramount Pictures).

For anyone in the day-to-day entertainment business, or the periphery, who is directly or indirectly tasked with managing video-based intellectual property, this book is a must-read. If you are a student, and are looking for a primer on the business, or a media executive who wants to better understand what that division across two buildings away does, and how it relates to you, this book is for you. The book is helpful to a wide range of groups because it pulls together theory and practice in a unique fashion, providing readers a history lesson of the market's evolution. And for anyone generally interested in how networks and studios make money—and put money at risk—from the TV shows and movies they produce, and the novel challenges they are facing today, this book will give you a unique overview—and even give you a glimpse into the future.

Going beyond the basic markets, though, Jeff then turns to how technology has disrupted traditional distribution channels, and how areas that were once secure and the lifeblood of the industry are under attack and could even disappear. As areas converge, access to content becomes more ubiquitous, and Internet-enabled devices allow users to consume content when, where, and how they want it, we all need to be smarter. Five years ago, the most daunting impediment was technology—how the content was stored, managed, and delivered. The challenge for nearly everyone involved in media is the business model—and how to migrate from fixating on the "way we used to make money" to the unchartered waters of changes in windowing, rental-supplanting sell-through, subscription services, cord-shaving, "cord-nevers," over-the-top streaming—and the list goes on.

When I testified at a U.S. Senate Commerce Committee hearing on the "future of video" in the spring of 2012, I commented that there would be more changes in the television landscape in the next 18 months than the past five years. I believe that now as much as I did then. We are witnessing warp-speed changes in consumer content consumption habits, spending patterns, and demand for access to content by any means or device. The common refrain "the consumer is in charge" is spot on. Just as all of us became online travel agents and American Airlines' Sabre booking system had a near-monopoly on travel reservations, programming networks' chokehold on what and when you watch is quickly fading away. In 2011, theater attendance for feature films was the lowest in 16 years. All of this leads to change. Whether it is a DVR, VOD, cable programming, content you purchase, rent, or can access at no cost, coupled with millions of choices versus a few dozen during prime time just 10 years ago, working in media and managing revenues is not for the faint-hearted—or inexperienced. Jeff's book provides excellent insights and real-world observations on how change is a threat if you do not act, but also opens the door to vast opportunities if you make smart, informed, and expeditious decisions.

Acknowledgments

First, and most importantly, I would like to thank my family, including my wife Eve and sons Charlie and Teddy. I spent many long hours writing, and deeply appreciate their tolerance, patience, and support.

As noted at the outset of the book, the business side of the entertainment business is often apprentice-based in terms of learning. Beyond family and friends, there are a lot of people I would like to thank for their help, for being willing to bounce ideas off, contribute quotes, or review sections, as well as educating me (and serving as mentors, past and present) and simply offering encouragement: David Anderman, Ed Anderson, Tonik Barber, David Barron, Eric Besner, Peter Bradley, Alex Carlos, Chris Carvalho, Ed Catmull, Alex Collmer, Jason Donnell, Mike Dunn, Marion Edwards, Louis Feola, Jeff Fino, Bill Gannon, Alexander Goethal, Lynne Hale, Jim Hedges, Katarzyna Lasota Heller, Michael Hoff, Carrie Hurwitz, Ben Johnson, Barry Jossen, Jayant Kadambi, Jack Kennedy, Graham Kill, Cathy Kirkman, Michael Knobloch, Germon Knoop, Michael Kohn, David Krall, Josh Kramer, Kevin Kurtz, Julian Levin, Peter Levinsohn, Michael Lopez, George Lucas, Rich Lyons, Larry Marcus, Gary Marenzi, Jamie McCabe, Sean McGinn, Mary McLaren, Jim Morris, Jim Mullany, Ned Nalle, Daniel Paul, CJ Prober, Tom Quinn, Gordon Radley, Jesse Redniss, Hal Richardson, Curtis Roberts, Howard Roffman, Stuart Rosove, Ted Russell, Craig Sherman, Pablo Spiller, Eric Stein, Steve Swassey, Sophie Turner Laing, Michael Uslan, Pedro de Vasconsoles, Kul Wadhwa, Jim Ward, Tom Warner, Tom van Wavern, Blair Westlake, Catherine Winder, and Kevin Yen.

Also, special thanks in this second edition to Mark Zabezhinsky, who helped as a research assistant (and probably took on more than he bargained for), Blair Westlake for so kindly providing a foreword, and Wade Holden and his colleagues at SNL Kagan for providing industry data.

And, of course, everyone at Focal (including those formerly at Elsevier and now with Taylor & Francis), including especially Elinor Actipis, Emma Elder, Paul Gottehrer, Peter Linsley, Lauren Mattos, Dennis

xxi

McGonagle, and Chris Simpson, as well as Charlotte Hiorns and Kelly Derrick at Florence Production.

Finally, opinions in this book are Jeffrey Ulin's personal opinions and expressions, and do not represent the positions or opinions of any of his past, present or future employers.

CHAPTER 1

Market Opportunity and Segmentation
The Diverse Role of Studios and Networks

More content from this chapter is available at
www.focalpress.com/9780240824239

1

Introduction

This book provides an overview of how the business side of the television and motion picture industry works. By the end of the text, readers will gain a practical understanding of how a film, television, or video project moves from concept to making money. Stars make the headlines, but marketing and distribution convert content into cash. To explain how the system works, this book charts the path that entertainment content takes from development to financing to distribution, and attempts to demystify the submarkets through which a production is exhibited, sold, watched, rented, or otherwise consumed. In summary, this book explains the process by which a single idea turns into a unique piece of entertainment software capable of generating over a billion dollars and sustaining cash flow over decades. I will also attempt to put into context the growing array of Internet and other new media opportunities that are altering how we watch content and blurring the lines of how we define categories of media. Since the publication of my first edition, the introduction and mass adoption of tablets, along with the emergence of apps, has accelerated the trend toward on-the-go and on-demand access to the point where digital distribution systems have moved from being labeled as disruptive to representing the future of the market. What I will explore in this book, and what all media companies continue to struggle with, is why it is so challenging to make as much (if not more) money through these new avenues as traditional outlets.

With the potential of generating great wealth by creating and distributing content also comes great risk, and motion picture studios today can be seen as venture capitalists managing a specialized portfolio. In contrast to traditional venture capitalist investments, though, film investors risk capital on a product whose initial value is rooted in subjective judgment. Valuing creativity is tough enough, but investing in a film or TV show often asks people to judge a work before they can see it—a step back from the famous pornography standard "I know it when I see it." Bets are accordingly hedged by vesting vast financial responsibility over productions in people who have developed successful creative track records. Focusing too much attention, though, on creative judgment as opposed to marketing and financial acumen risks failure, and managers who can balance competing creative and business agendas often become the corporate stars. Analysts seeking trends may promote "content is king," but in the trenches success tends to be linked with marrying creative and sales skills.

As a result of this mix, there is no defined career path to breaking into the business or rising to success within it. Unlike attending law school and rising to partner, or business school and aspiring to investment banking, leaders in the film and TV world are an eclectic group hailing from legal, finance, producing, directing, marketing, and talent management backgrounds. Without a clear educational starting point or defined career path, how do these leaders and entrepreneurs learn the "business"?

Beyond what I hope will be a "we wish we'd had this book" reply, the simplest answer is that many executives learn by some form of apprenticeship. As an alternative to starting in the mailroom, which will always remain both a legendary and real option for breaking into the entertainment business, this book will equip readers with a basic understanding of the economics and business issues that affect virtually every TV show and film. Behind every program or movie is a multi-year tale involving passion, risk, millions of dollars, and hundreds of people. In fact, every project is akin to an entrepreneurial venture where a business plan (concept) is sold, financing is raised, a product is made and tested (production), and a final product is released.

While this sounds simple enough, the potential of overnight wealth, a culture of stars, and the power of studios and networks serve to throw up barriers to entry that segment the industry and make the entertainment production and distribution chain unique. The emergence of online and digital distribution is changing the equation, enabling cheaper, faster production and seemingly ubiquitous and simultaneous access to content; whether sustainable business models evolve to generate the bulk of revenues from these new platforms or these outlets simply serve as supplementary access points for content remains the question of the day.

What is certain, however, is that to understand these new avenues one has to understand the historical landscape. Traditional media (film/TV/video) still accounts for over 90 percent of all media revenues, and the success of online/digital ventures will be tied to how opportunities relate to existing revenue streams. The exploitation of media is a symbiotic process, where success is achieved by choreographing distribution across time and distribution outlets to maximize an ultimate bottom line. Media conglomerates have developed a fine-tuned system mixing free and paid-for access (TV versus theaters), varying price points (DVD sales and rentals, pay TV, video-on-demand), and windows driving repeat consumption—a system that will generate far more money (and therefore sustain higher budgets) than an ad hoc watch-for-free-everywhere-now structure. It is because the Internet offers the chance to dramatically broaden exposure, lower costs, and target finely sliced demographics that the two systems are both attractive and struggling to merge in a way that ensures expansion rather than contraction of the pie.

Market Opportunity and Segmenting the Market

A reference to the "film and TV market" is a bit of a misnomer, because these catch-all categories are actually an aggregation of many specialty markets, each with its nuances and particular market challenges. The rest of the chapters of this book detail exploitation patterns common across product categories, such as how a property is distributed into standard and emerging channels, while this chapter first outlines the range of primary markets and niche businesses. I will also try to highlight differing risk factors and financials that are explored in greater detail later in the book, but here I want to focus on the diversity of the market and how it can be segmented. In fact, the simple process of segmentation illustrates the diversity of the business and how studios can be defined as an almost mutual fund-like aggregation of related businesses with differing investment and risk profiles. It is because of this range of activities and the way a studio can be characterized that business opportunities tend to be "silo-specific"; a successful business plan in the entertainment industry is likely to focus on limited or niche risk profiles and financials. Except for the launch of DreamWorks (which ultimately retrenched to primarily focus on film production), it is rare for any entity to try to tackle the overall market from scratch.

Defining Studios by Their Distribution Infrastructure

There are a finite number of major studios (i.e., Sony, Disney, Paramount, Universal, Warner Bros., Fox, and MGM), and the greatest power that the studio brings to a film is not producing. Rather, studios are financing and distribution machines that bankroll production and then dominate the distribution channels to market and release the films they finance.

Accordingly, the most defining element of a studio is its distribution arm—this is how studios make most of their revenue, and is the unique facet that distinguishes a "studio" from a studio look-alike. Sometimes a company, such as Lionsgate or Miramax in its original iteration (when run independently by Bob and Harvey Weinstein), will have enough scale that it is referred to as a "mini-major." This somewhat fluid category generally refers to a company that is independent, can offer broad distribution, and consistently produces and releases a range of product; again, though, what largely distinguishes a mini-major from simply being a large production company is its distribution capacity. Any company, studios included, can arrange financing: there are plenty of people that want to invest in movies. In this regard, the film business is no different than any other business. Is the production bank-financed, risk/VC-financed, or funded by private individuals? (See Chapter 3 for a discussion of production financing.)

What is different with studios is that they will not invest (generally) in a film without obtaining and exercising distribution rights. This is because they are, first and foremost, marketing and distribution organizations, not banks. Sure, they buy properties, hire stars, and finance the films they elect to make; however, to some extent this can be viewed as a pretext to controlling which properties they distribute and own (or at least control). If the project looks like a hit, it is captive, and the studio, through its exclusive control of the distribution chain, can maximize the economic potential of the property. If the property fails to meet creative expectations, however, the studio has options, from writing it off and not releasing the property, to selling off all or part of the rights as a hedge, to rolling the dice with a variety of release strategies.

So, beyond money, which anyone can bring, and creative production, which an independent can bring, what is it about distribution that separates studios?

What Does Distribution Really Mean?

Distribution in Hollywood terms is akin to sales; however, it is more complicated than a straightforward notion of sales, given the nature of intellectual property and the strategies executed to maximize value over the life of a single property. Intellectual property rights are infinitely divisible, and distributing a film or TV show is the art of maximizing consumption and corresponding revenues across exploitation options. Whereas marketing focuses on awareness and driving consumption, distribution focuses on making that consumption profitable. Additionally, distribution is also the art of creating opportunities to drive repeat consumption of the same product. This is managed by creating exclusive or otherwise distinct periods of viewing in the context of ensuring that the product is released and customized worldwide.

In contrast to a typical software product, the global sales of which are predicated on a particular release version (e.g., Windows 98), a film is released in multiple versions, formats, and consumer markets in each territory in the world.

5

Figure 1.1 represents what I will call "Ulin's Rule": content value is optimized by exploiting the factors of time, repeat consumption (platforms), exclusivity, and differential pricing in a pattern taking into account external market conditions and the interplay of the factors among each other.

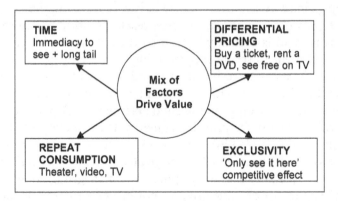

Figure 1.1 Ulin's Rule: Four Drivers of Distribution Value

Launching content via online distribution presents monetization challenges because simultaneous, nonexclusive, flat-priced access does not allow the interplay of Ulin's Rule factors: use of online platforms tend only to drive value by exploiting the time factor. To earn the same lifetime value on the Internet for a product that would otherwise flow through traditional markets not only must initial consumption expand to compensate for a decline caused by cutting out markets in the chain (or reduced because a driver such as exclusivity is removed), but also it must compensate for the cumulative effect of losing the matrix of drivers that have been honed to optimize long-term value. When thinking about Internet opportunities and different distribution platforms, keep in mind these elements and ask whether the new system is eliminating one or more of the factors: if the answer is yes, then there is likely a tug of war between the old media and new media platforms, with adoption slowed as executives struggle for a method of harmonizing the two that does not shrink the overall pie.

Importantly, the impact of eliminating one or more drivers does not change the value equation in a linear or pro-rata fashion. In the evolved ecosystem of exploiting windows, the legs work better together and the elimination of a driver has an uncertain, although inevitably negative, consequence on monetization.

For example, as I argue in more detail in Chapter 7, a persistent video-on-demand (VOD) model is a natural outgrowth of enabling technology and the long-and-wide (everything-available-now) tail (Figure 1.2); if, as a further consequence, a form of persistent VOD monetization undermines exclusivity or eliminates the concept of time segmentation (such that content is always available), then ultimate content value can be severely undercut (Figure 1.3). In such a scenario, the platforms creating gating access to content may bolster returns, but the individual content provider is unlikely to ever reach its prior equilibrium of value. This trend is currently hidden by the gold rush of new services vying for content to secure programming in the short term; however, value is being maintained by either traditional exclusivity or a form of quasi-exclusivity by the club of new platform/service leaders, and if exclusivity starts to truly evaporate and persistent VOD takes hold, then value will fall below the prior benchmarks. This is necessarily the case when the second and third bites at the apple (e.g., video revenues), which have often been equal to or greater than the first bite, are no longer viable (or as viable). It is a product of managed window systems optimizing the mix of value drivers—not in a persistent VOD model— that such subsequent bites can be bigger.

6

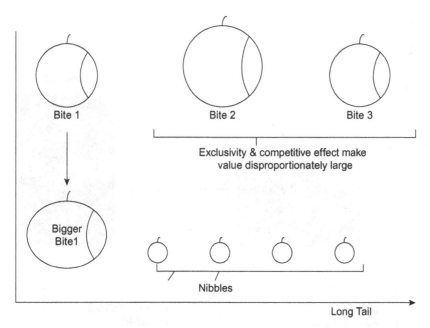

Figure 1.2 The Long Tail

Although the realization of the long tail has been ballyhooed as good for content, I am arguing quite the contrary in terms of content value. A consumption shift to infinite shelf space (what I will dub the wide tail, or the online platypus) and infinite shelf life (the long tail) does not automatically enhance content value. In fact, the result is quite the contrary. Despite easier, better, broader access to all content, if that access is achieved via elimination of a driver, then Ulin's Rule means that lifetime value for a content provider will actually diminish.

As earlier noted, the one counterweight to this decline is an upfront expansion of consumption, but it is unlikely that more people watching or buying at launch can compensate for reductions suffered in traditional downstream windows. Additionally, to those arguing for the elimination of windows and forecasting that a fully open system would engender more people consuming earlier—unshackled from the barriers thrown up by content distributors to window and therefore withhold content per the consumer's creed that programming should be freely available whenever you want it, wherever you want it, however you want it— I need simply to point out that media consumption today is already heavily front-loaded. As discussed in Chapter 9 regarding marketing (and elsewhere throughout the book, including Chapter 3 regarding

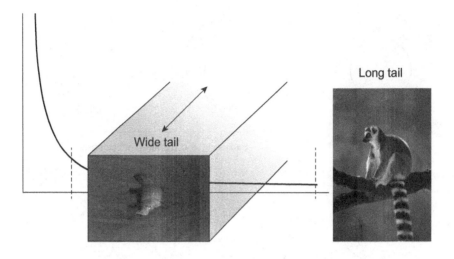

Long tail

Wide tail

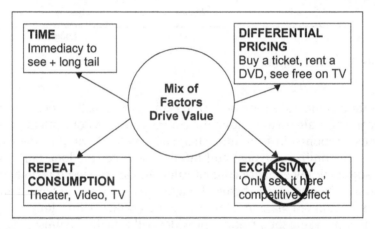

TIME Immediacy to see + long tail	**DIFFERENTIAL PRICING** Buy a ticket, rent a DVD, see free on TV
Mix of Factors Drive Value	
REPEAT CONSUMPTION Theater, Video, TV	**EXCLUSIVITY** 'Only see it here' competitive effect

Figure 1.3 Persistent VOD: a Natural Outgrowth of the Platypus and Long-tail Effect, coupled with Elimination of a Value Drive, Reduces Content Value

experience goods, and Chapters 4–6 covering the theatrical, video, and TV markets), few, if any, other businesses spend so much money in an effort to launch brands overnight. The media business, in part as a strategy to combat piracy and in part to propel a number of the value drivers, including immediacy of viewing/consumption, spends inordinate amounts of money and energy exciting consumers to stampede the box office and other downstream launches; when all possible tactics are already utilized, and the vast majority of box office and video revenues come within the first two weeks of launch, it is quite legitimate to ask whether there is any additional consumption that can be driven upfront, let alone whether the net would be so much wider that it could substitute for shrinking viewership in later windows. (Note: while TV is not an exact parallel, given the need to sustain consumption over episodes, similar efforts are made to launch series to as big an audience as possible, with the goal of creating a significant enough base to leverage for continued viability.) (See also discussion of binge viewing in Chapter 7).

Again, the window system is inherently an optimized system for lifetime management. With online, though, the tail is wider (my online platypus effect), but not necessarily longer for product most want to see: video enables greater depth of copy than theatrical, pay TV fills up airtime with hits and misses, and cable has long exploited viewing of niche product still driving demand but not worthy of premium placement (e.g., *Nick at Nite*). The challenge is that it is counterintuitive to admit that value can go down by providing more content with easier access.

Simply, while our platypus coupled with a long tail may posit infinite shelf space and infinite content, in the real world there are not infinite buyers and infinite advertisers to match this availability. (Note: This effect is often depicted in the context of monetizing Web pages, where websites similarly trend toward infinite; see also Figure 6.3 on page 308 regarding this effect.) Moreover, because new content is generally more valuable (sorry, most long-tail business model proponents), more long-tail content, if niche, likely means that it is fighting for already marginal dollars—the wide tail then only complicates matters by adding infinite competition to an already marginalized tail. It is because of all these factors that Ulin's Rule and the maximization of distribution value is more complex in practice than the simple diagrams above—throughout this book I will attempt to dissect the many moving parts and how each key content revenue opportunity contributes to the whole and is adapting to new digital permutations and challenges.

Range of Activities—Distribution Encompasses Many Markets

To accomplish the feat of releasing a single property in multiple versions and formats to a variety of consumer markets, a huge infrastructure is needed to manage and customize the property for global release. The following is a sample listing of release markets, versions, and formats.

Specialized Markets Where a Film is Seen:

- movie theaters
- video and DVD/Blu-ray
- pay television
- pay-per-view television/video-on-demand (PPV/VOD)
- free and cable television
- hotel/motel
- airlines
- non-theatrical (e.g., colleges, cruise ships)
- Internet/portable devices/tablets

Formats:

- film prints (35 mm, 70 mm, 16 mm)
- digital masters for D-cinema
- videocassette (though disappearing rapidly)
- DVD/Blu-ray
- formatted (and often edited) for TV broadcast (video master) and
- compressed for Internet/download/portable devices

10

Versions:

- original theatrical release
- extended or special versions for video/DVD (e.g., director's cut)
- widescreen versus pan-and-scan aspect ratio
- accompanied by value-added material (commentary, deleted scenes, trailers)

The need for different markets, formats, and even versions creates a complex matrix for delivery of elements. Moreover, as technology affords more viewing platforms, the combinations can grow by a multiple; for example, because DVD was additive to video (at least initially), the product SKUs increased by a factor of this doubling of the distribution channel times the number of versions released. Take this formula and compound it by all major territories in the world, and the complications of supplying consumer demand involve complex logistics.

The following illustrates this point. Assume a studio or producer has a family genre movie, such as *Avatar* or *Spider-Man*, that will be released "wide" in all traditional release channels in all major markets in the world. How many different versions of the film do you think need to be created, marketed, sold, and delivered? In my first edition, I described how the number can quite easily equal 150 versions across the range of release platforms, and possibly even more. That statement was premised on an assumption that the movie was initially released in theaters, in at least 20 major markets around the world, requiring upwards of 20 different film-print versions. The growth of digital cinema, though (see further description in Chapter 4), has dramatically increased the number of versions. The complexity is a function of multiple competing digital cinema systems and the growth of 3D, where there is a technical challenge in standardizing lighting levels; the upshot is the requirement of color timing to harmonize the appearance across different systems and, to some extent, managing the logistics of customizing per theater to assure consistent exhibition. For the DreamWorks animation film *How to Train Your Dragon*, the *Hollywood Reporter* estimated that there were 2,342 3D digital files (across a myriad of 3D projection systems, including Dolby, Master Image, RealD, and Xpand), and quoted Jeffrey Katzenberg as noting that "We now have a higher degree of complexity needed to put the right version of the movie in the right system in each theater."[1] As systems inevitably consolidate and converge over time, this matix of prints will shrink, but for the time being, with films such as *Avatar* released in more than 90 international versions (47 languages, and specialized versions required across digital 2D screens, 3D versions, and IMAX venues), my prior total of 150 different versions could conceivably be reached solely from theatrical prints.[2] Figure 1.4 below assumes:

- the movie is initially released in theaters, in at least 35 markets around the world
- the movie is released worldwide in the home-video market on DVD and VHS, and that consumers are offered a range of formats, such as a letterbox version (a "widescreen" version that leaves black on the top and bottom of the screen) and a "pan-and-scan" version that is reformatted from the theatrical aspect ratio to fill up a traditional square television screen (note: VHS releases and pan-and-scan are largely phased out, but the analogy remains, as for example, there will be Blu-ray and traditional DVD SKUs)
- the film is released into major pay TV markets worldwide (channels may have different specs)
- the film is edited for broadcast on major network TV channels
- the property is compressed for Internet/download and streaming viewing
- miscellaneous other masters, with different specs, are needed for ancillary markets such as airlines

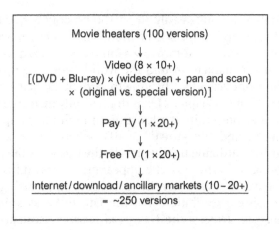

Figure 1.4 Volume and complexity of Release Versions

Relative Size of Distribution Revenue Streams

In the following chapters, I will discuss each of the key sub-markets in detail, but it is helpful to put the different revenue streams in perspective. Figure 1.5 illustrates the major revenue streams that have collectively generated upwards of $50 billion in each of the last several years.

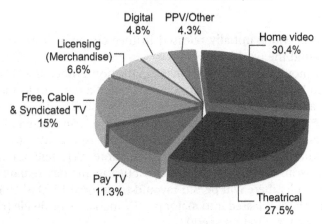

Figure 1.5 Motion Picture Distributor Revenue Streams

Overhead

Not every new format or element above adds significant new complexity, but to manage just the theatrical distribution chain, which represents only a portion of the distribution channels, requires significant overhead. Within each of the primary divisions (theatrical, pay TV, free TV, video), there are several key functions that need to be staffed. (Note: Digital/online can be structured as an independent division or coordinated and absorbed among divisions, such as when video also manages electronic sell-through sales.) Typically, there are dedicated sales, marketing, and finance staff plus general management; to the extent there is a formula, every subsidiary office in an overseas territory would replicate this general structure.

To extrapolate cost, let us assume 10 people per office with an average salary of $100,000, and that salary costs represent approximately 60 percent of the office's budget, with SG&A expenses accounting for the other 40 percent. That would represent a budget of approximately $1.7 million per office. Assuming 12 offices, this represents $20 million of overhead per year for a film or video division; the United States remains the largest and most fiercely competitive market in the world, with overhead costs (including international oversight) that can represent a significant portion of the worldwide overhead numbers.

13

Arguably, the foregoing is a conservative snapshot, for upwards of 1,000 people can be employed worldwide at a major studio across the divisions comprising the distribution chain. To illustrate the size, simply take a key individual territory as an example. A major operation in France could easily have 50 or more people, depending on structure and product flow, with an organizational infrastructure as seen in Figure 1.6 (excluding personal assistants/administrative support).

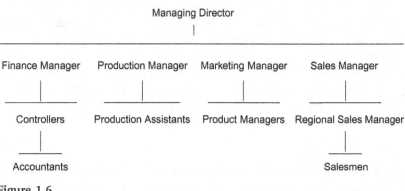

Figure 1.6

Usually, the largest number of people is in the sales area, and a geographically dispersed area with hundreds or even thousands of individual accounts to cover could comprise half of the overall headcount. (Note: in some cases, there could also be dedicated legal, although legal and business affairs tend to operate at headquarters.)

Pipeline

The overhead required to run the distribution apparatus cannot be justified without a sufficient quantity of product to market and sell. This relationship is fairly straightforward: the more titles released, the greater the revenue, and the easier to amortize the cost of the fixed overhead. Stated simply, if there were $50 million in distribution overhead, an independent releasing five films per year would need to amortize $10 million per film, whereas a larger studio releasing 25 pictures would need to recoup only $2 million per picture in overhead costs.

Studio distribution is the organization and function that matches the content pipeline with the challenge of delivering that content to every consumer on the planet—multiple times.

Complexity + Overhead + Pipeline = Studio Distribution

The above infrastructure and needs is the underbelly of the studio system, and what studios do better than anyone else is market and distribute film product to every nook and cranny of the world.

Need for Control

The other piece of the equation is control, which requires a more hands-on distribution approach than would otherwise be acceptable in an OEM or purely licensed world. Control can be viewed in terms of a negative or positive perspective. The need for control in a negative sense exists as a watchdog feature, providing security to producers and investors and others associated with the project, and assuring that the project is looked after properly. Control in a positive sense means that proper focus can be brought to distribution, thereby increasing the revenue potential on a particular project. Arguably, in the Hollywood context, these can be of equal importance.

Negative Control

Films are very individual, with stars, producers, and directors so vested in the development, production, and outcome that they have enormous influence over detailed elements of release and distribution. When travel was less ubiquitous than it is today, and revenues from international markets were a nice sprinkling on top of United States grosses, attention may not have been as significant; however, when a top star or director is likely to hear about (or even see) what has happened to his or her film in Germany or Japan, they will generally want the same rules applied in local markets as in Hollywood and New York. The only way to police this is on-the-ground control, making it less likely to cede supervisory control in major markets to mere licensees. How can the studio boss look his or her most important supplier in the face and pledge, "we'll take care of you" if he has passed the baton locally?

Executives will not risk their careers on "he'll never know about it," and the danger of discovering noncompliance has ratcheted up with every improvement in communications technology. A couple of years ago, I speculated that if an advertisement that required Tom Hanks's approval was improperly handled in Spain, a competitor could take a picture of it on his cell phone and transmit it to his agent in Los Angeles over a wireless Internet connection instantly. Now, with the advent of Twitter and other blogging/microblogging sites, the risk is even greater, for an issue or incident can go viral almost instantly, effectively bypassing damage-control safeguards. If you were counting on Mr. Hanks for your next picture, or if this represented a breach of your contract for a current picture in release, would you risk it?

Positive Control

By positive control, I simply mean that focus will usually lead to incremental revenue. Sub-distribution or agency relationships, by their nature, yield control to third parties, and studios tend to have direct offices handling distribution in their major markets. Only with this level of oversight can a distribution organization push its agenda and maneuver against its competitors, who are invariably releasing titles of their own at the same time and to the same customers. This direct supplier–customer relationship is what studios offer to their clients—a global matrix of relationships and focus that an independent without the same level of continuous product flow cannot support.

The Independent's Dilemma

An independent may not care as much about some or all of these issues, for it may have less entrenched relationships or be more willing, by its very nature, to take on certain risks. It still, though, has to release its product via all the key distribution channels (e.g., theatrical, TV, video) and into as many territories as possible around the world. To raise money, it may make strategic sense to license rights (often tied to a guarantee), which in turn usually has the consequence of ceding an element of control, as well as some potential upside; to the independent, though, securing an advance guarantee or accepting that less direct control may forfeit revenues at the margin may greatly outweigh the burden of carrying the extra overhead. In essence, they can beat over 70 percent of the system, but they cannot match the pure strength and reach of the studio distribution infrastructure. And to many people, especially on big movies with powerful producers and directors behind them, a pitch of "almost as good" simply is not good enough.

Joint Ventures

The pressure to fill a pipeline and bring down per-title releasing costs while guaranteeing the broadest possible release is great, and even defining of what makes a studio. Despite the fact, however, that costs come down in a linear progression relative to titles released, the total overhead is still a very large number; such a large number, in fact, that it has frequently led to the formation of joint ventures. A joint venture may only need an incremental amount of extra overhead, if any, while perhaps doubling or tripling the throughput of titles. In the above studio case, a joint venture could easily increase the title flow from 25 to 60, bringing down the per-recoupment number in the above scenario to under $1 million per title to cover the overhead.

Studio joint ventures grew in the 1980s with the globalization of the business. The number of titles a studio released fell within a relatively static range, and even a significant percentage increase in product still meant a finite number of major films (e.g., 20 or 30). What changed dramatically was the importance of the international markets. In the early 1980s, the international box office as a percentage of the worldwide box office was in the 40 percent range, then grew to over a 50 percent share by the mid 1990s, by the mid 2000s had grown to more than 60 percent,[3] and by 2010 started to approach 70 percent (e.g., 68 percent in 2011; see Figure 1.7 and also Table 4.1 in Chapter 4). (Note: In 2010, foreign sales accounted for roughly 70 percent of total receipts, both for industry and for the movie *Avatar*.[4]) The splits, of course, are picture-dependent and, in extreme cases, can have an international share close to 80 percent, with Universal's *Battleship* having an international share of nearly 79 percent, and Fox's *Life of Pi* around 80 percent.[5] But the overall trend is clear, especially for box office hits with international stars and franchise recognition.[6] With the emergence of China as a major theatrical market (see Chapter 4), this trend of international box office

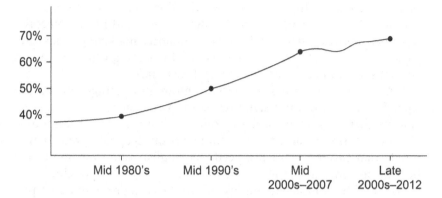

Figure 1.7 International Box Office as a Percent of Worldwide Box Office

dominating global box office is poised to continue. Moreover, in instances, films are now starting to be released first overseas, a trend that was anathema just a few years ago. In the spring of 2012 (leading off the summer season), Disney debuted its hit *The Avengers* first in key international territories, and Universal followed suit, launching *Battleship* overseas. In an unprecedented step, and telling trend, the U.S. was the last major theatrical territory in which *Battleship* was released.[7]

17

When individual territories outside the United States started to represent the potential, and then the actual, return of tens of millions of dollars, the studios needed to build an infrastructure to manage and maximize the release of their products abroad. Moreover, this matured market by market. First, the growth of the international theatrical market warranted the expansion. Shortly thereafter, with the explosive growth of the videocassette market in the 1980s and 1990s, including the 1990s expansion of major United States retailers such as Blockbuster to international markets, studios needed to mirror theatrical expansion on the video side. Distribution of videocassettes (now DVDs and Blu-rays) and of movies into theaters utilizes the same underlying product and target consumers, but the similarities stop there; the differences of marketing a live event in theaters versus manufacturing a consumer product required different manufacturing, delivery, and marketing, and with it a different management infrastructure.

Three studios joined together to form United International Pictures, better known in the industry by its abbreviation UIP. Headquartered in London, UIP was historically a joint venture among Paramount Pictures, Universal Pictures, and MGM (MGM later dropped out, but the volume of titles remained high as DreamWorks titles were put through the venture). The three parties shared common overhead in the categories described above: general management, finance, marketing, sales, and legal. Additional efficiencies were gained by sharing office space and general sales and administrative budget cost lines.

What was not shared is perhaps more interesting—the parties shared costs, but did not share revenues. A cost-sharing joint venture is a peculiar instrument of fierce competitors in the film community. Natural adversaries came together for two common goals: protection of intellectual property and the need to establish sales and marketing beachheads around the globe for as little overhead as possible. Both goals could be completely fulfilled without sharing revenues on a per-product or aggregate basis; perhaps more importantly, the structure of the business likely would not have permitted the sharing of revenues even if this was a common goal. Because each film has many other parties tied to it, with complicated equity, rights, and financial participation structures, it is unlikely that all the parties who would need to approve the sharing of such revenues would ultimately agree to do so.

Why, for example, would Steven Spielberg and Universal all agree to share revenues on its film *Jurassic Park* with Paramount or MGM? Similarly, why would Paramount Pictures and Tom Cruise want to share revenues on *Mission: Impossible* with Universal? The simple answer is they would not, and they do not. Every one of these parties, however, has a vested interest in the films released under a structure that: (1) minimizes costs and therefore returns the greatest cash flow; (2) protects the underlying intellectual property and minimizes forces such as piracy that undermine the ability to sell the property and generate cash; and (3) maximizes the sales opportunities.

Once this formula is established, it is relatively easy to replicate for other distribution channels. UIP, for example, spun off a separate division for pay TV (UIP Pay TV), a market that exploded in the early 1990s. The same theatrical partners joined forces to lower overhead and distribute product into established and emerging pay TV markets worldwide.

Additionally, two of these partners, Paramount and Universal, teamed up for videocassette distribution and formed CIC Video (where I once worked, based in UIP House in London). CIC, similar to UIP and UIP Pay TV, set up branch operations throughout the world headquartered in the UK. Table 1.1 is a representative chart of countries served by direct subsidiary offices.

In addition to direct offices, the venture would service licensees in countless other territories. These are examples of territories typically

Table 1.1 Countries Served by Direct Subsidiary Offices/Territory

Australia	Malaysia
Brazil	Mexico
Denmark	New Zealand
France	Norway
Germany	South Africa
Holland/The Netherlands	South Korea
Hong Kong	Spain
Italy	Sweden
Japan	United Kingdom

managed by studios as licensee markets: Argentina, Chile, Colombia, Czech Republic, Ecuador, Finland, Greece, Hungary, Iceland, Indonesia, Israel, Philippines, Poland, Portugal, Singapore, Taiwan, Thailand, Turkey, Uruguay, and Venezuela. (Note: This is not an exhaustive list.) Whether it makes sense to operate a subsidiary office or even to license product into a territory at all depends on factors including market maturity, economic conditions, size of the market, and the status of piracy/intellectual property enforcement. Many of the largest developing markets, which historically have been licensee territories throughout most of the span of the era of joint ventures, including Russia, China, and India, are being transitioned by studios into direct operations. Russia serves as a prime example, as rapid economic growth propelled the theatrical market from insignificant to among the top 10 worldwide markets in just a few years.

19

UIP and CIC, although among the longest lasting and most prominent joint ventures (UIP was formed in 1981), are simply examples, and many other companies similarly joined forces in distribution (e.g., CBS and Fox formed CBS/FOX Video, partnering to distribute product on videocassette worldwide).

Demise of Historic Joint Ventures

None of UIP, CIC, UIP Pay TV, or CBS/FOX Video exists today in their grand joint-venture forms. First, UIP Pay TV was disbanded in the mid 1990s, then the video venture CIC was largely shuttered by 2000, and finally UIP's theatrical breakup/reorganization was announced in 2005 and implemented in 2006 (though the partners still distribute via the venture in limited territories). Why did this happen?

The answer is rooted partly in economics and partly in ego. The economic justification in several instances was less compelling than when the ventures were convenient cost-sharing vehicles enabling market entry and boosting clout with product supply. In the case of pay TV, for example, the overhead necessary to run an organization was nominal when compared to a theatrical or video division. Most countries only had one or two major pay TV broadcasters; accordingly, the client base worldwide was well under 50, and the number of significant clients was under 20.

This lower overhead base, coupled with growing pay TV revenues, made the decision relatively easy. Additionally, given the limited stations/competition and the desire to own part of the broadcasting base, the studios started opportunistically launching joint or wholly owned local pay TV networks. Over time, services such as Showtime in Australia or LAP TV in Latin America, both of which are owned by a consortium of studios, became a common business model. Fox was among the most aggressive studios, replicating its successful Sky model in the UK and owning or acquiring significant equity stakes in the largest number of pay TV services worldwide. The Fox family of global pay networks grew to include the following major services:

- BSkyB—UK
- Star—Asia (including Southeast Asia, India, Mideast, China/Hong Kong)
- Sky Italia—Italy
- LAP TV (partner interest in Latin American service)
- Showtime—Australia (partner in PMP, pre-Foxtel interest)

The logic behind the breakups of CIC and UIP are a bit more complicated, and are seemingly grounded as much in politics as economics. In both instances, the companies called on thousands of clients, and the range of titles from multiple studios virtually ensured the entity of some of the strongest and most consistent product flow in the industry—a fact that is critical in a week in, week out business. A video retailer is more likely to accept better terms and take more units from one of its best suppliers, knowing that a blockbuster it is likely to want will always be just around the corner. This strength of product flow, however, also turned out to be a problem with local competition authorities.

UIP was forced to defend anticompetitive practices allegations for years, and formally opposed an investigation by the European Union Commission (Competition Authority) in Brussels that threatened sanctions and even the breakup of the venture. Some argue that the EU

Commission's claims were politically bolstered by member states with protectionist legislation and quotas for locally produced product. In the end, UIP was successful in its defense, but the company was always a political target and forced to be on guard. While CIC was not similarly subject to an EU Commission inquiry, as a sister company it was always conscious of the issues.

In addition to theoretical arguments regarding anticompetitive behavior given market leverage, these types of joint ventures were always in the spotlight for specific claims. One of the most active watchdogs has been the competition authority in Spain. In 2006, the studios were fined by the Spanish authorities on a theatrical claim. *Variety* reported: "In the biggest face-off in recent years between Hollywood and Spanish institutions, Spain's antitrust authorities have slammed a €12 million ($15.3 million) fine on the sub-branches of Hollywood's major studios in Spain for cartel price fixing and anticompetitive coordination of other commercial policies."[8] Cases such as this only make operators of a joint venture among studios all the more paranoid.

Competition concerns aside, these ventures always had the maverick studio boss looming over them, wary that his or her film was somehow disadvantaged by treatment of a competitive partner's title. The defense to this type of attack is that there will always be a competitive film, and better it be in the family so the headquarters can work to maximize all product; at least in a venture it is theoretically easier to schedule releases and allocate resources so that one studio's product is not directly against another partner's product (although, in practice, pursuant to antitrust/ competition rules studios cannot share release dates). Ultimately, no matter what argument is made, the concern comes down to focus: every studio wants its big title pushed at the expense of everything else, and this is hard (at least by perception) to achieve in a joint venture. As the markets matured, and the international theatrical and video markets continued to grow as a percentage of worldwide revenues, many studio heads wanted unfettered control and dedication for key territories.

Many have argued that the breakup of these ventures simply for dedication and control is economic folly. These joint ventures had been releasing major studio hits for decades without discriminating one over the other. In fact, they could not discriminate, for the partners were always wary of this, and any significant diverting of focus or resources to one partner versus another would not be tolerated. Moreover, focus/dedication would have to yield a return that recovered 100 percent of the overhead now borne by the studio that had been allocated to its partner(s) previously. In a 50/50 joint venture, that means recouping an equivalent of 100 percent more than it needed to previously (e.g., if

$20 million in total overhead, the studio now needed to recoup the full $20 million rather than only $10 million), and in a partnership with three parties it was even worse. These are pure bottom-line sums, for direct picture costs were already allocated by title. It is for this reason that politics comes into the equation. Clearly not all product will have an uplift to cover the additional overhead costs, but by the same measure never again will an executive of Studio X be fearful that he or she left money on the table for a major release because resources were diverted to a competitor's film.

Branding and Scale Needs: Online Giving Rise to a New Era of Joint Ventures?

Perhaps the Internet and new digital delivery systems are fostering a new era of joint ventures. Today, global reach need not be achieved in an iterative fashion by rolling out international subsidiaries; rather, given unprecedented online adoption rates (e.g., YouTube, Facebook), companies are competing in a kind of virtual land-grab and teaming up for services that offer instant scale.

As discussed in Chapter 7, NBC/Universal and Fox partnered in 2008 to launch Hulu; by combining the breadth of programming from these two networks/studios, the on-demand service was able to offer diversified, premium content on a scale to support a new distribution platform. (Note: The joint venture expanded in 2009 when ABC became a third partner.) Similarly, looking to innovate within the on-demand space, Paramount, MGM, and Lionsgate in 2008 (each looking for alternatives to their historical Pay TV output deals with Showtime) formed the joint venture Studio 3 Networks, branding its distribution service "Epix." Epix, a hybrid premium television and video-on-demand service, bills itself as a "next-generation premium entertainment brand, video-on-demand and Internet service," leveraging diversified content from its partners and providing multiplatform access to satisfy the new consumer who insists on viewing content anywhere, anytime.[9] Both of these services followed the major studios' initial foray into the online space, where MovieLink and CinemaNow were launched as joint ventures to download films, but for a variety of reasons never achieved hoped-for adoption levels (see Chapter 7).

Studios as Defined by Range of Product

Although I will continue to argue that the distribution capacity and capability of a studio in fact defines a studio, this is not the popular starting point. Most look at a studio as a "super producer," with the financial muscle to create a large range of product. Given consolidation of most TV networks into vertically integrated groups, this range of product is further diversified by primary outlet (e.g., made for film, TV, online). Although I may refer in some of the examples below to only one category, such as film, the premise often holds across media types, which accentuates the distribution diversity under the broader media groups.

Quantity

It is instructive to compare a studio to an independent on two basic grounds: quantity of product and average product budget. On these two statistics alone, it would be easy to segment studios. From a pure quantity standpoint, studios have the greatest volume of product. MPAA member companies collectively tend to release in the range of 150–200 new feature films per year, and while the total number of independent films released is usually more than double that number (approximately 400 per year, for a total of approximately 600 films per year released in the United States), the independent releases tend to be on a much smaller scale and capture only a sliver of the total box office receipts (even if, as of late, they are capturing more of the awards glory); moreover, no individual independent releases more than a handful of movies per year. (Note: A good example of a top independent, often releasing pictures gaining recognition at film festivals, is Samuel Goldwyn Films.) Table 1.2 evidences the consistency of the trend regarding number of films released per year.

Viewed from the standpoint of an independent producer, whose companies tend to be dedicated to the output of individuals (e.g., a producer or director), even the largest and longest tenured independents are limited to the number of films their key players can handle in a given period. New Regency, headed by Arnon Milchan, Imagine Entertainment, led by Brian Grazer and Ron Howard, and Working Title Films, run by Tim Bevan and Eric Fellner, are three of the largest

Table 1.2 Number of Films Released Per Year in the U.S.[10]

	2008	2009	2010	2011	2012
MPAA Studios*	168	158	141	141	128
Others	470	399	422	468	549

* Includes subsidiaries

Table 1.3 Examples Films Produced by Leading Independents

New Regency	Imagine Entertainment	Working Title
Famous Films	*Famous Films*	*Famous Films*
Mr. & Mrs. Smith	Apollo 13	Four Weddings and a Funeral
Pretty Woman	A Beautiful Mind	Bridget Jones's Diary
L.A. Confidential	The Da Vinci Code	Notting Hill
2010 Releases	*2011 Releases*	*2012 Releases*
Knight and Day	Tower Heist	Les Misérables
Love & Other Drugs	Cowboys & Aliens	Anna Karenina
	J. Edgar	Contraband
	The Dilemma	Big Miracle
	Blue Crush 2	

and most consistently producing independents over approximately the last 20 years. New Regency has long been affiliated with Fox, while both Imagine and Working Title have distribution output deals with Universal. Table 1.3 lists samples of films over the last few years from each, as well as a couple of the films that catapulted each group to "producer stardom."

The point regarding quantity becomes self-evident and simple—only a larger organization that aggregates talent can produce on this larger scale. By corollary, to aggregate talent (e.g., producers and directors) the same organization needs to defer to talent on many issues, including the physical production of films. Coming full circle, the consequence of this aggregation is the resulting scale to take on different risks, including maintaining distribution overhead.

Range of Labels and Relationships

Range of Labels

One simple way to boost output is to create a number of film divisions. Almost all of the studios have availed themselves of this strategy, which segments risks into mini-brands and labels that usually have very specific parameters. These parameters are often defined by budget limit, but can also be differentiated by type of content. Fox, for example, created Fox Searchlight, which specializes in lower-budget fare, and similarly Universal created Focus; these are examples of smaller labels that take advantage of part of the larger studio infrastructure, but otherwise are tasked with a certain quantity output at lower budget ranges to diversify the studio's overall portfolio.

Divisions and smaller labels are not strictly limited, though, to lower-budget films. Disney, for example, diversified into: (1) Walt Disney Pictures, which is generally limited to family and animated fare; (2) Touchstone, which is generally a releasing-only arm; (3) Hollywood Pictures; and (4) Miramax, which, when run by the Weinsteins, was a large, internally diversified studio releasing a comparable number of pictures in a year to the balance of the sister Disney labels.

Table 1.4 is a chart of some of the specialty labels under studio umbrellas and examples of the pictures made and/or released. This list used to be nearly twice as long, but driven by the 2008 recession, a number of labels have either been shuttered or sold off, including Paramount's Vantage (*There Will Be Blood*), Disney's Miramax (*The Queen, No Country for Old Men*), and Warner's Warner Independent (*Good Night and Good Luck, March of the Penguins*). In fact, the *New York Times*, looking at the pending 2013 Oscars ceremony, noted, "the number of films released by specialty divisions of the major studios, which have

Table 1.4 Speciality Labels Under Studio Umbrellas

Studio	Labels	Example of Films in Sub-Label
Sony	Columbia Revolution Sony Classics	*Friends with Money*
Fox	20th Century Fox Fox 2000 Fox Searchlight	*Slumdog Millionaire, Juno,* *The Tree of Life*
Disney	Walt Disney Pictures Touchstone Hollywood Pictures	All Pixar releases (e.g., *Finding Nemo, Cars*)
Warners	Warner Bros. New Line	*The Lord of the Rings* trilogy
Paramount	Paramount MTV/Nickelodeon	
Universal	Universal Focus Features	*Brokeback Mountain, Jane Eyre*

Table 1.5 Breakdown of Fox Domestic Box Office

Label/Releasing Arm	Division B.O.	% of Total Studio B.O.
20th Century Fox	$1.1 billion	72
Fox 2000	$272 million	17
Fox Searchlight	$162 million	10
Fox Atomic	$7 million	1

backed Oscar winners like *Slumdog Millionaire*, from Fox Searchlight, fell to just 37 pictures last year, down 55 percent from 82 in 2002, according to the Motion Picture Association of America."[11]

Taking a snapshot from a few years ago at the height of specialty labels, with the exception of Paramount (where DreamWorks' pictures—prior to its separation and move to Disney—accounted for a substantial percentage of the studio's overall box office), the principal arm rather than the specialty labels accounted for greater than two-thirds of the studios' overall domestic box office. Fox was a typical example. Table 1.5 is a breakdown of its total $1.56 billion 2006 domestic box office.[12]

Range of Relationships

In addition to subsidiary film divisions that specialize in certain genres or budget ranges or simply add volume, studios increase output via "housekeeping" deals with star producers and directors. Studios will create what are referred to as "first-look" deals where they pay the overhead of certain companies, including funding offices (e.g., on the studio lot), in return for a first option on financing and distributing a pitched property. (See the companion website for a discussion of first-look deals and puts.)

Range of Budgets

Studios produce and finance projects within a wide range of budgets, with the distribution pattern creating a bell-type curve bounded by very low and very high budgets at the extremes; the average in this case represents the majority of output, expensive product in any other industry, but in studio terms midrange risk. An example of a high-budget label is Paramount's former relationship with DreamWorks, where Dream-Works had the freedom to independently green-light movies with budgets up to $85 million, and reportedly up to $100 million if Steven Spielberg was directing.[13]

Low Budget   It is possible to produce a film for under $1 million, as the proliferation of film festivals demonstrates. Technology has also brought the cost of filmmaking down, making it accessible to a wider range of filmmakers. Easy access to digital tools and software for editing is revolutionizing the business. Studios have the choice of commissioning lower-budget films directly, or, as discussed above, creating specialty labels focusing on this fare. Although there is no per se ceiling for low budget, the category implies a budget of under $10 million, and generally refers to under $5 million or $7 million.

Under the Radar   What is truly under the radar is a moving target. With the cost of production escalating, films under $30 million, and especially under $20 million, have a different risk profile and can be categorized as "under the radar." It may often be easier to jump-start a film in this range, and some studios will allow stars to dabble in this category for a project perceived as more risky (e.g., out of character). I do not mean to imply that this is a trivial sum, or that making a project in this range is easy. Rather, executives tacitly acknowledge that in the budget hierarchy there is a category between low and high budget that sometimes receives less scrutiny.

27

High Budget   High budget is now a misnomer, for a typical budget is in fact high and people search for terms that differentiate the extremes, such as when a film costs more than $100 million. Accordingly, it is in this very wide range of somewhere above the then current perceived cutoff for a higher level of scrutiny or approval matrix to authorize ("under the radar" where the project is in a lower risk category) and $100 million that most films today fall. According to MPAA statistics, the average cost of a major MPAA member studio movie in 2007 was $70.8 million.[14] (See Chapter 4 for 2010/2011 estimates by SNL Kagan).

Franchise or Tentpole Budget   There is no formal range for this term of art, but when someone mentions "tentpole," the budget is invariably more than $100 million, sometimes more than $200 million, and the studio is making an exception for a picture that it believes can become (or extend) a franchise. Moreover, a tentpole picture has the goal of lifting the whole studio's fortunes, from specific economic return to driving packages of multiple films to intangible benefits. These are big-bet and often defining films, properties that are targeted for franchise or award purposes. Modern-day epics fall into this range, with *Titanic* leading the way. In other cases, films with a perceived "can't fail" audience may justify an extraordinary budget, such as franchise sequels: Warner Bros. with *Harry Potter*, Sony with *Spider-Man*, and Disney with *Star Wars* and Marvel (e.g., *Iron Man*) fare. *Variety*, discussing the extraordinary number of big-budget tentpole sequels in the summer of 2007, noted that "five key tentpoles have an aggregate budget of $1.3 billion," and continued: "Production costs continue to climb precipitously at the tentpole end, with *Spider-Man 3*, *Pirates 3* (*Pirates of the Caribbean: At World's End*), and *Evan Almighty* redefining the outer limits of spending. Last year's discussion of how far past $200 million *Superman Returns* may have gone seems quaint by comparison."[15] What may have seemed exceptional a few years ago is now commonplace, and the summer is invariably stocked with high-budget sequels. Summer 2012 was no exception and included, among others, *The Avengers*, *The Dark Knight Rises*, *The Amazing Spider-Man*, *The Bourne Legacy*, *Madagascar 3: Europe's Most Wanted*, and *Men in Black 3*.

This category of if-we-make-it-they-will-come blockbusters is a driver for the studios. There is frequently guaranteed interest and PR, cross-promotion opportunities galore, sequel and franchise potential, pre-sold games and merchandise, etc. Additionally, as discussed in other chapters, these tentpole pictures stake out certain prime weekends and holiday periods (e.g., in the U.S., Memorial Day, Christmas, Thanksgiving) for release, and virtually guarantee the sale of other pictures in TV packages of films.

Why there is this range of budgets is again economically driven. All films can succeed or fail beyond rational expectations. Higher-budget films cost more because "insurance" factors are baked in: a star, a branded property, groundbreaking or spectacular special effects, and action sequences are all assumed to drive people to the theater (although, as discussed in Chapter 3, the highly variable nature of box office success is generally not tempered by such factors). With the extra costs come extra risks, as well as the need to share the upside with the stars/people/properties that are making it expensive in the first place. Accordingly, every studio dreams of the film that will cost less and break through—perhaps less glitzy, but driving more profits to the bottom line. Every studio would take 10 *My Big Fat Greek Weddings* or *Slumdog Millionaires* over an expensive action hero film. (In fact, the film *Last Action Hero*, starring Arnold Schwarzenegger, was Sony/Columbia's big bet in 1993, but significantly underperformed at the box office, with a domestic take of $50 million against a reputed budget of close to $90 million, as famously chronicled in the book *Hit & Run* in the chapter "How They Built the Bomb."[16])

28

The Internet Wrinkle The Internet is allowing people to experiment with production at costs that are, in cases, so low that it is redefining what low budget means. It is hard to compare most online production to other media because the format has generally been shorter-form. As people continue to experiment, whether producing content intended only for Web viewing, hoping to utilize the medium for lower-cost pilots that can then migrate to TV, or producing series developed for on-demand viewing, it will be interesting to see whether budgets rise to match quality expectations of other media (as we are seeing with online originals from leaders such as Netflix and Hulu) or whether the Internet will drive a different cost structure (as has historically been the case) linked to new and evolving online content categories (see Chapters 3 and 7, including discussion of online leaders branching out to produce original content in Chapter 7).

Pipeline and Portfolio

Range of Genre and Demographic

While economics drive a portfolio strategy in terms of budget range, marketing drives the product mix in terms of sales. Accordingly, product targeted at different genres is produced to satisfy a variety of consumer appetites:

- action
- romance
- comedy
- thriller
- drama
- historical or reality-based stories
- kids and family
- musical
- adult entertainment

These categories may seem obvious because they have become so ingrained. Simply check out the shelf headings at your local video store (if you can still find one), search categories for VOD options, or read film critics' reviews—descriptions are peppered with Dewey decimal classification-type verbiage to categorize films. If the film is not easy to peg, then use a crossover term such as chick flick, or combine phrases such as "action thriller" or "romantic comedy." Retailers' and e-tailers' creative labeling of shelves/sections and endless categories for awards further add to the lexicon of segmentation.

At some level, the categories become self-fulfilling, and demand is generated to fill the niche pipeline. How many romantic comedies do we have? If the studio cannot supply the genre, it starts to become more of a niche player, which can start to affect perceptions, relationships, and ultimately valuations. Categories come into and out of vogue (e.g., musicals), and about the only category where it has always been accepted to opt out is adult entertainment.

Range of Type/Style

If a portfolio strategy is not complicated enough, then draw a matrix combining different types of budget, genres, and relationships, and then layer on styles and types. Film style classifications include live-action movies, traditional animation, computer graphics-generated, etc. Today, even format comes into the mix, with 3D another variant.

These categories are more technical or process-driven, but serve to create yet another level of specialization or segmentation. For a studio, it is not enough to stop, for example, at the "kids market." Conscious decisions need to be made about a portfolio within this limited category —how many titles, what budget range, how many animated versus live action, is there a range of budgets within the animation category, etc.

Other Markets—Video, Online, etc.

This proliferation of product cutting across every possible style and range has served to create outlets and demand for product beyond what is released in theaters or produced for TV. Demand in the children's market, linked to the growth of home viewing starting with videocassettes, spawned the "made-for-video" business. At a video store, it became nearly impossible to discern whether sequels or spin-offs from films and name brands (*Aladdin 2*, *The Scorpion King 2*, *The Lion King 1½*, *American Pie 4*) were made for the movie or video market. (Note: The growth of this segment, and specific economics, are discussed in more detail in Chapter 5.)

Finally, online is expanding the production palate, with producers creating original product that ranges from features to shorts. In theory, distributing original Internet content should fall outside the studio system, for any producer with a website can stream content to anyone; hence, with the Internet enabling independence, why pay, or team, with a studio? The reason is that accompanying the near-zero barrier to entry with Internet distribution (bandwidth/site infrastructure is still needed) is the challenge of infinite competition and clutter. Accordingly, not only are networks and studios beginning to produce their own content, but they will start to affiliate with independents that need marketing assistance (and/or financing, as costs increase with talent inevitably demanding more in relation to growing revenues, or higher quality thresholds are sought). In fact, associating with a brand is one of the easiest ways to rise above clutter and attract viewers, and there is every reason to expect that, over time, studios/networks will add a portfolio of Internet originals, complementing the diversity found today in traditional media platforms. (See Chapter 7 regarding new growth of originals within online aggregators.)

Brand Creation versus Brand Extension

Finally, in terms of looking at the creation of product to fill the studio pipeline, one needs to look at the desire to find a branded property. Everyone is looking for that "sure thing," and a property with built-in recognition and an assumed built-in audience theoretically lowers risk and gives marketing a jump-start.

Aside from the new idea, there are four treasure troves of ideas that serve as the lifeblood of Hollywood: the real world, books and comics, sequels, and spin-offs. I will only mention the real world in passing, given the obvious nature of creating dramas either set in historical settings or adaptations of real-life events (e.g., *The King's Speech, Saving Private Ryan, The Pianist, Argo, Zero Dark Thirty*). However, it is worth noting that the explosion of user-generated content on the Internet (e.g., YouTube videos) is defining an entirely new source of material that producers are trying to exploit, as well as migrate to other media.

Books and comics are the largest source of branded fare. In fact, try to find a bestseller with a strong lead character today that is not being adapted (or at least optioned/developed) for the screen. Table 1.6 is a very small sampling.

Brand Extension: Sequels

Sequels are a relatively new phenomenon looking over the last 100 years of film in that these rights, while reserved by the studios, were not considered very valuable until the success of *Jaws* and *Star Wars* in the 1970s proved otherwise. George Lucas recognized the inherent value of sequels with *Star Wars*, and by retaining sequel and related rights to the original property built the most lucrative franchise in movie history. It only takes someone else making billions of dollars before others catch on, and today rights in sequels and spin-offs are cherished and fiercely negotiated for up front. In fact, of the top 25 films of the Box office in 2012, roughly two-thirds were either sequels or some form of derivative adaptation, with 7 of the top 10 being part of a series.[17]

Table 1.6 Examples of Film Adaptations of Books and Comics

Book	Film
Robert Ludlum books	The *Bourne* series of movies
Harry Potter books	*Harry Potter* movies
Tom Clancy books	*The Hunt for Red October*
John Grisham books	*The Pelican Brief, The Firm*
The Hunger Games books	*The Hunger Games* movies
Jane Austen novels	*Pride and Prejudice*
The Da Vinci Code	*The Da Vinci Code*
J.R.R. Tolkien books	*The Lord of the Rings* movies

Comic	Film
Batman	*Batman* series of films
Spider-Man	*Spider-Man* series of films
X-Men	*X-Men* series of films
Superman	*Superman* series of films
Iron Man	*Iron Man* series of films (plus *The Avengers*)

A successful film can become a brand overnight, and since the 1980s, and especially the 1990s, the mantra has been once a movie reaches a certain box office level, executives immediately start thinking about making a sequel. Table 1.7 shows some prominent examples.

Sequels have become such a successful formula—of course they are not a guarantee; witness *Babe: Pig in the City*—that they have given birth to "prequels" and simultaneously produced sequels. Sequels used to be thought about in terms of what happens next: do they live, do they live happily ever after, what's the next adventure . . .? Because movies are fantasy-based and have no boundaries, prequels are now becoming popular. In these movies, the audience learns how a character grew up— often without the famous actors from the original films even appearing. The *Star Wars* prequels (*The Phantom Menace, Attack of the Clones*, and *Revenge of the Sith*) serve as the most striking examples, absent stars such as Harrison Ford, Mark Hamill, and Carrie Fisher.

Additionally, with expensive films and effects, producers have started making more than one film in a series simultaneously to amortize costs. *The Matrix Reloaded* and *The Matrix Revolutions*, for example, were made together and were released six months apart in 2003 in the summer

Table 1.7 Examples of Films and Their Sequels

Original Film	Sequel(s)
Jaws	*Jaws 2, Jaws 3 . . .*
Rocky	*Rocky II, Rocky III . . . Rocky Balboa*
Star Wars (Episode IV)	*The Empire Strikes Back (Episode V), Return of the Jedi (Episode VI), Episodes I, II, III,* pending *Episodes VII, VIII, IX*
Raiders of the Lost Ark	*Indiana Jones and the Temple of Doom, Indiana Jones and the Last Crusade, Indiana Jones and the Kingdom of the Crystal Skulll*
The Terminator	*Terminator 2: Judgment Day, Terminator 3: Rise of the Machines, Terminator Salvation*
The Mummy	*The Mummy Returns, The Mummy: Tomb of the Dragon Emperor*
Home Alone	*Home Alone 2, 3, 4*
Pirates of the Caribbean: The Curse of the Black Pearl	*Pirates of the Carribean 2: Dead Man's Chest, 3: At World's End, 4: On Stranger Tides*
Spider-Man	*Spider-Man 2, 3, The Amazing Spider-Man*
Die Hard	*Die Hard 2, Die Hard with a Vengeance, Live Free or Die Hard, A Good Day to Die Hard*
Harry Potter series	*Harry Potter 2, 3, 4, 5, 6, 7, 8*
Batman series	*Batman . . . The Dark Knight* trilogy

and at Christmas. *The Lord of the Rings* trilogy was green-lit by New Line Cinema to be made as a production bundle, and the more recent *The Hobbit* films, *An Unexpected Journey, The Desolation of Smaug,* and *There and Back Again,* are being filmed back to back in New Zealand (to achieve certain production efficiencies), with anticipated respective release dates by Warner Bros. of December 2012, 2013, and 2014. Similarly, Disney committed to making both *Pirates of the Caribbean 2* and *3* at the same time, thus being able to keep the cast and crew together.

Brand Extension: Spin-Offs

The classic spin-off is when a character from one film/property is used to launch an ancillary franchise. In television, one of the best examples is *Frasier*. The Frasier character, played by Kelsey Grammer, appeared in *Cheers*, and when *Cheers* wound down the network launched *Frasier* as

33

a new series. As most classic TV watchers know, Frasier was a pompous psychiatrist who was among the cast of support characters who regularly hung out at the Boston-based bar on the earlier *Cheers*. In the new show, the premise was that he has moved home to Seattle and practices psychiatry via hosting a local radio call-in show. The difference between a sequel and a spin-off should be quite clear. A sequel to *Cheers* would be, for example, a *Cheers* movie or *Cheers* reunion show where we saw what happened down the road.

An example of a movie spin-off would be *The Scorpion King*. *The Scorpion King* stars the villain from *The Mummy*, but does not continue with the other main characters, nor does it continue the quest or love interests pursued by the hero/main character in *The Mummy* or *The Mummy Returns*, played by Brendan Fraser. In fact, the distinction between *The Mummy Returns* and *The Scorpion King* paints a good distinction between a sequel (the former) and a spin-off (the latter). (Note: Not having worked on these, it is possible that in the specific contracts for these films they were not treated this way and were negotiated differently.)

34   Brand Extension: Remakes

A remake provides another category of brand extension, albeit one that is used less frequently than a sequel or spin-off. An example of a remake is *Sabrina*, where a classic film is remade with new lead actors and actresses. The original film, starring Audrey Hepburn, Humphrey Bogart, and William Holden, was remade using the same lead characters, same principal storyline, and same general locations, but the former cast is now updated with Julia Ormond, Harrison Ford, and Greg Kinnear.

Remakes are less common for a simple reason: it is natural for audiences to compare the remake with the original, and if the original is strong enough that it is worthy of remaking, then the new film better be strong enough to stand up to the original. Still, the formula of starting with a classic and substituting current stars seems a formula and risk often worth taking. Again, this is a classic example of brand extension with another variation on risk analysis.

Crossover to Other Markets: Sequels and Spin-Offs

Finally, there is the catchall crossover category where properties migrate across media:

- films spawn TV shows (e.g., *M*A*S*H*, *My Big Fat Greek Life*, *The Young Indiana Jones Chronicles*)

- TV series spawn films (e.g., *Star Trek, Miami Vice, The Flintstones*)
- games spawn films (e.g., *Lara Croft: Tomb Raider*)

Sometimes a property becomes so successful and spawns so many permutations that it is nearly impossible to distinguish what came from what. The original *Star Trek* series certainly led to the success of spin-off series such as *Star Trek: The Next Generation*, but with further spin-offs and sequel movies from both the original series and spin-off series, the boundaries become blurred (and are becoming more so all the time, with a prequel to the *Star Trek* series, simply titled *Star Trek*, released theatrically in summer 2009, with its follow-up *Star Trek Into Darkness* launched in 2013). Maybe this is like the show's mantra of "to go where no one has gone before" because the cumulative weight of episodes and movies has led to a *Star Trek* franchise that is bigger than the sum of its parts and almost unique in the business. It is, in fact, an example of brand extension where the brand has outgrown its origin and taken on a life of its own. (It certainly seemed that way when I attended a Royal Premiere in London of a new *Star Trek* film starring the cast of the TV series *Star Trek: The Next Generation*, and an actress playing an alien doctor sat next to Prince Charles during the playing of "God Save the Queen." If this is not an example of the international reach of brand extension, then I don't know what is.)

Windows and Film Ultimates: Life-Cycle Management of Intellectual Property Assets

While the following discussion focuses on film, most original linear media has now found additional sales windows outside of its launch platform. TV shows are now released on DVD, downloaded, seen on cable, watched in syndication, and accessed online/via on-the-go devices. The ability to adapt linear video content to multiple viewing platforms—at different times and for differentiated prices—is the essence of the Ulin's Rule continuum, which allows distributors to maximize the lifetime value of a single piece of intellectual property. A property such as *Star Wars* or *Harry Potter* can generate revenues in the billions of dollars over time, taking advantage of multiple consumption opportunities that at once expand access to those who did not view the production initially and entice those who did watch to consume the show/film again and again. This unique sales cycle is the envy of games producers, who have still not innovated material downstream sales platforms, as well as the challenge of the day for how best to utilize the

Web. The following overview focuses on film, but highlights the key points of consumption that all media needs either to leverage, or compete with, depending on where one sits in the chain.

Film: Primary Distribution Windows

It is common to tie up the rights to a movie for five or more years shortly after it has been released in theaters, and, in cases, before the movie is even released. In some cases, movie rights may be committed for more than 10 years. Carving out exclusive shorter periods of exploitation ("windows") during these several years creates the time-sensitive individual business segments that form the continuum of film distribution.

Typically, a film will be launched with a bang in theaters, with the distributor investing heavily in marketing; the initial theatrical release engine then fuels downstream markets and revenues for years to come. After theatrical release, the film will be exclusively licensed for broadcast, viewing, or sale in a specified limited market for a defined length of time. The following are the primary windows and rights through which films have historically been distributed:

36

- theatrical
- video and DVD/Blu-ray
- pay television
- free television
- hotel/motel
- airline
- PPV/VOD
- non-theatrical
- cable and syndication

The above are the main distribution outlets, and do not represent the full reach of exploitation of the rights in a film. For example, rights to create video games and merchandising are not listed above, as they are labeled ancillary exploitations (see Chapter 8).

Film Revenue Cycle

The following depicts the historical film revenue cycle:

Theatrical → Hotel PPV → Home Video → Residential VOD

→ Pay TV → Free TV

The length of each of these windows and whether they are exclusive or have a period of nonexclusive overlap with other rights is relatively standard, but far from fixed. With the advent of new technologies and platforms, there have been more window shifts in the last few years than probably in the prior 25 (see below, including the sections "Shifting Windows" and "New and Changing Windows," regarding recent shifts and experiments in window patterns). Because intellectual property rights are, in theory, infinitely divisible, the crux of the economics is what layering will maximize the ultimate return on the property. Everyone in a segment is fearful of a different right cannibalizing its space, and accordingly the language of windows and distribution is all about holdbacks, exclusivity, and the term to exploit the rights. As a general rule, distribution is all about maximizing discrete periods of exclusivity. This is the heart of the clash with Internet opportunities, for the greatest successes of the Web tend to be tied to free and ubiquitous access.

The succeeding chapters will discuss the relevant windows in all of these categories, and the economic influences that have caused the windows to evolve into their jigsaw places in the pattern. As a brief overview here, the historical windows above can be summarized as follows (see also Figure 1.8 below regarding historical windows, and   **37** Figure 1.9 on page 41 regarding changing patterns.):

Theatrical: 1–3 months, with a holdback of 6 months to home video.
Hotel VOD/PPV: Short window, 2–3 months, prior to home video.
Home Video: Continuous window, with holdback of 6 months before pay TV and shorter holdback (1+ months) before residential VOD.

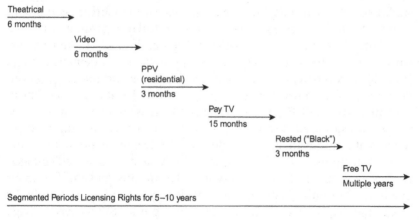

Figure 1.8 Historical Film Windows

Residential VOD: Historically, 3+ months post video, but given online pressures now often simultaneous with or 30 days post video.

Pay TV: 1–1.5 years, sometimes with multiple windows, between video and free TV, with an 18-month holdback to free TV. Often includes a "black" period following the pay window where the property cannot be exploited and is "rested."

Free TV: Multiple-year window, with length, holdbacks, and carve-outs for secondary pay windows deal-dependent, and also dependent on the type of free TV outlet (e.g., network versus cable versus syndication).

International Variations

In the United States, and in most countries, windows are negotiated between parties and freely movable—no laws could stop a producer from releasing a movie on DVD on the same date as its theatrical release. In fact, 2929 Productions has done just this and espouses this release strategy (see below). However, a few countries regulate windows to create order and to protect the local film industry.

France is the best-known example, and the windows for video, pay TV, and free TV exploitation relative to theatrical release are all set by law. Historically, pay TV was prohibited from broadcasting a picture prior to 18 months following its theatrical release in the territory, a movie could not be released on DVD prior to six months following the theatrical release, and there was a mandated three-year holdback from theatrical release to free TV. Accordingly, while an American studio that releases a hit movie in the middle of the summer will ensure that the DVD comes out for the fourth-quarter holiday gift-giving period domestically, the studio could not in parallel take advantage of the Christmas traffic in France. There is renewed debate in France today regarding windows, especially given the growth of video-on-demand. In 2011, French legislation imposed the same rules on subscription video-on-demand services (SVOD) with respect to investment requirements and quotas (e.g., on-demand services must devote 50 percent of their catalog to European content, and overall 35 percent to French films) as applied to pay services, yet as *Variety* noted, the windows do not match, thus putting these services at a disadvantage: "But although VOD sites share many of the same obligations as TV channels, they don't have the same advantages. For instance, the pay TV window is at 10 months and the free-to-air one is at 22 months. Subscription VOD is way behind at 36 months."[18] Over time, legislating windows that would put an SVOD service (e.g., Netflix)—which is effectively competing with pay channels (see Chapters

6 and 7)—at a distinct competitive disadvantage will inevitably be influenced by a fierce mix of economics and local politics.

Life Cycle and Ultimates

Assuming one entity controls all the distribution rights and has autonomy to set the property's exploitation, then the goal will be life-cycle management to maximize the return on the property through its various windows. This is obviously harder than it sounds; in big corporations, divisions often run autonomously and even compete with each other. Moreover, divisions and individuals who are compensated by quarterly or annual performance may be unwilling to look at the big picture if that means sacrificing their revenue for the sake of another division—especially if a current revenue stream is secure and other revenue streams are either speculative or still subject to performance. Would you jeopardize a bonus or meeting your department's financial goals to preserve a downstream upside for which neither you nor your department would directly financially benefit?

Accordingly, senior management needs to set priorities, boundaries, and rules governing the exploitation of windows. From a macro and accounting perspective, companies and owners of intellectual property assets need to project the revenue over this life cycle; the sum total amount expected through all relevant windows over a defined period (which period could be a planning cycle internally, or may be a specific defined length of time as required by accounting standards) is called the film's ultimate and, as discussed in the companion website to Chapter 10, is required for tax purposes in amortizing film costs and expenses.

Shifting Windows

Collapsed Windows and Protecting Windows

2929 Entertainment, the maverick entertainment company founded and run by billionaires Mark Cuban and Todd Wagner (formerly having started Broadcast.com and selling it to Yahoo!), has created a vertically integrated chain combining production financing (via its Magnolia Pictures), theatrical exhibition (by its Landmark Theatre chain), and TV (via its HD Net movie channel). They have backed various directors/producers, such as Steven Soderbergh and George Clooney, and have lobbied for "day-and-date" release across multiple distribution platforms, including video and theatrical. 2929 Entertainment's "triple bow" in movie theaters, cable, and DVD of Steven Soderbergh's *The Bubble* in

January 2006 was the first test, and proved little: "With grosses of some $72,000 from 32 theaters, most owned by Cuban and Wagner's Landmark Theatres, the results of the much-watched experiment showed that simultaneous release may be better at selling DVDs than movie tickets."[19]

Despite this first trial, Todd Wagner and others have publicly spotlighted the inefficiencies in the market, and in so doing made a number of interesting points. In particular, he has questioned: (1) Why would you want to spend marketing money twice, first to launch a movie theatrically and then for video—would it not be more efficient, and therefore profitable, to combine spending and release a video simultaneously? (2) Why should consumers who may not want to see a movie in theaters, or did not have the time to see it in theaters (as theatrical runs are becoming shorter and shorter), or could not afford to take the family to see it in the theater, have to wait six months to see it on video? Would it not be nice to be part of the water-cooler conversation while the film is in release and is topical?

Some of these arguments are sacrilegious to various industry segments, not to mention counter to the Ulin's Rule value matrix (especially regarding repeat consumption). Most theater owners predict the end to their business if they do not have a protected window, and a consumer could on the same day choose to buy a movie on PPV/VOD or rent it on video rather than seeing it in the theater. Perhaps the greatest power of windows is the marketing pitch "only available here," a message that is diluted, if not fully undermined, when exclusivity is lost; moreover, for a distributor, initial consumption must expand enough to offset the loss driven by collapsing repeat consumption windows (e.g., DVD), a proposition that is both risky and unproven. Nevertheless, with 2929 Entertainment's strategy, and general flux in historical windows with the advent of new technologies and shifting consumption (e.g., growth of residential and online VOD), an interesting experiment is being played out that, at its core, challenges the pillars on which the studio system is based.

New and Changing Windows

2929 Entertainment's strategy is not an isolated example: distributors are considering changing windows all the time (Figure 1.9 shows typical patterns). In early 2006, for example, Fox announced the introduction of a premium hi-def VOD window just 60 days after a film's theatrical release.[20] At around the same time, IFC Entertainment announced IFC in Theaters to debut select independent films via Comcast's On Demand service on the same day that the movies were theatrically released in cinemas.[21] IFC has since expanded its strategy, releasing

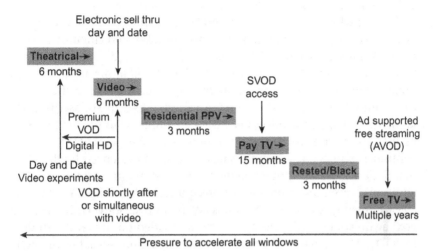

Windows in Flux

Figure 1.9 Changing Window Patterns

films on VOD and all other key platforms simultaneously with their theatrical release. The strategy pioneered by IFC and Magnolia created buzz in 2011 when the film *Margin Call* (starring Kevin Spacey) essentially doubled its U.S. box office ($5.3 million) with concurrent releases across key VOD cable services as well as Amazon and Netflix (VOD estimated at another $5 million), proving, at least in the indie-budget category, that VOD can be additive.[22] An earlier test that extended windowing challenges to the Internet realm was ClickStar's (a company backed by Intel and actor Morgan Freeman) attempt to pioneer the downloading of feature films. In part to combat Internet piracy and avoid illegal downloads of films, ClickStar announced plans to make its films simultaneously available for Internet download with theatrical release.[23] ClickStar experimented with a couple of broadband day-and-date releases, partnering with AOL, for example, to release *Lonely Hearts* (featuring an ensemble cast with stars such as John Travolta and James Gandolfini). The company did not succeed with the dual-release strategy, and rumors existed that theaters would not support the product given the windowing. Whether, in fact, windowing tussles were the prime causal factor (as opposed, for example, to the films themselves), the notion of on-demand Internet premieres, which may have seemed futuristic just a few years ago, is now not only feasible, but potentially poses one of the greatest threats to movie windows by any technology recently created. The question is no longer whether this can happen, but rather what is the appropriate window for Internet access.

As typified by the ClickStar example, quiet boycotts by competitive chains to Landmark's 2929 Entertainment releases, and cinemas refusing to book movies when DVD releases are accelerated too close to the theatrical premiere (as happened with Fox's *Night at the Museum* when major chains in the UK and Germany boycotted the film in the face of the planned DVD release in mid April after its Christmas theatrical launch),[24] changing windows is always a gamble, with the length of an exclusive theatrical run among the most sensitive elements. The trend continues, with VOD being the latest culprit, as evidenced by the 2011 Ben Stiller/Eddie Murphy comedy *Tower Heist*. In an effort to generate additional revenues in the face of precipitously shrinking DVD income (see Chapter 5), a number of studios (Warner Bros., Sony, Universal, and Fox) again strategized creating a "premium video-on-demand" window (PVOD). The concept of PVOD is to make a film available on VOD services (e.g., cable VOD) relatively soon after its theatrical release for a comparatively high price—the high pricing, on the one hand, being the premium charged for access well in advance of the customary VOD window, and, on the other hand, being somewhat of a disincentive ensuring that masses will not take advantage of the opportunity to undercut the theatrical window. In the case of *Tower Heist*, Universal planned to make the film available to certain of its affiliated Comcast cable subscribers for $59.99 three weeks after its theatrical release (i.e., at Thanksgiving, 2011, just shortly after the film's November 4, 2011 theatrical debut).[25] Even though portrayed only as an experiment, several U.S. chains, including Cinemark and National Amusements, openly expressed their intention to boycott the film if Universal followed through, which caused Universal to pull the plug on its test. Whether or not it played into that decision, it seemed ironic that the film's director, Bret Rattner, had earlier in the year signed an open letter sponsored by the National Association of Theatre Owners (NATO) criticizing early home video release of movies. The *LA Times* noted of the dust-up, "The move is an embarrassing reversal for Universal, which did not say when it would attempt another similar release. It is the latest development in a growing feud between studios and theater owners over the thorny issue of how soon movies should be made available to consumers at home after the films open in theatres."[26] Despite technological changes, the turf of windows, being the lifeblood of certain businesses, tends to be defended at all costs by those who are threatened.

What no one questions today, however, is that the increased variety of windows is creating more competition than ever before, and as a corollary leading to the compression of windows, acceleration of revenues (with most films now staying in theaters only a handful of weeks), and greater risk. Moreover, as discussed throughout this book, new technologies and distribution platforms are not only causing window juggling (e.g., on-demand access now not only via cable, but also on tablets and other Web-enabled devices), but threatening to undermine the entire window system and with it the fundamental economic underpinnings of the business.

Television: Channels Defined by Range and Quantity of Product Plus Reach and Specialization

Distribution is obviously very different in the TV arena, as a network or cable channel is the distribution channel itself rather than a conduit to decentralized points where consumers view a product (i.e., movie theaters). Accordingly, the question "what is a network?" has a more tangible answer than "what is a studio?" (and further falls more into the regulatory and legal area). Chapter 6 discusses this line in more detail, and for the purposes here I will limit the analysis to the parallel issues, such as range and differentiation of product and how segmentation plays out and even defines channels in the TV world. (Note: Here, I am focusing on the TV channel/network as a whole, and for the moment putting aside access to select TV content online and via VOD access through a growing array of on-the-go and other devices; again, see Chapters 6 and 7 for the changing TV landscape and what TV means in the new ecosystem.)

Defining Networks by Product, Reach, and Range of Budgets

Aside from the technical or legal definitions, networks, like studio entities, are defined by diversity, quantity, and reach. Marketing, scheduling, and affiliating a common trademark across the breadth of disparate content then help create a wraparound brand, leveraging goodwill to enable cross-promotion and awareness.

By diversity, I mean that programming, while specialized at times, caters to the overall audience and covers a broad spectrum: news, kids, sports, talk shows, dramas, sitcoms, etc. A channel could fulfill legal and regulatory (e.g., FCC) bells and whistles for carriage, time devoted to education, and other criteria, but the consumer base would not equate it with a "broadcast network" without the rhythm of a morning show, followed by daytime and kids, followed by news, followed by primetime, followed by late night . . . that defines the viewing public's day. In essence, networks are defined by their diversity rather than specialization, with specialization limited to style, feel, and demographic targeting.

If this description is accurate, it poses a challenge in translating the network brand to the Internet, where the linear rhythm and differentiated programming by time period fully disappear. In a VOD world, the brand becomes more a symbol of quality, the "network seal of approval," a filter from clutter. Even if one views the Web as the great equalizer—removing the power of the gatekeeper for those with time to select content via discovery—there are a lot of people who trust that gatekeeper to deliver programming true to a brand they trust.

In terms of reach, the footprint needs to capture a critical mass of households, which in network terms means national coverage. What is "national," and whether coverage needs to be via terrestrial over-the-air broadcast rather than via cable or satellite, are issues for legislative fodder. Finally, regarding quantity, consumers associate networks with unparalleled numbers of original programs, in essence putting them at the vanguard of entertainment (see Chapter 6 for detailed discussion of network hours, definition of reach, etc. and Chapter 7 regarding the increasing output of original content by online services putting them in more direct competition with networks/cable channels).

The point I am trying to make is that absent the formal definitions, networks and studios are remarkably similar. They stand out against independents or pretenders because they have an indisputable edge in terms of ability to reach viewers and in the quantity and diversity of product that they supply to viewers. Like the studios, the desire for hits and the cost of filling the pipeline rationally leads to diversification of product across budgets, genres, and suppliers. The same issue of brand creation versus brand extension applies, with the same economic forces driving the choices. Also, the desire to tie up talent and secure first looks at the hoped-for next hit shows is the same. Even the portfolio strategy defined by genre (e.g., comedy, drama, reality) is similar in the decision process.

What principally differs is how the genres are defined, how product specialization has uniquely evolved in the TV market, how product specialization and cable have come to drive niche channels, and how product distribution infrastructure is important, but not defining, in TV

Table 1.8 Film and Television Genres

Film/Motion Pictures	Television
Action	Morning
Romance	Daytime
Comedy	Soap
Thriller	Primetime
Drama	Kids
Historical or reality-based stories	News
Kids and family	Late night
Musical	Sports
Adult entertainment	Movies

(on this last point, the same forces that led to joint ventures internationally in theatrical and video generally did not exist in TV, given the limited points of sale).

Television Genres: Defined by Time Slots

Traditional television is now a 24/7 medium, and programming is primarily driven by ratings. Accordingly, product is developed to cater to the audience that is most likely to be watching during a specific period of the day—a driving force, and constraint, that is wholly absent in defining genres in the film world (and, as earlier noted, is also absent when accessing TV via VOD services, posing a novel challenge to the historical landscape).

45

In the left column in Table 1.8, I have listed the genres highlighted for motion pictures, and in the right column I have listed key genres for TV. It is actually quite interesting to see, side by side, two industries that are so closely aligned, and the difference in the driving categories for programming. Of course, this is an oversimplification, but the larger point holds true: traditional TV is mostly time-based, and each time segment has its own demographics and related ratings targets. (See Chapters 6 and 7 regarding changes to this historical positioning, and asking questions such as what TV means in a VOD world.)

Product Differentiation within Time Slots

Networks' product portfolio strategies therefore deal with setting lineups by days of the week. A station will rarely, for example, target all drama or all comedy and instead diversify its portfolio by targeted evenings. This is self-evident from simply looking over TV listings, where a viewer will pick out an evening of sitcoms (e.g., CBS programming *The Big Bang Theory* and *Two and a Half Men* back to back) or a pairing of favorite dramas.

Bundling like-type shows also allows a hit show to create a halo effect, providing a strong lead-in or lead-out for surrounding series (another factor eliminated in the new VOD construct). When a new show following a hit fails to retain a threshold percentage of its lead-in audience, then almost inevitably it will be in trouble, sending programmers scurrying to juggle time slots and better hold the audience (see Chapter 6).

Range of Budgets

Ratings and advertising dollars spent are the lifeblood of TV and ultimately determine budgets. As is obvious, space with less demand, and fewer eyeballs, necessitates lower budget content targeted at a smaller, often niche audience; in fact, outside of primetime hours, one of the great challenges of TV is how to fill up the rest of the space. A range of budgets is a natural outgrowth of time segmentation, and the only real issue is how elastic budgets are within already predefined budget ranges. A network may pay millions of dollars per half hour for a primetime show versus another primetime show with a modest budget, but both of these shows will fall within the same high-budget primetime category and be viewed independently from budgets for daytime fare.

Product Portfolio Strategy: Brand Extension versus Brand Creation

Brand Extension and Brand Creation

The same concept discussed above with respect to film applies to TV, but less frequently, or perhaps less overtly. While it is easy to list a series of books that are translated into movies, the same task is harder in TV. The trend is strong when it comes to classic kids' comics and properties (e.g., *Spider-Man*, *Batman*, *X-Men*), but far fewer adult series are spawned from books and other media.

Economically, it is not obvious why this is the case; TV could similarly benefit from a large launch bolstered by high pre-awareness of the subject. The reason therefore seems to lie more in the format, as TV, given its rigid time periods, is inherently more formulaic and less forgiving. A compelling series, with full story arc and punctuated cliffhangers, needs to be told in a repeatable pattern in 22 minutes (for a commercial half hour slot) or approximately 44 minutes (for an hour program).

Table 1.9 Sources of Top TV Shows and Movies

Top Films and Source	Top TV Shows and Source
The Avengers (comic)	*NCIS* (original)
The Dark Knight Rises (comic)	*CSI* (original)
The Hunger Games (book)	*The Office* (U.K. original, U.S. remake
The Hobbit: An Unexpected Journey (book)	*Survivor* (original)
The Twilight Saga: Breaking Dawn – Part 2 (book)	*American Idol* (original)

The quick pace of comedies with strong fanciful hyperbolic characters tends to lend itself to this structure, but generally novels do not. The books that do tend to be translated are those with strong characters in a genre that already works well on TV, such as a detective series. Robert Parker's private detective was successfully brought to TV in the series *Spenser: For Hire*—yet even it seems an exception in the category (and when exceptions are found, such as in the case of HBO's hit *Game of Thrones*, they tend to surface on Pay TV, which already caters to productions that are more akin to a miniseries in scale and scope). Most new TV series, and the vast majority of hits, are truly fresh properties that depend more on the associated creative talent (including the cast) than on an existing brand. Table 1.9 compares some of the top movies versus TV shows from 2012, and the difference is clear.

What serves as fodder for TV are new concepts to drive an old formula. The sitcom with the seemingly mismatched husband and wife, the new reality series, the hospital drama, the disease-of-the-week TV movie, the new cop show, the sexual tension (he or she never meets the right girl or guy) sitcom—these formulas work. Much to the disdain of TV critics that pine for something out of the mold, network TV is much more dependent on mining old formulas than mining brands.

Segmenting Driving Specialized Cable Channels

The ultimate portfolio strategy is not only to segment properties within a network, but have enough critical mass of product to further segment properties into specialty channels. The maturation of the cable market in the 1980s created additional shelf space, leading to a proliferation of specialty cable channels in the 1990s. By the year 2000, a U.S. market that 25 years before was defined by the big three networks (ABC, CBS, and NBC), plus public television and limited UHF local stations, had dedicated channels that few could have imagined (see Table 1.10).

Table 1.10 TV Channel Demographics/Specialities

Demographic/Specialty	Channel
Kids	Nickelodeon
	Noggin
	Cartoon Network
	Disney Channel
	ABC Family
	PBS Kids Sprout
General sports	ESPN, ESPN2
	Comcast Sports Net
	Fox Sports Net
Golf	Golf Channel
Weather	Weather Channel
Women	Lifetime
	Oxygen
Animals and nature; world wildlife and culture	Animal Planet
	Discovery Channel
	National Geographic Channel
News and finance	CNN
	CNN FN
	MSNBC
	Fox News Channel
Shopping	Home Shopping Network (HSN)
Food	Food Network
Travel	Travel Channel
Comedy	Comedy Central
Independent film/classics	Sundance Channel
	IFC
	AMC
Science fiction	Syfy Channel
Music related	MTV
	VH1
History	History Channel

I refer to the above channels as "channels" rather than networks, for they generally fail the diversity test and have a limited scope of original programming, even if national carriage satisfies reach and around-the-clock programming satisfies duration. At heart, these are genre-specific channels that program to limited demographics. Because the majority of the above channels are owned by their parent networks and studios, however, the individual channels can be seen as part of a portfolio strategy within large media groups.

In terms of influence, it had long been assumed that cable channels, because of their narrow focus, could not compete head-on with networks. That used to be true in terms of overall ratings, but within specific demographics the genre can overwhelm network clout. The kids' area is perhaps the strongest example. Nickelodeon and Cartoon Network, for example, have become such powerful brands that for years they have consistently beaten network ratings in key children's time slots. The force of 24/7 kids' shows and cartoons is, in fact, so strong that I have had network executives bemoan that they cannot compete—the cross-promotion opportunities and targeted marketing dollars are so large next to what a major over-the-air network can muster with only a few hours a week dedicated to the kids demographic that the network is often put in a position that it accepts second-class status and is fighting for incremental rather than leadership share.

Additionally, as further discussed in Chapter 6, cable networks are increasingly moving to develop original programming. Recent examples include dramas and comedies on F/X such as *Sons of Anarchy* and *It's Always Sunny in Philadelphia* (the network originally helping pioneer the space with *The Shield* and *Rescue Me*), as well as *The Closer, Leverage*, and *Franklin & Bash* on TNT, *Eureka* and *Ghost Hunters* on Syfy, *Psych, Royal Pains, White Collar*, and *Burn Notice* on USA, and *Mad Men, The Walking Dead*, and *Breaking Bad* on AMC. More frequently, these shows are drawing ratings directly competing with networks, especially in specific advertiser demographics, that can equal or surpass traditional network shows.

Television Windows and Life-Cycle Revenues

The concepts of windows and life-cycle revenues discussed above regarding film also apply to original television programming.

In terms of windows, TV series will have an exclusive run on a broadcaster and then may be licensed into several "aftermarkets." Additional markets include:

- cable—if launched on network or pay TV (e.g., *Sex and the City* on TNT post HBO);
- syndication—licensed market-by-local-market if enough episodes are available to strip; usually requires a minimum of 65 episodes (a new development is online syndication, either viewed by dispersed embedded players such as via Hulu, or to multiple sites);
- video—TV series are licensed by "seasons" for consumption on DVD/Blu-ray;
- download/Internet—TV series available for download on iTunes or Amazon, plus other services; and
- PPV/VOD—TV series available after initial broadcast, now for free, rental, or purchase, such as free-on-demand via Hulu, or via aggregators such as Amazon, Netflix, and Apple (additionally, apps such as HBO Go are enabling new permutations of on-the-go subscription video-on-demand viewing, though, as discussed in later chapters, VOD access now tends to be accelerated upfront and, as such, can be viewed both as a threat to earlier windows and a downstream second-bite opportunity).

50 Chapters 6 and 7 describe these windows in more detail.

Unlike the film revenue cycle, where windows are set in a fairly rigid and consistent time frame, windows for TV are more dependent on success and aggregating sufficient episodes for licensing into downstream markets. For example, if one assumes a hit series for which there are at least 65 episodes, a window pattern may appear as in the equation below.

TV broadcast → Residential VOD/PPV → Internet re-broadcast

→ Video release → Downloads → Syndication

These windows are shifting, with residential VOD (and now, though still in flux, PVOD), for example, accelerated, and new models for "catch up" tested on the Internet, including free Internet VOD (via streaming; again, see Chapters 6 and 7). Additionally, some services have tested allowing viewers to buy next week's episode early on a VOD basis; some broadcasters in Europe have experimented offering a "season pass," whereby a subscriber pays for the ability to watch all episodes of a series prior to their TV debut (with the restriction that the most one can skip ahead is to see the next new episode early); and Netflix is premiering its first original series, allowing subscribers simultaneous access to all episodes and thus enabling "binge viewing" (see also Chapter 7).

Are the Current Shifts in Windows Forewarning the Collapse of the Window Construct?

Given how the studios and networks have historically controlled the pipeline for product, both in terms of content creation and distribution, it is interesting to ponder whether current Internet-driven shifts in content creation will force similar shifts in distribution patterns. The open nature of the Web has led to a democratization of content such that virtually anyone can post anything. Will this inevitably force distribution to follow in such a way that we will eventually see a world without windows? I asked Blair Westlake, Corporate Vice President of Media and Entertainment Group for Microsoft, and former Universal Pictures senior executive, how he viewed this clash, as he has a unique perspective interacting among all the major studios and media players:

As we look back over the past several years, so much has changed, and yet, so little has changed.

By that I mean we have seen significant advances in technology, including broadband household penetration and speeds, albeit we are still far from the reach of broadband being on par with over-the-air television or cable/satellite/telco delivered video.

The proverbial "business model" is proving to be the single biggest challenge both content owners and distributors face.

Is it likely, or realistic, to believe that as more and more content is available to consumers—much of which will be at little to no cost for them—both wholesale and retail pricing/costs will remain status quo to those enjoyed in the "traditional" model?

Will advertising play a bigger role, as subscription fees, both those paid to channel owners by distributors, but also the fees consumers pay for cable/satellite/telco distributors?

What business models will take-hold and deliver the kind of revenue to all those in the food chain to continue to build delivery systems and create the quality content consumers have come to expect?

In the U.S., TV Everywhere, an initiative announced by Comcast and Time Warner in June 2009, was intended to give video subscribers access to all the content for which they are already paying, to see it on any device, not just their set-top box. A fantastic initiative that seemed to address so many issues, and yet one that has proven to be a slow rollout and have even slower consumer take-up. Recent reports show less than 20 percent of U.S. households even use it. One can speculate on the reasons, but one has to assume a significant factor in the relatively low adoption levels is changing viewing behavior and ever-expanding choice through means other than traditional distributors.

A world of "cord nevers"—young consumers who opt never to subscribe to cable—will have its own implications on business models.

Will we see the windows for motion pictures continue to shrink? Will channel bundles be broken into more manageable (i.e., cost) sizes? Will linear TV be pushed to the side and nearly all content be available on-demand? Will the DVR become the equivalent of the rotary dial phone? These are just some of the changes we may see.

Those who are prepared—and get ahead of the change—will prosper. Those digging in their heels determined to keep the status quo will be challenged.

We have all too often heard the "you don't want to be in the buggy whip business" metaphor as Henry Ford introduced the Model-T. The evolution of delivery and consumption of entertainment is changing exponentially.

(TV) Life Cycle and Ultimates

Life-cycle management is just as important with a TV series as with a film, because a successful TV series can run in repeats/syndication indefinitely. However, the "long tail" of syndication is giving way to the long tail of the Internet, with downward revenue pressures from more diverse and earlier exposure. Accordingly, planning is more complex in an area that was already challenging for planners that needed to estimate whether a show would even survive enough seasons to reach a critical episode threshold for syndication. In terms of ultimates, the same concept applies in that financial planners need to aggregate all potential revenue streams—a process that has also become much more complex with the release of TV series on DVD/Blu-ray and the new technology windows emerging (TV series VOD and downloads did not exist prior to 2006). How value is captured watching episodes via social networking sites such as Facebook soon promises to add yet another layer of modelling.

Internet and Other Digital Access Points

Throughout this book, I will discuss the impact of online and new digital exploitation avenues on traditional revenue streams—all of which goes into the calculus of ultimates and what value can be derived from an individual piece of content. Given the dynamic times and excitement around new platforms, delivery methods, points of access, and even new types of content, there is a tendency to hype new media/digital over the existing system. However, the evolution of "convergence" can only be understood in the context of grasping the nuances of how the current, finely honed systems of distribution work to maximize revenue potential. New digital and online-enabled opportunities are part of the overall fabric, and as certain platforms reach or move past their consumption peaks (e.g., DVD sales and revenues), distribution executives need to carefully balance what is incremental revenue, whether they risk trading higher margin for lower margin sales, and whether new media opportunities even hold the potential of being substitutional for the billions of dollars now seemingly at risk. I asked long-time TV veteran Hal Richardson, currently President of Paramount Worldwide Television Distribution, and former DreamWorks Head of Television Distribution, for his perspective on old versus new media, and he provided an excellent summary of the relative growth and maturation curves:

53

For the past 30 years, the two largest and most important ancillary revenue streams for motion picture distribution have been home entertainment (VHS cassettes and DVDs) and television (the licensing of movies to pay television and broadcast and/or basic cable networks). These distribution activities deliver tens of billions of dollars in revenue annually to motion picture producers and distributors. These distribution businesses are mature, and year-on-year revenue growth has begun to flatten with respect to television and decline significantly with respect to home entertainment. It can be argued the increased availability of motion pictures through digitally delivered alternatives may have accelerated the flattening of the growth curve for traditional ancillary distribution. Unfortunately, at least so far, the incremental additional revenue generated through new media distribution (download to own, DTO; electronic sell-through, EST; transactional video-on-demand, TVOD;

subscription video-on-demand, SVOD; and free video-on-demand, FVOD) has not provided increases in revenue at the same volume and velocity as revenue has decreased from shrinking DVD sales. In other words, the flattening of the growth in old media distribution is not being completely replaced by the incremental revenue generated by new media digital distribution. Video rental has been growing over the past few years, driven by Redbox and, to a lesser extent, Netflix, in the U.S., and transactional VOD revenue has been increasing, particularly from Internet-based services (iTunes, Amazon, and Vudu). Standalone SVOD operators (primarily Netflix and Amazon), delivering their services "over the top" (OTT) directly to consumers over the Internet rather than through cable or satellite distributors have begun to aggressively pursue motion picture licensing deals. However, some analysts have questioned Netflix's ability to sustain their current level of capital investment in content. The trick, which all distributors of motion pictures will need to master, is how to prudently manage the continuing maturation of traditional ancillary distribution while continuing to enfranchise the unquestioned potential inherent in digital distribution through new media; all within the context of continuing to grow the overall revenue generated by this continuingly evolving array of opportunities for consumers to enjoy motion pictures.

54

Online Impact

Given this interplay of old and new media, at the end of each chapter (excluding Chapter 7), I will summarize some of the key ways in which the Internet and new/digital media applications are influencing the area discussed. While challenging in this introductory overview chapter to distill select trends, I nevertheless want to highlight the following:

■ Online and other digital media applications, such as downloads and streaming VOD (including subscription video-on-demand access), are dramatically influencing and changing the historical windowing patterns of films and TV; this trend is being exacerbated by an expansion of on-the-go platforms (e.g., tablets and apps), enabling consumers portable flexibility to watch when and where they want.

■ The notion of what is a "network" is an intriguing question in the online space, as the trademark brands that are grounded in linear programming tailored to defined time periods struggle for relevancy in an inherently VOD environment.

■ Studios, whose strength is unparalleled distribution infrastructure and reach, are grappling with how to retain dominance in an online world, where infrastructure needs are now commoditized and minimized, and where a sole producer with a website can achieve equal reach.

■ The diversity of production and portfolio strategies that define studios and networks remain just as important in an online world, but the question remains whether online and new on-the-go outlets will prove an expansion of the portfolio or come to turn the whole system on its head.

■ Content distribution joint ventures, which were formed to defray costs in establishing global beachheads for distributing film, TV, and video, and then declined when international markets grew to the size of justifying control of local operations, are back in vogue in the online space. The breadth of content enables instant scale in branding new on-demand platforms (plus, a single access point affords the potential of global reach), though new joint ventures are apt over time to face similar challenges to those that led to the demise of most traditional market JVs (e.g., rivalries between partners once the particular JV market reaches maturity).

55

CHAPTER 2

Intellectual Property Assets Enabling Distribution

The Business of Creating, Marketing, and Protecting an Idea

More content from this chapter is available at
www.focalpress.com/9780240824239

The process of creating a property for production and sale, though often perceived as more fun than building a standard widget, is still very much a business proposition. Being an art, there are exceptions and patrons who may ignore the commercial aspects; however, the production business is predominantly a for-profit endeavor. This means business choices are made even at the root stages of creating content. (Note: For an interesting perspective on "art for art's sake" and the conflict between creative endeavors versus business, see Richard Caves's book *Creative Industries*.)

This chapter will explore some of the business choices surrounding the development process (e.g., What should be made and why? Can we sell it?), as well as address the business and art of marketing and selling an idea (aka, pitching). While nuances are different, the principles of selling creative ideas are no different than any other business. What differs are the risk factors, as captured famously by Oscar-winning screenwriter William Goldman's famous rule about the correlation between a developed idea and commercial success: "Nobody knows anything."[1]

Finally, it is the underlying nature of intellectual property that allows pieces of content to be divided and licensed in a myriad of ways, enabling the distribution side of the business. The essence of distribution is then figuring out how best to carve up and exploit rights (whether traditional or relating to new online and digital outlets) in a way that maximizes the return on the whole. Given that the parceling and licensing out of rights derives from the underlying intellectual property rights and rules governing their exploitation, it is important to understand some of the fundamentals of how the legal framework functions to authorize, foster, and protect a vibrant market for content.

The Development Process

In a sense, development and distribution are the bookends to exploiting media content. Development kicks off the cycle, and can be likened, in part, to product development. First, an idea or product is roughed out and analyzed. After beating up the idea a bit, a decision will be made to archive the idea or invest in a prototype. The prototype will be built, and likely go through a few iterations of refinement before testing. Finally, after testing and debugging the assembly line, the product will be marketed and shipped. Unfortunately, the analogy is far from perfect because a creative good is subject to infinite variance, and the outcome is largely unknown until the property is produced and then distributed for viewing.

57

Further underlying the challenge of development and the "nobody knows" principle is the concept of creative products as experience goods (see Chapter 3 for further discussion), such that an individual cannot truly know if he or she likes something until he or she consumes it. If you accept this proposition, then development and distribution may be less bookends than the blind leading the blind. This, I would argue, is where economic "what ifs" and reality clash, for there are no doubt methods to improve the odds: I digress a bit below into issues of pitching and marketing ideas, because methodology matters, I describe certain breaks with orthodoxy, because some have figured out a way to beat the supposed impossible system (e.g., Pixar), and I relate distribution, because it is stuck with optimizing the result in the face of waiting for the consumptive verdict on the experience good.

Development in Stages

With a creative business, the first stage of development is generating a range of ideas for projects. This could mean that a single individual originates concepts, or in the case of an organization, such as a network or studio, development executives take pitches from "creatives." Whatever the context, a variety of ideas will rise to the top, and there is a winnowing out of concepts until finalists are selected. Once there is a choice regarding which to pursue, the "development process" begins in earnest: an idea is taken from concept to script (the prototype). Once the script is written, it will need refinement, which can mean many drafts, and may even require fresh blood in the form of different writers (redesigning and refining the prototype). Once the script is ready, the similarities stop, because it just is not possible to test a script.

The TV industry has solved the problem with the concept of a pilot, which pushes the prototype concept out one step. Pilots are still risky and expensive, but clearly short of the full investment of a 13-or-more-episode commitment. There is no exact parallel in film, although executives try to review and test at relevant stages. Dailies and rough cuts are scrutinized, and decisions made to fix problems as soon as possible, even if that means reshooting; on occasion, directors will also utilize animatics to rough out the story (see further discussion in the section "Mock-Ups and Storyboards", page 67). Online is more akin to TV (and may in fact be TV of the future—see Chapters 6 and 7), and pilots can be created, although the medium is still evolving, and everyone is struggling to figure out what content works best and whether the medium is better adapted to testing content for other media (e.g., TV) or for creating new forms of self-sustaining online properties.

Development in the Context of Distribution

I talk about development for the same reason that William Goldman laments that writers are infrequently consulted or involved after tendering a script, even though it is their blueprint and nuance that grounds the project. The quandary is: Why do elements so inextricably interdependent become so separated in the production chain? It is a peculiar Hollywood (and perhaps, more generally, creative production) practice that first the executive producer, then the writer, then the director knows best; as the responsibility baton is passed, judgment and authority over the whole tend to be transferred, too, often disenfranchising a key guiding force. Perhaps this explains the passion over credits (and the need for public thank-yous), which, at a root level, ensures that each contribution continues to be valued. In the continuum of segmenting value (or input), distribution and marketing rarely have input at the development stage, even though each represents the beginning and end of the chain and is ultimately dependent upon one another. Is there a way to fix the chain, or is William Goldman correct that inherent in the creative process "nobody knows," and so no one is worse off from a system that may allow somewhat isolated inputs in an otherwise collaborative endeavor? Can it not be argued that this structure jeopardizes the whole while fostering a culture of plausible deniability by being able to blame the producer or "suits" on failure ("it was the product," "marketing screwed it up," "they didn't know how to handle it . . .")?

Vesting Control with the Director, and Pixar Breaking the Mold

Sometimes a radical break with orthodoxy can lead to success, and here, and later in the chapter, I will cite Pixar as an exception driving true innovation. I was honored to have Ed Catmull, president and cofounder of Pixar, speak at my Media and Entertainment class at the Haas School of Business (Berkeley), and asked him the straightforward question: What, if anything, does Pixar do differently that has led to the unbroken streak of hit after hit? After all, no one in the history of the motion picture business has a batting average anywhere near that of Pixar's, starting with *Toy Story* and continuing with virtually every film since. His answer was, at once, simple and earthshaking: Pixar, essentially green-lights people, not projects, and puts its faith in directors to come up with a story and see it through. In an article titled "How Pixar Fosters Collective Creativity" in the *Harvard Business Review*, Mr. Catmull punctuated this very point:

59

We believe the creative vision propelling each movie comes from one or two people and not from either corporate executives or a development department. Our philosophy is: You get great creative people, you bet big on them, you give them enormous leeway and support, and you provide them with an environment in which they can get honest feedback from everyone.[2]

Directors such as Brad Bird (*The Incredibles*), Andrew Stanton (*Finding Nemo*), or John Lasseter (*Toy Story*) will know the next picture is "theirs" and proceed with a mini-team to develop a handful of ideas from which one is chosen. Of course, there is debate over ideas, and the ability to beat up concepts and refine as a team, but Pixar's ability to build up a "creative brain trust" (as Catmull puts it) that can check egos and collaborate with brute honesty for the benefit of the whole is no doubt unique. Clearly, there are multiple factors at play, but one common thread rarely mentioned or given credence is the continuous link from concept to completion.

I always hear a similar theme from luminary directors such as George Lucas, a vocal proponent of protecting the director's vision, and he is, of course, right, as long as the director acts responsibly. The problem is that ceding too much control to a director without the ability to manage the budget has often been the bane of Hollywood. For those who want to read the ultimate business management disaster story, Steven Bach's classic *Final Cut* recounts how director Michael Cimino's *Heaven's Gate* (made following his multiple-Oscar-winning film *The Deer Hunter*) virtually brought down United Artists' studio (note the book's subtitle: *Art, Money and Ego in the Making of* Heaven's Gate, *the Film that Sank United Artists*).

Is There an Optimal Feedback Loop?

Coming back to distribution: Is it not possible to create a better relationship among distribution, marketing, and development than already exists, or innovate a new methodology, much as Pixar has achieved, at least on the development front? On the one hand, any creative executive will bristle at "suits" telling him or her what to do—often rightly so. But there is a difference between input and decision, and as long as the creative executives have final say, would it be productive for them to have input from those people responsible for selling what they plan to make? Would any other business decide to put a new product into production without direct feedback from the people responsible for bringing it to market? At some level, this is the filter that is supposed to be provided by studio heads, but they have their own predilections, and may have scant experience on the sales and marketing side. When I was CEO of the animation studio Wild Brain (producer of multiple TV series), I stayed relatively hands-off from the development meetings, but once a slate was recommended, I used to refer to myself as the "are you out of your mind" filter. The issue was: Am I the best person to fill that role, or is that a fair expectation for anyone?

There are, obviously, plenty of examples of trying to create a productive feedback loop, and the challenge is balancing the yin and yang of these different sources of studio power. I was fortunate enough to create a TV show that became a hit on Disney Channel, a preschool animated series called *Higglytown Heroes* (featured on Playhouse Disney). When Disney was evaluating the rough idea, and then after focus testing a trial, it involved a number of divisions, most notably merchandising. The question was: Could this lead to successful toys, etc.? As described in Chapter 8, merchandising can be a driver for production, and in the case of children's fare, particularly animated fare, this is often the case. Here is an example of the end-sellers becoming involved at the outset, so that the whole team is vested in success. However, is the tail wagging the dog here, and, as creative executives will argue, should merchandising and similar considerations be driving or diluting the creative, when an equal argument can be made that too much input such as this will homogenize creativity and doom a production? Not an easy call, but, again, I would argue that constructive input is always a good factor, as long as lines are drawn. It is the ability to balance such factors and make the correct call that is the art of surviving as a studio chief.

Is Online Different?

Development for original online media, while talked about as new, has been around for more than 15 years. Again, referring back to Wild Brain, in the late 1990s, the studio produced a range of online original animated series in Flash (Figure 2.1)—many of which premiered on Cartoon Network's online Web Premiere Toons.

The difference with online "series" then and now tends to be length, as Web-original series are often only a few minutes long, tailored to the surfing mentality of online viewers; although less a factor today, Web series running times were originally limited due to connectivity concerns and bandwidth costs for streaming.

61

Also similar today is the tendency to view shorter Web content as a live development test: successful series may be picked up as TV series, and the total development costs are relatively small, because a company can produce multiple Web series for less than the cost of a TV pilot. While there are instances of pickups, such as *Sophia's Diary* by the UK's Channel 5 from online and social networking site Bebo (developed for TV by Sony Pictures International TV), where the series had become an online sensation, this is still an infrequent exception, and most Internet fare is targeted and designed for a different viewing experience (and, in fact, *Sophia's Diary* subsequently returned for additional seasons to the Internet via Bebo). Time will tell whether convergence applies and Web series become a viable laboratory for traditional TV, but, at least to date, the success has been sparse. As discussed in Chapter 7, online leaders, including Netflix, Amazon, YouTube, and Hulu, are now all starting to branch out into original programming. With the stakes raised and such leading companies competing both with each other and traditional media (e.g., pay TV), it is likely longer-form and high-quality content will raise the online bar and lead to more TV-like programming, truly blurring the lines between Web and TV development and programming.

Another trend that is evolving is producing complementary second-screen programming, where original content tied to an ongoing television

Figure 2.1

series is developed to augment the brand and increase engagement. USA Networks, the leading basic cable network for original programming in the U.S., with hits ranging from *Burn Notice* to *Psych, White Collar* and *Suits*, has created a variety of online extensions of its series. One prime example is the hit series *Psych*, where the network produced a companion online piece, *Hashtag Killer*, helping to bridge seasons and provide a new form of lead-in to new season launches. (See also Chapter 9 regarding marketing and USA's Club Psych.) I asked Jesse Redniss, SVP Digital at USA Network, and responsible for the network's online initiatives, how the development process had changed given new opportunities tied to the second screen, and he noted:

A great deal has changed in the last six months to a year. We have seen a lot of success in our synched show experiences—*Hashtag Killer* and *Psych* was just such a colossal success, not just for the show, but for the network as a whole. That season, we launched *Hashtag Killer* leading into the season. We are trying two-screen participation on *Suits* and *NCIS*. Our development process now routinely includes meeting with our producers and writers to identify the shows that have the potential for that type of activity. We like to do everything, though, as a handcrafted opportunity—it's like creating batches of bourbon: every story is carefully crafted. It is really important that we don't homogenize our gamification and transmedia experiences. We want each experience to be a uniquely important story.

63

The ability to dovetail shorter-form online originals with successful series is, in part, enabled by the dual advantages of built-in branding (leveraging crossover marketing) and lower production costs. This helps distinguish experiments, such as USA has launched, versus simply using the Web as a lower-cost test bed—in fact, a pure lower-budget (i.e., lower investment risk) strategy may actually prove an impediment to shows being picked up on TV. This is because an inexpensive show without the budget to attract top talent may only be able to pull in limited revenues from nascent Web advertising. This, too, will evolve, with top directors and producers starting to test the Web experience. Marshall Herskovitz and Ed Zwick (*Thirtysomething*) produced *Quarterlife*, an original online series debuting on Myspace, which then was touted as the first high-profile U.S. Web series to make the jump to broadcast when it was picked up by NBC. After a disappointing launch, however, the show was quickly canceled.[3] Another high-profile early trial was ABC's *In the Motherhood*, starring Leah Remini (former star of *King of Queens*) and Jenny McCarthy (MTV), which, in March 2009, tried to make the leap from Web series to network sitcom. This online series, which was reputedly higher cost than typical Web fare, combined top talent with a Web-sponsorship angle, as the successful online series was backed by Unilever and Sprint and produced by WPP's entertainment affiliate, Mindshare Entertainment.[4] These advantages, though, failed to catapult the show to success on network. A variety of companies continue to seek programming that can bridge the online–TV channel divide: Comedy Central, in 2012, commissioned a couple of TV pilots, including a Will Ferrell-produced viral Web series, *Drunk History Across America*,[5] and *Tiny Apartment*, based on a Web series of the same name.[6] Additionally, Nickelodeon ordered 21 episodes of *Fred: The Show*, a short-form (11-minute episodes) live-action comedy focused on the Fred character made popular on YouTube.[7]

These types of experiments will continue, and Web series will, on occasion, cross over, but the struggle, in part, is symptomatic of the premise discussed above: the Web is a different medium, with its own viewership quirks. Producers, whether those starting with the Web or those with success in other media trying to adapt, are challenged when figuring out how to make an online original successful, let alone strike a chord that will create equal or greater success in the longer-form, linear, and largely formulaic outlet of television. While many are eager to point to crossover potential, and even discuss how transmedia storytelling can change how we conceive of programming, the fact is that Web series remain extraordinarily niche. It is not surprising that outlets such as Comedy Central are mining the Web for edgy content that complements its lineup, with an upside of breaking through; however, this still is relegated to experimental, despite the continued growth of Web viewing and the dramatic expansion of access points (e.g., tablets) over the last few years. Save for the recent foray into originals by online leaders such as Amazon, Netflix, YouTube, and Hulu (see Chapter 7), I had to search harder to find examples of Web-inspired TV pilots and shows in writing this revised edition than I did back in 2008.

What I believe could become a trend is creating online spin-offs from successful TV fare. In theory, if there is strong online marketing tied to a series, and networks such as USA Network are able to build a targeted community and communicate with registered users, then that community should be able to sustain original programming. I again turned to Jesse Redniss and asked whether he foresaw series migrating to online once network ratings diminished to the point that the show could not be sustained on-air, and yet there was still a strong enough community of viewers that could support the series in the less demanding and more niche world of online viewing. He agreed this was likely a future trend, and noted:

There is a lot of opportunity for this strategy to lead to spin-offs or even online versions of a show. We are already developing many secondary storylines around our shows. This past summer, we launched "Neal's Stash" (tied to *White Collar*). *Suits* has "Suits Recruits." *Covert Affairs* has "Sights Unseen." If we get to a point when a show is too cost-prohibitive to keep on the air but there is a model where we can keep it through digital distribution through other mediums, it is definitely a possibility we will move in that direction. *Arrested Development* is a great example of this already happening.

(Note: See also Chapters 6 and 7 discussing elements of the future of TV, including, for example, aggregators launching online originals and continuing series cancelled on-air, such as Netflix's production of a new season of *Arrested Development*, and Hulu's plans to bring back classic soap operas such as *All My Children*.) Whether looking at how networks view the online opportunity, or the broader scope of content coming from the sea of creators leveraging the Internet, what is undoubtedly clear is that the Web, which has a barrier to entry of virtually zero, fosters an extraordinary variety of creativity. With no gatekeepers, anyone can post just about anything. Moreover, in the flat world of the Internet, ideas can come from anywhere, and individuals can be influenced by trends and ideas in a virtual world. Great artistic movements have often dovetailed with the congregation of like-minded creators in a location, such as the art schools in Paris. Today, an individual interested in *X* no longer needs to travel to *Y* to be part of the *Z* movement, and can be tapped into ideas and influenced by a circle of friends who have never met in person. We are truly at ground zero of this new melting pot, which, in theory, should spur innovation.

A fascinating corollary to this unparalleled access to global peers and elimination of filters to express creative concepts is that the content can be critiqued by anyone, with a feedback loop of favorites, top picks, etc., rising to the top from online voting and metrics. Figure 2.2 shows a form of network effect, where popularity is driven from the masses in an inverted pyramid from the historical development process.

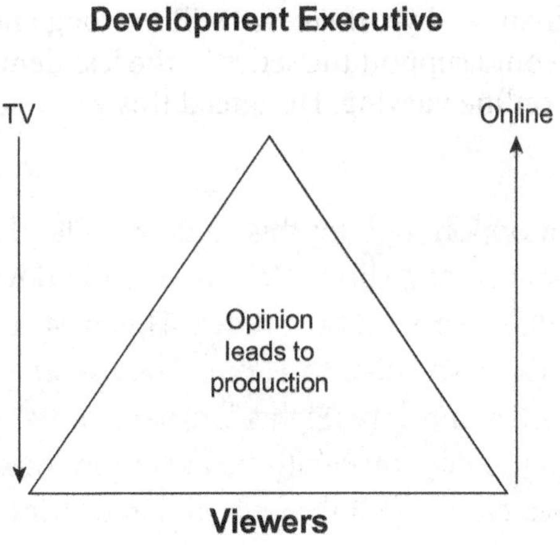

Development Executive

Figure 2.2 The Network Effect

Development Guidelines

When there is a filter, and "gatekeepers," there will typically be a series of questions asked in selecting an idea/concept to develop. What those questions are, however, is not formalized: no standard checklist exists, and unquestionably lots of executives go on their "gut." If that does not sound scary, it should. The companion website outlines a number of threshold questions (e.g., Is the idea sustainable, or "big enough"?) that illustrate the filtering process that film executives may employ, and an idea that can run this gauntlet will improve its odds of moving from concept to production. The companion website also addresses the related issue in selecting projects of market timing, where questions such as "Is the genre hot?" or "Is there a growing demographic?" are addressed.

Development Costs

Development costs money, both in terms of hard costs and labor. A typical development department would have the following line items in its budget:

- people/overhead
- fund for writers
- fund for acquisitions/options
- legal costs for negotiating deals
- travel and entertainment costs

- marketing costs
- rent, phones, and general office costs

More importantly, it is a department of all costs and no revenues— *development is a pure overhead category.*

The ratio of properties produced to those developed is never 1:1, and, in fact, the ratio can vary dramatically from company to company. A 5:1 or 10:1 ratio is not extraordinary, and it is easy to see how costs can mount up quickly. This is especially true once projects enter script stages, where screenwriters cost, at minimum, tens of thousands of dollars per draft, and often in the hundreds of thousands (even reaching sums in the millions with superstar writers). I have been involved with projects that were green-lit with development costs ranging from under $100,000 to several million, and no one was trying harder in one scenario versus another. In all cases, the unspoken focus remains on ROI, with higher development costs justified by the belief that certain "proven" talent will more likely lead to a project's success.

The development process requires many stars to align, including the clicking of the underlying creative, the satisfying of various egos and executives, and the luck of timing. Simply put, there is no magic formula. What most outsiders perceive as relatively easy, to insiders is recognized as a very difficult, often frustrating and time-consuming process. As Jim Morris, former president of Industrial Light & Magic and producer of Pixar's *Wall·E* (as well as general manager of Pixar Animation Studios) told me, "I've never met a director who was trying to make a bad movie."

Mock-Ups and Storyboards

In the quest to implement systems that reduce costs and risks, and stage phases before full production costs are committed, directors are always seeking new tools or systems. As noted previously, the concept of pilots tempers risk in TV, but there is no similar scheme in film production. Certain projects, though, and especially animated features, lend themselves to mock-ups. Detailed storyboards together with temporary voice tracks can be pieced together to gain a sense of timing and story—it is at this stage of "putting it up on reels" that the producer can gain a glimpse of whether the characters, humor, etc., are working as intended. Additionally, this can become a milestone after which approval of the more labor-intensive and expensive production phase of full animation and lighting a film may be green-lit. With technological advances, this process can now be computerized, and it is possible to construct an animatic for any type of film. While, on occasion, this may prove helpful with effects-intensive projects where, concepts are difficult to visualize, it is not utilized in most instances, given the dependence of live-action films on actors' performances.

Optioning Properties

An option has evolved as the standard means of acquiring film and television properties. Not unlike an option in other markets, an option in the media context represents an economic compromise, balancing issues of time, exclusivity, value, and uncertain conditions of moving a project forward.

Accepting the proposition that with books, comics, and life stories there is a limitless source of ideas for projects, the market has developed to value these ideas while putting constraints on the time an acquirer can take to turn the property into a film or TV show. The owner of a book, for example, may be thrilled that someone wants to turn it into a film, but also wants assurance that if he or she entrusts that process to a producer, he or she will deliver. What happens if the producer starts working on a script but the script does not progress as hoped for, or, worse, the producer (if not a studio or network) is unable to secure financing and distribution? Months or years can pass, so there needs to be a mechanism in place to dissolve the relationship and help find a new partner.

Efficiency of Options

Producers who develop properties are ultimately middlemen. They are an efficient source of developing content for studios and networks (and now online outlets) in that they scour the world for interesting ideas. Producers, together with agents who package creative talent and properties, then bring other talent into the mix, evolving and ultimately transforming the idea into a production; however, producers know that for every project produced, their office is littered with many more properties that died along the way or are in limbo. In essence, a producer acquires a property believing he or she can then add value to it and sell it to a third party who will distribute and finance the production (even if he or she contributes financing, he or she will ultimately need a broadcast or distribution partner). Because the odds are significantly against any optioned project actually making it to production, the producer acquiring the property wants to invest as little upfront in the option as possible.

The option market functions as efficiently as other option markets, governed by the simple principle of supply and demand. If a property is not famous and/or has limited exposure, few people are likely to be competing for the rights; the option price will be low, and, in cases, can even be zero. For a book by a well-known author who has had other properties successfully translated to film, the price can be in the millions. The elasticity of the price is then tempered by factoring in subjective elements such as: (1) Is there other value in the parties working together, such that it is worth lowering or raising a fee to close the deal? (2) Is there a strong belief that the party has a better chance of securing financing and distribution, therefore increasing the odds this project will make it to production? (3) Is there a synergy between the parties or related products or divisions?

Options effectively balance this time–money–uncertainty continuum by carving out a middle ground protecting both property creators and acquirers from respective downsides (predominantly, time on the creator side, and risked capital on the acquirer side). The option agreement also sets out a formal agreement for success, ensuring who has what rights and financial stake assuming the project moves forward to production and release or broadcast.

At a certain point, the option holder needs to make a commitment to buy or release the property. All option contracts have a "purchase price," and the option holder has the right to acquire defined rights in the property (usually all rights, including copyright ownership) by paying an agreed sum before the expiration of the option period. This is where real money is paid. While option payments are often in the low thousands of dollars, purchase prices tend to be in the hundreds of thousands or millions of dollars: this is the transfer of ownership. (See the companion website for a short overview of option contracts.)

Marketing Ideas (aka Pitching)

There are no set rules or formulas for pitching an idea, but there are certain conventional practices that seem to have evolved. This is ultimately not magic, but pure marketing. How do you grab someone else's attention, get him or her excited about an idea, and convince him or her that your idea is the one worthy of their time and investment?

Also, movies and television are consumed in a short period relative to the time it takes to read a book. Accordingly, at some level, they are formulaic to ensure that the audience has been sucked in and brought through a roller coaster of emotion within a short period of time. (The companion website delves into a bit more detail on the strategy of setting up pitches, who should make the pitch, and what materials may be appropriate.) In the next section, I will simply address the rhythm of how film story beats are crafted, and provide an example illustrating some of the threshold questions a development executive may need to navigate on the road to green-lighting a project.

Rhythm of the Story, Walk Me Through the Story

All films have what are referred to as "story beats," which are a very rough equivalent to acts in plays or musicals. They define the pace and the emotional arc that the story takes us through. In marketing a story, a good creative executive should be able to address the following items when explaining and trying to sell his concept.

What are the main story beats? The creative executive should try to make sure that a story has enough twists and turns and depth to satisfy the following type of hierarchy:

- Once upon a time . . .
- And every day . . .
- Until one day . . .
- And because of this . . .
- And because of that . . .
- Until finally . . .
- And ever since then . . .

What are the main plot points? Namely, what are the dramatic twists that change the direction of the story and/or character? Think about how many times you have seen a movie and things are going along fine until . . . someone dies, someone is attacked, someone is kidnapped, or something precious is stolen. Then, something needs to be found or someone saved or avenged—we are drawn into the story.

Toy Story as an Example

- *What is it about? In two or three sentences, whose story is it and what happens?*—It is a story about a boy's favorite toy, a cowboy doll named Woody (and all the toys are alive!). When Woody loses his leader-of-the-toys role and is abandoned in favor of the newfangled spaceman toy, Buzz Lightyear, Woody ousts Buzz. Woody ultimately redeems himself and reclaims his cherished position by leading the other toys to rescue Buzz from the jeopardy Woody has put him in.
- *Make me care: What is the lead character's goal?*—Woody is driven to make Andy (the boy) love him and be his favorite toy—Woody

wants to be left on Andy's pillow and taken on trips, not thrown in the closet to gather dust.

- *Who are the lead characters? What is the personality of the lead characters?*—Woody is a lovable jokester. Buzz Lightyear is a haughty, by-the-book Mountie in space gear who you know has a soft spot (because, after all, he is a toy).
- *What is the core conflict? Who is the villain, or who or what opposes the protagonist?*—Buzz Lightyear threatens Woody's position (stature, life, etc.)
- *What changes? How has the key character grown/transformed, what lessons have been learned, what are the consequences for the story's arc?*—Woody comes to like and respect Buzz, not view their relationships as a "me-against-him" contest for Andy's attention: there is room for both.
- *Who is it for? What is the target demographic?*—Kids of all ages.
- *What is the best analogy for the story? Is it like Superman meets . . .?*— (The more original, the harder it is to come up with something.)
- *Who would you cast? Who would make your perfect lead, friend, villain?*—It would be Tom Hanks as Woody and Tim Allen as Buzz Lightyear.
- *What is the setting? Where does it take place?*—It takes place in a stylized, animated version of an American suburb.
- *What is the tone and style? Is it a comedy, or is it action . . . is it a live-action mix?*—It is a comedy adventure, produced entirely in computer graphics animation.
- *Can you capture the spirit with a one-line premise?*—What if all your toys were alive?
- *What are the two (or more) driving plot points? What spins the audience around from Act I to Act II, and Act II to Act III?*

1. Buzz arrives on the scene, instantly upsetting Woody's world and security.
2. Buzz is put in jeopardy: left behind outside the house and needs to be rescued.
3. Woody to the rescue.

Protecting Content: Copyright, Piracy, and Related Issues

Ideas in their raw form are not protectable. It is only when they are committed to writing or a tangible form of expression that they transform from a thought or verbal description to a concrete expression of that idea that is afforded copyright protection. The following is not meant to be a legal primer, but a brief introduction to the main vehicles used to protect the expression of creative content. Most critically, by properly protecting an idea, one creates property, namely a piece of intellectual property—it is the development and exploitation of individual pieces of intellectual property around which the entire film and television business (and, by extension, online content business) is based.

Copyright

Copyrights are the primary and historical method by which intellectual property in the film and television business is protected. The idea of copyrights is rooted in the United States Constitution, which states: "The Congress shall have Power . . . To promote the Progress of Science and useful Arts, by securing for limited Times to Authors and Inventors the exclusive Right to their respective Writings and Discoveries."[8]

Copyright Law Basics

(Note: The following discussion tracks U.S. law, but global copyright laws mirror the same basic pattern.) The specific copyright law is contained in federal law, which covers both what can be copyrighted and what rights are granted by copyright. In terms of the "what," the law enumerates several categories of "works of authorship" and specifically includes "motion pictures and other audiovisual works"—a category that easily encompasses film, video, television, etc.[9]

In terms of the rights affixing to copyrighted works, the law then defines a bundle of exclusive rights that an author possesses by owning the copyright to his or her work. These rights include the right to copy, distribute, perform, and display works, together with the right to make derivative works (e.g. sequels); more importantly, these are the rights that enable the licensing and exploitation of movies and TV shows (all video-based content), and ground the distribution side of the business. As codified, the specific language of the law grants copyright owners the right:

1. to reproduce the copyrighted work in copies or phonorecords;
2. to prepare derivative works based upon the copyrighted work;
3. to distribute copies or phonorecords of the copyrighted work to the public by sale or other transfer or ownership, or by rental, lease, or lending;

---

4. in the case of literary, musical dramatic, and choreographic works, pantomimes, and motion pictures and other audiovisual works, to perform the copyrighted work publicly; and
5. in the case of literary, musical, dramatic, and choreographic works, pantomimes, and pictorial, graphic, or sculptural works, including the individual images of a motion picture or other audiovisual work, to display the copyrighted work publicly.[10]

There are, of course, nuances to the application of these general principles (e.g., international applications), but a detailed discussion of copyright law is far beyond the scope of this book; however, I do at least want to mention the doctrine of fair use. Basically, "fair use" is an exception category that expressly allows certain uses of a copyrighted work without the permission of the owner, including for criticism, news reporting, teaching, and research.[11] Moving from this high-level description to a practical set of rules is more complicated, as the law includes a set of factors by which fair use can be judged, such as how much of the work is used/copied in relation to the whole, and what is it being used for. A body of case law has evolved dealing with the enumerated factors and how they are to be balanced; nevertheless, it is easy to imagine the complications and arguments arising in the fair use context, and how case law has had to evolve to define mind-boggling permutations. Simply pose the question: What is news?

The final two points I want to highlight about copyright regard length of protection and divisibility of content. In terms of length, the duration of copyright protection has changed over time due to amendments in the act, with studios and other owners of key brands lobbying for extensions. An extension in 1998 was, at the time, jokingly referred to as the Mickey Mouse extension, due, in part, to vigorous lobbying efforts by Disney, which faced Mickey Mouse entering the public domain. (Note: U.S. copyright for movies is now generally for the life of the author plus 70 years, or in the case of corporate authorship, the earlier of 95 years after publication or 120 years after creation.) Perhaps the most important element of copyright ownership in terms of distribution is that intellectual property is divisible; namely, any or all of the exclusive rights vested in the copyright owner may be transferred or licensed separately. Hence, the licensing of various rights, such as rights for TV exhibition or online streaming, are grounded in copyright and enable the distinct licenses that embody the windowing of content. Moreover, it is the infinite permutations of licenses that create the different distribution rights discussed throughout this book.

73

Grant of Rights and Digital Complications

In the context of digital rights and new technology, it is interesting to note the evolution of the language "whether now known or hereafter devised," which is frequently used in a grant of rights. This language developed as a direct result of technology. Methods of exploitation continue to be invented that creators of content could not have envisioned when producing the original work. When David Lean made *Lawrence of Arabia*, the studio could never have anticipated that one day that film would not only be shown in theaters and possibly TV, but that it would be stored "in the cloud," and viewed on DVDs, over the Internet, and by digital file sharing. Inevitably, when a new delivery medium generates significant revenues, people will argue that this area was not covered by the original contract or grant of rights and is reserved. This argument was quite common when the videocassette market emerged. Accordingly, this catch-all language grew to protect against rights that the original owner might later claim were reserved, because the rights/market never existed at the time of the grant.

Nature of Copyright Allows Segmenting Distribution Rights—Licensing Content Rights is Complicated

Coming back to an earlier point, revenues are derived from multiple distribution streams (theaters, TV, video, merchandising, online, etc.), and it is the ownership of copyright and the nature of intellectual property that allows rights and revenues to be segmented and applied separately to each of those distribution streams. The copyright owner of a film could, in theory, parcel off each possible distribution right to a different party, creating one license for pay TV, one for free TV, one for film clips, one for a soundtrack album, and on and on. In fact, it is this divisibility that allows the interplay of factors outlined in Ulin's Rule, discussed in Chapter 1, where the value of a single asset is a function of maximizing value by balancing time, differential pricing options, exclusivity, and multiple platforms for repeat consumption.

Complicating the challenge of segmenting rights into bits are the dual factors that licenses can be bounded in multiple ways (e.g., exclusive versus nonexclusive, in perpetuity versus limited periods of time, worldwide versus in discrete territories), and that third parties often retain stakes in, or approvals over, the use of the content being licensed. While, at one level, there is an owner (who may or may not be the creator) and a consumer, between the two is a labyrinth of rights, inputs, and approvals. Licensing content is fundamentally complicated (see Figure 2.3).

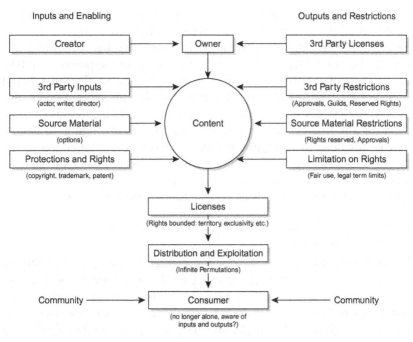

Figure 2.3 Licensing Content is Complicated

Copyright in the Digital Age—New Laws and Evolving Boundaries

The 1998 Digital Millennium Copyright Act (DMCA) represents a major overhaul of U.S. copyright law, and among its several provisions was an attempt to promote Internet access by insulating carriers from claims based upon content they helped transport but did not screen/review. An ISP or phone company would be reluctant to carry messages and content over its lines or network if it could be sued by someone based upon carried content. The section of the DMCA that provides for the limitation of liability—in fact, a bar on monetary damages—for copyright infringement (a "safe harbor") was thrust into the public spotlight by a $1 billion suit by Viacom against YouTube (see also the discussion in Chapter 7).

The practical application of the law has been to insulate service providers from liability from third-party postings on websites (which have recently grown exponentially with user-generated content, and social networking sites), and YouTube and others argue that as long as they are acting to "take down" infringing content when placed on notice, they should be able to avail themselves of the law's safe-harbor protections. In 2010, the court found in favor of YouTube, supporting this key tenet of the DMCA and ensuring that sites acting responsibly to take down content would be shielded from infringement lawsuits based upon content uploaded by third parties. Despite this ruling (which also upheld the DMCA underpinning an appeal in 2013)[12], many continue debating the line of what is fair use and what is infringing—a debate that is not new, as elements of this line have been challenged in the digital space before (e.g., in the context of peer-to-peer file-sharing services) and will likely persist so long as technology innovations enable quicker and easier methods to access content and blur lines.

Peer-to-Peer File Sharing, Piracy, and the Seminal Supreme Court Grokster Case

It is in the file-sharing space—first highlighted in the music industry by Napster, and then in the film space by Grokster, Morpheus, Kazaa, and other similar services—where peer-to-peer file-sharing services raised novel copyright issues. At stake was whether certain activities were non-infringing legitimate copyright activities or pirate activities that could result in damages or even criminal penalties.

Peer-to-peer networks allow disparate computer users to share electronic files of content. Peer-to-peer systems differ from other systems in that they are not funneled through a central server, but rather operate by sharing information directly between the different computers tapped into the system. If a popular file, such as a copy of a movie not yet publicly available, is on a computer, then others who are notified of the availability can start swapping bits to download and simultaneously share that file. The advantages are speed, as data is parceled out in bits, and cost, since there are no central bandwidth or server storage costs; in fact, it is the free access and remarkable efficiency of the systems that led them to grow so rapidly. Peer-to-peer networks and technology grew so fast that some articles estimated that upwards of one-third of all Internet traffic in 2006 utilized BitTorrent, a highly efficient peer-to-peer technology initially created by its whiz-kid founder as a publishing tool.

Anxious to avoid the chaos and downturn experienced in the music industry (which, to some extent can be bounded as the time between when Napster skyrocketed until Apple's iTunes offered a legal and compelling download alternative), the studios, acting through their trade organization, the Motion Picture Association of America (MPAA), were keen to resolve the legal landscape and prevent a Napster-type scenario in the film and video business. (Note: P2P and piracy issues are global concerns, and the MPAA works in concert with its sister arm, the Motion Picture Association (MPA), whose focus is international markets.) There was a sense of urgency, for, as broadband penetration continued to increase, there was a belief that it was simply a matter of time before compression and storage enabled larger video files to be downloaded quickly and easily. Fortunately for the film and TV business, a major U.S. Supreme Court case (Grokster—see below) clarified the field and curtailed the spread of illegal peer-to-peer video file sharing before some of the technology issues improved enough to enable simple mass-market adoption.

The seminal case addressing the peer-to-peer issue, supported by the MPAA, was *Metro-Goldwyn-Mayer v. Grokster, Ltd.* (popularly known as the Grokster case). A unanimous Supreme Court decision (June 2005) prohibited the Grokster service, and sent notice to peer-to-peer services that encouraged illegal downloads that they would be held accountable and shut down. The services could not argue that they were neutral bystanders while culpability rested with the actual users downloading files. Justice Souter, in delivering the opinion, summarized: "We hold that one who distributes a device with the object of promoting its use to infringe copyright, as shown by clear expression or other affirmative steps taken to foster infringement, is liable for the resulting acts of infringement by third parties."

The Grokster case also revisited elements of the famous Sony Betamax case, which enabled the videocassette industry and the upgraded technological iterations, including DVD, that followed. In Chapter 5, the landmark Supreme Court case of *Sony Corp of America v. Universal City Studios, Inc.* is discussed in the context of permitting home use copying via videocassette recorders (VCRs). The underlying issue in that case was whether Sony, a manufacturer of VCRs, was liable for infringement when VCR owners used their VCRs to tape copyrighted programs. The court held no, arguing that "time-shifting" (recording a program to view at a later time) was a fair and non-infringing use; in essence, the video industry was saved by the Supreme Court's reasoning that because a VCR was capable of "commercially significant non-infringing uses," Sony (i.e., the manufacturer) was not liable for copyright infringement.

This history is important because, in the Grokster case, the Supreme Court had to revisit elements of Sony to assess whether peer-to-peer copying represented a similar fair and non-infringing use. In finding in favor of the studios, it first set the moral or value equation, noting, "The more artistic protection is favored, the more technological innovation may be discouraged; the administration of copyright law is an exercise in managing the trade-off."[13] In a sense, it was an easy case because the facts showed "a purpose to cause and profit from third-party acts of copyright infringement";[14] in an opinion so politically charged, the court likely did not want to stray further than necessary, and in some ways took the easy path in relying on somewhat egregious facts tipping the scales in favor of defining the activities as infringement.

In so doing, however, the implications were clear and the path was set. The real world does not wait like law-school professors to argue the nuances: Grokster had lost, induced copyright violations via peer-to-peer file sharing were considered illegal, and services such as Grokster were henceforth branded pirates.

Wrinkles from Cloud Services, Remote Storage, and On-Demand Catch Up

For a brief period, the "Cablevision" case (*Cartoon Network et al. v. CSC Holdings, Inc. and Cablevision Sys. Corp.*) threatened to put a new spin on the Sony Betamax case when a U.S. District Court (Southern District of NY) ruled that there was a copyright violation in enabling DVR recordings via remote servers—in essence, the copyright owner's rights of exclusive reproduction and public performance rights would be violated by the process of ingestion buffer copies and server playback copies. Ultimately, the Second Circuit reversed the decision, holding that neither buffer copies (essentially transitory copies) nor the server copies (enabling consumers' playback/viewing) were directly infringing.[15] This was an important ruling in the digital sphere, for cloud and streaming services are dependent upon remote servers, which all involve elements of transitory storage—were it not for this outcome, services such as Amazon VOD and UltraViolet (discussed in Chapters 5 and 7) could have been undermined.

Another spin on storage and access arises from a Fox lawsuit against Dish Network for its serviced called AutoHop. The service automatically records the whole schedule of the four major U.S. broadcast networks, making the programming available to subscribers for a week afterwards, and further enables users to push a button to skip ads when taking advantage of catch-up viewing. Fox, in 2012 filings for an injunction, argued that Dish's actions amounted to "wholesale copying of Fox's copyrighted programming in order to offer its subscribers an on-demand library of commercial-free programs, in violation of copyright law and its contractual obligations."[16] At issue, in part, in the case was a new variant of whether the storage of content for later viewing was akin to the type of fair use that was sanctioned by the Sony Betamax case. These examples, and other similar cases that will no doubt arise as companies try to store and funnel content for on-demand applications, serve as a reminder of the struggle between content owners/distributors and those seeking to gain iterative rights to satiate the appetite of viewers craving evermore flexibility in viewing.

Beyond Sony and Grokster

The Web knows no geographic boundaries, and accordingly Grokster can be seen as merely a starting point in a global battle to curb Internet piracy. As discussed briefly below, and also touched on in Chapter 7, the MPAA and MPA work on enforcement and education worldwide, trying to defeat safe havens. This is a particularly challenging problem because a few individuals with powerful servers (e.g., capable of tracking which computers have downloaded file elements), can literally set up anywhere and cause significant damage from remote locations.

Technology Titans versus Hollywood

The focus of shutting down pirate bays/sites overseas has unexpectedly pitted Hollywood against technology leaders: the debate is now about Internet censorship versus Hollywood's legitimate concern about Internet piracy. House and Senate bills, including the Stop Online Piracy Act (SOPA), backed by Hollywood and the MPA, would have enabled the Justice Department to obtain court orders requiring U.S. Internet service provides (including search engines, ad networks, and payment processers) to block foreign websites linked to online piracy. In December 2011, cofounders of Google (Sergey Brin), PayPal (Elon Musk), Yahoo! (Jerry Yang), and eBay (Pierre Omidyar) joined with other Internet pioneers in signing "An Open Letter to Washington" (republished in several leading publications, including the *New York Times*, *Washington Post*, and *Wall Street Journal*), attacking the legislation and likening the chilling effect as allowing the U.S. government the power "to censor the Web using techniques similar to those used by China, Malaysia, and Iran."[17]

The backlash caused by the open letter snowballed into a series of online protests, including a coordinated effort on January 18, 2012 whereby thousands of sites, including Wikipedia (English language), shut down their services for a day in protest to raise awareness (Figure 2.4).

The actions effectively stopped the legislation in its tracks, and the SOPA bill was pulled and debate halted shortly afterwards. A few months later, the European Parliament overwhelmingly defeated the Anti-Counterfeiting Trade Agreement (ACTA), which called for Internet service providers to enforce copyrights. While sounding benign, echoing the themes that upended SOPA, those against argued that its passage would lead to a form of Internet police. Sounding similar alarms, and

79

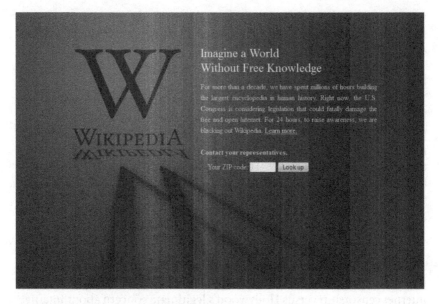

Figure 2.4 Wikipedia, January 18, 2012

politicizing the issue, opponents after the votes stood holding placards reading "Hello Democracy, Goodbye ACTA," with the *International Herald Tribune* publishing a symbolic photo of the lawmakers celebrating the defeat under a sub-headline reading "Internet Freedom Groups Rejoice in Victory as Media Firms Lament Vote.[18]

Beyond enforcement/piracy issues, permutations of content distribution in the digital realm continue to lead to new debates and novel issues. The next iteration of copyright debate arose not in the download/file-sharing medium, but in the area of digital access to streaming video on services such as YouTube (e.g., applying the DMCA's notice and takedown provisions to user postings of third-party copyrighted content, which had grown in scale, as highlighted by the earlier mentioned lawsuit filed by Viacom against YouTube/Google) and in access to programming in remote servers (e.g., the Cablevision case, with its implications for cloud-based services).

Streaming Live TV—the Threat of Enabling Cord-Cutting

Cord-cutting, the process by which viewers can gain access to TV programs over the Internet without subscribing to cable TV, is the essence of much of the over-the-top market (see Chapter 7), and an obvious fear for cable providers and over-the-air broadcasters whose channels are retransmitted via cable. A number of companies have experimented with how to grab free broadcast signals over the airwaves and make them accessible via the Web; however, when media mogul Barry Diller (who counts among his accomplishments the creation of the Fox network) invested in start-up Aereo, the networks took particular note and sued. Aereo provides users a tiny antenna that picks up broadcast signals, allowing them to gain access to channels over the Web—which the networks argue is rebroadcasting their programming without paying license fees. Although the argument is couched in these legal terms, the underlying concern is the economic loss, and, in describing the beef, the *Hollywood Reporter* noted: "The prospect of cord-cutting worries broadcasters who fear that since nobody is measuring those who watch Internet streams, ad buyers won't pay up for them without a verifiable ratings system."[19]

Because these systems also include DVR capability, arguments harken back to Sony. Aereo, playing the "we're just an extension of permitted technology" card, issued a statement to Venture Beat defending its position, and the legality of accessing over-the-air broadcast signals with an antenna and enabling an individual to make a recording for his or her personal use; interestingly, they went so far as to specifically cite the Cablevision case (which, as noted above, authorized the recording and playback of individual recordings via a remotely located DVR).[20] The stakes were then significantly raised when the U.S. Court of Appeals refused to shut down Aereo, and NewsCorp's COO Chase Carey proclaimed that if the courts continued to sanction Aereo's model, he would entertain taking the Fox Network off the air and converting the network to a paid channel: "This is not an ideal path we look to pursue, but we can't sit idly by and let an entity steal our signal. We will move to a subscription model if that's our only recourse."[21] The publicity ripple soon caused others to support the threat—Univision agreed with Carey, and CBS CEO Les Moonves announced he was considering disconnecting their freely available signal and opting for cable in areas where Aero was operating.[22] Given the overall attack networks feel they are under from OTT operators and other digital access means, it is not surprising that they will fight fiercely to preserve turf via the type of absolute boundaries that legal or regulatory lines can preserve. (See also Chapters 6 and 7 regarding the variety of threats that TV is under from OTT providers.) Cases such as those noted involving Aereo, AutoHop, Cablevision, and YouTube are continually setting new boundaries in the evolution of copyright law (and related communications/regulatory rules)—a process that is likely to be ongoing for years, with questions about display, access, storage, and copying all pushing the edge of legal doctrine that is struggling to keep pace with the changes enabled by new digital and online applications.

Trademarks

Trademarks complement copyright in the context of protecting a film or TV property: whereas copyright will protect the whole as well as fundamental elements, trademarks serve to protect elements of the property that identify the brand, and, in turn, can brand specific products that have distinct value as a result of the association with the brand. For example, the movie *Toy Story* is the subject of copyright protection, but the name of a key character (e.g., Buzz Lightyear) will be separately protected to brand a Buzz Lightyear action figure toy or a *Toy Story* T-shirt featuring a cast of characters. Trademarks are denoted by a word, name, or symbol that identifies the source of a good and differentiates it from another good; consumers are accustomed to seeing a *"™"* notice, indicating a property claim on the item. For a detailed discussion of trademarks, an easy reference guide can be found at the United States Patent and Trademark Office's website.[23]

Trademarks as Anchors of a Merchandising Program

Trademarks in the entertainment arena are very important when a property is used to sell commercial merchandise (see Chapter 8 for a discussion of merchandising). *Batman* action figures, Mickey Mouse T-shirts, *The Lord of the Rings* puzzles, and *Star Wars* toy lightsabers are all examples of merchandise where the product is branded by its association to the related film or film character. The trademark on the merchandise, in the form of a word, name, or symbol, indicates to the customer the source of that product.

(The companion website includes a brief discussion of the administration of a trademark program, together with a short overview of patents and their application in the production/distribution realm.)

Piracy and Fighting Illegal Copying and Downloads

Piracy is a fancy word for copyright theft, and historically piracy of content was limited to illegal copies of prints and tapes. Namely, antipiracy efforts were focused on stopping people from going into theaters and camcording a film to make copies, or from obtaining a copy

82

(legally or illegally) of a videocassette and replicating that copy without a license for additional sale. The digital age creates a plethora of new piracy categories, from making digital copies to sharing files. The MPAA and film studios mince no words about equating piracy with theft:

Movie pirates are thieves, plain and simple. Piracy is the unauthorized taking, copying, or use of copyrighted materials without permission. It is no different from stealing another person's shoes or stereo, except sometimes it can be a lot more damaging. Piracy is committed in many ways, including Internet piracy, copying and distribution of discs, broadcasts, and even public performances.[24]

Digital theft has grown so rapidly that MPAA member studios' losses from illegal downloads now rivals or likely exceeds bootlegged piracy losses. (Note: regarding scale, an MPAA study in 2006 found that of an overall estimated $6.1 billion loss to MPAA studios in 2005, $3.8 billion was from "hard-goods" piracy, such as illegally manufactured or copied DVDs, but that approximately $2.3 billion was lost to Internet piracy, such as illegal downloads.[25]) Quantifying the effect of piracy, either substantiating an amount of lost revenue in a sector or the overall impact on the economy, is extremely challenging, but, in the context of supporting SOPA, the MPA, in a press release, suggested a staggering number: "According to the Institute for Policy Innovation, more than $58 billion is lost to the U.S. economy annually due to content theft, including more than 373,000 lost American jobs, $16 billion in lost employees earnings, plus $3 billion in badly needed federal, state, and local governments' tax revenue."[25]

It is impossible to overstate the industry's concern over illegal downloading, hence the MPAA's stance in the Grokster case. When Warner Bros. released *The Dark Knight* (2008) despite robust advanced efforts to protect prints and keep the film from illegal streaming sites, media measurement firm BigChampagne, as cited in a *New York Times* article titled "New Wave of Pirates Plunders Hollywood," estimated that the movie had been illegally downloaded more than seven million times worldwide by the end of the year of release.[27] There is little doubt that established losses as a result of illegal downloads and streaming will in time, dwarf losses from "hard-goods" piracy (if, in fact, this has not already happened).

Among the most recent examples of taking down Internet pirate sites, and perhaps the most public case since those of Napster, Grokster, and Pirate Bay, is the shutting down of Megaupload and the criminal prosecution of its notorious founder Kim Schmitz (aka Kim Dotcom). Flaunting his wealth via online videos cavorting in yachts and private jets, and operating out of a 25,000-square foot mansion in New Zealand worth more than $20 million, some of the facts reported about Kim Dotcom and Megaupload include: (1) the site at its peak being the 13th most visited site on the Web, with upwards of 180 million users; (2) accumulating wealth of more than $200 million and earning more than $40 million in 2010 alone; and (3) causing, according to the racketeering and criminal copyright infringement complaint, in excess of $500 million in losses to copyright holders (including all of the six major Hollywood studios).[28] What is interesting about Megaupload (beyond the obvious) is that Kim Dotcom exploited the same technology that is disrupting traditional distribution. Megaupload encouraged people to "rip" digital copies of content and then upload them to its site; the company would then leverage cyber-lockers to distribute content to users for download, allowing a certain amount for free and then charging by tiers (e.g., $13 per month of $78 per year) as if it were a legitimate service. In essence, Megaupload utilized distributed servers and cloud service to solve storage and download issues, yet did not play on the same level playing field as other services enabling digital lockers (e.g., Amazon), which (as discussed in Chapters 5 and 7) are changing the nature of video rental, transactional video-on-demand, and on-the-go access; namely, they stole rather than licensed the content, and then unjustly profited from the exploitation. Some argue that the case may be challenging to prove because it is being pursued on criminal grounds rather than a civil action. Regardless, few question that the service enabled blatant copyright infringement, and the case and the profile of Megaupload evidences how the fight against piracy has had to move to new frontiers.

While Megaupload provides an example of mass-scale piracy, there are countless smaller operations where pirates defeat security systems (e.g., hacking smart cards, card-sharing servers) and offer services (e.g., free access to pay TV) and lower-cost subscriptions as if they were legitimate cable or pay providers. When cheap set-top boxes can download Internet streams (often utilizing software illegally designed to defeat security systems/encryption) and offer both legitimate and pirated content, it can be challenging to bring prosecutions—an issue that is especially troubling when mom-and-pop pirate services offer subscriptions to hundreds, thereby profiting handsomely but operating on a small enough scale that authorities often cannot devote resources to thwarting the newest culprit in a never-ending game of whack-a-mole.

Are There Innocent Infringers, or is All Piracy Bad?

When thinking about piracy, an interesting facet is that the pejorative term has become a catch-all for a variety of actually quite different behaviours—some of which could be aptly likened to innocent actions rather than criminal acts. Stuart Rosove, while VP Marketing for Irdeto (a global media distribution technology company that, among a variety of services, provides content security), described how Irdeto has developed an approach to help its customers, which looks at the spectrum by segmenting piracy into different baskets (see Figure 2.5):

Most people think of a pirate as a malicious ill-intentioned individual. In this evolving digital ecosystem, that's simply not the case anymore. The Piracy Continuum is a proprietary framework (trademarked and owned by Irdeto) that accurately describes the mechanics of the market and provides Irdeto customers a corporate governance perspective on the market, enabling them to better manage threats and capture opportunities. The continuum expresses the variety of "pirate types." Each one, in many ways, has intent to capture content, but each has very different motivations.

85

The existence of the continuum, coupled with increasingly sophisticated and professional looking pirate sites, is making combating the problem increasingly challenging. CommunicAsia, in discussing Irdeto's Piracy Continuum (Figure 2.5), noted in an article entitled "Some Pirates are More Equal than Others": "In many cases, the sites offering pirate content look fabulous and carry big-brand well-trusted advertising. Sometimes they even charge for access. So how's a person to know?"[29] (Note: As a disclaimer, during the writing of this second edition, I changed jobs and currently serve as general counsel of Irdeto.)

When pirate sites can attract perhaps innocent customers and charge for access to content they themselves have not legitimately/legally acquired, the stakes for fighting piracy take on an even greater sense of urgency—this is no longer an example of opportunity costs (how much revenues are lost to pirates), but a more quantifiable theft perpetrated

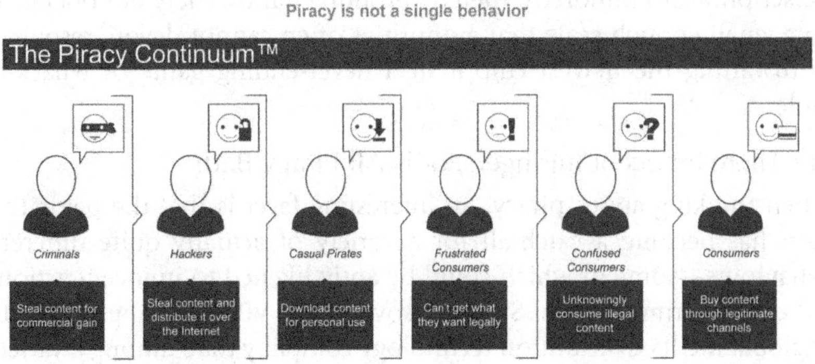

Figure 2.5 The Piracy Continuum

© Irdeto 2012; www.irdeto.com

by those so emboldened (e.g., Megaupload) that they have the chutzpah to charge subscription fees.

Fighting Piracy

86 The MPAA is the principal agent for fighting film piracy, and all of its member Hollywood studios contribute a percentage of film revenues to fund the organization generally. A sizable portion of the MPAA's budget is then specifically targeted toward bolstering copyright laws and funding global antipiracy efforts. Many of the MPAA's employees in its antipiracy efforts are former law enforcement officers who have experience planning raids and working with local, national, and international law enforcement agencies.

The MPAA fights piracy by employing a variety of tactics. In its own words, from the "Piracy and the Law" tab on its website, the organization notes that "it takes a multi-pronged approach to fighting piracy, including educating people about the consequences of piracy, supporting the prosecution of Internet thieves, assisting law enforcement authorities to root out pirate operations, and encouraging the development of new technologies (e.g., encryption) that foster legal Internet and digital media uses"[30] (see Figure 2.6). In a form of technology battling with technology, to counter piracy, studios and other content suppliers are employing a range of tactics beyond encryption, including embedding markers into product (e.g., watermarking), and requiring digital rights management (DRM) systems. (See Chapter 7 and the online supplement for a further discussion of DRM.) Additionally, altering windows to release product day-and-date is, at once, a market response to the reality of piracy, as well as an attempt to blunt its impact.

LIGHTS.
CAMERA.
BUSTED.

Figure 2.6 The MPAA Fights Piracy
Reproduced by the permission of the Motion Picture Association of America

As noted above, the losses incurred from quantifiable piracy are staggering, and are made that much worse when factoring in opportunity costs from markets that have either not matured or are simply unavailable due to piracy factors. Most of the video market in China and Russia is lost to piracy. Given that these are among the fastest-growing major economies in the world, and present some of the greatest upside for growth to the Hollywood studios and networks, the efforts to fight piracy there are among the highest-priority items of the MPA. China and Russia have begun to mature on the theatrical side, with both countries posting some of the largest market gains for box office revenue in the world (see Chapter 4); video and TV, however, continue to lag behind, especially in China, elevating intellectual property and piracy to key issues in trade negotiations at the political/government level.

How to turn a pirate market into a legitimate market is obviously a tricky equation. To succeed against legitimate distribution, pirate prices need to be lower—the essence of piracy is earlier, or at least simultaneous, access and lower prices. Lower prices, though, mean lower margins, not to mention limited distribution to the extent major retail channels enforce stocking legitimate product. If you can show pirates a way to improve distribution and increase margins as a simple business proposition, they will start seeing that working with the rights owners will yield more money. Like a diplomat talking to the enemy, product suppliers sometimes need to work with pirates to help convert them. This is what started happening in select markets, with key suppliers first accelerating windows to start competing with pirates (starting to erode their market share) and then working with the "pirates" to establish new and higher sustainable price points. Through this process, markets can start to evolve legitimate distribution.

Of course, diplomacy only goes so far, and the surest way to stop piracy is via legal enforcement. In the digital sphere, this is a never-ending battle, pitting content creators and distributors, through trade organizations such as the MPAA, against pirate sites such as Megaupload. Because the scale of the battle is global, and pirates can literally operate from servers based anywhere, the challenges are enormous, and local government cooperation is necessary to shut down even the most egregious offenders. Although many countries may have laws on the books that seem tough, those laws are only as good as the willingness of local authorities to enforce them. When those vested with defending the value of content then work to support laws with a stated goal of making it easier to thwart pirates and bolster copyright protection find themselves rebuffed—such as occurred with the SOPA and ACTA legislation—it strikes a nerve. Approaching the issue with a mentality of "How could anyone be against this?" it seems almost unfathomable that legislation inherently designed to prevent theft can be struck down in the name of democracy. This is a stark example of complications arising from media distribution over the Internet, and how a gulf has opened in a matter where parties should, in theory, be natural allies. Google, as discussed in Chapter 7, is investing heavily in original content and channels via YouTube, and in no manner endorses copyright theft. Content producers and distributers alike understand that legitimate distribution and the prevention of piracy is the bulwark that preserves content value—without protecting the ecosystem, key drivers in Ulin's Rule fall apart. How to reconcile this agreed principle (piracy is bad) with the utopian promise of an open net (net neutrality) is simply proving to be more politically challenging than anyone in the media business ever imagined.

I asked Kasia Lasota Heller, current chair of European Digital Media Association (EdiMA), an organization focused on the digital industry,[31] how she saw the sides coming together in the future:

> In her opinion, the recent battles and disagreements here are not about the protection of copyright, but have more to do with the relationship between generations. The older generation is used to waiting patiently for content to be accessible in the traditional sequence: cinema, rental, pay TV, and public TV, and the current system of distribution offers access to content according to a schedule of distributors. The younger generation, on the other hand, wants to benefit from the digital technology that makes it possible to access desired content whenever and wherever a user wishes to, namely as soon as a work has been created, and on a medium of the user's choice. Kasia firmly believes that a step in the right direction in the fight against piracy would be to make it possible for users to access the desired content according to the users' wishes in terms of timing, medium, and payment method. If stakeholders fail to start down that path, it will be to the detriment of consumers, and piracy is unlikely to decrease.

This issue is further discussed in Chapter 6, in which I suggest that the Hobson's choice of accepting piracy or succumbing to the preferences of consumers to have content earlier (and via sources they choose) can be akin to window blackmail if viewed on a by-distributor basis. Should HBO have to offer its next hit to those without a cable subscription, or else be subject to piracy? Forbes suggests just this, and even states that when looking at rampant piracy of *Game of Thrones* in the face of overwhelming demand, HBO only has itself to blame for not making it easily available on alternative platforms such as Netflix.[32] Perhaps piracy, markets, and a generational clash will ultimately force distributors' hands, but delay in access (i.e, windows) is not a plot to tease would-be viewers, nor an invitation to piracy; rather, as described throughout this book, windowing is a tried-and-true and arguably optimized system that is crucial to how content is monetized and, as a corollary, financed. Is granting a company who has invested $100 million in a movie (or millions of dollars in TV episodes) the right to decide where, when, and how to offer that content to customers somehow wrong, or indeed trumped by those who feel they are entitled to that content earlier, for less, or even for free? Unfortunately, beliefs of entitlement on both sides have created a stalemate between factions that need each other to achieve their goals—thus becoming a classic political dilemma, frustrating younger consumers and leaving producers and distributors to scratch their heads.

Online Impact

- The lower cost to produce original online content has led to the use of the Web for online pilots; these pilots can be tested both for Web use and potential crossover to television.
- Online is the fastest growing area of piracy. This has created industry action to contain peer-to-peer file-sharing services enabling the illegal copying of content; efforts to thwart digital piracy have also led to tagging content in new ways (e.g., watermarks), accelerating breadth and timing of releases, and putting focus on DRM and encryption technologies. Laws designed to help stop piracy and enable the legitimate distribution of content, though, have run into unexpected roadblocks from those espousing net neutrality—fearing the slippery slope of Internet police or censorship, even at the expense of stopping clear pirates.
- The Web is enabling increased risk-taking, as less is at stake given lower entry costs in online programming; the net result is lower and fewer barriers to entry and the democratization of content.
- There is an increased pool of creativity from the flat world and global Internet access: development no longer needs to be local; an artist need not go to an enclave to network, interact, and absorb trends; anyone can receive feedback from anywhere (the next hit could come from a kid in New Delhi as easily as from Hollywood).
- The Web provides an instant feedback loop: voting for "best" creates a pyramid effect, forcing up and validating favored content via a type of instant network effect.
- The evolution of the Internet is pushing the boundaries of copyright laws, with new digital applications continuously creating novel issues (e.g., mini-antennas redistributing broadcast signals over the Web, legality of copying elements in remote cloud servers).

CHAPTER 3

Financing Production
Studios and Networks as Venture Capitalists

Overview

This chapter will discuss how film and television projects are financed, **91** including how the money is raised and secured and what piece of the pie parties retain for their investment. I will argue that, to a large degree, Hollywood studios are simply specialized venture capitalists with the return on investment (ROI) strategy premised on limited but large bets. The discussion of traditional film and TV financing is in stark contrast to original Internet production, which today remains heavily dependent on venture capital or other private backing, given the nascent (though growing) video advertising market and speculative returns; with the advent of online leaders moving into original production (see Chapter 7), though, these differences are likely to narrow, and, on the assumption that online "networks" such as Netflix find success and compete more directly with traditional TV channels, then inevitably there will be a measure of convergence.

Standard Hollywood movies have become extraordinarily expensive: the average cost of a studio-released film is now roughly $70 million, and when then adding marketing and distribution costs, the sunk cost per project typically exceeds $100 million[1] (see Table 9.5 in Chapter 9). Moreover, all studios have a certain number of event or "tentpole" pictures per year whose total production and marketing costs will be well in excess of $100 million. In fact, as highlighted in Chapter 1, certain pictures can even have budgets exceeding $200 million. In 2005, Universal's *King Kong*, directed by Peter Jackson, was reported to have a budget of $207 million.[2] In 2006, *Variety* reported *Superman Returns* from Warner Bros. passed $200 million as well. By 2007, multiple pictures (e.g., *Spider-Man 3*, *Pirates of the Caribbean: At World's End*) were reputedly cresting this mark.[3] By 2012, exceeding the $200 million mark was no longer unusual, with the following movies all reputed to be in this range: *John Carter*, *The Dark Knight Rises*, *The Avengers*, *Battleship*, *The Amazing Spider-Man*, and *Men in Black 3*.[4] Perhaps this level, though, represents the limit that studios can bear (especially with declining DVD revenues), for even *Avatar* was reputed to cost in the $230 million range (though, when combining marketing, the total production and marketing costs were estimated at more than $380 million).[5]

TV financing costs are tempered by the ability to stage commitments (e.g., pilot, episode commitment by season), and while the risks are therefore smaller, the numbers for network shows and movie-like pay TV series (e.g., *The Sopranos*, *Rome*, *Game of Thrones*) can nevertheless be in the tens of millions across a season.

Principal Methods of Financing Films

As with any other business, there are innumerable ways of financing the production and release of a film. The following is a snapshot of the most common financing schemes, with each category discussed in detail later in this chapter.

The first, and perhaps oldest, method to fund production is via studio financing, where a major studio simply foots the bill itself. Even when a studio pays, however, there are often issues about how it raises the money and whether it reduces the risk by syndicating a portion of the financing or selling off parts. A second form of financing involves schemes pursuant to which independent producers secure capital either to co-finance or fully fund a picture; this can involve bank financing, pre-sales, completion bonds, negative pickup structures, and complicated debt and equity slate financings.

Another scenario employed by independent producers, though limited to a subset of extremely wealthy and powerful producers (and, as a corollary, successful), is simply to shoulder all the risk and self-finance pictures. This is the scenario sometimes referred to as a distribution rental model, such as the deal between Lucasfilm and Fox for the *Star Wars* prequels (*The Phantom Menace*, *Attack of the Clones*, and *Revenge of the Sith*), the much-speculated-about deal between Pixar and Disney (before Disney acquired Pixar in 2006), and allegedly, DreamWorks' relationship with Disney.

Finally, in an apt analogy to the venture capital world, productions can sometimes have "angel" financing, where a wealthy third-party entity or individual may simply underwrite a production. This was the case with Robert Zemeckis' *Polar Express*, which, as discussed in more detail later, was significantly underwritten by real estate mogul Steve Bing.

A level of complexity is introduced in most financings because the structure is rarely a pure form of the methods previously described. Coproductions, for example, are a common vehicle to share risk, and can take place within any one of the structures; moreover, the term coproduction itself is much ballyhooed and little understood. It can mean anything from a sharing of rights to a legal structure tied to formal government subsidies and tax schemes.

Principal Methods of Financing Online Production

There is not much to summarize in this area because there are no well-developed models in the online space akin to film and TV. Today, the principal method of financing online production is to secure funding from friends and family or venture capitalists (VCs) willing to advance funds against a stake in the website/production company. Very few companies are breaking even in this space, and the VCs are frequently betting on building up sites and "mini-channels" rather than focusing on funding a specific individual piece of content. Sites such as funny ordie.com (Will Ferrell and Sequoia Capital-backed) and comedy.com (Dean Valentine, former Prexy UPN) are seemingly content aggregation plays that likely rest on the strategy that the brand/site will be worth more than the sum of its parts. Accordingly, we can surmise that the goal, as with all VC-type investments, is an IPO or sale based on future multiples rather than value based on a piece of content's current cash flow. The online space is better understood if one views the space as a clear playing field in which entrepreneurs are launching hundreds of new networks, each vying for reach and brand adoption.

Another strategy—though less popular today than a few years ago, which speaks volumes in itself regarding what networks think about the threat to their series from short-form originals—is for the larger media groups to fund online sister divisions, attempting to incubate new content that may create crossover synergies, as well as developing self-sustaining niche channels and hits. Funding for shows in affiliated divisions is advanced by the larger company and then recouped by revenues garnered through advertising, sponsorships, and product

93

placements (see also Chapter 9 for a discussion of product placements versus promotional partners).

It is product placements, though, that appear to be the most sought-after method to, in part, finance shows and mitigate risk. Often credited as helping to launch the trend, UK site Bebo's *Kate Modern*, for example, secured upfront funding via embedded product placements (e.g., character wears a particular shoe brand) and sponsorships; sponsors included Microsoft, Procter & Gamble, Warner Music, Paramount, and Orange. The UK's *Guardian* reported that these sponsors each paid up to £250,000 for placement in the show, with each sponsor paying "... based on the amount its brand is integrated into the storyline, which includes monitoring the number of times it appears in the video and is mentioned in the script."[6] More recently, the original Web series *Dating Rules* (Figure 3.1) integrated products from Ford (Ford Escape car) and Schick (Quattro razor for women) into its second season, which debuted on Hulu in August 2012 (after a successful launch of the six- to eight-minute episodic web series at the beginning of January 2012).

While product placements can be lucrative, the downsides are the risk of dating the show (as a brand may change or be phased out over time), the challenge of compromising the creative to integrate the brand, and the need to lock the advertising far in advance, given production timelines. Moreover, rather than being innovative, the focus on product

94

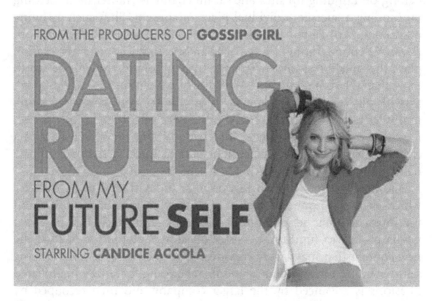

Figure 3.1

placements smacks of back-to-the-future thinking, as it was "soaps" that backed TV in the early days; if the analogy holds true, then product placements should give way to more traditional forms of advertising as the market matures (which is now happening, albeit more slowly than many predicted).

Not only are traditional "commercials" becoming commonplace online, with video advertising commanding significantly higher CPMs than display ads (and the very presence of these ads making online programming feel more akin to traditional TV) but, for the first time, a landscape exists where original programming can garner direct advertising revenues with the potential of covering production costs— although with a still immature market for online originals, and big players willing to deficit fund productions to bolster and differentiate their brand value, generally only a fraction of the costs are today being recouped (and why even major players are employing hedged strategies as they dip their toes into the challenge of producing and monetizing original programming). As video ads become accepted, and views are expanded by syndicating content offsite to capture more eyeballs (i.e., producers do not care if you watch the show on their site or Hulu, as long as they capture a material share of video ad revenues wherever you watch), then online revenues will increase and the overall experience/business will come to parallel traditional TV. As discussed in Chapter 7, this is already starting to occur, with Hulu, Netflix, Amazon, and YouTube all launching original production, and trying to siphon off advertising dollars from traditional TV via "digital upfronts." The question will be, then, one of ratings, with metrics tied to views, impressions, and engagement (e.g., click-throughs, text messages) versus ratings points, and the strength of content setting market prices for CPM rates.

Currently, however, there appears to be a disconnect between CPM rates for TV and online, with content owners often claiming premium content is undervalued online, while online networks, in contrast, assert that the same content is priced at a premium to offline media. Although this should be a simple comparison, in fact the two positions are difficult to reconcile because the rates are priced independently and each has different advantages and disadvantages. In the case of offline, the "live" effect of programming and its scale in simultaneously reaching a mass audience commands a premium despite the relative inefficiency of targeting a diffuse (even if generally demographically targeted) audience without direct online-like metrics to track delivery. With online, the advertising can focus delivery and virtually track one-to-one relationships that should command a premium; however, online content's value is diluted relative to offline because the same scale of mass delivery is only reached (if at all) in fragmented impressions over a long period of time (e.g., 10 million people may be reached over a week or month, rather than simultaneously). Accordingly, valuing what advertising rates should be when similar (if not identical) content is delivered online via free streaming versus the rate for free television delivery is not as straight-forward as it may appear.

Arguably, as referenced in Chapter 6, online is more comparable in delivery to TV syndication, and, over time, some convergence in valu-ation between these markets may emerge. Even then, the parallels are not exact, in that TV syndication tends to be focused on local pricing (as advertising may be sold market by market), while online syndication of premium content on the Web is not only local, but potentially global. In the end, to some degree the analogy between the experiences (which are not identical) is like comparing apples and oranges, while recog-nizing there are strong correlations (both fruits, both healthy), as well as differentiating nuances (green and red apples, mandarin oranges). With all these moving parts, it is not surprising that producers of original online content struggle to build monetization models against budgets and initially launched shows with the relative certainty of sponsorships driven by product placements.

When writing my first edition, I asked Jayant Kadambi, founder and CEO of YuMe networks, one of the top online advertising platforms and networks, and a leader in the video advertising space, whether he thought we would soon see convergence between online and offline pricing, or whether the markets would continue to set rates independently. He advised:

Providing a comparison or correlation between online media spending and offline media spending will only help increase the scale, reach, and breadth of online advertising. If an offline advertiser spends $100,000 to reach an audience and receives a GRP of 52, then the natural question before the advertiser spends $100,000 online is: What is the GRP equivalent? Think about purchasing an apple in the U.S. for $1. Intuitively, we know whether that is expensive or not. If we spend 400 drachma for an apple in Greece, the immediate reaction is to convert back to USD to see if it is expensive. So, whether there is convergence in the pricing, models between online and offline will eventually be influenced by the net value the advertiser sees in each medium.

But there definitely will be correlation models between the two media outlets.

This dichotomy still generally holds true, and the challenge has become exacerbated by the nature of fragmented viewing. How are ratings or value to be captured in a world when viewers are interacting with multiple screens simultaneously? By 2012, Nielsen reported the following simultaneous usage between TV and tablets:

- At least once per day: 45 percent
- At least several times per week: 69 percent
- Never: 12 percent

And what were we doing while also watching TV? According to Nielsen, looking at the general population, we were looking up information, e-mailing, visiting social networks, and not all the time seeking information relating to what we were watching (Table 3.1).

Table 3.1 Activities Engaged in while Watching Television[7]

Activities	General Population* (%)
Checked e-mail site during the program	61
Checked sport score	34
Looked up coupons or deals related to an advertisement I saw on TV	22
Looked up information related to the TV program I was watching	37
Looked up product information for an advertisement I saw on TV	27
Visited a social network site during the program	47

* Tablet owners aged 13 and over.

Other studies point to similar engagement shifts in today's multi-screen world—the same technology that enables a tangential yet deeper dive into related information (e.g. looking up a brand of clothing character X is wearing, or facts about the author), also allows the viewer to veer off course and engage in wholly unrelated activities (e.g., checking in on Facebook). What then is the value of fragmented engagement?

I talk about this a bit in Chapter 6 regarding television, and pose the same question here: Does it make better sense to measure engagement (an Internet model, where concrete actions such as click-throughs and conversions can be tangibly measured) or reach and frequency (traditional advertising metrics), and if the answer is, to a degree, both, then how is value further parsed knowing that engagement in today's world means one eye on something else? Again, as discussed in Chapter 6, the advertising world has moved slowly, simply capturing viewing a program at different times (e.g., live and when viewed on a DVR within X days of initial airing), and now faces the more daunting challenge of capturing value when content is consumed well outside the historical "appointment viewing" norm, and instead: (1) over a more extended period (time-shifting at will); (2) over multiple devices; and (3) in the context of multi-screen, simultaneous activity. What should a rating mean in this world, and how long will advertisers and media outlets agree to a standard based on what some claim is anachronistic sampling and varied engagement levels of those that (by the sampling statistics) are assumed to be watching in the first place? Nielsen has announced the marginal step of trying to capture Internet streams connected to TVs in expanding the construct of TV households, while pledging to try to develop ratings data that would further capture viewership on portable platforms (e.g. tablets);[8] however, this is merely recognizing the obvious migration of viewing programming "off TV" and does not address the related and equally vital issues of harmonizing value amid systems utilizing varied advertising methods (including none in the case of certain subscription streaming services), allocating value when multiple screens may be simultaneously used, and capturing direct engagement. (See also related discussion in Chapter 6.)

Variety of Financing Methods as a Response to Difficulty and Risks in Predicting Success of Experience Goods

As a premise to discussing financing, it is important to digress into certain economic theories that lurk behind the allocation of risk and the disproportionate importance that marketing has in the media and entertainment business. Film and television are classic experience goods, as distinct from ordinary goods. An experience good is a product that the consumer cannot accurately or fully assess until consuming it, whether that is via watching a film or TV show or reading a book.[9] Given the nature of creative goods—that nobody knows what will be a success—and the fact that you cannot really know whether you will like a property until you digest it yourself, it is natural for us to look for signals and references to make better bets before investing our time. These references and signals can come from sources as disparate as award recognition, critics' picks, and word of mouth (or blogs, a new media form of word of mouth). In the end, we are all searching for a trusted source that improves the odds we will make a good choice. The problem is that a good choice is highly personal, and mapping external sources of information regarding a creative good onto an internal measurement, while having to choose among a dizzying range of product (sometimes referred to as infinite variance) from which we will pick a small sample to spend time with (consume), seems an almost impossible proposition.

The issue is made more complex when one considers that the external signals are imperfect. Statistics show that awards are often poor predictors of commercial success, with trends and voting-pool demographics (which the consumer may not share) skewing results. One only needs to look at the disconnect recently between Best Picture Oscar nominations and commercial success to see the pattern. Of the top 15 box office films of 2008, including the top five, *The Dark Knight*, *Iron Man*, *Indiana Jones and the Kingdom of the Crystal Skull*, *Hancock*, and *Wall·E*, none were nominated for Best Picture (though this comparison, to be fair, should exclude *Wall·E*, which won for Best Animated Feature; note, I am using this older year because the example comes from before the Academy expanded the nominations for the Best Picture category, in part to combat the fact that few box office hits were being nominated). In fact, of the pictures nominated for Best Picture Oscars in 2008 and 2009, only one picture each year (*Juno* and *The Curious Case of Benjamin Button*, respectively) had a United States box office greater than $100 million. The pattern was essentially continued in 2012, with *Skyfall*, *The Dark Knight Rises*, and *The Avengers* all generating greater than $1 billion at the worldwide box office, yet none of the films garnering a Best Picture nomination; in fact, none of the top 15 grossing films worldwide were nominated.[10] Perhaps this lack of correlation is a function of the line between movies as an art form versus a commercial endeavor; industry-sponsored awards shows tend to focus on underlying skills and performance attributes, of which subset of inputs are simply another source of signals. When art and entertainment value do overlap, though, such as with a blockbuster that is also a best picture winner, then this may be one of the few cases where signals are clear.

Critics are another source of information, but this information is only as good as your personal mapping to a critic's choice: How often have we said "I disagree with that opinion," or were disappointed with a recommendation? Accordingly, we tend to try to adjust the critics' picks by integrating bias, countering with whether there is a better correlation to types of films they have liked where we agree, etc. Additionally, as also discussed in Chapter 9, it is unclear whether online sources of information that aggregate reviews (e.g., Rotten Tomatoes) and social networking sites that exponentially disseminate opinions actually improve personal decision-making or interject a cacophonous web of biases requiring more sophisticated (or perhaps arbitrary) filtering. Even affinity for actors might pique interest, but it does not help that much (even your favorite actors can be in a clunker).

Finally, word of mouth is the mother of all external signals, and it is the watercooler buzz and positive recommendations that marketers so covet. The danger here is that trends follow herd behavior, and experience goods inherently lend themselves to bandwagon and cascade effects. This is because even with imperfect information (needing to consume the good yourself to really know if you agree with the pack/like it), consumers have to balance internal and external inputs without knowing which judgment is correct. Richard Caves illuminates the problem by what almost seems like a riddle. If you see John buying good X, and you have an independent sense you will like X, you will follow your hunch and go with the flow (and the same pattern holds in reverse with rejection). But what happens if your internal sense differs from the external recommendation and the signals cross each other out? What do you do? If we were to assume the outcome is determined by a coin flip, it can start a trend—if heads you buy, then you agree with John, and the next consumer will see two positive signals, even though in reality there was only one. The problem cascades such that a trend can appear even though the sum of the individual collective gut picks may come out the other way.[11] This helps explain, at least in part, how it is easy to wonder how everyone loved or hated such and such, and yet you felt just the opposite coming out of the theater.

It would be an interesting research exercise to study whether social networking sites materially improve signalling. If recommendations are coming from a trusted set of friends, and you have mapped your "likes" onto recommendations, should these external signals trump your internal hunches if not in alignment? Clearly, this is the message social networking sites such as Facebook want its users to accept. The problem is that the information is still imperfect, and the variables that go into whether you ultimately like show X or movie Y are highly subjective and personal—likely influenced by the best external signals you can find, but sill not fully determined by them. This is simply the inherent challenge of experience goods, and while social networks no doubt improve signals (which is unquestionably valuable), they cannot, in and of themselves, defeat the experience good problem.

Combining the factors of information cascades, infinite variance, experience goods, and imperfect signals, it is no wonder that success of product is highly variable, risk is extreme, and that assorted financing schemes have evolved to try to combat the problem. In trying to solve the question whether there are strategies that may temper the risk inherent with movies, and sampling over 2,000 films, economists Arthur de Vany and David Walls concluded that box office revenues have infinite variance and that they do not converge on an average because the mean is dominated by extreme successes (blockbusters). As far as mitigating risk, they conclude it is impossible:

> We conclude that the studio model of risk management lacks a foundation in theory or evidence. Revenue forecasts have zero precision, which is just a formal way of saying that "anything can happen." Movies are complex products and the cascade of information among filmgoers during the course of a film's theatrical exhibition can evolve along so many paths that it is impossible to attribute the success of a movie to individual causal factors. In other words, as Goldman said, "Nobody knows anything."[12]

101

It is because risk cannot be fully mitigated that participants (studios, producers) have evolved varying financing mechanisms as a way of distributing that risk. I will also argue in Chapter 9 that the nature of experience goods underlies the importance of marketing, which can help signaling and at least try to influence a positive cascade of information.

Challenge Exacerbated in Selecting which Product to Produce

The previous section focuses on the process by which consumers grapple with experience goods in making decisions, but the related challenge of financing is to predict that very outcome before the experience good is even made. The ultimate challenge of financing is that someone is asked to judge this creative value proposition at a root sage without adequate inputs to make the decision required. This is a nearly impossible task.

Additionally, it helps explain why the development process is so murky, protracted, subject to second-guessing, and littered with projects that "almost got made."

This quandary is also, in part, why so much emphasis is placed on backing those with successful track records; it is also why some executives continue to seek a repeatable system to implement and become frustrated realizing that, indeed, some development/production elements are formulaic (e.g., plot points and acts in a script, needing conflict and character growth) and yet the formulas do not necessarily lead to success.

Alas, as noted in Chapter 2, there are no golden rules or right answers in selecting creative goods before they are produced to stave off a single bomb or a more cataclysmic result. The combination of intrinsic risk, the increase in the number of films with $200m+ budgets, and the trend for revenues to be front-loaded with ever shorter theatrical runs (see Chapter 4), has even led luminaries like Steven Spielberg and George Lucas to predict the end of the business as we know it. In a panel at USC's School of Cinema Arts (2013) Spielberg noted: "There's going to be an implosion where three or four or maybe even a half dozen mega-budget movies are going to go crashing into the ground, and that's going to change the paradigm."[13] It is the nature of the business, though, that big productions carry big risks, and from *Heaven's Gate* (see Chapter 2) to *John Carter* and *The Lone Ranger* (2012 and 2013 releases), some are always pointing to "bombs" that in extreme cases could risk the associated studio.[14] If experience goods were merely widgets, then an assembly line would work. However, because creative goods are subject to infinite variety, and nobody knows with certainty what will work—especially at the root stage before a project is infused with its creative spark—what is most coveted and compensated is creative talent backers believe will infuse a project with pixie dust.

Studio Financing

Classic Production–Financing–Distribution Deal

This is the standard deal where a producer brings a developed picture to a studio and the studio agrees to fund production and marketing costs, as well as distribute the film. The difference between this structure and a pure in-house production is that in an in-house production, the studio has already acquired the property and then simply green-lights the project, engaging a producer on a work-for-hire basis. While a production–financing–distribution (PFD) deal may entail an assignment of the underlying rights to the studio in return for agreeing to move forward, typically the deal starts with an independent producer who has acquired the rights to a property, developed it, attached key talent, and then "sets it up" at the studio. This is also the stage where agents often play a critical role, by specializing in "packaging" talent (and take a packaging fee), such that a studio is presented with a turnkey project ready to produce.

In return for financing production and distribution, the studio typically acquires all copyright and underlying rights in and to the property, as well as worldwide distribution rights in all media in perpetuity. (Note: There may be select guild mandated reservations of rights.) While this may sound extreme, the studio is shouldering all the financial risk and the producer will be making both upfront fees in the budget, as well as have a back-end participation tied to a negotiated profits definition (see Chapter 10). Accordingly, this is the classic risk–reward scenario, where full financing vests the distributor with the upside and ownership.

Studio Financing of Production Slate; Studio Coproductions

Regardless of whether a studio enters into a PFD agreement or some other structure on a particular picture, from a macro standpoint, studios need a strategy to finance their overall production slate. The simplest and oldest method of financing is via bank credit facilities covering a slate of films. Disney, for example, worked with Credit Suisse First Boston (2005) to structure its $500 million Kingdom Fund.[15] As the business continues to grow riskier and more complex, however, studios have sought a variety of methods to secure production financing, acknowledging that they need to cede some upside to offset the enormous risks taken. Investors, too, though, are focused on the risks, especially as technology has altered the landscape and DVD revenues (historically a cash cow buffer) have significantly declined (see Chapter 5).

Coproductions

When a studio wants to offset risk, it will often enter into a coproduction relationship with another studio. In such a case, each studio will agree what percentage of the budget it will contribute, and will, in turn, keep certain exclusive distribution rights. The simplest and most frequently used mechanism is to split domestic and foreign rights. On occasion, this scenario arises when the project involves talent tied to different studios (e.g., famous director vs. lead star), and the only way to move forward is sharing.

Sometimes, however, during production a studio will become nervous with escalating costs and decide to limit its risk by selling off a piece. The most famous example of this is the film *Titanic*. The movie was originally a Fox production, but as costs spiraled and the studio became increasingly nervous (at the time, there was even talk that the whole studio could be in jeopardy if the film bombed, given the investment), Fox elected to sell off part of the film to Paramount. It was rumored that Paramount invested a fixed sum, allowing the picture to be completed, and ended up with a 50 percent share of the picture, even though its investment was ultimately less than 50 percent of the costs. With the film going on to break all box office records, the deal made by then-studio head John Dolgin was regarded as one of the shrewdest of its day.

A more detailed discussion of coproductions follows, but it is discussed here as a financing mechanism by a studio to spread risk or marry talent, as opposed to the later strategy where a coproduction is a necessary vehicle to raise the money for production in the first place. (Note: Studios can also employ the same strategy as discussed in the section "Independent Financing"; namely, selling select rights or markets.

Debt and Equity Financings

Another mechanism by which a studio will finance films is via stock or other equity/debt offerings. Pixar, for example, went public and was able to use its proceeds to co-finance its pictures with Disney. DreamWorks Animation's public offering similarly allowed it to finance films and secure below-market distribution fees, and ultimately remain independent when its parent, DreamWorks SKG, was sold to Paramount (December 2005). This is a difficult strategy because: (1) there are off-the-top offering costs that can be significant; and (2) investors are usually looking for a particularly strong track record or brand, which can be hard to illustrate with a diverse studio slate (something that both Pixar and DreamWorks Animation achieved within the niche of computer graphics-based animated films).

Off-Balance Sheet Financing

A mechanism similar to equity financing, in that funds may be raised from a diffuse pool of investors, is a limited partnership. This structure differs, however, in that, as opposed to raising equity capital, it is referred to as off-balance sheet financing. The first and most famous examples were the Disney-backed Silver Screen Limited Partnership offerings in the 1980s.

In 1985, Disney, through broker E.F. Hutton & Company, offered 400,000 limited partnership interests for a maximum offering of $200,000,000. The prospectus, under the use of proceeds section, listed the items shown in Table 3.2 (under the maximum offering scenario).

Table 3.2 Disney Prospectus

	Amount	Percentage
Source of funds		
Gross offering proceeds	$200,000,000	100
Use of funds		
Public offering expenses		
Selling commissions	$17,000,000	8.5
Offering expenses	$3,500,000	1.75
Operations		
Film financing	$179,500,000	89.75
Total use of funds	$200,000,000	100

The prospectus footnoted the film financing line as follows:

Funds available for financing films will be loaned pursuant to the
Loan Agreement and invested in the Joint Venture to pay film
costs, which include direct film cost, overhead payable to Disney
and to the Partnership for the benefit of the Managing Partner
and a contingency reserve. Disney and the Managing Partner will
receive overhead of 13.5 percent and 4 percent, respectively, of
the Budgeted Film Cost (excluding overhead) of each Joint Venture
Film and 3.75 percent and 1 percent (which is included in the
loan amount), respectively, of the direct production costs (plus
interest) of the Completed Films . . .

(Note: The summary reflects the initial offering of $100 million and
200,000 units, which was then amended two months later to double the
offering.)

It is an interesting exercise to read through these summary terms,
which define distribution fees, requiring Disney's Buena Vista distribution arm to fund minimum marketing expenditures in releasing each
film and allocate revenue disbursement. One item that is both obvious
and not obvious (because it is not highlighted) is that the investment
is cross-collateralized, given that the unit investments apply to the slate
of films rather than to an individual film. As previously noted, this
would be difficult to achieve in other instances, but because "Disney" is
perceived as a brand and the offering limits the budget range and nature

of the pictures, using revenues from multiple films to pay out a single investment can work.

Studios Leveraging Hedge Fund and Private Equity Investments

In the mid 2000s, hedge funds—loosely regulated investment vehicles for wealthy and institutional investors, often requiring a minimum investment of $1 million or more—flush with cash started cozying up to financing opportunities that covered a slate of studio pictures. Beyond simply seeking new investment outlets, another factor potentially driving the new studio–hedge fund (and private equity) partnerships was the quickly changing technology landscape. As release windows started moving, and iPods, DVRs, and the Internet ushered in a new era of digital downloading and access, investors familiar with technology plays were oddly more comfortable investing in the same landscape that was making the control-it-all studios less comfortable with their distribution roots and forecasts. Both were players in high-stakes games, and it was hardly a surprise they should ultimately team up. To the extent studios were already acting like VCs, why should they not play by the same rules as professional VCs and take in private equity groups in a syndicate as partners?

106

What has changed in the last few years is that there has been a renaissance of outside non-bank film funds. It is difficult to draw bright lines, however, among these funds, in that the line between individuals ("angels"), major private equity-type funds, and independents has become somewhat blurry. I will still discuss each of these variations below, but Table 3.3 is an outline of a sampling of funds (excluding production companies with exclusive studio deals, such as Village Roadshow and New Regency, which could be deemed mini-majors and are discussed separately below, and only including some select examples of funds tied to individual backers that are more generally discussed below under angels).

What is interesting about this new range of funds is that there is competition among pioneers of hedge-type funds (Legendary and Relativity), individuals who in today's culture of billionaires can act as if they were a fund unto themselves (Fred Smith, FedEx founder; offspring of Oracle founder, Larry Ellison), and funds helmed by former studio/network chiefs (Jeff Sagansky and Hemisphere). Moreover, a common evolving thread is that these players are seeking more control, either demanding to have certain approvals over titles, or, once achieving a certain scale, morphing into independent producers masquerading as would-be mini-majors (e.g., Legendary, Relativity). The danger in coming to the table with so much money, and goals of

Table 3.3 Examples of Funds[16]

Fund Name	Principal	Size of Film Fund	Studio Partners	Examples of Films	Misc.
Legendary	Thomas Tull	$700 million	Warners	*The Dark Knight, The Hangover, Inception*	Pact ends 2013; Legendary entered into a new five year deal with Universal, launching 2014
Skydance	David Ellison	$350 million	Paramount	*Mission: Impossible – Ghost Protocol, Star Trek Into Darkness*	Son of Larry Ellison (Oracle CEO)
Cross Creek	Thompson Brothers	$260 million+	Universal	*Black Swan, Rush, The Ides of March*	Louisiana oil and gas family
Emmett/Furla Films	Randall Emmett and George Furla	$250 million	Multiple	*Lay The Favorite, The Tomb*	With Envision Entertainment, leverage Russian oil and real estate ventures
Relativity Media	Ryan Kavanaugh	$600 million+	Universal	*Bridesmaids, Safe House, Cowboys & Aliens*	Going independent
Hemisphere Tentpole	Jeff Sagansky	$200 million+	Multiple	*The Smurfs, Men in Black 3*	Partners with Winchester Capital Partners
Media Rights Capital	Modi Wiczyk and Asif Satchu	$350 million	Multiple	*Babel, Bruno, 30 Minutes or Less*	
Dune Capital	Ex-Goldman Sachs partners	$500 million	Fox	*Avatar, Rise of the Planet of the Apes*	Reputedly funds 35 percent of all Fox films
Alcon	Fred Smith	$550 million	Warner Bros.	*The Blind Side, Dophin Tale*	
Annapurna Pictures	Megan Ellison			*True Grit, Zero Dark Thirty*	Daughter of Larry Ellison (Oracle CEO)

becoming studio-like entities, is that it undermines the inherent concept of funds. At their essence, funds are seeking to employ some hedge strategy, spreading risk across a range of projects, deferring the choice of films to the development experts, and targeting an upside resulting from diversity, balance, and partnership. Hollywood has always been a magnet for "dumb money," and without a sufficient spread and portfolio there is no objective evidence that this new spigot of investors will prove any more successful than co-financing vehicles of the past. Many of these investments—even if calculated risks—still fall within the ambit of passion-driven financing, and with the concentration of so much wealth by a select few, there is simply a greater pool today of people who can risk greater sums.

Whether these investors can strike deals that mitigate their risks, in an environment when returns are less predictable because of diminishing home video revenues (see Chapter 5), is pending—clearly investors will try to negotiate prior recoupments, seeking some return before talent is cut in or before the studio takes its fee (see Chapter 10). However, studios have seen it all, and with more competition they will likely hold out for deals that share the upside but avoid cutting into their own safeguards of taking fees off the top (again, see Chapter 10). This is because, while a studio may share 50 percent of the upside with finance partners that correspondingly fund 50 percent of a film's budget, the most attractive part about these deals is that, historically, they were all about money. This is in stark contrast to the approach of a true mini-major or key production company supplier (e.g., Revolution and Spyglass previously at Sony, Village Roadshow with Warner Bros., and New Regency at Fox), where the independent is taking creative and production control, and even certain distribution rights alongside investments.

Universal's Prexy-COO Rick Finkelstein noted of the historical hedge fund deals to *Variety*: "You retain worldwide distribution, you retain complete creative control, you've got a financial partner and you're allowed to take a distribution fee. The economics are quite attractive."[17] Echoing this sentiment, Paramount's CFO Mark Badagliacca stated: "We like it because it's a slate deal without giving up any rights."[18]

So how do these deals work economically? Although each has its nuances, in the simplest scenario a studio and fund would each share production costs 50/50. In parallel, the studio and fund would similarly share profits 50/50. The issue then became: How are "profits" defined? In this instance, all revenues (except potentially certain ancillaries) would likely be accounted for—namely 100 percent of video revenues as opposed to a 20 percent royalty—and apply in the gross revenue line.

108

Table 3.4 *Batman Begins* ROI Example

United States box office	$205 m	
International box office	$166 m	
Total box office	$371 m	
Rentals	$185 m	Assume approximately 50 percent theatrical box office
Video	$180 m	Assume approximately $18 net wholesale × 10 million units worldwide
Net video	$100 m	Assume approximately 55 percent margin
Television	$65 m	
Total revenue	$350 m	Rentals + net video + TV
Production costs	-$150 m	$75 million returned to hedge fund (if pre P&A)
P&A	-$105 m	Assume approximately 70 percent production cost
Distribution fee	-$52 m	Assume approximately 15 percent revenues
Profit	$43 m	Revenues − costs (P&A + production + distribution fee)
Hedge fund	$21.5 m	Assume 50 percent share

In terms of expenses, the studio would usually take a reduced distribution fee (10–15 percent as opposed to 25–30 percent). Also, the studio would often fund print and advertising (P&A) costs and recoup those first, together with its distribution fee, out of gross revenues.

Table 3.4 is a simple example, taking the United States and international box office numbers from *Batman Begins* (box office from www.boxofficemojo.com).

If the fund put in $75 million (50 percent of estimated production costs) and received $21.5 million, that would be a 28.6 percent ROI; if they also had to fund 50 percent of the P&A, however, then the total investment would jump to $127.5 million and their return would drop to 16.8 percent (still high). (Note: These returns do not include leverage effects, where true equity returns would be higher, assuming a mix of equity and debt.) On this logic, the investment would make sense. However, a couple of key items need to be factored in. First, the above is probably a rosy picture, for it assumes no gross players, no interest, etc.

Factoring in these costs/expenses, the profit probably dips to single digits (for a detailed discussion of profit calculation, see Chapter 10). Second, this assumes all the revenues come in upfront. In fact, certain TV revenues will come in years downstream, and factoring in the time value of money, the return per year becomes a much smaller amount. Finally, this is one picture, and this hit needs to cover losses on other films: if the return is not more than 20 percent on a hit, then arguably it is going to be difficult to show a return across the portfolio.

Accordingly, the *Wall Street Journal* quipped in an article titled "Defying the Odds, Hedge Funds Bet Billions on Movies": "Yet in a business where the conventional wisdom says that 10 percent of a studio's films are responsible for 100 percent of its profits, even a passel of Harvard Business School graduates may not be immune to the pitfalls faced by nearly every investor to have hit the intersection of Hollywood and Vine."[19] The *Wall Street Journal* article continued to highlight the limited return on investment, and cash flow issues previously described:

> The problem is that under the terms of most co-financing deals, the new investors are often the last in line to get paid. Once exhibitors take their half of ticket sales, many studios take a distribution fee of 10–15 percent of what's left from the box office. Then, the movie's production and marketing costs are paid back, and any A-list actors or directors pocket their shares. After that, the revenue-sharing process begins and it continues for the next five or more years as revenue flows in from DVD sales, pay cable showings, and toy or other merchandise sales.[20]

To Include or Not to Include Tentpoles in the Slate—Do Limited Slates, and the Relatively Small Size of all Slates, Doom Fund Investments?

The studios are obviously quite savvy in the deals they choose, and frequently withhold their perceived best assets from financings that would require a material sharing of upside. It is therefore not surprising that hoped-for tentpoles such as *The Chronicles of Narnia* and *Pirates of the Caribbean* series were withheld by Disney from a 2005 co-financing deal, and that Sony excluded *Spider-Man 3*, the James Bond title *Casino Royale*, and *The Da Vinci Code* from its former Gun Hill Road deal.[21] (Note: As in most financings, there is more than meets the eye, and it is possible that the Regal Entertainment backing of Narnia and MGM control over James Bond could have forced an "exclusion" because neither of these stakeholders would likely want a further dividing of the pie.) A more recent example was the 2011 negotiation between Warners and Legendary, which limited Legendary's investment in *The Dark Knight Rises* to 25 percent from what was reported to be the traditional 50 percent stake in Legendary's investments in Warner Bros. films. The *Los Angeles Times*, talking about Warner film group's president Jeff Robinov's strategy, noted about the pending *Batman* sequel: "Because it is expected to be a hugely successful blockbuster—*The Dark Knight* grossed $1 billion in 2008—Robinov did not want to give away a big piece of the profit . . ."[22]

In fact, what is surprising is not the exclusion of major franchise pictures from sharing, but the very fact that certain major tentpoles, such as *Batman* and *Superman* (though the franchises had both waned, and the studios were hoping for a comeback) were included in the first place. Their inclusion is what arguably started to attract the most attention in the space.

One could have predicted at the outset, based on simple economic patterns, that this cycle would have to come full circle; namely, hits pay for misses (the above-quoted 10 percent rule), and excluding some of the more likely hits from an overall slate dooms the success of a fund. It took only a short time for the inevitable cycle to start reaching an early maturity.

111

Poseidon, which reportedly cost $150–160 million to produce, grossed only $22.2 million in its opening weekend, leading to the questioning of Virtual Studio's strategy and a *Variety* headline: "Sea Change at Hollywood Newbie: *Poseidon* Capsizes Fund."[23] Other funds started to fare similarly, with Legendary Pictures-backed (Warners deal) *Lady in the Water* (M. Night Shyamalan) and *Ant Bully* (Tom Hanks-backed) underperforming. Quickly, hedge funds were on the defensive, reminding investors about the underlying portfolio strategy.[24]

But how long would it take for rational economics to right the *Poseidon* tainted ship? This was not a mutual fund with hundreds of stocks diversifying a risk portfolio; even the largest of the funds was small, with no more than 20–25 pictures in the mix. Nevertheless, the first arguments were focused on differentiating one pool from the next, rather than to address the fact that all the pools were too small to provide a true hedge against risk. Investors, no doubt trying to defend their strategy, first argued that one film did not undermine a portfolio strategy, and then as large films in the portfolio started to underperform, distinguished their pools from others by challenging the scope of the slate. *Variety* noted: "Wall Streeters said Virtual may be more exposed than the other funds by co-financing such a small slate."[25]

Because excluding some of the most likely hits, by definition, increased the risk profile, it was therefore not surprising that funds started to reconsider the composition of portfolios, with the organizer of the Universal and Sony deals with Gun Hill Road going on record that new studio deals would involve a studio's full slate of pictures.[26] No longer would it be so easy for studios to create off-balance sheet financing of $100 million-plus pictures while excluding other key titles.

Of course, a big hit will change all perception, for the amount of money a single film can generate may justify an entire slate investment. Legendary's share in *The Dark Knight*, which became the number 2 box office film of all time (at that time), surpassing half a billion in the United States (compare to previous *Batman Begins* example in Table 3.4) theoretically could have earned it upwards of $250 million over time (and much more if they participate in certain ancillary revenues such as merchandising). Note that the increase in return is more than a linear relationship, because after a certain point additional revenues are not matched by additional costs (i.e., the production and print and initial advertising costs are fixed, so imagine the above *Batman Begins* example but simply double the revenue lines). It is because a single hit, which may represent less than 5 percent of the total portfolio (based on number of films) can potentially recoup 50 percent or more of an entire fund's risk that investors tend to ignore the relatively small pool size. Based on statistics, a sample size of 20 may not be large enough to ensure consistent deviations and therefore tempered risk, but one has to remember that these are not random samples, and placing bets with proven producers should positively skew results, as long as all titles are included. A studio will rarely go zero for 10, but as discussed previously, taking some of the best picks out of the mix may change the equation from a predictable statistical spread to more luck-based metrics.

In the merry-go-round of co-financing logic, arguments have now come full circle, as a 2012 *Variety* article titled "Slate Debate: Investors Now Get to Pick and Choose" noted with respect to some of the current funds discussed above: "In the past, many moneymen blindly financed slates of films they didn't pick themselves . . . Now, many co-financing arrangements involve fewer films and allow studio partners like David Ellisons Skydance Productions and Jeff Sagansky's Hempisphere, for example, to have more leverage in choosing which films to partner on— especially among tentpoles."[27] While ensuring participation in major tentpoles makes sense, the logic of fewer films and selecting those films speaks more toward becoming a producer (high risk) than actually managing a fund (diversified, hedged risk).

112

Independent Financing

Independent financing is a catch-all term that refers to a myriad of financing schemes, and is generally distinguished from the above discussion concerning funds because funds invest across a slate, and much "independent financing" applies on a per-project basis. The common thread is that: (1) money is sought to actually pay for production, requiring that cash is advanced before the project starts; and (2) that the source of funding is, at least in part, from a party other than the distributor. This occurs in two very simple cases: when the producer cannot obtain the studio's commitment to fund production, or when the producer does not want to take the studio's money because it can keep something that the studio would have demanded. The "what it keeps" can range from creative control to a larger share of the pie (by bringing money to the table) to retaining specified rights. (Note: While some of the following discussion can apply equally to television (e.g., pre-sales), the bulk of independent financing and the overview below applies in the context of funding films.)

Most cases of independent financing are because the producer needs money to make or complete his or her project. Although there are no bright-line categories, the following are typical methods of financing:

- foreign pre-sales
- ancillary advances
- negative pickups
- bank credit lines
- angels
- crowdsourcing

Although some of these mechanisms, such as pre-sales, are the tools of structuring coproductions, I discuss the nature of coproductions separately below, and here focus on some of the line item issues of how the underlying rights are divided and treated. I have also included crowdsourcing schemes, such as via Kickstarter, which is a relatively new and still evolving source of production financing.

Foreign Pre-Sales

Foreign pre-sales are either full or partial sales of specified rights in a particular territory. For example, it may mean theatrical rights only, or theatrical, video, and TV rights in a territory. These sales can be structured either as percentages of the budget or in fixed dollar terms. Moreover,

Table 3.5 Hypothetical TV Show Finances

Network/Pre-Sale Partner	Territory and Rights	Pre-Sold as % of Budget	$ Pre-Sold
Pan-European broadcaster	Europe cable	15	52,500
French network	France	25	87,500
German network	Germany	10	35,000
UK network	UK	5	17,500
Italian network	Italy	5	17,500
			210,000

the deals may be structured on a quitclaim basis (outright sale of rights in perpetuity) or on the basis of an advance, where the producer shares in an upside after the licensee distributor recoups its investment per a negotiated formula. Table 3.5 is a hypothetical example for an animated television show budgeted at $350,000.

114   In the above example, if a producer could obtain this level of commitment, it would have 60 percent of its budget secured while still having the balance of the world (United States, Asia, Latin America) available. Depending on the deal structure, the broadcasters may commit to a percentage of budget, rather than a set license fee, which can be advantageous if the budget increases; in fact, in theory only, it is possible to sell more than 100 percent and be in profits before production.

A wrinkle on the above is that not all contributed amounts fall into the same category. Some broadcasters/partners may put in their amount as a straight license fee, others may make contributions contingent on it being a coproduction (requiring a certain amount of localized production/elements and control), and yet others may allocate their contribution between a license fee and an equity investment. To take this example further, the French amount may require a French coproduction, where the government-backed CNC actually contributes an amount and the French broadcaster contributes the balance as its license fee. In this instance, the French network may not demand an equity investment, and may simply acquire broadcast rights since its investment/cost has already been subsidized. The German amount may or may not include an equity component. If the broadcaster demands equity, it could be 50/50, for example, where $17,500 of the $35,000 would be considered an equity investment; namely, they would hold a 5 percent equity stake in the profits. Finally, one partner, such as the Pan-European Broadcaster, may require ancillary rights, or a stake in ancillary rights, as opposed to a stake in the whole. If they were granted European merchandising rights and a fee, then the producer may only have a secondary income stream from merchandising.

There is no obvious outcome, with a continuum of stakeholding moving up and down depending on the percentage of ownership, percentage of budget covered, and range of rights retained/granted by the producer. The final deal may cover enough of the budget to move forward, grant third parties 40–50 percent of the overall equity in defined revenues, and grant others a different percentage of merchandising or video. The endgame is obviously to cover the production budget and retain as much of an equity stake as possible.

Ancillary Advances

I touched on ancillary advances above in pre-sales, but it is important to differentiate between primary and ancillary rights granted. Table 3.5 was predicated on licensing the television broadcast rights to a television show. By ancillary, I mean other downstream revenues, such as from merchandising or video. Because these downstream revenues are dependent on the success of the primary revenue source (e.g., there will likely not be merchandising on an original TV property until it is a hit), these amounts are speculative. Accordingly, these are harder advances to obtain, and will usually be discounted given the uncertain value.

Negative Pickups

A negative pickup is a deal structure where the distributor guarantees the producer that it will distribute the finished picture and reimburse the producer for agreed negative costs (i.e., production costs), subject to the picture conforming to terms detailed in the negative pickup agreement. With distribution and reimbursement of production costs secured, the producer will then borrow money from a third-party lender using the reimbursement contract as collateral.

The advantage to the distributor is cash flow and the elimination of risk: nothing is paid until the picture is completed to the satisfaction of stipulated contract terms. The advantage to the producer is a greater measure of independence—the terms of the negative pickup agreement will often impose less creative control than if the studio distributor were directly overseeing production—and the elimination of certain financing charges, such as studio interest. (These charges may not be market rate, and may continue to accrue until recoupment, which is set back to the extent distribution fees are taken out first, leaving less cash available to recoup production costs.)

Under a negative pickup structure, the distributor would have approval over all material elements of production. Such approval rights may include approval over the budget, production schedule, the script, all above-the-line talent (i.e., principal cast, director, writer, producer), and contingent compensation granted (e.g., net or gross profit participations). In addition to approval of the creative and financing elements, the agreement will grant the distributor the right to approve delivery specifications. Such specifications will include, for example, that the picture will have a running time of not less than X and not more than Y, and that it will have a rating not more restrictive than "R".

In both the negative pickup structure and in any structure involving loans from a third party, securing a completion bond will likely be required. A completion bond is a contract with a designated completion bond company that can ultimately take over production and complete the film in the event of a producer default. These companies engage reputable producers, and will monitor the cash flow and progress of production against specified milestones. Of course, all parties will do whatever they can to avoid takeover, but in the draconian eventuality that a producer is failing to deliver, these companies will step in and manage the balance of production. Completion bonds can be quite expensive and are calculated on a percentage of the budget, usually in the range of a few percent. Examples of what may contractually trigger a takeover might include:

- Over budget: If the picture is materially over budget (e.g., if final estimated direct costs are estimated to exceed the budgeted costs by X, excluding costs of overhead, interest, and the completion bond fee).
- Over schedule: If the picture is more than X weeks behind schedule.
- Default: In the event of a material default.

Third-Party Credit—Banks, Angels, and a Mix of Private Equity

Bank Credit Lines

If a producer has a sufficient track record and consistent volume of production, a direct bank credit line may be able to be secured. This will often take the form of a revolving credit facility, and, depending on the structure, may cross-collateralize revenues from pictures to secure the overall facility. The economic advantage to a bank line is that it is all about money. The bank will only be concerned with the financial securitization and recoupment of its loaned sums and will not want to retain rights. Accordingly, this is an advantageous structure to retain the copyright, foreign and ancillary rights, and therefore upside in a property.

It is also possible to structure a bank line as "gap financing," where only a percentage of the budget is needed. This is a typical scenario where pre-sales and advances against ancillary revenues (such as a merchandising advance from a toy company) cover a significant amount of the production budget, and the bank line covers the bridge or gap to fund 100 percent of the costs. In this instance, the bank line will almost always come in first recoupment position, which gives the lenders comfort. In essence, they can look to 100 percent of the revenues to cover 20 percent of the budget, lowering the risk. Nevertheless, films are inherently risky, and obtaining a bank loan, even if for limited gap financing, is not easy; moreover, the documentation and legal fees can be quite considerable, constituting another expense to be built into the budget.

Mini-Majors and Credit Facilities   117

Similar to a bank line of credit, producers, directors, and independent studios with a sufficient track record can raise enough money to create a "mini-studio." This was the case when Joe Roth, former production head at Fox and then Disney, launched Revolution Studios. Combining a variety of distribution output deals, including theatrical distribution via Sony, Revolution raised over $1 billion for film production before a single picture was made. Similarly, when Harvey and Bob Weinstein left Miramax (the company they had founded and sold to Disney), they were able to launch a mini-studio with their new The Weinstein Company—a proposition that was only possible with the combination of distribution deals and significant third-party financing.

To an extent, this is an independent's dream, and it is common to see a mixture of distribution deals and bank credit facilities funding production (set in place with the security of the distribution arrangements). Another prominent example was Merrill Lynch's half-billion-dollar backing of Marvel Entertainment, the comic book company whose characters include Spider-Man and X-Men, when it was still an independent (pre acquisition by Disney). (Note: The line between this type of deal and the previously discussed private equity/hedge fund-backed slate financings can be fuzzy; I have separated Marvel here because it was an example of an independent brand raising financing, as opposed to a deal directly leveraging studio distribution.) In May 2006, Merrill Lynch took out a full-page ad in the *International Herald Tribune*, boasting:

Marvel Entertainment knew that by creating their own film studio they could profit directly from their legendary comic book characters rather than licensing the rights. But they lacked the production facility to achieve their vision. That is, until they talked to Merrill Lynch. We structured a transaction hailed as the "best Hollywood has ever seen," using Marvel's intellectual property as equity to raise $525 million—enough to bankroll up to 10 feature films. So now Marvel has full creative control over these characters. Not to mention their own destiny. This is just one example of how Merrill Lynch delivers exceptional financial solutions for exceptional clients.[28]

Almost 20 years ago, the "mother of all studio financings" at the time was the 1995 creation of DreamWorks SKG. A studio, promising to be on the scale of a major, not just a mini-major, was launched from scratch by combining the track record of legendary producers and directors (Steven Spielberg, Jeffrey Katzenberg, David Geffen) and backing by an enormous investor with Paul Allen (Microsoft cofounder), reportedly investing $500 million. Its initial credit facility was replaced by a $1.5 billion financing deal in 2002:

DreamWorks Announces New Financing

Los Angeles—DreamWorks LLC today announced that it has closed two major financing transactions totaling $1.5 billion. The new financing consists of a $1 billion film securitization—the first of its kind in the film industry—as well as a $500 million revolving credit facility. Together, these financings replace the Company's existing financing arrangements at a substantially lower cost of capital and extends the Company's access to debt capital until at least October 2007.

. . . The securitization uses a unique structure that finances expected film revenue cash receipts from DreamWorks' library of existing films, as well as from future live action releases. According to the terms of the securitization, funds are advanced after a film has been released in the domestic theatrical market for several weeks, at which point the film's revenue stream over a multi-year period is highly predictable. In part, this predictability allowed the transaction to gain investment grade status from the two leading rating agencies . . .[29]

It is accordingly not surprising that if an entity with an unproven track record but lots of cash can join the co-financing game, that a large independent with a sustained track record ought to be able to arrange significant financing for its own slate. This trend was started, in part, by Revolution, but has now expanded to a myriad of independents, such as Village Roadshow and Summit Entertainment. The amounts these companies are now able to raise are on par with studios, and gives the original DreamWorks financing a mundane air. Summit, of *Twilight* fame, had negotiated a $750 million refinancing in 2011;[30] then, post Lionsgate's acquisition of Summit, Lionsgate sought a new credit line of equal amount in 2012.[31] Village Roadshow, the independent with perhaps the longest track record—having distributed pictures via Warners since the late 1990s (and with a library at the time of its new financing of over 65 films)—secured $1 billion in financing in 2010, enabling it to produce films such as *Sex and the City 2*.[32]

When companies such as DreamWorks, Lionsgate, and Village Roadshow can raise in the hundreds of millions of dollars, and even secure revolving lines up to $1 billion, to finance their slates, it would seem there is a fine line between production company and studio; however, remember, as discussed in Chapter 1, that a key defining element of a studio is global distribution infrastructure—developing, producing, and financing product goes a long way, but product still needs to be marketed and distributed globally, and through all channels. As difficult as it may seem to grasp, $1 billion in financing does not in itself create a studio. Expanding to this next level (as well as diversifying production to cover other major markets, including TV) is extraordinarily difficult, as was borne out by the original DreamWorks SKG ambition.

Angel Investors

Similar to a venture capital structure, the film business tends to attract wealthy individuals that want to invest in pictures. These types of deals vary widely, but there seem to be a couple of consistent themes. First, the investor, while wanting a return, has a secondary objective of passion/fun/ego, and will accordingly take a producer or executive producer credit; of course, this is not unfair, in that much of the role of an executive producer can be putting together financing. Second, the investor is usually contributing a sizable amount of the budget. These individuals are high-stakes players, investing likely for high risk, high reward, rather than just as a gap financier. In fact, there is often a personal passion for the project, and the angel investor may be putting in money because, simply, he or she wants to make the film.

A high-profile example of an angel-financed film is *Polar Express*. Steve Bing, heir to a real estate fortune who turned to entertainment, partnered with Warner Bros. to back the Robert Zemeckis-directed (*Back to the Future, Forrest Gump, Who Framed Roger Rabbit?*) animated holiday film *Polar Express*, starring Tom Hanks. The film was considered risky given its $165 million budget (with some reports speculating it was more than $200 million) and pioneering motion-capture animation technique (to give a unique look and range to animating human characters). Warner Bros. hedged its risk by partnering with Bing, as *Business Week* reported: "And even folks at Warner Bros. are said to be thrilled that multimillionaire Steve Bing, who aspires to be a big-time producer, has put $80 million into the film. He's also covering half the $50 million or more in marketing expenses, according to a source with knowledge of the deal. Says the source: 'If it tanks, it won't leave Warner with that much of a hole [thanks to Bing].'"[33]

Sometimes the lines between an angel and a fund can blur, as seems to be the case with Alcon Entertainment. FedEx founder and CEO Frederick Smith teamed with Alcon founders to launch *My Dog Skip* (initially headed to DVD), and then went on to become an equity partner in a multi-picture financing deal, reportedly worth $550 million, with Warner Bros.[34] Another example where the line is blurry between a production company and an individual is billionaire Philip Anschutz, who backed Walden Media as an independent studio, financing generally family fare such as *The Chronicles of Narnia* (originally with Disney). As was depicted in Table 3.3, there are many new entrants in this arena, including Oracle founder Larry Ellison's kin Megan and David Ellison, who respectively launched Annapurna Pictures and Skydance. There are countless similar stories given the allure of Hollywood—most of them are simply less high-profile and outside the public eye.

Crowdsourcing

Crowdsourcing is a relatively new phenomenon, enabling individuals to contribute to projects via the Internet. What companies offer are perks, sometimes phrased as "VIP elements," rather than actual stock or profit participations in projects. Two of the largest sites that focus on media productions are Kickstarter and Indiegogo. Kickstarter, which bills itself as "the world's largest funding platform for creative projects," allows anyone to post a project, and then with a ticking clock waits to see if all of the financing is contributed. If the financing goal is not reached, then no money is accepted and the project does not move forward—in its website section on "How Kickstarter Works," the site explains that the all-or-nothing method is designed to protect everyone involved, and bluntly proclaims: "This way, no one is expected to develop a project with an insufficient budget, which sucks."[35] In contrast, Indiegogo offers content creators to select either a fixed-funding or flexible-funding scheme, where, again, in the fixed scenario if the goal is not reached, then no fee is taken, and no money accepted (all contributors are refunded). Pursuant to the respective websites, the companies/sites charge a percentage fee from the funding total (e.g., 4 percent or 5 percent, which is only collected on a fixed-funding goal if the threshold is met) and a market rate credit/payment processing fee; Indiegogo charges a higher rate (9 percent) on funds raised for "flexible funding," where the creator keeps whatever is raised without a threshold needing to be met.

Neither financing site takes equity ownership in projects, and are designed to allow creators to democratically raise money by outlining a project and setting a goal. In return for contributions, funders receive different levels of rewards tied to donation level. For a game, for example, a contributor might receive a downloadable copy once published, or for a larger contribution perhaps a signed copy of an element from the developer, or some form of direct engagement with the developer/producer (e.g., a lunch or conversation).

Historically, these sites tended to fund niche projects, with tens of thousands of dollars raised; however, in 2012, Double Fine, a San Francisco games company, broke through the clutter and defined the potential of crowdsourced project financing. Posting a description of a game it wanted to make and seeking $400,000, in February 2012 Double Fine raised $800,000 within the first eight hours, over $1 million by the next day, and within a week of posting nearly $2 million. Double Fine could accordingly boast that it was the first independent studio to fully fund a game via Kickstarter. Although Double Fine is the exception, it does prove the case of an independent with a track record and following able to crowdsource its fans and finance future productions.

Similarly, Kickstarter is being leveraged by Hollywood independents, such as Bret Easton Ellis (author of Less Than Zero, and producer of The Informers) and Paul Schrader (screenwriter of Raging Bull and Taxi Driver, and director of American Gigolo) for their movie The Canyons. They are utilizing Kickstarter, essentially, for gap financing, seeking $100,000

121

to complement their own investments in the project.[36] In return for contributions, the following are some examples of what a donor can receive: at the lowest tier, for $1, a contributor will receive a high-resolution poster download; for $100, they are offering tickets to a private cast-and-crew screening, together with a copy of the DVD (or Blu-ray); and, for $5,000, Bret Easton Ellis will read and review your novel, post the review on an international blog or website, and you will be granted an associate producer credit on the film. In a short timeframe, Ellis and Schrader reached their target and more (generating $159,000 against a posted target of $100,000).

Although neither Kickstarter nor Indiegogo allow direct equity investment in a project, in order to avoid securities laws violations, many crowdsourcing proponents have advocated a loosening of the regulations to enable smaller companies to raise capital via more micro-finance means. In March 2012, as part of the JOBS Act passed by the U.S. Congress, a section entitled "Entrepreneur Access to Capital" attempted to pave just this path. The law includes a specific crowdsourcing exemption, allowing private companies to raise up to $1 million per year, and sanctioning capital-raising via the Internet through websites registered with the SEC. (Note: There are various conditions attached, rules are being adopted, and many are concerned about the abrogation of historical protections and the potential for fraud, which has caused the crowd-sourcing community to preemptively set standards via the Crowdfunding Accreditation for Platform Standards self-policing policy.[37])

What is interesting about the new regulations, coupled with the growth of crowdsourcing generally, is how to define the actual investments. If, for example, an individual gains a specific benefit from the transaction, such as a copy of the to-be-produced product, then the fundraising is akin to a pre-sale; similarly, if there is a bundled benefit for a higher-tier donation (e.g., contribute $20 and Company X will provide you a downloadable copy of Y when it is complete, and for $100 you get the copy plus a value-added item, such as a signed animation still from the director), then the pledged financing can be construed as an advance purchase. Crowdsourcing is really the inverse of using credit cards (Figure 3.2). The credit card industry created consumer liquidity by enabling purchasers to buy a product (and take ownership/access) now while paying later; whereas, with crowdsourced financing, company liquidity is created by taking payment now while pledging to deliver the product (transfer ownership/provide access) later. (Note: In accounting terms, this is the difference between an account receivable and a deferred liability.)

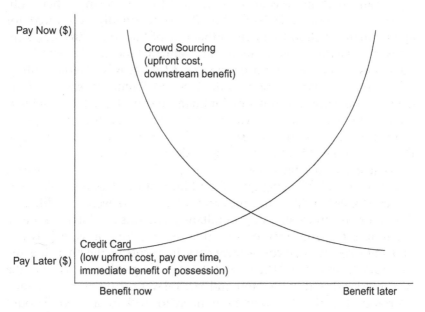

Figure 3.2 Crowd Sourcing Funding—For Consumers, the Inverse of Credit Card Financing

Leveraging Production with International Coproduction Financing—the Wachowskis' Experiment with Cloud Atlas

International coproductions are the norm with films originating in Europe, as domestic markets often cannot support the full costs of a high-budget film, especially when the cast/production is associated with a particular language. The film *Cloud Atlas*, an ambitious project of Andy and Lana Wachowski, the sibling team behind *The Matrix* series of movies, pushed the limits of independent international productions. With a reputed budget of $100 million and a blockbuster cast including Tom Hanks, Halle Berry, and Hugh Grant, among others, the film was a German–American–Asian coproduction not only with multiple locations, but also multiple principal crews and directors. Asian investors contributed more than one-third of the budget (approximately $35 million), which included substantial investments from South Korea (Bloomage Company, a Korean film distributor), Singapore (shipping magnate Tony Teo), Hong Kong (major film distributor Media Asia

Group), and China (Beijing film company Dreams of the Dragon). Significant financing was also contributed from Germany, where subsidies (e.g., German Federal Film Fund) reportedly accounted for approximately $18 million; given that one of the film's directors, Tom Tykwer, is German, the head of the German Federal Film Fund was quoted as saying, "From our perspective, *Cloud Atlas* is a German film." Add to this that Warner Bros. is the U.S. distributor (at least as of the date of production was not a major financial contributor), the movie is a classic independent film, with sources cobbled together from global sources, set in multiple overseas locations, with investors from Asia, Europe, and the U.S. alike claiming pride of ownership.

What makes the financing truly unique, however, is that to weave this creative and financing quilt for a film that involves multiple interrelated stories (in different times and places), there were two different film units and crews shooting simultaneously. This production scheme maximizes the efficiency of shooting, with actors moving between different roles, even on consecutive days. In discussing the financing, the *New York Times* noted: "The idea of shooting on parallel tracks, with the Wachowskis directing one unit and Mr. Tykwer the other, grew from a realization that the stars were more likely to work for a steep discount if the shoot could be finished in half the time. Actors also play different roles in different time periods, keeping them busy and, on certain days, turning stars into extras."[38]

Rent-a-Distributor: When a Producer Rises to Studio-Like Clout

The rent-a-distributor model is rarely used and limited to producers with enough of a checkbook and a track record that they can pay for production costs and bargain for reduced distribution fees.

The most famous example of this model is Lucasfilm's deal with 20th Century Fox for the three *Star Wars* prequels, *The Phantom Menace*, *Attack of the Clones*, and *Revenge of the Sith*. Due to the success of the original *Star Wars* trilogy, George Lucas had the financing and leverage to pay for the three prequels himself. Fox was reputedly investing no direct production costs, receiving a negotiated fee for distributing the *Star Wars* films.[39] This arrangement of only earning fees without taking any risk, while the producer, in essence, utilizes the studio's distribution operations (e.g., theatrical, video) and maintains the upside for having financed production, is often unfairly characterized as risk-free to the studio. By unfairly characterized, I mean that this premise tends to ignore the opportunity costs; Fox took on the responsibility and management of releasing these films, which was significant because they were destined to become the event titles of their respective years and require appropriate associated management and overhead time.

Presumably, the only reason a studio would agree to take on this level of time commitment is if: (1) it was important to have a relationship with the talent and/or property; and (2) if it believed, even with no or minimal upside ownership stake, it could earn significant distribution fees. This latter point underscores that the films in question need to be of mega box office stature, which leads to the corollary benefit of the studio leveraging one of the most desired films in its portfolio. While packaging is theoretically illegal under antitrust laws prohibiting tying arrangements, if Studio X comes to a client with a slate of pictures and one of those pictures is a must-have picture, the wheels are greased for the other releases. All of these elements were satisfied: Fox had been the home/distributor of the original *Star Wars* films, clearly wanted to maintain a relationship with George Lucas, believed each film had the potential to generate hundreds of millions of dollars, from which it could generate significant fees, and was ensured of multiple tentpole releases anchoring its summer slate over a number of years (from which it could directly or indirectly leverage other films).

The reason a producer would want this type of deal is to maintain the upside and keep control over the property both creatively and economically. Talking about the arrangement, *Business Week* noted of Lucas's control of the prequels: "He retains the rights to dictate marketing, distribution, and just about everything else about how they'll be seen in theaters."[40] The deal was the envy of every producer that could afford to bankroll his production, and before Disney acquired Pixar the distribution deal being negotiated was publicly referred to as a "Lucas-type distribution deal," where Pixar would pay Disney a modest fee and retain the upside profit.

Applying the above test, Disney was in a similar position with Pixar as Fox was with Lucasfilm: Disney wanted to continue its collaboration with Pixar (one of the most successful in studio history), believed it would earn significant fees from distribution (even with a significantly discounted distribution fee), and with the track record of past Pixar films knew it would have a series of must-have hits that would help leverage its other films and businesses. The one significant difference, however, was that while Fox and Lucasfilm had been successful partners, Fox was not a brand inextricably tied with Lucasfilm. In the case of Disney–Pixar, the fact that Disney is a consumer brand heralded as synonymous with successful animation and that Pixar, for years, had been upstaging them

125

and could have become a competitor was clearly a factor. One could argue that the deal took on overtones beyond pure current economics, and that more than a distribution relationship was needed to restore Disney to its glory and market leadership in the animation space. To the extent that Disney may not have been willing to take a sliver of the pie on a successful animated film as opposed to holding the full upside (including character/franchise rights to cycle through theme parks and other vertically integrated divisions), the scales were simply tipped in favor of a purchase (ironically, after Disney spurned a rent-a-distributor deal with Pixar and acquired the animation powerhouse, a few years later it acquired Lusasfilm).

Finally, even with all the clout in the world, a producer still needs the product distributed and cannot afford the massive overhead of a worldwide theatrical and video distribution team. Despite whatever Hollywood-hugging one may witness, this is a relationship driven by necessity, not love. It is this remaining underlying tension that fuels the passion for new distribution mediums, now enabled by digital technology, and holds the ace card of a producer bypassing the studio distribution system and going directly to the consumer. It is only the theatrical/video/TV infrastructure, marketing expertise and clout, and associated overhead costs that pose obstacles and require a partnership between production and distribution. What those who want to bypass the traditional studio system and distribute directly often fail to recognize is that the studios are quite good at what they do. Studios have become adept at efficiently creating brands overnight and repeating this feat on a regular basis. The infrastructure is not something to be dismissed lightly, for it is to the success of a film what an efficient supply pipeline is to a manufacturing endeavor; moreover, as discussed in Chapter 1, the efficiency is created by scale and cannot be repeated easily, if at all, on a one-off basis.

Reduced Distribution Fees are Key to the Deal

While the relative advantages detailed above are all important, it is key to remember that the heart of a pure distribution arrangement is the producer's ability to lock in a below-market distribution fee. For this to work economically for both parties, it needs to be primarily a financially driven relationship and not a competitive one.

While market rate fees can be 30 percent and higher, a rent-a-distributor deal where the producer is providing all the financing can drive down fees to single-digit levels. DreamWorks Animation, in its SEC filing, noted that it had an 8 percent distribution fee with DreamWorks studio.[41]

While this could be perceived as a sweetheart deal between affiliated entities, it apparently set a benchmark for Steven Spielberg. When DreamWorks announced its split from Paramount in October 2008, backed by a reported $1.3 billion in financing from India's Reliance Communications and debt raised by J.P. Morgan,[42] it lined up a distribution deal with Universal, the studio where Spielberg made *Jaws* and began his career. Commenting on the deal, the *New York Times* noted: "Under the terms of the seven-year deal, Universal will distribute up to six films a year, according to a statement by the studio and the film executives. Universal will receive an 8 percent distribution fee, according to a person briefed on the negotiations."[43] Shortly after this deal was announced, however, the Universal relationship fell apart and Dream-Works instead teamed with Disney, where the studio announced it would release 30 films over five years under its Touchstone Pictures label. Evidencing the difficult climate of raising financing at the time (even for Spielberg, the ultimate luminary in Hollywood), as well as the sensitivity of how low studios were willing to reduce their distribution fees, the *New York Times* later reported that DreamWorks would instead be paying a 10 percent distribution fee: "The percentage is more onerous than the company had expected at Universal."[44]

Funding Ensures Tapping into 100 Percent of Revenue Streams

As briefly discussed above, one of the principal advantages to funding all or a percentage of costs is that it tends to eliminate "Hollywood accounting" (see Chapter 10) and allows the backers to look to all revenue streams for recoupment and profits. Net profits definitions and participations are structured to define only a certain pot of revenues, such as video only being accounted for at a royalty percentage rate, rather than 100 percent of revenues. By partnering with a studio, a co-financier, if smart, stands in the same shoes as the studio; namely, they will recoup out of the same revenue streams and at the same time.

Television: How and Why Does it Differ?

To understand television financing, it is important to grasp that there are several micro-markets that are fundamentally different in their economics. While all TV is focused on attracting eyeballs, and methods of monteizing those eyeballs (ratings or capturing subscribers), cable, network, pay TV, and syndication all behave a bit differently. The following is a short overview, with the details of TV economics discussed in Chapter 6.

Network, Cable, and Pay TV Financing

Network

Network television is the most ratings-sensitive of all TV, for historically 100 percent of the revenues from a broadcast show are generated from advertising dollars tied to ratings. This creates cutthroat competition for eyeballs, and fractions of a percent of a ratings point can make or break shows. Network primetime shows are the most expensive to produce, with budgets in the millions of dollars; network license fees rarely cover the budget, but can exceed 50 percent of the budget. Accordingly, a TV production is usually faced with a healthy deficit. It would not be uncommon for a production budget for a primetime one-hour drama to be over $2 million, and if there were 10 episodes ordered and the license fee covered half the budget, the production would be in the red $10 million or more (and if a full "season" of 22 episodes is ordered, this will more than double). The only way to recover this deficit is from off-network revenues, including DVD sales, international broadcast licenses, syndication (see Chapter 6 for more detail), and new online and digital revenue streams (see Chapter 7).

It is because of this high risk, and the fact that few shows make it to syndication to recoup, that network shows are generally produced by parties with deep pockets—the studios and networks. The strategy is much like that of films: diversify production, hits pay for misses, and the vast majority of profits come from select properties that are breakout hits.

Cable

Cable is interesting because it is a hybrid. Cable networks earn money from two sources: advertising and carriage fees. Advertising works exactly like network, with inventory sold in the open market and dependent on ratings. The advantage cable has is that, in addition to advertising revenues, the networks are paid by cable operators to be carried on their system. In years past, some stations had to pay the cable operators to be carried, but currently the economics have flipped and almost all cable networks with material national reach are paid by the carriers. The issue is the amount of the fee, which can vary dramatically.

The basic economics are that the cable system will negotiate a per-subscriber fee, which is then paid on a per-month basis. If a network,

128

for example, is carried in 50 million homes and is paid an average of $0.10 per subscriber per month, then it would receive $60 million per year. Another network with similar reach, demanding $0.50 per subscriber per month, would reap $300 million per year ($25 million × 12 months). Because many major networks with national carriage now approach closer to 85 million homes, the numbers can be staggering. At the $0.50 level, this translates into over half a billion dollars on an annual basis. On the flip side, the cable carrier then offers consumers a "basic pay package," which bundles channels and takes the aggregate cable fees paid by consumers and reallocates the pool to acquire access to the various channels in the cable bundle. If a particular channel is in greater demand, such as ESPN, then it will have a higher per-subscriber fee than a channel that is less critical to the average basic pay subscriber. What has become interesting in recent years is that cable stations have managed to markedly increase the license fees paid for carriage through the success of original content. As further discussed in Chapter 6, cable networks such as AMC, on the strength of original series (e.g., *Mad Men*, *Breaking Bad*, *The Walking Dead*) have altered their profile and increased their fees—to the tune in AMC's case, which was previously a bastion for older reruns, where operators pay in the range of $0.40 per subscriber per month, and on a base of 80 million subscribers can earn an estimated $30 million per month just from fees.[45]

The fees paid by the cable operators ultimately allow cable stations to be a bit less ratings-sensitive and to make larger episode commitments. The one element the cable stations generally do not have, however, is the upside of syndication. This is because cable itself grew up as an aftermarket, and tends to be the home for shows after network. Network shows go to cable or syndication, but there are few, if any, examples of shows moving upstream from cable to network. As more and more cable stations venture into original programming to differentiate themselves, there may be a secondary market that evolves for the best of these shows (a clear opportunity for online); until that time, the economics of cable rest on advertising, allocated carriage fees, DVD sales/VOD rental, digital downloads, and international sales.

Pay TV

Pay TV differs the most dramatically; instead of advertising dollars and ratings, these "networks" are directly dependent on subscriber fees. To a degree, this insulates the networks from direct ratings pressure. This fact, coupled with greater creative freedom due to different regulatory restrictions (being outside of "free TV" standards and practices), allows a range of programming that cannot be shown on cable or network, and has led to innovative hits based on violent or sexual themes, such as *The Sopranos* and *Sex and the City*. How many episodes a pay network wants to commission is simply an exercise in allocating a relatively fixed/known programming budget created out of its subscriber-funded revenue stream.

As for subscriber funding, the economics are an extension of the cable per-subscriber fees detailed above. In the case of cable channels, the per-subscriber fees are generally in the cents per subscriber, as a portion of the fee consumers pay for cable is allocated by the carrier among the various networks. In contrast, the carriers can afford dollars per subscriber for pay stations, since they pass along the cost to subscribers who pay a specific upcharge for access to the pay network. Basically, consumers can opt in and out of whether to subscribe to HBO, Starz, and Showtime, and the number of consumers that opt in and what they are willing to pay for the channel has a direct correlation on the channel's funding and programming budget.

What is interesting is that pay TV did not historically seek or depend on an aftermarket. With the new trend of certain shows "sanitized" for basic cable, plus the boon in DVD sales from TV season box sets, pay TV hits seem to have the best of all worlds: high subscriber fees, minimal ratings pressure, international sales, DVD sales and online downloads, VOD rentals, and secondary runs on cable plus potentially online.

Deficit and Risk Continuum

Logically, based on the revenue sources coming into cable, network, and pay TV programming, the risk continuum is fairly simple (see Figure 3.3).

Pay TV broadcasters know their budgets, and if a show runs a deficit it is because the cost/episode is greater than the allocation the service has given the show; this may happen if there is an expectation of downstream revenues, and a conscious decision to run an upfront deficit simply to sustain a high production budget. In the basic cable scenario, ratings and advertising are still a material component, and because of the lack of aftermarket syndication opportunities, shows need to pay

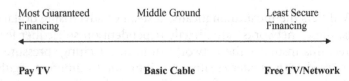

Figure 3.3 The Risk Continuum

for themselves upfront. A deficit may be sustainable under the theory that a critically acclaimed show raises the basic cable network's profile (as described above in the case of recent AMC hits such as *Mad Men*), and thus ultimately its per-subscriber carriage fee. This is a reasonable assumption when targeting more niche audiences, but an assumption with limited elasticity given the supplementary need of advertising revenues based on ratings performance. Network show financing carries by far the highest risk, as all revenue is dependent on performance and advertising dollars tied to ratings.

TV and Online's Relatively Lower-Risk Profile

Television programs are less risky to finance than film for several key reasons. First, the upfront investment is simply not as high, as TV episodes are in the low millions of dollars rather than the average $70 million cost (pre P&A) of the average studio film. Second, the marketing costs of launching a show are materially lower; although there can be significant PR and off-air promotion costs, a significant part of achieving audience awareness is on-air promotion. Even if house ads are considered opportunity costs, the number is small next to the amount overall media spends to launch a major movie. Third, networks create pilots and test shows before launching series—while movies may be tested with audiences and tweaked, there is no pilot stage, and a movie release is akin to all bets on the pilot. Fourth, TV series rarely receive full episode commitments, with broadcasters waiting to order more "product" until they see how the show is performing. Finally, in the case of cable and pay TV, there are built-in revenue streams, creating a cushion; this is in contrast to a movie, where literally no one can show up.

Online

Financing shorter-form online programming ratchets down the risk yet another level. Compared to television, budgets are a fraction, which is due both to the fact that programming is shorter and the cost per minute of production is significantly less. While the cost-per-minute differential may narrow as efforts are made to improve quality (see Chapter 7, regarding online leaders such as Netflix moving into original content), the shorter format most producers are adopting will continue to provide an advantage (although, it is possible on a cost-per-minute basis it could become more expensive, given there are less minutes to amortize, and series costs tend to be front-loaded). Accordingly, the sampling nature of the Internet coupled with shorter pilots means that online production may indefinitely remain lower risk versus film and television, provided that upsides materialize. One could argue that today the risks are higher because the revenue side remains immature and there are few proven models/examples of profitability, regardless of how low production costs may be. This is why the business launched predominantly with VC-type backing, and why we have not seen the development of similar financing structures as in other media.

I previously asked the CFO of ABC, Jim Hedges (recently stepped down in 2012 after more than 15 years with the network), how he viewed the landscape and whether we would see online financing mechanisms start to mimic those found in TV and other traditional media, and he advised:

We're at the beginning of real change in how consumers view television content. And the change is significant and will provide great new opportunities for media companies.

Historically, viewers consumed television content on the big three networks when it was programmed by a network executive. There were no other options. If you missed your favorite show Thursday at 9 p.m. on ABC, you had to wait for the repeat or you just missed it.

Today, consumers are programming their own "networks" by using the many options available to them, including watching it "live" on the network, watching it on their DVR, their computer via the Internet, by downloading a purchased episode from iTunes, or on their mobile device. In the very near future, video-on-demand will also be another option available, and there will be others that follow. They can also buy the DVD of the season's episodes shortly after the season ends.

All of these new platforms provide the opportunity for viewers to consume the shows they love when they choose to, wherever they are—all with the potential to increase viewing. Historically, fans of hit TV shows only watched six episodes on average. If that average increases with all of these new opportunities to view, then media companies can monetize the additional viewing.

Some of the new platforms also have the added benefit (yet to be realized) of being able to target advertising to specific demographic and psychographic breaks, in large part because we'll be able to know something about that consumer, either by tracking where they go online or by asking them who they are. This should result in more efficient return on investment for advertisers, as well as higher ad rates for media companies.

In terms of financing, I believe the traditional methods will remain as viable options for big media companies. For online productions, I think it will be split into several buckets of financing: big media companies will finance online productions in a similar way to productions created for the linear television platforms, and may use online as a new development ground for TV shows; small production companies will develop and produce online content in a nonunion environment, funded by venture capital and other traditional sources; user-generated content will continue to grow as the price of entry continues to drop, although it appears to be difficult to monetize this content in the near term.

VC Analogy

All of these factors combine to make financing TV a much lower-risk proposition than movies. Networks (and new online "networks")still function in a private equity-type role, financing a slate of projects where hits pay for misses. The fundamental economics of attracting consumer dollars is similar: performance translates into ticket sales with movies and to ratings and/or consumer demand for the channel in TV. Also, the number of movies a studio will release and the TV shows a "network" will back are in the same order of magnitude (ones and tens, not hundreds or thousands of different properties per year). Therefore, acting as a VC, educated bets will be placed on a relatively small sampling of projects, with upfront investment significant and an expectation that the majority of projects may fail or lose money. The hits, however, can have staggering ROIs in the hundreds of millions of dollars. Should broadcasters not therefore be classified as a specialized form of VC or private equity investor financing a variety of projects they help nurture, but not directly produce/manage?

To the extent this analogy is accurate, then it is also fair to query why a range of financing mechanisms have not evolved in TV similar to film. In short, there are no obvious answers. It may be that broadcasters have sufficient financing and that there is no need to cede the windfall syndication/long-tail profits on hits (having learned their lesson from the days of fin/syn regulations, where producers earned more than the broadcasters) (see Chapter 6). Also, it may be that timing plays a significant role (the return on TV is less immediate given the need to build up a library of episodes to syndicate over several years), that opportunities are limited by the absence of slate deals (networks pick up shows one by one), or that staged pickups, coupled with guaranteed license fees, apportion risk into manageable buckets.

The Wrinkles of Coproduction

Coproductions, as described earlier as in the case of *Titanic*, are structures designed either to share financial risk or to bring together financial and creative parties in a form of joint venture. Coproductions are challenging because they usually involve a partner by necessity rather than choice: if you do not need to hedge the financial risk or could acquire the creative yourself, then a coproduction should not be considered. Some of the most successful coproductions are partnerships between arch-competitors who come together simply out of fear or necessity.

I will divide coproductions, other than instances of coproductions between two major studios to hedge risk, into three principal groupings:

■ Case A: A party invests in a production in return for an equity stake
■ Case B: A party invests in a production in return for distribution rights
■ Case C: When there is creative collaboration between parties on a production

Case A: A Party Invests in Production in Return for an Equity Stake

The simplest scenario to understand is a 50/50 coproduction, where both parties fund a production equally and profits are also shared equally (and paid at the same time). Even in a 50/50 split, however, if both parties bring different assets or expertise, it is likely that underlying rights may be divided by contract such that only defined elements are actually split 50/50. For example, it is possible to allocate copyright ownership, back-end participations, and defined exploitation rights in a different ratio even if both parties funded 50/50 and the goal is to roughly equalize net profits from aggregate revenue streams. Accordingly, a 50/50-funded deal could vest copyright 100 percent in one party, or vest a lesser percentage of the profits in one party if that party were compensated in other ways, such as having exclusive distribution rights in a category and keeping 100 percent of a corresponding distribution fee. I have been involved in deals, as yet another iteration, where one party funded

134

virtually 100 percent of the production costs, the parties shared copyright 50/50 (actually an awkward construct pursuant to copyright law), and the back-end revenues were split in a complicated formula.

The core principle, though, is usually a sharing of upfront costs and therefore risk in return for some ownership stake. The tricky part is ownership, which can mean anything from ownership of the underlying intellectual property, to rights to exploit various distribution rights, to an income stream driven off of a contractual definition of specified revenues/profits. Because each of these categories is then divisible into a myriad of options, the permutations can be diverse and complicated—nice fodder for entertainment lawyers and analysts alike.

Case B: A Party Invests in a Production in Return for Distribution Rights

It is not uncommon for a deal in which one party acquires select distribution rights to be characterized as a coproduction, especially when the value of such distribution rights is considered a significant part of the overall financing. Accordingly, a significant pre-sale or rights acquisition deal can rise to the level of a coproduction when the acquiring party advances or otherwise guarantees a significant percentage of the budget in return for the acquired rights. This is especially true when principal rights are acquired for a region. For example, if Producer A is producing a television show and Distributor B acquires rights to distribute or directly broadcast the show throughout Europe, then Distributor B may be informally or formally referred to as a coproduction partner.

The collateral impact is that downstream sub-distributors may also then consider themselves coproducers, especially if the show has status attached to it, even though Producer A would neither have a direct relationship with the sub-distributors nor consider them coproducers (but merely licensees). This may occur, for example, where a European-wide distributor licenses a show to a local network, and that network portrays itself on flyers and other literature as a coproducer. Because in this case a coproducer does not actually mean anything, it is akin to a status ranking where the broadcasting station wants to confer status or significance to its role. It would be highly unusual for this to happen in a simple license, but if they did commit and advance money early in a partnership with the broader European-wide distributor, there is at least an argument.

The underlying reason for speaking about this type of scenario in coproduction terms is that Distributor B has taken a significant risk, committing early and upfront to the show and playing a material role in the financing of the production budget. Depending upon the exact percentage, and the relationship between the parties, the distributor may also have some creative input to ensure the end product works in its territory.

What is ultimately interesting in this scenario is that a third party, by committing to buy a property before it is finished (or, in cases, before production even commences), can be treated as a partner even if they neither acquire any rights to the underlying intellectual property (i.e., copyright) nor any back-end interest in the property. The entire investment and relationship is bounded by acquiring territory-specific rights, with revenues limited solely to such rights.

Case C: When There is Creative and/or Production Collaboration Between Parties with Respect to a Production

This is a common scenario when parties pool different skill sets. A good example of this would involve outsourcing physical production, or certain elements of physical production. This is the typical pattern in animation, where an American studio, again for simplicity called here Producer A, commissions/develops and oversees scripts and story-boards, and then sends the packet to an overseas studio in Asia to produce the actual cel or CG animation. This pattern is dictated by economic efficiencies and realities. A United States network, for example, may be more inclined to buy a show if it is written by local talent it is comfortable with and helmed by a director it knows; however, there may be acceptance or even lack of interest where the ultimate physical production occurs. In contrast, the overseas studio may have little or no development expertise or reputation, but instead can offer lower production costs due to labor-rate differentials or local government tax incentives. By teaming up, the coproduction arrangement maximizes its opportunity to license the show to a United States network while lowering the production costs.

The above scenario could easily be structured as simple work for hire, or outsourcing. However, if financing is desired, the overseas studio may contribute toward the budget either with direct cash or discounts to labor rates; namely, investing sweat equity for a stake. Accordingly, if Overseas Studio B wants to retain an equity interest, wants to retain local or regional distribution rights, or needs to retain certain rights to qualify for subsidies or tax credits, then the deal could be structured as a co-production. Moreover, if it is perceived that each party will have a better chance of striking a good local license for broadcast of the property, splitting the distribution rights so that Producer A and Overseas Studio B handle their local markets, a coproduction becomes natural.

Hybrid and Example

It is possible to combine one or all of these options into a variety of hybrids. For example, Producer A could own the underlying copyright and IP 100 percent, but still team up with a partner with specialized production expertise and related distribution connections; Partner B, for its part, may have significant creative rights, retain an equity interest in the revenue stream of the production, invest directly or indirectly (e.g., discounted production fees), and also keep select distribution rights. This crosses over all categories above: there is creative collaboration, there is an equity investment in the project, and certain distribution rights are acquired. One can easily see this scenario in the context of a publisher, for example, that owns a famous book but wants a partner to produce a series for TV and help distribute it to networks.

The following is an illustrative example. Publisher A owns a book about a green tiger that has a moderate following. Distributor B, based in Europe, loves the book and wants to finance a low-budget movie, believing it will be a great kids' video property. The budget is $4 million, but Distributor B can only afford an investment of $3 million. Publisher A has an affiliated animation division, and both parties believe they will be compatible partners to creatively produce and distribute the movie.

There is a shortfall of $1 million in the overall budget, but 15 percent of this ($600,000) is for customary producer's fees and another $400,000 is from a 20 percent overhead markup on $2 million of below-the-line production costs. Publisher A realizes that if they forego any margin and markup and produce literally at cost, they can get by with the $3 million cash and make the movie. They decide to do this, but only as long as they share the copyright and have a deal that gives them the appropriate upside for their investment.

The coproduction deal may therefore be struck as follows:

- Publisher A and Distributor B share copyright 50/50 (or retained 100 percent by A)
- Distributor B has worldwide distribution rights for a fee of 25 percent
- Publisher A invests $1 million in foregone markups ("sweat equity")
- Distributor B invests $3 million in cash.
- The parties agree to share profits based on the ratio of investment (75/25)
- Publisher A has a back-end creative percentage for the rights (X percent of net)

137

```
$10M revenue – $6M costs
   (A gets its $1M, and B its $3M + $2M marketing costs) =
   $4M net revenues
   (Publisher A would keep $1M, and Distributor B $3M)
```

Figure 3.4

If $10 million in revenues is received, what is the split of the pot? Let us assume there are $2 million in other costs (marketing, etc., beyond the production costs) and the $10 million is net after taking out the 25 percent distribution fee off the top (see Figure 3.4).

In the above example, the split would change to 67.5/32.5 if there were a creative participation of 10 percent. Publisher A would then take $400,000 from the net revenues, leaving the parties to split the balance of $3.6 million 75/25; Publisher A's share would be $400,000 + $900,000 (25 percent of $3.6 million), which represents 32.5 percent of the $4 million net revenues. This formula would then become more complicated if the parties split up distribution, such that one party held Europe and the other party the rest of the world. In such an instance, there could be recoupment out of the revenues of their income streams, with shared upside in overages; if one party has recouped before the other, the sums over recoupment may go to recoup the unrecouped party until everyone has had their initial investment returned.

I could go on and on with further wrinkles, making this needlessly complex. The point is that when two parties share rights and underlying financing, the arrangement can range from very simple to formulas that, in the end, only the participation accountants may fully understand how to apply. The formulas become inherently complex when there is an actual or perceived inequality of either money invested or rights owned. Up front, some of the key hurdles to overcome include:

■ Should a party have an equity investment equal to the percentage of the budget they funded, or is there a dilution formula applied from the beginning because one party's non-cash contribution needs to be valued? This is the case when one of the parties contributes the property/intangible creative elements for which they need to be compensated. Accordingly, if one party puts in 60 percent of the money, and the other 40 percent, that 100 percent may only recoup against 90 percent if the creative partner is separately granted 10 percent as inalienable compensation for the creative.

- Should a party be entitled to dollar-for-dollar weighted value for foregone margin, such as reducing or eliminating a producer's fee? The project could take a year or more to make, and the producer's fee would have been the profit margin—it may seem easy to say that was not real money, but the company may have foregone profitable work to invest in this project, for which it earned nothing.
- What happens when one party recoups before another, if the rights have been divided up? Is recoupment cross-collateralized so that both parties get the benefit of the other's rights for recoupment, and then the splits adjust later, or is each party dependent on its own rights to recoup its own investment?
- Who owns/controls the property? Does one party, by virtue of a greater investment, have say over future exploitation/derivative productions?

The sharing of creative production, on the one hand, and financing/distribution, on the other, is always complicated. Look what happened to Disney/Pixar, and that was a relatively straightforward arrangement where who did what in terms of financing, distribution, and production was very clear. Few people talk about *Finding Nemo* as a coproduction, but in certain structural terms the deal could easily be characterized that way. Financing was shared 50/50, but because copyright was not shared in the same way, it was often simply characterized as a distribution relationship in the press.

Online's Relatively Low Coproduction Quotient

There are few examples of coproductions in the online context because creative tends to be homegrown, costs are relatively low, and a key driver is the ability to produce and distribute independently. Because of the current immaturity of the revenue side, however, as more producers strive to deliver higher-quality online content (thus driving up costs), capital risked will increase and coproductions will inevitably emerge. Said another way, the more online original production comes to look like TV, the more likely similar coproduction structures will develop. In fact, because the chance of success should not dramatically increase with an increase in budget (assuming "nobody knows"), one can posit a proportionate relationship between the increase of production costs and the chance of forming coproductions (see Figure 3.5).

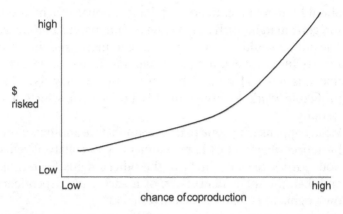

Figure 3.5 The Coproduction Quotient

Government-Backed Coproductions: International Schemes and State Tax Subsidies

International Foreign governments often provide tax incentives to bolster local production. These take all sorts of forms, and can be implemented at a national or regional level.

In certain cases, such as in the *Cloud Atlas* example above, a local government or fund will literally pay for a percentage of the total budget. Australia is one of the more aggressive regimes promoting local filming, and it is estimated that roughly 12 percent of the budget of *Superman Returns* was saved by local tax schemes/breaks.[46] France's CNC sponsors a variety of schemes to assist the French film industry, with layers of incentives permeating production and sometimes tied to local quotas. In the animation area, for example, French animation studios have a distinct cost advantage over American competitors, as between increased fees from local broadcasters for qualifying local production plus CNC subsidies, it is common to cover over one-third of a production's budget through incentive-based schemes. Europe, in particular, has a flourishing coproduction tradition, in part from the 1992 European Convention on Cinematic Coproduction, which sanctions productions that cross borders within the EU to partake of subsidies offered by all participating EU countries.[47] Canada also has a particularly robust incentive system tied to an intricate system of tax credits, in part driven by its small domestic market when compared to the United States.

It is impossible to summarize all the worldwide programs, but there seems to be a rhythm of different countries luring production and then pulling back, with production moving around the globe seeking the best deals of the day. Germany, which had been very active with film tax funds in the 1990s, is now less aggressive. Starting a few years ago, Singapore, via its Media Development Authority and Economic Development Board, became focused on providing incentives for local Asian production. (As a disclaimer, I have personally been involved in a couple of significant deals in Singapore over the last few years linked to government-backed initiatives.) The recent filming of *The Hobbit* trilogy included a showdown between director Peter Jackson and New Zealand authorities. The government ultimately yielded and granted various financial incentives to keep filming in New Zealand (motivated, no doubt, by bolstering the local economy combined with recognizing the tourism and positive PR benefits the original *The Lord of the Rings* films brought to the country): "The National-led Government controversially changed employment laws and granted tax breaks amounting to $67 million to Warners in 2010 after director Sir Peter Jackson warned *The Hobbit* franchise could be moved to countries where it was cheaper to film."[48] The debate over granting these incentives became a national cause célèbre, and attracted worldwide interest—in the end, the investment seemed to pay off, as a *New Zealand Herald* article sub-headlined "Majority Back $67 Million in Tax Breaks Given for The Hobbit, as Bank Estimates $1.5 Billion in Revenue Retained" noted that most people were fine granting the incentive so long as the country would more than recoup the amount provided (a not-very-surprising result, and hardly a ringing endorsement for underwriting costs if actually risky).

Abuse of Systems and Credits   Cinar, an animation studio that was publicly listed and known globally for such hits as *Babar* and *Arthur*, provides an example of how tax incentives and subsidies become so integral to production costs that people will bend the rules to comply. One of the tenets of many international schemes, including in France and Canada, is the tying of tax credits to hiring local talent; namely, the government is allocating money to stimulate local work, and imposes specific quotas that must be met as a quid pro quo for qualifying for the tax packages or other subsidies. These are often applied on a "points system," where the production must have a certain number of local points: engaging a Canadian director is worth X points, Canadian writers Y points, and so on. Depending on the scheme, it becomes difficult to secure enough qualifying points without the majority of key talent being local. Cinar admitted wrongly claiming tax credits listing writers as Canadian when, in fact, the scripts were written by American writers— this and other improprieties then came to light during an investigation that led to the firing of the founders, tax fraud claims, and the delisting of the company from Nasdaq. The moral is simple: follow the rules, especially when taking government money.

United States-Based Schemes   Just like foreign governments have established tax and other schemes to stimulate local production, various states have implemented programs to attract filming. I am always asking people: "Why are you filming in Oregon, Michigan, etc.?" only to catch myself when realizing it has little to do with the physical location and everything to do with the cross section of the environment working and local incentive programs.

The amounts granted can be extraordinary because most schemes are tied to percentages, which means, as budgets go up, so does the taxpayers' commitment. Controversy followed Brad Pitt's movie *The Curious Case of Benjamin Button* (Paramount and Warner Bros.) when it created local tax credit obligations of over $27 million as the film's budget climbed to a reported $167 million.[49] (Note: The criticisms of *The Curious Case of Benjamin Button* may fall into the "can't win" category, as part of the goal was to create local jobs in the post-Hurricane Katrina economy.) Most states offer credits tied to production cost rebates for amounts spent in-state, typically ranging from 15 to 25 percent. Louisiana's program, however, initially offered credits tied to the entire budget, and therefore captured costs, including some costs relating to stars, that may have been incurred outside the state; this has now been changed, and credits are tied to in-state production spending.[50]

The justification for such credits is creating local work and jobs. However, some argue that low-cost production will migrate, that taxpayers will wise up to funding other people's productions, and that the employment created is short-lived. Regardless of the spin, the essence of the programs is that state taxpayer money is being used to fund production, and it is a difficult calculation to assess whether the local stimulus generates more money than is spent. The *New York Times* summarized:

Some, like Michigan, simply refund a percentage of expenditures to the producers. Others, like Louisiana's, issue a tax credit that can reduce the taxes a producer pays or be sold to someone else. Either way, the state gives up revenue that otherwise would be collected to put money in the producer's pockets . . . critics have sharply challenged the notion that state subsidies for the film business can ever buy more than momentary glitter.[51]

States that are able to create a steady stream of production no doubt create local jobs; the challenge is not trying to match each new aggressive scheme to keep those jobs, as someone globally will inevitably offer a better deal in an attempt to steal production away.

Online Impact

- Online production has created a wave of venture capital money funding niche channels.
- Risks associated with producing original online content, which is still an immature market, should theoretically create coproduction structures to help defray that risk (despite generally lower production costs); as budgets increase and more original premium content is produced online, coproduction arrangements mimicking TV are likely to grow.
- The lower cost of online content may come to threaten traditional financing mechanisms.
- Oddly, the online and digital world has had less impact on film and TV financing than in distribution and revenue areas.
- Traditional financing schemes are not being applied to online production because despite the by-title risk in film and TV, distribution revenue streams for traditional media are relatively "bankable," whereas a dependable Internet revenue model has not evolved to support related financing.
- Crowdsourcing is evolving as a new means of financing production, tapping into the 1:1 relationships enabled by the Web and finding some success in harnessing the power of core fans to contribute to products they want to see.
- While the growth of video advertising is making online viewing more akin to TV, there is a lack of harmonization of advertising metrics; the culture clash or ratings points versus CPMs, coupled with the nature of online viewing being a form of syndication, creates a value gulf that continues to make comparing financing and programming in the two ecosystems more like comparing apples and oranges. The challenge is being further exacerbated by multi-screen viewing, which has not been materially factored into standard advertising metrics; a further challenge is assessing value if viewing is measurably fragmented, with consumers often keeping an eye on something else (e.g., a social network), while still tuned to a program.

143

CHAPTER 4

Theatrical Distribution

144   Unlike the market for traditional packaged goods where the goal is often to sustain and grow a household brand over time, the film and television business operates by media blitz to try to create new brands overnight. A movie can become a brand unto itself, and what business other than the film business strives to create a new brand over a weekend? The time, money, and effort expended to create public awareness of a film in its opening weekend is staggering, and has become the front edge of criticism by artists who bemoan the subjugation of art to the beast of box office grosses.

Because a major studio film frequently needs to recoup better than $100 million between production and marketing costs—with the average cost of a studio film approximately $70 million and the average marketing costs approximately $35 milllion[1]—openings are critically important. (Note: These amounts were published by the MPA a few years ago, and while not recently updated, they still serve as one of the few "hard data points" published in the industry; as discussed in Chapters 1 and 9, SNL Kagan estimates that the costs were similar to these prior benchmarks, with the average studio film having a negative cost of $72.3 million in 2010 and $66.6 million in 2011, and domestic print and marketing costs of approximately $40 million; see Table 9.5 in Chapter 9.) One of the most interesting developments of the maturation of the distribution market is that the more important the revenue streams outside of box office have become, the more important the value placed on the box office. In other businesses, the thesis would be that as traditional outlets were overtaken by new channels of distribution, one might see the original outlets dwindle in importance and, in cases, be phased out entirely. Not so in the film world.

With the growth of other markets, and the potential for combined revenues from TV, video, merchandising, and new media sources to surpass revenues from movie theaters, the bellwether of box office has grown in importance. The reason is twofold, and relatively simple. First, the success of the box office continues to be an accurate barometer for the success in subsequent release markets. Second, the media frenzy surrounding theatrical release drives awareness that is amortized over the life cycle of the product and drives consumption months and even years later.

In terms of the influence of the Web and digital technologies on the theatrical market, while there are clearly major changes in exhibition and production systems (e.g., HD cameras and digital cinema), perhaps the most significant impact the digital revolution is having on theatrical exhibition is the way movies are marketed. Budgets for online marketing are growing, virtually every movie has its own website and Facebook page, and marketing executives are trying to generate "buzz" by pushing out trailers and other information to YouTube and an array of social media sites. Additionally, review sites such as Rotten Tomatoes aggregate critics' opinions and reduce nationwide diverse reactions into a single, homogenized scorecard: What percentage of reviews are positive or negative? The ability to broadly market via leading websites and social media sites while narrowly targeting demographics via niche sites and seeding blogs and microblogging outlets is revolutionizing movie marketing—ask anyone under 25 today whether they check out a film first on the Web or on social media (where they may focus on "likes" or more specific recommendations from friends) as opposed to looking at a newspaper, and they are likely to sneer that you even posed the question. Although I could delve into these influences here, I simply want to highlight the impact, and instead address most of these factors in Chapter 9.

Theatrical Release as a Loss-Leader

Basic Definitions and the Uneasy Tension between Distribution and Production

Theatrical release simply means the exhibition of a film in movie theaters where revenue is derived from members of the public buying tickets.

The "gate," or the revenues derived from ticket sales, is what is referred to as "box office." The amount of money that the distributor keeps from the box office receipts is called "film rentals."

Box office can sometimes lead to misleading numbers when preparing macro-statistics on industry growth and trends because box office captures only a cumulative number. There are a myriad of ticket prices and discounts reflecting regional and local differences and accommodations for seniors and kids. Basically, the box office is an excellent measuring stick and the ultimate source of revenue, but it does not provide marketing data on who the consumers were or even how many of them attended (a concept that seems anachronistic in the age of social media, micro-blogging, and Web metrics). Box office over a period may have gone up, but that could mean that attendance was down while average ticket prices were up. Because of this ambiguity, some countries choose to measure trends by "admittance"; namely, how many people attended (i.e., tickets bought). This is customary in France, where the value of certain down-stream rights is pegged to attendance rather than revenue figures.

Theatrical release is the first trigger among film windows, and because a film can be rereleased, the most common trigger is the "initial theatrical release." How long a film stays in movie theaters is a factor of the film's performance, and studios negotiate picture-specific deals with each theater into which a film is booked. Depending upon clout and stature, the distributor (e.g., the studio's theatrical distribution arm) may be able to negotiate for guarantee or hold weeks, securing a set minimum period of time the film will be in release; guaranteed minimum weeks are obviously risky propositions for both sides, because if a film flops, the theater will want to drop it quickly and show something new, and the distributor will be reluctant to spend marketing dollars for fear of throwing good money after bad.

In extreme cases, the driving force may be neither of the negotiating parties, but the film's director or producer who secured a release commitment from the distributing studio. Lack of trust inevitably fuels the relationship, because producers and directors who have put years of work into a project want as many guarantees as possible that their film will have the best possible chance to succeed. Cries of "they didn't know how to handle the film" and other excuses are rife in Hollywood, in part because a project shifts 180 degrees in responsibility from delivery to release. During production, the director and producer are kings, and in almost total control over hundreds of people and millions of dollars. Once the film is delivered, the distributor is in near total control. An often-uneasy partnership is borne, and in failure it is easy to point a finger at the other party.

146

Distributors may be burdened with certain expectations, politics, and commitments, but basically function to make tough, on-the-spot business calls. Also, as suppliers, and factoring in their need to maintain good relationships with exhibitors, it does not behoove a distributor to keep a movie in theaters longer than makes sense. The relationship factor is then weighed together with opportunity costs (when the distributor could be substituting a more profitable picture) and the fact that the distributor is spending real money each day a film is in major release in marketing dollars to support cross-media campaigns.

The Theatrical Release Challenge—Locomotive for Awareness While Profits Remain Downstream

The other wrinkle is that, weekly box office numbers aside, there may be a marketing justification to keep a film in theaters. Because film rentals will rarely recoup a film's investment, the theatrical release can be seen as a loss-leader to create awareness of the property for downstream video, TV, and other rights. In fact, looking at the ultimates for the film (i.e., lifetime projections of all revenue sources), most distributors are reconciled to losing money through this stage of exploitation. Accordingly, the distributor is not running a straightforward break-even analysis in trying to decide whether to keep a film in theaters versus pulling it (balancing opportunity cost versus continuing marketing costs); this calculation is coupled with a more complex marketing analysis, taking into account consumer impressions, market awareness, and impact on providing the bang to fuel subsequent exploitation. Namely, there cannot be much of a long tail without a launch.

147

Ultimately, those in charge of distribution are almost always in an awkward position—they have virtually no input in the creative product, and yet are responsible for opening the film (in tandem with the marketing department) and literally charting its destiny. A distributor must make a good picture great, and somehow find a way on "a dog" to pull enough box office out quickly to recoup some investment before the public sours; moreover, it needs to achieve this within a context of not really knowing what the reaction will be (given the "nobody knows" quandary of experience goods).

Hedging Bets and Profiling Release Patterns

The film *Titanic* provides another good example in this context, as it posed a dilemma for the distributor and studio having to make high-stakes calls without the benefit of knowing how the audience would react. The reviews before opening were dicey, and the picture was well known in the Hollywood community to be suffering from budget problems. In fact, rumor had it that Fox was so nervous about the budget that it was desperate to sell off rights and reduce its potential downside, which it ultimately did with Paramount (see Chapter 3).

Selling off the upside and mitigating its potential downside turned out to be Paramount's gain, as the reviews were wrong and the picture became the all-time box office champ (until director James Cameron one-upped himself with *Avatar*). More than a box office champ, the film also defied the odds and played throughout the summer, staying on the charts for almost a whole year, ending up at $1.8 billion in worldwide box office ($600 million United States, $1.2 billion international).[2] When a film continues playing like this, beyond a typical pattern where most films would see a decline, it is referred to in industry lingo as "it's got legs."

In trying to select the right strategy, a distributor needs to profile its film and match the pattern of release to the nature of the film. This is really the ambit of marketing (which, again, is discussed in detail in Chapter 9). Briefly, however, for a picture where word of mouth is important, the film may only be opened in select venues for buzz to build. Assuming success, the picture then expands locations as its reputation grows, as was the case for Sony's release of Katherine Bigelow's *Zero Dark Thirty*, launching in New York and Los Angeles before Christmas 2012 and then expanding in mid January. (Note: The initial limited release still satisfied eligibility for 2012 Academy Award contention, which can sometimes be a strategy to debut films in the holiday period and then expand in the New Year, given announcements of Oscar nominations occur early in January.) A staged release was also the strategy for Clint Eastwood's Best Picture Oscar-winning film *Million Dollar Baby* (2005). Warner Bros. believed they had a strong picture, even one that might be Oscar caliber, but the women's boxing theme and euthanasia twist needed nurturing to attract broad audiences. This strategy of building buzz before widening the release is also sometimes used when a film may be perceived as an art or period piece (e.g., some of the earlier Miramax pictures, such as Merchant Ivory Productions), as well as when a picture is perceived to appeal to more of an intellectual crowd. Woody Allen films would fall into this latter category, and tend to open in big cities, including his hometown and frequent film backdrop Manhattan, before broadening after hopefully generating buzz and critical acclaim.

148

The more typical strategy is to open a picture wide, taking as much box office upfront as possible when consumers are enticed into attending through the large upfront marketing campaign creating awareness.

History and Market Evolution

Consent Decrees, Block Booking, and Blind Bidding

The current exhibition environment has come full circle from 50 or more years ago when most of the major studios owned theaters and vertically integrated the production–distribution–exhibition chain by preferentially selling to their own theaters. This included Paramount, MGM, 20th Century Fox, Warner Bros., and RKO. As a result of complaints by independents, the Department of Justice sued these five studios, alleging anticompetitive behavior, and won a landmark case. In 1948, the Supreme Court in *U.S. v. Paramount* et al. forced these defendant studios to sign a consent decree and divest themselves of theater ownership, while retaining distribution and production.

In addition to forcing divestiture, the consent decree reached beyond the theater-owner defendants and brought the remaining major studios (Columbia, Universal, United Artists) within its ambit regarding certain booking practices. At that time, studios routinely engaged in what is referred to as "block booking," where the license of one picture was tied to the license of other films; in the extreme case, a producer/studio would pre-sell its entire slate of films for a year to a certain theater or theater chain. One tenet of antitrust law (at least at the time of the case) is that you cannot "tie" products, where a party uses the economic leverage of one product to force a buyer to also buy a second unrelated product that it does not want.

The justice department naturally saw block booking as anticompetitive, and outlawed the practice as part of the consent decree. Going forward, distributors were forced to sell films picture by picture, and theater by theater, with all theaters having a right to bid and compete to exhibit a film.

Another practice that was prohibited by the consent decree was "blind bidding." Blind bidding is just as it sounds: a distributor would make a theater owner bid on a film and agree to terms without the benefit of seeing the movie first. This was a particularly onerous practice given the inherent challenges of handicapping creative goods. The decree proscribed this practice, and the new law mandated that all films needed to be screened before being sold or put out to bid.

Multiplexes and Bankruptcies of Major Chains

A number of factors led to a spate of bankruptcies of several major chains following boom years in the 1990s. Probably the biggest contributor was the simple fact that screens grew at a pace that far outstripped the rise in movie attendance. According to the National Association of Theater Owners (NATO), in the period from 1988 through 2000, the number of screens in the United States rose to approximately 37,000 from 23,000, representing a 61 percent increase, while theater admissions only rose by about 36 percent. The trend then leveled out, with screens flattening out and coming down only slightly from a 1999 peak to 36,000 + as of the mid 2000s.[3]

This growth was spurred by the phenomenon of multiplexes, which could leverage common infrastructure (concessions, ticket sales, ushers) across multiple screens, and vary theater size, allowing them to match capacity to demand. This was a compelling economic proposition, but the eight- to 10-screen expansion seemed tempered compared to the next iteration of megaplexes. AMC, which originated the multiplex from a modest two-theater experiment, started the megaplex trend in 1994, building a 24-theater complex in Dallas. The megaplexes included now-common features such as coffee bars, stadium seating, and video arcades, and soon everyone followed.[4] The total number of theaters ultimately contracted, as exhibitors abandoned leases and consolidated screens into larger multi-screen venues; according to NATO, the number of locations actually contracted from 7,151 to 5,629 in the decade following the advent of multiplexes (e.g., roughly from 1995).[5] The contraction, though, was not enough to counter the larger issue of a massive increase in screens, high operating costs from new megaplexes, and smaller percentage increases in ticket sales and price of tickets.

The net result was too many empty seats and too much overhead, a formula that led to the bankruptcy over time of most of the major chains, such as Loews Cineplex Entertainment, Carmike Cinemas, United Artists, General Cinema, and Regal Cinemas.[6] In a sense, the economics of stadium theater venues are . . . like stadiums. Most of the time capacity is empty—some estimate that theaters operate in the range of 10–15 percent capacity (meaning most seats are empty most of the time)—and the key is maximizing consumption during peak full-capacity events (i.e., hits). This pattern means greater pressure than ever on turning over screens, as operators want something fresh to drive the audience, unable to afford to wait for a middling performer.

By 2013, the trend of declining screens had been halted, led largely by the growth of digital cinema (see below). For a roughly five-year period, the total screens in the U.S. has hovered around 39,000 and according to the MPAA 81 percent of all the U.S. screens in 2012 were in venues with eight or more screens—the new order is clearly the mega-multiplex, and probably more surprisingly is digital, with digital screens now representing 83 percent of all U.S. screens.[7]

The Digital Divide and Digital Cinema

The Growth of Digital Cinema

George Lucas and Lucasfilm helped pioneer D-cinema by shooting *Star Wars: Episode II – Attack of the Clones* digitally and releasing the film on 60-plus digital screens in North America in 2002. Much like Lucas had pushed sound presentation with his THX technology and business, D-cinema offered the potential of consistent picture quality. Given the lack of uniform standards, infrastructure, and others to come on board quickly, by the time *Star Wars: Episode III – Revenge of the Sith* came out three years later (May 2005), the amount of digital screens available had not appreciably increased.

151

With the studios banding together and setting standards in 2005 under the Digital Cinema Initiative (DCI) consortium, and the theater owners through NATO then building on the agreement and agreeing to specifications, the landscape was set for quick adoption and there was renewed hype. Despite this momentum, though, as of Christmas 2008 there were reportedly only approximately 1,000 screens out of the 35,000-plus screen universe in the United States equipped for digital projection.

Trying to make sense of the glacial adoption, I asked Tom Quinn, senior director of worldwide distribution for Lucasfilm—who managed multiple digital releases with different studio partners, and has had a catbird's seat to watch the evolution of D-cinema—why he thought adoption had not yet, at that time, materialized. He advised:

The promise of D-cinema is undeniable from a long-term cost savings point of view for both studios and production companies. The challenges have been: Who will pay for it and whose technology will be used? As a comparison to what we witnessed in the home video industry, first with VHS versus Betamax, and more recently Blu-ray versus HD-DVD, the issues are much more complex. Exhibitors don't really believe D-cinema will drive more ticket sales, and unless there is an impact on a game-changing scale as moving, for example, from cassette to DVD or black-and-white to color film motivating the consumer, they don't feel they should be the ones bearing the costs of converting cinemas. Added to this is a system that has been virtually the same for 100 years and continues to work well—the "don't fix what isn't broken" mentality is hard for the studios to overcome. This is especially true given the high upfront costs of conversion and the fact shifting technology could be outdated soon after multi-component systems, including servers, projectors, etc., are installed.

Against this backdrop, and just when it appeared that it could take years for momentum to build (even though most in the industry were continuing to herald the benefits), the tide turned—and what nobody could have anticipated was, once the trend started to take hold, how fast the overall landscape would shift: by mid 2012, more than 27,000 screens in the U.S. had been converted to digital, and the *Hollywood Reporter* ran the shocking front-page headline, entitled "Fox Eyes End to 35 mm Film Distribution in U.S." The article began: "Fox has become the first major Hollywood studio to officially notify theater owners that it will distribute all of its films domestically in a digital format within the next year or two, bringing an end to 35 mm prints."[8] Supporting this shift was the fact that by the end of 2012, there was a near-complete turning upside down of the digital screen penetration chart: from only 14.2 percent of all U.S. screens in 2008 to 83 percent of U.S. screens by 2013. Further, the MPAA, in its 2012 Theatrical Market report, noted that as of Q1 2013, more than two-thirds of the total 130,000 global cinema screens had been converted to digital (a combination of either 3D or digital non-3D).[9] (Note: In U.S. screens by type, MPAA notes that in 2008, 5,515 were digital (both 3D and non-3D) out of 38,834 total screens, while in 2012, there were only 6,789 analog screens out of a U.S. screen universe of 39,918.)

When I asked Julian Levin, who headed the DCI and serves as executive vice president, digital exhibition & non-theatrical sales and distribution at 20th Century Fox, whether this was over-exaggerated or whether we truly would see prints go the way of 8-track tapes, he noted:

Elimination of 35 mm prints is already underway, and Fox has already stopped supplying 35 mm prints to several markets in Asia.

Furthermore, the U.S. will probably stop using 35 mm prints in 2013, and many other international territories are sure to follow in the next few years. Once digital projection gained traction, with the added benefit of 3D, the point of no return came very quickly, faster than most would have perhaps imagined just a few years ago. The phase out will obviously be market-dependent, but when you reach more than 80 percent conversion of screens within certain markets, the move to all-digital starts to become self-fulfilling and, certainly, prints will become a thing of the past in many territories in the next 2–5 years.

How did this happen? First, it is instructive to look at the absolute numbers. Figure 4.1 is a parallel chart of historical penetration and forecast growth as predicted by 20th Century Fox while the tide was turning. Figure 4.2 is a parallel chart of historical penetration and forecast growth as predicted by 20th Century Fox for the international market.

Adoption of this scale required incentives to invest in the infrastructure, and the DCI was able to forge extremely productive partnerships between the content providers (i.e., studios) and exhibitors. The partnerships implemented what became known as "virtual print fees" to fund and amortize the cost of converting traditional cinemas to digital screens. The cost of conversion was reportedly very high—in the range of $80,000–100,000 per screen—and required some form of partnership/incentive scheme. A type of catalyst was needed, not simply because of the absolute costs and other obstacles that had hindered adoption, but also because conversions were being urged during a period of market turbulence (namely, how would cinemas fare overall in the face of digital disturbance and new forms of access to content) and not long after the time that the majority of major exhibition chains had emerged from bankruptcy. Addressing the macro industry costs, *Time* magazine, in its annual (2006) "What's Next" issue, interviewed George Lucas for an article titled "Can This Man Save the Movies? (Again?)"[10] and succinctly attributed the delay to theater owners: "When they hear the word digital, they reach for digitalis. Already feeling the hit for the 13 percent slump in moviegoing over the past three years, they aren't eager to spend the more than $3 billion or so that it would cost to convert approximately 36,000 film projectors to digital."

The virtual print program was designed to solve the inertia by looking at the differential between the cost of a physical print (such as $1,000)

153

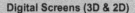

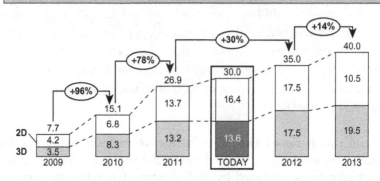

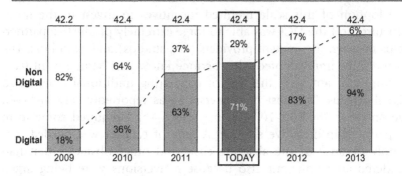

Figure 4.1 Historical Penetration and Forecast Growth as Predicted by 20th Century Fox for the U.S. Market

Courtesy of 20th Century Fox.

and the lower cost of a digital print and contribute the savings (or at least a part of the theoretical savings) into a pool. The specifics of how that savings was funded was then the subject of negotiation, but the key element is that rather than simply pocketing the savings, the interested parties agreed to impute costs as if physical prints were still being used and utilize that related pool of money to incentivize and fund conversions.

Again, I turned to Julian Levin, who advised the following regarding the implementation of these virtual print fee programs:

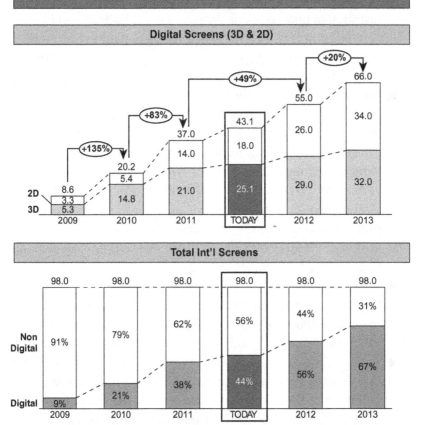

INTERNATIONAL DIGITAL SCREEN PROJECTIONS

Digital Screens (3D & 2D)

Total Int'l Screens

Figure 4.2 Historical Penetration and Forecast Growth as Predicted by 20th Century Fox for the International Market

Courtesy of 20th Century Fox.

In connection with financing the cost of digital projection systems around the world, Fox has made enormous efforts to create a business model that was extremely fair to exhibitors and with distributors contributing significantly to the cost. The business models varied and have evolved. Fox has created the following options for exhibitors:

- Fox has closed a good number of deals with third-party integrators in the U.S. as well as internationally (some regionally around the world). These integrators would then arrange a structured financing scheme and contributions to the system cost and financing charges would be paid by distributors upon booking each movie on each screen (a "virtual print fee," or VPF). These deals tended to be complex and required full transparency to recoupment (over 8–10 years), at which point the entire system cost be paid off.

■ Fox also made available "direct-to-exhibitor" deals, which were simplified, allowing an exhibitor to deal direct with Fox should the exhibitor elect not to go with a large third-party integrator. These deals tend to be structured where the exhibitor arranges the financing and Fox pays VPFs for a certain period of time, at which point the VPFs stop. These arrangements are subject to individual exhibitor issues, import duties, customs, taxes, and a variety of moving parts so the cost varies from one exhibitor to another and from one country to another.

■ In certain cases such as France, Italy, Germany, and Norway, the government got involved and provided a structure that exhibitors and distributors could participate in. Fox made accommodations for each of these nuances and guidelines.

■ Once the systems are paid off toward 2020, distributors should benefit from some 35 mm print cost savings, and exhibitors will have the benefit of automation, alternative content, live broadcast, and a host of other electronic efficiencies.

In summary, exhibitors have had ample opportunity to select what plan they prefer, and for those exhibitors who are still not prepared to move (quickly), they could well become a casualty of the global conversion to digital projectors.

The combination of virtual print fee incentives and related schemes (and one would suspect benchmarks requiring certain levels of conversion), spurred the market on from incremental growth to upwards of 1,000 screens/month, and the resulting overall shift in the market landscape as depicted in the charts above. At the same time, the introduction of 3D films, which require D-cinema, provided a further accelerant—a process that was helped significantly by *Avatar*, which put 3D on the map (see a further discussion regarding 3D below).

Benefits of D-Cinema

D-cinema refers to the process of exhibiting a movie in a theater by digital projection rather than via a film print. The incentives are multifold.

First, most believe that once economies of scale are reached (a driving factor behind the virtual print fee programs) that D-cinema will dramatically reduce the cost of distribution, with the cost of a D-cinema delivery a fraction of the cost of striking and shipping prints. Second, a digital copy does not degrade like a film print, in theory offering a perfect copy with pristine picture and sound each time; in layman's terms, "no scratches." Third, because of the costs, prints are often "bicycled" such that the first-run prints from larger cities and multiplexes will move to smaller towns after a few weeks. These locations are known as "second run" and their customers are forced to wait for new releases; eliminating print costs would expand distribution and bring films to these locations sooner.[11] Finally, installation of D-cinema allows a digital infrastructure that can convert cinemas into multipurpose venues capable of special event programming, including 3D-film and live-event simulcasting (e.g., sports events, concerts, live theater/opera simulcasts).

Systems, Standards, and the Challenge of Keeping Pace with Technology Advances

D-cinema requires four elements that did not exist historically: a digital projector, a server holding the movie on a file, a digital master, and a delivery mechanism to transfer a copy of the film onto the server (Figure 4.3). Over time, the costs will come down, and the economies of scale in converting the market has already materially reduced the average cost of converting screens; nevertheless, as discussed above regarding virtual print fees, significant upfront investment is required from all sides. The exhibitors need to install projectors and servers (which collectively make up a digital projection system), while the distributors need to create D-cinema masters and standardize delivery mechanisms to clone the master and upload a copy to the in-cinema server.

Standards are, not surprisingly, challenging to cement. This is, in part, due to politics—different groups, such as NATO (exhibitors trade organization) and the DCI, originally promulgated their own standards—and differing opinions on key experience elements such as resolution quality. The de facto resolution standard was JPEG 2000 ("2K"), although many have subsequently pushed for 4K projectors. An interesting question arises as to whether at some point improved resolution is actually a negative: some believe that the 4K resolution is too high, creating an almost artificial, hyperreal, and defect-visible level.

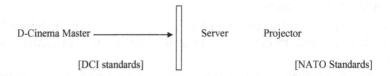

D-Cinema Master ⟶ ⎜ Server   Projector

[DCI standards]   ⎜   [NATO Standards]

Figure 4.3 The Elements of D-Cinema

Even if the 2K versus 4K debate is resolved (and architecture was put in place accommodating both), issues of frame rate and what is needed for 3D create new wrinkles (e.g., if 60 frames per second is desired and installed base of D-cinema is 48 frames per second, then down-conversion is required).

Technology ever marches on, and today there is discussion of laser projection technology, with the benefit of projecting brighter images. It is unlikely we will see the scale of investment again in the near future to upgrade cinemas, but all parties will continue to struggle with the line of improving the experience versus the costs associated.

158

Theaters on the Ropes—3D and Needing a New Hook

Against the backdrop of increasing piracy, potentially declining box office (as vicissitudes change the outlook every year or two, though 2012, helped by four different films cresting $1 billion at the box office—*Skyfall*, *The Avengers*, *The Dark Knight Rises*, and *The Hobbit: An Unexpected Journey*—saw an increase for the first time in two years, both in terms of absolute attendance and domestic box office revenue),[12] and increased competition from other media sources (including streaming and down-loading to portable downloadable devices), there is a frequent chorus of calls to save the movies. At times, talking about the business almost as if it were a dinosaur, articles and experts often cite reasons for moviegoing (aside from quality arguments) ranging from "movies are produced for the big screen experience" to "movies are a social experience." The point is executives were becoming defensive and people, particularly theater owners, were concerned. What will bring people into the theaters in record numbers when consumers have a 50-inch LCD TV screen with high-definition content and theatrical-like surround sound? Even studio heads acknowledge the high costs to a family to go to the movies versus renting (babysitter + four tickets + parking + food = $100 versus DVD or VOD rental at less than $5). Although the deep 2008/2009 recession seemed to reverse the trend, as going to the movies proved an escape from economic gloom (as had happened historically), all of the foregoing challenges remain, and no doubt the theaters will need to continue to provide an enhanced and differentiating experience to the moviegoer.

D-cinema, and in particular 3D, was heralded as offering just this value-added experience. Beyond all the historical good reasons to go to the movies, and the quality upgrade of digital cinema, 3D was marketed as something new—one could claim it was back-to-the-future, 3D glasses and all. The argument was the glasses were better this time. Moreover, 3D was perceived as enough of a differentiator to raise ticket prices, to as high as $25, which would both offset the higher production costs of 3D plus help theaters defray the costs of digital conversion. In practice, the premium charged for 3D tickets is about $2–4 more than for traditional 2D, with this differential seemingly now somewhat universally applied. Regal, for example, added $3.50–4.00 for its venues that exhibited *Monsters vs Aliens* (2009),[13] and AMC in Los Angeles charged $4 more on both adult and children's tickets in 2012.[14]

A group of prominent directors, including Peter Jackson, George Lucas, Robert Zemeckis, James Cameron, and Robert Rodriguez all spoke out in favor of 3D and the theatrical experience. Some even started developing 3D projects or converting prior films into 3D, waiting to avail themselves of the new technological possibilities. Here was something that could not be matched in the living room. By 2007, James Cameron announced all his future films would be 3D (his first non-documentary movie directed since *Titanic* being *Avatar*), and Robert Zemeckis seemed to be following suit. Disney, which announced that all its future animated and Pixar films would be released in both 2D and 3D, even tried to co-opt the medium in its marketing by branding new releases as being in "Disney Digital 3D." For the first time, significant numbers of 3D films were being produced (e.g., Warner's *Journey to the Center of the Earth*, Fox's *Avatar*, Lionsgate's *My Bloody Valentine*, DreamWorks Animation's *Monsters vs Aliens*), but the danger remained that production was well ahead of digital screen conversion, leaving distributors in a quandary and forcing the dual exhibition of the pictures intended exclusively for 3D in standard version simply to obtain enough screens for a wide release.[15] DreamWorks Animation, betting big on 3D and having converted its pipeline to 3D productions, was able to expand 3D screen counts to 2,000 for its March 2009 release of *Monsters vs Aliens*, making it the broadest new 3D release while still falling well short of stated goals for a majority of screens exhibiting the film in 3D.[16]

As indicated by the statistics above, all of this changed within a couple of years. The digital transition had taken shape, and then the industry was jolted awake, first by the juggernaut of *Avatar* (becoming the all-time box office king, and garnering upwards of 70 percent of its box office from 3D releases), followed by the huge success of Disney's rerelease of *The Lion King* in 3D ($172 million worldwide, and $94 million domestically).[17] The conversion costs for 2012 high-profile launches of classics, including *Star Wars: Episode I – The Phantom Menace* and *Titanic*, were easily justified, and luminary filmmakers were unabashed with praise and predictions. In an advertisement run by the International 3D Society (www.international3dsociety.com), George Lucas lent his support to the organization's "Make it 3D" campaign: "Digital 3D technology is revolutionizing filmmaking the way sound did in the 1920s. It will someday become the big-screen standard for presentation, with 3D replacing 2D the way color replaced black-and-white. It's just a better way of looking at movies."

In some sense, the 3D success and the conversion of screens to D-cinemas were symbiotic. On the one hand, a couple of high-profile pictures, the most prominent being *Avatar*, demanded the conversion, because 3D requires compliance with D-cinema specifications. On the other hand, among the benefits of baseline D-cinema conversion was then the relatively simple upgrade to offer 3D—and therefore exhibit moneymakers such as *Avatar*. To offer 3D in addition to D-cinema requires a lens that pulls across the projector and creates the polarization and depth; this, combined with the polarized glasses, which divides the 48 frames per second intwo two, creates the 3D effect. Accordingly, a theater needs both the equipment and the glasses—an incremental cost that is currently funded and passed on via the higher ticket prices charged for 3D admissions. Overall, the growth in 3D screens has been astounding, and largely parallels the phenomenal growth of digital screens generally: according to the MPAA, there were only 2,536 3D screens globally in 2008, with the number climbing to 45,545 by the end of 2012.[18]

It is too early to predict the outcome of the 3D trend—certainly, effects laden event films such as *The Hobbit: An Unexpected Journey* benefit from the premium pricing and lend themselves particularly well to the format, but the race to make everything 3D seems to have cooled. In 2012, the number of 3D releases dropped (from 34 to 28), but clearly there is a trend to produce in significant quantity, and for certain types of films it will be an expectation of fans.[19]

Distributor–Exhibitor Splits/Deals

The following discussion analyzes how money that comes into a theater from customers is split between the exhibitor (theater) and distributor (studio). Figure 4.4 illustrates the theatrical distribution chain, but if

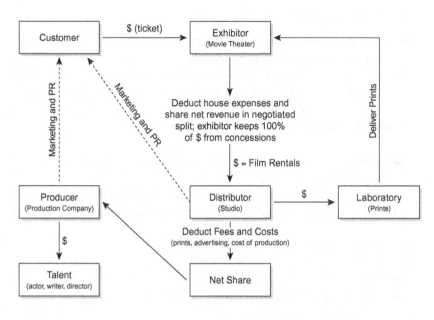

Figure 4.4 The Theatrical Distribution Chain

161

one looks past the moving parts, the key element in terms of theatrical revenues and returns is the simple link between the cinema and booking studio.

Components of Film Rental

The amount of money that the studio/distributor keeps from the box office is all-important, because this is ultimately the "at-the-source revenue." The industry rule of thumb is that the studio keeps roughly 50 percent of the cumulative box office: But how do you get there? Almost all exhibition deals are based around the following concepts:

- House nut: The theater's overhead costs, including rent, maintenance, utilities, labor costs, equipment, insurance, etc.
- Film rental: The distributor's share of the gross box office receipts
- Runs: Lingo for how many theaters a film is booked in (but can also denote the first run of a picture)
- Guaranteed weeks: How many weeks a theater commits to a film
- Zones: The level of exclusivity in the market is defined by competitive versus noncompetitive zones.

90/10 Minimum Guarantee Deals

The 90/10 deal used to be the standard, but is now used in a minority of instances. Nevertheless, they are still found, and are instructive in terms of how the concept of house nuts are applied and impact film rental calculations. When a distributor has screened a film for the major exhibitors and is ready to offer them the picture, the booking negotiation will usually address the following elements:

■ Playing time is the number of committed weeks (sometimes in two-week increments)
■ Percentage split of box office, after deduction of specified house nut
■ Minimum percentage/floor for distributor from box office, by week

Accordingly, a deal could look like the following:

■ Playing time: eight weeks (at high end)
■ 90/10 over $5,000 house expenses, with the following minimums:

- Week 1: 60 percent
- Week 2: 55 percent
- Week 3: 50 percent
- Weeks 4–5: 45 percent
- Weeks 6–8: 35 percent

Let us assume that the film brings in $40,000 in box office in week one, compared to another film with the same deal bringing in $10,000. How are the splits calculated?

Film One:

$40,000
−$5,000
───────
$35,000
───────

$31,500 @ 90 percent
$3,500 @ 10 percent

Minimum floor calculation: 60 percent of $40,000 = $24,000

Since $31,500 > $24,000, the distributor keeps $31,500

Exhibitor keeps $8,500 ($3,500 + $5,000)

Film Two:

$10,000
-$5,000
———
$5,000
———

$4,500 @ 90 percent
$500 @ 10 percent

Minimum floor calculation: 60 percent of $10,000 = $6,000

Since $6,000 > $4,500, the distributor keeps $6,000

Exhibitor keeps $4,000 ($10,000 – $6,000), and loses money

Years ago, revenue guarantees would sometimes be applied against the splits, such that, in addition to minimum floors, there would be minimum guarantees. Not only is this practice gone, but true holdovers are a bit of an anachronism; a holdover clause used to trigger an automatic extension for another week (often on a rolling basis) in the event the box office for the picture exceeded a stipulated threshold in the prior week. Today, however, holdovers are dictated by pure economics, and as discussed later, a non-performing title will likely be "kicked out" regardless of contractual provisions to the contrary.

Aggregates: Alternative to 90/10 Deals with House Nut

An aggregate deal is one in which the distributor and exhibitor negotiate a fixed split of the gross box office receipts and do not apply/deduct a house nut. The economic incentives behind this deal largely include doing away with calculating the house nut (by ensuring the exhibitor will not earn less than its nut) and simplifying the accounting; the logic is that if, after all the line-item calculations, the distributor knows it is likely to keep 50 percent, why not just agree to 50 percent? There is, of course, a risk that money could be left on the table, but the bet is that within a narrow band, revenues will even out over time. If the spread were 10 percent, this would not work, but if the parties, through experience, know the spread may only vary by a couple of percent on a certain type of picture, then the risk may be considered nominal. Perhaps the best way to illustrate this is with an example.

If an exhibitor plays a major film that is likely to sell out regularly over the first week or two, it does not mind paying out on the 90/10 split—its nut is covered, and the seats are filled with patrons buying

163

candy and popcorn. At any point that the minimum floor is triggered, however, the distributor is eating into the exhibitor's house nut. Accordingly, the exhibitor has to ask itself: Would I prefer to book the film where I may not keep my full nut, or should I book a different film where I keep my full nut? This may sound like a simultaneous equation, in that there should be no difference if both movies initially perform well. However, there is a difference with major pictures that may take multiple screens, and where the nut applied may vary per screen. By applying a fixed split, the exhibitor is theoretically assured that its revenues will not fall below its nut.

Splits may then be negotiated in a number of ways. If the exhibitor has the leverage, then the rental percentage will be lower. Additionally, one can imagine cases making the calculation extremely complicated, such as in creating a scale of aggregates in which the flat splits change over weeks, stepping down similarly to the previous minimum-floor 90/10 deal. In this hypothesized instance, negotiations could trade off upfront versus downstream percentages. If the distributor achieves a slightly better deal up front, then it will likely give something up on the back-end, somewhat evening out the equation. At this point, though, one has to question whether there is any efficiency or incentive to move to an aggregate.

Having come full circle, if all that happens is the net dollars are somewhat evened out, why bother? Again, the simple answer that no one will admit to, but probably strikes close to the heart, is ease of administration: a flat deal is easier to calculate and administer. Another reason could be that to book multiple screens in a multiplex (and stick the exhibitor, with the potential opportunity cost of booking incremental screens that may yield better economics with another film), the distributor may want to offer an incentive. That incentive is the aggregate, which, on the surface, is calculated in a way that would otherwise somewhat match the expected return of a firm-term deal, yet by its formula ensures, in theory, that the exhibitor does not risk a split below its house nut. The distributor forfeits incremental revenue equal to the delta between the aggregate split and any higher amount it may have earned on a different deal, but theoretically makes up the difference by expanding its release with the additional screens. (Note: The notion of additional screens expanding the pie is a theoretical statement, for it assumes that the box office is actually generated, which may not happen; and it fails to take into account the incremental print costs of playing that additional screen.)

Firm Terms versus Settlement

Despite contractual sliding scales (90/10 deals with minimums), the reality of the theatrical box office is that distributors and exhibitors have a symbiotic relationship and will often move off the letter of the contract. The contract with a sliding scale is sometimes referred to as "firm terms," because there is a clear formula used for calculating film rentals from the box office gross. In contrast, "settlement" is just like it sounds: at the end of a picture's run, the parties will sit down to evaluate performance and agree on a percentage. If this smells like a scene from a movie with people haggling in a back office, that is not too far from what can happen. The theatrical distribution business harkens back to the days of arm wrestling and handshakes, and in many cases it devolves to relationships and hard-nose negotiations.

Because distributors have a slate of films, the negotiations need to stay within the bounds of precedents and customary practices. Again, the parties need each other, and it is to neither side's long-term advantage to fleece the other. Whether horse trading numbers of screens, or holding over a print longer than the pure economics of that particular film may justify based on that isolated film's performance, there are lots of moving parts and chits to accumulate. When a studio promises a producer it can open a film to a certain breadth, or keep the film playing long enough to reach a certain total, it may need to do some juggling to achieve that goal. By splitting up the pie via settlement, there is obviously more flexibility; unfortunately, there is also more mystery. Ultimately, settlement can only influence results at the margins, because if the results strayed too far from firm terms, then one title would benefit at the expense of another and the system would break.

Four-Wall Structure

To "four wall" a movie means to literally rent the venue. In this scenario, the studio distributor will agree to a weekly rental amount and then keep 100 percent of the box office. This is the one scenario where film rentals are equal to box office. (Note: Given the extraordinary costs, in theory, any accounting should either allow the deduction of some form of house nut from the gross revenues or else allow a true flow through of the costs.)

A four-wall deal is unusual, but still occurs. It can come up in a case where the distributor wants a unique venue and this is the only way to ensure its film will be played and will not be dropped early. Another situation when a four-wall deal may make sense is when parties cannot agree to floors and splits; if a distributor was unwilling to accept the terms countered by an exhibitor, and the splits were too low, it might roll the dice to take on the house nut and keep the full gross. In theory, this situation is most likely to arise with a unique venue, possibly with a single screen, that has a high operating cost.

Release Strategy and Timing

There are no hard-and-fast rules regarding releases, but the following are a few of the critical factors taken into account.

Factors in When to Release

Day-and-Date

Films used to release in the United States and then open internationally weeks and even months later. Much of the delay was due to practical limitations: it would take time to complete the foreign versions (dubs and subtitles), and publicity tours were much easier to orchestrate in a staggered fashion.

With the globalization of the world, instant access from the Internet, and growing threats from piracy, more and more event films are being released simultaneously around the world—in film parlance, a "day-and-date" release. A day-and-date release allows for focused publicity, and affords international territories to capture the momentum rather than release a film when core fans are aware they are seeing the picture downstream. Moreover, for very large titles, it allows the release to become eventized. The largest contributing factor, though, is the ability to defeat piracy, an issue that many obsess over, given the potential for instant and global copies on the Internet.

International B.O. versus U.S.

As discussed in Chapter 1, in terms of windows generally, an increasingly important factor is the growing international box office relative to the whole pie. The numbers for international keep growing, as demonstrated in Table 4.1 from the MPAA's statistics (based on U.S.$ billions) showing a 32 percent increase in international box office from 2008 to 2012.

When international box office invariably starts to account for the majority of worldwide box office, and in extreme cases represents 70 percent or even 80 percent of the total, then the issues of day-and-date, piracy, and the ability to adjust marketing campaigns take a backseat to the absolute numbers; it is not that these other factors are no longer

166

Table 4.1 MPAA Theatrical Market Statistics (Global Box Office All Films)

	2008 ($)	2009 ($)	2010 ($)	2011 ($)	2012 ($)	% Change 2012 vs 2011	% Change 2012 vs 2008
US/Canada	9.6	10.6	10.6	10.2	10.8	6	12
International	18.1	18.8	21.0	22.4	23.9	6	32
Total	27.7	29.4	31.6	32.6	34.7	6	25

Data reproduced by permission of the Motion Picture Association of America, www.mpaa.org.

important, but rather that strategy decisions become disproportionately influenced by the relative returns.

In 2012, without knowing what the results would be—remembering the mantra of "nobody knows anything"—Universal and Hasbro took the then-unusual step of releasing hoped-for summer blockbuster *Battleship* overseas before the U.S.—a strategy that was initially lauded, as the film (estimated cost $209 million) took in about $227 million internationally (63 territories) before the U.S. debut. *Variety* summarized: "Universal hoped to get a head start on the busy overseas summer schedule by launching *Battleship* internationally more than a month before the U.S. The tactic appeared to work—at first. During its world tour, *Battleship* surpassed overseas tallies of *John Carter* ($210 million) and *Wrath of the Titans* ($217 million) and now stands as the year's fifth-highest grossing international release."[20] Unfortunately for Universal and Hasbro, *Battleship* launched in the U.S. to only $25.3 million the weekend prior to the Memorial Day holiday weekend, and with total domestic forecasts being downgraded to less than $60 million, Universal's president of domestic distribution (Nikki Rocco) was quoted in the *Los Angeles Times* as stating: "This is not a total disaster," in an article that started: "The box office debut of *Battleship* looked like a very different board game: Trouble."[21]

John Carter, which was held up as a disaster for Disney, and led to vicious publicity, a $200 million write down, and the departure of its distribution head Rich Ross, had a comparably lopsided international total: of its $282.2 million worldwide box office, $209.7 million, or 74.3 percent, came from international markets.[22] Although

167

both of these examples can be held up, on the one hand, as failures when measuring the domestic totals of films costing more than $200 million, on the other hand both films earned more than $200 million internationally. Only in Hollywood could a $200 million run be deemed a failure, and this is in large part due to the heavy PR and historical focus of domestic performance; in contrast, if the films had generated more than $200 million in the U.S. and had underwhelmed internationally, it would not have made headlines, nor likely triggered collateral consequences.

This dichotomy of bashing a film if it underperforms in the U.S. without giving due credit to international success, and therefore overall performance, is inherently irrational, and will inevitably lead to a change in how releases are perceived. Over time, day-and-date releases, or even the pattern of foreign first and then domestic, will become the norm, and performance will be looked at on a global scale. Distributors will then look at which markets over- or underperformed—which happens today on all films anyway—and adjust models and future marketing expenditures and forecasts accordingly. One would posit that with all these rational steps, PR will follow suit, and less emphasis will be placed on domestic performance as an overall benchmark of success. (Note: In fact, 2012's *Life of Pi* (Fox), while often cited as an exception, is a good example of international dominance in an instance where the film was hailed as a success both in the U.S. and worldwide, striking such a chord with global audiences that its international box office was roughly 80 percent of the worldwide total.) Focusing first on overseas results, though, given the Hollywood celebrity culture and nature of the beast, will take the longest to evolve. Expect huge successes in China to be hyped and followed, and U.S. performance to be overanalyzed and held up as a barometer for years to come.

Competition

All studios scrutinize the competitive landscape, as the cleaner window and the less competition, the better. Competition can be segmented into a number of categories.

First, there is competition from other product being released by the same studio/distributor. This is obviously the easiest category to address, and while studios will downplay this issue (under the rationalization that if they were not competing against their own film they would still be competing against something), there is obviously no reason to tax bandwidth and potentially compete against oneself. The second category is direct competition within a targeted demographic or genre. For example, if a major Disney animated movie is releasing, it probably makes better sense to pick a different time frame and not try to divide the animation audience; of course, given the cutthroat competition, there have been conscious attempts to directly release against a similar film in attempt to crush the competition and sustain an upper hand in the market. Additionally, competitive titles may afford an opportunity to counter-program, and a niche or differently targeted film may be able to provide an alternative to certain demographics, and in instances of box office dominated by tentpoles, may even be able to draft off the overall box office uplift. Finally, there is a fear factor—a big enough film that may monopolize the box office. This is especially true in cases of sequels, and often distributors will steer clear of event films, such as the next *The Hobbit* movie; if enough people move away, then opportunities arise to counter-program to targeted demographics.

Outside Factors (Events of National Attention)

Outside factors play a very important role; films are not simply competing against other films, but also for consumer dollars against other media. It is generally believed that certain events of national importance can siphon off attention and impact box office. Such events may include national political elections and major international sporting events, including the Olympics and the World Cup. These are all planned events that can be factored when planning release dates; however, in an increasingly connected and seemingly unpredictable world, news events, including wars and terrorist attacks, can also create reasons for last-minute juggling.

While the potential influence on diverting attention from the film is real, another key concern is the increased difficulty of marketing a property against these juggernauts of public attention. For example, media will be harder and more expensive to place at the peak of an election cycle. Accordingly, there can be a double hit: releasing a film in the window of an event of national importance will likely make it more expensive to reach desired awareness levels, and even if awareness targets are hit there is a risk that consumers will opt to spend their time and money on the national event that only occurs once every few years.

Acceleration of Revenues

Today, all focus seems to be on opening weekends, with distributors then modeling an ultimate box office based on an extrapolation from the initial week(s) and assumed declines. Historically, films could play for months, and it was not unusual for a blockbuster hit to play through, and even beyond, a season such as the summer. As the number of films made and released grew, competition grew with it. There are a number of interrelated factors that evolved, all feeding on each other, which accelerated this process and led to the compressed revenue cycle of a film taking in a higher and higher percentage of its overall revenue in the first 2–3 weeks of release.

First, people started to focus on opening weekends and records, putting pressure on openings. Marketing dollars were therefore allocated to open a film as large as possible—even if a film's box office had a sharper week-to-week decline at the beginning than it may have had with a debut on fewer screens. The initial larger box office could make up for this drop and theoretically push the cumulative total higher than an otherwise narrower release would have yielded.

Second, with more and more films, the spacing between major movies shrank. Competitive windows have narrowed, and studios now look to all 52 weeks of the year to find the best competitive free window in which to release; moreover, the jockeying is all critical. Go out against the wrong film and you could be done in the first week, as it is extraordinarily rare that a film that is opened wide and does not perform to expectations then gains in a subsequent week. The system is designed not to let this happen, as a new movie is always on its heels, and if a film does not perform, someone else will take its screens. The exhibition business is ruthless and all about filling seats, not second chances.

Accordingly, distributors are looking to maximize shorter and shorter runs: What am I likely to open up against? What am I coming after? What is coming after me? Each of these factors can dramatically influence the film's performance, and while there might have been months or at least a month between major titles, with the volume and budgets in current Hollywood this is now measured in weeks. A film that has two or three relatively clear weeks is now blessed, and as late as the mid 1990s this was hard to fathom.

The net result of the acceleration of revenue not only puts inordinate pressures on distributors and content owners, but has a disproportionate negative impact on theater owners. As described previously regarding rentals and weekly minimums, the longer a film plays, the more the split shifts to favor the theater owner; accordingly, theater owners are losing more of their upsides because they lock into revenue schemes where the upside is in downstream weeks that, at worst, no longer exist and, at best, have lower box office revenues to split. In discussing the plight of theaters, *Forbes* noted: "But the fact that films 'play off' and leave theaters faster is poison to the owners. It means that even if overall box office is constant or increasing, owners can be earning much less revenue. One *Titanic*, which didn't open particularly well, but played for weeks, is worth more to theater owners than five successful films, each of which earns one-fifth as much."[23]

Exacerbating these pressures are key holiday weekends and the built-in expectations of sequels (which often gravitate to these dates as a safe haven, given the usually high budgets). Opening in holiday periods when people have more free time to go to the movies has become a cultural tradition. In the U.S., Memorial Day weekend, Fourth of July, November (to play into Thanksgiving), and Christmas have become prime real estate. If a studio has a picture they view as a sure thing, they will leak out that date early and try to stake out that turf. Although the track record vindicates this strategy, because competition tends to cluster around these dates, it may not be the best strategy; to wit, *Batman—The Dark Knight* opened in mid July 2008 and went on to become the then-second highest grossing theatrical title of all time. Finally, what often is not talked about, but can be the most influential factor, is superstition. If a film (or director) has had good luck with a date, the studio may want to stick with that timing. I have seen many cases where a date seemed odd relative to the foregoing logical factors, only to realize it was the "director's date" or was when the original film launched (in the case of plotting a release date for a sequel).

171

The Online and Digital Speed Factor

Pressure from Review Sites

It was already harder to open a movie with "word of mouth" in a world when slow buzz from the watercooler conversation could be replaced by instant access to national reviews by a site such as Rotten Tomatoes. Only a couple of years ago, the concern was that before a movie opened, potential viewers were privy to whether a majority of critics liked it or not. Today, though, if someone wants an opinion from a more trusted source, they are apt to check out opinions not just via aggregate review sites and on their favorite blogs, but also through a web of social media outlets (e.g., from Twitter to Facebook). This new instantaneous and filtered-for-your-tastes feedback is just another factor compressing timelines: the immediacy and breadth of information makes it hard to hide a bomb, while providing an extra impetus to crash the gates if people are raving.

Online Release

One alternative is to release a film online, either simultaneously with theatrical release or as a substitute unique outlet. In November 2007, director Ed Burns decided to release his $4 million movie *Purple Violets* on iTunes. Commenting that there was "not enough money to market the film, not a wide-enough release to even make a dent in the moviegoing public's consciousness," he pioneered releasing the film via iTunes, reportedly the first time a feature film was debuted on Apple's download service.[24]

The model of launching a film online rather than theatrically has, to date, proven risky. The theory is that the online world provides instant access everywhere, and enough of a stampede to watch online would justify cannibalizing theatrical revenues. However, with 35,000 screens in the U.S. and most of the American population within a short drive of a theater, is a bit easier access really a compelling enticement? There are obvious consumer experience differences between seeing a movie online versus in-theater, plus serious economic hurdles, including: (1) theaters' willingness to boycott films that go online and do not grant an exclusive theatrical window; (2) the risk of further impact on the DVD market (on *Purple Violet*, "video distributors had offered lower-than-expected advance payments for the film's DVD right out of fear that its availability on iTunes would cannibalize home-video sales");[25] and (3) the fact that online marketing has not yet been proven successful as the sole vehicle to market a film (though, given the ability to demographically target with more efficient buys, someone is apt to take this risk and perhaps demonstrate a tipping point).

Records Are Not What They Used to Be— Dissecting Opening Weekends

An interesting fact about holidays and openings is that the record book is now more of a microscopic statistical analysis, with lots of people holding bits of records, the accounting segmented to spread the glory. There are now records for biggest one day (which I am proud to have been part of when *Star Wars: Episode III – Revenge of the Sith* opened to just over $50 million, only to see the record fall to *The Dark Knight* in 2008), but even that record has now been split into biggest Thursday opening versus biggest Friday versus biggest Saturday, with Saturday generally the biggest day for a film opening. *Star Wars: Episode III – Revenge of the Sith* leveled out the equation (at least for a while— all records are eventually broken) when its Thursday was bigger than any prior Saturday, but it was only a matter of time before new boundaries were set.

Much more complicated is the notion of the weekend box office. As noted earlier, weekends are customarily calculated as the Friday–Sunday box office. However, holidays skew the mix and can be four or six days. What is the period when Fourth of July falls on a Wednesday? This naturally leads to debates over the "highest weekend," highest four-day weekend, highest holiday weekend, and highest four-day holiday weekend. Beyond holiday, there is the issue of studios opening "event films" earlier. This helps build buzz for the film leading into the weekend, as well as having the corollary impact of expanding the weekend box office: what a film has grossed by Sunday night. And we are not yet done!

A further wrinkle occurs with sneaks and screenings. Sometimes a film will have a very limited release earlier in the week to build some awareness. This was the pattern with Russell Crowe's *Cinderella Man*, released on Friday June 3, 2005. The film actually hit some theaters in major markets for a special sneak the prior Sunday. While it is clear that this gross should not be counted in the following weekend, the line becomes blurred when a film opens midweek. Opening on a Thursday is now relatively common, and the Thursday numbers may or may not be included in the weekend. The studio will position the higher number as the weekend (taking it as a "four-day"), but the trades are likely to split that out and report the three-day and four-day numbers (since there are different records, and presumably it makes things more interesting).

The final issue has to do with midnight or late-night screenings that occur with huge event films. If you want to get picky, where does the 12:01 a.m. or 11:59 p.m. showing fit, and should these be separate or aggregated into the day or weekend? The only clear answer is that it all goes into the weekly gross and ultimate gross. I have not actually counted the permutations, but you should get the picture. To outsiders, it may seem a bit petty, like the multiple boxing crowns. Within the industry, however, it is like chum to a shark. It is an interesting exercise to go to Box Office Mojo and look at a top film and its "chart" section. For *The Hobbit: An Unexpected Journey* (2012), for example, I counted more than 50 types of rankings, and weekends are now tracked by calendar period (e.g., fall, December, holiday), opening periods by two-, three-, four-, five-, six-, seven-, eight-, nine-, and 10-day grosses, and consecutive (and nonconsecutive for good measure) weeks at number one—spin and bragging rights for all.

This would not be so important if it were not for the press and financial market expectations. The press will jump on box office and hit the ground running on Monday morning. Studio stock prices can rise and fall on these stories, as was the case when DreamWorks Animation released *Madagascar* on Memorial Day weekend, 2005. The film's performance was closely scrutinized, as it was the first release following the company's IPO, and analysts were watching carefully to gauge whether *Shrek* was a phenomenon, or whether the studio could repeat with blockbuster after blockbuster like Pixar. (Note: To be fair, there was further pressure in that just several days before, DreamWorks announced adjustments to its video numbers for *Shrek 2*.)

Against this backdrop, when *Madagascar* opened to $61 million, which is by anyone's standards a huge number, it was still not up to hyped expectations: "Shares of DreamWorks Animation hit a new low Tuesday, dropping more than 9 percent as some on Wall Street deemed as uninspiring the domestic haul of $61 million that *Madagascar* garnered in its first four days at the box office and Lehman Bros. downgraded the stock."[26] In an equally extreme, and more recent, example, *Men in Black 3*'s $70 million four-day Memorial Day weekend 2012 domestic opening led to the *Hollywood Reporter* opening its front-page banner article, entitled "MIB3 Opens Biggest, but Doubts Remain," as follows: "Despite a $203.2 million worldwide opening, the jury's still out on whether Will Smith threequel *Men in Black 3* can recoup its $230 million production budget and hefty marketing spend. The Sony tentpole grossed a modest $70 million ... compared with the $75 million to $80 million that the studio was anticipating."[27]

174

Studio Estimates

What is a bit mysterious is how that "weekend box office" is calculated. It seems difficult, if not impossible, to have final weekend numbers on Sunday (for the press to write about the weekend) without the benefit of Sunday's full figures. The studios, accordingly, have to estimate box office; however, the studios have been doing this so long and know their clients (theaters) so well that they can extrapolate a market number with a fairly reliable measure of precision. Although the potential for gamesmanship exists, there are built-in incentives to keep reporting as accurate as possible; the studios want to avoid having to report that they overestimated and take down a number.

What does all this have in common? The big opening, which puts pressure on the splits and dogfights for screens and locations, also brings us back to the aggregate concept.

Table 4.2 is a hybrid example: assuming $100,000 in box office in week one, a decline of 50 percent to $50,000 in week two, a further decline to $30,000 and $25,000 in weeks three and four, a decline to $10,000 and $7,500 in the next two weeks, and two more weeks at $5,000 and $3,000.

Table 4.2 Box Office Revenue

	Box Office
Two weeks @ 60	(.60 × $100,000) + (.60 × $50,000) = $90,000
Two weeks @ 50	(.50 × $30,000) + (.50 × $25,000) = $27,500
Two weeks @ 40	(.40 × $10,000) + (.40 × $7,500) = $7,000
Balance @ 30	(.30 × $5,000) + (.30 × $3,000) = $2,400
	Total Rentals = $126,900

Theatrical Booking

Locations, Types of Runs, Length of Runs, Frenzy of Booking

While other facets of the distribution business, in particular pay TV and video, have changed dramatically over time, the theatrical booking business maintains much of its decades-old practices. This is a business of having to turn over thousands of screens and theaters every week, steeped in relationships at both head office and local booking office levels. There is almost the feeling of a never-ending poker game: cards are shuffled and dealt every week, some cards are traded in, and when final bets are placed everyone is waiting to see who has the high hand on the weekend.

Zones and Types of Theaters

Theater bookings in the United States follow relatively standard patterns. The entire country's theater count is broken down into regions, cities, and districts, all falling under the management of the domestic theatrical distribution arm of a studio. This is typically managed in a regional structure, where a head office will manage multiple geographic regions such as the South, West, etc. Each region will, in turn, have a regional manager with an army of booking agents underneath him or her.

By having this level of management, the theatrical distribution arm will literally have a direct relationship with every single theater in the country, which totals around 4,000 locations with more than 35,000 screens.

In large urban areas where there are multiple cinemas within relatively close physical proximity, the theaters may be districted into zones or regions. These are not formal/legal classifications, but rather informal designations tacitly acknowledged by the individual theaters (or chains). If you are booking a film in a Regal cinema on Main Street, it may be accepted that you do not then book your film in the theater across the street at AMC's multiplex, thus granting the theater a measure of exclusivity over its competitor. With the advent of multiplexes, and in particular the growth of large multiplexes, the level of jockeying has shrunk over time.

While focus is on multiplexes and optimizing top theaters (true top-performing theaters are often referred to in industry parlance as "guns" or "gun theaters"), there are a couple of other categories that come into play. For example, drive-ins always want top pictures, especially in summer months, and threshold decisions need to be made whether drive-ins will be single or double bills (as they tend to book double features), and whether the film will play day-and-date with multiplexes or move over to drive-ins at a later date. For so-called "second-run" theaters, often located in smaller towns, prints will be bicycled over to the local cinema after it has had its multiplex/wide launch. Accordingly, along with economic splits, zones, and lengths of runs (see next section), theatrical booking departments also have to deal with the placement patterns of first run versus second run versus specialty (e.g., drive-in) venues. (Note: Drive-ins and second-run theaters are becoming some-what of a rarity, and accordingly the foregoing description is more of an historical anecdote, though still obviously illustrative of the broader issues in jockeying for screens.)

Booking: A Last-Minute Frenzy

When it gets down to a week or so before a film opens, it is a literal free-for-all. In a matter of days, a film can go from zero bookings to more than 3,000 theaters and 7,000 screens. During this booking time, it is all-out war, with distributors giving theaters terms, including the splits, the number of weeks, etc. In busy times, such as between Thanksgiving and Christmas and in the summer (especially Memorial Day through to the Fourth of July), every weekend is precious, and competition for locations and screens is extreme.

Even though distributors cannot book a theater until the exhibitors have seen the movie (as a result of the prohibition on blind bidding), it is fully impractical to wait until two weeks before a movie release to structure a game plan for booking thousands of venues. Long before the screenings take place, the distribution team will look at the population of theaters and competitive landscape of films and plot a strategy for locations and screens. Because this is done on a weekly basis, the parties are aware of each other's general tactics and preferences, and relationships have evolved. Accordingly, if Disney is about to release a Pixar film, or Fox has a large action/star-driven vehicle, they will have a strong educated guess as to which theaters they are likely to target and be able to book in downtown Chicago. Much attention is obviously focused on securing prime venues. Not all theaters are equal, and every distributor wants to lock up its top "gun" site.

It is almost like Las Vegas, because there can be a feeding frenzy, and yet it is all about placing bets—nobody knows how any particular film will actually perform. That is where exhibitor conventions (e.g., ShowWest) are so important. They sell to the theaters and make them believe before selling to the consumers. The theater proposition is much simpler than the consumer: no matter what anyone tells you, the theater owners are often single-mindedly focused on traffic. "How many people will a film drive to the venue to buy popcorn?" is the bottom line. Forget about art, reviews, or actors. It is a business.

As an example, put yourself in the place of a theater owner with a screen in downtown Chicago. If you are offered a film starring Tom Cruise or Leonardo DiCaprio at an X percent aggregate, such as 55 percent with second week at 50 percent, would you take that film versus a new CG animated film from a leading producer with two 50 percents? And what if you also had another film with a 90/10, with a sliding scale of guarantees/minimums? What would you choose and what are the variables you would take into account?

Adding to the craziness of bookings are "exception" markets and theaters, where rent costs of a prime venue are so high that theaters may be treated on a different economic basis. There is endless jockeying and side exception deals to manage, where the incentive is actually to strike fair deals for both sides. While it is a cutthroat business, it is also a 52-week-per-year business where it does not behoove a distributor to force a deal that would cause a theater to lose money. There are many more misses than hits, and the distributor is likely to need a favor from an exhibition chain to open a movie that has poor reviews or otherwise looks in trouble.

Length of Runs

Another factor in booking is the length of the run. Arguably, this is the single most important factor other than the splits, and it influences the splits, given that they are tiered over the run. The following are the typical engagements:

- six- to eight-week deals (less common)
- four-week deals
- two-week deals

Much of whether a deal falls into one category or not defaults to custom and practice. Certain towns (or locations) may be profiled as "eight-week towns," and this is the standard deal for a picture of a specific profile. These weeks denote a "minimum run period," and end up serving only as guidelines, both on success and failure. If a picture is still performing well and yielding returns greater than competitive/alternative product, logically it should continue to hold screens and keep playing. In the out weeks, there will be a floor for splits for which the picture will not drop below regardless of how long it plays. As noted earlier, a film such as *Titanic*, which played for weeks and months on end, while a boon to the distributor, is an even greater prize for the exhibitor—seats continue to be filled, and all at splits (if a 90/10 deal) favoring the theater. On the flip side, if a film is not performing, it may be kicked out early, with the distributor "granting relief" (see the section "Being Dropped", page 184).

Prints and Screen Counts

When booking theaters, distributors book both locations and then actual screens at those locations. To state the obvious, there are many more screens than locations, and for a major movie the ratio can be a multiple (e.g., 2:1). The number of locations/theaters is therefore the less interesting fact in terms of economics: the actual screens dictate both applicable house nuts/allowances, as well as the number of physical prints needed.

Prints can be very expensive, with an estimated average of approximately $1,500 per print for a major motion picture released widely through the studio system. (Note: Among the factors discussed above under D-cinema adoption is the opportunity to dramatically reduce these costs.) Of course, there are many variables that may go into a negotiation with a lab, including the type of film stock used and the length of the film (prints are still literally priced by the yard and deals are quoted in dollars or cents per foot). This does not sound too bad, until you run the numbers and extrapolate out worldwide costs for mega-movies that have a broad release, such as a *Shrek* or *Spider-Man* sequel. It is a trade secret how many screens were booked for *Shrek 2* and *Spider-Man 2*, but let us assume there were upwards of 3,500 locations and take an average of two screens per location. That could yield more than 7,000 screens. For the sake of simplicity, assume some backup prints would be made for key locations, and the total print run was 7,500. The 7,500 prints multiplied by $1,500 per print is $11.25 million. And this is just for the United States, and does not include all the pre-print mastering and quality assurance services that would be on top of this variable figure—when Fox talks about converting fully to D-cinema and eliminating physical prints, the studio is eyeing millions in savings (eventually, post contributing virtual print fees) while marketing the improvements in quality.

As earlier noted, historically, films played longer and did not open as wide, which meant that prints could be reused; a film might open in a major city, and after it had played a while it would then move to a smaller town or location. The benefit to the distributor is there is no incremental cost. However, when a film opens very wide and a distributor tries to garner as much box office up front as possible, then the opportunities for reusing prints are reduced. Moreover, prints could be reformatted to be used internationally in same-language territories, allowing the "bicycling" of assets worldwide and amortizing these sunk costs over more runs. With the move to event films and day-and-date releases, these opportunities are also eliminated.

One net result of a major, wide, day-and-date release is to dramatically drive up the print costs—yet another factor that makes D-cinema, which can radically reduce these costs, attractive.

179

Per-Screen Averages

Partly as a consequence of multiplexes and booking multiple prints at a single venue, the concept of per-screen averages is often misunderstood and, at best, inconsistently applied or quoted. Trade journals and general industry lingo will often refer to per-screen averages, but the use of "screen" is a misnomer. Per-screen averages quoted in the trades and viewed for distribution decisions are actually often per-location averages.

It is not rocket science to compare competitive per-screen averages, as common reporting systems will report gross box office dollars and pretty accurately estimate the number of locations played. The math is simply total box office divided by number of locations. As a rule of thumb, an average of $10,000 or higher is extremely good, and a picture starts to lose momentum as the number dwindles into the low thousands and even less.

Although analysis is not taken down to the per-seat level, it is possible to back into the numbers and understand why this average is such a good barometer. Let us assume the following:

Assumptions:

- Average ticket price: $7.00
- Average theater size: 300 seats (probably high, but makes math easier)

- Five showings per day
- One print per theater
- Standard three-day weekend calculation

Potential Gross: $7 × 300 = $2,100 × 5 = $10,500 per day

Per Weekend

The screen average can then be segmented by these periods. Because the lion's share of the weekly gross of a picture comes in on the weekend, this is the customary measurement for screen averages. The weekend is considered "three day," meaning Friday–Sunday.

3 × $10,500 = $31,500 potential weekend gross

A film that has a $10,000 weekend per-screen average would indicate that fully one-third of all potential seats for all shows for the whole weekend were sold. At five showings per day, that takes into account 15 showings, which means that, on average, all of the primetime showings would need to be nearly sold out (assuming roughly five to six are at peak hours) to achieve this number, or that they could be 75 percent sold out with a smattering of audience at non-primetime dates.

When you start to see per-screen averages well above $10,000, both intuitively and empirically, it means that people are coming to the movie at multiple times (day and evening). This is generally only achieved with a wide demographic.

Of course, these numbers can be deceptive. The variables discussed previously can dramatically skew the results (as can demographics, where a kids movie will have lower average ticket prices). For example, the number of prints on average per theater (i.e., screens) will have the most profound impact, with the number of show times per day having the next most. Of course, the more showings and the more prints typically indicate a major film, and should boost the per-screen average. If a film opens very wide (large number of prints) and the per-screen average is not high, you will be able immediately to conclude the release is in trouble. The problem is that there may not be much time to adjust, especially if marketing expenditure has been front-loaded. Finally, the above assumes a flat ticket price, but children's prices and matinees also influence the maximum potential gross (as can the new trend of premium pricing for 3D).

Interlocking

Interlocking is the practice of running two screens off a single projector/ print. This practice is discouraged, and in most cases prohibited, by distributors. There are concerns about accounting, as splits and nuts are based on per-screen deals, and interlocking usually takes place for overflow demand rather than regular show times. There are also quality concerns, given the very nature of interlocking. Ultimately, fear of being mistreated overrides the economic efficiency of saving a print. In a true crunch, however, it is fair to assume that a blind eye may be turned. The chance to have another full house and additional gross is likely to hold sway at the margin.

Decay Curves and Drop-Offs—Managing the Release

Once the film opens, it becomes part art and part science in terms of managing locations and screens. What everyone focuses on are the week-to-week decays, in particular the decays from weekend to weekend. Regardless of how one defines the days of the opening weekend, for a decay curve you need a like-to-like comparison, and a Friday–Sunday benchmark is used.

It is unfair to refer to these charts as simply "decays," because, depending on the release strategy, a film can actually increase from week to week. A picture that has a strategy of starting small and building an audience through reviews and word of mouth will expand locations. It may start at 100 theaters in major markets, and then wait to release wider nationally. The dream scenario is to open wide and have virtually no falloff, or even an uptick. This rarely happens, but occurred with *Shrek* in 2001, where its second weekend was nearly identical to its opening weekend (three-day to three-day, as one weekend was Memorial Day). This zero decay immediately indicated to DreamWorks that it had a major hit on its hands. The original *Shrek* grossed over $267 million, becoming the top animated film of all time at the point (yet another way to slice a record).[28]

Most films, however, follow traditional decays, meaning there is a relatively predictable pattern of drop-offs. The industry rule of thumb is that if you open well (namely, large!), a drop-off of approximately 50 percent in week two is anticipated. If the film drops significantly more, such as 60–70 percent, then one initially assumes that the marketing worked to drive people into the opening, but that the film may not have been well received—either word of mouth, or reviews, or competition took the wind out of its sails, and once this happens it is virtually impossible to recover. (Note: Given competition and accelerated box office takes, a larger drop-off may not mean the film is in trouble, but simply, in the case of a blockbuster or tentpole, that the first week was so large it will represent a disproportionate share of the total. See discussion below regarding acceleration of box office.) If the decay is in the acceptable range or even less than expected (this is what every executive is hoping for), then the goal immediately becomes to keep the decay from week two to week three within the same range, thereby keeping the momentum.

Depending on the percentage and the competition on the horizon, this is also when key marketing decisions are made. Do you run a hype or review advertisement ("Two thumbs up," "Best picture of the year, according to . . .," "Number 1 at the box office")? There will usually be some marketing planned post release (called "sustain marketing"), but as films are becoming more and more front-loaded, much sustain marketing spending, especially in weeks past the first two or three weeks, may be allocated literally on the spot during the week.

Trend of Accelerated Decays for Blockbusters

The bigger the film and the bigger the opening, the steeper the decay will likely be up front. On *Star Wars: Episode III – Revenge of the Sith*, for example, the Thursday–Sunday "opening weekend" was over $150 million, with the following long weekend (Memorial Day) taking in $70 million at the box office. The pure three-day to three-day, however, was $108 million to $55 million (59 percent), representing an acceptable 50 percent drop.[29]

This is a typical pattern for a blockbuster, but one then hopes for the decay curve to flatten out. Because the numbers are so large, and there are so many prints and show times playing, there will inevitably be a large fall. As weeks progress, however, and multiplexes are only playing one or two prints for normal show times, and locations consolidate, the decay curve will hopefully flatten and the weekly drops will not be as precipitous.

As noted earlier, in terms of prints and multiplexes, this is where it is important to distinguish between locations and prints, and in terms of prints to distinguish between sizes of auditoriums within a multiplex (see "Move-Overs" below). When a film opens particularly wide and one sees a print count in the range over 7,000, there are almost always multiple prints in one location. Continuing with *Star Wars: Episode III – Revenge of the Sith*, on the weekend of June 2, 2005, for example, you could go to the movie listings and pull up a 16- or 20-plex, and notice that, in counting up the actual number of films playing there, it was only nine or 10, and similarly, in a theater half the size, namely an 8-plex, there were only six films playing. This is because event or would-be event films that were opened wide and had large demand played on multiple screens. One can assume that at the 8-plex playing only six films that both *Star Wars: Episode III – Revenge of the Sith* and *Madagascar* had multiple screens (two each); similarly, in the 16-plex playing only six films, one of the films may have had as many as four or five screens at one point, and potentially more on opening weekend.

Move-Overs

There is yet another variable to consider in understanding the print placements—the size of theater. In a 20-plex, for example, theater sizes can range from several hundred seats to a couple of hundred seats or less. While not all theaters are equal, similarly "not all prints are equal" in terms of potential gross within the complex. Thus, when a print of a film opens in the largest screen, after it has run for a week or two, demand will likely wane and the auditorium will play to fewer people per showtime; in the extreme, which happens quite frequently, a print will move from playing to capacity to sparse crowds fairly quickly. Keeping the print in the theater may make sense to the distributor who wants the largest potential gross ("I don't care if it's empty during the matinees and mid-week Joe, 'cause I want that gross on the primetimes ... ") in some scenarios. However, this will not make economic sense if the print/distributor is bearing the house nut; in fact, the print can lose money if the nut is significant.

183

The larger the auditorium, the larger the nut, so when demand wanes, the print "moves over" from a larger to a smaller screen. This has two benefits. First, as just noted, the smaller screen has a smaller house nut. Second, moviegoing is a social experience, and most people prefer to have a full house rather than an empty house—it is inevitably the crowd reaction and the shared experience of hearing screams, cries, quick intakes of air from being shocked, and even the occasional funny heckle that is part of the magic of the theater and makes seeing a movie in the theater fun. (Note: This also partially explains the preview and midnight screening crush of attendance, as it is just as likely that people want to see the film in an atmosphere charged with the same excitement they feel than that they have to see the film early. It is more the electricity and shared experience of the moment that likely drives most people than the bragging rights that they saw it a few hours or days ahead of someone else.) That social, collective experience simply cannot be replicated at home, no matter how nice a flat-screen TV and home theater environment someone has created—in the age of social media, where e-interactions masquerade as being social, but in fact can be experienced in isolation, Hollywood always touts the real collective social experience of theatre-going (also, please no texting or posting once the lights go down!).

Move-overs thus have multiple benefits to both parties, for economically having full auditoriums is beneficial to both the distributor and exhibitor. Similarly, if a multiplex is playing a film on multiple screens, and the percentage of seats filled per screen per show time starts to drop off, then a print will be dropped and the film shown on two screens rather than three, increasing the average capacity filled per showtime. Of course, the distributor wants to ensure that there are still sufficient play times for people to see the film, and it is the balancing of nearing capacity versus not turning away people (who may not return—carpe diem is the MO) that becomes the art of booking.

Finally, it is worth pointing out that all of these issues are tied to success. In the more typical pattern, a film will play one screen per theater location, and hold on for dear life to stay as long as possible before becoming dropped.

Being Dropped

184 Inevitably, every film leaves the theater, and it is hopefully after several weeks rather than several days. The fight to hold screens can be vicious, and several factors influence a film's staying power. These key factors include:

- The weekly gross of the theater. What was the film's box office the prior week and weekend?
- The weekly gross of the film relative to the competitive titles playing in the same complex. Are there other films in the theater (assuming it is a multiplex)?
- The quantity of new films opening in the week, and the perceived strength/demand of the new product. Is there an expected blockbuster opening that will command multiple screens in a multiplex?
- The number of screens in the complex.
- The number of weeks the film has been in the theater. Is it the first or second week, or is it now into multiple weeks being played?
- The terms. What is the rental percentage being asked by the distributor, and is there an applicable house nut?
- The contractual terms. Is there a minimum booking period?
- The quantity of competitive films in the marketplace that are "grossing." Are there several pictures holding over with strong to respectable grosses, in addition to new films opening up?

- What other pictures the studio has in release. All theaters want to keep each of the studios happy, and while there are no allocated slots, it may be difficult for Studio A to keep multiple screens (when some are marginal performing pictures) at the expense of a rival studio securing a screen.
- Studio pressures/expectations driven by direct economics—achieving performance thresholds, which could be tied to economics, such as achieving a box office number that may trigger improved economics in a downstream revenue (e.g., pay TV output deals tiered to box office thresholds) and by indirect economics tied to relationships (e.g., fulfilling promises to the producer/director/actor—"Are you fighting for my picture?").
- What investment the studio has in the film. Not all pictures are equal in terms of the studio's financial stake, and while every studio will tell you that it is fighting for every cent on every film, it is natural to question whether there is a bit more fight in a film where the studio has a bigger stake.

These are the type of factors influencing the decisions. They comprise a unique mix by blending straightforward economics, cutthroat competition, allocations (within and without groups), politics, ego, and differing agendas. A studio is very conscious both of relationships and performance, but when counting relationships, they are truly in the middle of two parties they need to please: the exhibitor and the producer. Although distributors have a tremendous amount of clout (without them, you simply do not get into the screens/theaters), they are between a rock and a hard place. During a release, they need to please the film-maker who only cares about his or her movie and maximizing its results (at the expense of anyone else's film currently in release) and the theater chains who could care less about a particular film and only truly care about whether customers are filling the seats.

Tension arises because the factors weighed by the two sides (theater versus distributor) are dissimilar. The distributor is weighing a nearly impossible matrix of agendas, ranging from pleasing a star, to recouping an investment, to juggling multiple pictures within a slate, to maintaining pole position relationship treatment with a particular exhibition chain of theaters. The exhibitor, however, has relative tunnel vision focused on attendance: they can remain emotionally neutral and have virtually no reason to care about the particular film, only focusing on whether people come and the theater is full (taking their split and raking in concession money).

Despite the potential for a dizzying complex matrix, the end result of what stays in a theater is rarely a complex balancing act. Instead, it is absolutely Darwinian, and the strongest pictures survive. After every weekend, the distributor looks at a report of how its pictures performed and how they performed versus the competition. Box office information is freely available, and there is little argument as to relative standings. In an 8-plex theater, the local booker and theater are acutely aware of their ranking. If there are eight screens, and Studio A has one picture that came in last (eighth among eight), then that picture is going to get dropped in favor of a new picture coming into the market (or adding another good performer in the market that may not have been booked originally). The one exception to this rule is that by contract, as well as industry practice, virtually every major studio picture gets the benefit of the doubt for two weeks. If a studio is opening a movie with a major star or for a major director/producer, it will secure at least a two-week run, and will be hard pressed to pull it before this minimum period.

The survival-of-the-fittest mentality can be tempered by a few factors, such as the ability to move over. Because of the "not all screens are equal" factor, a film that is underperforming may still hold in a smaller auditorium because its gross remains strong enough to stay in the complex relative to competition. Moreover, all of the factors previously stated then can, and do, come into play at the margin. Most of the decisions are clear-cut. If the gross in a complex is $1,200 for a week and all other films are $3,000 and above, there is not much room for the distributor to argue; moreover, the smaller the complex, the easier the decision. A single screen or complex with six or fewer screens can ill afford to carry its overhead without performing product—they need to attract bodies and cannot amortize across product. If a movie is not working, they need to move on, and move on fast. However, with larger complexes, there is likely to be a range of performances, and it is therefore easier to accommodate relationships. If you have a 16-plex and Disney or Universal needs a screen, is the exhibitor going to shut them out on a marginal picture when they have an every-week of every-year relationship? If the picture is truly a disaster, then maybe, but if the distributor is pleading, then how much of a sacrifice is the 120-seat screen when there are 15 other screens booked with (hopefully) better-performing titles?

At the margins, studios may start splitting show times to stretch a picture's run. As the picture declines, it may play to specific demographics where splitting prints may make sense for a particular week: "I'll play X in the matinees and Y in the evenings." This is a band-aid solution and rarely holds over into multiple weeks, but can make sense in the short

186

term when there are tough calls. Essentially, this is a "something is better than nothing" mentality, and having capitulated halfway, you know your run is on a short rope. However, in the Darwinian world, once you are out, you are out, and there are probably few to no incremental costs to staying in the extra week—the print is already there, and every incremental dollar of box office helps amortize that cost and climb toward profits.

Decay Curves and Predicting Box Office

There is a relatively predictable pattern to performance, and, as discussed previously, the name of the game is flattening out the decay curve so that the week-to-week drop-offs are as small as possible. All films have a decay because the nature of the business is to eventize a release, and marketing has to be somewhat, if not fully, front-loaded to create the awareness for people to attend. Word of mouth (which, by the way, feels like an anachronistic phrase in the era of texting and social media, but which I am assuming will continue to be used by the industry to capture the broader context of spreading opinions by communicating verbally or electronically) can build a film that is opened small and then expands, but one can argue that this is merely a bell-curve release pattern strategy, and the decay starts being measured from the peak.

187

Accordingly, a decay curve is built from both expectations and by comparing drop-offs to comparable titles. By comparable, it may be that a film is compared to another title of similar genre with the same star: How does a Woody Allen movie or an Adam Sandler comedy decay? If the film is part of a series or franchise, then the task can be easier: How will *Harry Potter 3* compare to *Harry Potter 2*? Thus, a studio may build a model taking the best comparables it can find and look at the week-to-week decays of that film; namely, by what percentage it dropped week to week in weeks X to Y. The film being measured will have to have its own base, but once it has a starting point (opening-week or two-week data), then it is possible to plot its performance against like titles. Week to week, you will measure whether you are above or below the imputed curve.

A challenge for marketing will be to keep the baseline up and keep stimulating the baseline with spikes of activity. The theory is that because a decay is inevitable, the higher the base, the higher the net result. If you started from $10 million versus $8 million and were likely to decay the following week by 40 percent in either scenario, then the following week would be $6 million versus $4.8 million (an incremental $1.2 million). Accordingly, if the prior week had been targeted at $8 million and there was marketing activity/expenditure green-lit to boost box office achieving

$10 million, the net impact is hopefully much greater than the $2 million; instead, it is the $2 million and the gap in week two (incremental $1.2 million), plus the incremental benefit in subsequent weeks.

This all assumes, however, that the decays are consistent (which is not the case) and that you can straight-line the falloff tied to the higher base; in fact, no one really knows whether a program will truly raise the base in a trailing manner. Additionally, no one really knows whether the impact will be temporary and there will be a larger drop-off the subsequent week where the decay is catching up to the prior equilibrium and tracking more closely to the film's "true demand" rather than the temporary demand that was stimulated.

Measuring the payoff or break-even is therefore tricky, and the easiest benchmark is to look at the isolated period. Will the incremental costs spent this week be recouped from the lift this week in box office and resulting rental dollars? If the answer is yes, then this is a pretty good bet, for there is a payoff with the potential upside of having lifted the base and gaining the incremental value in subsequent weeks (i.e., gaining the $1.2 million the next week).

188   Finally, it is worth noting that while the key decay curve to track is box office, it is also possible to track decays of both theater locations and prints. The final tools will therefore include a box office decay chart and a print and theater decay chart (Table 4.3).

Table 4.3 Decay Chart Example

Week	Weekly Gross	Cumulative Week Gross	Number of Theaters	Number of Prints
Week 1				
Week 2				
Week 3				
Week 4				
Week 5				

Residual Impact of Theater Ownership

A final wrinkle in the mix is theater ownership. It is natural to assume that a theater owned by Warner Bros., for example, is likely to give preference to a Warner title. Despite the breakup of vertical integration and the consent decree (see page 149, "Consent Decrees, Block Booking, and Blind Bidding"), as antitrust rules became relaxed in the 1980s under the Reagan administration, a number of studios began to acquire ownership interests in theaters again, in particular Warner Bros. and Paramount (Viacom). At the margin, this can influence a picture's placement, as issues of personal theater preference are likely to lose out to the pure economics of whether a rival studio-owned venue will afford you the best chance of a long run (especially if you know a competitive film from that rival studio is set to open in X weeks).

International Booking

The international market has grown to a point where it is common for a major studio release to have more locations booked internationally than domestically (though the numbers are relatively close); additionally, the international bookings may be more profitable on a per-print average. I have not seen a direct study on this, but it is empirically true: if the print count is relatively even, and international box office is a greater percentage of the worldwide box office than domestic box office, then each international print (on average) must yield a greater return/box office gross.

The reason for this is largely due to the clustering of population in urban centers and cities versus the diffuse, relatively rural and suburban population in the United States. It also suggests that there is international growth potential, although the shift in media and uptake of VOD and Internet is likely to encroach too quickly to let this theoretical experiment play out to its otherwise logical conclusion.

The international theatrical market has lagged behind the United States in a few areas, but that is now quickly changing. The U.S. market, accommodating the vast suburban sprawl that has come to typify the dispersion of population, had a boom in the 1990s building multiplexes. While this trend was mirrored internationally, the phenomenon of 16- and 20-plexes did not grow at the same breathtaking pace. In retrospect, this was good, for, as earlier discussed, virtually all the major U.S. chains filed for or flirted with bankruptcy. Cinemas internationally reflect the local culture, and while there is an element of standardization and copying, there are many cinemas in Europe, for example, that maintain the character of great art houses (though even these, in many instances, have been refurbished and split into multiple screens).

One interesting trend is that digital cinema took off more quickly overseas than in the United States. To a degree, this is a result of lag, for certain territories that recently or are just now upgrading are skipping intermediate steps and installing D-cinema. This is especially true in Asia, and in particular China. One has to be careful, however, in defining D-cinema as, in the rush to enter the market, a number of locations (at least initially) were utilizing projectors below the 2K projector standard endorsed by most studios as a minimum resolution.

How a Property Travels

It is important to bear in mind that each film is unique, and the genre, star, and director can have profound influences on how the particular picture will fare in a particular territory. An American comedy may not travel well in one place, an action star may have disproportionate popularity in a certain country, and a franchise may, for reasons obvious or inexplicable, be relatively strong or weak versus its domestic market or even a neighboring territory. In some cases, the reason may be linked to a local star, and in others it may be that a scene takes place locally, some of the filming may have taken place locally, or the subject matter may strike a particular chord culturally. In many cases, however, it can simply be a mystery why a film works better in one country than another; this is the job of the marketing division, and the litany of excuses is longer than the list of why a film succeeds.

190

The animation industry is a particular curiosity. It became the trend with Pixar and then DreamWorks Animation and Blue Sky (*Ice Age*) (and now a few others, including Sony) to cast high-profile stars as voice talent. However, when Tom Hanks does not play the part in the German dub, nor Eddie Murphy in Spanish, then those actors truly do not ever appear in the film. The marketing hook and performance that was so pivotal to the domestic campaign (and arguably success) are simply nonexistent. Somehow, this does not impact performance to the extent that one would guess it should. Perhaps the clout of Hollywood and the brand expectations from these studios are able to overcome this hurdle, and people come and enjoy the film anyway, in a classic sense of "not knowing what they missed." This may simply be a testament to the film's overall strength, or to the fact that when watching, viewers focus on the character and do not necessarily associate the character with a particular individual/voice. In certain territories, the voice-over actors tend to repeat, such that the person who dubs for Daniel Craig or Pierce Brosnan in Germany tends to do so for all their films; in essence, a permanent stand-in. This is the voice locally associated with the actor, and accepted. (Note: Because many want to see the original version, certain cinemas in major cities will play "OV" English language prints.)

Europe

The largest European markets include the UK, France, Germany, Italy, Spain, and Russia. The number of prints used for the markets is in the same order of magnitude for the UK, France, and Germany, but this does not necessarily correlate to box office performance. The number of prints may often be the highest in Germany due to its dispersed metropolitan centers. Unlike the UK, where a couple of cities such as London can dominate, Germany is more akin to the United States, with many "states" and major cities (e.g., Berlin, Munich, Frankfurt, Hamburg, Cologne), and requires a higher print count. For most U.S. films, however, the U.K. box office will be larger than the German box office. France, despite the concentration of population in Paris with its rich film tradition, also tends to have high print counts, frequently exceeding the UK. Print counts may be, from highest to lowest: Germany, France, and the UK, while the box office could be exactly the opposite, from highest to lowest: the UK, France, and Germany.

This potentially inverse relationship between bookings/prints and box office revenues simply highlights some of the challenges in managing and maximizing contribution from international territories.

191

Asia/Pacific and the Rise of China

The largest market for major Hollywood films for years was usually Japan, followed next by Australia and then South Korea. However, the explosive growth of China has catapulted it into the second biggest market in the world. In an article describing a Chinese group's purchase in May 2012 of the U.S.'s second-largest theater chain, AMC Entertainment, the *Los Angeles Times* noted: "Last year, China saw a 30 percent increase in box office sales to $2.1 billion. This year it passed Japan as the biggest foreign market for Hollywood films."[30] Fueling and tracking the growth in revenues from China is its phenomenal screen growth. Screens have doubled in the last five years or so to approximately 11,000, giving it the second largest screen count in the world next to the U.S. These factors, plus the obvious growth of the middle class and consumer culture led the *Economist* to predict: "China's box office revenues may overtake America's by 2020."[31] Already, China's box office is 25 percent of that of North America, hitting $2.7 billion in 2012 (versus North America's $10.8 billion), surging 37 percent from 2011.[32]

An example of the market's might was the April 2012 release of *Titanic 3D*, where the 3D rerelease of the original blockbuster broke the record for all-time opening, with an initial take of $67 million. To put that opening into perspective, the film had earned $44.5 million in the

U.S. over its first two weeks,[33] and the entire international opening in 69 territories garnered $98.9 million.[34]

I asked Mary McLaren, chief operating officer of theatrical for 20th Century Fox, to put the growth of China's market in perspective, and she advised:

The growth of China's box office is a phenomenal success story. In 2006, China was ranked number 12 in international box office; in 2011, they have moved up to become the number-two market internationally. When Fox released *Star Wars: Episode III – Revenge of the Sith* in 2005, China represented less than 2 percent of the international box office, delivering just over $9 million; today, the market routinely contributes more than 10 percent of a film's international box office. China was our second-highest-grossing international market on *Rise of the Planet of the Apes*, with $31 million in box office, and the number-one international market for both *Avatar* and *Titanic 3D*, delivering staggering box office results of $203 million and $148 million, respectively. The good news for the industry is that the trend looks to carry on as digital screen growth continues to expand, with digital screens doubling and 3D screens nearly tripling in the past 16 months.

192

The growth of the Chinese box office and new stature as a top market is more remarkable when considering how few foreign films are released into the market each year. The Chinese have historically enforced a strict quota system, limiting the market to 20 foreign films per year. After a meeting with U.S. Vice President Joe Biden and the waiting-in-the-wings future premiere of China, Xi Jinping, in the U.S. in February 2012, the countries announced a raising of the limit to 34 per year, with the caveat that the additional 14 movies must be exhibited in 3D (or other large-screen format). Seeing the next gold rush, many in Hollywood are looking to circumvent the system, seeking coproduction deals that would skirt the quotas if the films are classified as local. It remains to be seen how effective studios and others will be in implementing coproductions, for beyond the routine complications (see coproduction discussion in Chapter 3), the level of control either directly or informally ceded in the China context may be greater than most are willing to accept; typical coproduction deals revolve around financing and balancing creative and economic decisions among partners, but in China coproduced properties are further subject to censor review and control.

Together with a relaxation of quotas, the Chinese government also adjusted the rules in terms of box office splits. The above discussion, in terms of film rentals and different structures, never applied to China, as the government, along with limiting foreign films, also managed a controlled system that dictated foreign distributors participated in a share of ticket sales ranging from 13.5–17.5 percent. For the new 14 3D or IMAX films permitted, the government now raised that percentage to 25 percent.[35] Chris Dodd, the chairman of the MPAA, remarked on the landmark changes: "The industry has been living with the numbers in terms of percentages and quotas for 20 years ... it begged for a conclusion."[36]

Unlike the situation in Europe, the number of prints in Asia generally tracks revenues, with the higher print count representing the larger market and corresponding higher box office.

Latin America

By far the largest markets in the region are Mexico and Brazil, with Mexico dominating both in terms of box office and prints.

Boom International Markets Driving Increase in International B.O.

193

It is because of the phenomenal growth of major markets such as Russia, India, and now especially China—none of which were in the top 10 markets, nor even close to them, a mere handful of years ago—that the overall international box office, as discussed above, continues to grow as a percentage of global box office. The MPAA, in its 2011 Theatrical Market Statistics report, noted: "International box office in U.S. dollars is up 35 percent over five years ago, driven by growth in various markets, including China and Russia."[37]

As a follow-on, its 2012 Theatrical Market Statistics report published total B.O. estimates for the top 10 international markets (Table 4.4).

Concessions

The unwritten rule of the industry is that "the theater keeps the popcorn." For decades, producers, distributors, and everyone else in the food chain of profits has tried, without success, to add concessions into the revenue base derived from theatrical exhibition. The "popcorn," however, is considered sacrosanct and is reserved entirely for the exhibitor. As discussed previously and in Chapter 10, the revenue base upon which participations and profits are calculated includes only the distributor's

Table 4.4 2012 Top 10 International Box Office Markets, from MPAA Theatrical Market Statistics 2012[38]

Territory	2012 Box Office (US$ Billions)
China	2.7
Japan	2.4
UK	1.7
France	1.7
India	1.4
Germany	1.3
South Korea	1.3
Russia	1.2
Australia	1.2
Brazil	0.8

194   cut from ticket sales (i.e., film rentals, as previously discussed). The theater owner's cut from the box office and the concessions are a vital part of the macroeconomic picture, but these revenues are excluded even from the baseline of calculations.

Online Impact

- The online and digital world is profoundly influencing the release strategy and timing of theatrical distribution: piracy concerns, exacerbated by file-sharing services and the potential for ubiquitous initial instant access to a film, are driving studios to release films "day-and-date" worldwide.
- Sites that aggregate nationwide critics' reviews, such as Rotten Tomatoes, are providing summary scorecards, theoretically hampering the ability to open a movie slowly and build "word of mouth"; the nature of cumulative and instant scorecards, coupled with mass and new immediate feedback from social media and microblogging sites, further accelerating marketing timelines and putting additional pressures on box office openings.

- The online world affords a new, and still relatively untested, premiere release window, tantalizing some who could create sufficient demand to bypass the historical system and test online pay-per-view models.
- Digital cinema can deliver pristine quality and, in the long run, lower cost distribution—its promise is finally being fulfilled, with adoption rates soaring globally over the last few years, to the point that studios are beginning to phase out the use of physical prints. Although this movement developed independently of the online world, growing competition from other media remains relevant in efforts to improve and differentiate the theatrical experience (which has also stimulated the growth of 3D), while also lowering its cost basis.
- See also Chapter 9 for impact on marketing in the theatrical market.

195

CHAPTER 5

The Home Video Business

196

The ability to watch a movie or TV show at home on a videocassette, or DVD or Blu-ray disc, has had a profound impact on the economics of the motion picture and television business. Not only has the video market altered the consumer's consumption pattern of watching movies, but it has also changed the underlying financial modeling of whether a movie, and in cases TV shows, are made in the first place. Despite the rapid and wide market penetration of new technologies such as DVDs, it is a testament to the cultural impact of videocassettes that the studios, at least colloquially, still refer to their divisions as Home Video. In fact, the word "video" in this context has become a misnomer, a catch-all of sorts that conceptually captures the varied devices that have evolved allowing consumers to watch films on their television, over a computer, via game systems, or more recently via tablets and other portable means.

In terms of profitability, the video market has provided a boon to studios' bottom lines. While the profitability on a new movie is generally measured in a single life cycle (e.g., theatrical, video, television, ancillary and new media revenue streams), the video market has added the magic of reincarnation by inducing consumers to keep buying the same product again and again with each new technological upgrade. The net result is that home-video revenues (i.e., revenues from sales of physical discs) grew to represent about half of studios' total film revenue. Figure 5.1 below illustrates how, in the early to mid 2000s, video captured nearly half of a studio's revenue pie[1]; Figure 1.5 (see Chapter 1), in contrast, depicts how that percentage has dropped precipitously to roughly one third in the last five years or so.

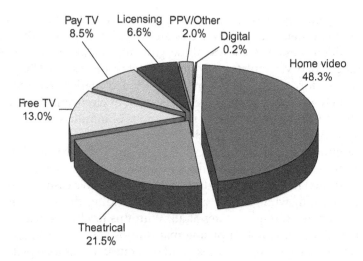

Figure 5.1 Studio Revenue Breakdown, 2007

Although this percentage has been steadily declining from its peak of roughly 50 percent of total revenues, the absolute numbers remain significant, and entering 2012 video still remained the single largest revenue segment (again, see Figure 1.5). Additionally, and quite important-antly, beyond capturing the biggest slice of the revenue pie and exploiting the churn factor, the studios have managed to keep a larger share of the video revenues. Typically, studios (and networks, as applicable) pay participa-tions based on a royalty percentage rather than accounting for the gross sums, which in turn makes video distribution uniquely profitable.

The evolution of the home video business is not over, and in this chapter I will review the genesis and growth of this approximately $14 billion market segment (down from a peak of $24 billion; see Table 5.1 on page 207), explore the radical changes that have taken place at retail distribution since the early 1990s, and discuss the underlying P&L models of how the business works and why videocassette/DVD/Blu-ray distribu-tion returns some of the highest margins in the distribution life-cycle chain. I will also review how this ancillary revenue source has spawned profitable original production (i.e., made-for-video), discuss marketing nuances driving home video consumption, outline some of the profound technical changes that have been catalysts for a reinvention of the category, and explore the impact that video release patterns/windows and piracy have had on the other parts of the business.

Finally, although new technology applications, including downloads and video-on-demand (VOD) access are inextricably tied to the future of the video market, I address these growing markets (together with watching video via tablets and other portable means) in Chapters 7 and 8, and focus here on the traditional video market. Nevertheless, I will touch on aspects such as the intersection of electronic sell-through (i.e., downloads to own) and the implications of infinite shelf space and depth of copy compared to physical retail sales.

In summary, this chapter will explain how and why the video business (again, here meaning physical discs as opposed to on-demand/digital permutations) has emerged to drive the largest positive cash flow of any studio division, while at the same time providing the safety net for studios to make certain pictures at all. With this level of vested interest in the business, it is not surprising that studios and networks alike are schizophrenic regarding download and other new technology platforms that are expanding video's reach while threatening to replace what has evolved into a pillar of the studio distribution (and financing) infrastructure.

¹⁹⁸ Compelling Value Proposition

To grasp the value-for-money proposition inherent in marketing a DVD of a hit movie, simply pause to think about one of your favorite recent films. That movie probably took over five years (and likely many more) to move from concept to release in theaters; over that period, hundreds, if not thousands, of people were involved in the production and release of the movie. On the financial side alone, and assuming the film is a major studio picture, it probably had an investment risk, including costs of producing, marketing, and releasing the film, of over $100 million. Wrap those years of hard work, incalculable passion and creativity, and dollars together and what do you have? You, the consumer, can take home a product that cost the studio over $100 million and years of work for about $20, and often less; better yet, you can rent the movie for about $3.

Whether renting or buying, the product is also perfectly tailored to the freedoms made possible via innovations in the consumer electronics industry: you can watch it when you want and where you want. This pitch is not often made overtly, but at a subliminal level, when advertisements say "own it today" or "bring it home today," they are saying you can own for $20 what it took us over $100 million to make, and you can watch it over and over for free and at your leisure. You do not have to go back very far when the concept of an average citizen owning a movie and watching it at home was beyond the grasp of reasonable expectations.

What other products can compete with the value of a video? Perhaps a record or CD of a concert, capturing the moment, are somewhat equivalent. If you had asked the people starting up studio video divisions, many of whom migrated from the record side, whether they would be happy to be as large as the record companies, they would have thought you were crazy. Certainly, it was not within upstart business plans that the revenues could come to surpass the music industry. It is not a stretch to state that video recorders and videos, and the improved technical iterations spawned, including most prominently DVD and now Blu-ray, have been considered the most important product invention to hit Hollywood since television. And yet, as grandiose and accurate as this statement may be, the pace of change in the online world has been so great that it is conceivable to view VOD access as quickly usurping the video mantle; VOD access, though, benefits enormously from the consumer renting culture spawned by home video, and to understand the shifts today and the economics of VOD access (whether à la carte or subscription, streaming or download) it is important to appreciate the models, history, and economics of video that paved the way for personal/home viewing. **199**

Accordingly, I will touch on a number of questions: How did video turn into big business? Where is the business headed, and why has it become the lifeblood of studio profitability? Is it possible that just as quickly as the video market grew to dominate distribution revenues, we are at the cusp of a decline so steep that in a few years, videos/DVDs/Blu-rays may disappear? Will the traditional video market be relegated to a historical footnote along with physical film prints, and be entirely replaced by on-demand digital media accessible via a range of new devices, including living room staples (TVs and game systems) and a host of portable devices (e.g., tablets)?

History and Growth of the Video Business

Early Roots: Format Wars and Seminal Legal Wrangling

The first consumer-targeted videocassette recorders were marketed in the 1970s, when Sony introduced the Betamax VCR. The introduction of the VCR faced the same chicken-and-egg dilemma that now seems commonplace with every new technology targeted at consumers' consumption of entertainment: Was there a match between the hardware and software base? When Sony's system was introduced, there was essentially neither software nor hardware available, much like the problem facing the launch of the DVD industry 20 years later in the mid 1990s.

To overcome such a hurdle, at least one party needs to take an enormous risk. In the case of the DVD, it was Warner Bros. leading the charge (see page 212, "Early Stages of the DVD: Piracy Concerns, Parallel Imports, and the Warners Factor"), but the true early pioneer of the business was Sony in the days of the Betamax introduction. Interestingly, and disproving the first-mover advantage, despite building the market (and to many having a superior format/product), Sony did not emerge as the leader.

Sony's visionary idea was that consumers would pay to be freed from television's broadcast schedule (sound familiar today?): the Betamax VCR would allow them to watch programs when they wanted, not as dictated by the network's broadcast schedule. The VCR was not originally positioned as a playback device for movies. Sony's CEO, Akio Morita, said at the time: "People do not have to read a book when it's delivered ... Why should they have to see a TV program when it's delivered?"[2] Accordingly, Sony marketed the Betamax VCR hardware player, which utilized a proprietary tape generically called the Beta format. Its marketing campaign echoed Morita's theme, pitching the player as a machine allowing consumers to "time-shift": consumers could record television programs and view them later at a more convenient time.

Whether history is repeating itself or technology advances enabling services such as Hulu are finally realizing Morita's original vision, it is clear we are now on the threshold of totally taking the programming out of the broadcast scheduler's hands. As alluded to in Chapter 6 and further discussed in Chapter 7, not only have DVRs made recording easier, but we can now envision (and, in fact, already experience) future iterations where TV is consumed in a playlist fashion, where viewers through VOD or other access select the programs they want to watch and then consume them according to their own programming schedule (which may be optimized or random).

Returning to the roots of the business, two factors greatly contributed to the explosive growth of the VCR market. First, and a point not often cited (and I will admit somewhat subject to challenge), the advent of the VCR was in the same general period as the emergence of cable TV in the U.S. Not only was the notion of time shifting attractive, but it was even more attractive in an environment of blossoming program choices. For decades, U.S. consumers were limited in programming choices to the three major broadcast networks plus a handful of local UHF stations; with cable TV came an explosion of choice.

Second, and more importantly, the ability to rent movies from video stores caught on like wildfire—the concept of building a library of tapes and renting tapes out for a price no more than a movie ticket proved revolutionary. Independent stores, which quickly gained the industry nickname "mom and pops," led the growth and proliferated throughout neighborhoods. It was an ideal small business, preying on pent-up demand and taking advantage of modest start-up costs (including the need for limited space); further, video rental was a cash business that built a loyal customer base virtually on its own via a regular supply of new product.

As great as this seemed for Sony and the new breed of video rental entrepreneurs, the whole notion of video rental seemed a looming disaster for the Hollywood studios who produced the films. The studios saw the VCR as a means of copyright infringement. The underlying economic fear was that individuals would copy movies and TV shows (and keep them for a home library), which would undermine the market to exhibit the programs on television. Universal's president, Sidney Sheinberg, upon seeing the Betamax time-shifting campaign, and fearing the loss of revenues that could lead from unauthorized copying of Universal's product, sued Sony for copyright infringement.

The resulting case, which was initially brought in 1976 and ultimately decided by the U.S. Supreme Court in 1984, was a landmark lawsuit that paved the way for DVDs, arguably saved the studio system, and is once again being pointed to as threatening the integrity of the distribution system (as new online services push the VOD envelope).

The Betamax Decision: Universal v. Sony

The ultimate finding in what has come to be known as the "Sony Betamax" case is that time-shifting via home copying for noncommercial purposes was permitted (in legal jargon, a fair use and non-infringing of copyright; for a further discussion of copyright, see Chapter 2). Before the Supreme Court reached this verdict, *Sony Corp. v. Universal City Studios*[3] went through a litany of phases, with each side supported by name-brand media allies. Universal was joined by Disney, who saw similar infringement of its copyrights and potential loss of television broadcast revenues. Sony was supported by the sports leagues, including commissioners of the national football, basketball, baseball, and hockey leagues; these leagues believed that VCRs were a benefit to live events, allowing fans/consumers to see games they would have otherwise missed. Another important Sony supporter was the Corporation for Public Broadcasting, believing that it was a good thing for children to be able to see educational programming and that VCRs promoted this end; further, it was endorsed by Fred Rogers, the star/producer of the classic preschool show *Mister Rogers' Neighborhood*.

In the end, after an eight-year legal odyssey, the Supreme Court reasoned that a significant number of copyright owners would not object to their content being time-shifted, that there was insufficient proof the ability to time-shift would undermine the value copyright holders would receive from licensing their content to TV (which proved to be true, as license fees increased over the following years), and therefore the Betamax was capable of "substantial non-infringing uses." Interestingly, the Supreme Court, in an almost prescient statement recognizing that new technological advances—advances like the Internet, file sharing, and VOD access via social media, of which it could not have been aware—would force it to consider the broader issues in the future:

. . . One may search the Copyright Act in vain for any sign that the elected representatives of the millions of people who watch television every day have made it unlawful to copy a program for later viewing at home, or have enacted a flat prohibition against the sale of machines that make such copying possible.

It may well be that Congress will take a fresh look at this new technology, just as it so often has examined other innovations in the past. But it is not our job to apply laws that have not yet been written. Applying the copyright statute, as it now reads, to the facts as they have been developed in this case, the judgment of the Court of Appeals must be reversed.

It was a close decision (5–4), and whether or not one agrees with the logic (or cynically believes that the court needed to craft a political opinion, allowing the flourishing video business to continue), the video business was officially sanctioned. By 1986, just a couple of years after the landmark Sony decision, combined video rental and sales revenues ($4.38 billion) exceeded the theatrical box office ($3.78 billion) for the first time. By 1988, rental revenues alone ($5.15 billion) exceeded the theatrical box office ($4.46 billion).[4]

Among the ironies of the case is how the party most vested in the case (Sony) ended up losing the battle for consumer dollars, and how the plaintiff (Universal) came to be bought by one of the hardware manufacturers that benefited from the verdict. Matsushita, the parent of the Panasonic brand, and sister company to JVC (together with non-affiliated Hitachi), developed and marketed the rival VHS format, which was incompatible with the Sony Betamax player. It was the VHS format that took hold and, by the mid 1980s, dominated. Video retailers did not want to stock alternate formats, and as VHS players became more dominant, more VHS titles were stocked and the spiral grew until Sony's Beta format was doomed. Within a few years of the *Sony v. Universal* decision, Sony threw in the towel and started manufacturing VHS players. Perhaps adding injury to insult, only a few years later the format war winner Matsushita bought MCA/Universal in an acquisition touting the merger of hardware and software.

The Sony Betamax case continues to mark an important turning point for the distribution of content onto in-home hardware, as well as serving as a precedent for the current age of digital age cases such as Napster, Grokster, and Cablevision (see Chapter 2).

The Early Retail Environment: The Rental Video Store   203

When videocassettes were new, and market penetration of VHS recorders was growing in the 1980s, the video business was almost entirely a rental business. By rental, I mean conventional rental stores such as Blockbuster Video or Hollywood Video (household brands that many under 25 may now not know).

At first, when the rental market was exploding, it was dominated by neighborhood video stores. The economics were relatively simple. The video store would buy units of movies from the studio distributor, and then rent the cassettes out to customers. The store would perform a simple break-even analysis of how many times a particular unit would need to be rented to turn a profit. There were some add-ons to mimic movie environment, such as selling popcorn or candy to take home with your movie. Marketing was relatively unsophisticated, led by film posters supplied by the studio distributors to advertise the hit and coming films.

As the business grew, chains formed and eventually dominated. At first, it was actually an acceptable retail strategy to be out of stock. If a store did not have enough units of a title, people would rent something else and come back for the other film; disappointment was a fundamental and accepted marketing strategy. This allowed the store to profit on two fronts: retailers could keep inventory down, not making risky decisions of possibly overbuying on a title, while virtually assured of repeat-customer business.

For a period, consumers seemed to accept the delay as part of life, and would happily rent a movie other than the one they had come in for. The out of luck, but somehow not entirely dissatisfied, customers would come back for the film they really wanted when: (1) the store called to let them know the title was back in stock (if they had placed their name on the reserve list); (2) at a somewhat random later date in the hope that they would be lucky and a copy would be available; or (3) at an even later date when they felt demand must have waned and they would have a really good chance that the title would be available to rent.

Amazingly, this lottery style mentality to renting did not dissuade consumers, and to some degree it helped fuel the growth and diversity of content offered by video retailers. Video stores recognized this phenomenon and were pleased for customers to rent a second- or third-choice title; as previously noted, this virtually guaranteed repeat business when the consumers returned the title they rented, but had not really wanted, and came back to rent the film they had come for in the first place. As a business model, this was almost too good to be true. Whenever one can make this type of statement, though, change is afoot. With the maturity of the business, impatience grew and consumers no longer accepted dissatisfaction as the rule.

Over time, rental stores became more competitive and needed to develop more traditional marketing campaigns to ensure customer loyalty. All types of schemes were implemented, from "rent 10 videos, get one rental free" loyalty programs, to store clubs that came with discounts, privileges, and mailings. More sophisticated chains divided customers into complex marketing matrixes, looking at who were frequent renters, casual renters, deadbeat clients, etc., and devising targeted campaigns to increase rental frequency and store loyalty. As the chains grew, they also started to advertise directly, advising customers "Come to Blockbuster and rent . . . ," growing their business with an injection of direct marketing dollars plus cooperative marketing spends set out in their agreements with the product suppliers. As in any other product category, choice, growth, and competition added complexity, and rentals started to have price differentiation. Examples of offers included: "buy two, get one for free" deals, keep the title for the same price for the weekend, and rent new titles at full price for one night while offering older titles for the same or lesser costs to keep for three or five days.

Finally, as a tangible example of the market maturing and retailers acknowledging that disappointing customers was not the best long-term

204

strategy, marketing schemes shifted 180 degrees to implement guarantees that new titles would be in stock (and, if not, the rental would be free). When a new title came out, there would often be pent-up demand similar to that which creates lines at movie theaters. To the "I'll wait to see it on video" crowd that had socially developed in response to the growth of the industry, the video release date was like a premiere. New titles, which a few years earlier would be gulped up the moment they hit shelves and be out of stock, would now be available in large quantities.

This marketing shift also had a direct economic consequence on competition. To satisfy demand, a store needed to have key new titles in sufficient quantity, which required a larger upfront investment. Whereas 10 or 15 copies may have been fine before, 10 times that number would now be required. An average retail price, which, at the time when rental was king in the 1980s and early 1990s, was approximately $70–$100, could change the inventory investment for one title from $700–$1,000 to over $10,000. Volume discounts may have allowed some lower average pricing, but the elasticity was not great and the net effect was pressure squeezing the smaller, "mom and pop" accounts. Not surprisingly, this timing coincided with increased clout from major chains, such as Blockbuster and Hollywood Video, which had begun expanding and gobbling up smaller outlets to become independent market forces. Between 1987 and 1989, Blockbuster grew from a 19-store chain to over 1,000 outlets, and in 1988, with just over 500 stores, became the country's top video retailer, with revenues of $200 million; growth did not slow down, and through further expansion and acquisitions the chain grew another 50 percent to 1,500 by 1991 before finally being acquired in a merger with Viacom in 1994.[5] The market was vibrant enough that, with enough stores, chains could go public, and rival video chains Hollywood Video and Movie Gallery both completed public offerings in the early 1990s.

And change was just beginning. The dominance of the rental store was about to give way to the sell-through market, with rental revenue sharing becoming an intermediate solution to lower-priced units in a still-vibrant rental market.

Transition from Rental to Videos for Purchase: Retail Expands to Accommodate Two Distinct Markets for Video/DVD Consumption

During the growth of the rental video market, a new pattern was slowly emerging that would ultimately overwhelm rental sales and even threaten to eliminate the rental store completely: direct sales of videos to consumers. In trade lingo, this became "rental versus sell-through." Today, the rental store seems to be facing extinction, combating the dual forces of downloads for purchase—"electronic sell-through"—and VOD access for rentals (both forces are discussed in more detail in Chapters 7 and 8, and serve as fodder for analysts who forecast new technology applications leading to the demise of historical markets).

The challenge in this earlier battle for survival was not played out as a public drama, as sell through was not initially perceived as a threat to rental's dominance. In fact, conventional wisdom questioned whether consumers would want to purchase a videocassette when it had become so easy and relatively inexpensive to rent a film. One threshold issue was: Would people really want to watch a particular movie more than once? The general consensus was no. Those customers who were passionate about a particular movie might rent it a few times, but for the rental store, which had invested substantial sums per copy of a title, there was every incentive to entice these fans back to re-rent the title.

For the video store, the game was still all about amortization of inventory cost based on turn: How many times did an individual cassette/copy need to be rented to break even? Obviously, it was an attractive business model to turn a copy many times rather than sell it once. Simply, if a copy of a blockbuster cost the rental store $50, and the outlet charged $5 per rental, the store needed to rent that copy 10 times to recoup. Moreover, because each film is unique, inventory obsolescence only applied to the physical materials (e.g., how long a cassette could be rented before the tape quality degraded to an unacceptable level). A title that had paid for itself could sit on the shelf as catalog inventory, providing pure profit for the indefinite future (subject to the number of copies originally stocked, as a store would obviously keep fewer copies in catalog than were acquired during the peak rental period of initial video release). In fact, one might say this was the first iteration of the "long tail" now so commonly discussed online. Accordingly, a hit title that needed 7–10 rental turns to recoup might have multiple future rental turns left, yielding more than a 100 percent return on investment on a per-copy basis.

If a title was able to generate over 100 percent ROI, then the business model to sell that unit was initially far from compelling. Ultimately, the model comes down to the simple elements of units and pricing. At the early stages, the cost per cassette made it difficult to create a margin allowing for markups to challenge the relative earning power of a rental unit. Even at a substantial markdown, such as to $20 inventory cost, the retail pricing was quite high; moreover, there was a disincentive to lower

206

Table 5.1 U.S. Retail Home Video Industry ($ billions)

	2002	2003	2004	2005	2006	2007	2009	2010	2011
Video Rental	8.3	8.2	8.1	7.8	7.7	7.0	6.0	5.2	5.0
Video Sell-Through	12.6	13.5	16.2	16.4	16.5	15.7	12.1	10.5	9.1
Total Video	20.9	21.7	24.3	24.2	24.2	22.8	18.1	15.7	14.1

pricing significantly when the rental business was thriving. A bigger obstacle, however, was simply the pattern of consumer consumption. The whole video market had exploded seemingly overnight, and people were used to renting, not buying. Something would have to fundamentally change to shift that pattern, including a dramatic lowering of inventory cost.

Not surprisingly, though, as in most consumer goods markets, prices inevitably started to come down. This was forced by pressure from large chains that demanded lower pricing for buying greater depth of inventory. More important than pressure from the rental stores, however, was the fairly rapid market shift from a predominantly rental business to a retail-dominated industry. Just like renting had before, buying videos became a quickly adopted consumer behavior.

By the time the DVD market reached its peak in 2004–2006 (see the next section), and as evidenced by Table 5.1, the percentage of sales for sell-through had shifted to close to 70 percent, whereas only a few years before the split was nearly even.

Key Factors Driving Growth in the Sell-Through Market

Among the key changes driving the growth of the sell-through market were: (1) the growing trend for consumers to collect videos; (2) the decline in pricing, allowing consumers to purchase titles for the same amount of money as (or at least not much more than) a record/CD; (3) studio efforts to sell mass volumes of select hit titles; and (4) the growth of the kids video business, initially led by Disney.

Examining these factors in a bit more detail, as the pattern of watching and renting videos matured, people started the habit of collecting titles. Although now accepted as commonplace, this was hardly an inevitable turn. Market research will tell that most purchased videos sit on the shelf: How often do you re-watch a movie that you have bought? For some favorites and classics, of course, the answer may be yes, but once collecting transitions from buying your favorite film to a habit, the answer will likely be different. And that is the key—becoming a habit—seducing you to purchase titles that do not quite make your top all-time list. As collecting became in vogue, studios started to mine their libraries and make older titles available, expanding the range of consumer choice. First there were books, then records, and now videos; in fact, the lingo that evolved was "video libraries." People started to buy videos, sometimes never even watch them, and keep them on the shelf as a new sort of trophy or archive.

And once a piece of media becomes a collectible, it becomes a gift, opening an entirely new marketing direction for sales. Studios, if nothing else, are brilliant marketing machines, and all video rights holders drove a truck through the opportunity to encourage sales as gifts. The fourth quarter is now the largest period for video sales (with the holidays an ideal time to launch gift sets and special editions), which is a far departure from the origins of the video rental business.

Second, and somewhat hand in hand, the market saw a reduction in pricing and a corresponding upturn in sales of mass volumes of a title. By the early 1990s, as the rental market was maturing and chains grew and consolidated, there was a rule of thumb that you could place 200,000 to 300,000 units of a key new title in North America. For a title that was not a hit or one without a star driving sales, this number could be halved, while a big hit might sell twice this number of units. The key point is that there was limited elasticity of volume in rental.

Studios salivated at the notion of selling millions of units of a title, and on big hits it became commonplace to run break-even comparisons to assess how many units would need to be sold at retail to justify a "sell-through" release (sales direct to consumer as opposed to rental). While sell-through means direct sales to consumers, what it implicates at the distribution level is a whole new set of pricing and a dramatic expansion of retail outlets. The retail infrastructure for direct-to-consumer sales had to be built, and the expansion of outlets to mass merchants, drug stores, supermarkets, record stores, and independents took years to mature. In point-of-sale terms, this could mean going from low thousands of outlets at video rental to over 30,000 outlets for direct-to-consumer sales.

The challenges that came with the sell-through market were the same as any other consumer product: inventory management, advertising, in-store merchandising, physical distribution, and order of magnitude issues in physical manufacture. This was a daunting and, at some level, risky challenge for an industry that was thriving on limited distribution to a finite group of key customers, and where inventory management (video rental was largely a no-returns business) was a relatively minor issue.

208

So, putting aside the growing pains of becoming another consumer product challenging soap for advertising time and store shelf space, the nuts-and-bolts question became: What was the multiple needed to sell at sell-through versus a rental release? An important, and to the studios somewhat comforting, element in the matrix was that rental was still important. On any title significant enough to justify a sell-through release, there was a built-in sale to all video stores. The studio could still sell its few hundred thousand units into the channel; it would simply earn a significantly lower margin, charging a wholesale price of $15–20+ as opposed to the highly profitable $50–70+ rental price. For a period, and for many years following in several international markets, there was even the ability to price differentiate. The supplier (i.e., studio) would charge a higher price for rental units sold to video stores, and create a separate, lower suggested retail price (SRP) for mass-market sell-through buyers.

The analysis was then a straightforward break-even equation, taking into account the sales uplift needed from a lower-priced good to surpass the revenue and contribution margin of the higher-priced, lower-volume rental units (with variable manufacturing and marketing costs factored in on the expense side). As a rule of thumb, it turned out that a title needed to sell a roughly 4:1 or 5:1 ratio to justify a sell-through release. **209**

The ultimate accelerant for the sell-through market was kids videos, in particular the emergence of Disney as a dominating force via its video division, Buena Vista Home Entertainment. Earlier, I pointed out the issue of whether people would watch a video repeatedly; the one area where this was clearly true was with children. Simply, kids would watch the same video over and over and over. It does not take a brain surgeon to recognize as a parent that buying a cassette for $20 that your kids will watch seemingly 100 times is a good investment. To the parent that can gain an hour or more of near-guaranteed peace and quiet, the value of the purchase is worth infinitely more than the cost. Hardly a babysitter could trump the satisfaction of a Disney video, and the combination of a babysitter and a Disney classic was as good a bet as there was out there.

Disney quickly recognized the gold mine that lay before it, and the timing not so coincidentally dovetailed with the reinvigoration of its animated film business. With hit after hit, commencing with *Beauty and the Beast* in 1991 and *Aladdin* in 1992 (see Table 5.2), Disney was validating a new market and spinning box office gold both in theaters and then again on video—a classic example of repeat consumption as a key factor in maximizing value per Ulin's Rule. Then, in 1995, *The Lion King* broke out of the box, reportedly selling a staggering 30 million units,[6] with reputedly 20 million units in its initial release window.

Table 5.2 Disney Animated Releases by Year

Year (Theater)	Title
1989	*The Little Mermaid*
1991	*Beauty and the Beast*
1992	*Aladdin*
1994	*The Lion King*
1995	*Toy Story*
1996	*The Hunchback of Notre Dame*
1997	*Hercules*
1999	*Tarzan, Toy Story 2*

The notion of 20 million units of a title had been seemingly unimaginable previously, and once the pattern of high volumes proved repeatable, there was no stopping. It continued for more than a decade, with *Finding Nemo* selling 20 million combined DVD and VHS units in its first two weeks of sales in November 2003, including 8 million on its first day of release for a record beating the prior *Spider-Man* tally.[7] Everyone tried to jump on the bandwagon, but during the 1990s growth spurt, Disney seemed to have a lock on printing money between box office success of animated titles and the amazing upside that the video industry provided.

Year after year, they continued to release a new hit, which became an instant classic given the numbers (though nothing again reached *The Lion King* heights) and had strong enough brand awareness to spur made-for-video sequels (see later discussion, "Beyond an Ancillary Market: Emergence of Made-for-Video Market).

The success of Disney videos catapulted the head of Disney's video division, Bill Mechanic, into executive stardom, and in the mid 1990s, he left Disney to become president of 20th Century Fox studios. In terms of animation, Mechanic never hit the peaks at Fox he experienced at Disney; acquiring Don Bluth studios and launching titles such as *Anastasia* helped Fox enter the lucrative market, but they failed to create a Disney-like brand engine from the genre. (Note: Fox eventually succeeded years later in building an animation brand via Blue Sky and its computer graphics hit franchise *Ice Age*.)

The Emergence of and Transition to DVDs

The video market has been nothing short of a cash flow godsend to studios and producers. After the initial growth of rental and the consumer acceptance of the direct-to-retail sales model, the market took off again. The next phase was the development of the digital video disc ("DVD," or in technical circles actually the digital versatile disc).

Technology had advanced such that it was possible to make a leap in video quality similar to the transition the record industry had gone through years before in converting from cassettes to compact discs (CDs). The CD quickly replaced the cassette when Phillips invented the digital encoding technology; the marketing thrust, and inevitably the driver in quick adoption, was that: (1) CDs were claimed to be indestructible (as opposed to cassettes, where the tape could get caught, jammed, or warped, permanently ruining the copy); (2) the sound quality emanating from digital encoding was a quantum leap forward from analog tape; and (3) CDs were smaller and therefore more portable than 12-inch vinyl records. While the random access convenience of just jumping from song to song on a CD was compelling (as opposed to fast-forwarding or rewinding), the notion of having a portable, near-perfect hiss-free and non-degradable crystal clear copy of music persuaded consumers. Sometimes, with technology, there truly is a better product, and CDs were a case in point.

I have digressed into the record business because the same forces were aligned against videocassettes. Different consortiums of motion picture studios, teamed with various consumer electronics manufacturers (e.g., Toshiba, Matsushita), pioneering DVD technology. They believed that the DVD offered the similar quantum leap from digital to analog quality that consumers had so overwhelmingly embraced in the record industry when moving from cassettes to CDs. As in the early days of the video-cassette, where format wars erupted between the Betamax and VHS formats, similar format wars took place on the DVD battlefront. Matsushita, the Japanese consumer electronics company (Panasonic brand) that had pioneered the VHS format and acquired Universal Studios (only to later divest majority ownership in a sale to Seagrams) was supporting one standard, whereas Toshiba and Warners were supporting another.

An entire chapter could be written about these format wars, but suffice it to say that given the investment, historical fallout from prior format disputes, and the potential market size, the studios banded together to "adopt" a format.

How Does a DVD Work?

The underlying technology of DVDs is compression, or the ability to take a huge amount of data and store it efficiently. Accordingly, there is a level of randomness, since there is a direct relationship between the amount of data stored and the end quality; the more information, the better the resulting output quality. The inherent problem concerning compression for DVDs is that the amount of information that needs to be processed for a moving picture is staggering relative to an audio file. For a movie, each frame needs to be stored, including all the elements, ranging from backgrounds, to characters, to colors, shading, audio, etc.

The quantity of pixels that need to be reduced to digital 0s and 1s to compress a color film image was, in fact, too great to fit onto a disc, which was a driving technical hurdle preventing the invention of a disc or technology that could mimic a CD for film. The breakthrough came with the notion of looking at the differences between frames and only storing the differences; in this way, the amount of data that needed to be converted and stored was dramatically reduced. DVD compression actually "cheats" by omitting data. The compression digitizes and stores new elements, but in terms of going from frame to frame, only differences need to be kept. This efficiency trick, combined with massively greater storage/data capacity compared to a CD, enabled compression of sufficient data to allow a typical film to fit on a single DVD disc.

212   Early Stages of the DVD: Piracy Concerns, Parallel Imports and the Warners Factor

At the Consumer Electronic Shows of the mid 1990s, gawkers and industry executives watching DVD demonstrations could intuitively grasp the leap in quality. DVD pictures were undoubtedly better, and the DVD offered the same type of ancillary upgrades to consumers that the CD had offered. Videotape often got stuck in machines, and DVDs eliminated those concerns, and were marketed with an aura of discs being "ultimate" and "permanent" (no one was talking about scratches, of course). Another user-friendly element was the elimination of having to rewind a tape. Rewinding a tape at the end of a movie is a universal nuisance, and some video rental stores even charged penalties if tapes were returned unwound. With a DVD, when the movie ended, you just hit a button—no rewinding, no hassle. As silly as it may sound, consumer market research regularly found the elimination of having to rewind as one of the most significant benefits of a DVD, which was statistically on par with the improved picture quality. Never overestimate the consumer!

A better mousetrap does not guarantee adoption, and in the case of the DVD, adoption was further hampered by studios' reluctance to market and sell properties on the new format: virtually all major studio executives recognized the benefits of the DVD, but concerns over piracy and parallel imports were sufficient barriers to move slowly, if at all.

The following was the cost-benefit matrix of the time:

Costs/Negatives:

- expenses to encourage consumer adoption
- need to manage duplicate inventories (video and DVD)
- piracy—DVDs held the potential of people making perfect digital copies
- parallel imports (see later discussion)

Benefits:

- better quality and durability
- favorable user-friendly features (e.g., no rewind)
- smaller packaging needs
- less expensive manufacturing costs, therefore higher margins
- ability to turnover library/catalog product by selling new format

Despite the apparent edge to the benefits, the inherent nature of the DVD as a perfect digital copy created significant anxiety at the studios. Intellectual property is the lifeblood of the system, and while video piracy was always a key concern, that concern heightened with digital copies. If just one person were able to make copies from a DVD, then, in theory, a pirate could have access to a digital master and illegally distribute perfect copies into the marketplace. This had the potential of undermining franchises, new releases, and entire studio libraries. The risk was simply too high, and until sufficient security was implemented most studios held back DVD releases of new titles (another form of windowing).

Adding to the problem was a concern about parallel imports. While it is commonplace to theatrically release a major movie on the same date worldwide (day-and-date release, as discussed in Chapter 4), this was rare to nonexistent back in the mid 1990s when DVDs were first introduced to the market. Parallel imports means buying goods in one territory and importing them into another. For example, if a movie were released in May in the United States, it might be planned for a release in Europe or Asia at Christmas, the same time the DVD of the title would be coming out in the United States. There was nothing to prevent a retailer from buying quantities of the DVDs in the United States and importing them to the market where the movie was just releasing in the theaters, or worse, in advance of the theatrical release. What would

213

happen if consumers could view (or worse, obtain) a perfect copy of the movie before it was even released in theaters? The potential of parallel imports had always existed, but, like piracy, the quality of digital copies heightened people's fears. The box office revenues in international territories were growing consistently, and the theatrical release was too important a driver of the entire studio system to risk.

A key strategy to combat this practice and enable the broader introduction of DVDs was the implementation of regional encoding. This was a process devised by the studios where DVD machines and related DVD software would only work within specific territorial boundaries. For example, a chip would be placed in a machine telling it that it was a "European" encoded player, and this player would only play a disc encoded as European. If you put a disc from the United States (encoded as a United States disc) into a European player, the codes would not match and the disc would not play. The studios managed to gain acceptance from consumer electronics companies manufacturing players (likely helped by Matsushita's relationship with Universal and Sony's ownership of a Hollywood major), and all parties agreed to a worldwide map.

214   Interestingly, regional encoding is akin to a form of hardware-based digital rights management (DRM), and was instituted to restrict how and where a consumer could play back a copy. Conceptually, DRM systems enable the same type of restrictions, but further open up a panoply of options down to managing how many times a product may be played on a specific machine (or overall). Regional encoding is still enforced today, and software bought in one territory will not play on a machine manufactured and sold in a different region. For those wanting to defeat the system, region-free players (which will play a disc regardless of which region it is encoded to) are available, but obviously for a premium price.

The net result of these fears, regarding piracy and the potential of undermining carefully orchestrated release windows, was that most studios were not releasing any titles on DVDs. Those studios that were entering the market were dabbling with older catalog titles where there was obviously no risk to current theatrical release. Sound familiar today? Again, history repeats itself, and the adoption of downloads or over-the-top releases of premium product and vesions (e.g, HD versions) has been slowed by fears of pirating a perfect digital copy (just like the introduction of the DVD); accordingly, content owners often lead with catalog titles to mitigate the risk.

One exception to this initial reluctance to release a broad array of titles on DVD was Warner Bros. The president of Warner Home Video, Warren

Lieberfarb, was among the earliest and most vocal proponents of DVD technology. Warners invested in a DVD authoring and replication facility, and simply believed that the DVD was such a superior technology that it was inevitable consumers would adopt the platform (not to mention the benefit of holding several related patents). For pioneering the technology, and championing its introduction against naysayers and those who wanted to delay launching, Warren Lieberfarb has been called "the father of DVD." Even within an incredibly competitive industry, people acknowledge Warners' leadership position as the catalyst for the transition to DVD from video. Most people forget, or were oblivious to, the significant risks to protection and window management of vital intellectual property assets that stalled and almost prevented the introduction of DVDs.

Influence of Computers: Cross-Platform Use of DVDs Speeds Adoption

One significant factor in the acceleration of DVD penetration was the crossover between consumer electronics players and computers. DVDs had an exponential increase in storage capacity versus floppy discs and CDs. (Note: A standard DVD holding a two-hour movie plus customary ancillary value-added materials (VAM) has roughly 9 GB of content, while Blu-ray boasts an increase to 50 GB.)[8]

As DVD drives slowly replaced other storage mediums on PCs, it was only a matter of time for convergence to take place. With a common software medium, consumers could store data, download pictures and music, and watch movies all with DVDs. Further, this convergence dovetailed with the increased penetration of laptop computers. It was now possible to bring a DVD of a movie on your laptop for a plane ride, jumping between spreadsheets and entertainment. History would repeat itself once again, with integrated systems used to drive adoption— Sony included Blu-ray players with its next-generation PlayStation 3 console system, hoping the consumer electronics product (this time a games system rather than a PC) would help drive adoption.

Recordable DVDs and Perceived Threats from Copying and Downloading

Once it became clear that DVDs were the medium of the future and would replace VHS cassettes, the next obstacle was the ability to record. For the same reasons that slowed the introduction of the DVD, piracy and economic fears tied to the ability to make digital copies, a recordable feature was delayed in the marketplace. It was one thing to allow a DVD, but the dangers ultimately seemed manageable without the ability of the consumer to burn copies of movies. As an accommodation to the concerns of the studios, the major consumer electronics manufacturers launched play-only DVD machines; when compared to the complexity of regional encoding, this was a relatively easy measure to assuage the software distributors.

Over time, however, pressures for recordable players overwhelmed this protectionist direction; moreover, the consumer electronics industry was not in a position to stop the computer manufacturers from deploying recordable drives. Memory and storage is the mantra of the personal computer industry, and computer manufacturers were inclined to encourage data storage rather than impede it. Whether music or digital camera/pictures, the new applications were growing at breakneck speed. It was unrealistic to expect that DVDs could record everything but visual entertainment software.

Giving the studios solace in terms of DVD burners becoming a standard accessory was the fact that movies are not easy to copy. The amount of data compressed is staggering, and it is cumbersome and complicated to copy a movie relative to a business file or music CD. Moreover, anti-copying mechanisms are encoded on films preventing the simple copying of a movie on DVD. The larger fear is the Internet, and while lengthy download times for movies (hours rather than minutes) seemed initially to pose a significant enough hurdle to give distributors comfort, technology again advanced and P2P file sharing exposed the underlying fear that had loomed with digital copies since the advent of DVDs.

At first, digital rights management systems (and the lure of new revenue streams) seemed to have progressed quickly enough to temper those fears and promise significant and ongoing roadblocks to the easy pirating of copies; however, it was this backdrop that caused the studios to take a strong stand in the Grokster case when the ability of P2P services demonstrated facility and scale for making pirate copies. This created the biggest challenge to the industry since the enabling *Sony v. Universal* case roughly 20 years before. (Note: See Chapter 2 for discussion of file sharing, P2P downloading technology, and the Grokster case in terms of the relationship to piracy and digital downloading.)

Intermediate Formats: Laserdiscs and VCDs

Finally, it is worth mentioning that, as in most areas of technology, there were intermediate steps between VHS and DVD adoption. Some may remember the laserdisc, which was dominated by companies such as Pioneer. Laserdiscs were about the size of an old phonographic record and had better clarity and durability than standard VHS tape; they were, accordingly, priced higher, and the early adopter videophiles built up collections of laserdiscs. Laserdiscs were still, however, based on analog technology and were ultimately doomed with the advent of the digital age. Consumers that always wanted the best available technology/presentation of the time built up collections, but the life of laserdiscs was comparatively short and the penetration of the hardware players relatively limited when compared with the mass-market adoption of both VHS and DVD and then Blu-ray.

Similarly, in Asia, and in particular Southeast Asia, a market grew up for video CDs (VCDs). These are CD size and look like DVDs, but simply have inferior compression and memory, and accordingly inferior picture quality. VCD distribution grew quickly in markets rife with piracy, and a consumer could usually find a low-quality and unauthorized version of virtually all studio blockbusters on VCD in the local markets. Because penetration grew quickly, it took some time for DVDs to supplant this market. However, with VCDs and laserdiscs both intermediate and inferior products to DVDs, these formats began to quickly diseppear; in fact, I suspect most readers of this book will never have heard of them.

217

Revenue Sharing—Consequence of a Hybrid Market and Aid to DVD Adoption

Revenue-sharing arrangements took off in the late 1990s. This was a scheme where the major studios gave the major video rental chains, such as Blockbuster and Hollywood Video, their titles on a consignment basis. Rather than charge $29–40 for a title, the studios deferred the upfront revenue in favor of a split of rental income. Although deals differed, it was reputed that a rule of thumb granted the studios 60 percent of the revenue from rental transactions; moreover, once a title had been past its peak release period, excess inventory was sold in-store ($5–15 range), with the proceeds shared between the distributor and rental chain.

Some have theorized that the introduction of revenue sharing was a gambit to increase DVD penetration, as the studios encouraged the shift away from VHS (in fact, some former video division heads have alleged just this tactic).

Once DVD penetration had hit mass-market levels, prices started coming down for both players and new release titles and revenue-sharing schemes waned. The *Hollywood Reporter* cited these factors and attributed the decline in revenue sharing to the increase of the consumer purchase market at the expense of the video rental store:

. . . Once DVD hardware market penetration reached about 50 million players in U.S. households by 2002, WHV and other major Hollywood studios began ratcheting down their rental revenue-sharing participation, while aggressively discounting the wholesale and retail price of movies on DVD. The new popularity of DVD, combined with low-priced hit new releases and classic catalog product, energized consumer spending on home videos, resulting in a national average household buy rate of 15 DVDs a year at an estimated price point of $19 or more each. That consumer action translated into triple-digit revenue gains at the studios. At the same time, the paradigm shift had reduced in-store foot traffic at video rental outlets nationwide, taking a huge bite out of gross consumer spending on movie rentals.[9]

Beyond an Ancillary Market: Emergence of the Made-for-Video Market

Direct-to-Video and Made-for-Video Markets

As video matured, and retail points of sale expanded, it became clear that there was an opportunity to release new/original product directly to the video consumer.

Paralleling the growth of the video market overall, the natural target base was the consumer buying the seemingly dizzying number of Disney videos. If it were possible to sell over 10 million copies of a movie such as *The Lion King* or *Beauty and the Beast*, would the same consumer buy a branded property that was not released in the theaters and was instead an original property for the home video market? With the benefit of hindsight, clearly the answer is yes. The simplest and most successful path was to create sequel properties. Disney perfected this almost to an art, and empowered a specific division focused on producing spin-offs. Examples of "video sequels" or spin-offs during this video renaissance included:

- *The Return of Jafar* (1994)
- *Aladdin and the King of Thieves* (1996)
- *Beauty and the Beast: The Enchanted Christmas* (1997)
- *Pocahontas II: Journey to a New World* (1998)
- *The Lion King 2: Simba's Pride* (1998)
- *Hercules: Zero to Hero* (1998)

- *The Little Mermaid II: Return to the Sea* (2000)
- *Lady and the Tramp 2: Scamp's Adventure* (2001)
- *The Hunchback of Notre Dame II* (2002)
- *Tarzan & Jane* (2002)
- *101 Dalmations 2: Patch's London Adventure* (2003)
- *The Jungle Book 2* (2003)
- *The Lion King 1½* (2004)
- *Mulan II* (2005)
- *Tarzan II* (2005)
- *The Fox and the Hound 2* (2006)[10]

Fox jumped on the bandwagon with titles such as *FernGully 2: The Magical Rescue*, as did Paramount, leveraging well-known characters and brands, such as *Charlotte's Web 2: Wilbur's Great Adventure*. Independents that had strong children's properties expanded their brand. A prime example was Lyric Studios franchise *Barney*; in addition to taking television episodes to video, live *Barney* concerts were perfect fare to release on DVD.

Perhaps the most successful example of a made-for-video property came from Universal Studios. Universal had theatrically released a film called *The Land Before Time*, executive produced by George Lucas and Steven Spielberg, to moderate success. Recognizing the inherent appeal of the characters, children's love of dinosaurs, and the franchise potential, Universal invested in video sequels. *The Land Before Time* franchise became so successful, and the potential for other made-for-videos was considered so high, that Universal created a new division called Universal Family and Home Entertainment. Headed by the former president of Universal's video division, Louis Feola, Universal produced a series of animated (e.g., *Balto: Wolf Quest*) and live-action (e.g., *Beethoven's 3rd, Beethoven's 4th, Beethoven's 5th, Slap Shot 2: Breaking the Ice*) properties under this banner. (Note: More current made-for-video titles include *The Scorpion King 2* and the *American Pie Presents* sequels (*Band Camp, The Naked Mile, Beta House*), the latter of which are estimated to have sold 1–2 million copies each.)[11] *The Land Before Time* property spawned more than 10 sequels, making it one of the most prolific and successful children's franchises in the marketplace.

DVD as a Fallback Release Outlet

"Made-for-video" titles are often confused with releases that may otherwise go direct to video. A title such as *The Land Before Time 3* is made for debut in the video market, but with the expense of marketing and releasing a theatrical film, studios soon realized that certain films

219

that did not pan out as planned could go straight to video. This outlet developed into an important revenue stream, given that there are many films made that never see the light of day in theaters or may have a very limited theatrical release to brand them theatricals (or otherwise qualify them for pricing tiers downstream delineated by output deals that have a theatrical release tier threshold). Interestingly, this has developed as a two-way street: there are also instances of film produced for the video market that come out well, and the studio may subsequently elect to release them theatrically. It is often hard to pinpoint these titles, however, for the distributor will likely be reticent to publicize that the title was originally intended for the video market for fear of souring the caché value.

Niche and Non-Studio Direct-to-Videos/Made-for-Videos

In addition to mainstream videos, the opportunity in the video market-place led to numerous niche opportunities. One of the strongest sectors was health and fitness/exercise. Swimsuit models and supermodels competed with the likes of Jane Fonda to release aerobic and other workout-related tapes.

220   Another burgeoning area was concert films. With the enhanced video and sound quality possible with DVDs, it became more attractive to sell a video from a concert tour or a specific performance to complement CD sales.

Finally, with the upside potential in the family/kids market, it was only a matter of time before toy companies capitalized on their key brands and expanded into the video market. Lego produced Bionicles, and Fox announced a partnership with Hasbro to produce and release titles based on several of its popular brands. I could go on and on talking about documentaries, music videos, and a variety of other genres, but the point is that DVDs opened up a new market for virtually all forms of content production.

Next-Generation DVDs: Blu-Ray versus HD-DVD—Format War Redux

In 2006, two new competing high-definition DVD systems were introduced pitting rival Japanese consumer electronics manufacturers against each other (again). Blu-ray, developed by Sony, and HD-DVD, developed by Toshiba, were pitted against each other, offering high-definition images (1080) and a remarkable amount of storage capacity (25–50 GB). Different partners lined up behind each, with Microsoft in the HD-DVD camp and a greater number of Hollywood studios (e.g., Disney and Fox) initially jumping on the Blu-ray bandwagon. Adoption was slow, however, as no parties wanted to be beholden to a format that might not win, the initial price points for players were high ($350+), and consumers were not convinced that the quality differential from standard DVDs warranted a pricey upgrade. Unlike earlier format wars, both sides tried to speed adoption by integrating the new players into other hardware: Sony including a Blu-ray player in each new PlayStation 3 game console, while Toshiba bundled its HD-DVD drives into notebook computers and Xbox 360 game systems.

It was a déjà vu scenario, with full-scale war between two major Japanese consumer electronics companies, billions of dollars potentially at stake, and the consumer caught in the middle, waiting out the format winner. With both sides having sold approximately 1 million units by the end of 2007, there seemed no clear winner in sight, and headlines abounded. This one was seen in the *International Herald Tribune* on New Year's Day 2008, just days before the annual mass gathering at the consumer electronics show in Las Vegas: "The Format Wars: Titans Stuck in a Stalemate—Despite Months of Tussling, No Clear Winner Has Emerged in the Battle Between Blu-ray and HD-DVD."[12] I was even part of the prior lobbying efforts, with studio partners and other vested parties alike courting Lucasfilm for an endorsement. What do you do when you have different franchises with different studios, and you do not know who may distribute your next film or TV series?

Then, suddenly everything changed and the battle was literally over. In February 2008, Warner Bros., the pioneer in traditional DVD, had been on the fence and then came out in favor of Blu-ray; within the same week or so, Walmart came out and announced it would no longer stock HD-DVDs or HD-DVD players. With the market share leader for DVD sales at retail and Warners both coming out in favor of Blu-ray, it shocked the market, and Toshiba pulled out.[13] No doubt, there was growing fear that delay could doom the entire industry, and if all the studios did not start lining up behind a common format, the danger existed that high definition would miss its window and be bypassed entirely by the growing download markets, akin to CDs being replaced by digital files.[14] In a sense, as typical with the introduction of new technology in the media, one battle had ended and another was just beginning.

Finally, one feature of Blu-ray put the physical media on a path to embrace the Internet—perhaps consciously designed to ensure a place working within the new Internet world rather than having to simply compete against it. "Blu-ray live" enables an interactive feature that allows viewers to simultaneously watch a film along with its director, seeing commentary and chat live while the movie is playing. Among the first tests of this component was an invitation to watch *The Dark Knight* along with its director, Christopher Nolan, and reportedly up to 100,000 people were supposed to be able to watch along together.

Blu-Ray to the Rescue?

Blu-ray is providing industry optimism after years of decline in the video industry—growing by roughly 20 percent in 2011, cresting $2 billion for the first time, and then seeing a 13 percent sales increase through the first half of 2012, Blu-ray sales are now material and mass market.[15] Part of the growth has been organic, but industry insiders acknowledge that *Avatar* helped fuel the growth, with Blu-ray sales of the film reaching 11 million units worldwide. With this market penetration, by the end of the third quarter, 2011 revenues from Blu-ray sales for the first time surpassed revenues from rental kiosks ($423 million for Q3 2011 from Blu-ray versus approximately $414 million from kiosk rentals).[16] This was extremely good news for the video industry, because margins tend to be higher from the sale of retail products than from rentals, and the only material growth in the prior few years had been from low-cost rentals, including, most importantly, Netflix and Redbox (see below for further discussion). Despite all this positive spin, it is important to put Blu-ray in context, as the increase in Blu-ray has been more than offset in declines in traditional DVD sales.

Product Diversification

In addition to the general video window of releasing a movie six months or so after theatrical release, it became economical to market other product at retail. Two major categories were exploited: catalog titles and television shows. As for catalog, every studio has a group of classics in its library, whether themed to stars (Betty Davis collection), awards (Oscar winners), or simply "classics."

When releasing these films, the practice of having the producer, or more often the director, create a special edition (e.g., director's cut) evolved. This could entail releasing an extended version of the film or re-editing parts that may have been cut out for theatrical release (often dealing with time constraints that did not apply to home viewing). Additionally, in some instances special editions would "clean up" elements in the master, given advanced technology (e.g., remastering, taking advantage of computer cleanup or digital sound), and in other cases the creator may have even produced new elements and re-edited the films. When George Lucas released the original *Star Wars* movies (*A New Hope, The Empire Strikes Back,* and *Return of the Jedi*) on DVD for the first time in 2004, all of these elements came into play: (1) all of the movies went through extensive cleanup, utilizing a computer digital restoration facility; (2) all of the movies included remastering sound elements; and (3) a few new elements were introduced, utilizing special effects to alter select sequences.

Another growth area was releasing "seasons" of television series. This became popular, initially, with longstanding hits such as *The Simpsons,* as well as fare that had developed a strong following on limited services such as pay TV but had not been exposed to a larger audience. HBO titles are a perfect example. Consumers that were aware of a show such as *The Sopranos* or *Sex and the City* but did not subscribe to HBO could rent entire seasons and watch them like a miniseries.

Soon, collections became the rule rather than the exception, and full seasons of top TV shows could be found on shelves: *Alias* from ABC, *24* from Fox, and the complete *Seinfeld*. By Christmas 2004, box sets abounded at retail, so much so that video distributors and retailers for the first time started worrying about saturation and how far the market could expand. Collections, special editions, etc. are all further illustra-   **223** tions of Ulin's Rule—distribution maximizes revenues through repeat consumption opportunities, tied to differential pricing and timing.

Maturation of the DVD Market and Growing Complexity of Retail Marketing

The DVD/Blu-ray/video supply chain, being tied to a physical consumer product, is far more complicated than the chain of licensing and delivery of movies and TV shows, respectively, to theaters and broadcasters. Figure 5.2 exhibits the key components of assimilating a variety of content into a product distributed in multiple SKUs and formats to outlets of fundamentally different character (rental versus sale), and marketed to the customer by both the distributor and point-of-purchase retailer.

Peaking of the DVD Curve and Compressed Sales Cycle

By the late 1990s, it was clear that DVDs were the format of the future, and in the ensuing years literally exploded. Growing from less than 10 percent in 1999, by the end of 2006 penetration exceeded 80 percent and had bypassed VCR penetration.[17] By 2003, annual DVD rental revenues exceeded VHS revenues,[18] and by 2005 the number of

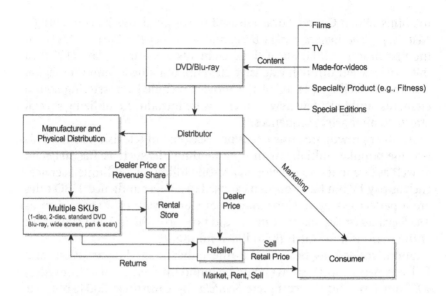

Figure 5.2 Complexity of DVD/Blu-ray Supply Chain

VHS units of a major title relative to DVD units was negligible. In fact, by 2005 many titles, such as *Star Wars: Episode III – Revenge of the Sith*, were released only on DVD.

With the growth of DVD, the balance between rental and sell-through started to shift dramatically toward sell-through. The durability and quality of DVDs, together with the ability to include special features (see discussion regarding VAM), made them ideal retail items, as well as perfect gifts. All of a sudden, it was not just Disney selling huge numbers of children's videos, but key titles from all studios were selling in the millions. And for children's properties, the numbers simply kept growing. *Shrek*, released in 2001, reportedly sold 2.5 million units in its first three days[19] en route to selling upwards of 20–30 million units worldwide, as did Disney–Pixar's *Finding Nemo*.

Depending on whose statistics one believes, the DVD/video market peaked somewhere between 2004 and 2006, and by the end of 2005 it was evident that the market was entering into a phase of decline, both on a by-title basis as well as overall. Given the size and importance of the home entertainment market in the media sector, this was mass-market news, as *USA Today* highlighted: "For the first time in home video's nearly 30-year history, sales and rentals slipped in 2005 as slowing growth of DVDs couldn't overcome falling prices and a dying VHS market."[20]

While, historically, home video revenue from most blockbusters equaled or surpassed that of their box office take, the trend seemed to have peaked. Describing the drop in conversion rate—the ratio of video sales to theatrical—*Variety* reported that the theatrical gross exceeded the DVD revenues of films such as *Batman Begins* and *War of the Worlds* (e.g., *Batman Begins* video revenues $170 million versus $205 million theatrical gross).[21] There has been a continuing decline in the DVD market ever since this peak[22] and, as noted and demonstrated by comparing Figures 1.5 and 5.1 (studio revenue breakdown in 2007 vs. 2012), the impact has been a steep fall in terms of the percentage of the overall studio revenue pie attributable to the video market (down to 30.4 percent from 48.3 percent). 2008 typifies the dramatic nature of the falloff, when there was a precipitous drop in new release volumes, estimated to be down close to 20 percent.[23] Illustrating the severity of the decline on a by-title basis over almost a decade, Table 5.3 lists the top-selling DVDs for 2003 versus 2008 and 2011 in the United States.

Given the overall importance of DVDs to the studio revenue base and ecosystem, this pace of decline continues to set off alarm bells; the cause can no longer be attributed solely to a recessionary climate, and the shift is putting even more emphasis on the future of electronic sell-through, subscription streaming, and other new consumption patterns in the digital space.

Compressed Sales Cycle

The other factor impacting the market maturation was an increasingly compressed sales cycle. This has been accentuated by the flood of additional product trying to take advantage of DVD dollars. Whereas only a few years earlier shelf space competition was between different hit movies, the largest growth sector became TV product and box sets; with a glut of new and catalog TV releases, together with made-for-DVD product, competition became fiercer, shelf space turned over more quickly, and sales cycles compressed. In a sense, the DVD retail cycle was beginning to mimic the box office, with revenues more front-loaded by the year, and films earning the majority of their video revenues within the first two weeks of release.[24] In fact, most studios acknowledge that the majority of sales on a title now come in this short period. The *Wall Street Journal* highlighted this shift: "a typical DVD release would rack up about one third of its total sales during the first week of release; the figure was even lower for animated movies, which tended to have longer legs. DVD sales would then steadily mount over weeks or months. But these days, DVD releases are generating a huge percentage of their total sales—typically over 50 percent and in some cases, up to 70 percent—in the first week."[25]

225

Table 5.3 Top Five DVDs of 2003, 2008, and 2011

Studio	Title	Date	Units
Disney	*Finding Nemo*	2003	26,000
New Line	*The Lord of The Rings: The Two Towers*	2003	21,050
Disney	*Pirates of the Caribbean: Curse of the Black Pearl*	2003	19,450
Warner Bros.	*The Matrix Reloaded*	2003	15,520
Universal	*Bruce Almighty*	2003	12,650
Warner Bros.	*The Dark Knight*	2008	12,385
Paramount	*Iron Man*	2008	11,375
Fox	*Alvin and the Chipmunks*	2008	10,560
Warner Bros.	*I Am Legend*	2008	10,125
DreamWorks Animation	*Kung Fu Panda*	2008	9,750
Warner Bros.	*Harry Potter and the Deathly Hallows: Part 1*	2011	8,565
Disney	*Tangled*	2011	7,635
Warner Bros.	*Harry Potter and the Deathly Hallows: Part 2*	2011	7,065
Disney	*Cars 2*	2011	5,340
Universal	*Bridesmaids*	2011	4,695

Note: Units are projected lifetime shipments of the film on home video.

This trend developed outside the pressures of new media, making the issue of how to window downloads that much more complicated. The DVD cash cow was set for a reversal of fortune, and no studio wanted to accelerate that trend. Unless downloads could be proven to add incremental value, let alone not cannibalize DVD, there was little impetus to experiment with key new releases.

Expansion of Retail Mass-Market Chains: Walmart, Best Buy, Target, etc.

Routinely selling more than 5 million copies of an A-title and, on occasion, over 10 million copies of select hit children's/family titles could only occur with the expansion of retail distribution. Video rental stores jumped on the bandwagon as a point of sale for DVDs, but their bread and butter remained rental, and the vast majority of sales took place at mass-market retailers.

Because DVDs as a software entertainment commodity offered a unique product with each release (as does a CD or video game), both suppliers and retailers quickly realized the marketing opportunities. Not only could DVDs sell in record numbers, but DVDs could actually drive consumer traffic into stores. If the next *Star Wars* or *The Lord of the Rings* movie were being released on DVD, customers would crash stores in droves. It was like Christmas time with each new major release.

Of course, nothing is that simple, and greater sales and expectations were also driven by increased marketing. To sell several million copies of a title, it is necessary to advertise the release, and advertising budgets for DVD releases multiplied several-fold. Studio video divisions became expert at running sophisticated P&L models, trying to gauge the saturation threshold after which increased marketing spend would not yield additional positive contribution margin.

Increased marketing expenditure could ultimately only be justified with concomitant retail support. Accordingly, retailers went through a maturation period as well, with more shelf space dedicated to DVDs. In-store marketing campaigns grew in importance, with dedicated in-store display packs, such as towers themed with images from the movie, adding additional capacity during a title's initial release. Executing a compelling in-store campaign involves elements including:

- posters
- additional signage
- stand-alone themed display towers
- placement of stand-alone displays and regular shelf placement (e.g., on new release end caps versus off-the-aisle placement)
- employee education
- in-store trailers
- dedicated retailer advertising
- trade advertisements
- store circulars in newspapers, etc

To achieve this type of coordinated campaign at retail, several economic incentives evolved. Industry practice developed such that studios offered an allowance for both market development and cooperative spending. Typically, studios will allow retailers to spend a small percentage of the wholesale revenue against their marketing costs directly

227

related to the title. Additionally, studios will allow another line item for cooperative advertising expenditure. Where these lines are drawn is a bit fuzzy, with cooperative advertising a bit easier to track, in that it is supposed to be allocated for actual advertising, whether print media, radio, or television. Cumulatively, a retailer may have a few percent of actual wholesale revenue to apply against its costs in advertising, marketing, and merchandising the title.

These sums are paid by the studio/video retailer, but in practice are administered as an allowance. The amounts calculated for marketing and co-op expenditures are deducted from the revenues otherwise due, yielding a net amount paid, thereby having a negligible cash flow effect. These are real costs, however, to the video distributor, and are a key line-item element of the overall video marketing budget, just as direct advertising creation costs and costs of buying media (TV and radio advertising) are costs driving the P&L analysis and ultimate contribution margin.

Retailer-Specific Implementation

Implementation of marketing programs is tailored at the retail level, typically tiered to the anticipated volume. In all markets, it is common to have a key account list, which will vary by studio and type of product (e.g., specialist account), but mainstream releases would typically include the following U.S. retailers (excluding wholesalers): Amazon, Best Buy, Walmart, Target, BJ's Wholesale Club, Borders, Circuit City, Costco, and Hollywood Video. (Note: A number of those outlets, including Borders, Circuit City, and Hollywood Video, have since filed for bankruptcy—a telling sign of the overall retail marketplace.) Depending on the title and studio, a select few top accounts, such as Walmart, Target, Best Buy, and Amazon, could easily account for over 60 percent of the total volume.

For the top-volume accounts, and on certain key new release titles, it may make sense to customize programs. Types of programs can obviously vary widely, but examples of specialized focus may entail:

- special product placement, such as guarantees of being positioned near the checkout register
- unique creative campaigns for posters, or buttons for staff
- rebate programs tied to individual purchases, such as point-of-sale rebates, or overall volumes
- discounts tied to sale of other purchases
- discounts tied to store gift cards
- customized packaging

- customized value-added offers (e.g., bundled merchandising, such as an action figure)
- special merchandisers, such as product towers
- special placement in circulars or flyers
- consumer prizes/sweepstakes

There is no limit to the creativity of a campaign.

Deals and programs will naturally depend on both the leverage of the title and market clout of the retailer. In many cases, it is the retailer, with the premium shelf space as the interface to the consumer, that can dictate terms. In fact, retailers with large traffic volume sometimes charge placement fees, such as to stock a video title in the end cap at the checkout lanes (e.g., charging a per-unit fee, and in extreme cases even holding a mini-auction and granting the space to the highest bidder).

Loss-Leading Product and Fostering Consistent Consumer Pricing

Another product of leverage is loss-leading a product. For a big enough title, it is not unusual for a retailer to deeply discount the title for a limited period if it is likely the special price offer will bring customers into the store. Many of the top accounts obviously carry a wide range of product, and the likelihood of additional sales if they can attract a customer into the store is high enough that sacrificing margin on a video title pays off. In extreme cases, the store is even willing to lose money on a title.

Although this sounds like a good deal to the video distributor (you can hear the video salesman gloating, "they want my product so badly they're willing to lose money!"), the trick to successful sales is managing the overall market, and one account can cause havoc. If a particular retailer dramatically undercuts its competitors, such that traffic is truly taken away from its competitors, then for the distributor the increased volume at that one chain better make up the difference. Otherwise, the distributor will be looking at lots of disgruntled customers who may want to return the product or may not be as accommodating on their next title or campaign. Remember, the wholesale pricing will have been relatively consistent, so a sale from Store X is relatively fungible to a sale from Store Y, and success is driven by making retail sales successful across the entire channel. No distributor wants to spend millions of dollars on an overall advertising campaign to support retail only to have one or two retailers undermine the overall effectiveness.

It is illegal to set onward retail pricing, and once a video is sold the buyer who bought in order to resell is free to set its price (U.S. first-sale doctrine, antitrust, price fixing); accordingly, a video distributor cannot prevent a specific retail account from pricing as they choose. A retailer could elect to give the DVD away for free, regardless of the price it paid for the unit to the distributor. If they want to lose money, that is their prerogative.

There is one accepted practice, however, that buffers this risk: establish minimum advertised price (MAP). A distributor is not obligated to financially support the retail marketing campaign, and there are certain quid pro quos established for committing to cooperative advertising and market development fund dollars. To be eligible for MAP contributions, a distributor may dictate that the retailer may not advertise the product for a price below $X. With this arrangement, the video retailer ensures a relatively consistent price band, yet the retailer maintains flexibility for the ultimate on-shelf price.

When MAP policies are set, they are almost always limited in time, such that on expiry the retailer is free to set and advertise pricing at will. In some cases, a distributor may strategically set MAP expiry to dovetail with a specific anticipated time of re-promotion or anticipated markdowns (especially if dealing with seasonal dates).

230

E-Tailers and Next-Generation Retail

Beyond the growth of mass-market retail, the video market has benefited from e-tailers such as Amazon stocking new and catalog DVDs. The growth of online shopping has been a boon for video, as DVDs were a natural complement to book sales, and Amazon has matured into a key customer for distributors. What is particularly helpful beyond actual sales is the predictive nature of online sites. E-tailers customarily take preorders for titles, and the relative volume of preorders can often be a good barometer of total retail sales.

Although e-tailers tend to thrive on margin, offering lower pricing given the absence of physical retail space, this is one area where the online stores can struggle to be the low-price leader. In an environment where mass-market physical retailers will, on occasion, loss-lead product to drive profit, and where competition between physical retailers is cutthroat, it may be a challenging proposition for an e-tailer to under-cut offline retail. What they can do, however, is more quickly implement temporary and targeted sales (namely, it is easier to change a price on-line than physically re-sticker physical stock, creating pricing pressure for their physical retail competitors by offering customers competitive pricing, coupled with convenience, preorder reservations, and targeted recommendations).

The Return of Rental and Transactional VOD as the Virtual Video Store

As sell-through retail video sales came to dominate the economics of the video market, it was unclear what the future of rental would be—in fact, at the time of publication of my first edition, the prior leading rental chains were struggling (and Blockbuster and Hollywood Video subsequently filed for bankruptcy), talk was all about the decline of the video market, and few were bullish about the prospects of a resurgence of video rental. Since 2009, however, the dual forces of rental kiosks, led by Redbox, and the growth of transactional video-on-demand (both from cable operators and from Internet-enabled streaming services such as Amazon and Netflix) have not only made the rental market viable again (at least in the U.S.), but have started an inevitable trend whereby rental will likely again come to dominate the video market. Although the scales have not yet tipped, I believe the somewhat irrational underpinning of the sell-through market (see prior discussion), combined with the efficiency of the realization of the virtual video store (whether via subscription streaming or transactional VOD), will force this shift. The growth of Netflix is a compelling example of consumer demand for rental, and yet Netflix as a subscription service is merely one option. Once access is improved via over-the-top systems (see Chapter 7), consumers become accustomed to having a choice among types of transactional VOD offerings (subscription versus à la carte), and vibrant competition diversifies the market (as is happening among Amazon, Netflix, Hulu, and new entrants such as Verizon and Comcast's Xfinity; again, see Chapter 7), there is every reason for consumers to embrace the virtual video store.

The only factor that could impede the virtual video store's inevitable success is if services cannot offer enough relevant content to satisfy and attract customers. Video rental stores succeeded because they truly stocked all the titles you wanted to see. If transactional VOD and streaming services fight for content and control titles exclusively, then some of these services could come more to resemble pay TV services than video stores—in Chapter 7, in fact, I argue that Netflix, known as a video company, is in fact more akin to a pay TV company, in that what is offered is subscription rental. Subscription rental when one company has all the content is the equivalent of a pay TV monopoly—in essence, this was Netflix's position, and offering the only viable service, combined with all the possible content, fuelled its spectacular streaming growth. When Netflix is no longer the only player, and if content is bid for and secured exclusively by a range of services, then there will be inevitable fallout. Content owners therefore face the conundrum of thwarting a monopoly (which Netflix was fast becoming) versus parcelling out content exclusively, which yields short-term gains (large minimum guarantees akin to pay TV), while to some degree risking the longer-term salvation of the virtual video store rental market (because a video store with only some of the content is a less compelling consumer proposition). Will consumers be willing to go to one service that has *Avatar*, and yet have to search a rival to find *The Hobbit: An Unexpected Journey* or *The Hunger Games*? Arguably, yes, but there is only so much fragmentation that will be accepted.

Redbox and the Growth of Kiosks

For years, video distributors have been trying to improve the accessibility of renting programs. Video kiosks were once predicted to be the rage, with vending-type machines located in high-traffic areas (e.g., lobby of large office buildings): customers would pay, get the DVD through a slot when it dropped out, and return it to the machine within a day or two. Although kiosks were found selectively worldwide, including in supermarkets and in international territories where retail space is at a premium such as Japan, video kiosks never caught on as projected—until the last five years. Growing out of kiosks within McDonald's restaurants, Coinstar, Inc. grew its U.S. base from just over 1,000 locations in 2005 to over 35,000 at the beginning of 2012 (see Figure 5.3); in fact, near the beginning of 2012, Redbox touted on its website that its kiosks had rented more than 1.5 billion discs, and that more than 68 percent of the U.S. population lived within a five-minute drive of a Redbox kiosk.[26]

How did it achieve this growth? In short, price. While Redbox was undoubtedly helped by finding a niche between Netflix switching its focus to streaming and the largest video rental chain, Blockbuster, going bankrupt, it nevertheless defied conventional wisdom to increase its DVD rental share in 2011 by 10 percent to garner 35 percent of the market and become the leader in the U.S.[27] Barrons, talking about the bargain that Redbox offers consumers, highlighted its price advantage and strategy: "Redbox had more than 500 million rentals in 2011's first nine months. In a tough economic climate, it isn't hard to see why. While the newly released move *The Help* can be rented at Redbox for $1.20 a night, it's for sale at $16.99 at Amazon.com (AMZN) and costs $4.99 to rent on Comcast (CMSSA) or Time Warner Cable (TWC)."[28]

Seeing the success of Redbox, Blockbuster, coming out of bankruptcy and now owned by Dish Network, started Blockbuster Express kiosks to compete—that bet paid off in 2012 when Coinstar/Redbox announced a purchase of Blockbuster's 9,000 kiosks for $100 million. Depending upon the number of Blockbuster kiosks Redbox maintains and converts

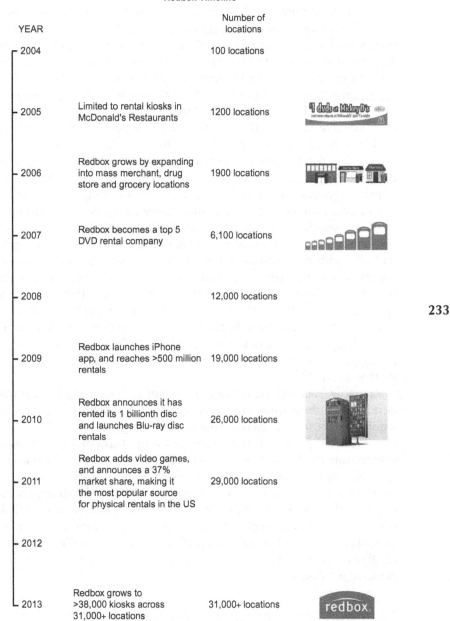

Redbox Timeline

YEAR		Number of locations	
2004		100 locations	
2005	Limited to rental kiosks in McDonald's Restaurants	1200 locations	
2006	Redbox grows by expanding into mass merchant, drug store and grocery locations	1900 locations	
2007	Redbox becomes a top 5 DVD rental company	6,100 locations	
2008		12,000 locations	
2009	Redbox launches iPhone app, and reaches >500 million rentals	19,000 locations	
2010	Redbox announces it has rented its 1 billionth disc and launches Blu-ray disc rentals	26,000 locations	
2011	Redbox adds video games, and announces a 37% market share, making it the most popular source for physical rentals in the US	29,000 locations	
2012			
2013	Redbox grows to >38,000 kiosks across 31,000+ locations	31,000+ locations	

233

Figure 5.3 Redbox's Growth from 1,000+ Locations to Approximately 30,000 in a Five+ Year Horizon

Data © 2012 Redbox (excerpted from Redbox.com/history)

to its branding, Redbox locations could grow to over 40,000 (in early 2012, the total number of kiosks still remained around 35,000, but by 2013 the numbers started increasing again).[29] This is an amazing turnaround in a market where DVD sales (Blu-ray and DVD) dropped 12 percent in 2011,[30] and led Redbox's SVP of marketing to boast: "We have more locations than McDonald's and Starbucks combined."[31]

The growth of Redbox and its comparatively low pricing prompted a new window debate. Studios had generally structured a 28-day holdback from video release to Redbox rentals. At the beginning of 2012, with its deal with Redbox set to expire, Warner Bros., looking to further protect the window for customers to either buy a new DVD or rent it via VOD, demanded that the holdback be doubled to 56 days; Redbox balked, and Warners cancelled its deal, believing that in the long run, $1 rentals would undermine the studio's profitability versus higher margins in the VOD and sell-through markets. Redbox, without a Warners deal, simply opted to buy Warner Bros. titles at retail outlets, still able quickly to stock its kioks with hits such as *A Very Harold & Kumar 3D Christmas*, and simply accepting a smaller margin than if it had the benefit of buying from Warner Bros. directly. When Universal's deal similarly came up for renewal (Q1 2012), the studio was rumoured to want to join Warners in requiring a 56-day delay, but ultimately backed down and maintained its 28-delay (i.e., holdback between when DVDs first are available for purchase by consumers to when they are made available for rental at Redbox kiosks).[32]

Arguably, succumbing to the pressures of Redbox and its low pricing is not in the best long-term interests of studios whose bottom lines would benefit from preserving the highest margin access to its product (i.e., Warners' position). The challenge for the frustrated studios, however, is how hard to fight when, to many, Redbox is a surprise buffer (if not godsend) against a declining market. Without Redbox kiosks, the studios could face the once-unimaginable notion of the disappearance of physical discs for on-location rental. The entire Redbox story and the behind-the-scenes strategizing with respect to its window (imagine, a window just for kiosk rental!) is a perfect example of the disruptive force of digital systems and the desperate effort of content distributors to preserve windows.

Netflix and the Growth of Subscription Rental

Although I discuss Netflix, and in particular its streaming service and access points (e.g., Roku) in Chapter 7, the service and company also has to be discussed here, given its roots in the video market.

Netflix's original secret sauce was to combine the inventory management and ease of access of the Internet with old-world fulfillment—the mail. A customer could scan a seemingly infinite catalog of titles (online viewing is not constrained by physical retail shelf space, i.e., the wide tail) and then simply place an order. Fulfilment was then quite clever: order one or more, and every time you returned a DVD you could select another one that would be shipped out to your home. The movies came in simple paper cases (without the bulky video box) with prepaid envelopes: just seal and return. Netflix grew dramatically from a 1998 launch with less than 1,000 titles to over 1 million subscribers by 2003, at which point it had delivered over 100 million DVDs (and, by 2007, over 1 billion).[33] This was essentially a virtual video store, and the only drawback was fulfilment delay. That lag did not turn out to be the obstacle some thought, perhaps due to the ability to order in volume, so it was possible to build an inventory at home and always have something ready to watch while you decided what to see next.

By 2006, Blockbuster was on the ropes and Netflix had passed the 4-million-customer mark. Blockbuster and other traditional video retailers had to compete directly, and Blockbuster launched a home delivery service, even going so far as to advertise the new option during the Super Bowl (February 2006). While achieving these numbers and starting to overtake the historical market leader Blockbuster may have seemed like success in itself at the time, Netflix's growth only started to accelerate. By 2009, it passed 12 million subscribers, and by mid 2011 that number had doubled to more than 24 million, making it the media industry's largest subscription business.[34] Netflix's stock rose in similar hockey stick fashion, hitting a high of nearly $305 in July 2011, before crashing to $62.37 just months later[35] after decoupling its physical and digital business and rebranding its streaming service to Qwikster.

Netflix's Qwikster Debacle

In less than a month's time in September 2011, Netflix announced and then abandoned a new brand, Qwikster, which will live on in business school case study lore—of what not to do. In the summer of 2011, as its stock hit an all-time high, Netflix announced: (1) that it was significantly increasing the price of its service that allowed customers to obtain DVDs through the mail and access unlimited streaming of titles online: instead of only $9.99 per month, customers would have to choose between now paying $15.98 for the bundled offering, or pay $7.99 per month month for streaming access only; and (2) that Qwikster would be the new name/brand for its streaming-only service. The *Economist*, in an article titled "Netflix Messes Up," described how Netflix, fearing "being left behind by technological change, like AOL with its dial-up service," saw its future in streaming, but failed to anticipate the customer hostility that led to jamming the company's switchboard with complaints, being deluged with hostile comments on its Facebook page, and causing the stock to plummet: "The company's reputation for top-notch customer service has been tarnished . . . Netflix has made a tactical error and treated its customers shabbily. It has also jumped too hastily into the future—as if Renault were to declare that electric cars are the future and rename its petrol car division Qwikmobile."[36]

The *Wall Street Journal*, citing famous branding mistakes such as Coca-Cola's failed introduction of "New Coke," stated: "Netflix joins a list of companies with embarrassing flip-flops," and graphically plotted the failed introduction against the company's falling stock price (see Figure 5.4). (Note: As discussed later, Netflix quickly rebounded and its streaming business grew to dominate, if not define, the SVOD business; see next section and also Chapter 7).[37]

236

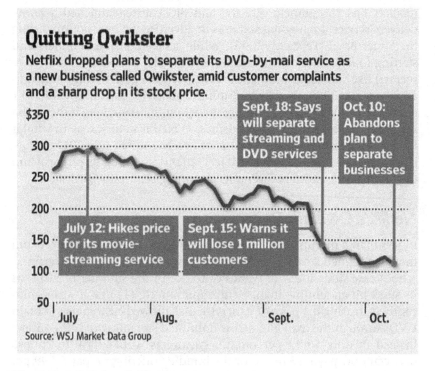

Quitting Qwikster

Netflix dropped plans to separate its DVD-by-mail service as a new business called Qwikster, amid customer complaints and a sharp drop in its stock price.

Sept. 18: Says will separate streaming and DVD services

Oct. 10: Abandons plan to separate businesses

July 12: Hikes price for its movie-streaming service

Sept. 15: Warns it will lose 1 million customers

Source: WSJ Market Data Group

Figure 5.4 Quitting Quikster

Reproduced by permission of the *Wall Street Journal*.

The Slow, Steady Decline of Netflix's Physical Disc Rental Business, and its Belief in Streaming Focus Vindicated

Although Netflix may have created marketing and branding sins that may take years to overcome, it was nevertheless correct in its core assumptions: its recent growth had been fueled by a surge in streaming customers, streaming was its future, and offering a competitively priced subscription streaming-only option would dovetail with ultimate consumer demand. Despite having subscription levels drop from a former high of nearly 25 million, in Q1 2012 the company still had nearly 22 million streaming subscribers, was on track to add streaming customers at the same pace it had seen a year earlier, and was seeing its total subscriber count climb back above 23 million.[38]

Netflix believed it had weathered the storm, and was managing the reality of losing traditional DVD customers, hoping to mitigate these losses and even grow by building its streaming base and expanding internationally. After losing 2.8 million DVD customers in the last quarter of 2011 and expecting to lose another 1.5 million in the first quarter of 2012, the *Wall Street Journal* noted that in an analyst call, Neflix CEO Reed Hastings admitted he has no plans to promote Netflix's traditional DVD business, and even stated: "We expect DVD subscribers to decline steadily for every quarter forever."[39] Against this forecast, but for the growth of Redbox described above, it would be easy to write off physical discs and begin drafting the obituary of DVD rentals; as described in Chapter 7, even Redbox is joining the streaming competition, partnering with Verizon for Redbox Instant, and it is entirely possible that, as quickly as kiosks grew, they could become obsolete. Arguably, the transition is inevitable (Why not even smaller kiosks, coupled with electronic outlets such as ATMs—plug in your USB and download?), and the only question is the speed at which customers without broadband access will delay the switch, given the large installed base of DVD players and the cheap rental options (e.g., Redbox) available. Technology has a way of increasing adoption faster than anticipated, and with nearly 1 billion people on Facebook, it would be hard to argue that the streaming generation has not already arrived. As for Netflix, with its new focus on streaming and further feuling subscriptions with the launch of original series (see Chapter 7), by mid-2013, its streaming subscribers grew to 30 million in the U.S., and nearly 38 million worldwide.[40]

237

Netflix's Next Big Challenge: The Cost of Content

As Netflix grew and became the proverbial 10,000-pound gorilla, two different pressures were bound to develop: competition would evolve, and content suppliers (who, as studios, were also would-be competitors) were likely to charge more for content, or withhold it altogether. Big media companies, at once grateful for Netflix as a buyer yet increasingly wary of its dominance, started to snipe. Jeff Bewkes, Time Warner's CEO, famously scoffed to the *New York Times*: "It's not like the Albanian army is going to take over the world." Time Warner was often quoted as raising concerns about deals with Netflix eroding the value of content. The CEO of TBS (a Warner company), Phil Kent, went so far as to openly warn those who would sell programming to Netflix to think about the impact on downstream syndication deals, advising suppliers that Netflix streaming deals were "going to have a significant impact on what we're going to be willing to pay for programming or even bid at all."[41]

First, suppliers started to withold content, including Sony Pictures Entertainment, and then Starz. Starz was a significant blow, for it was one of Netflix's earliest deals, struck in 2008 before streaming had mushroomed for what was reportedly $30 million per year.[42] Netflix essentially added the streaming rights for nominal amounts under the original deal, but if one now viewed Netflix streaming more akin to a pay TV service where pricing is on a per-subscriber basis (see Chapter 6), then the pricing would go up dramatically. The *Hollywood Reporter*[43] gave the example that at 25 million subscribers, Netflix would "pay 10 cents a sub for each month for Starz content—compared with the estimated $4 a sub Starz gets for its premium movie service from Comcast, DirecTV, and other multisystem operators . . ." While estimates of the value of renewing the Starz pact, which included Disney titles such as *Toy Story*, were speculated to be from $200–300 million (and Reed Hastings even being quoted as saying that $200 million per year "wouldn't be shocking"),[44] Starz ultimately elected to cut its ties, and its properties were removed from Netflix.

Although Netflix lost Starz, it added other content and continues to aggressively court content producers for rights. (Note: In an interesting twist in the evolution of Netflix and the industry overall, Netflix, as discussed in Chapters 6 and 7, has evolved into more of a pay TV company, offering a similar subscription aggregation service online as opposed to over cable, and as such is now competing with Starz for content, and wrestled the Disney output deal away in 2012.) Examples of deals concluded include:[45]

238

- 1,000 titles from Epix, reputedly paying $200 million for five years, outbidding an offer from Showtime for $175 million, with titles such as *Iron Man* and *G.I. Joe: The Rise of Cobra* streaming 90 days after Expix debuts in its pay TV window.
- Relativity films, including titles such as *The Fighter*, available within a few months of its DVD release.
- Disney/ABC television product, valued at over $150 million, including series such as *Lost, Scrubs, Desperate Housewives*, and *Hannah Montana*, where all six seasons of *Lost* are reportedly valued at $45 million.
- Fox television titles, although tilted toward cancelled series, including *Lie to Me, Prison Break, Bones*, and *Arrested Development*.
- Disney movies (including Marvel and Pixar) starting in 2017, at an estimated annual cost of $350 million.[46]
- Select Warner Bros.-produced network titles, such as *Revolution* (NBC) and *The Following* (Fox).[47]

Another factor in the rise of the cost of content is that the DVD rental market and the streaming market, though similar, are based on different rights grounded in different legal protections. While the core notion of physical DVD rentals versus streaming access is an example of the infinite divisibility of intellectual property (see Chapter 2), the difference is exacerbated by the first-sale doctrine. The first-sale doctrine, as earlier discussed, essentially holds that once a retailer sells a product, it cannot restrict the onward sale of that product—a tenet that underlies second-ary markets such as eBay. This is also the principle pursuant to which Redbox could walk away from Warner Bros. and simply elect to buy the titles from third parties post release to then stock in its kiosks. In contrast, since streaming rights are transitory and tied to a license, Netflix needs to negotiate for these rights. The *Economist* highlighted this issue in contrasting the ability of Netflix to start renting DVDs as soon as that window opened: "To stream a film via the Internet, in contrast, Netflix must strike an agreement with the studio or TV firm that owns it. As Netflix has become richer and scarier, negotiations have become harder. The company must wait eight or nine years to stream many studio films."[48] Further, other providers such as HBO "refuse to let Netflix stream their shows at all."[49]

Combining all of these factors, the net result is that content is becoming increasingly more expensive, and the days of acquiring streaming rights somewhat under the radar and without major competitors bidding are long gone. It is difficult to estimate Netflix's total cost for content, but the *Hollywood Reporter* quotes a Lazard Capital Markets analyst as predicting that the company will spend upwards of

239

$1.2 billion in 2012 for streaming rights,[50] and the *Wall Street Journal* estimated that, as of September 2012, Netflix had $5 billion in streaming liabilities for content, up from $3.5 billion the prior years.[51] Again, paying in the range of $1 billion for content sounds more akin to a pay TV service, competing with the likes of HBO. In fact, as more of Netflix's content skews toward television fare—a consequence of cost, and despite its efforts to be the aggregator of all movies and TV shows—Netflix is aware that distributors of premium television content will quickly become its chief competition. Netflix is famous for publicly describing its strategy, and in its "Netflix Business Opportunity" slide deck posted on its website,[52] it both describes itself as an Internet Network (as opposed to broadcast or cable), and under "Long-Term Threats to Netflix" highlights: (1) TV Everywhere, noting: "Great Internet apps on all screens for all existing networks, at no extra consumer cost, would eventually mean less watching of Netflix, less desire by networks to license prior seasons to Netflix, because they can self-monetize in their app"; and (2) "Our most direct competitor for viewing time will probably be HBO GO."

It is important to remember that the discussion started in the context of the decline of the home video market, and how Netflix and Redbox were, to a degree, white knights infusing cash into the video kitty. What is clear, however, is that regardless of Netflix's roots and its success with DVDs, the company does not see that as a viable long-term market and is focusing all of its efforts on building its streaming business—a business that more resembles, and by its own definition is, a new form of a television network. Neither Redbox nor Netflix are tempering the decline of the more lucrative sell-through market, and if these services, over time, morph more into streaming TV-like services, then it is highly unlikely that this expanded TV universe (even if a slightly different window, and therefore additive) can make up for the demise of the corresponding video market. Given the historical importance of the video market—almost 50 percent of all studio revenues at its peak—the implications of this seismic shift underlies studios' and networks' justified fear of the disruptive force of digital distribution, even as they move to embrace the inevitable new landscape.

Window Movements

There is no doubt that given the importance of DVD revenues, there has been pressure to tinker with the window. In analyzing the tug of war between competing media, *Business Week* summarized:

To capture that DVD gold, Hollywood has for years made its flicks available to TV viewers only through a carefully structured system of "windows." DVD retailers waited six months after the theater premiere; cable's and satellite's video-on-demand (VOD) got the film 90 days after that, and HBO and other pay TV services six months following VOD. But the windows have been slowly closing, and studios now ship DVDs to market sooner than ever before—on average, in 137 days (versus 200 days in 1998), according to DVD Release Report . . . [53]

While this may sound dramatic, I would argue that the shrinking of the window has been merely iterative; in fact, and perhaps not surprisingly given the continued importance of both the theatrical and video markets, the window for video release, while accelerating, has stayed relatively static for several years. Window protection is so important for theatrical releases that the cinema chains exert extreme pressure, and will even in extreme cases boycott studios that test closing the gap by accelerating a DVD release date too close to the theatrical release.[54] The movie cinema trade association National Association of Theater Owners (NATO) goes so far as to track the window/gap studio by studio, down to average days post release and "announcement" dates. Table 5.4 is a schedule of the video release window by year, as reported by NATO.

241

While there is significant experimentation with download/electronic sell-through and VOD windows (as discussed in Chapter 7), the DVD window, even if narrowing a bit, seems to remain a relatively stable fulcrum around which manifestations of physical and electronic video sales and rentals are trying to balance. As discussed above, there are changes in holdbacks to lower priced rental options, such as in the case of Netflix and Redbox, but this is generally fine-tuning around the broader DVD window; as services morph from being perceived as video rental to being more akin to pay TV, however, then the windows will shift more fundamentally—as is already starting to happen, including the introduction of a new Digital HD window.

I asked Mike Dunn, president of 20th Century Fox Home Entertainment, what he thought about the video window relative to expanding digital options, and he confirmed the continuing importance of physical media while highlighting the need to provide alternatives in order to fulfill the consumer's demand for digital access across a range of devices:

Digital is redefining home entertainment, with consumers' changing habits influencing the way TV and movies are delivered and enjoyed across a range of screens. While physical media remains a

Table 5.4 Average Video Release Window

Year	Average Video Release Window
1998	5 months, 22 days
1999	5 months, 18 days
2000	5 months, 16 days
2001	5 months, 12 days
2002	5 months, 8 days
2003	4 months, 27 days
2004	4 months, 20 days
2005	4 months, 18 days
2006	4 months, 11 days
2007	4 months, 19 days
2008	4 months, 10 days
2009	4 months, 11 days
2010	4 months, 12 days
2011	4 months, 5 days
2012	3 months, 29 days

NATO memo, September 27, 2012, Re: Average Video Announcement and Video Release Windows (as of September 24, 2012).

key part of the industry, with Blu-ray flattering large-screen, Wi-Fi-enabled HD and 3D televisions in the living room, the need to meet consumer demand for access across all their connected devices has fostered new momentum and innovation for digital downloads and electronic sell-through models.

At Fox Home Entertainment, we understood the potential for Blu-ray to demonstrate for consumers what was possible in digital. We heighten the relationship fans have with their favorite entertainment by making available new content through downloads and second-screen engagements. Not only could fans view TV shows and movies in stunning visual quality, but they could receive new narratives, unseen footage, and commentaries, as well as purchase in real time the clothes and accessories worn by their favorite characters. This willingness for consumers to engage and embrace

242

digital through Blu-ray, along with the evolution of portable devices on which content is enjoyed, seeded consumer interest and drove our leadership in new digital delivery models.

Our digital strategy supports fostering easy, affordable, and accessible ways for consumers to access their entertainment anytime and enjoy it across all of their devices. This approach is also leading to new business models, while fostering the evolution of UltraViolet and other ways for consumers to amass digital collections. In 2012, as an example, we launched Digital HD, which redefines electronic sell-through and combines for unique benefits: early access, affordable pricing, cloud storage, and availability across multiple devices. The Ridley Scott epic *Prometheus* was our first Digital HD title, and was available three weeks ahead of its physical media launch into the home market. With a single purchase, consumers can enjoy the movie on any screen in the highest quality possible. The success of the release, and others that have followed, demonstrate the opportunities that come with embracing what's next and appealing to what consumers say they want: convenience for our digital lifestyles.

243

Physical Disc Inventory Management and Impact on Pricing and Profits

Returns and Stock Management

Probably the biggest single issue impacting the release of a title into the sell-through market is managing inventory. Rental units are generally firm sales, and when a rental chain decides it is overstocked or inventory has reached obsolescence, it can either destroy the units or sell them. Sell-through units/DVDs are, however, no different than any other consumer product, and excess stock is most often subject to return.

There are multiple steps in inventory management, and I will briefly touch on the life-cycle sequence in which they occur: (1) initial shipments; (2) replenishment; (3) returns; (4) price reductions and price protection; and (5) catalog management. While managing this process has been the focus of video divisions for years, a move to digital distribution (whether streaming or EST downloads) eliminates the need to manage inventory, as well as the risk associated with insufficient or excess stock. If electronic/digital distribution were therefore wholly substitutional for physical discs, there would be no reluctance, and in fact exuberance, in shedding the burden of managing physical stock. It is because we are not yet at this point, though, and because video still remains a very significant revenue source (not to mention the impact these factors have had on the evolution of the market), that I will discuss them in detail below.

Parallels in Games Market

Before addressing these elements, though, I want to briefly highlight that the same issues apply to most packaged-goods entertainment, and especially to the video-game industry. The implications of the shift to digital distribution in the games market is heightened due to an advantage not found with video—not only can distributors of product made for the major console platforms (Nintendo Wii, Microsoft Xbox, Sony PlayStation) eliminate inventory risk if games are downloaded via online networks such as Xbox Live Arcade, but game distributors also have the ability to update games with patches, new levels, and character add-ons. Moreover, these same online distribution platforms enable networked playing and other interactive features, providing further additional benefits to transitioning.

Similar to the video scenario, these benefits do not come challenge-free, as digital distribution is simultaneously enabling new competitive download options. The games industry is watching carefully the growth of fully online portals such as Steam, which bypass the console platforms entirely and allow 100 percent digital PC access; there is less risk to the ecosystem at the moment with such outlets, however, as the content providers must first port the games for play on these platforms. The combination of being able to control whether to port games to non-console digital platforms, coupled with the generally inferior user experience versus utilizing controllers (though you can now buy plug-in joysticks, etc.), ensures, at least for the time being, that these online systems remain ancillary. The major console manufacturers who dominate the games market, having created a captive vertically integrated end-to-end ecosystem, can accordingly limit downstream applications via licenses and benefit from the fact that, unlike videos, games can be updated and expanded via digital downloads. This measure of control enables the same players to manage the expansion and integration of new download experiences—as discussed in Chapter 8, the threats faced by the old guard are more from social games, which leverage digital distribution and "freemium" business models. Although these new types of games may create some pricing pressure, it is generally considered

244

a different market, appealing to a different and expanded user base ("casual" games versus "core" games), thus holding more potential for market expansion than cannibalization. The end result is generally benefitting the games business, and the longer-term challenge will be how producers can maintain high product price points (pricing has always been artificially high, given the need to pay manufacturing fees to the console owners that keep manufacturing captive under the guise of proprietary patented systems and the need to recoup costs of developing upgraded next-generation systems). Digital distribution with games, as with videos, eliminates the physical disc costs, and it is harder to justify a high per-unit cost, even if that is tied to a licensing and system-access model. Accordingly, the games business, which has always benefitted from high pricing and margins, will benefit similarly from reduced distribution costs, but those same pressures will ultimately force lower pricing, with the danger that margins will fall as well.

Initial Shipment

This is by far the most important step, because miscalculations on initial placement will plague the title's performance all the way downstream. It is debatable whether it is worse to over-ship or under-ship, but if demand outstrips supply and a title has been under-shipped, there are really only a couple of issues to address.

First, the obvious consequence is lost sales, and opportunity costs are always the hardest element to accurately forecast. If the under-shipment is recognized early, by utilizing an efficient supply chain (see later discussion) it is still feasible to capitalize on demand. However, because marketing campaigns are designed to create intense demand on release, absent a honed and tightly managed supply chain it is obviously difficult to reach fully substitutional sales outside the window of coordinated advertising and retail marketing/focus.

Second, the distributor needs to confirm how feasible it is to quickly replenish inventory and mitigate lost sales. In the mid to late 1990s, this would have been difficult, but as the market has matured, so has the replication and distribution system. Today, single plants may be able to produce 1 million discs per day and deliver them nationwide to out-of-stock retailers within the week—full replenishment may not be possible literally overnight, but it is feasible in a matter of days. Again, days count when dealing with a coordinated marketing campaign; the consequences of being out of stock and replenishing late include: (1) losing retail placement position; (2) losing retail focus; (3) selling against a new competitive title; and (4) missing key sales days such as weekends or seasonal-specific dates.

If, in contrast, the initial shipment has glutted the market and it turns out the distributor has materially over-shipped, there is likely to be pressure to take returns. This leads to complex management challenges, including price-protection decisions, as discussed later. Moreover, over-stating revenues and having to reverse out-earnings due to returns is a serious problem and (as also discussed later) has been responsible for significant downturns in the stock prices of companies who miss their targets.

Replenishment, Fulfilment, and Logistics

The sophistication of the market largely dictates how replenishment works. In the United States, the video arms of the studios and supply chains of the replicators and distributors are models of efficiency. On a major release, a studio has visibility into its large direct customers to the extent that it can check sales periodically during the day. The inventory and sell-through numbers are constantly updated, and it is possible to see how a title is progressing on release early in the week and top up SKUs as necessary for the weekend. Replicators able to churn out hundreds of thousands of units per day (if not more) then further decide how many units to build at which stage of production, balancing finished-goods inventory versus elements needed for a quick turnaround on the assembly line.

246

As the sell-through business matured, the duplicators recognized that they could fulfill additional distribution functions. Not only could they make the physical good, but they could handle the logistics of sorting SKUs, packing the product, and shipping the product. This step is frequently referred to as "pick, pack, and ship," and involves the logistics of everything in the chain, from completion of the physical good to delivering the good to the retailer. It may seem simple here, but the process of sorting inventory for delivery to retailers is a mechanized art.

The management of the backroom logistics does not stop there, however. The replicator has now taken on the task of processing returns, repurposing stock, invoicing the client/retailer, processing related credits, and even handling some collections. Basically, the entire chain, from manufacturing, to delivery, to payment, can be outsourced, leaving the intellectual property owner to focus on marketing the product and setting customer-specific terms.

The less sophisticated the retail market, the harder it is to replenish efficiently—the replicators have the systems, but without the retail systems to report offtake efficiently, the distributor is left to place all its product up front. Otherwise, the distributor risks out of stocks without the ability to replenish; this is not a viable option when the product has a short shelf life, driven by a burst of front-loaded advertising to drive consumers to purchase in a relatively short window. As discussed previously, the decay curves for video sales are becoming steeper, with an ever-increasing percentage of total sales on a unit in the first couple of weeks of release. Again, this correlates to increased competition and the fight for shelf space, with most displays rotating out on a regular weekly or biweekly basis and restocked with the "new title of the week."

No matter how efficient the supply chain and replenishment logistics, there is no guarantee of sales and always a risk of over- or under-stocks. While the risk is not nearly of the scale as on the theatrical release (as theatrical results convert the product from a nobody-knows experience good to a property that can be more accurately forecast for subsequent market sales—conversion rates), significant risks, even if more bounded, still exist. Because of the marketing profile, the trend has been to over-supply to ensure against out of stocks, as well as secure optimum store display. While every distributor knows they need to ship in more than 1 million units to sell-through 1 million, the art is to narrow the gap as much as possible without jeopardizing sales—the greater the efficiency in this stock management, the greater the margins and profits.

247

Returns

Historically, distributors have negotiated returns provisions with retailers that tend to be account-specific. A customary provision, for example, may be that an account is allowed a returns provision of 20 percent. It is also possible to negotiate for zero returns (a "firm sale") or allow a retailer 100 percent returns. A 100 percent returns allowance usually occurs when either a retailer has enough clout to insist on this flexibility, or the retailer has agreed to take extra units and aggressively market the title. Regardless of what is negotiated, it is important to keep in perspective that these provisions may change after the fact—a retailer that has agreed to 20 percent returns and finds that the title significantly underperforms is likely to ask for relief and return a much higher percentage. If this is a key customer and the distributor has another title coming out the following month it wants to push, it may not be so easy in practice to rigidly enforce the hard 20 percent number. The success of a title ultimately depends both on the distributor and retailer market, and both parties need to juggle short-term performance versus long-term relationships. This is where friction arises with producers, as someone involved with a specific title will not accept the sacrifice of his or her title's performance to accommodate client relationships that may bear no direct impact on his or her film's video revenues.

Return Reserve

For accounting purposes, returns caps allow the distributor to take return reserve provisions; namely, in accounting for sales, a provision will be taken for returns based upon the contractual return allowance or a permitted reserve. When accounting for sales, there is always a gap, and several elements need to be reconciled: What has been shipped into the retail channel? What units have actually sold-through to date (bought by a consumer as opposed to bought by the store)? What number of units is likely to remain at retail for future/continuing sales? What number of units is likely to be returned?

Returns impact participation statements (see Chapter 10) and need to be looked at in terms of how returns are treated between the distributor and retailer, and how returns are accounted for between the distributor and the producer/participant. There may be separate deals, and this may not be (though often is) strictly a pass-through relationship. One can theoretically imagine a producer with sufficient leverage inserting a returns cap in its deals to protect against a distributor favoring a retail customer or making a decision based on retail relationships as opposed to strictly on the title.

248   There may also be contractual provisions regarding the timing of returns and reserves. In addition to or unrelated to a returns allowance percentage, the parties could strike a deal prohibiting returns for a period of time (e.g., no returns for 90 days or six months); this has the advantage of keeping the product on shelf, and may allow for increased sales over a different or incremental selling season that would not take place without the protection (shelf space otherwise ceded to a competitive title).

On the participant side, there may be a push to stipulate that returns allowances may only be taken for a limited period of time and then released; it is customary to negotiate periods during which returns reserves need to be liquidated. Because the reserves are allowed, the distributor will naturally take advantage of potential returns and keep the money (in anticipation of returned units); however, these returns may never materialize, and all the while the money is held and not paid over to the producer. This practice, which is equivalent to the concept of "float" in other industries, means that the negotiated reporting and liquidation periods can be quite significant.

Spotlight on DreamWorks Animation and Pixar in 2005

The issue of returns was highlighted in 2005 when both Pixar and DreamWorks Animation were hit with returns on, respectively, *The Incredibles* and *Shrek 2*.

The tempest was set off by DreamWorks statements and filings. In January 2005, DreamWorks Animation stated that it had sold 37 million units of *Shrek 2* worldwide. However, in March the studio reported that it had only sold 33.7 million units and that it expected the title to continue with a strong performance and sell over 40 million by the end of the first quarter. When the day of reckoning came in May, Dream-Works Animation reported that it had only sold 35 million units (not 40 million), and admitted that the rate of sales that propelled the title to the top video seller of 2004 did not keep pace into 2005.

The reporting caused DreamWorks Animation's stock to fall 12 percent on the disappointing earnings, and the entire issue of returns and slowing down of the video market started making headlines. The *Wall Street Journal* reported: "In just its second quarter since becoming a public company, DreamWorks fell short of earnings forecasts by 25 percent and its stock tumbled as Wall Street wondered why the mistake wasn't disclosed sooner."[55]

Beyond the hit in stock price and negative publicity, the misjudgement on sales and returns even led to lawsuits, which in turn made headlines:

Shrek 2 DVDs Subject of Lawsuit. Shareholders sue DreamWorks **249** alleging misleading projections. . . . A proposed class-action lawsuit, filed in federal court in Los Angeles today, seeks unspecified damages from DreamWorks Animation for allegedly misleading stockholders about prospects for sales of *Shrek 2* DVDs."[56]

In the wake of this news, Pixar warned that it would have larger-than-expected returns on *The Incredibles*; on June 30, 2005, Pixar cut its earnings per-share estimate for the second quarter from 15 to 10 cents, citing slower-than-expected sales. The issue became prominent enough that even the SEC started to examine the reporting process for each of these studios. Ultimately, the SEC's local arm investigating DreamWorks recommended that no enforcement action be taken, and *Variety* reported: "While the SEC itself still has to make a formal decision, recommend-ation makes it very likely that DWA will escape government sanction for failing to warn investors, before first-quarter earnings were announced last year, that returns on the *Shrek 2* DVD were running much higher than anticipated . . ."[57]

While the issue of returns seemed like a revelation to the press and some investors, the difficulty of managing inventory levels and balancing returns was nothing new to industry insiders. What had changed were two factors. First, as earlier discussed, there was a slowing down of sales in the industry, and within 2005 the market seemed to have hit its by-title ceiling; the overall market was still healthy, but with title saturation and withering competition the market appeared to be retrenching on the high end of sales. This was a trend that had been predicted, but the reality came quicker than anticipated and started to send shock waves through the market.[58] Second, with a microscope on the industry, there was the ability, in the case of both Pixar and DreamWorks Animation, to see the impact on a specific title. This transparency was rare, for studios would otherwise report numbers on a consolidated basis, and to outsiders it was impossible to glean the numbers or even trends on the basis of a single title. With *The Incredibles* and *Shrek 2*, there was no way to hide the line-item performance.

Format and SKU Variables

An important variable in managing inventory and returns is also managing product SKUs. In some cases, a video or DVD release will be split into pan-and-scan and widescreen versions. Typically, a traditional box-shaped TV screen plays a 4:3 aspect ratio, which is referred to as pan and scan. In contrast, the horizontal aspect ratio of widescreen, replicating the rectangular movie, is 16:9. The widescreen aspect ratio matches the way a movie has been shot and edited, capturing the full breadth of the scene. To create a pan-and-scan version, the filmmaker actually has to create and approve another version, because the picture cannot simply be squeezed into the other shape. Accordingly, a pan-and-scan version will often cut off images at the margins.

The advent of widescreen monitors and increased consumer market knowledge led to an increase in widescreen versions. For years, pan-and-scan dominated, as widescreen was limited to the "purist" consumer who wanted to see the picture as the director intended it/as seen on film, so elements and scope are not compromised (and would put up with the black bars at the top and bottom of the screen). With the market maturation, plus increased consumer awareness of formats and the growth of rectangular flat-screen monitors, the SKU balance started to equalize on "collector"-type titles. By 2003–2004, certain titles were selling a greater number of widescreen versions, a trend that had been predicted but until this point of intersection (DVD growth and alternate monitors) had not happened. With each year, the proportion continued to shift in favor of widescreen—in fact, widescreen has become the de facto standard with pan and scan set to disappear.

Finally, in terms of SKUs, studios started to offer special "2-disc sets" of key titles, with one disc containing the film and the other disc filled with bonus material (or, in video parlance, value-added material or "VAM"; see Chapter 9 for more discussion of VAM in the context of marketing). The extra material both justified a higher price point and had become a self-fulfilling expectation from the standpoint of consumer demand—once it was commonplace, it became an expected component. The net result of the bonus disc was the studio distributor had a choice whether to release one version including the bonus material, or two versions with the alternate SKU comprised of just the film disc. If two SKUs were released, this obviously complicated the release matrix: Would the physical packaging change? Would the artwork change to distinguish SKUs? Would the price points vary? Would the distribution points of sale change?

Today, the existence of "VAM" can be a differentiator helping justify the purchase of physical versions versus digital copies that frequently only offer the movie or TV show itself. In a world with cloud access and storage and digital rentals via Netflix and cable VOD, VAM offers premium content valuable to the collector and often only available with purchase.

Pricing, Price Reductions, and Price Protection

Pricing is not quite what it seems from customarily quoted numbers, and to understand the economics it is important to appreciate net pricing. The price charged by the retailer to the consumer is called the retail price. Because it is illegal to set an onward price, what is usually set is the SRP; MAP is a vehicle to influence the SRP, but ultimately there is market flexibility and neither the SRP nor MAP actually locks a retailer into a specific sales price. (Note: When you hear about a store advertising as a low-price leader, or matching in the market, it is important to discern between whether a specific store in the chain will alter pricing within the store to match a competitor, or whether the chain/store is actually advertising a specific price to the consumer. It is very different to claim you will match a price (where no figure is stated in the ad) and to actually advertise a specific price in newspapers and circulars.)

The price that the distributor charges the retailer is often called the dealer price, which is the video term for wholesale price. As a rule of thumb, the wholesale price tends to be roughly 60 percent of the SRP. The wholesale price is basically fixed across the U.S. market (in accordance with the Robinson–Patman Act); nevertheless, there can be marginal account differences in the wholesale price, as juggling can take place with marketing allowances (market development funds and cooperative advertising allowances) and tailored programs.

Like any consumer product, over time there are markdowns as new items enter the market. In the video sector, product is generally segmented into "new releases" and "catalog." When a product transitions from a new release to catalog, however, the price is not fixed, although generally product is re-categorized after its initial release cycle. The challenge of a distributor is to manage its library of titles, find ways to turn over its catalog titles, and maintain demand and premium pricing for the key titles in its library. Accordingly, segmenting the library becomes an important marketing proposition, and to generate demand and interest titles are often themed or grouped (e.g., marketed as classics, award-winners, part of director's collections).

In terms of life-cycle management, studio distributors are always running models (and conducting market research) comparing units and corresponding contribution margins at differing pricing; for example, will dropping the price from $19.99 to $14.99 generate sufficient incremental sales to outweigh the lower per-unit profit? Managing price is an art, not a science, and is influenced by factors such as the nature of the title, the competitive environment, retail pressures, inventory in the market, seasonality, life-cycle promotional opportunities, and rebate programs.

252   On a typical release, it would be customary to release at a higher price (but a price that hopefully yields maximum net profit/contribution, taking into account the matrix of pricing and volume), and then to reduce the price downstream; for example, if a movie came out at Christmas, and the video came out in late spring the following year, the price may be reduced in the fourth quarter for a Christmas promotion. If competitive product pricing is lower, there will be retail pressure to match, and subsequent price reductions will be implemented. All this activity may generate incremental sales, but there are two issues that need to be weighed. The first is that, except in rare instances, it is very difficult to raise a price—once it sinks to a certain level, it is apt to stay there. Namely, once in the bargain bin, it will be very difficult for the distributor to sell more units into a retailer at a higher price. The second key issue is price protection.

What is Price Protection?

Price protection is money paid by a distributor to a retailer when the distributor drops its wholesale price and sells more units into the market at a price below what it charged the retailer for the retailer's previously purchased on-hand inventory. For example, if Studio X sold units into the market at a wholesale price of around $12, such that Retailer Y generally priced the title at $19.99 to the consumer, and the studio had a promotion where it wanted to sell in more units of the movie at $9 to drive a retail price of $14.99, it might have a price-protection issue. The issue would arise because retailers would have current stock at the higher price, and would want to be equalized such that all stock had the same cost basis. To take in more units, it would insist that the studio pay or credit it back the difference between $9 and $12 on all units it had. This $3 difference is the price-protection payment charged to the distributor.

The retailer holds the leverage here. If the studio does not equalize the stock, the retailer would likely have the option to return its unsold product for full credit.

Price protection generally occurs in two scenarios. The first is when a title has been successful and there is an opportunity to sell in additional units, such as implementing a seasonal promotion dropping the price after the title has already been in the market for a period. Even with success, individual stores within the same account are apt to be out of stock and others to have excess units—in a perfect world, the retailer would stock balance, excess units would sell-through, and price protection would not be needed; however, the reality is the distributor is likely to bear the brunt of this evening out via price protection, which, if executed well, may only be a credit against new units sold in and would not incur any actual out-of-pocket cash payments. A second scenario can occur when a title has severely underperformed. If a title is not selling-through, and there is so much excess inventory that retailers are threatening to send it back (retailers will want to maintain whatever product is generating turnover and margin), then the distributor may need to drop the product's price just to keep it on shelves. If they can convince accounts to take in more units when the price is dropped, then there is the potential for netting the price-protection costs against the additional revenues from new units—a scenario akin to a successful title; however, if new units are not ordered or the units do not generate enough revenues to cover the price-protection costs, then the distributor may have to pay the difference in cash. Usually, return reserves will cover this deficit, but if price protection is needed to keep the title on shelf and the liquidation of return reserves (sums held to offset returns) provides insufficient funds, then the distributor can find itself in the lose-lose position of lower price (and therefore reducing its margin) and paying cash out of pocket for the privilege of cutting its margin. This can, obviously, be a disaster scenario.

Point-of-Sale Rebates

While price protection impacts the entire channel and effects a permanent pricing change, point-of-sale (POS) rebates are a mechanism to implement a temporary price rollback. A supplier may authorize a limited-time price cut, either across the retail channel or with specific accounts, which is implemented at checkout. To create an incentive for the retailer to reduce the shelf price from $19.99 to $14.99, a supplier may offer a $5 POS rebate, which will be applied at the wholesale price level, with the expectation that the full discount will then be passed along to the consumer, lowering the shelf price as just described. The advantage to the supplier is that they only need to credit the stores for units actually sold rather than on the entire inventory. This is a strategy frequently used for promotional sales, or during key holiday periods where the seller is trying to move units during periods of heavy foot traffic, but where the seller does not want to implement a permanent price cut.

Moratorium

Another tool that a distributor can use both to manage inventory as well as pricing is to put a title on moratorium. This means simply that the title is no longer available for purchase. By limiting supply, this may help stabilize either pricing or inventory levels, as stores may be less likely to return product if they are unable to later reorder units. Also, putting a title on moratorium may stimulate sales: "order now or else ..." Disney has used this strategy very effectively on its animated classics, advertising that a title is available for a limited period only, helping to spike interest and demand. The product is then literally rested until another cycle or perhaps another special version is later released.

Putting a title on moratorium is especially useful in the instance of multiple SKUs. This may help send a message to retail that the current version of a title will not be replenished (staving off potential returns), and further limits supply to clean out the channel before a different version is released. One of the goals is to avoid market confusion, so that the new version (e.g., a special edition) is the only widely available version, allowing focused marketing campaigns both at the retail and consumer levels.

Price Erosion and Bargain Bins

One of the most difficult elements in managing a title or catalog is dealing with price erosion. As noted earlier, new titles can command a premium price, but once the initial sales cycle has passed the product is perceived as older and will often be repriced in an effort to stimulate sales.

What counters price erosion is that, unlike consumer goods, which are fungible, every movie is a unique piece of software. There will only be one *The Godfather* or *Titanic*, and pricing does not need to drop for that film to compete because there is another identical product coming into the market; instead, pricing may need to move for the consumer to view the title as competitive against other similar films. If a competitor has a classics line that underprices its rival studios, price sensitivity alone may influence the consumer's selection.

Managing consumer expectations is tricky, and, as previously noted, once there is a perception that pricing is at a certain level, it can be difficult to move back up to a higher cost basis. Ultimately, pricing is based on brand and catalog management, and can be influenced by seasonality, new formats coming into play, inventory levels, and even corporate revenue pressures (e.g., dropping a price and stimulating sales can help achieve hitting an earnings target).

It is now common for certain retailers to sell older titles in "bargain bins," where consumers may buy DVDs for a couple of dollars. Even high-profile titles can be steeply discounted for promotions, as has been the case on Black Friday in the U.S., when some of the *Harry Potter* titles and *The Lord of the Rings* films could be found in the $5–6 range. This is a far cry from the former high-priced rental market, and many video distributors bemoan the price erosion in the market. The discounting may be fine if volume is stimulated, but if volumes do not meet projections and the pricing becomes a consumer expectation, rather than a limited promotion, then the high margins the business has enjoyed are put in jeopardy.

Ultimately, there are no other *Harry Potter* movies, so how and when to move price and launch promotions is the realm of brand management that makes the video market so interesting. Again, even though all films fall into categories, all individual films remain unique, challenging video divisions to hit targets by simultaneously macro- and micromanaging its catalog of product.

International Variations

Most of the information discussed in this chapter applies equally to the international marketplace, but there are both obvious and subtle differences. It is beyond the scope of this book to delve into territory-specific nuances, but I will try to highlight a few significant areas of difference.

Release Timing and Development of Market

Although video and DVD technology has been driven by European and Asian (in particular Japanese) consumer electronics companies, market

255

growth and penetration has been driven by software and Hollywood pressures. The international video and DVD markets have usually lagged the United States in terms of maturation and retail sophistication.

In terms of retail and consumer patterns, the DVD and Blu-ray market has generally mirrored the prior VHS sell-through market. In territories such as France, for example, where there was a long sell-through tradition and sophistication of key retailers such as the hypermarkets (Auchan, Carrefour) the DVD market has followed a similar pattern. Accordingly, key retailers such as the hypermarkets, or entertainment software chains such as Virgin Megastore or FNAC, tend to have the same challenges that exist in the North American market: How is the product merchandised? How is it displayed? What are the promotional campaigns? Is the price point appropriate?

Additionally, with sophisticated merchandising and placement usually comes quality reporting. The ability of the distributor to see through to actual consumer sales forces the development of state-of-the-art inventory management systems and distribution that allows quick, store-level replenishment. Stock balancing can occur on a daily, and at minimum weekly basis, affording the distributor to respond to consumer demand while maintaining a greater level of flexibility in creating product.

256

The ability to tinker with stock balances, replenish inventory, and top up manufacturing is only possible with this level of reporting from retail, and the parallel ability of retail to handle changes rapidly. The type of systems that can report and consolidate by-title sales at store and chain levels on a daily basis, however, are only justifiable with certain threshold volumes; in essence, the entire supply side feeds on itself with volume driving sophistication, and fulfilment, merchandising, and manufacturing capabilities evolving with demand. The United States is such a large market with diverse and distant retail distribution requirements that it developed this level of maturity quickly. That process has lagged in many international markets, but has now caught up in sophistication across the territories one would expect (e.g., much of western Europe, Australia). (Note: Not surprisingly, many of the trends discussed above, including, for example, the use of reserves and price protection, is similarly applied in the sales and stock balancing of other physical copies of packaged goods media, such as videogames; additionally, as the same mass-market retailers tend to stock both movies and games, inventory systems have improved and have, to some measure, converged —though movies/DVDs are still managed separately.)

Outside the pure supply chain, considerations such as competition and external factors in the local marketplace tend also to mimic the U.S. market. Regarding external factors, video releases may be tied to natural key sales periods, such as national holidays and vacation periods. As for the impact of competition, all distributors similarly analyze the release schedule of competitive product and date ("street date") their releases to try to secure the optimal window for sales.

Any and all of these factors are reasons why a DVD may come out on a different date in different territories. Weighing against these factors, however, will be concerns about piracy and parallel imports: once a product is out in the worldwide marketplace, there is a danger it may find its way to the local consumer before the product has been directly released in the country—an issue that is now exacerbated with Internet access, especially for English-language product.

Localization Challenges

The main challenge of international markets is the creation of language-specific SKUs. Each DVD will need to be authored and compressed like the United States, but across the rest of the world there will be multiple SKUs covering both dubbed and subtitled versions.

In addition to language versions, marketing campaigns will be tailored to the specific market as will, in cases, the packaging. Whenever a creative campaign is changed, and especially when it is uniquely tailored to a specific territory, there is inherent delay. Additionally, depending upon contractual requirements, time may need to be allocated to obtain approvals from talent, as well as for home office executives to coordinate their approvals with both international branches and the producer/ production company that made the film. Hopefully, these elements have been planned for (and lead times built into release schedules), but the potential for delays is obvious.

257

Pricing: Variable Pricing to Customers and Net Pricing

Pricing internationally can be a "free-for-all" relative to the U.S. market where distributors set the same dealer price for all customers and do not differentiate price based on volume commitments. Instead, distributors have to manage the retail channel by other means, including marketing commitment (co-op marketing and market development fund), returns policies, inventory placement, etc.

In contrast, historically in some European markets and specifically in highly price-sensitive retail markets, the distributors may set different prices for different customers. Not only can the actual dealer price vary, but there may be different discount schemes applied to varying accounts with variable pricing at each stage of the chain: retail/shelf price, dealer price, net invoiced price.

Table 5.5 Pricing Table

	SRP	DLP	DLP as % of SRP	Dis-counts* (%)	Rebate (%)	Net Price	Shelf Price
Germany	24.99	14.30		20	5	11	22.99
France	24.99	20.50		25	—	15.40	24.99**
UK	24.99	17.00		20	2	13.20	15.99

* May be further subcategories, such as cash discounts and standard discounts.
** In France, it is a regulated market and the shelf price—SRP.

Obviously, the distributor needs to ensure a certain range to avoid chaos and resentment in the marketplace. This is usually achieved by applying larger discounts to key accounts, which in turn often break out based on relative volumes. While this may all sound simple in practice, think about having to account for net pricing at the retail-chain-specific level, rolling up to the market overall, and then equalizing pricing by backing out applicable VAT taxes and harmonizing exchange rates. The simple question, "What is the price in the market?" could easily have different answers.

Table 5.5 is an example. Within each market, the distributor needs to customize its terms with retailers, and will generally fix both the SRP and the DLP; however, the wholesale price/DLP may have significant discounts applied that can be sliced in a variety of ways. There may be standard discounts and rebates, which may be within a continuum (e.g., standard discounts within a band of 20–25 percent), or the formula may be quite complicated. Some markets may apply layers of discounts, applying at chain level and tied to variables such as cash payment/payment terms. Accordingly, historical relationships, retailer-level commitment to placement and marketing, trading terms, payment terms, volumes ordered, and return provisions all factor into the relationship matrix and ultimate per-unit/per-retailer pricing structure.

Another factor that is quickly impacting pricing patterns is the Internet. By cutting out the middleman, certain e-tailers can effectively undercut traditional retail pricing. This puts pressure on margins, which comes back to the distributor in the form of physical retailers wanting additional discounts. In markets where differential dealer pricing based on volume commitments is legal, this can create enormous challenges in managing the market.

Video Economics and Why Video Revenues are Uniquely Profitable to Studios

The video business emerged as a kind of hidden caryatid holding up the theatrical film business on the back of its retail sales. While there is a general awareness of the importance of the video revenue stream (approximately 50 percent of the total revenue pie at its peak, and still among the most important overall revenue sources), what is less understood is that video is uniquely profitable for distributors and accordingly provides the studios with its most important source of positive cash flow.

Video Revenues

Video/DVD revenues grew to become so significant that for more than a decade they represented a critical if not the primary hedge strategy against the risk of making a film. There is an assumed floor for video units, and even a movie with disappointing box office results can earn significant video revenue.

How video revenues are calculated depends upon one's participation deal. From a studio standpoint, the calculation is straightforward:

(dealer price) × (net units sold) = video gross revenues

However, video revenues as regards third parties are often calculated on a royalty basis. This is the case for most participations (see later cash flow discussion), as well as in licensee arrangements. In the case of a studio licensing video rights to a third party in a territory where they do not distribute directly, the third party licensee is likely to account and pay on a royalty-per-unit basis (see the next section for further discussion on the basis and structuring of royalty payments).

Video Royalty Theory and Influence on Cash Flow

When the VHS video business first launched, videos were likened to an ancillary revenue stream such as soundtrack records. Following the record model, the conventional method of paying producers and artists was on a royalty theory: 20 percent of video revenues would be put into the general pot out of which profits would be paid. Seen generally as found money, this methodology was accepted and only later became the bane of artists who felt unfairly compensated from the windfall studios

259

were making on video sales. This remains an undercurrent of guild–studio tensions in residual negotiations, where guilds are wary of leaving Internet and other new media revenues on the table and repeating the sins of video deals past (see Chapter 7 for further discussion).

This royalty theory and calculation is a fundamental element in the calculation of net profits (see Chapter 10). In a typical studio definition of net profits, video is accounted for only based upon the 20 percent royalty from video net revenues. The other 80 percent of revenues are simply kept by the video distributor, creating a significant stream of free cash flow.

Why Uniquely Profitable—at Least in Perception

Video divisions appear uniquely profitable for two simple reasons. First, pursuant to accounting for revenues on a royalty only, the vast majority of revenues are shielded from participations and kept captive for the distributor. Second, as an ancillary revenue, the video division is not directly responsible for production costs; the division applies a gross margin calculation that, in terms of content production, generally only accounts for video transfer and mastering costs, as well as the creation of any bonus material. (Note: The studio accounting divisions will, however, keep track of all costs and revenues for creating film ultimates.)

Once fixed costs of mastering, authoring, and compressing material are recouped, video profits are based on the variable costs of manufacturing and selling-through units.

Setting Royalty Rates

While true revenue sharing breaks down video economics based on line-item revenues and costs, many video deals are royalty based and do not go into this level of detail and accounting. In fact, many royalty negotiations are simply haggling over a percentage or two, with the parties recognizing bands of historical rates or perhaps reverting to custom. However, there is grounded economic reasoning underlying rates, even if actual negotiations fail to delve into the detail. In theory, it is possible to deduct the assumed costs from wholesale revenue and arrive at an amount of profits available on a per-unit basis. From this number, the parties can then negotiate a percentage split of profits; the percentage that the producer keeps could then be expressed instead as a royalty based on the wholesale number. Table 5.6 is an example.

From this available profit, the distributor and producer will share in an agreed proportion; in this example, at a 50/50 split the producer

Table 5.6

Retail Cost	$24.99	
Dealer Price	$14.99	(at about 60%)
Cost of Goods	$3.50	(estimate)
Other Costs	$1.00	
Marketing	$2.25	(assume 15%)
Profit remaining	$8.24	(about 55% gross margin)

would keep $4.12 as its profit per contribution. Another way to arrive at this figure would be to ask what royalty rate on the dealer price the producer would need to receive the same profit. The answer is a royalty of about 27.5 percent (0.275 × $14.99 = $4.12). Similarly, if it were agreed that the producer should keep 60 percent of the profits, then the royalty rate would edge up to almost 33 percent (0.60 × $8.24/$14.99). What percentage each party keeps is the subject of negotiation and should reflect the relative values of what each is contributing. This is simpler in theory than practice when needing to weigh the relative value of content contribution versus distribution and perhaps financing.

While there can be many other factors in the negotiation, at minimum this is a credible way of examining how to split the pie. Moreover, even though this calculation is based on a myriad of assumptions, it has the end logic of simplicity. All the parties need to track is the wholesale price and the units sold in order to calculate, report, and pay a participation. This is infinitely simpler and less controversial than tracking all revenue and cost categories; moreover, it likely avoids auditing costs, which can multiply exponentially when adding on the complexity of multiple countries and currency conversions. (See Chapter 10, section titled "Online Accounting: Simple Revenue Sharing and the Net Profits Divide," for a discussion regarding Internet revenue sharing versus royalty accounting.)

Advances and Recoupment

Once a royalty rate is set, the other key item to agree on is an advance, if any. An advance will likely be due if the product is an acquisition. The amount of the advance will be a relatively simple calculation matching the expected unit sales multiplied by the revenue that will be due based on those sales—again, this is an easier calculation if it is based on a royalty per unit. The variables will be the royalty rate and the unit assumptions, and then what percentage of the total expected value should be covered by a minimum guarantee.

Table 5.7 Hypothetical Video P&L.

Revenue Side	Description	Sample	Assumptions
Gross Units			
Rental	Actual number of units shipped into the rental store channel	100,000	
Sell-Through	Actual number of units shipped into retail via direct accounts or wholesalers	900,000	
		1,000,000	
Gross Revenues			
Rental	Simple formula of wholesale price multiplied by number of units		$19.99 Shelf from $26.99 SRP
Sell-Through	Simple formula of wholesale price multiplied by number of units	16,000,000	$16 per unit wholesale
Deductions from Gross			
Returns	Returns either from defective units, or from accounts with returns rights	180,000	Assume 20% (of sell-through #)
Rebates	POS rebate incentives, or overall adjustments to wholesale price		
Price Protection	$ credited to lower COGs on unsold retail inventory, enabling price drop		
Net Units			
Rental	Units net of returns: units either sold-through or not returned/	100,000	
Sell-Through	Units net of returns: units either sold-through or not returned/returnable	720,000	
		820,000	
Net Revenue			
Rental	Adjusted net wholesale price multiplied by net units		Assume ~60% SRP ($16 wholesale price)
Sell-Through	Adjusted net wholesale price multiplied by net units		
Total	(Note: Another category could be revenue share)	13,120,000	DP × by net units
Cost Side			
Manufacturing Expenses	(exclusive of creation of product and any value-added material)		On gross units
Mastering and Menus	Navigation interfaces and menus		

Item	Description	Amount	Notes
Replication/Duplication	Physical cost of creating the DVD disc		
Packaging	The physical cost of labels, paper/sleeves		
Cases and assembly	The physical cost of the plastic box/case		
Miscellaneous (returns, obsolesence)			
Distribution Expenses			
Assemble and sort ("Pick and pack")	Supply chain cost of sorting and customizing units for delivery		
Shipping (freight)	Physical cost of transport and delivery to customer		
Returns costs	Cost of taking back and processing returns back into inventory		
Merchandising	Rackjobber costs who manage in-store displays and placement		
Miscellaneous (customer admin)		3,000,000	Assume ~$3 per unit On gross units
Marketing Expenses			
Trade Marketing	Marketing to DVD/video accounts (e.g., Best Buy, Walmart, Blockbuster)		
Advertising (sales kits, etc.)	Sales materials for the trade		
Point of Purchase (POP)	In-store marketing elements, such as standees, counter pieces, posters		
Consumer Marketing			
Advertising (online and offline media)	TV, radio and online spots/banners (cost of creation and placement)		
Promotion and Publicity	Press junkets, PR costs, hard costs of talent/exec travel to promote		
Research costs	Cost of pricing studies, focus groups, etc.	3,200,000	Assume ~$3.20 per unit (20% of $16 DP)
Sales Expenses			
Market Development Funds (MDF)	% of revenue allocation to aid retailer marketing and promotion efforts		
Co-op advertising	Similar to MDF, but tied to actual media placement (e.g., a retailer ad)		
Trade Shows	Allocated costs of attending trade shows: advance showing of product		
Miscellaneous (e.g., mailers)		960,000	Assume 5–6% of GR
Total Net Expenses		7,160,000	
Total Net Revenues – Total Net Expenses = Total Net Profit/Contribution Margin		13,120,000	
		–7,160,000	
		–5,960,000	

The next step is confirming out of which revenues the distributor will then recoup the guarantee paid. If it is a 50/50 costs off the top split of revenues deal, then it will take twice as long to recoup/reach overages than if the recoupment were out of 100 percent of revenues earned. This example, however, assumes a straight sharing without factoring in a fee. No distributor would likely agree to pay an advance, recoup the advance, and then start sharing profits without ever having taken a fee.

A further wrinkle on this is preventing a fee-on-a-fee scenario (i.e., double-dipping). The following is an example:

$300,000 advance and a 20 percent fee

20 percent fee on the advance = $60,000

20 percent fee with a $300,000 advance
= $375 to recoup, for it takes $375,000 of gross to recoup the advance plus the fee

Advance

1 – fee = gross necessary to recoup plus fee

$300/(1 - 0.20) = 375$

Video P&L

Table 5.7 is a hypothetical video P&L, which further exhibits the complexity of gauging the net profit amount and why royalties, being much easier to calculate and track, are instead frequently used. Additionally, below I describe in more detail several of the line-item cost categories.

Video Costs

Probably the best way to illustrate video costs is to walk through the costs at various stages of exploiting a new-release DVD or Blu-ray title. I will break this into three sections: building and encoding the DVD material, manufacturing the DVD, and marketing and distributing the DVD. Paralleling the complexity of the DVD supply chain, the logistics of creating, manufacturing, and fulfilling DVD orders is a complicated process. The DVD is an inherently complex product and the physical plants are high-tech, secure, impressive facilities that rival the efficiency of any assembly line.

Building and Encoding DVD Material

The first stage consists of two parts: what material will physically appear on the DVD, and how that material will be converted to compressed digital form. Regarding the materials, it is important to recognize on the cost side that a DVD involves much more than simply transferring a film or TV show to the DVD. The value of the market and ability to tinker after the fact have created a consumer value proposition mandating that the DVD (for a major title) offers something extra. That something extra includes vast amounts of VAM, as well as navigation. (Note: As discussed earlier, VAM may not be offered in rental options, and some consider VAM the differentiator justifying purchase of a title; essentially, VAM can be leveraged as a mechanism to preserve sell-through/ownership tied to higher price points in an environment when cloud access can otherwise eliminate the impetus to purchase.) The entry point to a DVD is called the menu, and each major DVD has a uniquely produced menu and interface to enhance the experience. This is the interface screen that asks whether you want to watch widescreen or pan and scan (if the particular DVD gives you a choice), has a play button, and lists the other options that the particular DVD may give you. This can include traveling to all sorts of VAM, jumping to specific chapters, hearing director or talent commentary, watching trailers or altering the presentation settings.

All of these choices are then integrated to a user-friendly environment that will thematically pull from the title. The page may be static, scrolling, or may have visual cut scenes that play and then dissolve into the static menu page. All of this obviously takes time and money, and depending on the budget and consumer expectations, very significant sums can be spent creating additional material and the navigational interface through which the consumer can explore the hours of extra content. Because of these features, the DVD has become an interactive product, allowing the viewer to customize his or her viewing experience and delve into extra features that can be much longer the actual content around which this VAM is built. It is not unusual for a major two-hour film to come with four or more hours of "bonus material."

Once all the elements are set (the title, the menus, and the bonus material), then all the material needs to be encoded. This step is called authoring and compression, which is technical lingo for transferring the material to the digital medium. There are specific authoring and compression houses who bid out product and create the masters from which the DVDs are then replicated. There has been a natural consolidation of video replicators and compression houses; in fact, some of the replicators have acquired authoring companies, thus allowing them to offer customers one-stop shopping through the production chain. Similar steps are required for online/digital versions delivered via broadband access, or cloud-based and other over-the-top distribution channels, as discussed in Chapter 7. In those instances, content is

265

ingested and transcoded as appropriate for delivery via servers that then provide VOD access through digital rights management software. DRM systems, coupled with additional security through transmission and playback schemes, then enable consumers to gain access to the content based upon whatever rules (How long is the access? How many times can a program be viewed?) are put in place and economic systems (e.g., rental versus sell-through) are offered.

The cost of authoring and compression has come down over time, with improvements in both technology and competition. One of the more significant costs comes from the international side, where different language masters require several different masters to be configured, authored, and compressed.

Manufacturing the DVD

Manufacturing costs are broken out into pennies—and pennies matter in a business with slim replication margins and unit volumes that can be in the several millions. Like any other good, the manufacturing costs of physical discs are a roll-up of lots of sub costs, since every DVD/Blu-ray is customized.

As a rule of thumb, usually half to more than half of the total costs come from the physical replication of the disc and the cost of the plastic DVD case (Amaray case). What the actual disc costs are per unit will vary according to vendors and market conditions. Many studios have overall long-term deals with replicators. The vendors benefit from having secure capacity filled, and the studios benefit by incentives to lock up their business. If a distributor is able to bid out replication on the "spot market," they may or may not strike opportunistic deals. If the manufacturing is in the peak period where every studio is pumping out DVDs for the fourth-quarter gift season, and capacity is constrained, then costs may go up. However, depending on the replicator, its particular flow of product from its studio deals may be up or down depending on the actual title performance (does the studio have three hit titles or three dogs?), and pricing may fluctuate given the actual capacity expected. One thing is for certain: every studio wants secure capacity with the absolute lowest price, which virtually ensures a consistently competitive market.

The following are examples of the types of elements in the manufacturing process that go into assembling a finished-goods price:

- physical disc replication, for which price may vary by the memory size of the DVD
- price of the Amaray case

- costs to create/print menus, sleeves, and then insert the material into the case
- spine labels
- security tags (different retailers may require different tags/configurations)
- booklet and disc insertion
- shrink-wrapping the finished product
- external stickers
- barcodes
- freight costs for delivery (if distribution bundled with manufacturing costs).

The above is the baseline, as the process can become more complicated for special gift SKUs, bundling product together (e.g., pack-in toy), or special cases.

One great advantage DVDs had, which helped spur adoption, was that the physical replication costs were low when compared to making a VHS tape. The costs continued to drop over time, so not only were more DVD units of a title being sold, but the margins based on manufacturing alone were in parallel going up. The timing, product, and type of DVD (e.g, DVD-9 or DVD-5) can all influence price. As noted previously, this is a negotiation of pennies, and it is the pennies that ultimately determine the margin and profitability of the DVD duplicator.

Electronic Sell-Through Advantage

Regardless of how low costs are pushed, a challenge the DVD market faces is that physical costs can never drop to the level of digital goods—where except for server and bandwidth costs, which are usually borne by the retailer (e.g., Apple, Netflix, Amazon), the manufacturing costs are effectively zero. Accordingly, a very compelling argument for downloads is the elimination of nearly all of the foregoing costs. Although limited costs such as compression remain, the cost reductions in delivery via electronic sell-through drop directly to the bottom line. The issue is then whether the same product is being delivered, and therefore whether pricing should be reduced. Often, downloads are priced the same as physical copies, but with no physical costs and without VAM, digital goods should cost less and yield greater margins. Until competition further develops or consumers balk at the prices and opt for physical discs, download services will likely continue to charge these premiums—initially justifying the lack of discounting on the cost of building market share and needing to amortize back-end infrastructure. However, over the long run, the pricing relative to costs is not rational, and we will

267

see prices coming down, including differentiated pricing based on the quality and volume of material.

Marketing and Distributing the DVD

(Note: The following is a summary overview of some key costs, but for a more complete discussion see Chapter 9.)

Marketing of DVDs entails two primary costs. The first is the consumer marketing and advertising campaign costs borne by the studio distributor. This entails the same types of categories as theatrical marketing, ranging from print ads, to TV spots, to online promotion—where online promotion itself is now diversifying to segment digital advertising promotion and leveraging social networks. Beyond paid-for media, advertising costs (again, like theatrical) also include posters, trailers, press/PR activity, and even junkets. As the upside for DVDs/Blu-ray has grown, the marketing campaigns have become that much more complex—often planned months, if not a year, in advance of the release.

The other major cost category is trade marketing, given the importance of incentivizing retailers both to execute at point of purchase and to advertise themselves, utilizing DVD/Blu-ray product to attract store traffic. As mentioned earlier, distributors will therefore offer market development fund and cooperative advertising allowances that the retailers may spend on in-store campaigns, circular advertising, and general promotions (including online banners, home-page and above-the-fold placements, etc.). These sums are variable and tied to a percentage of wholesale revenues: the more units bought, the more money available for promotion.

Sometimes, with a significant enough title, the retail campaign can also be stimulated with customized product or tie-ins. These can take the form of retailer exclusives, special product SKUs (e.g., double packs, packed-in merchandise), and rebate programs. If programs are customized by the retailer, then a key customer such as Walmart or Media Markt may be able to differentiate its offer and advertising, creating an incentive for the chain to advertise the product and perhaps feature the unique SKU in circulars. There is no limit to tie-ins, and with the release of the DVD for *Star Wars: Episode III – Revenge of the Sith,* Fox and Lucasfilm executed a unique program with Best Buy involving the Donald Trump television hit *The Apprentice;* the task for the contestants on the show was to build a display that would showcase *Episode III* and related product (Star Wars video game) at Best Buy stores, and then a version of the winning team's display would be utilized in select Best Buy retail outlets.

268

Finally, in very limited instances there may be the potential for promotional partners, akin to theatrical tie-ins. It is the bane of video marketing chiefs that, despite the size of video revenues, and the critical importance of DVD/Blu-ray sales in the life cycle of any title, such deals are the exception and not routine. DVD sales simply do not piggyback on marketing waves of theatrical release scale and are still largely viewed by consumer brands as ancillary.

The Future of Video

Technology is ever marching on and impacting the future of video; in fact, as quickly as DVDs appeared, it is possible to imagine them becoming as extinct as VHS.

iPods, tablets, and other digital storage devices demonstrate how DVDs could become supplanted with hardware capable of holding vast digital files. Imagine your library of DVDs all on one machine or storage box . . . an iPad can hold your library of music CDs, your lifetime collection of photographs, and your DVD collection. Conceptually, it is only a matter of storage, an issue that the studios (via UltraViolet) and companies such as Amazon are solving via cloud-based digital lockers (see Chapter 7). In my prior edition, I pointed to the prospect of this growth (noting future devices would hold not simply music, but also videos), but in many ways the future is already here, with devices such as Amazon's Kindle Fire, Samsung's Galaxy tablet, and the iPad (none of which existed at the first printing of this book in 2009), enabling personal digital video libraries.

How quickly these options will further erode the DVD/Blu-ray world is a matter of speculation. People still love browsing book stores, and there is an element of passion in collecting DVDs; however, it seems unlikely that the desire to collect boxes or a preference for physical artwork over thumbnails are strong enough forces to hold back the convenience (and, arguably, inevitability) of digital copies. One countering force is retail pressure, as key chains will have every incentive to slow the shift and try to thwart the demise of a multi-billion dollar product line. Whether, or how long, the DVD can coexist with the next generation of VOD, streaming services, and digital storage devices is ultimately up to the consumer.

I asked long-term industry veteran Louis Feola, former president of Paramount's made-for-home entertainment division (Paramount Famous Productions) and former president of Universal Home Entertainment, how quickly he expected the full digital transition to take place:

269

The film and television industry has endured a century of new delivery systems that, upon their introductions, were predicted to displace prior points of distribution. It was the rarest of situations when that actually occurred quickly. Business transitions and consumer adaptation simply take time. Digital and Internet technology will indeed overpower DVD and Blu-ray, and while no one can predict the future with absolute certainty, in the short- to mid-term brick-and-mortar and electronic will coexist. The industry will continue to maximize mature revenue streams while developing new revenue streams.

Online Impact

- An entirely new category of "video distribution" has emerged in the form of downloads, with purchases via an iPod, tablet, or other system now labeled as "electronic sell-through."
- "E-tailers" such as Amazon have developed a significant market share and are pioneering new ownership constructs, such as the ability to purchase content and maintain it in a remote digital locker; e-tailers are also putting pressure on retail pricing (given lower cost structure), as well as enabling new predictive release metrics via preorder commitments.
- VOD services (both streaming and download), available either over-the-top or through traditional access points, are threatening the existence of video rental, the sector that launched, and once was the entire, video business.
- Transactional VOD, whether subscriber-based as offered by Netflix, or à la carte via services such as Amazon, has made the virtual video store a reality; additionally, cloud-based infrastructure has enabled limitless depth of copy (wide and long tail) accessible via a multitude of connected/Internet-ready devices, posing a near-insurmountable challenge to traditional video rental.
- Online services are enabling greater depth of available titles, given the elimination of physical shelf-space constraints (wide tail).
- Linked online applications enable interactivity, such as a Blu-ray feature allowing a "live" version, where you can watch a

movie along with the director, who is simultaneously commenting.

■ Kiosks, such as those operated by Redbox, have created a low-price rental option that, at least temporarily, has defied those predicting the death of physical rental. Will kiosks, to retain relevance, become digital, such that consumers can download video content to devices with a flash drive/USB connection (or even phone) by simply plugging in (or downstream by near-field wireless)?

■ Piracy concerns from file sharing are, similar to the theatrical market, leading to more front-loaded day-and-date releases and the compression of the video sales cycle.

CHAPTER 6

Television Distribution

272   The TV market is both a primary and secondary platform for content. Although TV is traditionally thought about in terms of TV series and other made-for-television productions, TV programming is a quilt that also relies heavily on other product. Accordingly, beyond analyzing first-run programming, to understand the entire economic picture it is also important to review how television garners revenues for films and other intellectual properties that can be aired on television but were not originally produced for television broadcast.

This chapter focuses on traditional television, namely free television (commonly referred to as free over-the-air broadcast television) and cable/pay television. New technologies, such as cable video-on-demand (VOD) and Internet/OTT streaming, are blurring the lines of what has historically been categorized as "television" (see Figure 6.1), and this blurring and the emerging new media platforms for TV programming are only touched upon here and then discussed in greater detail in Chapter 7. It is worth noting up front, however, that the very nature of what we perceive as "TV" is changing so rapidly that at the end of this century's first decade, the landscape has completely transformed from what existed just a few years ago. Simply look at the new points of access that already exist (see Figure 6.2).

Against this backdrop, there are evident challenges, including windowing, as well as forecasting whether and how fast new media revenue streams will mature. I asked Gary Marenzi, former president of

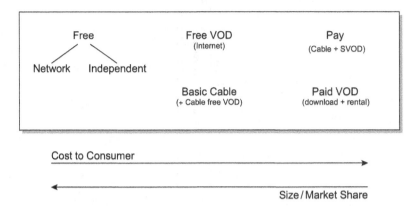

Figure 6.1 Types of Television

MGM Worldwide Television, as well as Paramount International Television, how he viewed this new landscape and how television distributors were adapting and tempering enthusiasm for new revenue streams versus the proven sources:

Digital/online-enabled platforms are becoming a major source of revenue for content providers, as more and more consumers (especially those under the age of 30) are utilizing their laptops, tablets, and smartphones as their primary sources of video content. This growth is obviously welcome and has helped to compensate for the decline in physical disc/DVD sales, but it requires the licensor to be extra vigilant in determining what rights are granted and for which exploitation windows. Obviously, licensors want to maximize their revenues from traditional sources like free television, so they'll protect these traditional windows against over-exposure by other media. But as media licensing opportunities continue to grow, the major content providers will stir up competition for pricier, exclusive windows regardless of the delivery configuration. The key for content providers is to maintain the value of their programming for every potential audience, so that priority will not change no matter how many new distribution options emerge.

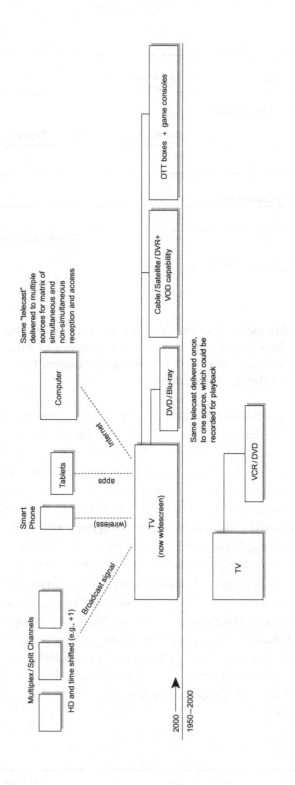

Figure 6.2 The Shifting TV Landscape

Table 6.1 Table of Broadcast Television Networks

Television Network	Founded	% of U.S. Households Reached	No. of Households Viewable	Type of Network	No. of Full-Power Affiliates	No. of Low-Power Affiliates and Transmitters
PBS	1969	99.00	105,579,120	Non-profit	349	342
ABC	1948	96.75	103,179,600	Commercial	229	266
NBC	1946	97.17	103,624,370	Commercial	226	338
CBS	1948	96.98	103,421,270	Commercial	215	299
Fox	1986	96.18	102,565,710	Commercial	203	202
The CW	September 18, 2006	96.18	102,565,710	Commercial	158 + 5 cable-only stations	11

Data from Wikipedia (http://en.wikipedia.org/wiki/List_of_United_States_over_the_air_television_networks). Excludes My Network TV.

Free Television (United States)

Free Television Market Segmentation

Free National Networks

The market is divided into terrestrial over-the-air national networks (NBC, CBS, ABC, Fox, and The CW) and cable or satellite-delivered television stations. Networks are somewhat complicated entities, however, in that a network is really a grouping of local television stations that are either owned by or affiliated with the parent network company. The FCC regulates station ownership to protect against the concentration of media ownership within markets, a construct that may become moot as market shares continue to erode and access to media from online and other sources becomes ubiquitous. There are several regulations, but the critical ones governing television station ownership are:

- National TV Ownership Rule: Prohibits an entity from owning television stations that would reach more than 39 percent of U.S. television households.
- Local TV Multiple Ownership Rule: Allows an entity to own two television stations in the same designated market area (DMA, as defined by Nielsen Media Research) provided threshold minimum of other stations in the market remain and at least one of the stations is not ranked among the four highest-ranked stations in the DMA.
- Dual TV Ownership Rule: Prohibits a merger between or among these four television networks: ABC, CBS, Fox, and NBC.[1]

Accordingly, the "big" networks are an aggregation of owned local TV broadcasters and affiliated stations, which cover all the major DMAs and reach nearly all the potential households in the United States (see Table 6.1). (Note: While reach has been relatively constant, it is interesting to note that services such as Nielsen have reduced their counts of TV households, a fact attributable to a census shift to the Web and evidence of cord-cutting (see Chapter 7); the reduction by Nielsen of households in 2011 was the first downsizing of total households by the ratings agency since 1990.[2])

The "network" only programs a certain amount of airtime for simulcast on a national basis, which generally includes the national news and a primetime schedule of three hours in the evening. In terms of original programming, this translates into around 22 hours per week (three hours Monday–Saturday, four hours Sunday, excepting Fox, which broadcasts an hour less in primetime). This is among the reasons why NBC's announcement at the end of 2008, amid the steep economic downturn, to eliminate original scripted programming in its 10:00 p.m. hour (EST/PST) was so dramatic (shifting a new Jay Leno talk show to its third primetime hour); this represented a shift of five hours out of 22, nearly a quarter reduction in original programming. (Note: The move, leading to a ratings decline, was generally considered disastrous and was quickly abandoned.)

The affiliates are generally obligated to run the network programming during these hours, but for the balance of the schedule they have a measure of flexibility whether or not to take the network-offered programming. The network actually markets and sells to its affiliates, trying to convince them to come on board for its slate. Economically, there are strong incentives to stay consistent with programming: the local affiliates gain the benefit of the brand (e.g., ABC or NBC), and the more shows it programs from the parent, the stronger and more consistent the brand. From the network's standpoint, it wants national coverage for its programming and will therefore incentivize the local stations to stay loyal to its slate.

Local Independent Stations

Alongside affiliate stations that make up a national network, there remain many local independent television stations. The recent disbanding of the WB and UPN (2006) for the new CW network freed up several local affiliates, creating a boon for the independent market, which for years had been in decline. In the 1980s and the early 1990s, there was a plethora of strong independents, fueling off-network syndication opportunities, but the growth of networks such as UPN, WB, and Fox gobbled up the prime independents and relegated much syndication to an afterthought following cable options.

Cable Networks

There are currently over 200 cable stations in the United States, with top-tiered channels bundled in "basic" carriage packages such that popular networks (e.g., Discovery Channel, ESPN, TNT, and USA) are provided in the overall fee charged to the consumer. This is distinguished from "premium cable," for which the consumer pays a direct incremental fee for access to specific premium channels such as HBO ("premium pay cable").

With the increased penetration of cable and satellite, many larger media companies have diversified programming by creating niche or specialized channels, and, as in the broadcast space, the independents have largely been consolidated. Examples of cable networks with national reach that are part of larger media groups include USA, Syfy, and Bravo (under the former NBC-affiliated family, and now all part of Comcast); Comedy Central, Nickelodeon, Spike, MTV (under the MTV Networks/Viacom family); CNN, TBS, TNT, TMC (under the Warners family); Fox Sports, FX (under the Fox/NewsCorp family); and ESPN, the Disney Channel, and the ABC Family (under the Disney umbrella). A good resource for television programming issues and for identifying a complete list of networks is the publication *Broadcasting & Cable* (see www.broadcastandcable.com, which lists upwards of 250 channels/networks). Beyond the pattern of large media producers developing or acquiring cable outlets for their content, it may be a new trend to see pure-play cable operators owning the cable networks carried over their pipe, in essence incubating their own viewers. Comcast, for example, before broadening its holdings with the acquisition of NBC Universal and its affiliated networks, was the parent to a variety of smaller services, including the Golf Channel, E! Entertainment, G4 (merged with the acquired Tech TV), and OLN (Outdoor Living Network, rebranded Fine

278 Living).

Free Video-on-Demand and Internet Access— What Does Free TV Mean?

It used to be that "TV was only TV," but with the advent of advertising-supported Internet access, such as offered by Hulu, and cable-free VOD (FVOD), the lines are blurring. In contracts, attorneys have to grapple with whether TV should be delineated by delivery mechanisms (e.g., analog, digital, free-over-the-air, terrestrial, satellite), and now dealmakers and attorneys alike need to categorize Internet streaming and other on-demand access. If a network such as NBC makes a show available for free Internet access on a non-NBC-branded site such as Hulu, or ABC makes a primetime show available via abc.com, or CBS makes its primetime series available for free viewing on cable free-on-demand, how should these be characterized?

As a consumer, you can access *Glee*, or *CSI* for no additional charge and watch the same programming with the same, or in most cases fewer, commercials. Because the start time for access is in the viewer's control (and the site even perhaps embedded into a personalized page on a social networking website), it is a form of VOD; moreover, because this VOD is not transaction-based (i.e., no direct fee to the viewer), but is advertising-supported, it is coming to be known as advertising-supported VOD (AVOD), a subset of FVOD. (Note: See Chapter 8 for more discussion on transactional VOD.) Whatever the label, free viewing at one's election is competitive with free viewing in accordance with a broadcaster's schedule.

Free TV is therefore becoming categorized not so much by where or how one watches, but whether the content is TV-branded and -produced ("premium content"). In the future, free TV will ultimately only mean programming broadcast on TV (or perhaps debuted or simultaneously launched on TV) in addition to being made available via other outlets, thus turning everything on its head. Today, we think of the other markets as emerging and competitive to TV, but if and when content is everywhere (and, by and large, the market is already close to this point), then free TV will become the limiting, not the defining factor, because unlike other platforms, broadcasters have retail-like limited shelf space: just compare 22 hours of primetime versus an infinite range of choice on-demand or via the Internet. The fact that a program at least was aired or launched on TV, or was produced for TV, may become the defining element of whether it falls within the notion of TV at all.

Metrics and Monetization Challenges

It is worth circling back to the discussion in Chapter 3 regarding the challenge of pricing advertising, and the difficulty of reconciling online versus offline pricing—in some ways, it is almost as mystifying as international currency conversions and trying to find equivalents, given many moving parts. The issue is important in the FVOD context because major cable operators are straddling the fence, pricing in one way now while looking to major growth and an upside if they can coax the ecosystem into capturing value via increased VOD viewing accompanied by dynamic ad insertion. U.S. cable giant Comcast is a good example. Speaking at a *Broadcast & Cable* summit, and noting that Comcast anticipates VOD advertising impressions on FVOD content to increase tenfold between summers 2012 and 2013, one of Comcast's executives noted: "We have 400 million monthly VOD views on Comcast. I'd love to have a dollar for every view."[3] FVOD revenue growth is enabled by dynamically inserting advertising into content called up by users, which makes the viewing experience feel more like live TV (as ads are not embedded in the content, creating the same repetitive loop each time a program is called). The catch is that the value of viewing those ads is still generally monetized via ratings, and captured within Nielsen Live+3 ratings windows; however, with dynamic advertising insertion and the ability to monitor by user, people are now starting to track data in different ways and looking at online impression metrics. The industry simply needs to rationalize and harmonize the systems, and once everyone can obtain consistent and reliable data from VOD sources (i.e., set-top boxes in terms of cable), then arguably different metrics than estimated (and aggregated) ratings ought to be used for valuing those VOD views.

This challenge was further highlighted in Chapter 3 when discussing the underpinnings of ratings, and the challenge of capturing downstream viewing from sources outside traditional TV, given the fast growth of watching via a myriad of devices, including game systems, tablets, and phones. Nielsen talks of the shift in "appointment viewing" whereby, historically, viewing and therefore ratings were grounded in capturing views at a particular place and time (with live sports being the prime example). However, they have asked the obvious question as to what happens when viewers can freely time-shift to when they want—how much viewing is taking place outside both the traditional metrics ("live") and then outside the "catch-up" window captured generally as Live+3 and at the outside as Live +7? Citing a new National People Meter Panel that is being trialed, Nielsen has reported findings that "just over five percent of viewing is happening in this beyond-7-day environment, with less than one percent for syndication. In fact, some of the top shows are adding up to an entire rating point in this expanded period."[4] My guess is that this 5 percent is well underreported because metrics have not been reliably developed to capture the plethora of devices where people are actually watching, and that the sampling is too dependent on traditional streams from DVRs, where catch-up started and is still most prevalent. The challenges are daunting in terms of harmonizing ratings and metrics, but no doubt more and more content is being consumed both off-TV and later (whether via one-off catch-up or emerging trends of binge viewing, whereby viewers will watch a series in marathon fashion). (See Chapter 7 for further discussion.)

Distribution Patterns and Windows: The Decline of Ratings for Theatrical Feature Films on TV and Evolution of the Market

Historical Window Patterns and New Technology Influence on Runs

The market for feature films on TV has historically been very strong, and for years a key sales benchmark was a license to one of the major national networks. In the best of scenarios, the market even provides four successive TV windows, allowing for millions of dollars continually flowing in for well over a decade:

- 12–18-month window on pay television (e.g., HBO, Showtime, Starz)
- 3–4-year window on network TV (e.g., NBC, ABC, CBS, Fox)
- multi-year window on cable TV
- multi-year window in syndication.

(Note: As discussed later, four windows today is extremely rare.)

Assuming this historical pattern, a theatrical feature film will typically be licensed to a broadcast network for debut approximately three years after its theatrical release. This allows an exclusive period for the theatrical run, followed by the primary video/cable VOD window and a pay TV license (see Figures 1.8 and 1.9 in Chapter 1). Up until the TV landscape shifted dramatically (see Figure 6.2), the "network window" was generally the most lucrative, as the networks simply had a larger reach and audience share, and could therefore pay more with the larger advertising revenues earned. To the extent value is allocated over runs, the initial airing would command the greatest value because audience ratings usually show a decline with each successive airing. Accordingly, network licenses are customarily for relatively short periods and limited numbers of runs, such as for three or four runs over three or four years. Depending on the film, the first run, if not all of the runs, will usually be in primetime.

The Internet and digital technology are complicating even this relatively simple construct, as the definition of a "run" (i.e., telecast) is transforming. If a broadcaster has a multiplex channel, such as NBC and NBC HD, are simulcasts on each only one run? What if there are time-delayed digital channels where the entire channel is shifted an hour or two (e.g., ITV + 1), thus expanding the hours programming is broadcast (Program X is on at 9:00 p.m. on Channel Y, and again at 10:00 p.m. on Channel Y + 1, with Y + 1 the exact feed/programming as Y, just shifted back an hour). Is the + 1 run considered part of the other run, or separate? And, finally, what about free streaming VOD repeats on cable or the Internet, where a show may be available for a limited time (sometimes referred to as a "catch-up") after the TV broadcast, allowing viewers to see the show if they missed it live or did not record it? Are catch-up runs separate runs, or is a run the live broadcast plus a week's catch-up access?

Setting the evolving and boggling matrix of the definition of a run aside, in certain instances, with exceptional films, the license may specify exact airing windows such as around a holiday period or in a cross-promotional window if the movie is tied to a larger franchise. This was

281

the case with Steven Spielberg's classic *E.T.*, where Sears sponsored the broadcasts and the film was licensed to play as a perennial on Thanksgiving. In the instance of a film series, such as *James Bond, Star Wars, Batman,* or *Spider-Man*, the license may be structured (or broadcasters may simply structure their schedules) so that airings take place around the promotional window for an upcoming new film in the franchise. Some believe that such an airing could detract from the theatrical release, but others ascribe to the theory that the TV broadcast helps cross-promote the film, and the film's marketing platform, in turn, helps cross-promote the TV broadcast.

Decline in Ratings for Films on TV

It is an acknowledged fact that ratings for films on TV have declined over time, and there are several factors frequently pointed to explaining the slide. Among these are the growth of DVD, the growth of other media options such as the Internet, fragmentation of the TV market with the growth of cable, waning tolerance for viewing films with commercial breaks, the ability to consume the film earlier via ancillary platforms such as VOD and PPV, the changing profile of network scheduling and programming (e.g., reality craze), and, of course, piracy.

It is no doubt also true that before the growth of the home video market, TV had a more dominating impact: there was a large audience that had never seen the movie, and no matter how big a film was at the theater, the reach of tens of millions of eyeballs on TV inevitably dwarfed the numbers that had physically seen the movie in cinemas. With movies selling in the millions across downloads, digital lockers, and DVDs, and the expansion of ancillary windows/access, including VOD, allowing earlier consumption, clearly prior exposure has contributed to the decline in ratings of films on TV. In the 1980s when a film played on television, this was its first and primary exposure after the movie theater; now, however, by the time a film is on free television years downstream from its theatrical release, there have been innumerable opportunities to "consume" the movie on a variety of platforms (and, regrettably, both illegally as well as legally).

Shared Windows, Shorter Network Licenses, and Clout of Cable

With the decline in network clout and the growth of cable channels, the traditional sequential TV windows are becoming more of an historical artifact. There are instances where films go to network, and then cable, and then syndication; however, it is now common for cable stations to

282

buy out network windows or to partner with networks on shared long-term windows with oscillating periods of exclusivity. The playing field is relatively level, and cable stations such as FX, USA/Syfy, TBS/TNT, Spike, Bravo, and the ABC family can compete with, and in cases are, the frontrunners to the networks, even in cases where the networks may be an affiliated sister company. Because the licensors are trying to garner the best deal for their specific film or package, the best option may cut across different studio lines and strange bedfellows can emerge.

Ranges of fees are tightly guarded, but Table 6.2 outlines several high-profile deals typical of the market's high end, and also illustrates how some films will share windows between cable and networks.

It is also worth highlighting that with the growing clout of cable, and especially in hybrid licenses where cable stations and networks may share runs, the licensed runs and period for networks are shrinking. Whereas it may have been typical to take three to four runs, scenarios now arise where a network may only take one or two runs.

Star Wars Example

I was personally involved in overseeing the licensing of the six *Star Wars* movies to TV. As of 2005, none of the films had aired on cable or syndication for several years, and *Episode III*, which was just launching in theaters, had obviously never been licensed to television. Given the unique nature of the saga, and knowing that there were no more sequel motion pictures planned for the future (at least that was the case at the time, before George Lucas turned the keys to the franchise over to Disney in his 2012 sale of Lucasfilm), it made sense to explore licensing all six films together. The highlight would be the television premiere of *Episode III*, supported with the first TV window for all of the films together. The final deal was made with Spike, at the time a relatively new cable network under the ownership of MTV Networks/Viacom, which catered to a male-skewing audience. Spike had rebranded itself as "the network for men," in contrast to women's branded networks such as Oxygen or Lifetime. The network had a variety of programming, but had been successful with franchise exploitation having been the home to the *James Bond* films. I cannot comment on the specifics of the deal, but it was significant, and *Variety* (without confirmation from either Lucasfilm or Spike) reported the package as being sold for $70 million.[5]

I relate this story not as a travelogue of deals past, but as an example of how interesting the TV market can be. At the outset of this deal, it probably would have been fair for analysts to speculate that the films would go to Fox, as historically movies of this stature would only debut on network; in fact, *Episode I* and *Episode II* had debuted on Fox. Cable

Table 6.2 Movie Licensing Fees

Film	Network	License Fee	Term	Source	Windowing/Notes
Spider-Man 2	FBC and FX	$50 million	10 years	HR, June 30, 2004; *Variety*, June 29, 2004	Rumored carve-outs for a second network window after first 3 years
King Kong	TNT and ABC	$26.5 million	8+ years	*Variety*, February 14, 2006	Noted $22 million TNT first 6 months + 50 months post ABC; ABC $4.5 million for three runs over three years following initial TNT exclusive window
Superman Returns	FX	$17–25 million		*Variety*, January 11, 2006	FX bought out window pre film's release in June 2006
Hitch	TBS	$25 million		*Variety*, January 30, 2007	
Avatar	FX	$25–30 million	6+ years	*Variety*, January 7, 2010	Standard windowing post HBO pay rights
The Hangover Part II	FX	$24 million		*Deadline*, May 31, 2011	Part of 13-title package

had grown to a point, however, and the market had changed substantially enough that *Episode III*, the film with by far the biggest box office of 2005 ($380 million in the U.S. and $848 million globally) and among the top box office films of all time (as of 2005, number seven of all time), was licensed to premiere on Spike.

There is no doubt this formerly network-dominated business had experienced a seismic shift when *The Lord of the Rings* premiered on TNT, *Star Wars* on Spike, and *Avatar* on FX. This is also a sign of healthy competition as the big four networks and cable channels jockey for positioning and programming.

Economics and Pattern of Licensing Feature Films for TV Broadcast

Films were historically licensed in large packages. The size of packages could vary dramatically, from a few films to hundreds—a traditional studio package of films would often include 25 or more films. A buyer would acquire all the titles for a "package price," with the titles having (usually) common numbers of runs and a common license period. There were always a couple of key lead titles, and buyers would be faced with the dilemma of potentially having to acquire a bunch of secondary titles simply to acquire the few titles they really wanted to program. With deals often going out several years, and with lots of airtime to fill up, this scheme satisfied buyers and sellers for years. The top pictures would be programmed in premiere slots, where premiums could be charged for commercial spots, and the other pictures could be used at off-peak times or even as filler. The art of valuing pictures within a multiple-picture package lies somewhere between absolute logic and litigation.

Packages are still common, but as buyers have become more selective, the number of pictures in those packages has shrunk, and the economics are more closely tied to true per-picture valuations.

So, how do you value a license?

Runs and Term

The most critical elements are the number of runs and term. There are certain industry-accepted benchmarks, and the jousting is then within these parameters. As noted previously, network television licenses are usually for a small number of runs such as three or four. This is largely due to the fact that, as earlier discussed, the definition of "network" accounts for those hours that are programmed by the network as opposed to given back to the affiliates; this inherent limitation puts a cap on inventory and programming space. A second limitation is that films are long—with commercial breaks, they take up a minimum of two hours of programming time, and can take up to three-hour blocks. Completing the matrix is the fact of diminishing returns: ratings typically decline with subsequent broadcasts, echoing the general TV pattern of higher ratings for new episodes/programs than for repeats.

Add up the factors of: (1) diminishing ratings with repeats; (2) limited inventory; and (3) requirement of large chunks of prime programming inventory space, and what you get is the need to space out broadcasts and cap runs. It does not really help to have the right to broadcast a film on network 10 times in three years because the network would never allocate that much space; the opportunity cost of foregoing a show that would likely draw higher ratings would force the network to omit runs. Moreover, for the licensor, if a film was played too frequently and the overexposure caused a severe dip in ratings, then the future value would be diminished. Everyone would lose.

The result is a mutual desire to manage runs in a way that maximizes ratings and returns. As a rule of thumb, playing a film on network, on average, more than once a year starts the downward spiral; accordingly, most network deals call for a couple of runs, and sometimes up to four, over a period of time that allows breathing room of, on average, at least a year between runs. A traditional network deal may therefore be structured as three or four runs over three or four years.

Cable licenses are more complicated, for there is more inventory space and the smaller audience share lends itself to more repeat viewings; cable, after all, grew up as a bastion for reruns, and only in recent years have cable networks invested substantially in original programming to differentiate themselves. The pattern in cable is more dependent on the niche and individual station philosophy, and some stations will literally play programming to death. What is typical across all groups is that the average number of runs is substantially higher—it is not unusual to see film deals with 10 or more runs of a title per year. This allows the cable network great flexibility in programming, and enables customized blocks, such as marathons, weeks focusing on subject matters, retrospectives, etc. The cable station is often branded as the "home of X," and for that to ring true it needs to appear enough to validate the identity. Airings once a year or so do not make sense, nor would there be (potentially) enough programming to fill up the schedule. As networks mature, they often realize that they have the same vested interest in not overexposing a property, and balance is ultimately struck.

It is important to note in this context that a run may not be what one expects of a single run; namely, before the layer of complexity created by Internet VOD or multiplexed channels, cable and pay TV required nuances on the notion of runs. A network run will be just as it sounds: a simultaneous broadcast aired by its network affiliates, run one time during the day. For cable, however, given the lower penetration and repeat programming as part of the landscape, runs may be defined similar to a pay television context with the use of exhibition days. An exhibition day is a 24-hour period (very specifically defined in a contract; for example, 12:00 a.m. until 11:59 p.m., and then within the box defined as an exhibition day there may be multiple runs granted). Accordingly, the cable broadcaster may have the right to broadcast a title two or perhaps even three times within that single day. Often, these runs are placed at unrelated times to fill up programming space, but in other instances there will be back-to-back runs (often marketed as an "encore" performance). The theory is that no viewer would watch the program twice in a day, and that the multiple start-time schedule will not undermine the value: after all, there are only so many exhibition days allowed. So long as the number of exhibition days is within customary bounds, and likewise the number of runs permitted within each such exhibition day is standard, then this practice is generally accepted.

287

Setting License Fees

It is only after sorting out the runs and years that it can then make relative sense to value the corresponding license fee. That is why it is so difficult to make direct comparisons on TV deals: the playing field is not level. It is not like dealing with DVD units, where there are bragging rights to absolute numbers (although this has its quirks, as discussed in Chapter 5, with performance influenced by pricing, returns, and inventory management) or the egalitarian barometer of box office. When you hear about a license value for a TV deal, it has to be put in context of how many runs, how many years, and if it was a stand-alone or an allocation of some sort was involved (now only imagine the complications wrought by trying to factor in online catch-up). Moreover, in a world of relationships and horse-trading, there may be political or timing elements that could further influence values.

Stripping out these other considerations, and looking purely at the underlying economics, the principles of valuing the license fee then becomes straightforward. The licensor will look to competitive product or historical licenses to set a range, and the licensee broadcaster will be running numbers on potential advertising revenues. The deal can thus be looked at on a macro level in terms of the gross fee, and then also be validated bottom-up by analyzing on a per-run basis (either straight-lining license fees per run or imputing a certain discount after a certain number of runs). At some level, this can be overanalyzed, because a buyer and seller will be negotiating here in a classic fashion trying to find common ground. Are you going to agree to $50,000 per run or not?

To gauge whether $50,000 per run is fair value, if one side perceives there is too much of a gulf and they cannot agree on terms, then the negotiation may take on factors that apportion risk. This often takes two forms. First, a licensor may agree to a percentage of barter, such as a deal that is part cash and part barter. In this scenario, a certain minimum guaranty is locked in for security, and the balance is tied to the ad sales. This is a cumbersome direction, for it requires being in the loop on the ad sales front, as well as the determination and cost of potentially auditing the revenues. Another, frankly easier path may be tying overages or underages to ratings performance. If the fees are ultimately tied to a certain expectation level, then tying a bonus to over-performing should protect both sides; the licensor will win by protecting an upside, and the broadcaster can easily afford the upside if they have earned a premium on the ad sales. Both of these scenarios significantly complicate a deal from a reporting, managing, and trust perspective.

288   Another method of valuation is simply to quote an industry-accepted range. On hit films, it was sometimes quoted as a "rule of thumb" that the license fee should be in the range of 10–15 percent of domestic box office; however, this percentage cannot be relied upon as an accurate benchmark, and to the extent there is a benchmark range, it tends to move over time. In the case of *Superman Returns*, for example, *Variety* said of FX: "The network has agreed to pay Warner Bros. Domestic Cable about 12 percent of the eventual domestic gross, with a cap at between $17 million and $25 million, depending on the contract's length of term and on whether Warners finds another buyer to share the window with FX." Although an older example, in reporting a license for *War of the Worlds*, *Variety* referenced this barometer in the context of a reputed $25 million fee:

That's a much lower stipend than the 15 percent of domestic box office, which used to be the benchmark for a successful theatrical-movie deal in the network window. But times have changed. Since *War of the Worlds* has grossed more than $230 million domestically, 15 percent would come to $34.5 million—an impossible figure for distributor DreamWorks to draw in a sluggish broadcast and cable marketplace for theatricals. . . . Bowing to the new reality, distributors have put a cap on the total license fee, which can start as low as $22 million and rise to as high as $27 million a title, unless the buyer gets more runs and a longer exclusive license term.[6]

Further indicating that there is likely an artificial ceiling in the market, *Broadcasting & Cable* magazine, in describing how FX was recently dominating the market, acquiring 28 of the top 50 box office titles in 2011 (including *Mission: Impossible – Ghost Protocol* and *The Girl with the Dragon Tattoo* as part of a $100 million 19-film deal), noted in the context of a further acquisition of *21 Jump Street* and *The Lorax* that: "Basic cable networks tend to pay 8 percent to 12 percent of domestic box office for premiere rights to theatricals."[7]

A final twist is licensing titles across channels within a larger group. If a particular film has crossover demographic appeal, together with a strong enough brand identity, then there may be a desire to play the title across multiple group-affiliated networks. This obviously adds another wrinkle to the analysis and value for runs. Moreover, this is an area where analysis paralysis can loom, and from a macro point of view many will simply split this into network versus cable; namely, how many aggregated cable runs are required across various cable outlets. It may be that certain discounts are taken, or that certain outlets are either ignored (given limited reach) or excluded on grounds of fit ("I do not want X on Y!"). The primary impact of aggregating potential licensees is that the fee will usually increase, given the greater exposure, and the time of the license will also be lengthened to allow for the title to be cycled through the different outlets without over-saturating exposure both on a single outlet and across the group. While it was only the syndication market that traditionally had very long licenses, one may now see 10-year licenses in this context.

First-Run TV Series

First-run TV series tend to follow a regular cycle of development and launch tied to network seasons. Although the growth of cable, including powerful pay networks such as HBO, have altered this, and some networks have gone to a year-round launch calendar, most network shows debut in the fall and are committed to following screenings of pilots in the spring.

Pitch Season and Timing

Pitch season is traditionally in the fall. The new network season has launched and, within a short span (in many cases, within the first two to three episodes), the broadcasters are already starting to evaluate which new shows will survive and whether to consider mid-season replacements.

After scheduling pitches ("pitch season"), the networks will then decide which ideas to green-light for a script, with the network's approval of the writer. The script will then be written later in the fourth quarter so the script would be ready to take to pilot in the new year. There is a brutal winnowing down of material, and only a small percentage of pitches are commissioned for scripts, and an even smaller percentage of scripts are then produced as pilots. The ratio can vary dramatically from company to company, with the economic incentive to maximize the percentage of pilots made from scripts commissioned. The Museum of Broadcasting once pegged the ratios as follows: "few scripts are commissioned, and fewer still lead to the production of a pilot—estimates suggest that out of 300 pitches, approximately 50 scripts are commissioned, and of those, only 6 to 10 lead to the production of a pilot."[8]

Pilots

290 Although expensive to produce, as discussed in Chapter 3, pilots are an efficient means to test a concept and evaluate a show before committing to a full series. To a degree, this solves the problem faced by theatrical films, and inherent in experience goods, of having to complete the movie before it can be screened and tested; theoretically, a pilot dramatically decreases the risk on a per-property basis because there is enough information to make an informed decision, yet the show is not so far along that it is too late to make changes.

Because pilots are the guinea pigs of a series, experimenting with location, premise, cast, timing, etc., they tend to be significantly more expensive than later episodes. Once a show finds its rhythm, it should become more efficient to produce (but for escalating talent costs), as episodes are produced in volume, and upfront costs of sets, costumes, and infrastructure can be amortized over the run of series. Although the amounts are now dated, the Museum of Broadcasting noted the following regarding costs and the risks at stake: "In the early 1990s the average cost for a half-hour pilot ranged from $500,000 to $700,000, and hour-long pilot programs cost as much as $2 million if a show had extensive effects."[9] Today, the cost of pilots is a multiple of those figures. In looking at the 2009–2010 pilot season, the *Hollywood Reporter* noted that with the downturn in the economy, the average cost of drama pilots had dropped to $5–5.5 million from a high of $6–6.5 million in 2008.[10]

Pickups and Screening for International Networks

The "network cycle" continues in the second quarter of the new year as network executives tinker with and test pilots with focus groups. By spring, decisions need to be made, and the networks elect which shows they will commission for their fall lineup. The timing is dictated by the "upfronts" (see more detailed discussion later, as well as discussion of emerging digital upfronts in Chapter 7), where the networks put on a dog and pony show for advertisers, unveiling their primetime lineups and securing large upfront buys for the bulk of the season's airtime. Virtually as soon as the lineups are locked, the networks host screenings for international buyers; the "LA Screenings" occur toward the end of May following the network upfronts and comprise a week when international networks cycle through all the new offerings. The LA Screenings have evolved into a significant market, given the growing importance of global license fees and the need for key broadcasters to launch series on a nearly simultaneous basis to avoid devaluation from piracy and potential early online glimpses.

(Note: There are other forms of first-run programming, such as TV movies and miniseries, both of which have generally fallen out of favor given costs and general programming economics (TV movies, for example, are now more common on cable networks, such as Lifetime, that can both match programming to specific demographics and heavily promote and rebroadcast the programs given their 24/7 control of airtime and limited original offerings). Given that these formats have become relatively niche programming, I will not address here, but simply point them out as another factor in market segmentation, as described in Chapter 1.)

Syndication Window and Barter

Syndication versus Network Coverage and Timing

Syndication used to be the Holy Grail for TV: once a program reached a certain number of episodes, it could be sold into syndication for fees that can dwarf initial licensing revenues, turning a deficit into profits. The traditional magic number for syndication is 65 episodes. This allows a station to run a program five days per week ("stripping") for 13 weeks, corresponding to half of a network season (e.g., September–December); with repeats, this quantity provides adequate episodes to run a series daily throughout the entire broadcast year. Although this can still be true, the market has shifted dramatically from the 1980s and 1990s, when

Table 6.3 Ratings and Coverage of Syndicated Shows (2006)

Program	Stations/ % Coverage	Ratings— AA %
Wheel of Fortune	488/98	9.2
Oprah Winfrey	521/99	7.6
Jeopardy	464/98	7.2
Dr. Phil	523/99	5.6
Entertainment Tonight	484/99	5.6
Judge Judy	473/97	4.8
Seinfeld	408/99	4.7
Friends	404/99	3.9

Variety, December 18–24, 2006; AA average refers to non-duplicated viewing for multiple airings of the same show.

syndication was king. This is due to a number of factors: the elimination of the fin/syn rules (see the section "Impact of Elimination of Fin/Syn Rules and Growth of Cable" later in this chapter for discussion), the growth of cable stations acquiring programming that used to be the staple of syndication, and the shrinking number of potential syndication buyers overall (by network groups such as Fox and the WB, now part of CW, aggregating stations and taking key independents off the market).

Before discussing these forces and the evolution of the market further, however, it is useful to clearly define syndication. Simply, syndication means licensing a program into the individual markets on a one-by-one basis. There are over 400 markets in the United States, and syndicators maintain dedicated sales forces to sell programming into individual stations. Table 6.3 illustrates a matrix of top-ranked syndicated shows, coverage achieved, and their ratings.

As discussed earlier, stations are either owned, affiliated, or independent; even affiliated stations have programming flexibility and only take a certain percentage of programs from their affiliated parent groups, thus having residual program slots to acquire other programming offered by the network (such as branded late-night shows or morning talk shows) or unaffiliated third parties. When all the network affiliates broadcast a program together, it reaches 95 percent or more of the potential TV households, thus creating the unique convergence of saturation market coverage and simultaneous broadcast. This is a cumbersome way, in essence, to stay live.

In contrast, syndication is the broadcast of the same program over non-affiliated stations at times programmed by the individual stations. Accordingly, it is possible in syndication to achieve the same market coverage and the same amount of time on the air. The profound difference is in missing that intersection of simultaneous broadcasts with full market coverage. This pseudo-live nature of a network broadcast is what makes it so powerful: the network can reach an enormous number of people with the same programming at the same time. This cross section allows for targeted marketing and scheduling, which in turn allows for targeted advertising. Despite the explosion of new media options, there is still no better way to reach a population of over 250 million people. Broadcasters know that a certain percentage of X demographic will watch the nightly news at 6:00 p.m. versus Y demographic for a sitcom in primetime. And the game is all about that sole fact: how many eyeballs of which type (here, young versus old, male versus female, kid versus adult) will see the program.

Syndication, in contrast, is still about drawing eyeballs, but the task can be more challenging when the promotion is solely at a local level.

There is no absolute magic threshold for coverage, but there is a certain quantum of coverage that rises to the level of "significant." That benchmark is usually in the 70 percent or more range. The composition of the coverage is often a hodgepodge of stations. It could mean an ABC affiliate in Denver and Dallas, a Fox affiliate in Los Angeles, and independent stations in Kansas City and Seattle. There are sometimes certain station groupings, such as the former "WB 100," that may license together, which can achieve a chunk of coverage in one deal.

Achieving a certain quantity threshold of coverage is critical for attracting advertisers, as many will not consider a program that does not hit an internal mandated coverage threshold (e.g., 80 percent of nationwide coverage). Beyond the absolute percentage, however, advertisers will look at both the quality of stations and the programming time. For a national buy, there will usually need to be a significant number of top stations in key markets. If, for example, there are no network-affiliated stations carrying the program in the top 10 markets (e.g., no network affiliates in Los Angeles, New York, Chicago), then it is obviously a hard sell. Sometimes this can be overcome with a strong enough station grouping, such as a percentage of Fox- or ABC-affiliated stations.

Because the syndication quilt will not achieve simultaneous broadcasts, advertisers will also be keenly interested in the time slots. It may be great to have a Chicago station, but if it is a CW station broadcasting a kids' show at 5:00 a.m., then the value is clearly very different than

293

had it been an ABC affiliate at 8:00 a.m. It is because of this particular challenge of trying to aggregate and secure advertising commitments across unaffiliated stations in less than full market coverage with non-synchronized broadcast times that anyone in this business needs a good advertising–sales team. The nature of the beast is such that it may be difficult or impossible to secure a national spot/advertiser, and that advertising needs to be sold on a market-by-market, broadcast-slot-by-broadcast-slot basis. Because syndicators may air a program more than once a week, the matrix of total telecasts becomes quite complicated to manage. (Note: See also Chapters 3 and 7 regarding the challenge of pricing fragmented online/Internet viewing, as akin to a form of national or global syndication, whereas traditional TV syndication sells advertising locally.)

Barter as a Solution to Fragmented Sales and Airings

Making this task of selling ads even harder is the speculative nature of viewership. Because of the fragmented placement, marketing can only be committed at the local level, and ratings are only meaningful within the discreet local market. Accordingly, what has emerged is a barter market.

The term barter syndication is often used in this context, and means a sharing of the advertising time. If a 22-minute program is shown in a 30-minute block, that may leave approximately seven minutes of advertising space to sell (excluding time reserved for station promos). The licensor of the program may "own" all or part of this time, and is betting on the fact that he or she can sell the space for better terms than he or she would otherwise receive for licensing the program outright. This is also a mechanism for the station to hedge its bets and lower program acquisition cost. It may be better for a station to pay $1,000 rather than $3,000 for a program and cede some advertising time to lower its costs.

In this instance, the station is obviously betting on a couple of factors. First, it is assuming that the value the licensor will achieve from selling the advertising inventory is less than the discount the station has granted. Second, the station is assuming that there is residual value/benefit to having the programming; it draws viewers to the station generally in the time period, viewers are not going to a competitor, and viewers may stay tuned in for other programming because of coming in the first place.

There are even instances of full barter, where the station pays nothing and the licensor achieves any and all financial benefit from selling the space it retains. In this situation, the station may reserve some spots and have a pure upside from selling inventory against no-cost basis.

Of course, there are always opportunity costs, and the buyer needs to value whether another program would create greater ultimate value.

As a result of the complexity and difficulty of clearing markets, and then selling advertising across a scattered broadcast pattern, specialist distributors have evolved. Two of the powerhouses in this space, for example, have been King World (now merged with CBS) and Tribune; additionally, given the scale, companies will sometimes further partner with other specialists, as was the case of syndicating *South Park*, where one company was responsible for market clearances and another for the ad sales.

Barter to the Extreme—Paying for Blocks of Airspace

The ultimate barter arrangement is the full auctioning off of airspace. This tends to occur in a couple of niche areas, such as certain children's programming.

A prime example of this practice was 4Kids Entertainment's arrangement with Fox. When Fox Family was sold to Disney, Fox opted to shutter its Saturday-morning Fox Kids animation block and instead lease the space. It struck a deal with 4Kids, the company that represented the merchandise licensing rights to *Pokémon* (and certain non-Asian TV rights to both *Pokémon* and *Yu-Gi-Oh!*), where 4Kids paid Fox $25 million per year for the airtime; 4Kids then sold the commercial space within its half-hour block and was betting that either its annual advertising revenue would exceed the $25 million, or if it ran a deficit its merchandising sales would take it into profits. In essence, the company rented the commercial space, viewing the broadcasts as a giant commercial for the brand that would then drive non-TV revenue. Perhaps only in children's programming, where robust merchandising programs may be a primary goal, can a producer set a strategy to use the show itself as a loss-leader to drive ancillary revenues. (See Chapter 8 for additional discussion of this 4Kids–Fox deal.)

Infomercials are another area where one sees negative license fees and full purchase of airspace. Here, a company is renting the airtime for a giant commercial. This presents even tougher economics than the 4Kids example, because an infomercial is not selling advertising against the airtime, and therefore needs to recoup 100 percent of the lease costs against product sales. At least in the 4Kids instance, there is the goal for advertising to recoup the rental costs, with the deficit in the worst case merely a fraction of the overall lease costs. For this reason, infomercials tend to air during inexpensive slots, because costs would become prohibitive during prime airtime.

295

First-Run Syndication and Off-Network Syndication

First-run syndication means programming produced for initial broadcast in the syndication market. These programs are often daily, unscripted shows such as talk or game shows (e.g., the original *Oprah Winfrey* show, *Wheel of Fortune*, *Entertainment Tonight*). In the 1980s, there was an upswing in the number of dramas that succeeded in syndication, with spin-off *Star Trek* series (*Star Trek: The Next Generation* and *Star Trek: Deep Space Nine*) and *Baywatch* pacing the market. (Note: *Baywatch* was an interesting case because it aired initially on NBC and was cancelled, but then continued with new episodes in syndication.) The nature of first-run syndication shows also leads to longevity not seen in other programming—two of the most successful syndicated shows have been *Wheel of Fortune* and *Jeopardy*; both premiered in the early 1980s and have been running for roughly 25 years.

In contrast to first-run syndication, off-network syndication refers to the playing of reruns of hit shows after they have finished their network runs (or in the case of multiple completed seasons for long running series). This captures the category of when shows such as *Seinfeld*, *The Simpsons*, and *The Cosby Show* are syndicated to independent stations. As earlier noted, it is only the most successful of shows, those that reach more than 65 episodes, and more frequently crest 100 episodes, that have the awareness and stature to succeed in this market. Achieving this status, however, is the ultimate mark of success, and is where TV shows have their true upsides.

One of the most famous examples was *The Cosby Show*, which led the networks ratings race in the 1980s, and in the 1986 network season had a record 34.9 rating on NBC (representing 63 million viewers at the time) *Time* magazine noted: "The show's success has created its own bonanza on the syndication market: *The Cosby Show* reruns, currently being sold to local stations, have earned a record-smashing $600 million, and the total could eventually top $1 billion ..."[11] This is the Holy Grail of television, and the success of *The Cosby Show* paved the way for its producer, the Carsey-Werner Company, to become one of the most successful independents in TV history: "Another hit show of the 1980s for Carsey-Werner was *The Cosby Show* spin-off *A Different World*, which aired on NBC beginning in 1987. The following season, 1988–1989, the company would accomplish the unprecedented feat of producing the year's three highest rated shows: *The Cosby Show* at number one, followed by *Roseanne* and *A Different World*."[12]

(Note: As an interesting footnote, the wealth created here allowed Marcy Carsey to partner with Oprah Winfrey and Geraldine Leybourne (former Disney and Nickelodeon executive) to found the Oxygen network, and Tom Werner was part of the group that purchased controlling interest in the Boston Red Sox baseball team.)

Aftermarket sales continue to be the lifeblood of television success today. The key market change is that whereas cable networks were originally simply competing with syndication for top programming, they are now the leading buyers. *The Sopranos* set a record, with an estimated $2.5 million per-episode license fee from A&E for an exclusive run off of pay TV (HBO). A few other examples, some also with fees greater than $2 million per episode, include: (1) *Sex and the City* to TBS for an estimated $700,000 per episode;[13] (2) *The Office* to TBS and Fox-owned and -operated affiliates for $950,000 per episode ($650,000 per episode for TBS);[14] (3) *Law & Order: Criminal Intent* to USA/Bravo for just under $2 million per episode; (4) *The Mentalist* for approximately $2.2 million per episode to TNT; (5) *NCIS: Los Angeles* for approximately $2.2 million per episode to USA;[15] (6) *Hawaii Five-O* for approximately $2.1–2.5 million to TNT;[16] and (7) *The Big Bang Theory* for $1.5 million per episode to TBS.[17] What is interesting in the foregoing *NCIS: Los Angeles* example is that this sale was achieved during the first year of the series, long before there were enough episodes to be "stripped" into typical syndication. This type of move, while unusual, is not unprecedented, as strong brands with spin-off series have similarly managed sales during their first seasons (e.g., *CSI: Miami* and *CSI: New York*, respectively to A&E for $1 million per episode and to Spike TV for $1.9 million per episode).[18]

Online Services Now Changing the Dynamics

It was inevitable, with the growth of streaming services such as Hulu and Netflix becoming leading gateways for both on-demand and secondary viewings (and thus akin to new types of networks), that Internet-delivered services would start to compete with cable for programming in the off-network/syndication window. In 2013, CBS hit series *The Good Wife* was sold in a complex window for what was estimated to be $2 million per episode in what I can best describe as a "syndication-plus" license window. The show was sold to Amazon, Hulu, the Hallmark Channel, and basic syndication, in a divvying up that allows certain seasons to be accessed via Amazon Prime (commencing March 2013) Hulu Plus to offer seasons on its subscription service (commencing September 2013), the Hallmark Channel to air episodes on basic cable (starting in January 2014), and weekend broadcast syndication airings being sold in (for fall 2014 debut).[19] The deal also has marketing implications, with availability on online services viewed as a potential catalyst for bringing in new viewers to current episodes. Deadline noted: "The rationale is that binge-viewing customers are so accustomed to such platforms, as evidenced by *Breaking Bad* on Netflix, it would send new viewers to *The Good Wife*'s original telecasts on CBS the way it happened with *Breaking Bad* on AMC, which has been sizzling since the series' previous seasons became available for streaming."[20]

(See Chapter 7 for further discussion of online streaming services such as Netflix and Hulu impacting television programming.)

Online's "Short Tail" versus "Long Tail" and Impact on Syndication

The ability via the Internet to monetize the long-tail value of content sometimes leads people to assume that the long tail creates incremental revenue; however, that may only be true if there is no additional upfront exposure or what I will refer to as the "wide tail" (or the platypus effect discussed in Chapter 1). The increased access points for TV programming and the ability to easily see a show you missed via free Internet, cable VOD, and expanded video and over-the-top VOD offerings (e.g., Netflix, Amazon) leads to such front-loaded exposure that downstream values are inevitably poised to drop. This is due to multiple factors, including fewer viewers who are watching a show for the first time in a long-tail window and less repeat consumption with greater access to more new programming in the wide tail. In my first edition, I noted we were already seeing the impact on pricing and revenues, and further predicted that the overall pie would shrink if the nonexclusive value of the wide tail did not equal the prior exclusive value of the long tail. I asked long-term industry veteran and president of Fox TV International, Marion Edwards, about the new TV landscape and whether she sees the pie expanding from Hulu-type services or whether easy access is serving to undermine pricing for reruns. She noted:

There is no doubt that the world of "free on-demand" (FOD), now primarily referred to as AVOD (advertiser-supported video-on-demand), as well as SVOD (subscription video-on-demand) viewing, whether accessed on a network-branded website, or on OTT services such as Hulu, Netflix, Amazon, or any number of smaller local services, all delivered via various platforms to the ever-growing number of devices, is having a major impact on the traditional revenue streams associated with the distribution business. The obvious upside is that, in the AVOD model, these services give the advertisers "unskippable" ads (which makes those ads more valuable), the networks have found a new way to allow viewers to "catch up" with shows they may have missed, and the viewers can watch programs when and where they choose. The SVOD model allows for consumer consumption of entire series (binge viewing) quickly after the first network run had ended and has pumped important revenue into the distribution stream.

The distributor, however, has the challenge of trying to make the program seem fresh and unique in a world where it has become ubiquitous, and to be mindful of the home entertainment value when consumers are very aware that programming is available for *free* quickly after telecast, and soon after first run on SVOD services. In addition, the new ask from broadcasters is to allow downloading for some period of time, instead of the streaming rights currently granted. We are already seeing the impact on the long-term value of TV programs in terms of relicense in the traditional aftermarkets. The emergence of digital terrestrial television channels as consumers of "library" series has helped retain value, but has not replaced the value of network relicense. How the overall economic model continues to evolve remains to be seen.

Impact of Elimination of Fin/Syn Rules and Growth of Cable

The huge off-network syndication revenues earned by producers such as Carsey-Warner were among the reasons that broadcast networks started to lobby against the elimination of the financial interest and syndication rules (fin/syn rules). Summarizing the history, the Museum of Broadcast Communications notes:

The Federal Communications Commission (FCC) implemented the rules in 1970, attempting to increase programming diversity and limit the market control of the three broadcast television networks. The rules prohibited network participation in two related arenas: the financial interest of the television programs they aired beyond first-run exhibition, and the creation of in-house syndication arms, especially in the domestic market. Consent decrees executed by the Justice Department in 1977 solidified the rules, and limited the amount of primetime programming the networks could produce themselves.[21]

These rules were contested for years, with producers favoring fin/syn fighting the networks, and were eventually relaxed and then fully eliminated in 1995. One of the reasons for the elimination was a belief that media competition, including from the growth of the cable market, had weakened the networks' prior dominance and that therefore the protections were no longer needed. This was true, to a degree. The combined TV market share for ABC/CBS/NBC in the time of the rules' promulgation in the 1970s bordered 90 percent, but 20 years later in the mid 1990s the share had dropped into the middle 60 percent. Nevertheless, the fear of vertical integration by major media groups, and the difficulty for smaller producers to deficit finance series in the hope of hits that would pay for misses, remains a challenging reality for independent producers who want to keep the back-end/upside in their productions. How easy do you think it is today for an independent producer to land a show on NBC and maintain ownership in the back-end syndication revenues that could lead to the type of upside reaped by Carsey-Werner on *The Cosby Show*?

Virtually any producer will lament that the result of changes in the fin/syn rules has been to shift leverage to buyers/networks. I asked Ned Nalle, former president of Universal Worldwide Television and executive producer of various series (e.g., *Legend of the Seeker* for ABC Studios, along with Sam Raimi, director of the *Spider-Man* films), if he agreed with this trend. He noted:

Mergers and relaxation of financial interest regulations have led to market concentration. Putting aside whether the quality of the content has improved, deteriorated, or stayed the same since the market contracted, it nevertheless means less competition among buyers for content. That means the leverage pendulum has moved decidedly over to the buyer, and away from the seller. It also seems to excuse that, absent more competitors breathing down his or her neck, a buyer can and will take more time to make a decision. The buyer will also exact more rights away from suppliers. It doesn't mean that worthy shows won't get ordered, and eventually be on the air. But shows may be commissioned for financial-interest reasons as much as creative or ratings merits. As the gatekeeper, a network can demand anything from an anxious producer, including distribution rights, financial interest, negative covenants, sequels, spin-offs, and certain protection before a producer might migrate a hit series to a network rival.

Basic Economics of TV Series

The TV business has always been one of deficits; namely, the license fees for a show rarely cover the cost of production, and the resulting deficit is hopefully made up in off-network syndication sales or other revenue streams such as DVD. This holds as true today as when the fin/syn rules were in force and Carsey-Warner was in its heyday. (Note: At that time, it cost approximately $500,000 per episode to make a standard half-hour comedy, which would typically run at a deficit of $100,000–200,000.)[22] The only difference today is that the gulf has grown, with the cost of production generally rising more than corresponding license fees. This is not surprising, given the erosion of network market shares and in the increased competitive environment.

The macro picture is therefore similar to the motion picture business, **301** where hits pay for misses, and success is based on a portfolio strategy. The buffer that has sustained the TV business recently is the expansion of additional revenue streams. In the children's area, as described before in the 4Kids example, merchandising opportunities are sought after to recoup a deficit. With respect to live action, the growth of the DVD market for television series, now augmented by online and portable revenues, such as downloads to tablets, VOD access via cable, and OTT services, has created an additional buffer to projected deficits following initial broadcast license fees. The *New York Times*, in part quoting 20th Century Fox Television co-president Dana Walden, analyzed how hit show *24* would likely not have been made absent DVD revenues:

. . . the costs of producing a drama like *24* had become so prohibitive that it probably could not be made today without the DVD sales. Though the studio would not release exact figures, each of the series' 120 episodes has cost just under $2.5 million to make, for a total of about $300 million. Licensing fees from the Fox Network are not believed to have exceeded $1.3 million an episode, for a total of no more than about $156 million. The rights to broadcast the series internationally have probably been sold for

$1 million or more an episode, for a total of at least $120 million. All told, that revenue—about $276 million—has not been sufficient to eliminate the deficit and provide a profit. DVD sales, however, have.

"The DVD opportunity on this series has enabled us to produce the show that is on the air," Ms. Walden said.[23]

This interdependency is the reason that the decline in certain sectors, such as the DVD market, has such a ripple effect. If DVD revenues materially decline (as they have), and revenues from new access points (e.g., downloads, VOD, and subscription rentals) are less than sub-stitutional for the drops in the markets previously essential for overall financing, then how is expensive-to-produce premium product to be funded? This is the question of the day, and why the economic interplay of Ulin's Rule can paint a frightening picture. This continuum also lies at the heart of the fight against piracy; while some fight against strengthening rules and enforcement, conjuring up the spectre of a regulated Web undermining free speech and access, the flip side is that if piracy goes unchecked and consumers can gain access to shows for free that are, in fact, supposed to be paid for, then the financing walls buttressing production come down and the quality of content tumbles with them. I know almost no TV or film executive that would disagree with this analysis, which is why it becomes all the more frustrating for studios and networks when laws designed, at their root, to address this problem are thwarted because of political movements grounded in free expression. The sad fact is that the same media executives believe fiercely in the same free expression, but somehow the message has become distorted and those that are actually allies have failed at cogently expressing common ground and outlining appropriate boundaries (see also discussion in Chapter 2).

Cable's Advantage and Move into Original Programming

The risk profile of a series is directly proportional to the number of likely revenue sources for recoupment. As discussed in Chapter 3, cable networks can theoretically take greater risks than the broadcast networks because they have a dual-revenue stream from cable subscriber fees and advertising. The cable fees are guaranteed, and create a production funding pool insulating a particular series from the direct impact of advertising revenue; the subscriber fees are tied to the overall network and brand, such that a hit series can help drive brand value, but a one-off failure will not change the underlying economics (other than, of

302

course, the impact on advertising for that show). This is one reason that cable networks are starting to offer more and more original programming: a hit or group of hits can help increase the brand value of the network and differentiate it to a greater extent than reruns. Accordingly, a series on a cable network can now draw from: (1) advertising dollars; (2) an allocation from cable subscriber fees paid to the network overall; (3) DVD revenues from box sets of seasons; and (4) emerging revenue streams, such as OTT rentals, subscription VOD, and EST downloads, to a growing array of tablets and other portable devices. A network series benefits from all of these sources except for the cable subscriber fees; however, that element alone can be so significant that the cable network can afford to take different risks and accept a lower audience rating.

The success of original cable series, as opposed to original series in syndication (e.g., *Star Trek*) has recently created an almost renaissance of original programming. The ability for non-networks to produce hit original series was proven by HBO, with hits such as *Sex and the City* and *The Sopranos*. Soon, non-pay channels realized they could enter the market as well, and the following is a snapshot of a few of the shows evidencing the trend of cable networks to develop their own franchises (of course, this had long been the trend with kids' channels such as Nickelodeon with *Jimmy Neutron*, etc.):

303

- USA: *Psych, Burn Notice, Suits, White Collar*
- TNT: *The Closer, Leverage, Franklin & Bash*
- F/X: *Sons Of Anarchy, It's Always Sunny in Philadelphia, Rescue Me*
- AMC: *Mad Men, Breaking Bad, The Walking Dead*
- Syfy: *Ghost Hunters, Eureka*
- Lifetime: *Army Wives, The Client List*
- A&E: *Dog the Bounty Hunter, Storage Wars*
- Disney Channel: *Hannah Montana, Good Luck Charlie*

In some cases, the show's ratings have been extremely competitive, with TNT's *The Closer* scoring network primetime-like numbers in a few instances (especially with season premieres). From dabbling, cable networks started to gain confidence in their ability to launch original series and began to leverage two inherent competitive advantages. First, cable stations could counter-program and start seasons in periods when the networks showed reruns. USA and TNT, for example, routinely air new episodes of series in the summer, enticing viewers who preferred new episodes to network reruns or replacements. Second, because cable stations program a full day, as opposed to a network that has limited primetime hours and must share promotional time with affiliates, the cable networks can cross-promote new shows literally nonstop; further, because they may only have a couple of original series, the promotion can reach channel saturation, optimizing marketing support to help shows break through the clutter. Accordingly, the cable networks tend to program their originals in sequence, rather than as a lineup, thereby maximizing promotion and always having something new (e.g., F/X will plug its fall original during its summer original series).

The issue now may become whether the market can absorb all these shows. As the market has matured, it may be, as *Variety* noted, that everyone needs to run faster just to stay in place:

The one-time vast wasteland of cable networks filled with repeats and wrestling has been replaced by a world in which even networks as small as Sundance Channel are producing quality first-run fare. No longer a band of misfits, basic cable's top nets are spending more money on original fare and making more noise with marketing—yet they aren't seeing their numbers grow. They're having to do more just to maintain the status quo.[24]

A Golden Age for TV?

The strength of quality content, however, has somewhat disproven this flattening hypothesis, as there are significant examples of cable shows lifting the entire network. *Mad Men* on AMC, basic cable's only winner of the Emmy for Outstanding Drama Series (not once, but four consecutive years starting in 2008) is a good example. Prior to launching hit originals, including *Breaking Bad*, *The Walking Dead*, and *Mad Men*, AMC was primarily known for older films and reruns, product that dovetailed with its original name (American Movie Classics). Leveraging cult followings, the network has been able to increase its cable licensing fees significantly (see Chapter 3 discussion of cable financing), with the *New York Times* estimating that AMC charges MSOs, like Comcast and DirectTV, upwards of $0.40 per month per subscriber—with national carriage and 80 million subscribers, that translates into $30 million per month for license fees, a sum that could not be commanded without viewers clamouring to see these select hits.[25]

The net result of more money to produce quality shows begetting more quality shows, while feeling a bit like a bubble, has in fact proven to be a virtuous cycle, lifting the quality bar to a point where many feel there is an unexpected renaissance in TV. Despite the competition from new digital and online sources (see also Chapter 7), the *New York Times* article "The *Mad Men* Economic Miracle" described this as television's "golden age" and waxed on that: "Networks have effectively entered into a quality war. Basic-cable channels have to broadcast shows that are so good that audiences will go nuts when denied them. Pay TV channels, which kick-started this economic model, are compelled to make shows that are even better. And somehow, they all seem to be making insane amounts of money."[26]

While all this is true, the digital competitive forces are lurking, and cable companies are well aware that cable bills have become extremely pricey and that they cannot simply keep raising rates (which is the only way to fund demands for increased subscriber fees, which are in turn commanded by cable channels succeeding with evermore original fare). Not only does cable have to fight cord-cutting by a new generation used to online access without forking out for cable bills, and expanding digital piracy of in-demand shows, but now the online companies are themselves getting in on the original content bandwagon. The production of original content by the online leaders that are aggregating content in the over-the-top space is a direct threat to cable, and exacerbates traditional media players' fears of their digital competitors. Chapter 7 discusses how services ranging from YouTube to Amazon, Hulu, and Netflix are moving into online originals; among a variety of impacts, this new range of programming, including from some of the services themselves that are starting to look like an aggregator of cable channels, will be competing both for viewers and advertisers, putting pressure on cable that the industry has never before faced. The foregoing quoted *New York Times* article, in talking about AMC and how cable channels spin cliffhangers from their original series into gold, mused that while Charles Dickens had to sell the next chapter in books (that were published in a serialized form), no one has managed to monetize cliffhangers like TV (and cable TV); the article could, though, have as aptly quoted from Dickens that for TV, today it is truly the best of times and worst of times.

Upfront Markets, Mechanics of Advertising Sales, and Ratings

Advertising is the lifeblood of free television, and networks essentially lease portions of their airtime to advertisers, charging rent based on ratings. Much like any other rental market, rates can be based on long- or short-term rates, with discounts applied to prepayment or longer-term security scenarios. To grasp the mechanics of the television advertising landscape, imagine you owned an apartment building where certain views commanded premium pricing (exchanging the notion of view for viewership), discounts were applied to someone leasing bulk space, such as an entire floor, and each individual unit in the building was a unique property that commanded its own rental rate (yet still had some rational relationship to all the other units rented). In this analogy, the TV upfront markets would be akin to long-term rentals, the scatter market would equate to monthly or weekly rentals, and ratings would be the cost-per-square-foot barometer for setting the rental rates.

Upfront Markets

There are a couple of times a year when networks pitch their new season lineups to advertisers, trying to secure commitments for shows before broadcasts. This obviously secures capital/commitments to underwrite production costs, the annual ritual of which has come to be known as the upfront markets.

The mechanism of the upfront markets is relatively straightforward. Broadcasters auction off their commercial space, referred to as "inventory," and receive guaranteed payments for the commercial space/spots. The buyers of spots obviously secure key placement for their products, as the upfront markets cover large commitments over long periods of time. Companies with a steady stream of advertising needs, such as auto companies or large packaged goods companies, will secure a range of spots that will then be allocated to specific products at a later date. Those companies buying large inventory and later allocating to clients tend to have products that need continuous marketing, and therefore do not need to have the first spot on *NCIS* on the week of November X. For this flexibility, they buy in volume and gain both the benefit of guaranteed delivery as well as a certain discount.

It is in part this guaranteed, and to an extent more flexible, income stream that was put in jeopardy with the U.S. auto company and broader 2008 economic crisis; without this revenue, the networks cannot afford a basket of staple programming and risks, with the collateral impact hitting everything from the concept of primetime (NBC's decision to substitute Jay Leno for scripted fare in its third hour) to sports. And there is a lot at stake with the US broadcast networks securing an estimated $9.2 billion during the 2012–2013 upfront market; CBS alone in the 2013–2014 market reportedly sold about 80% of its commercial inventory for $2.5–2.6 billion.[27] Evidencing the strength of cable, Turner in 2012 took in about $4 billion across its networks, with TBS and TNT accounting for an estimated $1.95 billion[28] (see footnotes for relative size of 2007 market). (Note: The 2007 upfront markets, by comparison, secured over $15 billion for the broadcast and cable networks (respectively, $9 billion and $6.5 billion).[29]

The spots will be sold on a cost-per-thousand-eyeballs basis (CPM). Spots can either be based on general ratings/viewership, or spots will be sold with a guarantee within a certain targeted demographic (e.g., certain rating in the 18- to 30-year-old demo). As noted previously, the seller has the benefit of secured sales and financing, and the buyer secures a certain number of guaranteed spots and eyeballs for their client base. The game is then in the pricing, with buyers trying to make efficient use of marketing dollars and the sellers/broadcasters trying to maximize the value of each second of commercial time.

Economically, what then happens is that the seller/broadcaster will guarantee a number of eyeballs, with the guarantee used to drive the price as high as possible. The rub then comes when a show either under- or over-delivers. If it over-delivers, then the buyer had a very efficient buy; it paid for X eyeballs and actually received a higher viewership than it bargained for. On the flip side, if a show under-delivers, then the seller has to make good on its guarantee and compensate the buyer for the show underperforming. This practice is literally known as "make goods." The seller will allocate additional spots or other value to make up the difference. A good example of this market is likely the first season of *Survivor*. The show was a much bigger hit than anticipated, and those buyers who had space on the show benefited from the over-delivery and had an efficient buy. The market then corrects in the next season/upfronts, where expectations are adjusted and the broadcaster will increase the charge for the show, raising the CPM for the targeted rating.

One interesting economic factor in setting rates is that while the market corrects, it does not correct radically such that year to year the CPM value proportionately adjusts to the prior year's ratings. A network that has had a strong run over several years will command a premium in its CPM base value, whereas a network that has been struggling historically but has just come off a strong year may not be able to increase its rate to "current market" overnight.

Why the CPM pricing of advertising inventory does not correct to market and more quickly discount or grant goodwill based on recent performance is a lesson of relative leverage and limited players. The same scenario would not play out in the brutal maelstrom of the stock market. A key differentiator here is that a network is not going to discount its pricing more quickly than it has to, and will fight every step to avoid erosion, arguing that any recent correction is a temporary dip and its new lineup will place the channel back on top. The buyer is more likely to accept this because the pricing is in relative rather than absolute terms, and they will ultimately only pay the "true" value of delivery once make goods are applied (if applicable).

Digital Upfronts

As discussed in more detail in Chapter 7, in 2012 online aggregators started to host events in advance of the traditional network upfronts,

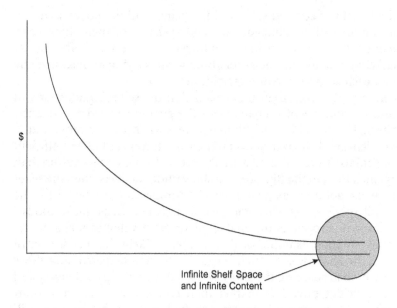

$

Infinite Shelf Space
and Infinite Content

Figure 6.3 Diminishing Value in Long Tail

trying to tap into advertising dollars for original content. With the expansion of programming, the question will now become whether advertisers simply adjust their allocation of media spending, or the expansion of content leads to an overall expansion of advertising. The former is the likely initial result, with advertising becoming more targeted. This is, in part, because, at least in theory, the number of advertisers does not expand with the quantity of content. Over time, however, there could be an expansion if niche channels/programming opens up less expensive advertising opportunities to companies that could not efficiently participate before—akin to what has happened on the Web, with Google AdSense pioneering the way. Finally, the last step in the cycle is a levelling off, with the long tail of content yielding less revenue, given the amount of content that continues to expand is still chasing limited buyers. This is depicted in Figure 6.3, and is the same effect sometimes referred to in terms of Web pages, which tend toward infinity (and also why, per Ulin's Rule, more content with easier access, as discussed in Chapter 1, does not necessarily lead to greater value).

Scatter Market

The opposite side of the upfront market is the scatter market. The scatter market is just as it sounds: in this market, companies can make specific buys for limited spots and placements. This market is needed when a buyer/advertiser has specific timing demands, such as the release of a product (e.g, the release of a film). If you want to advertise your product on a specific show on a specific night to either tie into a promotion or product launch, then you will likely be buying in the scatter market. The advantage the buyer gains is the specific timing and placement, but what they sacrifice is guaranteed delivery. The buy is at risk, and there will likely be no guaranteed make goods.

The process, art, and business of buying media is a complicated discipline, with millions of dollars at stake in increments of 15- and 30-second inventories. Perhaps the most cited example of advertising expenditure is the Super Bowl. Despite the claims of the demise of TV and new media impacting viewership, advertising on the Super Bowl continues to be vibrant, with fees charged per spot at the upfronts and total advertising spending continuing to climb—a 30 second spot in 2013 hitting a record $4 million.[30]

Understanding Traditional Ratings

Almost everyone uses Nielsen ratings as a barometer of the audience and demographics captured, and it is best to go to Nielsen Media for the relevant definitions. The website has an excellent glossary, and defines ratings, share, designated market areas, metered markets, etc. Nielsen explains the difference between a rating and share as follows:

- The terms rating and share are basic to the television industry. Both are expressed as percentages.
- Simply put, a rating tells how many people watched a particular TV program; it is the percent of households or persons within a universe (all TV households, or adults 18–49, for example) who are tuned to a particular program or daypart.
- A share expresses this same number of viewers as a percent of only the households or persons actually watching television during the program or daypart. Thus, a share is a percent of a constantly changing number—the number of homes or number of persons in a given demographic using television at that time. Shares can be useful as a gauge of competitive standing.[31]

Accordingly, if one looks at the entire U.S. market (defined as the universe of TV households, which approximates 110 million homes), a ratings point would be 1 percent of this total, which means, as a rule of thumb, that a 1 percent rating translates into just over 1 million people/homes.[32]

In Nielsen's glossary of media terms and acronyms, it further defines the metrics with specific formulas. Focusing again on the key measurements of ratings and share, Nielsen's formulas are as follows:

Rating (average audience):

$$\text{Rating \%} = \frac{\text{Audience}}{\text{Universe Estimate}}$$

Share (of audience):

$$\text{Share} = \frac{\text{Rating}}{\text{HUT}}$$

Households using television (HUT):

$$\text{HUT \%} = \frac{\text{\# HH with TV Sets in Use}}{\text{Total HH Universe Estimate}[33]}$$

In practice, ratings are dissected and used not only for an overall measurement, but also targeted advertising buys. Clients will want a specific delivery with a defined demographic, such as adults 18–49 or males 25–49. The pricing of the buys is then formulated by indexing the value of a ratings point to the population reached on a per-1,000 impression basis. Nielsen defines these CPP and CPM measurements as follows:

Cost per rating point (CPP):

$$\text{CPP} = \frac{\text{Average Unit Cost}}{\text{Rating \%}} \quad \text{or} \quad \frac{\text{Total Sch Cost}}{\text{GRPs}}$$

Cost per thousand (CPM):

$$\text{CPM} = \frac{\text{Media Cost} \times 1000}{\text{Impressions}[34]}$$

DVRs, Ad-Skipping, and the Threat to Traditional Advertising

DVRs posed an immediate and profound threat to the traditional television broadcast model because consumers could fast-forward through commercials. If viewers became accustomed to recording shows and zapping commercials, the value of advertising would be reduced, and ultimately the entire ad-supported model of free TV could be undermined. The statistics are shaky, but *Variety* noted: "it's generally accepted that 35–40 percent of people who watch programs played back on DVRs still sit through the ads."[35]

As DVR penetration approaches mass-market levels, it is creating new pressures, and as discussed previously, it is altering the way ratings are reported and advertising purchased.

Ad-Skipping

Ironically, as TV programming was first finding outlets on the Internet, one of the sales items for streaming content is that advertising could be embedded and not skipped; the market, though, has now moved on, with the ability to give viewers choices of ads (see Hulu discussion), and services differentiated by the flexibility (or not) and placement of advertisements. Thinking had thus come full circle, or perhaps even further: first, there was the fear of the Internet siphoning away consumers from TV, then the fear of ad-skipping undermining the entire broadcast infrastructure, then the Internet perceived as a savior to broadcast because commercials could not be skipped if watching a show via your computer as opposed to your TV, to ancillary revenues dependent on the mechanism for advertising being a differentiator. The one sure outcome is that the traditional television-advertising model is changing, and networks will need to find substitutional revenues as audience share declines from competing media options and advertising becomes more tenuous as more people can zap commercials.

I had an interesting conversation a few years ago with the founder of a technology company whose software enabled a TV-like interface via the Web. He mentioned that ad-skipping was overrated: ask people if they ad-skipped and then ask if they had ever, while fast-forwarding, stopped and rewound to watch something that caught their eye, and the percentage response was nearly identical. Why had the people stopped, rewound, and watched? Because the item was relevant. This simply created a need for better target marketing—something the Internet promised by feeding advertisements via customer-profiled databases (intelligent advertising serving), and a goal that TV advertising kept iteratively refining by slicing ratings into narrow demographic baskets.

I received a similar response recently from Alex Carlos, head of entertainment at YouTube, who believes online can improve the environment for advertisers and that ad-skipping is not the end of the story. When I asked about how he thought monetization of original content would evolve and how advertisers viewed the divide between ratings and CPM metrics, he advised:

311

Our ads are evolving all the time, but one thing remains the same: advertisers pay attention to the content that reaches their audiences. That applies to all channels, not just the funded channels.

We think online can change advertising for the better. Advertisers must create great ads that people want to watch. Over 60 percent of our instream ads are already TrueView skippable ads. That means that if a user doesn't want to watch the ads, he or she can skip it and the advertiser doesn't pay. The better ads and the more targeted we make them, the fewer people will skip. That's a good thing for the user and a good thing for the advertisers.

Not everyone is as forgiving, and the flexibility expressed by those hailing from the streaming/online side of the equation tends not to be found from those monetizing the network/traditional TV side of media. In 2012, Dish Network surprised many in the industry by enabling Auto Hop, a feature that allows viewers to automatically skip over advertisements. In May 2012, CBS, Fox, and NBC collectively sued Dish, and in a counterpunch Dish sued back, arguing that Auto Hop did not infringe any network copyrights.[36] The oddity of the case is that the adversaries have a symbiotic and mutually advantageous relationship: Dish is one of the networks' largest distributors, and the networks are similarly a key supplier of content to Dish. Nevertheless, the networks felt they had little option, with the issue similar to DVR manufacturer ReplayTV's ad-skipping feature that had been tried 10 years earlier; at that time, the networks similarly sued, and the collective pressure and difference in size essentially drove ReplayTV out of business.[37] Commenting about the lawsuit, NBC alleged: "Dish simply does not have the authority to tamper with the ads from broadcast replays on a wholesale basis for its own economic and commercial advantage," and Fox argued that wholesale ad-skipping could destroy the whole free TV landscape: "We were given no choice but to file suit against one of our largest distributors, Dish Network, because of their surprising move to market a product with the clear goal of violating copyrights and destroying the fundamental underpinnings of the broadcast television ecosystem. Their wrongheaded decision requires us to take swift action in order to aggressively defend the future of free, over-the-air television."[38] Regardless of the outcome, it is interesting to see the different philosophical underpinnings when viewing ad-skipping from the perspective of traditional broadcasters versus online pioneers—and it is accordingly not surprising, considering the advertisers themselves are somewhat caught in the middle, just wanting to efficiently promote products and capture associated metrics about effectiveness, that a gulf remains in harmonizing metrics and systems.

A New Ratings Landscape: Live + Ratings and Ratings on Commercials

A few years ago, the ratings landscape began shifting as a result of factors including DVR viewing, and networks were insisting on moving beyond the historical measurements. The argument was simple: "live" ratings no longer accurately reflected how many people "watched" TV. (Note: I put "watched" in quotation marks because this was the argument just a couple of years ago, but going forward I believe the system will have to evolve even further to capture "consumed" via all outlets.)

After a tug of war in 2006, when advertisers succeeded in maintaining ratings based on traditional metrics of measuring the viewers who watched a program live (wanting to preserve this lower base as long as possible, arguably knowing they were only paying for live but recognizing a larger audience ultimately was captured), the advertisers and networks agreed to a new system that was introduced in the summer of 2007. Calling the pact on commercial ratings and DVR viewing "the   **313** biggest sea change" in the TV ad business in two decades, *Variety* summarized:

Virtually all ad sales will be based on Nielsen Media Research's newly introduced commercial ratings—which measure the number of viewers who are watching ads, and not just the programs in which the ads air. . . . As a quid pro quo, the advertising business had to acknowledge the existence of digital video recorders (DVRs). Most major advertisers will allow networks to measure their commercial ratings by adding in viewing via DVR that occurs up to three days after the initial telecast. (The new ad standard was quickly jargon-ized as "C3," or commercial ratings plus three.)[39]

The introduction of the new ratings system, providing the average ratings of a commercial within a program (and, by corollary, an indication of how many ads were skipped), was introduced just around the time of the 2007 upfronts, delaying deals and creating unprecedented levels of uncertainty as parties were reluctant to commit big sums against a new and untested ratings system.

Despite the anxiety, most parties ultimately agreed to the new C3 system, as *Variety* highlighted: "NBC Universal last month cut a

$1 billion deal with Group M, the media-buying arm of ad giant WPP, which included sales based on the C3 standard for the Peacock and for its cable sibs . . . That deal more than any other set the precedent for the industry's broad acceptance of the C3 standard."[40] (Almost as a truism, *Advertising Age*, in a 2007 upfront study, posed the question "What is the most significant new trend that has emerged during the 2007–2008 upfront season?" to the following groups: cable, broadcast, buyers, planners, and clients. Every single category replied that it was the new ratings construct, and specifically the Live + 3 measurement.)[41]

The jury was out whether this new scheme would truly capture time-shifted viewing in order to more fairly represent consumption of a broadcast program—with DVRs now commonplace, and consumers' options ever-expanding in terms of access to programming, why not Live + 10 rather than Live + 3? Surprisingly, the numbers actually stack up. Nielsen, in its 2012 report on the state of the media, notes that: "42.9 percent of time-shifted primetime broadcast programming is played back the same day it was recorded," and that a staggering "87.6 percent is played back within three days."[42] The fact that the ratings agency have found a compelling way to measure the impact of time-shifting and give metrics to advertisers that validate the broader bear hug of reaching consumers within the "zone of initial broadcast" does not, however, solve some of the other challenges posed by new access points and multi-screens.

314

Live + Still a Limited Solution

While the new "Live +" system is an improvement because it more accurately gauges the total consumption of a program, advertisers that are focused on time-specific flights will want to discount or dismiss the added time, and accordingly will not want to pay the same rates. If I have a movie opening on Friday, and advertise on Wednesday, the value of a consumer seeing my advertisement the next week following the opening weekend (imagine Live + 7) is greatly, if not fully, diminished (especially if my ad was targeted to drive opening weekend box office).

The open issue is now reliability: "It's generally thought that 5 percent of auds leave during commercials, and that is built into the system of buying and selling." But what if the commercial ratings say differently? "Even a tenth of a ratings point equates to millions of dollars," noted NBC Universal's research president to Variety.[43]

Once the slippery slope is opened, broadcasters may find that they need to refine metrics even further. One direction would be to slice commercials more finely, measuring each commercial rather than tracking average commercial ratings. Many advertisers, however, are likely to go beyond ratings, realizing their statistics need to compete with the direct consumer information readily available online; conceptually, the advertiser wants the same type of tracking to measure the effectiveness of buys on and offline. One trend addressing this convergence is to track engagement; namely, tracking not simply whether a show is watched, but how much time is spent watching down to a per-viewer level. While conceptually this may be a more valuable indicator, given the recent seismic shift, and the fact even online metrics are not yet valued-based on duration, it is not likely this next iteration of valuation will be adopted in the near term.

Internet Intersection—Live + What?

As noted above, economic pressures are pushing for ratings and metrics to be more precisely calculated. This trend is no doubt accentuated by the gulf in online metrics versus TV ratings, where Nielsen ratings are based on statistical samples and averages, while the online advertising market has now become accustomed to exact, by-individual costs per click and by-user impressions. There are, though, two different issues at play here.   315

First, there is the "what" should be captured, as in the argument that TV ratings should account not just for live watching, but also capture a viewer watching the program time-shifted via his or her DVR (hence, the Live + 3 rating). But what about all the other points of consumption evolving: Should this rating not also capture watching the show via Internet free VOD or on a mobile or other portable device (whether simulcast or accessible on a VOD basis)? The expansion of access points for consumption will inevitably cause a further shift in this metric to capture a total consumption number within a fixed period. This is a point I have been arguing for years, and finally in early 2013 Nielsen announced both that it would expand households to include TVs hooked up to the Internet (capturing cord-cutters plugging in TV monitors, and accessing content via such services as Aereo) and that, downstream, it would also measure viewership on iPads and other portable/mobile devices (though offered no details as to how they would capture, measure, and aggregate data from such portable devices).[44] To date, this has not been forced because-cord cutting is still new and has only impacted TV households at the margin (though this is changing and starting to evidence a material impact; see Chapter 7). Additionally, while the market was in a "laboratory phase" and companies began experimenting with different ad constructs such as trying fewer advertising minutes (*Wired* noted: "While broadcasters cram eight minutes of advertising into a half-hour show, Hulu sells only two"[45]), increasing the CPM rates (value per ad) by not enabling ad-skipping (e.g., Hulu has been able to charge a premium, selling spots, according to *Wired*, for "two to three times the ad rate that the broadcast network commands"[46]), and even eliminating ads in the context of subscription services (e.g., Netflix), it was bewildering how to harmonize values—there is still no consensus on how best to capture "Internet views," but at least Neilsen is acknowledging the problem and pledging to tackle it.

This leads into a second factor, namely dovetailing value and ratings systems: Is CPM for the Internet the same as CPM for a network-advertising buy? (See also discussion on page 93, "Principal Methods of Financing Online Production.") Both are trying to track costs based on reach (CPM viewers). However, the TV ratings are based on statistical values, while the online ratings are theoretically based on direct, by-user clicks or impressions. It will be interesting as these two systems, both based on different assumptions and data, yet trying ultimately to track the same information, continue to converge.

Finally, it is worth in this context noting some macro-statistics as to just how big the online video market is becoming—growth that means
316   differences in how the systems capture value are amplified as more video is consumed online. At the beginning of 2013, comScore, via its Video Metrix service, reported the following online statistics for the month of January (all sums on per-month basis):

- 180 million unique monthly video viewers
- viewers watched/streamed 36.2 billion online views
- each viewer watched 19 hours of video
- there were 9.1 billion video advertisements.[47]

It is no wonder that online video advertising is now big business, that online networks are pushing for digital upfronts tied to new premium programming, and that key ratings services (Nielsen) are seeking ways to capture dispersed ratings.

Social Media Driving New Changes

While, for years, I have been predicting a need for a major ratings changes given these dynamics, it appears that new systems may finally be coming—but driven from social media, rather than focusing on Internet broadcasters or FVOD services, as one may have expected. Neilsen and Twitter have teamed up to introduce what they are calling the "Nielsen Twitter TV Rating." This metric will track not the actual number of people watching, but rather try to rationalize some of the otherwise cacophonous noise in cyberspace by "calculating the total number of people who tweet about a programme, as well as the number of people who see those messages." As the *Financial Times* noted in describing how the hit show *Glee* jumped from a Nielsen ranking of 74th place to second place when measured by Publicis's Optimedia metric "that analyses information from Facebook, Twitter and a range of other sources," this is part of a continuing attempt to objectively quantify "buzz."[48]

Because these metrics, though, are still based on an extrapolation, and are trying to draw an assumed correlation between conversations and actual watching, it may be that they only serve to create value in advertising extensions—such as sponsored tweets or placing Facebook ads and tracking impressions. The more fundamental challenge of actually capturing ratings across diverse viewing platforms remains.

Pay Television

While there are some similarities to the free television market in pay television licenses, the underlying economics are significantly different. The market is dominated by a very small group of broadcasters, the inventory space has an elasticity component given multiplexing, and values are not fully dependent upon ratings.

The U.S. market is dominated by three key players: HBO/Cinemax, Showtime/The Movie Channel, and Starz/Encore. HBO is by far the largest, with more than 20 million subscribers (excluding Cinemax). Because the economics of series was discussed previously, my focus below will be on film licenses and the macroeconomics of pay channel deals/programming.

Film Licenses and Windows

As discussed in Chapter 1, the film pay TV window is typically a year or so from theatrical release, and six to nine months following video release. This is heavily dependent on changing market conditions, and as pay services have grown and expanded channel offerings through multiplexing services, the windows have now become more complicated. Pay TV services are often granted second and even third windows, so that a couple of years or more of exclusivity are secured, punctuated over several years, where the first and most important window is 12–18 months long.

Pay TV license fees can run into the millions of dollars, and services recoup the costs by amortizing fees over high numbers of runs and directly charging consumers a monthly access fee. Because pay services are not ratings-dependent, they are focused on two primary items for value: satisfying the current subscriber base and attracting new subscribers.

Subscriber satisfaction is an interesting issue. A service may feel it can pick and choose content, but there may be a built-in expectation from subscribers that they will have access to certain films or types of product. If a service markets itself as the top pay channel, where "you'll get all the hits," it would not be delivering on its promise if it did not have the top three or four films of the summer—an issue that will become more prevalent as online subscription aggregators, such as Netflix, come to resemble traditional pay TV services and compete for content (see also Chapter 7). The value proposition is a bit different if focused on attracting new subscribers, and the challenge is whether the service is able to accurately correlate subscriber changes with the playing of specific programs.

318

Basis for License Fees: Calculation of Runs

License fees paid by pay TV services have almost always been based on a fee-per-subscriber basis. Accordingly, if the fee was $1 per subscriber and there were 10 million subscribers, the license fee would be $10 million. Carefully crafted legal language dictates how the subscribers are counted, with choices ranging from at the time of contract, at the commencement of the license period, or as of the end of the period. It is also quite typical to calculate the average number of subscribers over a monthly period and then take the average of those averages over a specified period or aggregate the fees based on a per-month calculation.

Because most pay services have grown over time (given the name of the game is acquisition and maintenance of paying subscribers), licenses often take this into account. One method is to take averages calculated over specified periods, and another is to simply impute a number. In a typical deal, the license fee may be specified as a certain minimum guarantee, with overages due if subscribers increase past an agreed threshold. In the prior example, the licensee broadcaster may guarantee the licensee $10 million, but also agree to pay $1 per subscriber for every subscriber over 10 million. Because subscriber counts can go down, this can cut both ways; however, as licensors covet minimum guarantees, it is less common to have reduction provisions. Similarly, pay TV licensees often refuse to grant a minimum guarantee tied to a current subscriber level, since this gives them no flexibility for a downturn. If instead the minimum guarantee is lower but overages apply, then everyone has hedged their bets and the fee should come out fairly.

Despite this logical pattern, as services grow there is a tendency to start moving away from the per-subscriber formula to more fixed fees; namely, once maturity is reached, the risk of leaving money on the table is reduced and simplicity wins out.

Calculating Number of Runs—Complex Matrix from Multiplex Channels and Exhibition Days

The final important element of a pay TV license deal is understanding the implications of increasing runs by the notion of exhibition days and multiplex offerings. In pay TV agreements, an exhibition day usually is defined in a manner that allows multiple airings of the film within a 24-hour period (similar to the discussion on cable runs, but it was in fact pay TV that established the pattern now being copied). Similar to the cable example previously described, it would be typical to allow a couple of airings within a day. (Note: As discussed below, subscription VOD applications, known as SVOD, are now granting subscribers on-demand access to programs within the pay channel, a trend that obviates the need for exhibition days.) The theory behind exhibition days is that the structure affords the broadcaster greater programming flexibility, offering its customers more choice. For the licensor, because the viewings are confined to within the same day, it is more akin to time-shifting, and as per custom has not raised issues of overexposing the product.

319

In terms of exposure, an area that needs to be managed is runs on multiplexed channels. Multiplexing is simply the practice of successful services offering expanded channels. Sky in the UK, for example, offers a menu of channels such as Sky Movies 1, Sky Movies 2, and Sky Cinema. Each of these channels will have a slightly different flavor and programming skew, and each of these channels may have other affiliated channels. Language defining an exhibition day will therefore need to take account of the runs within a day and which channels those runs can be taken on. This sum can ultimately lead to a dizzying number of runs.

If we were to assume, for example, that 20 runs are allowed on a primary movie channel, as well as each multiplexed channel, and were further to assume that the total number of multiplexed channels allowed were capped at five, then the total number of runs would be 240. This is calculated as 20 runs per channel × 6 potential channels × 2 runs per exhibition days.

Beyond Multiplexing—Apps and Pay TV On the Go

A major new trend that has emerged since the publishing of my first edition is the explosion of the app market, and with it the ability to extend access through apps. HBO Go now enables SVOD access outside of the hard-wired cable ecosystem, allowing TV Everywhere applications (see Chapter 7), whereby a subscriber can access HBO in a VOD format via tablets (e.g., iPad, Kindle Fire) and smartphones. Recognizing that an app can provide additional functionality and is inextricably tied to interactive access points, in conjunction with the second season debut of *Game of Thrones*, HBO updated its app to enable second-screen functionality. Viewers can now pause the main video and access a range of supplementary content, such as viewing maps, watching behind-the-scenes interviews with cast and crew, and accessing information alerts providing additional information on scenes or character relationships.[49]

A hit such as *Game of Thrones* exposes the economic conundrum that providers face in the app versus TV world: there are countless people that want to watch just that program and would pay for access via an app, and the producer/network (HBO) has to balance that foregone revenue versus its dependency on cable and satellite partners and the upside provided by using the hit series to drive subscriptions (where subscriptions require the consumer to pay for the broader suite of offerings). To date, Time Warner has been very clear that the economics do not justify enabling people to obtain HBO Go on an à la carte basis. This has two short-term consequences, both of which involve a kind of theft. (Note: Piracy is nothing new to pay TV operators, who have long implemented sophisticated conditional access encryption systems to thwart those who want their content without paying, or worse, those who want to hijack and redistribute the content, profiting from charging discounted rates and deceptively operating like an alternate pay provider. See also Chapter 2's discussion of piracy.)

The first theft is password-sharing, leveraging the fact that HBO Go allows subscirbers to have three separate accounts, enabling family members to watch different shows at different times at home. A much more serious problem is outright piracy–an issue that used to be more of a problem in the theatrical and DVD markets, but now is an enormous concern for TV. According to a Forbes article entitled "HBO Only Has Itself to Blame for *Game of Thrones* Piracy," the second season of *Game of Thrones* (2012) had been "downloaded more than 25 million times from public torrent trackers since it began in early April, and its piracy hit a new peak following April 30th's episode, with more than 2.5

million downloads in a day." The article attributed the piracy problem to the fact of huge demand, and that it was not available online on services such as Netflix or Hulu or, for that matter, to anyone without a cable subscription.[50]

Although there may be a case for offering the series as a stand-alone offering to increase its base, the issue smacks of entitlement and fails to accept the implicit underpinnings of Ulin's Rule. OTT access or stand-alone access is not a fundamental right, and HBO can choose how, when, where, and for how much to exploit its programming. The critical driver of exclusivity creates enormous premium value for its content with cable systems, and the security of carriage and subscription, both tethered to exclusivity, enables the financing of expensive unique content (*Game of Thrones* is more akin to a miniseries in production value). To argue that HBO is its own worst enemy and that piracy is your just reward for not making content more freely available via online access is what I would have to call window blackmail.

And yet, as unfair as all this sounds, it is a real problem and something that neither HBO nor other content providers can ignore in the long term. Currently, while painful, the losses can be tolerated because there has not been a tipping point toward app viewing. A *New York Times* article that focused on the danger of password-sharing also quoted HBO's co-president Eric Kessler as saying: "The vast majority of our viewing continues to be on the linear service and the on-demand service" (on-demand referring to cable VOD systems), before noting the following telling statistics 2012: taking HBO viewing as a whole, 93 percent of viewing is via TV, 6 percent through on-demand, and 1 percent through HBO Go.[51] The demand to see hit content that is not freely available is nothing new to HBO—plenty of consumers wanted to see *The Sopranos* without having to fork out for a subscription. What is new today is that apps provide a mechanism to monetize that content via a paid-for independent stream, and there will be a tipping point (akin to the desire to offer premium VOD on theatricals jumping the video window). HBO is a child of cable, but as OTT services such as Netflix and Hulu continue to grow, and if HBO can materially expand its base by offering direct subscriptions or even à la carte VOD access to series via other access points, there will be increased pressure to monetize that demand. In theory, there is no reason that the new aggregators could not compete with cable for access to content—in fact, it is already happening (see further discussion in Chapter 7). Conceptually, you could subscribe to HBO via Amazon as easily as through cable.

In this context, as traditional pay operators expand their access points, new security concerns are apt to arise; as providers diversify where and how users can watch content, there are more links in the distribution chain to protect against piracy. Given the relatively low percentage of users currently watching via new on-the-go junctions versus traditional viewing, one wonders whether providers are prepared to tackle the complications of having to protect multiple sources embedded in an ever-growing array of consumer devices (e.g., phones, tablets). I asked Graham Kill, CEO of Irdeto, one of the preeminent global companies providing security solutions to protect the content distribution ecosystem, whether in the new on-the-go construct companies are more or less focused on the issues of protecting underlying content and where he sees the market heading:

Pay media platform operators (like U.S. cable operators) ultimately want to keep their hard-won and very valuable (subscriber acquisition costs amortized and now high ARPU annuity revenues with relatively low churn) subscribers entertained via their brand's platform. They want to maximize the time and money spent on their platform for a consumer's entertainment needs. As those consumers want premium content on devices and settings of their choosing, beyond the living room and their TVs, these platform operators have mobilized to extend their linear and VOD offerings to multi-screens OTT.

The challenge to the business model, to date, has been adding value to the premium packages to avoid churn, so they have deployed security merely to "tick the box" on their studio content licenses to get access to that content. The security requirements for such content deployment are far from standard, and vary per device targeted for consumption. This makes for a confusing world for operators.

Many of us believe, and there are some early indicators to bear this out, that ultimately premium content provided OTT will be paid for, and more robust security regimes deployed to protect it and the platform operator (or studios direct to consumers) business models associated with it. However, that security will have to be less invasive and more flexible than traditional STB conditional access security in order to match consumer expectations using always-connected devices of various flavors.

322

The phenomenon of apps enabling additional video streams is, importantly, not limited to pay TV or even pure VOD access. The London Summer Olympics (2012) exhibited the potential of the new app-enabled world, with NBC complementing traditional broadcast TV with a myriad of apps to watch virtually any event. Its NBC Olympics Live Extra app allowed cable and satellite subscribers to access and stream live more than 35,000 hours of content, including 32 sports and all medal events.[52] The president of NBC Olympics boasted: "NBC Olympics Live puts the London Olympic Games into the hands of America's tablet and smartphone user, enabling us to once again use advances in technology to provide the broadest possible access to the thousands of hours of Olympic competition."[53] Following the games, NBC, in a press release touting a variety of records, noted:

- NBC Olympics Digital set multiple records with video streams, engagement time, and page views—nearly 2 billion page views and 159 million video streams.
- Cable, satellite, and telco customers have verified 9.9 million devices either on nbcolympics.com or on the NBC Olympics Live Extra app.
- This is believed to be the most device verifications ever for a single event in TV Everywhere history.
- The NBC Olympics Live Extra and NBC Olympics Apps were downloaded more than 8 million times.
- The NBC Olympics Live Extra is believed to be the most downloaded "event-specific" app in Apple's store history.[54]

Interestingly, NBC was less forthcoming with respect to monetization from apps and digital revenues, noting only: "During the 17 days of the London Olympics, nbcolympics.com, the mobile site, and the apps delivered unprecedented traffic, consumption, and engagement." This would tend to support the thesis that while app access is revolutionizing viewing, programmers are struggling to harmonize metrics and capture value tethered to consuming via devices other than traditional televisions. Today it is unclear how to assess simultaneous value across different mediums, how to derive a common aggregate "ratings" number from near-simultaneous viewing, and whether there may be more value in an aggregate measurement or via the sum of the parts of viewing via different screens. Because of these challenges, broadcasters are tending to report about the successes in niches benchmarked against past performance in those silos, while touting the

323

knock-on halo effect that is deemed to improve related channels measured by traditional metrics.

It will be fascinating to see whether certain value drivers underpinning windows can be parsed out and differentiate value within the construct of a live broadcast—the concept of apps linked to live events, in theory, can enable repeat consumption (live and VOD watching again, in essence controlling your own replay) and differential pricing (basic free, with value-added functionality coming with a price, such as an in-screen second window offering content such as commentary or information about an athlete). It does not automatically follow, though, that while drivers can create different experiences, they will then lead to enhanced monetization. Live events, by their nature, being the epitome of the time driver, represent a different type of intellectual property and experience, with value being driven by how and whether it is possible to differentiate experiences tied to simultaneous consumption. This happens in the physical world via different pricing tied to access (a front-row seat at a sporting event priced at a premium to the bleachers), and programmers are just beginning to experience how to slice and price digital seats.

One thing from all these questions and changes is clear: apps are starting to influence the ecosystem in a measurable way, and will continue to have a profound impact on the consumption of certain types of programming. Whether they become the focus of monetization, or simply a linking or value-added/enhanced feature set mechanism via which other methods of monetization extract value (FVOD, SVOD)—which I believe is the likely outcome—is still evolving.

Output Deals

Most of the above applies to the structure of a deal on a by-picture basis. However, most studio films are licensed via output deals. An output deal is exactly what it sounds like: a studio will license its entire output of product to a program service, thereby securing long-term and broad product distribution and revenues. The benefit for the supplier is a guaranteed exclusive supply of key product, thereby giving it a competitive advantage over a rival service.

Because these deals are difficult to negotiate and rely on averages (certain number of titles performing in different ranges over time), they tend to be for long periods. Fox, which has had a 25-year continuous relationship with HBO, re-upped its deal in 2007 for 10 years, with guarantees of over $1 billion, as reported in *Variety*:

The money HBO pays Fox for a movie comes out of a formula heavily dependent on the domestic box office gross of the movie. But over the long term, HBO will pay an average of $6–7 million each for the titles in the output deal . . . HBO regards theatricals as the lifeblood of its multiplex channels and its on-demand service . . . Fully 70 percent of the schedule of HBO and its multiplexes consists of theatrical movies.[55]

Output deals are similar to free TV packages, only larger and with less choice. They work because pay services need to fill up a 24/7 schedule, catering to an audience that is constantly expecting something new, and to an extent different than they may have selected on their own. The great benefit of a dominant pay service is that it shows everything. Of course, subscribers expect and demand the key major releases; beyond the lead titles, however, the pay services offer exquisite variety. There are so many movies released every week that truly only a professional movie-watcher could catch the complete variety of offerings. With the pay service, that movie that you did not want to pay for in the theater, or found not quite compelling enough to rent, or were embarrassed to admit that you really wanted to see, is offered up from your bed. I would argue that a pay service is close to the movie equivalent of your favorite radio station: you trust them to program the things you know you want to hear (see), but you are actually looking for the disc jockey (programmer) to introduce you to that new band (film) that you vaguely knew something about or may not have even heard of at all. Output deals put the catalog at the hands of the programmer. But, unlike the music analogy, you cannot flip to another channel if you do not like the schedule, because with content exclusivity it is the only channel. (Note: The level of discovery that pay services offer has been superseded by online options, providing another challenge to the business, given that viewers today are more apt to craft personalized playlists than accept the passive discovery that has so well served pay TV since its inception; see also discussion of viewers customizing their viewing experience in Chapter 7.)

As touched on in other chapters, the structure of how pay TV channels acquire content is starting to have a profound impact for online aggregation leaders. In Chapters 5 and 7, I argue that Netflix today, although putatively a video rental service, is in fact closer to a pay service—namely, it is a subscriber-based content aggregator. As these markets converge, companies have to do more to differentiate themselves (leading to online aggregators starting to produce original content,

325

following the pay TV trend, as discussed in Chapter 7); moreover, it is the $1 billion checks for content that the Netflix's of the world will have to keep paying in order to continue offering content on a scale comparable with the leading pay TV services. That competitive future, though, is already here. In Chapters 5 and 7, I reference forecasts that Netflix will already spend greater than $1 billion for streaming rights in 2012 (and that its streaming liabilities approached $5 billion).[56] Additionally, in a telling sign of market shifts, in the UK Competition Commission announced an about-face in its declaration of pay giant Sky's dominance—dropping its case and noting that the growth of Amazon's Lovefilm and Netflix were materially altering the competitive landscape for acquiring premium content (see also Chapter 7). In the U.S., Netflix outbid pay service Starz for its next movie package (starting 2017), with the *Hollywood Reporter* noting: "Financial terms of the deal were not disclosed, but those close to the situation said Netflix will be paying $100 million-plus more to Disney than Starz was paying each year, putting the price tag near $350 million annually."[57]

For the moment, the lines are still blurring, and some pay services are still willing to license to their would-be competitors (who are eager for content) to the extent deals bring in revenues, help extend brands, and reach different audiences (e.g., viewers watching via mobile devices). In 2012, Epix, a small pay TV movie channel (partnership among Paramount Pictures, MGM, and Lionsgate) struggling to gain carriage via a number of the major MSOs, switched allegiances, licensing 3,000 movies to Amazon, who were keen to add additional content to their Amazon Prime members via the Kindle Fire. Reuters reported: "Netflix had been paying $200 million a year since 2010 for exclusive rights to Epix movies. The exclusivity expires this month [September 2012], but Netflix will keep Epix movies on its service through September 2012. Netflix has the option to extend its nonexclusive use of Epix through September 2014."[58]

Economics of Output Deals

In terms of economics, the key items in an output deal are length of term and fee. Because of the unique nature of the pay TV market, and the mutual advantages previously discussed, these deals are invariably for multiple years, and in some cases upwards of 10 years. The service is incentivized by locking up a key supplier—again, giving it access to an enormous range of quality product while shutting out a competitor from product that may feature the hottest star of the moment or an award-winning film. In addition to the aforementioned Fox deal, HBO has had several long-term deals, including with Universal, Warner Bros., New Line, and DreamWorks.[59] Each studio therefore has the security of knowing it has a constant income stream regardless of the performance fluctuation of its slate. When financing a picture, it is not an insignificant element that the studio can count on a secure sale. The same logic suggests that similar titanic struggles over long-term deals could emerge in the online/digital space between key aggregators and content suppliers; as discussed in Chapter 7, there is a current land-grab playing out, with sellers benefitting from a wave of competition, and an equilibrium has yet to be reached, including in terms of deal lengths.

Coming back to pay TV, this would still not work if the economics did not balance similarly. In a typical structure, the pay service would have a baseline guarantee for films. The films may be designated within a band, such as an A, B, or C picture. Although these may be defined on strictly financial terms, such as by U.S. box office gross, conceptually, definitions can also include hybrid elements such as if a star or particular director is attached. In addition to a minimum, the studio will have an upside because fees will further be tied to financial performance. Different gradings will usually correspond to box office thresholds. If a picture achieves $50 million box office, that may trigger one fee, and if it is greater than $100 million, it will trigger a different, higher fee. (Note: As discussed in Chapter 4, this can provide a distributor an incentive to keep a film playing longer in theaters than the week-to-week numbers may justify, if a bit more box office will trigger a material threshold, such as can be the case with pay TV.) The pay services are generally fine with this structure; they are simply indexing their exposure/cost to the value of the particular film. What they want to ensure is that there is some rational cap, and that on an amortized basis they are acquiring a certain overall volume for a certain bulk price. This tends to work out, because the vicissitudes of the business ensure a range of hits and misses—to the extent that if someone has a string of hits, it may be more costly in the short term, but should help both parties in the long term. In terms of caps, the deals may set an artificial limit, such that a film can only earn so much. If the cap is $X for a film achieving $150 million or more of domestic box office, for example, this will be fine for a film around that number, but will actually disadvantage a film that may achieve $250 million. In theory, this is a risk the licensor takes (assuming a cap), and is one of the benefits that the pay service reaps: they get somewhat of a bargain (akin to an efficient upfront buy in TV) and are assured they are not gouged at the high end, and in return are pledging the security of taking volume regardless of overall performance.

Most output deals historically have incorporated escalating fees over time. This can be tied either explicitly to subscriber growth, ensuring that the per-subscriber fee is maintained as the key element setting price, or in an imputed fashion over time. In theory, this is no different than a landlord having a rent inflation clause in a long-term lease, ensuring that the payments keep pace with market pricing. Accordingly, a 10-year contract is likely to include material escalators. This is one area where the pay services have been squeezed at times. If the assumptions are wrong, then pricing can rise significantly above what market pricing would have been absent the output deal. The service may have been forced to take the risk to secure the product, because the studio would not entertain such a long-term contract without the security of increasing fees. Given these dynamics, pay TV is one of the few areas where it is not uncommon to hear about deals being renegotiated (though still vehemently resisted). Deals between online aggregators and content providers, to date, have not been for as long a period because the market is immature and no one is certain about the relative risks—accordingly, with the stakes high and uncertainty remaining as to where/how equilibrium will be reached, there is less standardization.

To add further wrinkles (to the pay TV context), if you can think of a variable, it has probably come up. Some contracts will have "gorilla clauses," allowing for special treatment of select films. Many deals will have carve-outs, acknowledging that rights may be split in a way where the studio may reserve the right to exclude a picture. In virtually all deals, there are notice periods; the studio has some measure of flexibility including a picture and must provide notice of inclusion by a specified date. To the extent there is some flexibility for inclusion, it may be tempered by volume commitments (so many A-titles per period), such that the true flexibility is at the margins.

Value of Individual Titles

The ultimate value paid is obviously a closely held secret. Because there is strong competition among three U.S. services, however, it is fair to hypothesize that the value bears some relationship to the free TV window, which is longer but also comes later. *Variety*, in an article describing Starz's acquisition of 500 movies from Sony's library, including *Spider-Man* and *Men in Black*, noted that for TV, "four-year-exclusive blockbuster titles in the first window can cost a network upwards of $20 million apiece." It then continues on the relative value of library titles to fill in pay TV slates, highlighting that "it's far cheaper. The typical nonexclusive library title will fetch in the neighborhood of $150,000."[60]

Another variable, in theory, should be some discount applied to the pay fee in an output deal, because unlike free TV it is a guaranteed sale. This is, again, an important element in financing. Accordingly, if one believes the free TV value should be $20 million, do the factors of: (1) discounting for a guaranteed sale; (2) prior viewing in an earlier window; (3) smaller audience reach; and (4) a shorter overall window cumulatively increase or decrease the value relative to free TV? Many of the factors should net others out, creating a vibrant marketplace with license fees that can be in the high millions of dollars per title.

Revenue Model and Original Programming

As discussed in Chapter 3, pay television networks derive revenues from the intersection of carriage fees and subscriber fees. Carriage fees are fees paid by cable or satellite operators for the right to carry the channel, and subscriber fees are the approximately $30 per month that a subscriber pays to receive the channel; in macro terms, these numbers are aggregated by the cable provider, passing along a much larger fee to the channel (dollars per subscriber rather than cents per subscriber), given the direct consumer-funded per-subscriber fees. Without delving into the P&L of a pay TV network, the economics are somewhat straightforward: simply multiply the number of subscribers by the average monthly fee for the gross revenue budget. At subscriber levels in the millions, this quickly becomes a big number, and to the extent the service is able to maintain and grow its base, there is a very secure continuous income stream. (Note: Let us assume $20 per month × 10 million subs; with these numbers, the gross revenue approaches $2.5 billion over a year.)

Pay TV is therefore similar to cable in terms of the TV distribution chain, where consumer dollars flow to the cable operator, which in turn passes along the revenues to the pay TV network. This is somewhat akin to cable (where a percentage is passed through, but the network then directly receives advertising revenues), and is fundamentally different than free TV, where no consumer dollars are passed directly to the network. Figure 6.4 helps frame the value chain.

What has been interesting in the evolution of pay TV is that the operators have come to realize that its suite of programming optimizes subscriber satisfaction when combining access to films (traditional route) and supplementing movie fare with unique original programming. Because U.S. pay networks operate outside primetime network FCC standards and practices regulations, they seized the opportunity to create adult-oriented programming: the programs you always wanted to see but the subject matter was either too crude or risqué for network or cable boundaries. In fact, HBO's advertising slogan was "It's not television, it's HBO." And they are right: you cannot see sex, which underlies *Sex and the City* (in its original/uncensored form), or graphic violence, as seen

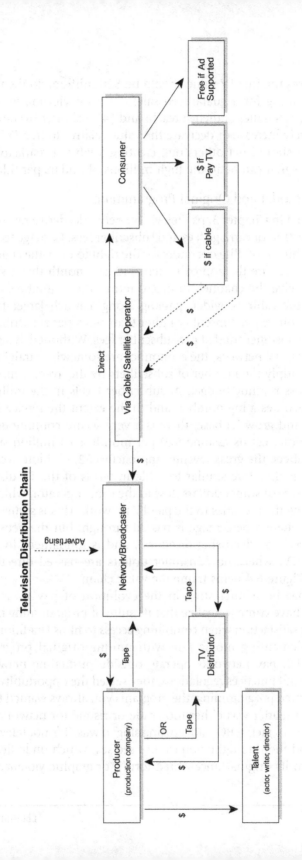

Figure 6.4 The Television Distribution Chain

in *Boardwalk Empire,* or explicit gay lovers, as seen in *Six Feet Under,* on free or cable television. Consumers are drawn to these shows, first and foremost, because they are great entertainment. What consumers may not pause to think about is that they are also watching racy dramas or soaps on HBO because regulations or customs prohibit elements that are central to these shows on non-pay TV.

HBO and other pay outlets have been very clever in taking strategic advantage of their positioning, insulated from competition (except by other pay networks) by law, to create original programming that you truly cannot see anywhere else. The other major pay services have, not surprisingly, jumped into the game following HBO's success: Showtime successfully launched *Weeds, The Tudors,* and *Californication,* while Starz, a bit later to the game, has joined the space with originals such as *Spartacus* and *Boss* (as well as, in 2010, backing the award-winning miniseries *The Pillars of the Earth,* adapted from the best-selling Ken Follett novel).

This strategy then has the knock-on benefit of being highly profit-able in the DVD/video market. The very nature of the gloves-off shows makes programming more akin to mini-movies. Positioned as a hybrid between TV series and the freedom of expression found in movies, these shows have been highly successful in the DVD market. Although now counted for and built into financial plans, these revenues are, to some extent, found money, as releasing TV series on DVD and now also into download, online subscription, and VOD rental markets was not a cornerstone of the decision to diversify into original pro-gramming in the first place. When a series happens to also translate to syndication, as has been the case with *Sex and the City* in a cleaned-up, edited version for TBS, it is, in theory, all profit to the bottom line. As earlier noted, in 2006, *The Sopranos* hit a record $2.5 million per episode in licensing second runs off HBO of the series on A&E. This is truly hitting the jackpot, and is revenue that cannot be expected from many other shows, because only shows achieving a certain level of success will be in demand for syndication/cable window, and also because not all pay TV original shows can be cleaned up (or otherwise translate well) for licensing into traditional free television.

The other key element of this programming is that it is somewhat ratings-proof, because original series on pay TV are not dependent on the advertising market, and accordingly are not slaves to traditional ratings (or at least not to the same extent). It is often said that the best job in town is the head of production or programmer for a channel such as HBO: high profile, good budgets, and minimal ratings pressure. Although this is obviously an exaggeration, it is truly within the

331

network's prerogative how long to keep a show, because as long as subscribers are holding steady or growing, there is no similar direct pressure on an individual show.

Original Programming Now the Cornerstone of Pay TV

The role of original programming on pay TV, as further discussed in Chapter 7, is instructive in terms of the maturation of the online aggregation space. For the pay TV services, they are in the third stage of maturity: (1) first, they built brands by aggregating content in the pay TV window, exploiting the repeat-consumption driver in Ulin's Rule and affording consumers a new form of content access; (2) then services, pioneered by HBO, added original programming (e.g., *The Sopranos*, *Sex and the City*, *Entourage*, to leverage not being constrained by FCC broadcasting standards and practices) to complement aggregated movies, utilizing original programming to drive subscriber growth while reaping dividends in ancillary markets (e.g., DVD sales); and (3) today, as pay channels leverage original programming not merely to drive subscribers, but defensively to stop subscriber erosion in the face of increased media options, expanded on-demand access, and the loss of status as the only aggregator in town. I would argue that today the reason viewers go to HBO is for original titles such as *Game of Thrones*, which have become the pay TV equivalent of primetime, and aggregated movies then fill out the schedule. Online aggregators such as Netflix are just emerging from a comparable first phase of maturity, and now have the challenge of succeeding in the second phase with original programs; however, these services will not benefit from the novelty of offering original fare, and face competition from deep-pocketed and experienced media companies who will not idly cede the online space (e.g., HBO, Showtime, Starz).

Moreover, it is not easy to succeed with original programming. HBO is the industry's bellwether, and its leading streak of success, and high-risk, high-reward strategy of financing its own shows and retaining the upside, has led to results such as $4 billion in 2010 and in various years reputedly accounting for 25 percent or more of Time Warner's total operating profit.[61] In tracking HBO's creative success with originals, talking about its latest challenges from companies such as Netflix, and chronicling its key series since launching originals, *The Economist* noted: "For more than a decade it has lavished good, smart product on its viewers, and in the process raised the entire industry's creative game."[62]

Nevertheless, a new battleground was borne in 2013 with Netflix's debut of original series and its garnering of fourteen Emmy award nominations. Netflix's and other online services' commitment to original fare (see Chapter 7), coupled with the fact that Netflix's subscriber count passed HBO for the first time (Netflix edging up to almost 30 million in the US by mid-2013) means that competition will remain vibrant with respect to the production of original context as well as acquiring third party content to aggregate.[63]

Aggregators Positioned for the Future

While pay TV services have an advantage in terms of brand value, customer base, experience creating hit original properties, and generally deep pockets to weather the disruptive forces from OTT services such as Netflix and Amazon, there are two new challenges that they face. First, the pressure to attract eyeballs is now more intense and challenging. Pay TV has long benefitted from limited or minimal competition among providers (see below regarding international and consolidation to monopoly providers) because subscribers wanted the full palate of content that could only be offered by aggregation. Today, with OTT services offering movies on demand, be it in subscription or à la carte fashion, the competitive landscape has fundamentally altered. As discussed in Chapter 7, no longer are pay services the only aggregators; rather, companies such as Netflix, which masqueraded as video services, are fundamentally subscription aggregators of premium content (sound a lot like pay TV?). In addition to heightened competition for viewers/subscribers, pay TV services now, as a corollary, also have increased competition for acquiring content. These new types of aggregators, themselves with deep pockets and large rivalling subscription bases, are also keen competitors fighting for content and their own output deals. Despite the importance of original content, pay TV services are, at their heart, aggregators of content, needing to fill up a 24/7 schedule while only producing a handful of hours. Additionally, the more a service looks like a video store (a concept that may feel quaint in a few years) and offers the full catalog of new content, while complementing that offering with key originals, the more compelling the value proposition to its subscribers. Accordingly, pay TV services, for the first time, are being challenged simultaneously on three fronts: original content, aggregated content, and competition for subscribers.

The good news for the services is that they are still well positioned in the ecosystem. They have the benefit of 1:1 subscribers, mimicking the advantage of online with direct knowledge of their customer base

333

(though clearly not as strong, given the cable or satellite provider middle-man interfacing with the consumer, though apps such as HBO Go promise transitioning this relationship in favor of the pay provider); they are aggregators at heart, which is in the strategic bullseye of a landscape where values for individual pieces of content are in flux; they are paid directly for their content, which, so long as they can maintain the demand, sets them apart from the pressure toward free and trying to monetize the ever-marginalized long and wide tails via advertising; and their positioning as an aggregator is again strategically well situated, given the movement overall toward VOD access (see also Chapter 7 discussing these factors). In many regards, of all media, pay TV is uniquely in the competitive crosshairs, with some of the most favorable positioning, as well as the most daunting challenges. My prediction is that leading services will emerge strongly from the current disruptive battles, blending their traditional offerings with new upsides by exploiting the crown jewels of original programming to a wider (and paid) audience while building direct-to-consumer engagements via apps (leveraging SVOD applications; see below) and select à la carte premium VOD offerings.

334

Flexible Pay TV: Subscription Video-on-Demand

Subscription video-on-demand (SVOD) is a relatively new application that can be applied in a few flavors. One variation is simply a functionality improvement on an existing service. This may be the case with a pay TV service that allows its cable/satellite subscribers to access programming at any time as opposed to the scheduled broadcast times. Accordingly, if HBO were to start a show at 9:00 p.m. on Monday, an SVOD application of its service would allow customers to access and watch the program at a time of their choosing (usually any time after the initial scheduled showing). Basically, it is converting a limited selection of programming, such as HBO's content for a month, to VOD access functionality.

Another variation of SVOD is via a computer. In this application, a service will allow a subscriber to download a show to his or her computer (with the transfer enabled by a security link or closed-loop Internet system). To the extent the residency of the program on the computer is time-limited (e.g., a rental), then it is a type of VOD, as opposed to a permanent download (i.e., ownership), which is then a form of electronic sell-through. (Note: The discussion here involves SVOD from pay cable services, and Netflix SVOD via OTT aggregation is discussed in Chapters 5 and 7.)

A further SVOD application is when program access is via a pay channel provider's set-top box (e.g., as occurs in various European markets). Certain highlighted content may be automatically downloaded/resident on the box ("pushed"), while other content needs to be accessed and then downloaded to the consumer ("pulled"). In the end, whether pushed, pulled, or otherwise, the goal of SVOD is improving the consumer's pay TV experience by making paid-for premium content accessible at any time. One can therefore envision SVOD supplanting traditional pay TV (in terms of films, this is merely an aggregation of content that could be available sooner except for the window). The next logical iteration is whether the customer will pay to have a subset of content available via his or her TV at an earlier date (put another way: Where is the line between transactional VOD and subscription VOD, and should premium aggregators that pay hefty guarantees be disadvantaged by having to wait for content?).

SVOD Window

To the extent this is all about the window timing, then the relevancy of pay TV channels comes into question. The pay TV services that have focused on original programming may end up protecting their brand based on differentiating content, for the repurposing of theatrical content that helped build their channels is unlikely to survive in an à la carte, on-demand world providing access on, or close to, the video window. Pioneering new applications by Amazon and Netflix (see Chapters 5, 6, and 7) are already enabling this vision, which in theory has to pose a serious threat to pay services (what's the real differences between HBO SVOD and Netflix SVOD other than the specific content available?). For the content supplier, this presents a Hobson's choice: failure to favor online/OTT VOD services may not give the consumers what they want, but failure to favor pay TV would give up guaranteed, very large revenue streams (see also Chapter 7). For the moment, given the sums involved and the need to maintain large advances as financing security in the face of declining video revenues, online aggregators (e.g., Netflix) are being treated akin to pay services, and as discussed earlier, competing head-on with historical pay channels.

The window and economics for SVOD simply track the underlying basic rights; namely, the window for an SVOD application of pay TV rights would mirror the consumer's pay TV subscription (although generally with no access to a show until it has been premiered on the service in its scheduled slot). The one exception to this would be to the extent parties want to limit viewing (protecting the value of pay

335

exhibitions), where SVOD availability could be windowed only to provide "catch-up" access. In this instance, the SVOD availability for a particular piece of content may be limited to a set period post the initial broadcast of the content.

Deal Term Overview (Pay and Free TV)

Although license agreements will obviously be quite detailed, when stripping away many of the legal protections and basic information governing the parties, the fundamental economic structure boils down to a relatively short list of items. While many of these categories have been discussed before, it is useful to view them in a checklist form.

Licensed Channels

In a pay TV deal, defining the range of primary and multiplex channels is critical. While focus may be on runs on a primary channel, there could be several additional multiplex channels (e.g., movie channel versus action channel, or other specialty theme). The multiplex options allow the broadcaster to amortize costs and increase the fees to the licensor; ratings are lower given limited coverage, but exposure may increase significantly. In some cases, there will be formal trade-offs agreed, such that one broadcast on Channel X may be substituted for one or more on Channel Y.

A free TV deal will generally be to a specific identified channel, such as CBS; however, as technology allows multiplexed options such as high-definition channels and even Internet carriage, the notion of a single channel actually existing as a branded channel that may appear in a basket of delivery and sub-branded channels will make this area ever more complex going forward.

Runs

As discussed earlier, pay TV has evolved in a more complex fashion, but with technical innovations allowing new possibilities with free TV, the concept of "runs" is fast becoming a more complicated issue. In pay TV deals, definitions can become almost ridiculously complex: defining numbers of runs per primary channel, runs per multiplex channel, conversion ratios to exchange runs between channels, aggregate runs on each type of channel (e.g., no more than X on primary and Y on each multiplex), and aggregate runs across the range of channels (e.g., no more than X cumulative runs across all of the licensed channels, including primary Channel X and multiplex Channel Y–Z). When layering on top of this matrix the fact that runs will be linked to exhibition days, which will typically allow two runs per exhibition day, and that exhibition days are defined by time limitations (e.g., a 24-hour period commencing . . .), calculating permitted runs and monitoring runs can become an exhausting and often unclear process. I have been involved in more than one situation where there were valid interpretation debates on permissible runs based on long-standing and seemingly clear definitions—and this all before the notion of viewing via an app.

Term

The structure of a license period can be straightforward, such as a fixed number of years, or complicated if there are multiple windows; a layer of complexity can be added to either scenario when the periods are tied to pending triggers, such as a specified number of months following yet-to-be-announced theatrical or video release dates. Additionally, beyond the actual window, there will often be blackout periods and defined pre-promotional windows.

The above scenarios, even in the case of multiple windows, assume fixed terms with the variable being the start date; however, because rights are bounded by both time and runs, a license period can, in theory, expire on a fixed or variable date (the variable is the last permitted broadcast). Agreements may therefore often be structured to trigger the end of the term on the earlier of the expiry of the fixed term or the last permitted broadcast/run.

337

Calendaring software will keep track of this matrix, logging in the fixed date and accelerating availabilities to the extent runs are taken early, which is frequently the case, as licensees will not wait until the last day or even month of a term to exercise broadcast rights. All of this can become more difficult to track if there are multiple windows, which can be similarly triggered by fixed periods or variable dates if tied to the expiry of another right (e.g., following expiry of free broadcast window X). This, in turn, may be likewise triggered by fixed and variable dates.

Taken together, calendaring and monitoring rights availabilities is a complex task subject to errors. The simple question of "availability" can cause lawsuits and relationship issues, as licensees are paying premiums and basing deals on rights that will be compromised if windows are misstated; there is nothing worse than finding that two clients, competitive with each other, both have rights to the same product at the same time. This is a never-ending headache for studios and is an area that is taken for granted, but is fraught with danger if not micromanaged to perfection.

License Fee

This is again straightforward if the fee is flat. However, to the extent there are potential overages involved, or if this otherwise has a contingent element, this can be quite complex. An overage definition needs to account for the difference between the minimum guarantee, which may either be flat or based on cents/dollars multiplied by a minimum stipulated subscriber basis, and the ultimate fee due, based on the actual number of subscribers multiplied by the agreed cents per subscriber base. The actual definition can become almost unwieldy in that the "actual" number is often pegged to the average number of subscribers in a month. The result can be akin to a complex bank interest calculation statement, with permutations of averages to refine the calculation.

Rights

The issues here can include:

- What is the territory? Is it physical- or language-bounded, or both?
- What languages are included? This may impact the definition of territory, such that rights may be both territorially and language-bound (e.g., such as a grant of rights for "French-speaking Belgium"). Further, language can have three tiers: the original version of the film (e.g., English language), as well as dubbed versions or subtitled versions.
- What formats/cuts are allowed? For example, will there be one or multiple versions of the product, such as an original version versus an extended director's cut, or is the release in standard definition or high definition?
- Are the rights just free TV or pay TV, or are there variations such as subscription video-on-demand (SVOD)?
- Do the rights licensed extend to channels being rebroadcast or accessed in VOD fashion via online sites, apps, or wireless systems?
- Are there technical limitations, such as curtailing digital transmissions?
- Are there carriage/delivery restrictions, such as via cable and satellite?
- Are single or multiple feeds permitted? This issue can arise in a multiplex situation or in territories with remote locations where a relay may be required for coverage in secondary areas.

338

International Market

The international markets have historically lagged behind the U.S. market in terms of maturation of both free and pay TV options, but that pattern is now changing.

History of Growth

Unlike the United States, many, if not most, international markets grew up with "state broadcasters." These were public as opposed to private channels that were either fully owned or controlled by the state, and accordingly funded by taxpayer money. Examples of such channels are the BBC in the UK, ARD/ZDF in Germany, and RAI in Italy. In some of these cases, funding is achieved through television license fees, where all citizens owning a television have to pay an annual TV license fee—a sort of tax. Even though I had been "in the business" for several years, I readily admit to the reality check of receiving my bill when I hooked up my television in London, and realized I was directly taxed to underwrite BBC programming. It is a common notion worldwide, but something of an anathema to Americans who have never experienced this system.

Not only did most countries have public broadcasters, but until the 1990s in many countries these were virtually the only broadcasters. As Americans were getting used to cable and an increasing number of channels, Europeans were just starting to auction off and authorize the first commercial licenses in the territories. In Spain, for example, the state network RTVE had dominated until the government allowed some of the first commercial licenses. The winners and resulting networks were free-to-air channels Antenne 3, which 10 years later became a leader in exhibiting movies on free TV (such as *The Lord of the Rings* and *Harry Potter* films), and Telecinco (Channel 5); additionally, Canal+ Espagne was initially granted a monopoly in the pay television space. There were, and still are, regional broadcasters, but the virtual simultaneous launch of three new national commercial networks had an obviously profound impact on the marketplace.

In the early 1990s, it was a renaissance for Hollywood studios and networks, for rather than having a handful of buyers limited by public-sector budgets, they all of a sudden had fierce competition from commercially sponsored national networks vying for viewership and profits. The pattern started in Western Europe, and then as the former Soviet bloc led to emerging democracies in Eastern Europe, competition and new stations started to flourish there as well. Hungry for programming, stations signed up massive output deals with studios and networks. Suddenly, the international TV divisions were no longer stepchildren, with hundreds of millions of dollars of revenues (at minimum) per year at stake.

The pattern continues as democracy spreads, broadcast outlets are freed from state control, and economies grow and build larger middle classes (e.g., Eastern Europe, India, Southeast Asia). However, the growth seen a few years ago in certain emerging markets, such as Russia, has slowed and TV distributors can no longer count on greenfield opportunities to substitute for declines in traditional secondary sales. I again turned to Marion Edwards, president of international TV at Fox, who confirmed:

> No market is emerging to equal licensing revenues of the core
> markets of Europe, and many of the markets considered 'emerging'
> in recent years have peaked and have turned to local programming
> to fill their schedules. Because we produce and distribute such a
> broad range of premium content, we're able to remain successful
> and relevant by supplying a variety of films, series, and formats
> for local production depending upon the mix that a particular
> territory seeks.

340

International Free Television

The economics of international free television, on territory-level basis, are not materially different than that of the domestic market.

License Deals

On the feature side, licenses tend to be for a fixed number of runs over a specified number of years. Also similar to the domestic model, license fees are fixed; on occasion, deals can be indexed to performance, if licensed in an output-deal-type structure. Barter, however, is rarely applied for U.S. product.

Finally, the pattern of packages that often typifies the U.S. syndication market has been frequently applied in the international context. Whether a package is set as part of an output arrangement, or simply as a stand-alone package, the economic underpinnings are the same. The buyer/station obtains throughput from a key supplier, and the seller has a guaranteed income stream indexed to theatrical performance; as important, the seller has secure placement of its titles, ensuring that underperforming films still find a home. This is a critical fact when circling back to the key value of studios: they are financing and distribution machines, and if they cannot ensure a producer or director that they will maximize revenues and license their films into all markets, then their role is severely compromised. (Note: Output deals apply more often to films than TV shows.)

The following 2007 deal between one of the two major German commercial networks, ProSiebenSat1, and Warner Bros., as described in the *Hollywood Reporter*, typifies this symbiotic relationship:

ProSiebenSat1 Group . . . has inked a long-term output deal with Warner Bros. International Television Distribution for the free-TV rights to at least 30 films per year, the company announced Thursday. A ProSiebenSat1 spokeswoman said the deal had a total worth "in the low hundreds of millions" of euros and a term of "several years."[64]

High Margin

International television licensing is extremely high margin, as the two principal categories of costs are relatively small. The first, and largest, is the cost of a sales force to license product globally. This will often involve layers as follows:

- Head office: management, marketing, and fulfillment.
- Regional office: regional heads/coordinators, often for UK, Western Europe, Eastern Europe, Japan, Australasia, and Latin America.
- Local offices: virtually all studios have multiple local offices in Europe, an office in Australia, and an office in Latin America.

The personnel are fixed costs, and accordingly the business can be managed simply by overhead cost. This infrastructure is a defining element of studios, as discussed in Chapter 1.

The other material cost is for delivery. International territories require different formats, such as PAL for Europe, as well as dubbed and subtitled tracks. While the licensee will often absorb some of these costs, it is not uncommon for the distributor to have to supply a foreign-language master. On top of the physical master, the licensee will need press kits, marketing materials, and occasional special-value features (e.g., customized intros or promotional pieces such as behind-the-scenes documentaries; such "VAM" is increasingly important as stations enable their own apps and websites offering supplementary material.). The matrix of elements can become quite complicated, and additional personnel need to coordinate the "trafficking" of elements (elements that need to be delivered in a time-sensitive manner, given local broadcast dates).

Further, any dubbing or subtitling will be specifically defined and subject to quality-control guidelines. Additionally, this becomes a significant economic issue, as dubbing can be expensive and who owns the dubbed masters is a negotiated point. It is not uncommon for a local broadcaster to invest in dubs for a TV show and to hold the right to those dubs. Accordingly, a producer who later wants to release in video via another distributor may not own or even have access to dubs of its own shows and may have to negotiate license fees for dubs to its own programs (for which costs, in turn, can influence whether the release is feasible).

In terms of the macro picture, though, the key element of the foregoing costs is that they are one-offs: a licensee will ultimately only require a single master. When comparing this to the video/DVD market or theatrical market, where variable costs for manufacturing units or creating prints run in the millions of dollars, the cost of delivery for TV is modest.

342

Crowdsourcing as Mechanism to Reduce Costs

Today, some of these costs are coming down by employing techniques such as crowdsourcing, tapping into local fans to create dubs—rather than view frustrated fans who want to see their favorite content in local language and "do it themselves" by posting self-created dubs almost overnight on the Web, companies are embracing this method rather than viewing the dub or subtitle creators as a type of pirate. Harnessing the community, and securing a level of quality control by having socially networked fans comment and self-police (akin to the Wikipedia model), content providers are finding ways to build communities and lower costs.

In 2012, Mozilla and the Knight Foundation invested $1 million in Amara (formerly known as Universal Subtitles), a pioneer in crowd-sourced translation services, to help the company broaden into dubbing videos. While the company provides tools for amateur videos, and is heavily used to translate YouTube videos, it is being increasingly leveraged for commercial contexts as well. Outlets such as PBS NewsHour and Al Jazeera utilize Amara, and given the ability to scale translations with essentially zero costs, it is likely that the use of crowdsourcing will become a staple for many broadcasters. (Note: There will inevitably remain some resistance at the premium content level where producers and distributors will be willing to underwrite costs to control the ownership and quality of the resulting materials.)

Repeatable

Unlike the theatrical market, where films are rarely rereleased, television is a somewhat evergreen market. New titles are obviously licensed, but library sales can also be very significant to the extent that markets continue to mature and add new outlets, such as secondary or tertiary channels that may be either cable- or satellite-delivered. The opportunities for continuing library sales lead to material revenues. Moreover, in cases of repeat licenses, element costs for delivery are either reduced or eliminated, leading to an almost 100 percent margin sale if overhead staff costs are not allocated out to the variable license.

It is a Big World

Probably the most significant factor in the international marketplace is the sheer size. As global markets have matured, it is possible to license product into more than 50 credible territories. Moreover, some of these have grown to the size that revenues, as a percentage of the United States, are high. Germany, France, Spain, the UK, Italy, Russia, Japan, Australia, and select other territories can all yield licenses in the millions of dollars. Accordingly, it is not a stretch to target achieving cumulative international sales that total or exceed U.S. sales. Of course, every market has its nuances. Add this truism to the fact that it is a relationship business and the value of maintaining a global sales force becomes evident.

Markets and Festivals

Most people think about Cannes when talking about film markets, but just as important, and perhaps more so in terms of money generated, Cannes hosts the two biggest worldwide television markets. Run by the Reed Midem organization, MIPCOM takes place in October and MIP in April. Although each market has certain ancillary events that distinguish it from the other, such as MIPCOM Jr. focusing on kids' programming just before MIPCOM in the fall, the markets are mirror images of each other, affording a biannual marketplace for worldwide TV executives to gather.

These are remarkably efficient markets attended by virtually every major program supplier and broadcaster in the world. Most of the studios and networks have major booths, and newcomers and wannabes can make an instant global impression. Gone are the peaks of lavish parties and spending, but for those in the business the markets have become a must-attend rite of season. I was honored to deliver a talk at MIPCOM tied into the release of the first edition of my book, focusing on the impact online was having on the traditional TV marketplace—as this edition evidences, the pace of change is such that I could speak each year and never run out of new topics to highlight.

For a period, there was a significant market in Monte Carlo in February, but with the U.S. domestic market NATPE falling in the same time frame and becoming better attended by international buyers, there were just too many festivals. Certain executives felt obligated to go to from NATPE, to Monte Carlo, to MIP, to the LA Screenings, and everyone admitted there was no compelling reason for this quantity.

Lack of Station Groups

One inefficiency in the international market is that there is a dearth of station groups that buy together across markets; in general, sales are made on a territory-by-territory basis. It would be attractive for a number of sellers to have "one-stop shopping" and license all of Europe or Western Europe in a single deal. A few companies have tried to aggregate station groups, such as CME, RTL, and SBS (since sold to a private equity consortium), but even in these instances many of the affiliated stations will acquire product independently. The reason is simple: countries have local sensibilities, and it is even more difficult to buy a program on the assumption it will work from Paris, to Frankfurt, to Barcelona than harmonizing a demographic audience from Sacramento to New Orleans. Even if demographics were aligned (e.g., targeting Generation X across affiliated stations), cultural nuances and differences make programming across borders extremely challenging. In a sense, it is a variation on the theme of the challenges of the euro.

Nevertheless, people will still try to aggregate station groups and more efficiently purchase content, and the purchase of ProSiebenSat1 in Germany by the same groups (KKR and Permira) that bought SBS (originally a Scandinavian broadcaster that branched out in countries such as Belgium, Hungary, the Netherlands, and Greece) was aimed at competing with RTL as the only other potential pan-European broadcaster. The *International Herald Tribune* commented on this scale:

The purchase of ProSiebenSat1, which operates five channels that draw 42 percent of all German TV advertising revenue, will bolster plans by KKR and Permira to create a competitor to RTL . . .

Analysts said KKR and Permira were likely to combine the German broadcaster . . . with the Permira-owned SBS Broadcasting, a Luxembourg-based group of 16 radio stations, 19 free channels, and 20 pay-TV channels.[65]

International Pay Television and Need for Scale

The economics of international pay television networks and the structure of license deals largely mimic much of the discussion above regarding the United States. It is high margin based on few costs beyond acquisition expenses, of which most other costs are fixed rather than variable. License fees are tied to fixed sums per subscriber, with overages applied against minimum guarantees. Windows tend to mimic those of the United States, with pay television's window accelerating to several months post video from an historical one-year-from-video holdback (still mandated in France), and runs defined in terms of exhibition days. Buyers and sellers attend the same markets as free TV, with MIP and MIPCOM as the primary international festivals.

The major difference is that while the United States is cable-dominated, many international services, such as Sky in the UK, are predominately satellite-delivered. Moreover, many of these services have been local pioneers, and the set-top box is actually tied to the pay TV service rather than the local cable carrier. The incremental hardware cost was initially a barrier to subscriber growth, but with the maturation of the market or discounted giveaways (and, in cases, even free) with signing up this is becoming less of a factor. What it does enable, however, is the networks to efficiently capture new VOD revenue streams because they already have the technical infrastructure in place to offer the services without a third party controlling the intermediate pipe/delivery mechanism. Additionally, although international services have quickly moved to digital delivery, enabled by the satellite-to-home delivery, there are limitations for interactivity; cable more easily enables two-way communication, whereas satellite is dependent on pulling down and manipulating a signal, but does not by its customary functioning enable a user to message back.

Finally, when talking about boxes, delivery, and positioning, a key challenge facing pay services—which have been inherently dependent on encrypted delivery and access via set-top boxes—is the competition from over-the-top services and boxes/technology enabling cord-cutting (see also discussion regarding cord cutting in Chapter 7).

Monopolies and Need for Scale: Product Monopoly versus Broadcast Monopoly

The other limitation of international services is simply the size of local domestic markets. There is limited elasticity in revenues derived from subscriber bases—it is great and steady when reaching a certain threshold, but if the base remains too low there is no way to increase revenues. A hit does not bring higher advertising dollars, and if the program has been acquired from a third party it may only become more costly downstream without the benefit of upside from corresponding increased revenues. This inherent cap on revenue against this lack of a cap on expenses leads to the result that international pay services need scale to survive.

In nearly every major international market, competition has not allowed networks to flourish, and in fact has almost crippled the stations. Cutthroat competition for Hollywood product and slowing subscriber growth, coupled with what I would argue is an inherent problem with scale when revenues cannot be increased in a linear way with programming success, has led to mergers in virtually every major market.

346 The push toward mergers has been fueled by infrastructure and programming costs, plus the desire to aggregate content so that the service can offer the same range of titles that the consumer has become accustomed to at the video store, and now on multiple devices (in an environment when many consumers are device-agnostic and simply expect ubiquitous access to programming anywhere, anytime). It is not uncommon to find monopolies in large territories, and for all practical purposes the key pay services in the UK, Germany, Spain, Italy, and South Africa have no material local competition. As of 2006, France joined this club with the merger of long-standing rivals TPS and Canal+ (though competition resurfaced in 2008 with the debut of FT-Orange's satellite pay services).[66] The result is an interesting dynamic: a monopoly negotiating with a monopoly—the only licensor with the rights to Film X licensing with the only pay TV broadcaster. So, who has the leverage?

Interestingly, neither and both. The services assume that each studio must agree to certain parameters—if pricing is cut for one, it will be for all. Similarly, the studios all attempt to take a most-favored-nations approach, for heads will roll if one studio accepts a cut only to find out that its rival did not. The only out is dissimilar product and length of term. These negotiations can therefore resemble a sumo-wrestling match and can be drawn out over long stretches. Agreements are eventually reached, though, because both sides ultimately need each other.

(Channels, even if a monopoly, still need content quantity and quality to attract and retain subscribers.) Fee escalators and pricing tied to bands of performance build in rational expectations and thresholds, and long-term output deals serve to provide mutual security both in terms of product flow and, to an extent, resource allocation, avoiding frequent protracted negotiations.

Table 6.4 shows countries that started with multiple pay TV networks that have consolidated into virtual local monopolies. This truly may be an example where a monopoly situation may benefit the consumer but not the supplier. Monopolies are never good for the program supplier, and usually lead to an increase in consumer pricing; however, as pay services are forced to compete against free services for viewers' time, as well as new media options, pricing has not increased dramatically. In fact, pricing has only so much elasticity against a universe with ever-expanding media options, and has a direct relationship with subscriber stability and growth. Accordingly, pay TV monopolies have evolved as a result of requiring scale for local survival, while being capped on abusing monopoly status vis-à-vis consumers by having to compete against other television options.

Interestingly, and in a very different structure from free television, in several territories the Hollywood studios have banded together to co-own the local pay TV networks: creating scale from the supply side. This is true, for example, in Latin America where LAP TV is a partnership among Fox, Universal, Paramount, and MGM, and Australia where Showtime, the channel of the Premium Movie Partnership (PMP), was a joint venture among Sony, Fox, Universal, and Paramount (pre-Foxtel interest). A partnership ensures a certain cap on programming costs, but similarly also caps the extreme upside. This is probably good over time for the studio owners, but potentially limiting to producers who are selling into an artificial market. Why would Universal approve a certain fee to a Paramount film whose producer is demanding higher fees when Paramount is unlikely to approve a higher fee to a Universal film? What likely results is a sort of most-favored-nations output deal structure, aiding network profitability at the likely expense of an occasional individual film. (Note: I cannot prove this, but it is a logical assumption based on the structure.)

Again, it is a Big World

The flip side to the growth of pay services worldwide and the potential of millions of dollars for a single film is the infrastructure needed to sell into these multiple markets. As outlined in Chapter 1, pay television launched similarly to joint ventures in theatrical and video markets.

Table 6.4 International Pay TV Monopolies

Territory	Original Pay Services	Current Pay Services	Evolution
UK	British Satellite Broadcasting Sky	BskyB	Merger of prior two
Spain	Canal+ Espagne Sogecable	Digital+	Merger of prior two
Germany	Premiere Teleclub (Switzerland)	Premiere	Merger
France*	Canal+ TPS	Canal+	Merged in 2006
	Orange	Orange Cinema Series	New France Telecom service in 2008
Italy	Telepiu Sky	Sky Italia	Merger of prior two
Japan	WOWOW Star Channel	WOWOW	Still competition

* There was a growing consolidation of Canal+ and Orange, with Canal+ having acquired France Telecom's Orange Cinema Series. However, the French competition authority, reviewing the ruling pursuant to which it had earlier authorized the merger of TPS and Canal+ in 2006, said no to this new consolidation and ordered Canal+ (as part of a ruling that allowed Canal+ to take over Bollore's free TV channels Direct 8 and Direct Star) to divest its holding of the Orange Cinema Series. The *Hollywood Reporter* described how the head of the French competition authority, Bruno Lasserre, "told French press on Monday that the Canal Plus–Orange Cinema Series deal 'restricts competition because it made Orange an ally of Canal Plus' and said that 'We want Orange to take back its independence.' The pattern in France demonstrates the natural economic pressures as described for market consolidation, though in this case held back by anti-monopoly legislative enforcement."[67] It will be interesting to see if this trend is reversed, following the pattern in the UK where the local competition authority decided not to pursue a further investigation of Sky given the increased competition from online services such as Lovefilm (see discussion in Chapter 7).

UIP pay television was a joint venture among MGM, Paramount, and Universal, literally mimicking the theatrical structure of UIP theatrical (and the video structure of CIC, although it was limited to Paramount and Universal). This venture enabled the studios to enter global markets with reduced overhead, and to offer a breadth of product that could literally launch a local network.

As the markets matured and revenues grew, the service was ultimately disbanded (after about 10 years). Today, every studio has pay television divisions and sales forces that can be staffed relatively thinly with the merging of worldwide services; PPV and VOD are often tied to these groups, as so many of the services are spin-offs from and owned by their larger pay TV parents.

Trendsetters and Market Leaders

Much like HBO in the United States, select pay TV networks have become a fixture on the local landscape, having a material impact on production and culture, and even growing into mini-studios. Two of the best examples are BSkyB in the UK and Canal+ in France. Among the oldest global pay networks, these channels attained early scale with millions of subscribers, enabling them sufficient cash flow to diversify into other production; in fact, both grew successful enough that they are perceived as true competitors to the free networks.

Canal+ grew so successful that it was the engine for Vivendi's acquisition of Universal Pictures (a combination that ultimately proved unsuccessful for a variety of reasons, including exuberance of Internet expectations, with Vivendi selling off Universal to GE/NBC). At its peak, Canal+ had acquired multiple networks across the globe, including:

349

- Canal+ Spain
- Canal+ France
- Canal+ Poland
- Canal+ Netherlands
- Canal+ Scandinavia (Sweden, Norway, Denmark)
- Canal+ Belgium (covering Benelux)
- Canal Horizons (French-speaking Africa)

For a period, this created the potential of one-stop shopping for many suppliers, although it is likely many executives would have yielded that facility to lessen the leverage of Canal+ in continental Europe.

On a much smaller scale, I will never forget the discussion I once had with a fledgling pay service in Eastern Europe in the early 1990s. Because consumers in the former communist country had been cloistered from Western entertainment, there was a voracious demand to watch new offerings. Pay services customarily cycle through movies on a multiple time/month basis (see discussion regarding runs), assuming that its audience will want to watch the new offering, and that with a repeating schedule, they will ultimately find a convenient time to watch. In the case of this territory, everyone watched the show the first time it was on, and the only way to satisfy the customers would have been to build a huge inventory and only show new programs (defeating the economic model).

Coproductions

The international market, unlike the United States, has a culture of coproductions. This stems, in large part, from the size of domestic markets and the need to aggregate markets to raise sufficient capital for projects. It is very common for multiple distributors or networks to fund percentages of a budget in return for local exclusivity plus a share of the overall profits.

As discussed in more detail in Chapter 3, a coproduction is a much-bandied term that can mean many things, including: (1) creative collaboration or a sharing of production versus distribution obligations; (2) co-financing, where more than one party invests in a production to share both risk and upside; (3) the sharing of distribution rights (e.g., a United States–European coproduction may mean that the U.S. investor acquires North American rights while the international party acquires European or all international rights, i.e. rights excluding North America); or (4) certain pre-sales scenarios (e.g., if one party acquires rights to a product in advance of completion or production, thereby creating financing security enabling production, it may consider the risk it has taken as justifying its position as a coproducer rather than a buyer).

While coproductions can be compelling, they are complicated, often cumbersome to construct and administer, and involve compromise. Inherent in the structure is a sharing of responsibility, something that often undermines the creative process. Just like the concept of "final cut," every production needs a creative master; when production is run by committee, or when groups are trying to compromise to accommodate local cultural differences (let alone whims or power plays), the end result often suffers. The more parties, the more these problems are exacerbated. If three or four parties are all funding a production as coproducers, and each has an expectation of creative input and authority, it can be a recipe for disaster. For those needing the money, this is a necessary evil. Many in Hollywood would never cede this level of control, and in fact the studio mantra tends to be to keep all control and all rights. Hence, co-productions are generally an international financing mechanism, and a staple of international TV production.

Case Study: The Kirch Group

Most Americans have not heard of Leo Kirch, even though he was a media mogul on the scale of a Ted Turner or Rupert Murdoch (well, maybe a mini-Murdoch). Similarly, most Americans have not heard of KirchMedia or Betafilm, but the Kirch Group's production reach spanned the globe and was behind the scenes of some of the more well-known shows—everything from the *Gone with the Wind* sequel *Scarlet,* to *Baywatch,* to *Star Trek* spin-off series (e.g., *Star Trek: The Next Generation*), to *JAG,* to coproducing/financing in Europe *The Young Indiana Jones Chronicles.*

What Leo Kirch achieved was total vertical integration in the German marketplace across TV stations, supply of TV product, and local production. At its height, the Kirch Empire, worth billions of dollars, was akin to wrapping NBC, HBO, Disney merchandising, and the largest local production company under one umbrella.

On the network side, Kirch built and controlled two of the three largest national free television commercial broadcasters: Sat 1 and ProSieben. On the pay television side, the group built the dominant pay television network, which, after a few iterations, is now known as Premiere. What was remarkable about the Kirch Empire is that Germany is highly decentralized and to gain national licenses it was necessary to gain buy-in from each of the autonomous regional areas. This was not wholly dissimilar to Fox aggregating enough local independent stations to form a national network. The difference in Germany is that when Kirch first built these networks, there were no other comparable national commercial networks: they were, in essence, creating the first commercial competition to the public broadcasters.

To feed the programming needs of the stations, and grow them, Kirch virtually monopolized the supply of programming from the United States. Early on, Kirch lobbied the U.S. studios, even bringing the regional stations they were trying to aggregate to meet people such as Frank Wells at Disney (at the time, co-head of Disney with Michael Eisner). Ultimately, they succeeded, and secured long-term output deals with all the major American studios. In a bold stroke, they created a duopoly. The only viable place for U.S. studios to license their product for top value became Kirch. In turn, Kirch had a monopoly on the programming put on its controlled networks. The result was a vertically integrated media empire that, for a period, controlled the television landscape in the country.

Over time, the Kirch Group built up one of the world's greatest libraries and largest integrated media companies in the world. An online encyclopedia summarized that:

By 1993, Kirch Gruppe had become the largest entertainment program provider for German-speaking countries, including Switzerland and Austria. The group was involved in all areas of the movie and TV entertainment business, such as production, synchronization, distribution, rights and licensing trade, movie and video rental, and merchandising. Besides owning about 15,000 movies and 50,000 hours of TV shows, Kirch's many production firms put out about 400 hours of new movies and TV programs per year.[68]

In addition to building a library of owned and licensed titles, the Kirch group built state-of-the-art technical facilities to store and archive the vast product accumulated. The technical group and storage vault at BetaTechnik became world-renowned, and many international producers used the facility to store negatives, prints, and masters, as well as to create foreign-language versions. The BetaTechnik storage vault looks like a scene from a sci-fi movie, with tall rows of film prints in a secure, clean, climate-controlled room reaching stories high, and mechanical computerized robots able to pull and access individual elements. When U.S. studios and leading producers wanted to archive treasured masters and prints, despite local options and promises of salt mines able to withstand nuclear strikes, many ultimately turned to Leo Kirch. If you want to find the old reels of a classic film, your best bet is not Hollywood, but Munich.

Like so many entertainment company stories, however, the reign of Betafilm and Kirch ultimately came to an end. KirchMedia's bankruptcy was nothing short of spectacular, with far-reaching consequences across borders. The *Hollywood Reporter* chronicled: "KirchMedia's bankruptcy in April 2002 was the largest in German post World War II history. Before it fell, the company built by Bavarian mogul Leo Kirch had the largest library of films and TV rights outside the U.S. studios . . . Observers estimate that when Kirch went belly up, the company's bad debts totaled €10 billion ($13 billion)."[69] The impact of the bankruptcy sent ripple effects through an incredible array of high-profile businesses and even governments:

- The banking world: HypoVereinsbank, Germany's second-largest publicly traded bank, and Bayerishe Landesbank (owned 50 percent by the Bavarian government) combined had loaned Kirch well over $1 billion.
- Kirch had employed over 10,000 people.
- Kirch held the rights to Formula One racing, and some worried it could destabilize the entire sport.
- Kirch held the broadcast rights to the German soccer league (and the worldwide broadcast rights to the World Cup), and missed payments could have thrown the sport into turmoil.

- It became a political issue, in that the Bavarian premiere Edmund Stoiber was the opponent in 2002 to Chancellor Gerhard Shroeder's re-election; speaking of the Bayerishe Landesbank's $1.7 billion in outstanding loans, *Time* magazine quoted Shroeder as saying: "This is not an indication of economic competence, but the opposite . . ."[70]
- Kirch owned more than a one-third share in Germany's largest publisher, Axel Springer Verlag.

There are many reputed causes, but two facts were, at minimum, catalytic forces. First, in an effort to build a digital pay service, Kirch tried to reproduce the strategy that had been so successful in free television: lock up rights. The difference was that by the late 1990s, the international markets had matured, studios had grown shrewder (and perhaps greedy), and the costs had ballooned. In 1996, for example, a 10-year deal with Paramount was announced for $1 billion.[71] Unfortunately, the field-of-dreams thinking did not lead to subscribers rushing to the service. Pay TV subscriptions did not come close to estimates, and the service, as described by *Time*, was losing money fast: "Kirch managed to sign up 2.4 million subscribers; the break-even point was 4 million. The company was losing more than $2 million a day and he borrowed heavily to keep it running."[72] Second, Kirch acquired the distribution rights to Formula One, another investment reportedly in the billions. This acquisition was targeted, in part, to gain monopoly-broadcasting control of the sport to drive viewers to its channels. A second and more controversial theory was that the group was also working to rescue EM.TV, a company that had a somewhat symbiotic relationship with the Kirch family of companies. Animation producer and distributor EM.TV was founded by a former Kirch executive, Thomas Haffa, and had a meteoric rise in value. Germany had never had a small market cap exchange such as the NASDAQ in the United States, and in the heyday of the Internet had launched a new exchange, appropriately called the Neur Markt. EM.TV was the star of the Neur Markt, going public, as described by *Business Week*, on revenues of only about $15 million and soon seeing its stock rise to into the multibillions:

353

EM.TV & Merchandising, a Munich outfit that may well be Europe's hottest company. EM.TV had a tiny $15 million in annual sales when it went public in October 1997. But over the past 10 months it has grown at an explosive rate as Haffa has spun deal after deal with the biggest players in the world of entertainment, from Walt Disney Co. to German media titan Leo Kirch. Its stock is up around 10,000 percent, to nearly $1,000 on Germany's growth stock exchange, the Neuer Markt. The stock carries a price-earnings ratio of roughly 90; Merrill Lynch & Co. estimates the company will earn $38.3 million this year on sales of $117 million.[73]

Part of its success was directly tied to Kirch, as EM.TV formed a venture and programming block called "Junior," which gave EM.TV the exclusive rights to Kirch's entire 20,000-title library of animated titles; for its part, Kirch helped land programming on its stations, guaranteeing distribution for the titles. EM.TV then leveraged this base with the fortunate circumstance that few, if any, major German media companies had ever been available to the public for investment; the two local giants, Bertlesman and Kirch, were both closely held private family companies.

EM.TV used its stock market value to go on an acquisition binge, first buying or acquiring investments in smaller animation studios, and then nabbing a big fish with the purchase of the Jim Henson Company. In a story on the cover of *Business Week* titled "The Cartoon King," Thomas Haffa boasted that they would rival Disney, and securing the prized Henson company was almost a metaphorical move to prove its ambition.[74] Several years before, after the death of Jim Henson, a pending acquisition of Henson by Disney fell apart in a public spat and now, nearly a decade later, the Germans had won the day. Of course, there was an enormous price: the reported sales price was $680 million, a figure that many insiders considered a significant premium over other market offers.[75] (Note: In an odd twist of fate, EM.TV ultimately sold Henson back to the Henson family (for a fraction of what it paid), who then turned around and sold the company to Disney, completing an odyssey that had the Muppets initially and then again in the Disney family of brands.)

The next deal was the straw that broke the camel's back. EM.TV, which up to that point had been a company focused on children's programming and drew strength from its merchandising abilities, diversified to acquire controlling interest in the sport of Formula One racing. In October 2000, EM.TV came under fire for irregularities in the reporting of earnings tied to the Henson acquisition, and the stock price crashed 32 percent in two days, and then shortly fell to less than one-third of its 52-week high.[76] Caught in a downward spiral, with insufficient cash flow to sustain operations, the company started selling assets.

The big prize was Formula One, which Haffa sold to Kirch. (Note: As another aside to the story, the German Neuer Markt, which had been based on the NASDAQ, eventually went out of business; although I have not seen it written about, EM.TV had been a significant percentage of the market's overall capitalization (e.g., several percent), and the failure of EM.TV started the spiral that led to the downfall of the whole market! Imagine a U.S. bankruptcy that actually helped take down the whole stock market and you can glean the enormity of the Kirch and EM.TV saga.)

The Formula One acquisition did not stem the tide of the digital pay services losses, however, and the collective weight of debt eventually put the once-dominant company into bankruptcy. Perhaps in a move to gain scale as global media partners were growing and perhaps to raise capital, given the slow subscriber growth (partially attributed to an expensive set-top box digital decoder), Kirch started offering small stakes in his empire for the first time; Silvio Berlusconi's Mediaset in Italy, Rupert Murdoch's NewsCorp, and German publisher Axel Springer all took small shares or had put options. When Axel Springer exercised its put option worth $670 million, and then Murdoch followed, the company, as described by *Business Week*, collapsed:

What went wrong? Everything, say industry execs and ex-Kirch employees. The set-top decoder cost $500, and Kirch stubbornly tried to pass the cost onto subscribers . . . Underlying pay TV's woes were the huge sums Kirch paid for rights to films and sporting events. His deals with foreign media companies obligated him to pay some $2.6 billion for films through 2006, West LB estimates. Vivendi is just one of the companies embroiled in litigation as it seeks to collect some $200 million from Kirch. Industry insiders believe he owes Paramount $100 million . . . Most important, Kirch had a 45-year history of borrowing big, betting big, and winning big. It was hard to imagine he would fail.[77]

(Note: At the time, Vivendi was the parent to Universal and Canal+.)

Within a few short years, both Kirch and EM.TV were reduced to shells of their former selves and the heyday of Germany as the key territory financing Hollywood television came to an abrupt end. The country, though, still remains one of the strongest TV markets. ProSiebenSat1, previously consolidated by Kirch (ProSieben had been founded by his son Thomas), was acquired by Israeli Power Rangers mogul and Fox Kids founder/co-owner Haim Saban. Saban, cash rich from the sale of Fox Family to Disney (since rebranded as ABC Family), cleverly bought during the tough days following the dual crashes of the Internet and Kirch, and in just a few years turned the network around and sold the group at the end of 2006 for more than $7.5 billion, a multiple of the purchase price.[78]

I have included this detailed background to illustrate a few salient points about the international television market. First, it is large. Once a stepchild of Hollywood, individual countries now have the scale to compete on a level playing field with the United States. Betafilm and Kirch produced and acquired quality programming in a quantity that rivaled any U.S. group. (Note: Betafilm today is once again a major producer/distributor.) Second, the market dynamics are no different than those found in the United States. Fierce competition for programming and eyeballs on networks leads to enormous risk-taking. Third, all Hollywood studios had deals with Kirch, gaining significant cash flow they could count on against production budgets. Fourth, the international TV market is a perfect example of the world economy. In the case of Kirch, a German company became a global media player that fueled and supported the cash flow of multiple Hollywood studios and producers. It acquired the TV rights to the second-most-watched sport in the world, and ultimately sold its leading network in bankruptcy to an Israeli-born entrepreneur (Haim Saban) who made his fortune on kids' and animated programming in the United States (having leveraged the fortune from *Mighty Morphin Power Rangers* into the building and sale of Fox Family). For Saban, his timing and navigation of the kids' programming space outwitted EM.TV. In the end, somehow, most of the key children's assets (the Muppets and Fox Family), ended up with Disney.

A New Landscape—Impact of DVRs, VOD, and Hardware

In 2005, a sea change began to take shape in the television landscape. From the inception of television through the first few years of the new millennium, the concept of television was relatively static. Viewers watched a monitor, and over time the quality of the monitor had improved, as had the channel offerings. From black and white to color, then from standard definition to high definition, from analog to digital, from square 4:3 to theatrical 16:9 aspect ratios, from stereo to home theater (and now from 2D to 3D), the viewing experience kept improving. Similarly, the quantity, and arguably the quality, of programming increased and improved from the big three networks, to tens of channels on cable, to hundreds of options via satellite. The range of programs available diversified exponentially. What fundamentally started to change in the beginning of the twenty-first century, however, was that the viewer could become the programmer. The world had evolved to a media mandate of "whatever you want, when you want it, and how you want it."

This change started with the Internet, and then the file-sharing capabilities enabled by Napster in the music/audio world. It was only a matter of time before digital compression improved enough and bandwidth became cheap enough that the same trends and demands emerged in video media. While DVRs had already started to become popular and improved user-friendly VOD options were integrated into the TV remote via the customer's cable or satellite box, the mid 2000s were a watershed period that ushered in an era of mass experimentation. Not only was VOD and DVR penetration growing quickly, but in a span of a year or so, virtually all networks and broadcasters were seeking ways to make their television programming available via Internet access, downloadable portable devices, and mobile phones—and this all before the further extension into apps and tablets. When the right models hit (e.g., iTunes, Hulu, Netflix), consumers adopted the new services/products with unprecedented speed.

Chapter 7 discusses the economics and emergence of these new distribution platforms in more detail, while the next section simply highlights a few of the new options that were poised to change the television landscape—overnight and forever.

TiVo and DVRs

First, there was TiVo, a revolutionary technology that allowed the pausing of live television. The essence of TiVo was that the technology converted a television into an easy, better, and virtually idiot-proof VCR—but not just a VCR that recorded shows, a type of digital recorder that allowed viewers to manipulate television shows as if they were being played via a VCR. Soon, the technology became more common, with cable companies such as Comcast offering bundled recorders with its service. The functionality initially enabled by the TiVo brand gave way in an OEM world to generic versions labeled digital video recorders (DVRs).

TiVo had the first-mover advantage in terms of digital recording technology, and in addition to being able to pause live TV and record

357

programs for playback with VCR functionality, the storage capacity enabled viewers to record a season of programs with the press of one button (record all episodes in the season of *X*). People that used TiVo became quickly addicted, but by 2005 the upstart Silicon Valley-based company was facing fierce competition from cable providers offering copycat DVR services. In particular, large cable providers such as Comcast aggressively marketed like-services at competitive prices with the marketing advantage of upgrading a captive installed base of customers. (Note: Comcast and TiVo then struck a deal to offer customers TiVo, meaning specific TiVo interface features.) As earlier discussed, the adoption of DVRs and resulting change in viewing patterns had such a profound impact that it led to a fundamental change in measuring ratings (Live +).

What is a bit hard to fathom is how quickly today new technologies lose their competitive advantage and simply become a commoditized feature set in digital devices. Today, the pausing feature of Tivo is a consumer expectation in any hardware (or even software) capable of exploiting the function. Of course, this is an area rife for patent claims, as evidenced by Apple's ire over features in Android smartphones.

The New TV Paradigm/VOD

Beyond the expanded access to programming enabled by free VOD (as discussed previously when asking the question "What is free TV?"), we are still in the infancy in terms of VOD applications. There is no reason conceptually that once viewers become more accustomed to VOD applications, they will not demand more personalized scheduling options: we should expect the TV paradigm to shift again to one where the viewer can be the programmer.

If I were to download 30 programs and pay for them (or select a cue of programs from free VOD options), some from TBS, some from CBS, some movies that were only available currently on DVD/video, some content from the Web, and store them for viewing on my hard drive (or set-top box, or iPod, or the cloud, or whatever), what would I call this compilation? Would it be my favorites? Would it be akin to a Netflix subscription where I paid to have 20 titles out at once for a fixed monthly subscription fee? Would it be akin to my having programmed my own mini-TV channel where I paid for the programming access? As technology puts more control in the consumer's hands, the boundaries defining TV become more blurred (again, see Chapter 7 for a discussion of the new paradigm).

Online Impact

- What is "free TV" is a rapidly moving target, with the development of advertising-supported AVOD services such as Hulu; additionally, key online providers such as YouTube, able to more finely target niches, are launching bouquets of original channels and even challenging conventional advertising practices with digital upfront markets.
- Where you can watch TV is evolving quickly, with networks offering "catch-up" VOD access on their own branded websites and via apps.
- Technology is shifting advertising metrics—DVRs have changed ratings tracking to "Live + 3," but how soon will we see "Live + Hulu"? Additionally, the standardization and flexibility of targeted/personalized streaming video advertisements is creating opportunities and challenges, with a mismatch in metrics between ratings and CPMs/engagement statistics.
- Piracy and global access to debuts via English-language websites is creating pressure to launch shows "day-and-date" internationally with the United States.
- Second-run repeat values, which historically drive long-term library values, are threatened because of wider, earlier repeat access from VOD applications (the pie may actually shrink and reduce ultimates if new revenues do not exceed resulting declines in syndication values).
- Multiplexing of channels is creating block-based time-shifting to add flexibility for viewer access (and quality flexibility with HD channels), enabling linear channels to compete more effectively in a more à la carte VOD world.
- Pay television is facing unprecedented challenges from OTT online services, such as Netflix, which may have roots in other markets (e.g., video) but at their core as subscription aggregators look much like a new breed of pay TV service.
- Apps are enabling direct-to-consumer distribution of TV content via a variety of business models (e.g., HBO Go via SVOD), expanding reach, enabling new levels of engagement/interactivity, and making second-screen viewing mass market.
- As more players enter the competitive landscape for providing and aggregating content, services are turning toward producing more original content as one of the few differentiators.

359

■ In the new TV paradigm, we can imagine the viewer becoming the programmer, aggregating a type of "favorites" list from a variety of channels and sources, and creating a personalized schedule.

360

Internet Distribution and a New Paradigm

On-Demand and Multi-Screen Access, Cord-Cutting, Online Originals, Cloud Applications, Social Media, and More

 More content from this chapter is available at
www.focalpress.com/9780240824239

The pace of change in the digital distribution of video-based media has been so torrid that much of what I discussed in the first edition of this book is fully outdated. Cloud applications had not penetrated the mass market, tablets did not exist, the app ecosystem had just been introduced, social media was in its infancy, and cord-cutting was not part of the vernacular. What is startling about the delivery and consumption shift led by cloud-based infrastructure, over-the-top access, personalization of TV, and streaming aggregators vying to become new networks is that this new paradigm follows directly on the heels of a period that was itself considered revolutionary. Traditional networks and video outlets, still critical and relevant as the prior chapters have illustrated, are akin to boxers having withstood a first punch that scared them, and a second blow that dazed—the pending question is whether, in fact, the cumulative shocks will ultimately create a knockout. The old boxer, wobbly but wily, is still upright because content continues to be king, and the most compelling content is vertically integrated within the old distribution infrastructure; moreover, traditional distributors are increasingly finding ways to license and exploit their prized content via on-demand systems and on-the-go outlets, using their leverage to turn would-be competitors into new revenue sources. The challenging question remains, though, whether we are approaching a tipping point when revenue from VOD access overtakes traditional sources, rather than the new channels of access being merely a new window to be carefully exploited and caged. If 2006–2008 was the period when the boxer climbed into the ring to defend his title, then I would argue the ensuing few years pushed him against the ropes; in the next several years, we will see that long-feared tipping point when the ropes come down and the digital distribution genie is no longer a pretender to the crown. The challenge to content owners, going back to Ulin's Rule, is to balance the streams and impose enough window discipline that persistent VOD is not the only window— for if it is, as discussed in Chapter 1 and throughout this book, then creators will see a continuing erosion of revenue, and the challenge of how to produce and finance premium content will become even more acute.

Not Very Old History—The New Millennium's Wave of Changes in Consuming Video Content

Before I discuss the impact of this wave of new changes (streaming aggregators competing as networks, advances in over-the-top access, cord-cutting, success of Internet-enabled and cloud-based services, professionals leveraging the broadcast-yourself model, social media and related personalized methods of consuming content, etc.), I want to take a step backwards to set the context. In my first edition, I started this chapter by noting: "The years 2006–2008 will be viewed historically as revolutionizing how consumers watched, accessed, and paid for video-based content. The explosion of video on the Web came about suddenly, fulfilling the promise of what many envisioned almost a decade earlier before the dot-com bust. Much of the change was enabled by technology, such as widely adopted DRM solutions, increased broadband penetration, and the advent of video-capable iPods and then iPhones." The confluence of several factors ushered in the digital revolution that threatened to upset and cannibalize traditional TV and video distribution:

- the "Googlization" of the world and proving the Web can be monetized;
- the YouTube and Hulu generation, instant streaming, and the emergence of free video-on-demand (VOD);

- the introduction of the video iPod and then the iPhone (and subsequently the iTunes App Store);
- implementation of reliable, flexible digital rights management (DRM) technology;
- traditional distributors, not pirates, legally making the market; and
- mass-market adoption of high-speed Internet access (fixed and wireless), together with the adoption of common standards.

User Experience Becomes King

Just as software drives hardware (content is king), compelling new user experiences (enabled by pioneering technology) tend to drive digital distribution channels, and there was a gold rush to develop platforms realizing the new on-demand, on-the-go paradigm. Apple, Hulu, and YouTube are among the companies that leveraged the serendipitous moment in time to launch the right site or products (e.g., YouTube offering free file hosting, together with a user-friendly interface for uploading and accessing content, at the same time allowing users to easily download the flash video application for free). The online video revolution was unleashed, and whether a new entrant (e.g., YouTube, Hulu) or market leader (e.g., Amazon, Netflix, Apple), all companies started experimenting with business models that could tap into but would not stifle the almost obsessive new consumer habits.

363

Rationalizing the Burst of Convergence

With so many moving parts, it is nearly impossible to clearly diagram this burst of convergence. Figure 7.1 is an attempt to capture the following key factors: (1) the online market is largely driven by deep-pocketed online market leaders in related sectors, not by pirates nor by traditional media distributors; (2) convergence is not business model-dependent, as subscription, rental, and free delivery models are all being deployed; (3) TV remains the Holy Grail to many, as whatever the primary viewing platform online market sector leaders are looking for ways to leverage content delivery to the TV screen (or, in cases, a second or third simultaneous screen, and as described later, trying to supplement offerings with original content and become TV itself); and (4) technology is enabling the migration of traditional media markets (e.g., TV, sell-through video, video rentals) into new online adapted versions of the traditional markets. (Note: For simplicity, I have omitted the further layer of delivery to TV via gaming systems.)

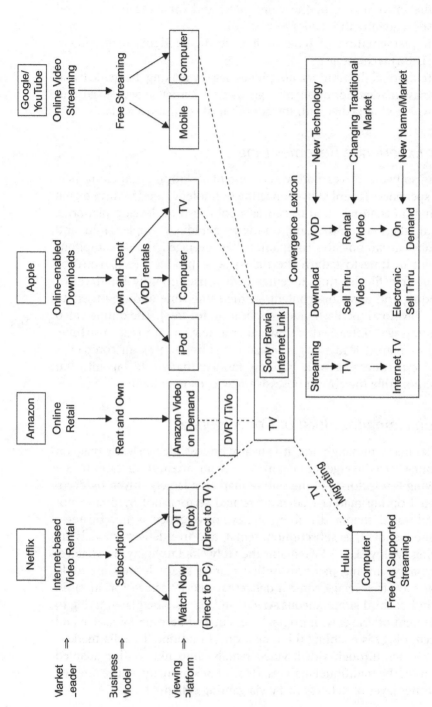

Figure 7.1 Market Segment Leaders That Pioneered New Technology Applications: Digital-Focused Companies Making the Market (2006–2008)

Again, it is important to emphasize that these were not small players angling to join the space. At the time, this represented the market leader in Internet-based video rental (Netflix), the market leader in Internet consumer shopping, including the top Internet site for DVD purchases (Amazon), the global pioneer in downloading media content transitioning from music to all media (Apple), and the top Internet search engine, whose stock had just made it the most valuable Internet company in the world (Google). Of equal importance to who was entering the market was who was not. Unlike the music space, there were no Napsters emerging as viable leaders. While some peer-to-peer companies may have been dominating Internet traffic, the upstarts were wannabes; funded by venture capitalists, the technology was not dominating the models, and in fact the technology was fast becoming a commodity and playing second fiddle to the larger brands. Perhaps the seminal Grokster case plus the earlier focus of the studios and the Motion Picture Association of America (MPAA) to squelch illegal downloads (and head off the woes that beset the music industry) together created a safe environment for companies to jump in and focus on the legal business. The issues debated were not the illegality of downloads, but the economic models of subscription versus pay-per-buy, adoption rates, conversion rates, etc. Against this landscape, the debate quickly became not "Would video downloads be viable?" but "Who would compete with Apple for the market, how fast would it grow, and would an economic model develop to rival iPod's flat $1.99 pricing for any download (an issue that now feels ancient, though only a few years old)?"

365

The key elements were that the product and technology were not perceived as intermediary, waiting for adoption of the next evolutionary product (as was the case with laserdisc before DVD); rather, the download market and portable devices enabling the market were perceived as permanent, with upgrades expected akin to the PC market. Just like the next laptop would be faster, sleeker, etc. (though at the time no one was yet thinking about the move to tablets), there was a built-in expectation that the next generation of downloads would be faster with more storage capacity. In a flash, the consumer adapted to the digital world, and did not even notice that content-viewing was being thought of in computer expectations rather than TV or video terms.

The new variety of offerings tempting consumers—from portability to living room convergence, from rental to ownership, from free to paid-for content—was dizzying and confusing. And yet, as we now know, the disruptive changes emerging were just the tip of the iceberg.

Fear Factor I: Panic to Avoid the Fate of the Music Industry

The quick pace of change and related murky legal waters initially cast fear among traditional distributors that the lifeblood of their business may be snatched away before they could even respond (with some arguing via illegal means). The crisis in the music industry, which was first paralyzed by online piracy and then rescued, in part, by iTunes, was threatening to similarly upend visual media as peer-to-peer services enabled file sharing of movies. Long-form video content, which previously had been thought to be somewhat immune given the inherent barriers of hour-plus stories and correspondingly large file sizes (i.e., a film cannot be divided into independent consumptive elements, like a record can be split into songs) was suddenly vulnerable. Whether melodramatic or not, the fate of media was perceived to be in the balance—and to many it still is.[1]

While there are no fully reliable statistics on illegal downloads versus legal buys, most industry insiders would admit that legal watching is simply a fraction of overall Internet viewing. At first, there was a proliferation of illegal services, and the motion picture industry, like the music industry before, had to contend with how to convert people to pay for something they were quickly becoming accustomed to receiving for free. The biggest danger came from peer-to-peer services that could virally distribute thousands of copies of a film almost instantly.

The threat of piracy, and the impact of the new breed of peer-to-peer services, was dealt with in 2005 by the U.S. Supreme Court decision in *Metro-Goldwyn-Mayer v. Grokster*; this case, discussed in Chapter 2, was a turning point for how Internet piracy would be perceived and contained. For here, it is simply worth reiterating that the peer-to-peer file-sharing services, such as Grokster, Kazaa, and BitTorrent, enabled individual users to efficiently share and download movies and other video content for free. There was enormous pressure, both at the government and industry level, to nip this in the bud and avoid a crisis similar to that experienced by the music industry prior to the white knight arrival of iPod and iPod lookalikes. Additionally, because the Web knows no geographic boundaries, it has become equally critical for foreign jurisdictions to act similarly. The Swedish Court's 2009 jailing of individuals behind Pirate Bay—a notorious site thumbing its nose at the notion of copyright protection—and the FBI's shutting down of Megaupload, paired with the indictment of its founder Kim Dotcom,[2] bolstered the trend fought for in Grokster.[3]

A key technological advance inherent to controlling piracy, as well as essential to managing the delivery of and access to content via the Internet, was the improvement in encryption systems. History is repeating itself: the prior fear was that DVDs provided perfect digital copies that could be pirated (holding back the introduction of DVDs), and now the same issues are surfacing via digital versions distributed through the Internet, with the scenario complicated by the need to authenticate specific devices and users. Licensors are anxious about their jewels being placed on someone's hard drive (or shareable device), and all the implications that go with that loss of control. Yes, the files are encrypted to ensure that your copy is truly on the end of a digital yo-yo, with the distributing service able to pull the strings to cut off the copy, pull it back after a set amount of time, and virtually control its ability to be played and copied (despite the fact it is stored on your computer, and now also on your tablet and in the cloud). All of this is critically important in the short term, but to many it is less important downstream, where they question the feasibility of imposing these levels of controls on consumers. To the extent people break the rules, services are shoring up safeguards and facilitating a path to market maturity where violators will hopefully be contained and be relegated to the same danger level as DVD pirates: a serious threat to be managed, but hopefully not a category killer (see further discussion in the companion website).

367

Finally, coming back to the urgency of thwarting peer-to-peer-enabled piracy, exacerbating the need for the studios to act and restore a sense of equilibrium, was the fact that change was taking place on the heels of the decline and peril experienced by the music industry. There was a feeling that this stage of change was somehow fundamentally different than prior iterative technological advances (which, despite previous fears, had served to expand total revenues); moreover, there was a realization that without action, the historical safety nets could not be counted on to preserve current markets.

Because everyone was unsure whether online would be an ancillary market or instead be the whale that could swallow the whole, as well as where lines should be drawn concerning viral access, people were scared and tending to take absolutist positions. With no obvious solutions, unproven monetization, different metrics than traditionally employed, fear of piracy, conflict between protecting valuable windows versus leveraging the Web's consumer marketing reach, and unprecedented adoption rates (e.g., YouTube, Facebook), media conglomerates at once acknowledged the changes were real and struggled to craft solutions that would expand rather than shrink the revenue pie.

Fear Factor II: Would On-Demand and Download Markets be Less than Substitutional for Traditional Markets (Pessimistically Discounting the Potential of the Markets Being Addictive)?

No matter what hype, until the on-demand and download markets approach revenue levels of the video market, they still represent secondary revenue streams. Video-on-demand is already perceived as the video of the future, and advertising-supported VOD (AVOD)/FVOD will be a critical element of TV going forward (see Hulu discussion on page 377), but the associated revenues from each remain a small fraction of the larger markets; moreover, it is not certain which markets will actually converge (is SVOD the same as pay TV?), nor whether different access methods will be complementary or whole segments will be eliminated. This is a critical issue given the Ulin's Rule factors outlined throughout: historically, licensing content through windows fostering exclusivity, repeat consumption, variable timing, and price points has optimized the pie. Because VOD can largely fulfill the consumer's appetite for access to all "when I want it, how I want it, where I want it," there was a simultaneous attack on not just the concept of windows, but more fundamentally the elements of exclusivity and timing upon which windows are constructed.

Economically, one of the key factors underlying this jeopardy is straightforward: online trends toward nonexclusive access, and TV licensing in particular is premised on exclusive windows. The much-hyped long tail of the Internet affords a broader platform for access to library titles than has ever existed before, but the long tail does not inherently prove enhanced monetization of that content. (Note: Most content people want to see already finds a home via traditional media (e.g., *Brady Bunch* reruns on Nick@Nite); see also discussion of marginalized return of the long tail in Chapters 1 and 6.) The jury is out. Even if access to a program and consumption dramatically expands, that would still not ensure greater licensed revenues than could be achieved from competition over exclusive rights. The threat presented by online is that expanded access and consumption could, for the first time, actually shrink the pie if that expansion is enabled by free and non-exclusive access. If windows are not choreographed and controlled but content is instead subject to the free-for-all of the Web, then many fear the bar will be lowered. Moreover, lower distribution costs, given the elimination of physical goods, does not guarantee higher margins, given the downward pricing pressures online.

In summary, the safety net that new technology would expand revenues—as had repeatedly happened, such as when video did not cannibalize TV, as early pundits feared—was in jeopardy, and executives in various sectors were left with the challenge of inventing a new market and revenue models or else, as in television, watch their repeat licensing revenues fall in the face of earlier online access that did not make up for their losses. Although people were witnessing a revolution of how programming would be consumed over the Internet as opposed to traditional TV, few were as prescient about the scope and speed as Bill Gates. At the 2007 World Economic Forum in Davos, Switzerland, he proclaimed: "I'm stunned how people aren't seeing that with TV, in five years from now, people will laugh at what we've had."[4] New markets and models have indeed emerged (e.g., catch-up via Hulu, subscription streaming via Netflix), giving hope that at least a balance can be restored. It is still too early to declare whether such new models will ultimately be additive. What is abundantly clear, though, is that consumers will demand multi-platform access, with repeat consumption in the future meaning consuming content via a smartphone, game console, PC, tablet, Internet-enabled TV, OTT hardware box, Blu-ray player, etc., in a pattern dictated more by convenience than a distributor-crafted linear sequence.

369

(See the companion website for more history, including "The Explosion of Video on the Web," "Change Could Have Been Even Faster (Speed and Quality as Limitations to Adoption and Downloads)," "To DRM or not to DRM," "Déjà Vu—Internet Piracy Control Measures Reminiscent of Fear of Perfect DVD Copies," "Common Platform—Behind The Scenes Accelerant," and "A Landscape Changed Virtually Overnight by iPods.")

Online Services Becoming "Networks"— the Move for Online Leaders to Compete with their Own Original Content

As earlier posited, VOD is blurring the lines of just what TV is, and I have long argued that Netflix, which is generally thought of as a video service given its DVD-by-mail roots, is more aptly compared to pay television; after all, pay TV, historically, is an aggregation subscription business, giving customers access to a variety of top programming for a fixed monthly fee. The market is now starting to prove this point, with Netflix acquiring Disney titles (available starting 2016), which had previously been with U.S. pay service Starz, for availability in the pay TV window. As a punctuation point on Internet services competing head-on with pay TV, the UK's competition authority Ofcom announced that it was ceasing its investigation into Sky's position of dominance in the UK pay TV market because the emergence of Lovefilm (acquired by Amazon) and Netflix had fundamentally altered the competitive landscape.[5]

As discussed in Chapter 6, though, there are critical challenges to the pay TV business, which, not surprisingly, are starting to impact the strategy of other aggregators: (1) cost of content is expensive, especially when trying to secure exclusive access (as noted in Chapter 6, a single studio's output deal can guarantee over $1 billion over an extended license); (2) aggregation in and of itself is not enough to retain customers, and to remain competitive pay TV services need to offer compelling original content; and (3) aggregating third-party content in a downstream window in an increasingly VOD world creates a bit of an identity crisis for a pure aggregator. Put another way, if an aggregator has to shell out big bucks for content, and at the same time sees its aggregation of content becoming a supplement rather than the driver of the business (How many people subscribe to HBO to get the movies they could have already seen in a prior VOD window versus those who want to watch *Entourage* or *Game of Thrones*?), what should their strategy be? The simple answer is focus on the driver that attracts and keeps customers: original content.

If this is the trend wrought by increasingly ubiquitous VOD access to content, then it was inevitable that other aggregation-based businesses started to modify their branding and offerings with original content. When I started to revise this chapter, based on the foregoing premise, I believed that leading services would launch originals—Netflix was among the first to announce, then followed by YouTube. In fact, in a draft, I had written, "I am not surprised that the likes of Netflix and YouTube in 2012 started to delve into originals; rather, I am surprised it took so long." Not long afterwards, Hulu and Amazon jumped in as well, saving me from this edition being immediately out of date on its 2013 release. Until recently, the U.S. market was the primary testing ground for this trend, but as the leading players branch out internationally the need for originals is becoming evident market by market. In the UK, *Televisual*, in an article entitled "Digital Giants Go TV Shopping," noted that Netflix, Amazon, and Hulu were all commissioning original shows to make their respective VOD services stand out. The article then went on to note of the testing ground: "catch-up services are proliferating and it is increasingly easy to access repeats on services such as YouView, 4oD and the BBC iPlayer—not to mention traditional services such as UKTV's suite of channels. So the leading players realized they have to offer something unique themselves in order to attract viewers. The move echoes Sky's strategy (though not its spend) of investing in original British content as part of its effort to stop churn and hold on to its 10 million-plus subscribers."[6]

The penultimate question, then, becomes whether streaming aggregators can migrate their brand, and how well in the future they compete head-on with, for example, HBO Go. Why should HBO not ask for the streaming rights to content they are already paying a premium price for, and position itself as the leader in aggregating streaming content (having been the innovator of subscription aggregation in the first place)? Maybe the battle lines will be drawn over timing (current content versus library), but this becomes a challenging difference to a consumer that no longer wants to wait.

Netflix, YouTube, Hulu, and Amazon Shift Gears

Netflix

In 2011, Netflix announced that it had partnered with Media Rights Capital and Academy Award-nominated director David Fincher (*The Social Network*, *The Girl with the Dragon Tattoo*) to produce a political drama starring Kevin Spacey entitled *House of Cards*. Reputed to cost $100 million to produce, Netflix is betting more than cash on its strategy of adding originals. After touting that total viewing exceeded 1 billion hours in June 2012, Netflix CEO Reed Hastings predicted via a Facebook post: "When *House of Cards* and *Arrested Development* debut, we'll blow these records away."[7] *Arrested Development*, though not a purely original series, is an interesting example of how online services are also providing a new market for series that were cancelled on traditional television (see also discussion of online and TV development in Chapter 2); whereas cable, on occasion, created a new home for series whose ratings could no longer justify a network run, online and on-demand platforms may now provide that second chance for successful shows with smaller, though avid, fan bases (*Arrested Development* having been a multiple Emmy award winner on Fox, with a cult following, while never achieving hit ratings).

Despite this promise (which no doubt has a white knight feeling to avid fans), Netflix's test with *Arrested Development* also provides an example of the challenges inherent in bringing back an older series. The ability to "tie up" actors for continuing seasons is both a staple and thorn

371

of producers, and once a series ceases production, the cast and crew scatter to new projects. This was one of the pivotal reasons that Netflix, when bringing back *Arrested Development*, had to announce that after one new season, it was likely it would not be able to continue the series, with CEO Reed Hastings even advising that it would be "one-off" and "not repeatable."[8] Launching a new series accordingly brings control and all the other associated benefits.

To move beyond an experiment utilizing only a small fraction of its content budget for original shows,[9] as well as compete with all the other services now following suit commissioning online original premium content, Netflix needs to commit to a substantial ongoing portfolio of original properties and leverage the shift in its offerings—a direction it signaled taking, with its chief content officer, Ted Sarandos, advising post the May 2013 launch of *Arrested Development* that Netflix planned to quickly double its volume of originals, devoting 15 percent of its budget to original programming, up from roughly 5 percent in 2013.[10] Clearly, though, even with limited fare, Netflix is starting to encroach on the turf of established pay channels much like it snuck up on the prior video market leaders. The *Wall Street Journal* acknowledged just this shift: "The move to start licensing original shows for its streaming service thrusts Netflix into more direct competition with premium-cable networks like Time Warner Inc.'s HBO, CBS Corp.'s Showtime, and Liberty Media Corp.'s Starz, which also run pricey original series alongside Hollywood movies."[11] If Netflix achieves even modest ongoing success with its original programming, I fully expect that this trend will continue and that Netflix will be increasingly viewed in "network" terms—in fact, this is already happening as reflected in reactions to Netflix's groundbreaking fourteen Emmy nominations in 2013.[12]

What was perhaps most interesting about the launch of *House of Cards* on Netflix (February 2013) was the debate it spawned about binge viewing versus traditional appointment viewing. Perhaps because the show's success could not be benchmarked against traditional TV since there were no ratings attached—no advertising, so nothing for Nielsen to monitor, a point which punctuates my earlier comment about the need for evolved metrics that capture and harmonize downstream viewing via a plethora of devices—analysts were looking to social media and other barometers to measure performance. In doing so, though, what became evident was the drop-off in conversation from binge viewing, as evidenced by the graph from Trendrr shown in Figure 7.2, as reproduced in the *New York Times*.

The headlines, interestingly, were not so much about the novelty of original content via Netflix, but rather about the viewing pattern

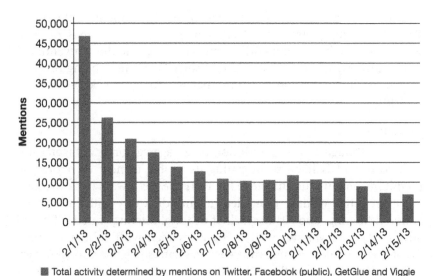

Total activity determined by mentions on Twitter, Facebook (public), GetGlue and Viggle

Figure 7.2 *House of Cards*: Social Media Decay Post Binge Viewing Launch
© Trendrr 2013, reproduced by permission of Trendrr.

that Netflix enabled by making all the episodes available at once: thus compressing the window and allowing binge/marathon viewing. Examples of headlines from the *New York Times* were: "Does the *House of Cards* All-You-Can-Eat Buffet Spoil Social Viewing?" and "Release of 13 Episodes Redefines Spoiler Alert"[13] The debate turned to how much the water cooler conversation helps market a show, whether a big bang launch akin to movies was better, or if there is an inherent benefit to the serial nature of TV. In analyzing the social media falloff, where trends indicated the debut would have put *House of Cards* among the top shows initially (at least measured by level of conversations) before its falloff, the *New York Times* noted: "Absent the long tail of online chatter, Netflix is missing out on the secondary bounce of people who want to catch up with the show when they see that many others are talking about it."[14] The *Times* also quoted the CEO of Trendrr, Mark Ghuneim, regarding the pattern: "That lack of scarcity, of windowing like traditional television, means that they aren't going to get those spikes in conversation … After you binge, you don't have a place to talk about it because everyone is on a different cadence."

It is far too early to tell what the ultimate effect and patterns will be, but this points to a classic disruptive concern when everyone is talking about windows, the long tail, and social media trends. What could be a further cry from the launch of a new network sitcom at 8:30 p.m. on Thursday evening? As online leaders morph into new kinds of "networks," not only is competition ratcheted up, but the conventional norms of how, when, and where we watch TV are now being blended in a new kind of online test tube that we do not yet know how to measure.

YouTube

YouTube, though not a subscription-based aggregator, is an aggregator at its core and is likewise migrating its profile to now offer original premium content. The challenge for YouTube has always been twofold: (1) it grew like wildfire grounded in pure discovery with little to no editorial filtering; and (2) the lack of editorial filtering scared off brand advertising that was wary of being associated with subpar content. Accordingly, while YouTube succeeded in establishing thousands (in fact, going into 2012, more than 20,000) of content partners with whom it shared advertising revenues, the associated advertising rates tended to be a fraction of those commanded by professional content.[15]

374 How to change this construct has been a continuing puzzle for YouTube, because user-generated content (UGC) is the heart of YouTube: content created by individuals and uploaded to the Web for anyone to see and potentially share. The company's early growth was directly correlated to the ease of uploading a video file, and continued when uploading images and video from cell phones created a new level of access and potential. A generation of citizen reporters was enabled, and suddenly nothing was private. A recording of Saddam Hussein's hanging exemplified that there were now, in essence, no limits to what could be uploaded and accessed. The new gatekeeper was editorial and search— not content creation, access, or technology—and its new owner Google was loathe to undermine the power of search. In its acquisition of YouTube, Google implicitly was betting it could crack the challenge of UGC. It knew the advertising categories were there, whether banners or video advertisements, and that the expectations of free, coupled with concerns about juxtaposing brand advertising next to unfiltered and "unprofessional" content (think silly pet videos), was an impediment to efficient monetization. Google simply had the deep pockets to experiment with models, inherently believing that, with an audience, it would solve the advertising issue much as it had pioneered success with its Chrome browser and Google AdSense.

I asked Alex Carlos, YouTube's head of entertainment, what progress had been made in capturing value from UGC, and he noted:

Huge progress. More than a third of YouTube's monetizable views come via our Content ID technology, which allows labels and movie studios to share in the revenue from user-uploaded clips. Record labels alone are earning hundreds of millions of dollars a year on YouTube. We see this becoming a significant revenue stream for the entertainment industry.

Even accepting YouTube's improved monetization of UGC, economically creating some form of editorial filter was inevitable, and accordingly the launch of "professional channels," while delayed, should not come as a surprise. This is simply the next evolution of YouTube trying to bridge the divide and be TV for the next generation.

In describing how YouTube does not merely want to be "like a TV network," but rather be TV itself, the *New York Times* asked the question that analysts had been wondering for years and that YouTube, wedded to its culture of discovery, had been resisting during its patient wait for enhanced monetization schemes: "But how much more could YouTube make if it could sell advertising based on predictable viewership for specific content—in other words, if it could adapt itself to the planning and budgeting cycles of the people who have real money to spend, and allow for the kind of advance marketing that the film and television industries depend on? So get used to channels. The only questions are what they will be and how well they will work."[16]

While the new U.S. channels are still developing, the scope and investment is sizeable: YouTube is creating around 100 new online video channels, with reports of $100 million to be invested in advances to content creators/providers; the list of celebrities involved is also significant, ranging from recording artists (e.g., Madonna, Jay-Z), to actors (e.g., Ashton Kutcher, Rainn Wilson, Sophia Vergara, Amy Poehler), to sports and extreme sports stars (e.g., Shaquille O'Neal, Tony Hawke), to cultural, self-help, and training gurus (e.g., Deepak Chopra, Jillian Michaels).[17] Further, the range of programming is designed to compete with the portfolio offered by cable providers, and includes news and fashion channels in partnership with major brands such as Thomson Reuters, the *Wall Street Journal*, and *Cosmopolitan*. In fact, as summarized by the *Wall Street Journal*, the ultimate breadth of programming will look a lot like basic cable: "The channels will span 19 categories such as pop culture, sports, music and health, entertainment tailored to African-Americans and Hispanics, animal lovers, mothers, teens, and home and garden enthusiasts ... In addition to generating about 25 original hours of programming every day, an additional 20 or so 'library

375

TV' hours, or existing content that may have been previously broadcast on TV, would be uploaded to YouTube daily on the channels."[18]

As part of launching (and monetizing) its new suite of channels, YouTube hosted "Brandcast" in May 2012; this was billed as YouTube's first major event at the advertising industry upfronts, and was targted to introduce the new YouTube channels and related Web brands to potential advertisers. As part of these upfronts, YouTube announced several new partnerships, including:

1. WIGS (www.youtube.com/wigs), a channel created/programmed by Jon Avent (*Black Swan, Risky Business*) and Rodrigo Garcia (*Albert Nobbs, In Treatment*) devoted to women's lives, featuring scripted series, unscripted content, shorts, and documentaries (with stars ranging from Jennifer Garner, Julia Stiles, and Virginia Madsen featured in initial series, and Jennifer Beals, Dakota Fanning, and Alison Janney committed to upcoming fare); and
2. a Team USA channel (www.youtube.com/teamusa), sponsored by AT&T, delivered by by the U.S. Olympic Committee, featuring original content relating to 2012 Olympic athletes, as well as potential Olympians and past heroes.[19]

As part of the press release announcing new partners and channels, and the hosting of Brandcast, YouTube boasted: "By the end of July, there will be 25 hours of new original content on YouTube each day."[20]

Against this background of new channel launches, I turned again to Alex Carlos, head of entertainment at YouTube, and asked whether YouTube perceived this launch and focus on new channels as reinventing TV, and how the company viewed the associated fund underwriting programming. He advised:

We're betting that the Internet is going to bring a new group of channels that's more niche and interactive than currently available. Our goal is for YouTube to become the defining platform for this next generation of channels.

Think about what we're all into today—we kiteboard, we do yoga, we paddleboard, we're into vegan cooking—we don't have channels that reflect that on TV because the start-up and operating costs are too high. That's why this complements the existing TV offering. Just as audiences shifted from broad to more narrow programming when cable came onto the scene in the late 1970s and early 1980s, we think audience will continue to shift—

spending more and more time with niche subject matter—because now the distribution landscape of online video allows for very discrete interests and audiences to be served. With YouTube, a whole new world of content can now make it to the screen.

The fund we created represents YouTube putting some skin in the game—it's small, but it's symbolic.

Not long after YouTube's announcement of its U.S.-based channels, it essentially doubled down its bet, announcing the launch of 60 new video channels in Europe. Making the announcement on the eve of the annual TV programming market MIPCOM (Cannes, October 2012), YouTube not only announced channels across the UK, Germany, and France, but also touted channel programming coming from industry heavyweights BBC Worldwide, Endemol (the Dutch company behind *Big Brother*), and Freemantle Media (*American Idol* producer, now part of Germany's Bertelsmann). The mix of channels and programming will mimic the portfolio goals of the U.S., ranging from major brands, to niche programming, to celebrity-led content—such as U.K. celebrity chef-produced "The Jamie Oliver Food Channel."[21] While the scope of YouTube's move appears grand, on a per-country level the investment is not particularly risky given the company's overall size. In the UK, where it has been reported the annual budget for original content is £10 million, Televisual, in quoting Pact's chief executive, referred to the amount relative to broadcasters ITV and Channel 4's budgets as "tiny," and continued on YouTube's hedged strategy: ". . . with YouTube providing an advance which they then earn back through advertising. Only then does YouTube split ad revenues with content creators."[22] Perhaps those seeking online funding and complaining about deal structures ought to read Chapter 10—I would love to find a distributor that started sharing upside before recouping a material part of its investment. YouTube and others investing in online content are still exercising prudence, and "new media" models are already starting to look a lot like traditional media.

377

Hulu

In the second quarter of 2012, in advance of the advertising upfronts, Hulu jumped on the original content bandwagon. In many ways, though, as an aggregator, it was the least obvious service to take the foray into development. This is because Hulu was started as a "catch-up" service for original programming, and its content consists of new original shows from its primary owners Fox, ABC, and NBC. Nevertheless, whether as a natural outgrowth of branding an aggregator as described above, or whether a necessary strategy to remain competitive vis-à-vis other key online services (e.g., YouTube, Netflix), Hulu announced that it was licensing 13 original TV series to be available exclusively online[23] (Note: The exclusivity element to drive value consistent with Ulin's Rule; UK's Televisual noting that Hulu "has a program acquistion budget of $500 million for 2012 and is keen to sign exclusive deals for content to differentiate itself from its competitors."[24])

Although there are no formal "digital upfronts," a trend started to emerge in spring 2012 of the online leaders making presentations and initiating de facto upfronts, in an effort to compete with traditional TV head to head and siphon off part of the upfront kitty to underwrite their online original content (see also prior YouTube discussion). Hulu kicked off this process, and announced five new "series" (and others in development), including:

1. *A Day in the Life*, a documentary series executive produced by Morgan Spurlock; and
2. *The Awesomes*, a Seth Meyers- and Michael Shoemaker-backed series set for 2013, pitched as "An unassuming superhero and his cohorts battle diabolical villains, paparazzi, and a less-than-ideal reputation as second-class crime fighters."[25]

By the beginning of 2013, Hulu confirmed its seriousness in the space, with an expanded lineup totaling 20 original series, including cop show *Braquo* about Paris cops on the edge (in the spirit of shows such as *The Wire*, *Southland*, and *The Shield*), *The Wrong Mans*, a comedy spy series coproduced with the BBC, adult animated comedy *Mother Up* (starring Eva Longoria), and Israeli drama *Prisoners of War* (in the spirit of *Homeland*).[26] Additionally, Hulu announced a deal with production company Prospect Park to bring back classic soap opera *One Life to Live* and *All My Children*.[27] If the soaps prove successful, it will demonstrate a major leap forward for online fare, given the seeming disconnect between the generally younger online demographic watching streaming content and the generally older demographic formerly wedded to afternoon soaps.

Regarding the apparent inconsistency in competing with its parent corporations providing new original content, the *New York Times* quoted Hulu's SVP of content, Andy Forssell, as noting that the company would work to "get stuff made and not compete with our partners."[28]

As discussed in Chapter 6 regarding TV, and as the trend tilts toward VOD consumption, it is interesting to speculate that there is nothing, in theory, to prevent experiments that launch shows first on Hulu and

378

then window them second to broadcast. In fact, this pattern could be an effective hedge against erosion of certain demographics, where it may be easier to market to audiences whose lives are spent disproportionately online and interacting via social media. Unlike the discussion of development in Chapter 2, where online series can, in cases, be thought of as testing grounds for pilots and series that may then leap the divide to broadcast, if Hulu's original fare becomes successful, then classic TV may truly become a syndication/downstream window rather than the production goal. It is also conceivable that, over time, Hulu could window to itself, offering subscribers to Hulu+ a first viewing opportunity before series then migrate either to its own free platform (AVOD-supported Hulu classic) or to traditional TV (see also later discussion of Hulu+).

In essence, hit content will prime the pump, and where it is then made available next will be driven by the then-available licensing choices; vertically integrated options are apt to influence the outcome when value is attached to brand-building, but will become less a defining factor as businesses mature and those financing content are simply focused on what option provides the greatest immediate return. We are a long way from lawsuits alleging one arm of a company such as Hulu has favored its sister service, but like lawsuits which challenge that conglomerates preferentially license properties to their affilaites (e.g., Time Warner licensing movies to HBO or Turner, where producers question whether the licenses are arms-length or higher fees could have been earned by licensing to a competitor), it is only a matter of time before we see the same arguments relating to online services (see Chapter 10 for a discussion of profits and such issues).

Amazon

Amazon, too, joined the group of streaming pioneers to announce its move into original programming. For its part, though, Amazon created a hybrid model not dissimilar to the crowdsourcing schemes discussed in Chapter 3 regarding financing production. Amazon announced that it would be soliciting ideas for comedy and children's TV programming: anyone can submit a proposal (e.g., pilot script), and, if accepted, Amazon will fund and produce the series, pay the submitter of the "winning" idea $55,000 plus royalties, and distribute the program via its online video service.[29]

In a sense, this scheme further extends the notion of democratizing content development, as discussed in Chapters 2 and 3 in the context of online access and crowdsourcing vehicles. However, to be fair,

379

Amazon Studios is no less a gatekeeper than a traditional network or studio, with the difference being you do not need a track record, agent, or friend to throw your script into the pool for consideration. In essence, the PR sounds great, but the odds of success are no better—everyone living in LA is pitching something, and Amazon is now simply another buyer, albeit with a new carrot and a bit of a new twist.

What may change the equation, however, is how Amazon claims it will monitor the process. The company initially advised that green-light decisions will be significantly influenced by user feedback when it allows users to watch animatics and video excerpts from proposed shows via Amazon Instant Video; nevertheless, it then plans to follow the tried-and-true process of producing pilots before commissioning additional episodes, and will have the overall development process shepherded by executives hailing from the traditional TV world.[30] As for the pilots themselves, which are reputed to cost in the range of $1 million each—putting the investment squarely between the lower costs of cable and the higher/closer to $2 million investment by broadcast networks for new comedies[31]—Amazon users will play a pivotal role in selecting series to go to production. Roy Price, Director of Amazon Studios, outlined the process for the first set of six pilots culled from more than 2,000 submitted ideas: "The six comedy pilots will begin production shortly, and once they are complete, we plan to post the pilots on Amazon Instant Video for feedback. We want Amazon customers to help us decide which original series we should produce."[32] Despite the lure of opening up the process to anyone submitting an idea, and punctuating my statement above that odds of discovery/success are no better than traditional development, the initial batch of pilots—including a scripted comedy show based on the *Onion*'s newsroom, to a series about four senators from *Doonsburry* creator/comic-strip legend Gary Trudeau called *Alpha House*—essentially all come from sources with media credibility/roots.[33]

Regardless of how one categorizes the odds, the Amazon development process is, at least by some measure, an application of inverting the development pyramid by funneling concepts from the wider user base to the development executive, rather than the development executive selecting the project and then marketing it to the broad customer base (see Figure 2.2, Chapter 2, and the related discussion).

Beyond pure originals, Amazon is taking a page out of its competitors' playbooks and also licensing content to diversify its portfolio of original offerings. For example, it announced that its Prime Instant Video would become the exclusive online subscription outlet for the PBS hit *Downton Abbey*.[34] Such arrangements (beyond again punctuating the value of the exclusivity driver in Ulin's Rule) ultimately set the stage for production extensions or joint ventures—theoretically, if viewership on PBS were to wane, then Amazon could step in and continue the show to a targeted online audience, a point discussed and postulated earlier in the context of the promise of online to sustain more limited but targeted viewing (though perhaps this is not the best example, as there may be no more targeted TV audience to begin with than fare for PBS).

Inevitably, Amazon, as well as Netflix, Hulu, and YouTube, will learn the challenge of launching production and development versus the success rate of crafting true and sustainable hits. Netflix in its initial foray (2013) already saw the vicissitudes, having its stock stock beaten up post the launch of *Arrested Development,* when the show was panned by critics (despite Netflix advising its subscribers consumed the episodes at a rate eclipsing *House of Cards*),[35] and then being hailed, when it garnered fourteen Emmy nominations to become the first streaming service to break the artificial ceiling and be perceived as a "player" in the TV space.[36] To the extent these online pioneers succeed, though, it will be a boon for production and significant expansion of creative outlets. In a world with endless niche cable channels, there is always room for quality content, and it will be enlightening to see who can crack the formula in the online streaming space and whether this will truly lead to new forms of self-sustaining networks or merely complimentary programming.

381

Traditional Search Engines and Everyone Else Creating Online Originals

Search Engines

With the major online entertainment providers such as YouTube, Hulu, Netflix, and Crackle (www.crackle.com, owned by Sony) moving into originals, it was not surprising for search engines, who have always wanted to provide diversified news and entertainment content to their user base, to jump on the bandwagon.

Yahoo!, which has been a leader in online news, launched a new Web series hosted by former ABC news anchor Katie Couric. The show, launched in May 2012, called *Katie's Talk,* includes interviews with topic experts and will focus on topics such as health, nutrition, parenting, and wellness.[37]

AOL, for its part, announced a more ambitious program, launching AOL On Network. The "network" takes the video library of content (already accessible via AOL) and themes programming into 14 curated channels, which will be supplemented by an array of original new series. The new series, announced during what AOL dubbed its "2012 Digital

Content NewFront"—its spin on crafting new digital upfronts to steal traditional TV's thunder, and some of its advertising dollars—included seven original shows, spanning scripted entertainment, reality, games, and news.[38] Among these shows were:

1. *Digital Justice*, a weekly reality series tracking digital forensic investigators working to solve cyber crimes;
2. *Little Women Big Cars* (debuted May 2012), a Web series about soccer moms striving to balance their schedules and family lives; and
3. *Nina Garcia*, in which *Project Runway* judge Nina Garcia helps women reclaim their swagger and mojo when they have lost their groove and embarked on a new life-changing phase (e.g., just had a new baby, stared a new relationship).[39]

Independents and Studios

The ever-maturing online video advertising market is increasingly enabling original programming made for the Web—producers now able to rely on more revenues than simply from integrated product placements (see Chapters 2 and 3) are developing shows with the Internet as the end and only outlet. The number of players and variety is increasing, and while slowly to date it will be interesting to see if the push into original content by online aggregators will stimulate the whole market, and if we will see renewed interest from traditional media sources that have so far only dabbled in the area. Sony produced *Sofia's Diary* for Bebo, Sony's Crackle has launched various Web series (e.g., paranormal thriller *The Unknown*), and *Big Brother* producer Endemol produced an interactive reality show *The Gap Year* (also for Bebo). Alongside such majors, new media studios such as Worldwide Biggies (launched by former Viacom executive Albie Hecht, who headed Nickelodeon programming and launched Spike), and Electric Farm Entertainment (whose founders include former CBS Entertainment president and co-head of Sony Pictures Entertainment Jeff Sagansky, along with *Lizzie McGuire* producer Stan Rogow) are examples of traditional media executives trying to match talent and programming to launch the next generation of online shows.[40]

Despite these examples, I had anticipated that original online series would have become more vibrant since the publication of my first edition, especially given the improvement in streaming delivery, increase in access points (e.g., tablets), and growth of streamed (and targeted) video advertising. However, as noted in Chapter 2 under the discussion of development, there are scant examples of success; programming has seemed to grow even more niche and, to date, talent guilds' fears of being

382

cut out of a new pie have proven unfounded, for there is generally not much money being made. Even studios with deep pockets that would seem able to risk development have generally shied away, dabbling at best; Disney's Stage 9, which was touted as a dedicated made-for-the-web production arm, launched a couple of short-lived properties (e.g., *The Squeegees*), and is symptomatic, as it was basically shuttered and folded back into the studio after less than a couple of years. Over time, though, there is little doubt that more, and better, online original content will be produced. In fact, as discussed in the context of key aggregators (e.g., Netflix, Amazon, YouTube, Hulu), this is now finally happening on a much grander scale—what we have not seen yet is crossover or hits, with online series still somewhat novelties. Nevertheless, with the amounts being invested and the ability of these deep-pocketed leaders to market and leverage the one-to-one relationships they enjoy with their bases, it is inevitable that something will break through—the issue is timing, and whether these companies have the fortitude to withstand the "nobody knows anything" risk to see through portfolios and become the next evolution of networks.

Finally, as the market evolves, it will be further interesting to see the impact on windowing. More and niche segmented channels open up opportunities to spin-off or continue programming (that might otherwise not be sustainable) to hyper-targeted audiences, and where a show may debut, migrate, or be viewed in a downstream window opens up a new matrix of licensing possibilities. Again, the notion of "what is TV?" is not easy to define as television morphs into a branding construct and is no longer defined simply by a single platform or appointment viewing.

Cord-Cutting: Over-the-Top, Apps, and Other Modes of Access

Dedicated Hardware Boxes

Since the days of Web TV (mid 1990s before its purchase by Microsoft), a Holy Grail has been the integration of the Web with television. With the advent of Nexflix's streaming service, the use of Microsoft's Xbox as a multimedia content hub (originally XBox 360), and the growth of Roku and Apple TV, the promise of streaming media boxes has largely been fulfilled. In addition to Roku, devices such as offered by Boxee easily enable customers to stream digital content and watch it via a TV or other screen/monitor. I have had the pleasure of watching Roku grow, and meeting with its founder (Anthony Wood) and former president (David Krall) in their Silicon Valley headquarters—for those who have not used Roku, the experience is the definition of plug-and-play. Simply plug the

Roku box in, select your home wireless network, and you have VOD access to streaming content such as Amazon VOD and Netflix, with full DVR control functionality (e.g., pause). When Roku invested heavily in advertising during the 2011 holiday season, brought down the price of its base box to $50, and had the hardware carried in mass-market electronic outlets, the brand began transitioning to mainstream use.[41] With a Roku box and other OTT devices, the virtual video store is truly realized, with inventory potentially dwarfing a retail outlet at your fingertips, loading and playing instantly.

I do not plan to offer a comparison of various devices here—there are plenty of online sources that can compare feature sets among competitive boxes. Rather, I simply want to emphasize general capability of the devices that enable the Internet-to-TV junction. I have also focused on Roku and Boxee here, not because of favoritism, but simply to illustrate the marketplace. Unless you are living in a cave, you know about Google and Apple, brands that permeate daily life and have changed the face of media. Roku and Boxee, though, are specialized companies focusing exclusively on this space; accordingly, they have either pioneered designs or user interfaces that cater to the core elements of easily porting content digitally/online to the TV screen, and are also likely more recognized by tech-savvy consumers (though you may hear more about Boxee, as it was acquired by Samsung in summer 2013).[42]

In the instance of both Boxee and Roku, both products are truly hardware/integrated software products that are, at least in design, content-agnostic; each box pulls content digitally and uses the TV merely as a display monitor, linking content from Web-based sources, as opposed to a TV that sources its content from the airwaves, cable, or satellite. Accordingly, both boxes allow users to pull movie and TV content from aggregators (e.g., Netflix, Vudu), and apps from the Web (e.g., Pandora, Flickr). In an effort to expand the content able to be pulled in, Boxee added an HD antenna to access live TV (grabbing the free digital signals of the major networks, and thus capturing a good chunk of live sports programming). The HD antenna connects directly to a small USB thumb drive that plugs into the Boxee device. (Note: Subtle legal differences in implementation have not made it the same target, to date, as Aero discussed in Chapter 2.) This represents the very definition of cord-cutting. While its marketing pitch in 2012 became "watch on TV, watch on apps" (to watch on TV, the company highlights that you either need the antenna or a cable connection), earlier website headings under live TV brazenly noted: "Broadcast + Internet = Easy Alternative to Cable." Boxee's website even advised: "Boxee intelligently blends live broadcast TV with shows and movies from the Internet to give you one interface for everything you want to watch ... Boxee

384

provides an easy alternative to high-priced monthly cable bills."[43] You can almost hear whispers of "snip, snip."

Finally, because the Boxee box/platform is content-agnostic and relies on software as "the brain," the box enables users to sort and interact with the content in the same way that users are manipulating connectivity on the Web. Accordingly, watching can become social, recommendations can come from friends and not just a cycling (and curated) TV guide channel, and content listings and queues can be personalized. (Note: In parallel to its connected TV product, Boxee used to offer a software download, enabling the same functionality via personal computers. In 2012, however, the company ceased supporting its software downloads, with its VP Marketing noting in a blog post: "We believe the future of TV will be driven by devices such as the Boxee box, connected TVs/Blu-rays and second-screen devices such as tablets and phones ... People will continue to watch a lot of video on their computer, but it is more likely to be a laptop than a home-theater PC and probably through a browser rather than downloaded software."[44]

When one thinks about the scope of what these new boxes enable, from the realization of the virtual video store to sorting and searching UI applications that more resemble a computer than a TV, there is a tendency to declare the future is here and that everyone will soon own a box. Remembering, though, the maxim content is king and that it is incredibly challenging to convince the mass-market user base to adopt yet another device that plugs in, means that the battle is far from over. In fact, I believe that despite the elegance and leap forward these boxes represent, by my next edition they could be viewed as iterative steps in the wasteland of media distribution. Why? Because the technology will have been integrated as a feature set into something else most already have: the TV. TiVo was revolutionary, but its core (and at the time revolutionary) application of pausing and recording live TV is now bundled into every DVR and cable box. Similarly, the enabling features of these best-of-breed hardware boxes will be integrated directly into TVs, or other devices connecting the living room (see the discussion under "Living Room Convergence")—the very fact that Boxee had the capability of being downloaded as software (regardless of the fact the company elected to abandon supporting PC downloads) implicates this slippery slope.

This migration was further highlighted to me in the summer of 2012, when I moved to Europe—instead of the "plug in" being my Roku box, sourcing and translating my wireless Internet signal, I plugged in a mini-receiver to the USB port in my Internet-ready TV, making my TV the multimedia entry point to the Internet, with key channels such as YouTube already preprogrammed.

In summer 2013, Google launched a variant to this gizmo with its Chromecast thumbdrive that plugs into a TV's HDMI port; in essence, Chromecast allows the user to search video on the Web via a mobile/ portable device or laptop, and then stream that content over the TV monitor.[45] To a degree, it reduces the OTT box to its barest form and defines plug and play.

In the chicken-and-egg conundrum of whether it is better to gain access to Web and app-based content via a plug in to the TV or instead gain access to TV by a plug in to a Web-based box, there is likely to be no absolute answer—it is hard to imagine the elimination of TVs, and yet cord-cutting is real and there will be a significant group that will prefer no cable bills and be watching content via over-the-air channels and the vast array of app-based programming available.

Again, if you believe content is king, and looking at the renaissance of high-quality TV being produced by cable as discussed in Chapter 6, strong originals will provide a buffer against cord-cutting; if, however, those originals are coming from online sources (as discussed above in the context of aggregators introducing originals), then that may further bolster cord-cutting. The consumer may save here, but there is unlikely to be a free lunch, as those same services are apt to erect barriers, such as offering content via subscription pay, to differentiate themselves— going back to Ulin's Rule, there need to be certain barriers (e.g., windows) to monetize content, and free access plus free content, even if AVOD proves more successful, is unlikely to sustain the production budgets, enabling high-quality premium content that so many people crave. Content will not be king in a cord-cutting world that does not figure out a way to enable value drivers to fund quality programming.

Multipurpose Boxes—Living Room Convergence and Home Network Hubs

The ability to access video over the Internet and then watch it over your TV has been perceived by many as the ultimate goal, and the premise of "living room convergence." At some level, convergence of platforms and content access would subsume all the different paths discussed in this chapter; accordingly, in my original edition, I was unsure whether to discuss Apple TV and other hybrid boxes under general market convergence, or rather in the context of download threats to the DVD market. Two facts now seem clear: convergence enabling simultaneous on-demand access to both online and offline content will continue, but the aggregation of access into one device is not likely to occur. Think more about access to TV and film content along the same lines as access to any content available on the Web: in a connected world, the ability to browse for what we want will become hardware-agnostic, and hardware will integrate flexible applications. It is no longer about playing a game or accessing TV via only one device, but about having access to Hulu, Netflix, Facebook, HBO, etc. via whatever device you may want to use, be that a TV, tablet, phone, or game console.

The advantage that devices that already connect to the TV have is just that: the TV monitor screen is still the best display medium, given size and integrated audio output. Apple's Apple TV may not have been the "killer app" people wanted, but regardless of the reason (e.g., people did not want another box), it was only one among a number of hardware solutions trying to provide the bridge. In a sense, it had been tried before (again, remember Web TV?), and whether the bridge is a new box or a feature in an existing box, in the long run there seems something a bit doomed about trying to create an interface to a television when the next generation of televisions can do it themselves (though innovative devices, bridging the Internet and TV, and enabling customization will undoubtedly drive new markets before such devices become standard integrated TV features, and a monitor is the access point to all).

One notable interface, though, where convergence is manifested today is via integrated games platforms such as Microsoft's Xbox Live Arcade (XBLA) and Sony's PlayStation Network (PSN); these systems/ environments enable both access to linear content and connectivity to millions playing interactive games. The growth of the Xbox Live platform (boasting more than 40 million members) and PSN (which has over 90 million registered users) and integrated ecosystems demonstrates a compelling application of living room convergence.[46] The lineup of content accessible via the Xbox 360 system, as an example, includes Netflix, Vudu, Hulu+, YouTube, HBO Go, and a variety of cable channels. In fact, Microsoft has announced that Xbox Live subscribers actually used the game console more for consuming entertainment than actual gaming—with *Adweek* quoting Microsoft's SVP of interactive entertainment as noting 18 billion hours of entertainment were consumed in 2012 by the service's more than 46 million subscribers.[47]

Not surprisingly, given this base and trend, and taking note of other online leaders launching original content, Microsoft too is augmenting its suite of offerings by producing original programming. In 2012, it hired former president of CBS Network Television Entertainment Group, Nancy Tellem, to become President of Microsoft's entertainment and digital media unit. A range of product is being considered, from high-quality pay-level content, to reality, series, alternative, and live programming (with how such product is monetized, such as potential add-on pricing to existing subscription costs, open to a variety of business models). Further, and talking about the possibility of transmedia applications and secondary storylines on second-screen devices, *Adweek* noted from an interview with Tellem that: "She saw episodes ranging from as short as 10 minutes to an hour and a half, multiiple episodes being produced, and using Xbox's interactive capabilities, be it the voice-and-gesture-enabled Kinect or the second-screen SmartGlass app."[48]

Original content aside, back to the box, the question Microsoft asks, rightly so, is: Why buy a limited feature box such as Roku when you can get the same content on the Xbox you already have? In terms of streaming and access, they are, in fact, comparable; the difference then lies in cost, user interface, space, and all the other features that drive a consumer to prefer one product over another. In terms of the question "Is living room convergence possible, and is it here?" the answer is yes; the question now becomes "What box/device do people want and, in terms of adoption, how many will they have?" Further, the question becomes one of "How many devices do you need (e.g., multiple TVs), and does the connection need to be fixed or can it be portable? Assuming your next TV has Bluetooth capability (or something similar), if an application such as Boxee software integrated into your tablet can be paired with your TV, enabling your tablet (or even cell phone) to act as your remote control, would that be enough? To some, yes; to the person also frequently connected to a gaming console, probably not; and to the definitive couch potato wedded to their remote, maybe somewhere inbetween. This last example, though, may be moot when the box itself is actually part of your TV.

Integrated Televisions: Internet Access Embedded within Your TV

In terms of television, for several years new sets were being conceived and built with enabling chips, such as evidenced by a deal announced in the summer of 2008 between Amazon and Sony. The then-named Amazon Video-on-Demand video store was placed on new high-definition Sony Bravia televisions. Today, there are multiple manufacturers making Internet-ready TVs, which, unlike boxes that connect via a video cable (e.g., HDMI cable), enable direct Internet access the same way your computer would connect (i.e., wirelessly, through a built-in port, antenna, or via an Ethernet cable). Once the Internet connectivity is established, then content is accessible via apps—Netflix, for example, is an app available on Samsung, Vizio, and Sony Internet televisions.

The limitation to most of the TVs will prove not to be the technology (the ability to access the Internet, and all the content that this implies, over your TV will become commonplace). Rather, the defining feature will become the user interface; complicated remote controls became the bane of the VCR industry—Roku succeeded, in part, because of the simplicity of its remote (minimal buttons and as easy as the plug-and-play hookup), and Apple redefined phones and tablets with its touch screen. Many were hoping that the original Apple TV would have created such a quantum leap, but a few years forward and most internet TVs are still controlled by complicated remotes or keyboards. Whether the next iteration brings touch screens, voice-activated controls (akin to Apple's Siri), or an entirely new approach, there is no doubt that TV manufactures will focus on pushing convergence and eliminating a box whose features it can seamlessly integrate.

Home Network Hubs and Multi-Screen Access— TV as the Tip of the Iceberg

Once apps and Internet functionality can be embedded into a television, then the next logical question is: Why stop there? If TVs in a networked and multi-screen world become just another type of monitor (though clearly the best one, given size, resolution, and audio), then it should be possible that the "junction box" can become more robust than anything we can imagine today. The future is likely to change the complexion of digital access in home to networked hubs. Whether Internet comes into your home via a high-speed phone connection or cable, the connection to a "box" is more apt to become a nerve center running a myriad of applications.

The first and most obvious iteration will be to enable TV Everywhere solutions within the wireless footprint of your home. We are already seeing this with applications such as AT&T U-verse, where content can move from one TV screen to another with linked DVR functionality; start a movie in the living room, get tired, and move to finish it in the bedroom. More than that, U-verse now allows the downloading of mobile apps to smartphones, where the consumer can browse TV guide listings, program his or her DVR, and even download content from his or her subscription packages to whatever device he or she wants. A content provider that already has rights to bring programming into the home is also in a better position (theoretically) to extend those licenses out via its hub, making the same content available via whatever device a customer may want to use for access (e.g., tablet, computer, smartphone) rather than being limited merely to the TV.

Once this capability is routine, then there is no limit to what digital applications may be enabled. Theoretically, anything that needs to be programmed or controlled could be linked via remote control smart access. Whereas iTunes is an integrated ecosystem for managing media, with content able to be stored and accessed via the cloud, why could it not run apps for other elements of your living room, or home overall?

Figure 7.3

© 2013 Apple, Inc.

390

Figure 7.4

© 2013 Apple, Inc.

Whether turning on or off a burglar alarm, lights, checking sensors in your kitchen, turning up the heat, or even tuning into a nanny cam, a hub tapping into the Internet and enabling remote or localized digital control is not a far-fetched notion. It will be media applications that first create the experience, but the digital remote control will then migrate to manage your entire connected home and life.

Third Screen: Smartphones as Hub, Even if Not Generally Categorized as "Over the Top"

Smartphones have been hailed as the next great distribution platform, and are commonly referred to as the "third screen." In my first edition, I posed the question: Why would a consumer need unique access to content through its mobile carrier versus gaining access to the same content via the Internet (which is accessible via its phone)? The answer, at that time, was that mobile carriers were trying to carve out a piece of the pie and provide a unique offering, and in some cases partnering to co-brand portals and gateways. Access was via a branded icon, which, if it did not require a download, would come bundled with the phone—"on deck." The introduction of the iPhone and the emergence of an app ecosystem have fundamentally changed the workings of this market. Apps, whether on tablets or smartphones, are becoming ubiquitous, and content providers are enabling direct access, such as via HBO Go. With the advent of the iPhone and explosion of the smartphone market, phones are, to put it simply, no longer mere phones. (Note: Neither Google's Android phones nor iPhones existed when the first version of this book was released, just a handful of years ago.) Instead, they are mini-digital hubs, a kind of home network on the go. A phone today can be a super remote control, programming and managing a local screen (i.e., your TV), a screen of its own (such as accessing content via iTunes or Hulu, or even live feeds) for watching content, and a personal computer, allowing you to surf the Web via a browser and then directly link to content (see Figures 7.3 and 7.4).

391

The potential for this market is just being realized. According to Nielsen's Three-Screen Report, comparing television, Internet, and mobile viewing, as of the beginning of 2008 there were more than 90 million mobile subscribers who owned video-capable phones (representing 36 percent of all U.S. mobile subscribers) and nearly 14 million people were paying for a mobile video plan (only a 6 percent penetration of mobile subscribers).[49] By 2012, the number of people watching on phones roughly doubled, with Nielsen reporting (though admittedly not a pure apples-to-apples comparison) that more than 33 million mobile phone owners watch video on their phones.[50]

Tablets and the New Multi-Screen World: Going Beyond the Notion of Second and Third Screen

Tablets have so quickly become part of the landscape, and as a hybrid between a laptop and a portable device offering the advantages of apps first found on smartphones, that the category has become the device of choice for watching content on the go. In fact, the versatility of tablets is such that the NPD Group forecast in 2013 that tablet PCs shipped would exceed notebook computer PCs for the first time.[51]

Like the trend innovated by Apple with the iPhone, the iPad was a brainchild of Steve Jobs and further cemented his already iconic status. While the iPad, and tablets in general, are attractive for a myriad of reasons, consuming video content is among their most compelling features—so much so that its screen is more important than the phone, and now underpins the concept of multi-screen access. The Kindle Fire complements Amazon's VOD and download options, with a harmonized ecosystem that rivals Apple's. Although at the time Amazon did not reveal public numbers, various analysts estimate the U.S. installed base to exceed 12.5 million units by the first quarter of 2013 (through two holiday seasons of sales), making it the most prominent Android-based tablet. In fact, *Venture Beat* ran an article estimating that the Kindle Fire's penetration had a reached a point whereby each tablet only needed to generate $3 per month in digital sales to yield a material profit.[52]

To fulfil consumer demand and expectations, every content distributor today has to find a way to seamlessly deliver to the multi-screen world, which now counts TV monitors (directly or via OTT services and STBs), PCs, tablets, smartphones, and game consoles. In just the tablet arena, this is a technically complex endeavor, given the growing variety of brand manufacturers, competing closed ecosystems (e.g., Amazon, Apple), and rival operating systems (e.g., Microsoft Windows, Google's Android, Apple's iOS).

Compare this to the environment not so long ago (depicted in Figure 6.2 in Chapter 6 where just TV and VCR are below the line), and it becomes a truism to say distribution today has become more complex. To producers and broadcasters, who are generally agnostic as to device, the opportunity for reach and making content ubiquitously accessible is groundbreaking. At the same time, though, this ubiquity is fraught with monetization challenges, as underscored by Ulin's Rule, and multi-screen access, no more than online access, does not guarantee increased profitability.

Growth of the App Economy—Access via Tablets and Smartphones

An entire book could be written about the explosion of the app economy and the phenomenon of tablets, and I do not plan to delve into the history and specifics of each of these categories. Nevertheless, a discussion of media access and distribution would not be complete without noting the impact.

The whole notion of "apps" was created when Apple launched its App Store in 2008, dramatically expanding the functionality of the iPhone—a classic example of utilizing software to drive hardware sales, though in this example profits flourished in tandem. The market adoption was nothing short of extraordinary, both in terms of companies leveraging the opportunity to develop apps, launching everything from new content to new businesses. Only nine months after the store's launch, Apple's SVP of worldwide product marketing announced in a press release: "The revolutionary App Store has been a phenomenal hit with iPhone and iPod touch users around the world, and we'd like to thank our customers and developers for helping us achieve the astonishing milestone of one billion apps downloaded."[53] By the start of 2013, in another press release, Apple recounted the following new milestones:

- Customers have downloaded over 40 billion apps, including nearly 20 billion in 2012 alone.
- The App Store has over 500 million active accounts.
- The third-party developer community have created more than 775,000 apps across the iPhone, iPad, and iPod touch.
- Since inception of the App Store, developers have been paid over $7 billion by Apple.
- The game *Temple Run* from Imangi Studios was downloaded more than 75 million times on the iOS platform in 2012.
- Two emerging game developers (Backflip Studios and Supercell) brought in more than $100 million in 2012 across their freemium titles *DragonVale* and *Clash of Clans*.[54]

The market pioneered by Apple soon saw copycats, just as happened with the iPhone (and with it, not surprisingly, a flurry of patent lawsuits). Soon there were apps tied to the Android operating system, and the market had become big enough on its own that categories of job definitions and statistics were being renamed to take account of apps, and Apple's CEO Tim Cook boasted of mobile apps that "Apple has become a jobs platform."[55] In terms of job growth, the *New York Times* noted: "A study commissioned by the tech advocacy group TechNet found that the 'app economy'—including Apple, Facebook, Google's Android, and other app platforms—was responsible, directly and indirectly, for 466,000 jobs. The study used a methodology that searched online help-wanted ads."[56] Regardless of whether you believe the detailed statistics, there was no doubt that the notion of an app economy had become real. Even with Apple taking a 30 percent share on app sales, developers could profit handsomely, and stories were emerging of programmers creating games and other apps making them virtually overnight millionaires. (Note: Such stories are always the PR draw, and those earning this type of money are obviously a small fraction of developers.) As discussed in various chapters (including Chapters 6 and 9 regarding TV distribution and marketing), the growth of the market enabled an entirely new category of marketing and cross promotion, and with the near-simultaneous rise of social media, distributors found an entirely new avenue beyond websites to both promote and distribute content (e.g., HBO Go, Facebook pages accessible via Facebook app).

Tablet growth spurred further adoption and convergence, as Samsung (Galaxy), Amazon (Kindle Fire), Barnes & Noble (Nook), Microsoft (Surface), and a host of other major consumer electronics companies (e.g., Lenovo, Toshiba) entered the market. As noted above, it is now likely that by the printing of this book, tablet shipments will exceed those of notebook computers—in a remarkably short period, app access via tablets has become mainstream, almost ensuring that the consumption and distribution vehicle will remain, even if the particular enabling hardware devices evolve or are superseded by some form of new technology in the future.

Although I am mentioning apps generally under the category of cord-cutting and alternate access, it is important to clarify that while apps enable portable access, they are what networks and cable operators hope will be an antidote to cord-cutting; as described in Chapter 6, TV networks are tying apps to subscriptions, so that if, for example, you subscribe to HBO, you can access that content off-network via the HBO Go app. This fulfils consumer demand for flexibility, but as discussed in other chapters, it does not necessarily satisfy the consumer that wants à la carte access to a hit show and does not want to pay for the bundled full subscription. This is where I have argued that there is no entitlement to access, and those that want PPV à la carte access early cannot, by fiat, change a window (and model) that has been designed to create cash flow to finance risky productions in the first place. Whether the ability of apps to offer easy PPV and VOD access is so tempting that it forces window changes (or else overwhelming demand will cause piracy to compromise the market) is still evolving, and different providers are experimenting with timing and tiers (see also, discussion below regarding international leaders leveraging apps). Apps, therefore, like many of the other Internet or digital changes, create another conundrum for distributors who see tremendous advantages (such as flexibility and a mechanism to blunt the effect of cord-cutting) and yet must tiptoe around the complications the new ecosystem breeds (e.g., should producers/networks tied to paid subscription models, where hit programs drive lifeblood subscription revenues, create a new form of windowing or access to leverage growing PPV demand?).

Overall Impact (Cord-Cutting)

It is difficult to find hard evidence demonstrating the effect of cord-cutting, but as noted in Chapter 6, Neilsen, in 2011, for the first time in over 20 years, revised downward its estimate of total U.S. TV households. In 2012, Nielsen dropped the number by 500,000 households,[57] but the prior year, when the revelation of a first-in-a-generation decline of TV Households was reported (dropping to 96.7 percent from 98.8 percent), the *New York Times* commented: **395**

> . . . young people who have grown up with laptops in their hands instead of remote controls are opting not to buy TV sets when they graduate from college or enter the work force, at least not at first. Instead, they are subsisting on a diet of television shows and movies from the Internet . . . [this] is prompting Nielsen to think about a redefinition of the term "television household" to include Internet video viewers.[58]

It is not surprising, recognizing that younger viewers are cord-cutting and watching via services such as Hulu and Netflix—and once so accustomed, perhaps never subscribing to cable, creating a new generation who do not cord-cut, but rather never cord-adopt—that Nielsen (as discussed in Chapter 6) is succumbing to the new reality and working to redefine ratings to capture Internet viewing.

Internet-Enabled Streaming Services: Amazon, Netflix, Hulu, and Beyond

Cord-cutting is real: consumption patterns are clearly changing, and more video content is being watched off-TV every year (and also further downstream in non-appointment viewing patterns). Table 7.1, from

Table 7.1 Monthly Time Spent in Hours:Minutes—Per User 2+ of Each Medium[59]

	Q3 2012	Q2 2012	Q3 2011	% Difference Year to Year	Hours:Minutes Difference Year to Year
On Traditional TV°	148:03	144:54	146:45	0.9	1:18
Watching Time -Shifted TV° (all TV homes)	11:30	11:33	10:51	6.0	0:39
Using a DVD/ Blu-Ray Device	5:17	5:13	6:18	−16.1	−1:01
Using a Game Console	6:38	6:26	6:51	−3.2	−0:13
Using the Internet on a Computer*+	28:58	28:29	28:33	1.5	0:25
Watching Video on Internet*¤	6:59	5:51	5:06	36.9	1:53
Mobile Subscribers Watching Video on a Mobile Phone^	5:25	5:20	4:47	25.0	1:05

Note: This table is based on total users of *each* medium. TV viewing patterns in the U.S. tend to be seasonal, with usage patterns different in winter months than summer months—sometimes leading to declines/increases in quarter-to-quarter usage.

Source: Nielsen, Cross Platform Report Q3 2012, Table 3.

Nielsen's Cross-Platform Report, indicates that while TV viewing continues to be strong, the largest growth rates for watching are on mobile and the Internet.

Netflix streaming grew *not on TV*, but watching via PCs. Netflix, in fact, succeeded by trying to make the application ubiquitously available— Netflix did not care whether you were accessing your account by your computer, over an Xbox, via a tablet, or through a box. In fact, it was the ability to get Netflix on your TV that initially drove Roku adoption. If you believe content is king, then Roku needed Netflix more than Netflix needed Roku, for Roku had little to provide unless paired with a diverse offering of content, whereas Netflix was like a steroid to any device via which you could watch streamed content. By the end of 2012, Netflix could boast of over 30 million streaming users worldwide, nearly 25 million in the U.S., and up from 20 million overall in 2010.[60]

Arguably, on-demand streaming is the most disruptive of all forces, as it leverages simultaneously the wide and long tail and makes access to content ubiquitous—it is accordingly not surprising that the industry has seen explosive growth in this sector.

Amazon: Digital Lockers, Remote Streaming Access, Downloads, and Bundled Subscription Streaming

Recognizing that download times were an inhibiting factor given the large file sizes of video-based content, services started to experiment with ways to combine instant access (to complete with online streaming) and ownership. Amazon launched its Unbox digital video service in 2006, and followed up with an enhanced version of the service, Amazon Video-on-Demand, in 2008 (now called Amazon Instant Video, or Prime Instant Video for Amazon Prime customers). At the time, Amazon was the first to pioneer cloud-based delivery and was attempting to offer a value proposition that was compelling versus DVDs. For my first edition, I had asked Josh Kramer, principal, business development and content licensing, Amazon Video-on-Demand, how he then viewed the market, and he advised, in part:

> One of the challenges Amazon has taken on is to make the ownership proposition in the digital sphere as compelling, if not more so, than the value proposition offered today by DVD and Blu-ray discs. A DVD has the inherent advantages of being highly transportable, durable, high quality, and playable on just about any TV anywhere, due to ubiquity of the DVD player. What does digital add to the value proposition? One key element is instant content delivery—giving customers access to their video collection, on whatever screen is most convenient for them. One of the ways we are working to deliver on this promise is through our cloud-based digital locker ("Your Video Library"), which aims to "unbind" content from a specific device, but instead associates the content with the customer him or herself, and the "domain" of screens to which he or she has access . . . we want to make it easy for the customer to buy a movie or a TV show, whether on shiny disc, or through a myriad of digital access points, and then make it easy for customers to enjoy their media whenever and wherever they want.

Amazon and others have now largely realized the goal of unbinding content, and what seemed revolutionary just a few years ago is now considered commonplace—and further has expanded as apps and tablets (including the Kindle Fire) represent the next iteration, and to a degree the epitome, of convenient, unbound digital access. Today's Amazon digital locker efficiently addresses the dual issues of file size (a handful of movies or TV shows could eat up the storage capacity of most computers and tablets) and the challenge of moving purchased content from device to device; moreover, because both downloads and streams are instantly available upon purchase from your "Library," it should not matter if you are at home, on a plane (assuming you have downloaded), or at a vacation ski home to access the program you have bought.

Of course, all of this infrastructure would be immaterial without content to offer, and Amazon, like its competitors, has been aggressively adding content. Beyond the originals discussed above, Amazon has the advantage of having been the leading online e-tailer for buying videos (see Chapter 5) and leveraged its positioning to sign up streaming partners. Beyond limited exclusives (e.g., *Downton Abby* from PBS, as noted earlier), Amazon, in early 2013, could boast of more than 150,000 titles across film and TV to rent or purchase, and was locking up content partners for its Prime member access. For example, it struck deals with: (1) Scripps Networks (HGTV, DIY Network, Food Network, Cooking Channel, Travel Channel) to allow subscription streaming access to the Scripps panoply of lifestyle shows (e.g., *Iron Chef*, *Chopped*, *House Hunters*, *House Hunters International*); (2) CBS to include various hit series (nonexclusively), such as *The Amazing Race* and *Undercover Boss*[61] (plus, as described in Chapter 6, *The Good Wife*, in a hybrid deal that also saw some rights go to Hulu and syndication); (3) A&E Networks to stream hits *Pawn Stars* and *Storage Wars*; and (4) Time Warner for Turner's *The Closer*.[62]

Specific content aside, Amazon has basically thought about all the contingencies of where and when you watch, as well as what gateway device you may be using for access, and created a three-way matrix: buying content, paying à la carte for rental videos, and leveraging subscription streaming (rental) by bundling with its Prime membership. It is instructive to look deeper at Amazon's rules, which provide a kind of guide to the new distribution order. For example, in the Amazon Instant Video Usage Rules found under "Videos" on Kindle Fire tablets, the company spells out that for streaming content, "You may stream purchased videos online through your Web browser and through Kindle Fire, compatible Internet-connected TVs, Blu-ray players, set-top-boxes that are compatible with Amazon Instant Video." Cognizant of the ever-expanding access points, and wanting to be ubiquitously available (competing for the same reach as competitors such as Netflix and Hulu+), Amazon is at once pushing its captive platform (Kindle Fire) while expanding its competitive reach. Then one needs to look at the restrictions tied to renting and owning. If one owns (i.e., Purchased Videos), then the access is infinite, either streaming from Your Library or launching a download, Amazon noting that viewing periods are "Indefinite—you may watch and rewatch your purchased videos as often as you want and as long as you want (subject to the limitations described in the Amazon Instant Video Terms of Use)."

Not surprisingly, rental is more complicated, as DRM protocols and other usage rules will attach to these more transient rights. For example, while only being able to download the content to one device, there is some flexibility in porting content with a Kindle, as you can start watching a download on your Kindle Fire and then finish steaming it via a different compatible device (so long as it is not simultaneously playing on multiple devices). When I first looked up the usage rules under Amazon Instant Video Terms of Use, there was an almost Freudian slip indicative of the complexity of implementing DRM—the posted rules noted of playing on not "more than once device." Viewing periods in rental are, not surprisingly, bounded (as restrictions will be set in the licenses with content suppliers), with restrictions on the macro-window of how long you have to start your rental post paying (e.g., 30 days) and how long you have to complete watching once you have started (e.g., 24 or 48 hours).

Finally, the third leg of the Amazon viewing stool is Prime Instant Videos, permitting Amazon Prime members—where a Prime membership costs $79 per year and affords members free two-day shipping on all e-commerce orders highlighted as eligible for Prime, plus unlimited instant streaming of movies and TV shows made available under Prime Instant Videos—the ability to watch content without any window restrictions (other than the content being available to Prime members). Amazon Prime Video is thus a kind of free-subscription-streaming-on-demand service akin to free video rental, provided as a value-added benefit to its Prime members. Given that Prime membership was originally, and remains primarily, an e-commerce financing option (pay $79 and get unlimited two-day service, where customers have to estimate the break-even on shipping costs and their yearly orders), granting quicker delivery to eligible products, Amazon is cleverly leveraging and cross-marketing to its customer base to build user traffic for its Instant Video service. Once hooked, an Amazon convert who has a Kindle Fire will see the holistic benefits of flexibility: ability to stream or download a video instantly upon purchase, and to enjoy the currently boundless storage of a remote digital locker or freedom of a resident copy should the manner of his or her on-the-go viewing be at a time when he or she may not have Internet connectivity.

The entire value proposition is highly compelling, and yet while this adds value to Amazon as well as the consumer, how will this fungibility play into the longer-term profitability of the producer/content supplier? The ability to so easily "watch and rewatch," as Amazon states, is no doubt fantastic for the consumer, but the ease of repeat consumption undermines that particular monetization driver (even if ownership has always enabled, the portable and remote flexibility reduces the chance of paid-for repeat consumption/need for multiple copies) and access via so many devices punctuates a measure of nonexclusivity (undermining part of the exclusivity driver, even if only here tied to Amazon). A content supplier previously would salivate at the segmentation of re-consumption and types of devices, which would create additional monetization opportunities tied to the additional consumption. All the while, though, this ease of consumption for viewers is not accompanied by higher or even any additional fees—the only extra money being made is from the hardware device manufacturers or content access points/platforms (e.g., www.amazon.com, Kindle Fire store). Moreover, Amazon is able to loss-lead its hardware, given its customer base, provide quasi-free subscriptions to undercut the value being paid for other subscription streaming services (e.g., Netflix), and influence consumption choices through its recommendation engines. In a nutshell, Amazon's offerings highlight the conundrum faced by content suppliers today, unable to turn a blind eye to what consumers crave, yet unable to capture new revenues in as profitable and efficient a manner as they have historically driven through the value drivers sustaining traditional windows.

Netflix

Another example of the same type of enabling of the virtual video store is Netflix's service, which first allowed users to access and watch movies and TV via their computers, and was then expanded to direct-to-TV applications. As initially launched, the consumer was offered instant electronic delivery, via streaming to the PC, of a rental DVD rather than having to wait for the DVD in the mail. The next iteration was a version announced in partnership with TiVo (fall 2008), where the Netflix Watch Instantly streaming rental service would be included within TiVo's suite of offerings. The stated goal was for a consumer to order a movie from Netflix via the remote control, which would be streamed directly to the

TiVo box/TV. As discussed, though, and in the spirit of covering every angle of living room convergence, Netflix was closing deals to deliver streaming programs not only via TiVo, but also through the plethora of evolving devices, independent set-top boxes (e.g., Roku) and next-generation game console systems (e.g., Xbox Live). Regarding consoles, shortly after its implementation, Netflix issued a joint press release with Microsoft, proclaiming that over 1 million users had downloaded the Xbox Live application from Netflix in less than the first three months of the partnership, and that Xbox Live users had viewed over 1.5 billion minutes of TV and movie content.[63]

As discussed elsewhere throughout this book, Netflix has also aggressively been acquiring (and launching its own original) content to maintain its position. This is an expensive proposition, and in questioning whether the billions being invested in content by services such as Netflix and Amazon in digital rights will be justified by the audiences they are building, the *Wall Street Journal* highlighted of the amounts: "Netflix committed to pay an estimated $300 million a year for exclusive rights to stream Walt Disney Co.'s films after 2016. Even before that deal was announced, Netflix had $5 billion in streaming content liabilities as of September 30, [2012], up from $3.5 billion a year earlier."[64]

Before this spending spree, I had asked Steve Swasey, then Netflix's vice president of corporate communications, how the company viewed all the experiments in the market, and whether in terms of streaming content to the living room there was space for multiple players and models or whether we would see more convergence. His response (2009) was prescient and still holds true a few years later:

Netflix is at the forefront of offering its customers the same type of services via online streaming and other applications that it has always provided—in terms of implementation, we believe content is king, and our business model is grounded in offering convenience, selection, and value in equal measure regardless of the delivery mechanism. It's clear to us that the consumer has a strong appetite not just for new releases, but for product in the "long tail"—this was clearly demonstrated to us on Oscar night (February 22, 2009), when 1.8 million DVDs were added to customers' queues, encompassing over 45,000 different titles. With new technology, we are simply able to diversify access to the long tail (and new content) via a subscription rental model tied to streaming as well as physical DVD. We now offer access through a variety of platforms, including the Roku box, and the more hardware partners, the easier it is for consumers to watch the content they want.

We believe the combined DVD and streaming subscription rental, enabled by the Roku box or through our other hardware partners, can live in a healthy way alongside other options, whether free video-on-demand services such as Hulu and YouTube, or pay-per-view access offered by Amazon or Apple. This is really no different than the brick-and-mortar world of rental video outlets, mass-market sell-through outlets, and television all coexisting, and what we are seeing is a transition of these models from the physical to the online world. It doesn't matter whether you label our Internet streaming delivery as subscription rental or a type of subscription on-demand service, because, at essence, it is the same model as DVD rental, providing great selection, ubiquitous content, and convenience to the customer. However, the more we can expand that principle—again convenience, selection, and value—the better, and the next step beyond access via physical set-top boxes is to integrate our streaming feature directly into televisions. At CES, we just announced partnerships with both LG and Vizio, whereby future TVs will embed the Netflix streaming application, and we expect to see this next-generation product out within the year.

Hulu and Hulu+

Hulu, as also discussed in Chapter 6, pioneered free streaming catch-up television by leveraging content from network partners and then innovating online syndication access together with new advertising models. The structure and service was quickly a big hit, as only roughly six months after launch, Hulu could boast providing 142 million streams to 12 million unique visitors, making it, according to Nielsen Online, the "sixth-most-popular online video brand in the United States, surpassing online video networks operated by ESPN, CNN, MTV, and Disney."[65] By spring 2009, roughly a year post launch, it had leapfrogged the competition to become, according to Nielsen Media Research, the number-two most popular video streaming site behind only YouTube.[66] Further, comScore reported that Hulu's video views surpassed 332 million, and its unique users had nearly tripled to almost 35 million.

(Note: Ranking it a bit lower relative to competition, placing it in both categories behind YouTube/Google, Fox Interactive Media, and Yahoo!.[67])

The site had become so big, so quickly, that Disney bought into the venture (May 2009) to become an equal-equity partner, adding its content from ABC.[68] The deal represented a significant strategy shift and potential game-changer in the space, as Disney altered its go-it-alone position of driving viewers to www.abc.com, while creating a near-network monopoly (only CBS missing, until Hulu struck a deal to carry CBS library series in 2012) to compete with the leading sites, such as YouTube, born of the online world.

Another unique feature of Hulu is that while the company promotes viewing at its website (www.hulu.com), from day one it embraced distribution partnerships. One of the radical departures Hulu innovated from the get-go was providing embed codes, enabling users to show its programming within their own sites and allowing the programming to virally circulate.[69] Hulu thereby enables third-party websites to embed its player into their sites, a practice now accepted as common, but at its inception it was considered a radical model and led to over 6,000 websites distributing Hulu content when only in the beta test phase. This is a significant departure for the network owners (Fox and NBC, and now also ABC), who thrive on driving viewers to a distinct location. The Hulu model casts the distribution net as wide as possible, with where and how Hulu is accessed as a second thought to offering a range of premium content free to viewers. Hulu is the quintessential example of convergence: while positioning itself as Internet TV, it is a kind of hybrid that can be thought of as VOD, free TV, and Internet TV. It is not surprising that its window pattern is not obvious for unaffiliated content licensors, especially when Hulu offers no license fees/guarantees but rather a cut of advertising revenues generated via its diffuse distribution (making the model to the content owner more like syndicated television).

After a couple of years of growth, Hulu launched a companion subscription service, Hulu+, which by 2013 had grown to 3 million subscribers paying $7.99 per month.

I asked David Baron, Hulu's VP of content partnerships, why, with the success of free streaming (the AVOD service), it made sense to branch out with a subscription service and how Hulu+ differs from the basic free service. He advised:

Hulu+ provides a number of advantages in the marketplace over our basic AVOD service. For consumers, there may be additional

403

content that is not available on the free service, as well as expanded access. While you can only watch the free Hulu service on PCs, Hulu Plus is accessible via a range of connected devices, including game systems, set-top boxes, smartphones, tablets, and connected TVs. Hulu+ also creates a dual revenue stream, with more revenue available to the content owners, which we believe is ultimately a better model for the industry. We've generated over $1 billion for our content providers since our founding, and today more of this money is coming from our dual-revenue-stream subscription service. Given these benefits to the consumer and content provider alike, we think we have a great runway ahead of us—as our advertising business expands, our programming diversifies, and our subscriber base continues to grow.

Even with success that has been heralded across the industry and is fodder for business-school case studies, Hulu faces significant challenges: a potential Achilles heel is that Hulu is beset by the benefit and burden of being a joint venture of networks seeking an upside while still incentivized to protect content value on their captive brands and channels. This dichotomy was highlighted when *Variety* obtained a confidential internal memo in the summer of 2012. The memo reportedly described debates among its owners that could lead to:

- retracting exclusivity for current content, which, for example, could enable partners such as Disney and Fox to license programming to competitors such as YouTube (content that has been exclusive to Hulu, driving its growth);
- holding back certain content to bolster and differentiate network sites such as www.abc.com (whereas before Hulu was entitled to all the content on dedicated network sites);
- taking back certain syndication rights, allowing parent networks rather than Hulu to distribute content to key third-party sites such as AOL and Yahoo; and
- questioning the limited advertising inventory, and pushing for additional spots on Hulu (limited and user-toggled choices for how and what ads to watch, having been a driver in Hulu's growth).[70]

Many have speculated that these tensions between the disruptive upstart service, whose revenues and user base continue to expand, and the independent goals of its owners led to the eventual exit of Hulu founding CEO Jason Killar (early 2013). Joint ventures are challenging constructs, in media often driven by the desire for new land grabs; as discussed in Chapter 1, many media joint ventures, even if still economically sensible, have fallen victim to the competitive desires of owners with the strength to go it alone once beachheads have been established and markets move to a different level of maturation. It will be interesting to see how the dynamics play out at Hulu, which, in a very short period, has successfully implemented new business models and established significant brand equity.

Regardless of the politics, and rumblings of IPOs and different exit strategies, the fact is that Hulu, as much as any other streaming service, has changed the face of television and how it can be consumed. Hulu+ is an extension of that trend, but the extent to which the company is able to continue drawing upon its backers for content, as opposed to competing independently in the overall marketplace for programming, will be an interesting process to watch evolve. Perhaps because of some of this uncertainty, yet also driven by the same forces of differentiation that are driving its online competitors, Hulu is betting heavily on original content (see above discussion). Today, we are seeing the birth of new pay TV services online and it would not be surprising if a streaming model that was originally fuelled by AVOD and catch-up programming comes to be driven as much, if not more, by subscription models—in the online world, where consumers still view content in shorter bits, perhaps a model will be proven where a mix of high-quality original series mixed with catch-up TV attracts a base that heretofore lived on a diet of movies interspersed with original dramas.

International Services

It is beyond the scope of this book to delve into all the new international services trying to follow the success of pioneers such as Hulu, YouTube, Netflix, and Amazon. In cases, these U.S.-based services are trying themselves to expand internationally, either through organic growth or acquisitions (e.g., Amazon's acquisition of the UK's Lovefilm). Beyond infrastructure, the most paramount challenge is simply building a compelling local library of content with the requisite streaming rights (a challenge that those in the business recognize as daunting). Nevertheless, there are services now launching regularly. As an example, Vivendi (which formerly owned Universal) is launching "Watchever" in Germany, a subscription streaming service being offered for €8.99 per month. Watchever (www.watchever.de) boasts that customers "will be able to watch entire seasons of award-winning U.S. series, blockbusters, and international art house films via Internet on a wide range of devices," and that those customers "can choose their end device from Web-enabled television sets (Smart TVs or other TVs connected to game consoles), PCs as well as Mac computers, notebooks, tablets, iPads, or iPhones."[71] An interesting component of the offering is that to overcome instances when no Internet connectivity will be available, the service allows subscribers to transfer content to "offline mode" and then access the programming via iPads, Android tablets, and iPhones.

Channel Streaming Apps (as Opposed to Accessing a Single Piece of Content) and Murky Legal Ground

There are a myriad of services enabling you to watch live TV of global channels via streaming. This is a fast-evolving space, and again my intention is not to highlight a particular service, but to comment on the nature of the offerings. For those who have not tried the exercise, simply go to the Web and create a general search for streaming TV channels; a surprising number of services pop up.

The goal of many of these services is putatively to offer domestic broadcasters the ability to move beyond local reach to a global audience. Without the need for satellite or cable infrastructure, channels can find a new audience, create new themed/branded multiplexed channels for additional content that may not fit within time constraints of existing channels, and expand brand identity. Of course, monetizing the channels is perplexing, as advertising beyond the local geographical footprint is not easily captured, the channels themselves would claim the rights to sell (and retain) advertising against broadcast content, and the streaming services are not generally paying for carriage akin to cable MSOs. Moreover, there are a myriad of related regulatory and legal issues involved (e.g., rebroadcasting rights, content bounded to territory restrictions in licenses with channels, copyright concerns as surfaced with YouTube)—and questions of bandwidth charges and net neutrality implications further complicate carriage downstream.

Nevertheless, opportunities seem to exist as regards accessing global networks whose signals/programming are captured and streamed. This has been made even easier via apps aggregating channels, such as the former version of TVU, providing a kind of global TV guide: Install, scroll through the seemingly limitless menu of network, cable, and other channels, select, and instantly have the channel streamed to your tablet. The challenge is distinguishing pirate from legitimate services, as most networks would not permit retransmission or so-called Web carriage absent compensation (see uproar over Aero in Chapter 2).

(Note: Accordingly, it is unclear whether there is permission to offer channels in many cases, with services seeming to link to published sources/stream first, and then offer to take down channels that object. A downloadable app offered in the Kindle Fire store, USTV, for example, noted on opening up the app: "If owners or producers don't want your channels to appear in our product, please send us your requests, we will remove corresponding channels from our application." While certain networks/broadcasters may allow channel streaming to the extent the costs of tracking down and stopping services from aggregating their channels is too cumbersome (if viewed from a whack-a-mole standpoint) and viewership is low given the generally inferior quality of the streams, as technology improves delivery and more consumers access the content, this is apt to become more of a future battleground than monetization opportunity, and legal fodder for the limits of linking.)

"Virtual MSOs"

Also in the mix, and somewhere between streaming of live channels and creating a suite of on-demand channels, is what is being referred to as virtual MSOs. These companies are seeking to aggregate linear TV channels (i.e., offer a package of channels just like you have via a cable subscription) and deliver them via broadband connections, thus competing directly with cable and satellite operators. It is rumoured that the likes of Apple, Sony, Google, and Intel are all involved in different schemes to create an MSO via broadband/IP; additionally, it is possible that the new Verizon-Redbox service may be targeting a similar play.

While the cost of delivery may be negated by transmitting over the Web, there are myriad challenges to launching a successful virtual MSO. One pivotal issue is simply the cost of content, as carriage deals tend to involve marathon negotiations that can also carry billion-dollar price tags. In discussing the obstacles facing Intel, for example, *Variety* noted: "Add in the complexities of coming to terms on an entirely new business model, one that can't violate the most-favored-nation clauses in place that prevent programmers from giving Intel any advantage over top MSOs like Comcast."[72] *Variety* further notes among the challenges: "No doubt Intel is keeping an eye on the debate over network neutrality, the principle that broadband providers can't give preferential treatment to any one source of data."[73]

The final results of channel delivery over IP will likely be determined, in part, by lobbyists and regulatory stuctures, as there is too much at stake to have the existing airwaves upended by a free-for-all over the Internet. It is beyond the scope of this book to delve into FCC regulations, politics, and the net-neutrality debate. What I simply want to highlight is the direction the market is evolving, the high-stakes battles being forged, and the ultimate leverage that owners of key brands and channels will have—this is one area where content will, to a large degree, remain king, for MSOs, whether real or virtual, are only forms of pipes charging a toll for access to content, and again, whether traditional or virtual, those holding licensing rights to key content will extract premiums for inclusion and packaging.

Cloud Services and Networks Enabling Everything, Everywhere

UltraViolet and TV Everywhere

TV Everywhere is a user-friendly phrase for a verification protocol that enables a TV broadcaster to verify that a user (seeking IPTV streaming video feeds of its cable content) is a subscriber to the broadcaster's service; in simpler terms, when Comcast and Time Warner announced the initiative, the goal was to enable cable subscribers to stream TV shows for free over the Internet. All you need to do is download an app (e.g., from TBS or TNT) and verify via a login that you are a paying customer of the cable subscriber. TNT went so far in the fall of 2011 as to run an advertising campaign featuring late-night host/comedian Conan O'Brien telling viewers to download TNT and TBS apps on their phones and tablets and start watching their favorite episodes online and on-demand.[74] Although HBO Go (part of the Time Warner family) is run independently from TV Everywhere, it helped pioneer the app method of watching cable shows online. Benefiting from advertising offline on HBO, as well as the growth of tablets/multi-screen options, Time Warner CEO Jeff Bewkes boasted in December 2011 that the app had been downloaded "5 million times and streamed over 98 million programs since its launch last year."[75]

TV Everywhere is, according to some, cable's grand design to thwart cord-cutting and retain cable subscribers. It is also perceived as a counterattack to the growth of Hulu, Netflix, and Amazon, providing free online access to shows as a value-added service with your cable subscription. For these reasons, and fear of "big cable," critics have attacked the move as anticompetitive. It is not necessary, though, to look at TV Everywhere in terms of a defensive position—the fact is that this distribution promises very large revenue gains to the content providers. Streams contain the same advertising as in the original cable broadcasts, and these online streams are aggregated within the Nielsen Live + 3 day ratings.[76] Now, if you watch a hit Turner show on your iPhone or iPad via the app, within three days of the original broadcast, the advertising revenues increase. A Needham & Co. analyst, as quoted in the *Hollywood Reporter*, projected that this could add $24–48 billion to the TV ecosystem over a few years, suggested that the largest content owners could see upwards of $10 billion per year increases in advertising revenue, and stated that these amounts ". . . dwarf any near-term revenue streams from digital platforms (Hulu, YouTube, etc.) . . . Additionally, these are low risk dollars as adding services to the TV bundle suggests additional revenue rather than economic cannibalization."[77]

The technology enabling the efficient deployment of TV Everywhere-type solutions is inevitably cloud-based. It is a complex technical task to deliver content to multiple screens; there are issues of security, authentication, and monetization, and cloud platforms enable content providers to deploy shows to varied platforms, and to scale deployment (ensuring the accessed show is properly and timely delivered in the right format, to a specific authenticated device) as new devices emerge and markets evolve. Different providers are experimenting with solutions, whether purely cloud-based or hybrids, and turning to software security companies focused on media technology, such as Irdeto and NDS (Cisco), to provide and secure delivery applications.

409

International Leaders Leveraging Apps and Providing Content Anytime

An interesting fact regarding the "everywhere" multi-screen concept is that before it became in vogue in the U.S., international companies were already pioneering the trend. In particular, Sky in the UK (a division of NewsCorp) had launched Sky Anytime (which later was rebranded Sky Player), which, as discussed in Chapter 6, enabled content to be both pushed and pulled to a box, and leveraged the satellite infrastructure of the Sky network. By the time the U.S. cable carriers announced their TV Everywhere ambitions, Sky had again rebranded as Sky Go and was now pioneering delivery leveraging the new app construct. With the Sky Go app, subscribers to the Sky service could now access content via games systems (e.g., Xbox), mobile phones, PCs, and tablets. Moreover, Sky started to migrate the bundle of cable packages into the Sky Go ecosystem, where content access was tiered to corresponding subscription levels. For example, a variety of live TV channels is offered, but not all channels may be available via the simple Sky Go app, and broader Sky subscription packages may be required. To ensure the widest adoption, Sky Go, for example, is also available for non-Sky TV subscribers on a PPV basis.

Because Sky has always been one of the global pioneers in terms of pay TV—adapting to new platforms, and broadcasting overall—I turned to Sophie Turner-Laing, its managing director of content, and longtime Sky executive, and asked: (1) whether embracing the multi-screen world and making the Sky app accessible via a range of devices, from game systems to phones and tablets, if the viewer base is expanding and thus bringing in more revenue, or if the old base is just being segmented; and (2) whether non-subscribers should be able to access key pay TV content on an à la carte PPV basis, as to some this takes away a carrot to growing and keeping the subscriber base. She advised how the app was indeed proving additive, and why enabling new tiers/types of access should not be viewed as a threat, but rather how Sky is opening up new distribution opportunities:

Sky's position as a market-leader is down to the way it combines the best possible content with cutting-edge technology that enhances the viewing experience and makes it easy for customers to watch TV on their terms. Our mobile service, Sky Go, is a great example of that. It's attracting over 3 million unique users a quarter, and growing, and we're continuing to expand the content available and extending it to reach more devices. New services like Sky Go offer even more value to existing customers from their subscription, but they also provide another reason for people to join Sky and help us to grow our overall customer base. We also recognize that we can monetize this success, which is why we have launched a new subscription service, Sky Go Extra. For a small additional charge, customers have the ability to download TV shows and movies to view offline and they can register two additional devices for Sky Go. It's still early days, but we're excited about this opportunity.

We see the growth in new forms of distribution as an opportunity rather than a threat. As well as enabling us to add greater value for existing customers, it also allows us to reach a whole new group of customers. That's why we launched our own Internet TV service, NOW TV, which is available via a wide range of connected devices. Customers can currently buy a monthly pass to watch Sky Movies. The next step will be the launch of Sky Sports this Spring, with customers able to buy day passes that offer access to all six Sky Sports channels for 24 hours. We believe that the launch of Sky Sports on NOW TV is an exciting opportunity. This is a way for us

410

to reach new customers by bringing a whole host of sports to an even bigger audience. Developing NOW TV alongside our market-leading Sky service positions our business well to deliver for customers and enjoy future success.

UltraViolet

The UltraViolet consortium is the flip side to TV Everywhere's offering, providing a multi-platform solution to stem the slide of DVD sales. Instead of authenticating that you are a cable subscriber, and then accessing shows via your phone or tablet, anyone who buys a DVD or Blu-ray enters an authentication code and can then watch that content anywhere it can be digitally delivered (e.g., computer, phone, tablet, Web-enabled TV). A consortium of 75 companies, including studios Paramount, Universal, and Sony, together with technology leaders (e.g., Microsoft, Intel), retailers (e.g., Best Buy), and streaming leaders (e.g., Netflix) banded together to offer consumers value-added digital ownership of the physical DVD asset—the motto becoming "buy it once, play it anywhere."

The technology, mimicking what Amazon pioneered with its Amazon VOD cloud-based service, provides users a digital locker to store purchased content; simply access your locker, and watch your movie from nearly any device, and any location. Disney, not part of UltraViolet, developed its own proprietary digital locker system, Keychest, to similarly offer purchasers ubiquitous access via digital devices with Internet connections. A number of people have questioned whether these cloud-based lockers will catch on, pointing to barriers such as entering authentication codes. While the UI issues may become paramount, the larger issue is in implications for windows. Whereas TV Everywhere is putatively a catch-up service able to expand the penumbra of the ratings shadow to more accurately capture and monetize "current viewing," digital lockers tied to purchased products effectively give away future viewings for free. While it can be argued that ownership of DVDs permitted this anyway, a critical element of Ulin's Rule is repeat consumption, and making repeat consumption easier without any additional monetization shrinks the pie. Perhaps if true, as argued in Chapter 5 regarding DVDs that few people actually watch DVDs repeatedly, this will not matter, and the economic effect of saving the DVD/Blu-ray market outweighs this concern. Regardless, UltraViolet without an additional revenue stream or premium on DVD pricing appears more of a defensive step targeted at stopping market erosion and granting consumers the flexibility required in a multi-screen VOD world.

411

Short-Term Renaissance for TV Programming Sales

The net result of TV Everywhere solutions, combined with the launch of new services ranging from Redbox/Verizon and Xfinity Streampix to compete with Hulu, Netflix, and Amazon, as well as Walmart's Vudu, Apple's iTunes, YouTube, and BestBuy's CinemaNow, is to drive up demand for content. In the short term, the industry's drop in DVD/Bluray revenues is being somewhat masked by growth from online/streaming deals. The content sellers (e.g., studios and networks), adept at windows and masters of exploiting the value in Ulin's Rule driver of exclusivity, have been deftly parcelling out content. The *New York Times* noted that a Lazard Capital Markets analyst estimated: "Netflix spent $937 million for streaming rights in 2011 and will pay $1.8 billion in 2012, as deals activate for CW shows like *90210* and DreamWorks Animation movies and TV Shows."[78] The total streaming liabilities are much higher: as noted earlier, Netflix's streaming liabilities for 2012 ballooned to $5 billion (as estimated by the *Wall Street Journal*).[79] Additionally, as mentioned in Chapter 6 regarding television, the lines are even being blurred by certain pay services, such as Epix licensing content to Amazon and Netflix—extracting increased revenues from competitive buyers, that are driving up pricing, even if those same buyers could be viewed as would-be competitors aggregating content on a similar subscription basis. Tribal logic of "the enemy of my enemy is my friend" has nothing on the politics and strategies of Hollywood.

While some are jumping for joy and view these new fees as a harbinger of a new market reality, the *New York Times* reporter Brooks Barnes is right to ask both whether this frenzy is a bubble: "Will movie streaming hurt other parts of the entertainment business, by speeding the demise of the DVD, for example, or by denting the ratings for regular TV?"[80] Windows and distribution, as painstakingly evidenced throughout this book, are part of a broader ecosystem with many interrelated parts. There is no doubt that this influx of competition to a market that was previously defined by Netflix and a handful of others, enabled by OTT solutions and amplified by the growth of tablets, is driving up content demand and, with it, prices. If content providers can maintain the elements of Ulin's Rule, including, importantly, exclusivity, within this new paradigm, then there is indeed hope to stave off decline—and even see an upside if growth proves additive above the declines wrought in the traditional TV and DVD markets (though, given the discussions in the preceding chapters regarding monetizing the video market and its scale, actually creating additive value will be daunting). What is less clear and needs further study is the online platypus effect described in

Chapter 1, and whether everything being available at once will have an overall cannibalizing effect. Content is subject to a competitive effect, as is demonstrated by numerous examples, including vying for clear marketing windows to launch new product (see the discussion in Chapter 9, "Marketing"); moreover, as posed in Chapters 1 and 6, an infinite tail and infinite shelf space cannot be matched by infinite advertisers and buyers, and as a result revenues are front-loaded against premium content and decline (leading to marginalized returns), the further out content finds itself on whatever type of tail.

There are far too many moving parts, new players, new experiments, and divergent economic forces at play to state an obvious conclusion. The hype of current bidding wars, yielding a temporary and some might argue irrational boon to content sellers lucky enough to leverage a land grab by would-be aggregators, is just one stage in the online streaming market sorting out a new equilibrium, which itself will impact the balance of the overall distribution ecosystem.

Bypassing Everyone: Direct from the Creator

Distributing a program direct to the consumer is every producer's dream. **413** This was the promise of YouTube (broadcast yourself), but the challenges in returning a profit are generating revenues from advertising (which requires infrastructure and revenue-sharing) and competing with the clutter of millions of other offerings. What if a producer or director could cut out the TV network or theater, and sell the movie/show directly to consumers for a per-viewing fee (akin to a movie ticket, but executed via VOD)? In theory, the barriers to entry have been minimized (manage a website, enable streaming/delivery via off-the-shelf technology, engage a payment processor) and the challenge becomes marketing: What will drive viewers to the site and convert them to purchasers? A big enough brand can assume that it will attract its core fans, solving the demand side of the equation; the remaining business issue is opportunity costs of direct distribution versus partnering with a major provider that bolsters sales by marketing exposure and cross promotion to its general/broader audience.

Louis C.K. Experiment

In December 2011, comedian Louis C.K. decided to experiment with the system, betting that he could make a significant return and charge his fans less to see a special by offering it to them directly. Simply by going to his website, consumers could pay $5 to download his concert film *Live at the Beacon Theater*. In 10 days, Louis C.K. generated more than

$1 million, with his website directing users to buy the special via PayPal, and noting: "No DRM, no regional restrictions, no crap. You can download this file, play it as much as you like, burn it to a DVD, whatever."[81] After four days, he had sold more than 110,000 copies, and by Christmas that number had doubled.[82] Louis C.K. paid for the production of the video (approximately $170,000) and website (approximately $32,000) himself, with these production costs largely covered by the ticket sales bought by the two audiences seeing the live show, which was filmed, and then edited; assuming the full costs were roughly a budgeted $250,000 (e.g., including payment processing fees), that created enough free cash flow to pay $250,000 in bonuses to staff, donate in the hundreds of thousands of dollars to charity, and still retain well over $200,000 in profit.[83]

What the numbers do not tell is how successful the project was versus making it available via a major broadcaster or cable outlet; perhaps Louis C.K. would have been paid a few million dollars with no risk. However, by this direct distribution method, he: (1) generated a bastion of goodwill with his fans (who paid only $5 for access, versus what would have been a multiple of that, perhaps up to $20 via traditional access via a major media company); (2) retained full control over the project, including marketing; (3) retained the ownership/ intellectual property rights; (4) made a sizeable profit; and (5) set the table for a repeat performance. Now knowing the system works, there is every reason to believe future iterations could be more broadly marketed, and the net profits could challenge the return from selling the special to a pay network (which would simply package the program and promote it to the same targeted consumers). Although clearly higher risk and more work, having proven the viability others will test this model, especially producers who have a strong brand following and can market to their core fans.

Power to Create Stars

Given the ability to sell content directly to consumers (e.g., Louis C.K. example), and the ability to broadcast yourself without going through a gatekeeper (e.g., YouTube), it would seem that the Internet should be churning out stars. However, that, in fact, is not generally the case. In my first edition, I asked then-head of YouTube's content partnerships, Kevin Yen, why the Internet had not yet led to the "discovery" of new celebrities. If one thinks about reach and frequency of a television network, YouTube's reach can be deemed as nearly on par with the 100 million or more TV household market, and arguably, given video views, certain demographics are consuming content at a similar or greater rate.

Why, then, has no Jerry Seinfeld or Oprah Winfrey emerged from the Internet, and can those with success online ever hope to reap the financial windfall stars achieve in traditional TV? Kevin advised (2009) that, given the infancy of the Internet, we need to be patient, and as the medium matures and successes migrate into mass-market culture, we will indeed see, and are already seeing, signs of creating stars and those stars benefiting financially:

The power of YouTube to generate stars is real. Already, several musicians have been discovered on YouTube then signed to major labels, and creative talent on YouTube are receiving pitches nearing or even exceeding a million dollars. As marketing dollars continue to flow online and traditional media companies embrace the power of community-procured stars, this translation of YouTube celebrity into real-world financial gain will increase in frequency and intensity. Overall rising ad sell-through rates and individual talent deals, combined with concerted promotion that often accompanies both, can systemically trigger virtuous cycles that fuel fame and fortune to levels of success impressive by any measure.

415

What Kevin postulated has evolved, and certainly people are translating viral YouTube success into monetary rewards. However, arguably, most of the successes on YouTube (at least in North America) continue to be niche celebrities, and there are scant examples of people gaining crossover fame and fortune solely from YouTube followings. A hyped case from 2011, for example, was then-13-year-old Rebecca Black, whose *Friday* music video was viewed over 100 million times; she was able to parlay this exposure into commercial ties with networks and leading online sites, with the *Friday* song performed on Fox's *Glee* and a series of videos, *Friday or Die*, being commissioned by www.funny ordie.com.[84] While this video may have gone viral and created a moment of fame, that this is a key example of "success" is a case in point why the curation of content helps bubble up hits and why YouTube, in order to generate more revenues, moved to launch a series of professional channels.

What YouTube has more successfully spawned in terms of "creating stars" is a fully democratized casting call, enabling promising performers to be noticed. Perhaps the best example is Justin Bieber, the teen phenomenon whose Vevo-hosted content reputedly crested 2 billion views.[85] Before Bieber reached this exalted status, though, he needed to be discovered and promoted via more traditional media. According to lore, a talent scout saw postings of Bieber performing cover songs on YouTube, and he was signed by Usher to his recording label (interestingly, Usher similarly broke through and was discovered as a young teenager—Usher was discovered on *Star Search*, a star curation engine in the pre-streaming era). The virtuous cycle of fame continued to reinforce Internet viewing, making Bieber a star in digital and traditional media.

Interestingly, there may be more examples of wannabes becoming celebrities in less mature international markets, where YouTube provides a differentiating platform in an environment of otherwise limited media choices. At the end of 2012, the *New York Times* ran an article entitled "Internet-Driven Fame and Fortune for Mideast Comedians," describing how a local heart surgeon had become the host of a *The Daily Show* look-alike political satire show (*El Bernameg*) on Egyptian TV (and no, this is not a parody of Albert Brooks' parody film *Searching for Comedy in the Muslim World*). According to the article, Dr. Youssef filmed clips in his laundry room parodying the deteriorating political situation, which led to tens of millions of views and a show that migrated to network TV, bringing comic relief to previously taboo topics, ranging from extreme religious views to political corruption. Describing his appearance as a guest with John Stewart on the real *The Daily Show*, the article noted: "Mr. Youssef said there was more money in comedy than cardiology. It seemed like a joke, but similar examples of Internet-driven fame and fortune are cropping up across the region, from Egypt to the United Arab Emirates . . ."[86]

Personalization and Socialization of TV—Playlists, Recommendation Engines, Social Watching, and Tools for Content Interaction

To date, consumption of video/TV has been passive, with the programmer setting the schedule (i.e., appointment viewing); even with VOD applications, the user generally has to sort through a dizzying array of titles, with "hot" or "new" titles marketed near an entry point to entice an impulse purchase. Not surprisingly, new apps are being developed daily that put the power of programming in the viewer's hand. This can take the form of turning your smartphone into a remote control, enabling you to sort through content and drop it into a playlist for later viewing, discovering content in a manner akin to what Pandora pioneered for music listening, or following recommendations by friends and influencers.

The notion of turning your smartphone into a TV remote control, with the app also learning your preferences so as to recommend other TV shows you may like, is at minimum a compelling notion. It is not surprising, then, to see both large companies and start-ups alike trying to realize this vision. AT&T U-verse, as discussed earlier, has added apps, extending its in-home box to being connected via smartphones. Peel (www.peel.com) is an example of another company pioneering the capacity. It started by providing complementary hardware in the form of a pear-shaped ornament that is synched along with your phone to your local WiFi network—to implement a "smart remote." Beyond controlling your TV via smartphone touch screen, and recommending programs by learning preferences in the same manner as websites are filtered via behavioural targeting, the app includes social features to share what you are watching. The newest iteration eliminates the need for additional hardware (the "pear") and instead utilizes integrated IR blasters embedded into next generation smart phones and tablets. IR blasters, in essence, replace your DVR remote control, emulating the function and allowing the phone (via an app) to serve as the remote to your TV, cable, and satellite access. Already, Peel is powering this capacity in Samsung and HTC smartphones and tablets, is working with various **417** OEM manufacturers to make this standard on mobile devices (and is starting to look globally, not simply in the U.S.), and forecasts that this capacity could be a part of over 100 million devices within a year. Philip Poulidis, CRO of Peel, told me: "This is a game changer as it basically puts an IP address on remote controls and the power of recommendations in the hands of tens of millions of consumer living rooms. Not to mention the valuable data that we will have access to real-time user TV viewership and preferences." (see Figure 7.5).

My point is not a sales pitch for Peel (in line with my economic comments throughout, I was excited about the free app, yet was not quite ready to purchase the pear hardware); rather, this is an example of how interacting with content is becoming more social and more personal, turning the channel guide on its head.

Concepts such as Peel and AT&T U-verse applications, though reinventing the remote, are generally tied to the fixed channels available via cable/TV listings (in fact, the app imports your cable channel guide in order to control it). To take the next leap in personalization, the options need to encompass the reach and long tail of the Web. Services such as Squrl do just this, porting the concept of DVRs for video on the web; search the Internet, as well as content aggregators such as Netflix, Hulu, and YouTube, and drop your choices into an organized collection of queues or galleries for viewing. (Note: The whole notion

Figure 7.5 Your phone as the New Remote Control

Reproduced by permission of Peel.

418 of search is yet another wrinkle, as various companies, ranging from Blinkx, to Michael Eisner-backed Veoh TV (with software functioning akin to a Web browser, but then generating video playlists), to Google (reportedly experimenting with voice and video search) trying to engineer a leap beyond keyword-based indexing.) This truly converts the channel guide to an iPod-like playlist, enabling users to sort and store content to watch later. Again, because TV is essentially a passive vehicle, whether people will adapt to actively becoming their own programmer is unclear; networks have long survived as curators and recommenders, even if that is achieved via persistent marketing.

To the extent that viewers embrace the concept of personal discovery, coupled with personal programming, it further hampers the ability of content creators to market and introduce new programming; worse, this could create the inverse of a virtuous cycle for content creators. With less ability to create overnight brands, the reach of new content diminishes, and so necessarily will its upfront value and the funds available to make the content in the first place. Discovery may be a key driver in personalization, but it is also a euphemism for risk.

The third leg of the personalization stool is an enhanced recommendation engine. You might think you know what you like by discovery (which has its limits, given the nature of experience goods, as discussed in Chapter 3), and may be influenced by friends via their choices (which has the risk of wrong-way cascades, as also discussed in

Chapter 3), but in the words of the Spice Girls, what do you really, really want? There are various forms of "curation" in terms of recommendation engines, but the two largest baskets seem to be ones that focus on third-party recommendations and opinions, and ones that focus on internal preferences. An example of the first is an Amazon-type engine that serves up suggestions based upon your history of preferences; a twist on this is Twitter or Rotten Tomatos, where you may elect to follow people or a sum of reviewers, whose comments (theoretically) are influencing your opinion (because you have elected to follow them or seek their rating). These are all responses to the experience goods dilemma earlier discussed. In the social media-focused world, opinions from friends are highly prized. Upstart video sharing site www.chill.com, for example, markets watching videos from people you care about via a hybrid strategy pushing video recommendations to you from friends (classic sharing) and from people you choose to follow (akin to Twitter). (See also the discussion of social marketing campaigns, and Gruvi, in Chapter 9.)

What about the other side of the experience good quandary, and recommendations based upon your instincts and likes rather than extrapolated from third party opinions (even if those are filtered opinions from people you trust)? Put another way, is there a subliminal way to make recommendations better, attacking the "DNA" of your personal likes? That is exactly what Pandora invented with its Music Genome Project®, a system that looks at the attributes of a song across hundreds of traits to form the DNA of the song. Additionally, Pandora layers on playlist technology, including advanced highly contextual collaborate filtering based on the billions of "thumbs up" and "thumbs down" it has received. Not surprisingly, others are attempting to mimic its success with other kinds of media content.

It is too early to tell what will succeed in this new space, but after looking at Jinni (www.jinni.com), an app that attempts to apply a genomic methodology and Taste Engine, I asked Larry Marcus, managing director at Walden Venture Capital, who was a founding investor in Pandora and backed its founder Tim Westergren all the way through its IPO (in fact, somewhat famously, as over one hundred VCs had previously turned down the initial pitch and the company was limping along on the fumes of its last credit card debt), how he viewed personalization in the TV market as opposed to music:

TV has very different dynamics than music: live content like news, sports, and appointment-TV (like primetime series or award shows)

419

drives large swaths of viewing. Music is consumed a song at a time in few-minute pieces, versus TV, which is consumed a show at a time in 22+ minute pieces, or even in multi-hour pieces via movies or season passes to a series. For example, if someone discovers a show they love, they might order or buy or rent a whole season from iTunes, Amazon, Netflix, or their video service provider. So TV-based recommendation is lumpier in need and applies to only a portion of the content. Lastly, TV has a smaller corpus of consumable content, is consumed in different ways so fundamentally has a different set of needs and values.

Social Watching

I mention the marketing benefit of social watching in Chapter 9, but it is important to note here how social media sites are becoming an important new access point for viewing. To the earlier question about ratings, "Why not look at Live + Hulu when evaluating appropriate metrics to capture true engagement and viewership?", can now be added: "What about Facebook?" YouTube, in posted statistics on its website, noted of social media watching: "500 years of YouTube video are watched every day on Facebook, and over 700 YouTube videos are shared on Twitter each minute."[87] The numbers are mindboggling, and when more professional content is able to be accessed via social media sites, whether from embedding media player widgets or simply enabling real estate, proper metrics for capturing value will again be challenged. For example, in a few years when viewing content via a social networking site may be commonplace, should the value be captured by "ratings" at the source of viewing, be captured via direct user impressions or clicks, be captured by passing through the engagement on the player (e.g., a Netflix or Hulu player sitting within Facebox, much like Netflix now sits as an option via OTT boxes such as Roku) to the source of the "broadcaster" serving up the content, or be captured and indexed to user engagement (so that if a user "likes" or "shares" the content, there is a premium added for direct engagement with the content)?

420

Already, start-ups such as Milyoni are enabling social viewing, and offer films from partners including Universal, Lionsgate, and Starz Media via a customable interface (see Figure 7.6).[88] The company also claims that its carriage of *The Perfect House*, a film made for Facebook, was the first full-length feature to play exclusively on Facebook, and that with the film *Marley* it enabled the first ever day-and-date theatrical release of a film simultaneously on Facebook.

Figure 7.6 Social Viewing Enabled by Milyoni
Reproduced by permission of Milyoni.

User Interface and New Tools for Personalization

Again, like the promise of many new gizmos and functionalities, user interface is critical and can galvanize demand—as Steve Jobs famously proved, sometimes the consumer does not know what he or she wants, and until the iPhone launched, phones had potential that simply had not been harnessed. The concept of personalizing TV is not new, as evidenced by Skype founder Niklas Zennstrom's launch of Joost and his prediction that "the television is becoming more difficult to distinguish from the computer screen, and yet there has been almost no real technical innovation in the television itself . . . On the simplest level, the History Channel should know that I prefer to watch ancient Greek history, but it should also allow me to interact and engage with others watching."[89]

Although Joost's vision, dating back several years, represented the coming together of a global application to see and even interact with whatever you want, when you want it, organized in favorites lists of how you want it, with good quality and instant access, the service stumbled after initial hype (shifting gears, for example, to a Web-integrated player rather than a download solution). (As a further interesting anecdote, in 2007 Viacom made an investment in Joost, seemingly validating the promise of the Web for distribution, even while it was suing YouTube.

New tools and types of content are starting to emerge and converge. First, companies started to offer simple editing systems, allowing users to make mini-movies, digitally editing and uploading with an ease that seemed unimaginable a few years earlier. Second, companies realized that with facile editing and unlimited content, users could create "mash-ups" combining elements of their own content with third-party content. Yahoo! bought the editing system Jumpcut, and technology start-up Eyespot signed deals with Lucasfilm and the NBA. I could never have imagined a few years ago that I would run a site enabling mash-ups, and being pitched proposals to stimulate engagement by challenging users to create their favorite amputations from *Star Wars* scenes. Managers overseeing brands realized that, properly structured, they may be able to better engage their customers by offering their own material to be edited by fans, or even combined with fan material.

Additionally, an array of widgets, applications, and functionalities on social networking sites has become a phenomenon; the sandbox will continue to be expanded, as giving consumers new tools to interact with, modify, and personalize content is a trend still in its infancy. The great challenge for media content in a number of these contexts is artistic integrity, and we are seeing the evolution of boundaries in terms of how far a creator or owner (and the law) will allow individuals to manipulate their work. In instances, fully open platforms have evolved, with Wikipedia as a prime example of encouraged modification and Creative Commons enabling open licenses and granting creators simple toggles such as "share alike" and "attribution" within a rules-based open framework for free content licensing.

Old Guard Tries to Adapt—Studios' Failed Bids to Offer an Online Service; Brick-and-Mortar Retailers Try to Offer Complementary Online Solutions

Limited Studio Attempts to Make the Download Market

Recognizing the potential of the market and the need to have legitimate platforms to counteract piracy around the onset of the online video explosion, the studios launched their own Web-based download services. The largest was MovieLink, a service co-owned by the following consortium of studios: Sony, Universal, MGM, Paramount, and Warner. A competitive service, CinemaNow, also offered a range of studio product.

While pioneers in providing a legal option for movie downloading, neither of these services—both hampered at the time by slow download speeds and starting up during the heyday of the peer-to-peer services that were eventually shut down by the Grokster decision—caught on, and adoption remained limited. Whether the problem was functionality, piracy, pricing, or available content does not matter, as part of the early strategy was for the studios to simply show they were offering a legal alternative to pirate peer-to-peer sites. In the end, with the platform showing increased promise and piracy curtailed, MovieLink was acquired by Blockbuster in the summer of 2007 to provide its download solution.[90] (See the companion website for more on this.)

Physical Retailers Offering Competitive Online Solutions

The challenges in the media space are no different for physical retailers trying to craft digital solutions than in other areas of retail. Namely, the woes of the traditional book store or record store are no different than toy stores or travel agencies, except perhaps a bit more acute; this is because media properties, often being intangibles (intellectual property), lend themselves uniquely well to digitization and digital consumption. A virtual tire will not do much for your real-world flat, but a portable, indestructible, comparably or lower-priced digital version of a TV show will not only be substitutional, but in the eyes of many consumers a preferable product option. Coupling this real world to digital conundrum of suppliers with the fact that their e-tail competitors (e.g., Amazon, Google/YouTube, Netflix) are some of the stars of the Internet (that have also redefined the world of logistics), it is a daunting challenge—and one that they are more often than not losing. In some instances, the only way companies have found to compete is to acquire companies as a market entry hedge against the inevitable erosion of their traditional businesses.

Walmart provides a telling case study. Recognizing the peak of the sell-through video market (see Chapter 5) and the corresponding threat to its lucrative (and market-leading) DVD business, in late 2006 Walmart introduced its own download service. The guinea pig title was Warner's *Superman Returns*, as *Variety* summarized:

423

Deal allows Walmart customers to download the film for use on portable devices for $1.95, computers for $2.95, or both for $3.95, in addition to the cost of the DVD, which retails in Walmart stores for $14.87. The retailing behemoth, which accounts for 40 percent of DVD sales, said it hopes to expand the pricing model to other titles ... Deal marks Walmart's attempt to convert its enormous walk-in DVD customer base into download films.[91]

This launch and hodgepodge pricing was symptomatic of the confusion in the market—the pricing model was clunky compared to the simplicity of all songs for $0.99 (the iTunes pricing then in effect). What the retailers were doing was trying to add comparable value ("we have it too") as opposed to something revolutionary.Clearly, the studios were taking a cautious approach. Discussing the fine line between online adoption and maintaining a vibrant DVD business at retail, Jeffrey Katzenberg, CEO of DreamWorks Animation, was quoted in the *Wall Street Journal* as saying: "We must not undercut our bread and butter ... The consumer decided when VHS was obsolete ... Not the hardware manufacturers, not retail, not us."[92] The same article that quoted Katzenberg went on to describe the awkward position both Walmart and studios found themselves in, and the retailer's reluctant entry into the digital market as highlighted by its dilemma with Disney: "After Disney announced a deal to provide television shows to Apple's video iPod, Walmart threatened not to carry the DVD version of the hit Disney Channel movie *High School Musical*, according to people familiar with the situation. After talking it through, Walmart ultimately relented and carried the DVD in its stores."[93]

Capability to offer downloads is one thing, but turning the new business to profitability is another. Walmart was entering the same murky waters of its competitors, hedging its bets against the future. Like everyone else, they would have to wait and see whether the new revenue streams would be additive or substitutional for its traditional business. Walmart, it seemed, quickly made up its mind: not much more than a year after it struggled with Disney and launched digital distribution, Walmart abandoned its experiment. The reasons for its abandonment were likely manifold, but one interesting point sometimes referenced is its DRM requirements were tied to playing content via Windows Media Player. This factor essentially precluded content from being watched on iPods, the then hardware platform of choice for watching downloaded content.[94]

Fast-forward to 2010 when Walmart re-entered the market with its acquisition of Vudu, beating out competitors such as Blockbuster for a reported price tag of more than $100 million.[95] Vudu, at the time a Silicon Valley start-up, began as a set-top box manufacturer; for the reasons discussed above (and counter to the strategy of some of the OTT device manufacturers discussed above that went fully in the other direction), namely the challenge of connecting yet another box to the TV and recognizing the migration of building the technology into TV sets and other connected devices as an app, Vudu shuttered its hardware box and integrated its cloud-based service with leading consumer electronics manufacturers such as Samsung, Toshiba, and Vizio. By Christmas 2011, Vudu included its VOD service into gaming systems (Xbox 360 and PlayStation 3) and tablets, placing it alongside the likes of Netflix and Amazon on the panoply of devices pioneering the OTT market. Additionally, Vudu added the flexibility to either rent (e.g., $0.99) content or download, and marketed availability of titles as the same day as DVD (since, for windowing, it positioned itself as an on-demand online rental outlet, not offering subscriptions, even marketing Vudu as same day versus Netflix DVD being 28 days later).

We are still in trial stages of companies working to leverage their online versus offline user base, but some initiatives for the 2011 holiday shopping season began to illustrate the type of cross-promotional campaigns that may become marketing staples. Walmart offered a $5 Vudu credit to buyers of certain DVD and Blu-ray titles (e.g., *Megamind*) in its retail outlets, leveraging in-store traffic over Black Friday.[96] GameStop, the leading independent games retail chain, had earlier pioneered programs such as this (and has a strategic advantage through user registrations tied to game exchanges and the robust online market), and it was accordingly not a surprise. What will be interesting is whether these key retailers continue to utilize different branding in their offline versus online presence (GameStop versus Impulse, Walmart and Vudu). The answer may be more in the consumer awareness of the brand itself—Netflix's attempt to separate its businesses and utilize different branding (i.e., the 2011 Qwikster debacle) did not work, while Walmart was likely aware of its prior failures and different customer bases and kept the unrelated Vudu moniker for its online presence.

425

Revenue Models and Economics: Multiple Systems Coexist, Just Like the Offline World

It is important to recognize that there is not a "right" model—advertising-based, subscriptions, transactional VOD, and downloads are all different economic models tied to different consumer preferences. At the beginning of the online media boom, various people were betting on certain models dominating (e.g., subscription versus pay-per-view), searching for a kind of magic formula to be matched to online consumption; history, though, has shown this not to be the case.

The quick market penetration of the iPod (though it grew up in an environment without other choices) and growth of Amazon's cloud-based offering is strong evidence of the viability of the pay-per-download/ownership model. One can equally argue that Netflix is evidence of the successful application of a subscription service (although, a rental one). The ultimate answer is less likely to turn on whether subscription, advertising, transactional rental, or pay-per-download models are the best, but on customer interface, reliability, security, marketing, pricing, and range of content offered; as noted earlier, user experience matters, and top experiences drive successful online distribution platforms. In theory, in a world where convenience and choice are the mantra, rival services with these opposing models (and compelling user experiences) will both be successful. Inherent in choice is the notion that a sizeable consumer population will want the ease of one-bill subscription, while another grouping will want the control feature of à la carte pay-per-download choice. Just as retail sales, rental, subscription, and other media coexist offline, there is no reason that a similar rental, purchase, free on-demand construct cannot similarly coexist in the online arena—a prediction posited by Netflix and others, and which has been borne out in the last few years.

Streaming: Fundamentals of Monetizing Internet Advertising

Despite the growth of many Internet sites, it remains a challenge to convert traffic into revenues, and especially profits. Chapter 6 describes a number of trends in advertising, including the emergence of FVOD, including AVOD, as the online equivalent of TV (hence the phrase Internet TV); the companion website includes a brief overview of the nuts and bolts of the advertising market/metrics as opposed to the structure of the FVOD window. For here, I will simply note the chart in Figure 7.7, which depicts the value chain of different types of advertisements (e.g., banner versus video) within the AVOD continuum.

AVOD Takes Off—the Hulu Generation

Hulu successfully pioneered an AVOD model leveraging network content; namely, TV shows and other premium content were available

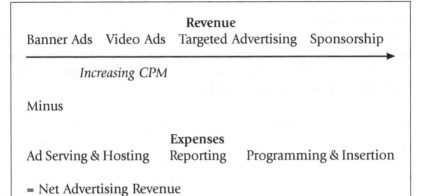

Figure 7.7 Value Chain of Advertisement Types

for free streaming, with revenues earned through the sale of video ads. As discussed in Chapter 6, Hulu believes "less is more," and grew serving a few video advertisements per 30-minute episode, in contrast to nearly eight minutes of advertising typically cut into a network commercial half hour. By restricting advertising and prohibiting ad-skipping, the service can charge a premium per ad, as well as offer a more compelling viewing experience.[97] Not only are there fewer ads, but a unique feature debuted by Hulu is allowing viewers to select among advertising options before a program rolls (e.g., electing to watch a longer pre-roll advertisement, such as two minutes before the program starts, rather than have the show interrupted with a couple of shorter advertisements spaced interstitially).[98]

In retrospect, looking at the historical growth of YouTube (free), coupled with ever-increasing broadband penetration and the growth of WiFi access, it was only a matter of time before professional content supported by free advertising mushroomed into a large TV-like business. Video advertising, with its short content and higher value, could be easily streamed, making what was already the standard for advertising offline the optimum form of advertising online—but even better, given the ability to target streams. Hulu was arguably the first and most compelling service to leverage this new paradigm, coupling free advertising with on-demand access.

Looking beyond its success to date, though, Hulu's AVOD monetization challenge is a microcosm of the overall challenge of the Internet with content: How can services blend the value of equal streams over diffuse locations (see next section) and time versus the live effect of television? Namely, how much are 10 million viewings in "syndication" worth versus live?

In my last edition, I asked David Barron, VP of content partnerships for Hulu, what he thought about the comparison to TV syndication and what Hulu was doing differently that was making it successful in monetizing the new space. He advised:

> To compare what Hulu is doing to TV syndication, you first have to understand that TV syndication is just one of many windows in the lifespan of a piece of content. Traditional entertainment companies have always relied on windowing content, whether by platform, time, technology, territory, etc. Hulu is proving that there is another viable window of free on-demand that can live alongside other distribution windows such as TV and electronic sell-through. For current network programming, the on-demand period extends for some number of weeks post initial TV airing, thereby extending the period viewers can watch their favorite show. For library content, the new on-demand window allows people to discover programs that either haven't been available for a long time, or weren't available in their market, and therefore provides a new revenue stream for the content producer. Of course, these are all businesses in development, and therefore the rules are changing regularly.
>
> In terms of how Hulu may be better exploiting this opportunity, including the long tail of library product, we create a great environment for people to enjoy long-form premium video, and whereas others have focused on user-generated content or, in cases, quantity over setting a quality bar, Hulu recognizes that entertainment is impulse-driven and we want to make it very easy to watch high-quality premium content in an equally high-quality environment.

Transactional VOD

Walmart's Vudu, Amazon's VOD rental program and cable-based rentals are examples of VOD pricing. As discussed in Chapter 5, this is the realization of the virtual video store with an infinite tail and infinite content. Price differentiation is now akin to models previously seen in the heyday of physical rental stores. Vudu, for example, offers tiered pricing tied to standard versus high definition and even 3D, as well as a "movie of the day" for only $0.99 and $2-for-two-night. Amazon similarly enables tiered pricing—all an easy option when distributing via cloud-based infrastructure that can deploy a particular format of a particular show to a specific device. Cable VOD options, such as offered by Comcast and other global providers, follow suit, and offer rental options often tied to format (high definition versus standard definition) and availability (new titles priced higher than library ones).

This type of pricing is optimal to a content owner/provider, for it can set its price (charging a premium in instances), can directly track and audit consumption (there is a discrete rental transaction), and brings in immediate revenue from the purchase transaction. The limiting factor is the same as in the offline world: window timing and demand to drive actual purchases versus free consumption.

Pay-Per-Download (Ownership)—Macro Issues of Downloads

In my first edition, I noted: "I can easily posit that players will begin to differentiate themselves via pricing, types of pricing mechanisms (e.g., pay-per-download versus subscription), and willingness to carry content exclusively and pay guarantees. (Note: Although, to the extent online outlets are akin to retail locations, then nonexclusivity and no guarantees make continued sense.)" This is now largely the case, and fixed pricing models (e.g., $1.99 per download, as Apple pioneered with iTunes) are footnotes of an immature and captive market.

As I forecast, in the long run it is irrational to pay the same fee for a five-minute Pixar short as for an hour-long episode of a hit primetime TV show—pricing tiers had to evolve, taking into account how recent a show is, what genre/category it comes from (e.g., a short, TV show, music video, feature film), and whether the transaction is based on a rental or purchase model.

The one fixed-fee model that so quickly built the market via iPods had to yield, given the interplay of factors in Ulin's Rule. Differential pricing is one of the key tools driving maximization of content value over time; rational economics posits that the inequality of value per purchase, and the crossover of so many different types of content that are differentially priced and consumed in the non-digital retail space, will favor price differentiation in the online space.

Another key factor influencing pricing trends includes loss-leading software to drive hardware: the download market has to be viewed in terms of related hardware sales. Apple could afford to price songs and video via what constituted an arguably illogical price matrix because, on the one hand, the content was a bit of a loss-leader for driving hardware sales, and on the other hand, simplified pricing helped develop a market that otherwise was slipping away to piracy. However, once the related hardware and software markets matured and competitors started to make inroads, there was inevitably a shift toward greater price differentiation indexed to varied types of content. It was the unique construct of a virtual monopoly on hardware by Apple, coupled with the broadest content availability that initially distorted the overall market. By the time Amazon introduced its Kindle Fire, price differentiation was common and the key was developing an easy consumption platform. Accordingly, rather than software loss-leading to drive hardware, as was arguably the case with Apple, the online market was growing so big that one could argue that Amazon was loss-leading its Kindle hardware to drive online purchases (whether in the growing video market or its grounding and historical e-tailing business).

An oddity that results from the shifting market ambitions in the download space is that one might expect guarantees to secure content in a scramble to establish positions. However, inclined to support market growth at the expense of piracy, and recognizing that initial revenues will, at best, be incremental, content owners were apt to view the EST distributor simply as a new kind of retailer. Instead of worrying about returns, the issue is allowable margin, with the calculus the wholesale markup (i.e., discount form SRP) converted from a retail dealer price to a distribution fee. Because the retailer and distributor are the same entity, the revenue splits (e.g., 70/30) are arguably artificially low, given that 30 percent is an amalgam of the retailer margin and the distribution fee. Let us compare online margin with retail (Table 7.2; excluding cost of goods), and assume: (1) in both cases the same distribution fee; and (2) that the customer price is lower online (which is the expectation, given no packaging and incentive to purchase).

This is a hypothetical evidencing how both sides win and keep as much revenue as possible from retail, even when pricing is lower. The actual splits will find an equilibrium based on these and a variety of other inputs, including leverage, timing, volume, quality of content, etc.—all like the traditional market.

Finally, because there are fewer fixed costs, with cost of goods negligible relative to DVD/Blu-ray manufacturing, managing inventory, and physical delivery to thousands of points of purchase, most revenues drop to the bottom line and margins are high for both sides. This is a further benefit and a fact that may explain the relative quick adoption

Table 7.2 Online versus Retail Margins

Video at Retailer	Electronic Sell-Through
SRP $29.95	SRP $17.99 (assume ~10% < retail shelf)
Wholesale $18 (assume ~60% SRP)	Distribution Fee $5.40 (assume 30%)
Shelf Price $20.00	Content Owner $12.59 (assume 70%)
$2.00 Retailer Profit	
Retailer Margin 11% (2/18)	
Distribution Fee $5.40 (30 × 18)	
Net to Owner $12.60 (18–5.40)	
$12.60 is the same:	Content owner keeps $12.60
	EST distributor foregoes 100% of retail margin, and takes this as a price discount to consumer
	If a "retail margin" were imputed on top of the distribution fee, such as 10%, then distributor would keep $1.80 + $5.40 = $7.20
	@ $7.20, the split would be 60/40

431

of simple revenue sharing splits. EST services could therefore afford to drop the price and still yield the same net margin to content owners as traditional retail.

Subscription: Better for the Service than the Content Owner?

As discussed in Chapter 6 relating to pay TV (and is somewhat obvious), the key calculus in a pure subscription model is whether the revenue from a subscriber base exceeds the cost of content. In a world without significant competition, and when content is offered nonexclusively to a range of platforms, the equation works remarkably well for the service (think Netflix streaming growth around 2011). However, as soon as competition is introduced and players jockey for content access—namely, the current state of the industry—everything obviously becomes more challenging. Aggregators are likely to watch their margins shrink as the costs of content acquisition far outstrips subscriber growth and the ability to increase pricing (if at all, with pricing pressures pointing the other way as services vie to undercut the other in a fight for subscribers). Because most analysts are looking at a subscription service and its profitability, and because revenues on a per-show basis are confidential and rarely reported, analysis tends to focus on total subscription revenues and total costs/operation costs; this, however, fails to account for the producer side of the equation and the impact that a fixed subscription cost has on the array of content aggregated.

A key limitation to certain subscription services providing a programmed basket of content is the diminishing returns to content providers. This is becauase an aggregation model is akin to cable. An aggregator (e.g., mobile phone, online, MSO) that charges by subscription, for example, only takes in a fixed amount of revenue regardless of the amount of content: revenues are subscribers multiplied by the monthly fixed fee ("monthly subscriber revenues"). If a subscriber pays $15 for a certain variety of content choice, by expanding that choice (e.g., doubling the number of available programs) the provider takes in no additional revenue. Accordingly, if there are 10 channels of content on a platform, then the operator is paying those content holders out of monthly subscriber revenues. If the channels go up to 20, and the operator is still only taking in monthly subscriber revenues, then the amount available per content provider goes down (X/20 instead of X/10).

The only way to counter this is to charge more as content choices go up, much like cable companies offer tiered subscriptions. The problem is that cable is limited to 100+ key channels and the pricing tiers can match the relatively limited universe. In a download, digital environment content choices are limitless (long and wide tail) and consumers are going to demand greater and greater choice and flexibility. However, there will be a natural ceiling for price increases; the tier charges will cap out while the demand for more content choices will continue to expand (Figure 7.8). This will inevitably be difficult for operators aggregating content and offering subscriptions to manage. Either they will squeeze the content providers—where top content driving subscriptions will still command a premium, but the average provider will see pressure to accept less rather than more even with subscription volume increasing— or they will have to limit content and segment offerings into genre silos (TV shows, sports, etc.) and price by tier. In contrast, pay-per-download services simply have to negotiate a split with the content provider.

This is the challenge facing companies such as Netflix, which, as described earlier, now has to pay much more for its content, but cannot similarly raise its pricing; it can justify squeezed margins so long as subscribers increase and increased costs can be rationalized

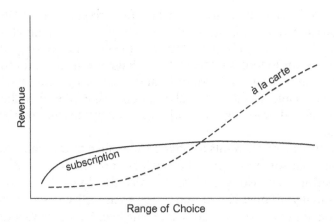

Figure 7.8

as an inevitable consequence of remaining competitive. Currently, the competitive effect of the land grab is masking system weakness, but once an equilibrium is reached suppliers of average content are likely to be the next ones seeing their margins pinched.

433

The foregoing scenario focuses on a pure subscription service, but a hybrid service such as Hulu+, which couples advertising with subscription fees, is more akin to a basic cable model. The dual revenue stream promises to provide upsides and security to content owners and a measure of flexibility for operators to confront the challenge illustrated in Figure 7.8. In theory, this mix of blending AVOD revenues with a baseline secure subscription rate should provide the same advantages online as has benefited cable channels offline and help solve part of the long- and wide-tail dilemma.

Finally, it is fair to assume that services will go beyond the simplicity of fixed-priced subscriptions and add more flexibility to defeat this challenge: offering subscription rates to content (like pay TV services) and the choice of à la carte pay-per-product options and subscriptions. Subscriptions will accordingly become more complicated, mimicking the pay TV or cable models where there will be tiers of content.

Differentiating between Tiers of Content: Cable Bundle Pricing Goes Online

As noted earlier, including under the discussion of TV Everywhere, as traditional pay TV operators and new entrants push diverse content offerings out for ubiquitous access, it is natural that tiered pricing will evolve. Perhaps some companies, where free access is in their DNA, such as YouTube, may not apply this model to their channel strategy; nevertheless, they will have to deal with the fact that offering 100 niche channels starts to look a lot like cable. What consumers get for free, what comes with a "basic" subscription, and what programming requires a premium charge is a fundamental question—especially when these same entities are all moving into original content to differentiate their offerings.

Any provider who wants to offer a wide range of content, taking into account that some of it may be original and that to succeed with an aggregation play (long and wide tail) the breadth of content is conceptually infinite, has to find a way to amortize costs of providing the programming—content does not come free. Accordingly, as discussed earlier in the context of the Sky Go ecosystem (in the UK), the Sky app indexes content access to different packages. Some channels may be free, but other content requires an ante (whether via VOD access or premium subscription). Any company that looks or feels like a virtual MSO or content aggregator will face the same challenge. While some may leverage existing businesses and amortize costs as an extension (either as a loss-leader to enter the market, or as an incentive to diversify to prevent erosion), at some point the content access needs to be funded. And so, for anyone who loves the notion of cord-cutting and expects to migrate to an online system to shed their cable bill, they are apt to find either a new version of their bill, or be seduced by seemingly free access only to find that they are paying, once again, via their à la carte choices. Namely, Netflix can be accessed via an OTT system, but you still have to pay for Netflix and the more its business becomes like a pay service, and the more online aggregators function like virtual MSOs aggregating a dizzying array of content, the more these companies will need to find a way to pass through content costs.

Dearth of Bold Experiments

Radical experiments with revenue models that implicitly break down or eliminate windows are rare, in part because so much is at stake. There are, accordingly, few examples in the TV space of fully accelerating access akin to the way Mark Cuban and Magnolia have collapsed the theatrical and video window (see Chapter 1). As discussed above, the download for rental, purchase, subscription, and advertising-supported models may compete with each other, but largely mimic the consumption ranges familiar in the offline world (rent, buy, watch for free). The interesting question for those who believe in free flexible access is not simply "Why shouldn't content be available simultaneously?", but "Why shouldn't it be available early?" In fact, this has been posited and some of the boldest experiments in terms of pricing have taken place in Europe, not the United States (see also Chapter 6). Interactive television services, such as Maxdome in Germany (owned by pan-European broadcasting group ProSiebenSat1) were starting to offer viewers the opportunity to see an episode early for an upcharge: if you do not want to be left with a cliffhanger, pay a couple of euros and you can see next week's episode early. Adreas Bartl, head of ProSiebenSat1's German operations, noted in an interview with TV Europe that: ". . . for an extra amount of money episodes have been available on Maxdome before their run on regular television, so if you were really interested in *Lost* and could not wait until the following week for the next episode, we did some good business with this."[99] Additionally, Maxdome offered a "season pass," where a viewer could pre-pay for early access throughout the season; to preserve demand for the regular broadcasts, however, consumers were not able to jump ahead more than one episode. This innovative approach to access (though admittedly a VOD application or a hybrid, and not a download model) was also catching on in the UK and France, with Britain's Channel 5 selling passes (£40) to download episodes of *CSI* before it hit television.[100]

435

The challenge with this model is economic—there may be incremental revenue, but this capacity undermines the "who shot JR?" effect, where a cliffhanger drives masses to watch a show that resolves the mystery. It should be a simple analysis to deduce what number of people need to subscribe to/buy the shows early to equal the value of what an exclusive premiere will yield with a rating of X. The difficulty in practice, though, is that both options are by their nature compelling, and both the buy rates and ratings are moving targets. As discussed earlier in the context of Netflix's debut of its first online original series, *House of Cards*, the subscription service allowed users immediate access to all episodes, enabling users to jump to the next episode and further with "binge viewing" of the whole season in marathon fashion—this is the first significant parallel experiment in the U.S. I am not going to repeat some of the issues discussed in that context, and here simply want to highlight the expanding sandbox and the fact that save for these examples most distributors have been loathe to tinker too much with leveraging the serial nature of television to monetize television series. (Note: What is starting to evolve, though, are networks allowing earlier seasons of episodes to be available online, tapping into the binge-viewing pattern enabled by streaming services, as a way to expose series to new potential viewers; those finding the show for the first time in the long-tail (and quickly "catching-up" via marathon consumption) are then hopefully converted to viewers for original on-network new season telecasts.)

Following all this logic, it is an interesting theoretical question why an earlier window has not arisen for theatrical releases. It would be possible, for example, to charge a premium to rabid fans of a franchise to see an early screening of the next instalment of a series (e.g., *Twilight, Harry Potter, The Hobbit*); if customers will pay a premium for 3D, it is logical they will pay a premium to see a movie before the rest of the world (e.g., charge for private screenings). Almost any movie executive would have a visceral reaction to such a suggestion, for it is iconoclastic and not only cuts against the ingrained economics but also has pejorative moral overtones in being somewhat antidemocratic. There is no law, though, requiring equal access to content, and a recording artist can play a venue of 50 seats as easily as a filmmaker could charge for a private showing. The impediments (egalitarian free and equal access arguments aside) are rather economic, and come from fears on the upside and downside of the action. On the upside, the biggest challenge of film releases (as discussed in Chapter 4) is marketing, and creating sufficient awareness and buzz to create the overnight brand such that it continues and permeates into the long tail; moreover, as an experience good, there is always a significant risk to success and thus any type of staggered release can kill demand pressure if reaction is negative. In short, the marketing challenges are already great, and to add into the mix an extended campaign (which costs more) and the risk of poor word of mouth (before the masses can judge for themselves) is arguably enough by itself to tip the scales. An equal if not paramount concern, on the downside, is that once out the film will inevitably be pirated; accordingly, studios want to bring in the most amount of money as quickly as possible after initial release. The net result is that unless a mogul is willing to roll the dice (which is a harder thing to do when answering to shareholders and markets), the type of early TV window tested in Europe and now by Netflix is likely to remain a strategy limited to TV, and even then generally limited for fear of undermining marketing advantages tied to cliffhangers. (Note: This discussion is different than the premium VOD window discussed in Chapter 1, which charges a premium for early access but has been criticized by exhibitors (i.e., theater chains) as risking cannibalizing ticket sales.)

436

Resistance to Disruptive Change: Studios Suing Rather than Embracing; Talent Guilds Fearful of Being Cut of Pie

Internet Viewing and Immediacy of Content—the YouTube Generation and the Studios Conundrum

The Emergence of YouTube and its Acquisition by Google

Digital technology accelerates adoption rates so dramatically (see discussion of scaling and joint ventures in Chapter 1), that usage outpaces the rules of the road, which still need to evolve to address the new landscape. This is happening now in the context of Facebook and social networks as regards privacy. When YouTube took off, the issue was posting content owned by a third party, and what was considered copyright infringement. To put this in context, it is important to take a step back and frame the success and impact of YouTube.

At the same time that iPods were fueling the adoption of downloads, free streaming video services led by YouTube were experiencing exponential growth and consumer acceptance. Figure 7.9 is the growth curve for YouTube, exhibiting at the time unprecedented growth from start-up phase to over 80 million users per month in a 2–3 year period.

In fact, the growth was so rapid (again, at the time, as opposed to the new benchmarks set by Facebook and Twitter), and YouTube had catapulted so far ahead of its competitors, that it was acquired by Google for $1.65 billion in October 2006—an enormous deal, given that YouTube was reputedly losing money. The *Hollywood Reporter* quoted Ken August, principal at Deloitte Consulting, commenting on this dynamic: "It's a huge price for a company that isn't profitable . . . It's a reflection in general of the huge interest in video on the Internet."[101] In fact, the deal was reminiscent of the high-flying deals of the dot-com days before the first bubble burst in 2000, as the move was driven by traffic—where Google's own Google Video lagged behind—with the assumption that monetization would follow. (Note: YouTube has only continued to grow, with statistics posted on its website in 2012 noting that more than 800 million unique users visit YouTube each month, watching more than 3 billion hours of videos on YouTube each month, with 72 hours of video uploaded to the site every minute.)

Not only was this deal risky, given the money paid for a company that was reputedly not yet profitable, but YouTube carried litigation risks. Certain videos on the site were from content companies that viewed the

437

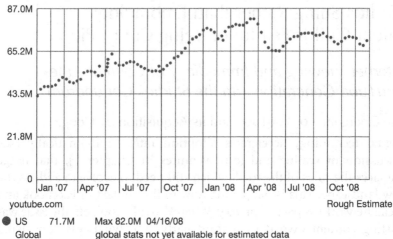

Monthly U.S. People 01/07–12/31/08

youtube.com   Rough Estimate

● US   71.7M   Max 82.0M 04/16/08
  Global   global stats not yet available for estimated data

Figure 7.9 Growth Curve for YouTube

site as infringing its copyrights, and were requesting YouTube to "take down" the material. This remedy, in theory, would insulate YouTube from copyright infringement liability under the Digital Millennium Copyright Act (see also Chapter 2).

A mitigating factor argued by Google/YouTube was the promise of implementing filtering technology. While significant progress had been made in "audio fingerprinting technology," which would compare music to catalogs of copyrighted songs and enable the automated identification of infringing material that could then be taken down, progress on implementing a video system was lagging. Tensions and stakes were thus extraordinarily high, and a Universal Music spokesman commented in the *International Herald Tribune* on companies' actions to prospectively cure the problem and ignore the past: "The copyright law doesn't give people the right to engage in the massive infringement of our content to build a thriving business and then, after the fact, avoid exposure by saying they will prospectively start to filter . . ."[102]

Although it was not clear whether YouTube would be weighed down by the type of copyright infringement problems that led to the demise of Grokster and other peer-to-peer sites, there was a significant difference in this context. Google/YouTube was not a pirate and pledged to clean things up. It was viewed as the type of player that could legitimize the market, much like Apple had done in the music space, and developing and implementing filtering technology was, at minimum, an effort to take a best-practices approach. In fact, YouTube not only made good on its pledge of implementing filtering technology, but also innovated what it calls its "Content ID" system. Utilizing this tool, any publisher has the right to tag its content to identify its authenticity. On its website, adjacent to a section entitled "Copyright Education," YouTube explains that owners posting video may: "Choose, in advance, what they want to happen when those videos are found. Make money from them. Get stats on them. Or block them from YouTube altogether."[103]

Viacom versus Google/YouTube

Perhaps it was inevitable given the high stakes of distribution, the Hollywood-produced copyrighted programs appearing on YouTube, and Google's seemingly overnight leap to market leader that a nasty fight would erupt. In March 2007, just months after Google's acquisition of YouTube, Viacom sued Google for $1 billion.

The amount itself was a statement, but the suit alleging "massive intentional copyright infringement" was a serious counter-punch to failed negotiations over the uploading of clips to YouTube from popular Viacom shows. Instantly, the case was cast as battleground central for old versus new media; moreover, the suit promised to be the seminal case in the evolution of copyright law, following the Sony Betamax case and *MGM v. Grokster* (see also Chapter 2). In the end, as discussed in Chapter 2, the U.S. District Court in 2010 sided with Google, ruling on summary judgement that YouTube was protected by the "safe harbor" provisions of the Digital Millennium Copyright Act, shielding it against copyright claims by its implementation of take-down provisions to remove infringing materials when put on notice. Although Viacom is appealing, most view the summary judgment as a clear ruling. The ire of the studios (or at least of Paramount/Viacom) is evident in a comment after the verdict from Viacom's general counsel Michael Fricklas: "YouTube and Google stole hundreds of thousands of video clips from artists and content creators, including Viacom, building a substantial business that was sold for billions of dollars . . . We believe that should not be allowed by law or common sense."[104]

Marketing Benefits: The Elephant in the Room and the Studio Dilemma

One of the oddities of the tug-of-war playing out in debates around what content users may permissibly upload is that while studio and network executives deride online sources that enable the playing of their content without permission, a large number of executives—and often from the same companies—advocate utilizing highly trafficked online sites for marketing. To the distribution boss, a clip or episode played without permission is taking money away while, to the marketing boss, the exposure of content to tens of millions of people with a viral effect is driving awareness and interest. Harmonizing the positions, however, is far from simple, and continues to present a conundrum.

I turned again to former president of Universal Worldwide TV and independent producer Ned Nalle and asked him how he viewed the marketing benefit compared to the risks. He sees a substantial turnaround from a few years ago when providers were more negative, lamenting that "no producer is getting rich off Internet delivery of his series," broadband was perceived as siphoning viewers away from traditional broadcasters, and advertisers were underpaying because of the immaturity of the system (and inability to reliably measure viewing):

> The convenience of Internet content delivery offers producers several advantages: the first is free marketing. Audiences can sample a debutante series on the bus, in flight, at lunch; not just at home. Positive experience on their portable screens can impel new devotees to the broadcast or cable channel that airs new episodes of that show at a regularly scheduled time.
>
> More importantly, broadband delivery advantageously enables a transfer of power from the broadcaster to the viewer. Binge viewing, which made a weekend event phenomenon from catch-up viewing on network series such as *24* and *Lost*, now becomes the great product attribute of video-on-demand.
>
> Many thought Netflix would thrive or fail delivering movies. But much of that service's recent value proposition was bolstered less by films, but instead because it granted instant consumer access to full seasons of TV series episodes. Were Netflix ever rebranded as "Nettube," the new moniker would be justified as on-demand streamed delivery of multiple seasons of a television series extends the subscriber's commitment to that branded service (as well as competitors like Amazon Prime Instant Video, HBO Go, Showtime On-Demand, Hulu+, YouTube, Vudu, etc.) Series streaming enable enables viewers to catch up and gorge themselves on an entire cannon of episodes (e.g., *Vampire Diaries*, *Downtown Abbey*, *Game of Thrones*, *Homeland*, *The Following*, *Revolution*), with total disregard to when network programmers decide to schedule

440

or cancel the series. Even with some delayed availability, once each episode becomes streamable, the privilege of subscription empowers the viewer to seize control from the network schedulers.

For the streaming service, the customer engagement for compelling TV series far outlives a single movie. For intellectual property owners, consumer access replenishes coffers. Subscribers pay the streaming company, who in turn compensate the copyright holder. Producers no longer reach ends-of-product life cycle when their serials (such as the examples above) don't repeat well in a second broadcast run. For years, there was a good reason why local TV stations didn't pay up for rerun rights to serialized dramas. With story outcomes known, serials didn't rate. But this old model assumed a paradigm of weekly or daily scheduling at a specific time of night, where the viewer is beholden to the scheduler. Currently, second-run serials seem to find new purpose when programmed back to back by a viewer with a remote control device. Missed plot points are easily recovered by scanning backwards. When the CW Network sought salvage value in its serial reruns in 2011, Netflix came to its garage sale, flush with subscriber cash.

441

Streaming services delivered by the Internet, and pay TV channels that originally entered the home from satellite or cable, are not dissimilar. Like HBO and Showtime before them, streaming channels have begun to finance exclusive content (e.g, Netflix's early offering, *House of Cards*) at sizeable license fees. Regardless of delivery method, in Netflix, YouTube, Amazon Prime, and others, content producers have found additional, rich customers for dream projects. More customers are usually welcomed by any business.

How Online and Download Revenues Became the Focus of Hollywood Guild Negotiations and Strikes

The potential for rapid revenue growth from online streaming and downloadable transactions has become a critical topic in the overall compensation of talent. Members of Hollywood guilds remember conceding issues and participation in the early days of video, not recognizing what an important element those revenues would become for film and television properties. The fear of "never again" has driven entrenched bargaining positions, and served as the emotional lightning rod for negotiations between the WGA and SAG with the Alliance of Motion Picture & Television Producers (AMPTP). Essentially, even though online and downloadable revenues are paltry today compared to sums historically generated via traditional outlets, actors, writers, and directors all want to protect themselves as these revenues grow—especially if they grow rapidly and start to cannibalize the monies that they have fought so hard to protect in past guild agreements.

To read about the issues in the press, it is easy to think that everything is unfair, and residuals are the lifeblood of compensation. In fact, as discussed in Chapter 2 regarding the compensation of writers, it is important to recognize that residuals (and what is fought over in guild new media negotiations) represent just one element of the overall compensation pie, and in many cases a relatively small fraction of the total compensation an individual will earn with respect to a particular project. While securing fair compensation for reuses and ensuring that digital media exploitation does not undermine revenue streams previously fought for has obvious logic, this is arguably an area where emotion and perceptions of just compensation play disproportionately to the actual compensation at hand.

Does Abandoning the Historical Residual System Make Sense?

A dramatic twist emerged in the summer of 2007, when the AMPTP, represented at a press conference by the heads of three networks (Warner Bros., CBS, and ABC) publicly called for a complete overhaul of the almost 50-year-old system of residuals for writers, actors, and directors. The Web was clearly at the heart of the debate, with the studio and networks initially rebuffing any attempt to extend residual-type payments to Web, download, streaming, and other digitl media exploitations.[105]

What started as debate about extending residuals to online/new media revenue streams, was seized on as an opening to turn the whole system, perceived to be out of whack, on its head. Warner Bros.' Barry Meyer, serving as spokesman for the AMPTP group, was quoted in *Broadcast & Cable* lamenting that fixed payments were being made when projects were still in the red and arguing that production costs need to be recouped before paying out residuals:

"The goal," Meyer said, "is to find a way to recoup the sizeable investment in movie and television programming before there is a sharing of profits with anybody. Why . . . does the model work that says you have to reuse that product trying to recapture a loss? Why isn't there a model that says once the investment is recovered, maybe there should be a higher percentage paid of the profits? . . . It is clear to us that those old models don't work anymore, that models based on reuse of programming before you've ve recouped your costs, or any semblance of costs have been recouped, don't work anymore. And we think that the study we're asking for has to look at that."[106]

Countering the AMPTP view, the guilds, deeply suspicious of "Hollywood accounting" (see Chapter 10) outright rejected the notion that a profits-based system could be fair. SAG's president bluntly noted that they did not need a study to show that a sharing mechanism based on profit accounting "would be inaccurate, unreliable and unfair. Talent can't be asked to share the profit risk when creative artists have no control over what projects are made or how they are budgeted—particularly for promotion and advertising."[107]

In the end, probably recognizing that scrapping residuals was too severe a change, the studios backed down a bit and the parties agreed to formulas in both streaming and EST contexts.

443

After the DGA and WGA settled their differences over the treatment on "new media" residuals and, respectively, agreed to new collective bargaining agreements (2007), SAG elected not to follow suit and was stalled in protracted negotiations with the AMPTP. Oddly, despite the difficulty in reaching an overall accord, both sides were in apparent agreement regarding a residual formula for the principal new media categories: (1) when a consumer pays to view a TV show or movie via a new media platform, including in the instance of downloads-to-own (EST); and (2) when a producer makes a TV show available via advertising-supported streaming. SAG's website, under a special bulletin pertaining to the negotiations, advised that if a TV show "were to be streamed on the Internet, it would have 24 free streaming days . . . Then, after the 24 days of streaming, they would have the right to exhibit the episode for two 26-week periods if they pay 3 percent of the applicable minimum for each 26-week period. In the case of a day performer who works one day, that comes to approximately $22 for each 26-week period . . ."[108] The calculations can become complex, as in the instance of EST the SAG website additionally noted: "the casts would share in 5.4 percent of 20 percent of the DGR (distributor's gross receipts) up to the first 50,000 units downloaded for features and up to the first 100,000 units downloaded for television programs."[109]

I need not elaborate on the arcane workings of the Hollywood collective bargaining agreements (which are about as easy to follow as the arcane accounting of net profits, which is discussed in Chapter 10 and similarly divvies up shares of shares of receipts), which over time will continue to haggle over splitting the online and download pie; the point is as first noted, in that even while immature, revenues associated with digital/streaming of content are a lightning rod, and guilds are adamant about participating in what they correctly perceive as a growing pie.

444

CHAPTER 8

Ancillary Revenues

Merchandising, Video Games, Hotels, Pay-Per-View and Transactional VOD Roots, Airlines, and Other Markets

More content from this chapter is available at
www.focalpress.com/9780240824239

445

This chapter combines a bit of a hodgepodge of revenue streams, but that is because an intellectual property asset, by its divisible and malleable nature, lends itself to being exploited via endless permutations, associated with a dizzying array of physical products, and distributed by any platform capable of attracting eyeballs. Given this open-ended sandbox to bring in additional dollars, in exceptional cases revenues from "ancillaries" can become the proverbial tail wagging the dog, generating more money than the property in its original incarnation. Merchandising, a category that could mean a thousand different products (ranging from toys, to games, to apparel), is what one tends to associate with ancillary revenue. I will accordingly devote the bulk of this chapter to merchandising (in the broad sense), and while it is beyond the scope of this book to delve too deeply into the games business, I will both touch on games as they relate to film/TV ancillaries and also discuss elements of social gaming. The evolution of data analytics, which is ever being fine-tuned by the gaming world, will inevitably influence all media consumption metrics and related advertising tracking and pricing.

Notwithstanding the importance of merchandising in the film and television world, in the context of distribution, a series of ancillary streams have carved out additional niche windows for exploiting content. The most prominent of these include:

- hotel/motel
- pay-per-view
- video-on-demand (VOD) (here focused on its roots, briefly touching on Internet VOD, as OTT services are generally discussed in Chapter 7)
- airlines
- non-theatrical.

I will only cover these markets in broad concept, in part to illustrate their relative relationship to the more important revenue drivers. What is interesting is how the landscape has changed: in my first edition, I included transactional video-on-demand within this section, but have now moved the discussion of transactional VOD to the video chapter (as VOD has, as predicted, become the new face of rental video), a discussion of SVOD to Chapter 6 (as subscription VOD has become akin to pay TV), and Internet VOD to Chapter 7 (as part of the description of streaming OTT services). In the new order, VOD is truly everywhere, and as discussed throughout the book the increasingly ubiquitous access to content in an on-demand manner is collapsing the value drivers in Ulin's Rule and putting unrelenting stress on the historical window system.

Finally, a quick note about online revenues—it would be fair to add online generally into this mix of "ancillaries," because many view online as just another additive revenue stream. However, I am treating online as a separate almost "super category," focusing on how it is impacting mainstream and ancillary revenue windows alike. In summary, that is the challenge of convergence: Are revenues from downloading a TV show to an iPod or streaming content to a tablet ancillary revenues, or rather new kinds of digital exploitation changing the very character of traditional markets (electronic sell-through supplanting DVD retail, and streaming content challenging the nature of what is TV)?

Merchandising

Merchandising revenues can be so significant that this ancillary market actually becomes the primary revenue stream targeted. Many animated properties originate from toys or with the intent of generating toy sales, with the producer sometimes viewing the cartoon (and, in extreme cases, its telecast) as a marketing expense. The challenge is that mer-

446

chandising revenues can be even more fickle than the film business, with toy vendors wary of the high risks even when dealing with name properties.[1] Basing toys on a movie runs a dual risk that the movie will work and then that the movie's performance can be converted into retail success with products based on the movie and its characters.

And yet, when a merchandising program takes off, it can be extremely big—in select cases, even bigger than all other traditional media streams combined. I had the privilege of cross-promoting videos with *Star Wars* merchandise, the all-time leader in merchandising sales from a film property. Commenting on cumulative sales generated over 35 years since the debut of the original film, the *Hollywood Reporter* summarized: "Over the span of *Star Wars'* lifetime, $20 billion and counting of licensed goods has been sold, this on top of the $4.4 billion in tickets and $3.8 billion in home entertainment products."[2]

Transmedia

In the era of social networking and digital versions of content, trans-media has been ballyhooed as a new buzzword for extending stories into other media and platforms; in general, the term refers not to sequels and remakes, but rather the production of new stories and content via different platforms and media, which serve to expand the fabric and experience of the core content. Whether this is fundamentally different than the notion of migrating a property into a franchise that is larger than the sum of its parts is difficult to define. Those trying to frame transmedia exploitation may argue that the difference is in planning: independent tangents are enabled from the get-go in an effort to create a broad, immersive experience where storylines are not linked, yet all tie together because of common grounding (which, in legal terms, reflects all the related properties being derivative works). No doubt, digital media helps enable these different threads. I would argue, though, that big enough franchises spawn an end result akin to transmedia storytelling, whether the end result is designed or simply evolves from opportunities to monetize different elements.

Star Wars, again, provides a good example. The following are some of the key tentacles of brand extension:

- Toys: Toys such as action figures and lightsabers have been a staple consumer retail product for decades, defining the franchise as an evergreen.
- Books: Searching the Web, one can find more than 100 different books (excluding graphic novels and comics) expanding upon the

Star Wars universe, ranging in age demographics (e.g., young adult) and segmented by timeline (before or after *X* period of "history" in the saga). Additionally, the books include longtime relationships with leading brands such as Random House and Scholastic, several *New York Times* bestsellers, and estimates of more than 160 million copies of books in print.[3]

■ Video games: LucasArts was among the top independent games publishers for almost 20 years, with *Star Wars* games both tying into and expanding the *Star Wars* universe. (Note: LucasArts was closed in 2013 post Disney's acquisition of Lucasfilm.) Lego alone has sold more than 15 million units of the *Lego Star Wars* video game, and the MMO *Star Wars: The Old Republic* (developed in collaboration between LucasArts and Electronic Arts' BioWare), launched during the 2011 holidays, sold more than 2 million copies in its first two months, and according to the *Hollywood Reporter* about 1.5 million people were paying an average subscription of $15 per month during Q1 2012.[4]

■ Theme park rides: *Star Tours*, a staple flight simulator ride at Disney theme parks globally, debuted in 1987, and was then revamped in 2011.

■ Education: There have been multiple *Star Wars* learning products over the span of the franchise, including in the last few years a range of interactive educational games from leading children's educational software company LeapFrog.

■ Television: The franchise has led to a series of documentaries, ranging from behind-the-scenes productions to Discovery Channel's *The Science of Star Wars*. Additionally, the hit animated series *The Clone Wars* was among Cartoon Network's top shows since its debut in 2008, averaging 2.2 million daily viewers, and has ranked as the top show for the boys 2–14 demographic.[5]

Arguably, books, video games, and television series taking characters and themes in different and new directions, in different media, often set in different time periods, enabling different and often immersive experiences yet all grounded in common iconography, is a form of transmedia storytelling. What is new today, however, when people often refer to transmedia, is the launching of a "franchise" with different elements from conception, enabling viral growth, which helps define and build a franchise. The formal definition of transmedia, or whether the tail wags the dog (or vice versa), though, is less important than the ability of intellectual property to be molded into different forms, formats, product, and media, which all can be independently monetized.

As Risky and Lucrative as the Film Business

What Properties Can Spawn Successful Merchandising Programs?

Most successful film- or TV-based merchandising programs are built around either franchise properties or properties targeted at the kids/family demographic such as animated features. To the extent that a property crosses over to both categories, namely franchises and kids, then the potential is that much greater. This is why films based on comic books have become so hot, and why brands such as Marvel have seen a resurgence. Even with this type of triangulation, nothing is a sure thing. *Batman* has been a success story, and more recently *Spider-Man* has hit its stride, but product based on *Superman* has struggled by comparison.

Star Wars has been the industry's leading and enduring success story, somehow managing to strike a continuing chord with multigenerational fans and collectors. It is a legendary industry story how Lucasfilm was caught by surprise by the product demand back in the 1970s following the launch of the original film. Demand was so high that toy company Kenner shipped empty boxes with vouchers for product that would be shipped later. This story is instructive to illustrate (again) the similarity of vicissitudes to the film business; namely, the market is hit-driven and no one can fully predict what will catch on and when. Accordingly, the business tends to segment into two major categories: established properties, where the merchandise becomes part of a larger franchise management program, and newly released properties that launch with the hype of presumed success (e.g., a new Pixar film).

It then becomes the challenge of major product providers, such as toy companies, to place large upfront bets. The two largest U.S. toy companies, Mattel and Hasbro, are heavily courted by every studio and network, because having a major toy program in place not only validates the expectations for an upcoming release, but also provides cross-promotion via the brand marketing of the toy company. It is like joining a craps table, but now there are more people betting on the roll, with the energy and expectations feeding on each other; moreover, the drama is heightened by the fact that everyone gets only one roll (the film's opening box office, or a TV series initial airings).

The Difference with TV

In many ways, merchandising driven off of TV is a much better business. This is because, with a continuing story, it is possible to hold back and see how a property is performing before ramping up too far. It is not

449

unusual to wait for the second season of a series before launching major product; the time delay allows programs to be built around what the merchandisers now know is a hit. Moreover, with TV there is the ability to keep the property in front of its consumers week after week. The combination of a more calculated risk and a longer tail should produce a healthier ROI, a fact further buttressed because TV production costs should be lower than film costs.

Among the great success stories in this space is *Power Rangers*, a series/franchise that became so strong that it (together with thousands of hours of other animated content controlled by Saban Entertainment) allowed producer Haim Saban to launch and co-own Fox Kids with NewsCorp; Saban then netted a huge personal payoff (in the billions) when he sold the kids cable network to Disney (which then rebranded the network ABC Family).[6] (See Chapter 7 for a discussion of how these profits were leveraged to make billions more with the purchase and sale of one of Germany's leading commercial TV networks.)

Another prime example over the last 10–20 years has been an explosion of anime-based properties, including *Pokémon*, *Yu-Gi-Oh!*, and *Dragon Ball Z*, hitting U.S. television (properties that are, in turn, often derivative of manga magazines and graphic novels). Nintendo's *Pokémon* turned into a phenomenon, becoming such a figure of pop culture that it appeared on the cover of *Time* magazine and the *New Yorker*, and a gigantic Pikachu balloon floated through the Macy's Thanksgiving Parade.[7] As an aside, I remember meeting the woman in Tokyo who created the signature yellow pocket monster character Pikachu, and autographs were so in demand that she regularly kept stickers with her to sign. In terms of numbers, *Pokémon* sales figures were daunting: from over 1,000 licensed products, it is estimated that global *Pokémon* merchandise sales exceeded $5 billion. And these numbers are from legitimate licenses—in 1999, Nintendo of America, the licensing agent for *Pokémon*, asked a New York court to crack down on pirates, alleging they were losing $725 million per year from counterfeit goods.[8]

It is the hope of these types of returns that excites the executives at all channels focused on kids programming. At Nickelodeon, *SpongeBob SquarePants* sustained a successful merchandising program for years. Disney uses its Disney Channel airtime to keep key characters fresh, such as with a CG-animated Mickey Mouse; moreover, it is also able to cross-promote items through its theme parks, networks, videos, etc., thus creating purchasing demand among each new generation of toddlers. Disney has also been able to expand its success into the teen demographic, as evidenced by its Disney Channel special *High School Musical*. This TV musical and its sequels (e.g., *High School Musical 2*), per *Variety*, "have sold nearly 15 million CDs, 50 million books, 4.8 million video games, and spawned stage shows, concerts, and an ice tour." In terms of financial return, at the height of the *High School Musical* frenzy (2009), Disney targeted $2.7 billion from *High School Musical* and *Hannah Montana* products.[9]

In contrast, name a successful TV or film merchandising program not aimed at kids. There are a few, such as around *The Simpsons* and *South Park*, but outside of these edgy shows where the merchandising leverages the cult appeal of the show, there are hardly any examples. Dramas, police shows, action movies, romantic comedies, sitcoms, and even niche genres such as horror do not lend themselves to converting property interest to product purchases. Why? Arguably, it is all about time, focus, and independence. As people grow older and are more independent with their choices, with more influences competing for their attention, marketing messages are diluted, and the desire to affiliate with a character or item becomes less compelling. Simply, think of a graph, where the Y axis is range of choice and influences, and the X axis is age. The older you get, the more choices and the more exposure. In contrast, children watch hours of certain TV shows each week (if not each day), and a particular property is more integral to their lives.

451

Chicken and Egg: When Merchandise Drives TV

As outlined in Chapter 6, on occasion producers will pay for airspace and take on the risk of selling the commercial inventory to guarantee a broadcast slot. This risk tends to be limited to instances where there are strong ancillary revenues, such as built-in merchandising from an established brand, where the P&L is not simply based on advertising sales. A prime example several years ago was 4Kids Entertainment's deal with Fox (4Kids holding TV merchandising and broadcast rights to *Pokémon* and other hit anime titles).

According to 4Kids Entertainment's annual report, "The Company, through a multi-year agreement with Fox, leases Fox's four hour Saturday morning children's programming block. The agreement, which commenced in September 2002, requires the Company to pay annual fees of $25,312 through 2006."[10] The annual report continued:

The Company, through a multi-year agreement with Fox, leases Fox's Saturday morning programming block from 8 a.m. to 12 p.m. eastern/pacific time (7 a.m. to 11 a.m. central time). In January 2005, the Company changed the name of the Saturday morning programming block from Fox Box to 4Kids TV. The Company provides substantially all programming content to be broadcast on 4Kids TV. 4Kids Ad Sales, Inc., a wholly-owned subsidiary of the Company, retains all of the revenue from its sale of network advertising time for the four-hour time period.[11]

Fox secured over $100 million over four years without any risk, presumably on the assessment that it could not sell $25 million of advertising per year in this space or otherwise net better than this amount after programming costs. The network's bet seemed to pay off based on the 4Kids report, which lists advertising media and broadcast revenues for 2002, 2003, and 2005, respectively, as $11.2 million, $22.54 million, and $24.1 million. In addition to running a deficit on the airtime, 4Kids had programming costs to amortize. And yet, as the report further noted, the company's belief that TV exposure would drive other revenues tied to the already established franchise justified the risk: "The ability of the Company to further develop its merchandising, home video, and music publishing revenue streams were significant components of its evaluation process which resulted in the decision to lease the 4Kids TV Saturday morning programming block."[12]

452

In the context of leveraging well-known brands with strong merchandising lines, the 4Kids Entertainment strategy of broadcasting new (and inexpensive-to-produce) series on network to drive awareness for ancillary revenue streams was a bold play. However, absent this context the notion of paying for production, receiving no license fee (and, in fact, having a negative license fee given the lower ad revenues versus the cost of the airtime), and betting the entire economics on ancillary revenues may carry worse odds than gambling.

Most Extreme Example: Toys Programming a Whole Network

The natural extension of the 4Kids experiment with Fox and programming a block of TV content is to take over and program an entire channel. With exposure difficult and a few key players controlling the network flow, both independents and toy companies recently changed strategy and have opted to become both the programmer and owner.

In 2009, Hasbro bought 50 percent of Discovery Kids to launch The Hub, a new children's network with a reach of approximately 60 million subscribers. While Discovery continues to manage advertising sales, programming is the responsibility of Hasbro—meaning that a toy company is leveraging a major cable network to promote its brands (e.g. *Transformers*), with animated series such as *Transformers Rescue Bots* and *Transformers Prime*.

Another example of a children's production company launching a network is PBS Kids Sprout. The channel originally launched in 2005 as a partnership among Comcast, HIT Entertainment, PBS, and Sesame Workshop. HIT Entertainment, launched originally as the overseas television arm of the Jim Henson Company (Henson International Television), had gone public and bought the iconic U.K. brand *Thomas the Tank Engine*. The new network enabled HIT to have a direct television outlet via which to air series and cross-promote its brands. (Note: In 2011, Mattel bought HIT Entertainment, bringing not only *Thomas the Tank Engine*, but global brands *Barney* and *Bob the Builder* under its umbrella; however, HIT's ownership interest in Sprout was not part of the transaction. This makes sense given the educational focus and mission of PBS and Sesame Workshop, which would arguably have been in direct conflict with having one of the two largest toy companies (Mattel) as a major owner.)

In A World of Apps, Do Toy Company–Network Partnerships Make Sense?

Given the growth of the app space, and the rise of brands such as *Angry Birds* into global franchises, it will be interesting to watch whether the appetite for toy companies to invest in linear television programming continues. Rovio, the Finnish developer of *Angry Birds*, riding the crest of over 500 million downloads (mobile and online) reportedly turned down a $2.5 billion bid from social games pioneer Zynga at the end of 2011.[13] This phenomenal growth in under two years is an example of digital power—the downloads combine use across cell phones, tablets, Web browsers, and computers, and according to Rovio users engagement was a staggering combined playtime of 200,000 years and 400 billion in-game bird launches.[14] Because apps and TV measure metrics so differently, it is difficult, if not impossible, to compare like-for-like value; nevertheless, if one were to harmonize a metric of user engagement, no doubt *Angry Birds* would come out near the top, if not a clear leader.

The number of toys and other merchandise that *Angry Birds* spawned would be the envy of any toy company. Rovio targeted sales of 20 million *Angry Birds* toys at Christmas 2011, and in an interview with *Forbes*, GM North America Andrew Stalbow noted the following statistics in highlighting the company's efforts on bridging the digital and physical world in 2012: "We're selling over 1 million plush toys every month. We have apparel in stores like Walmart and JC Penney. We have three new books in stores now—the cookbook and two dootle books. We had the number one 'most searched for' Halloween costume."[15]

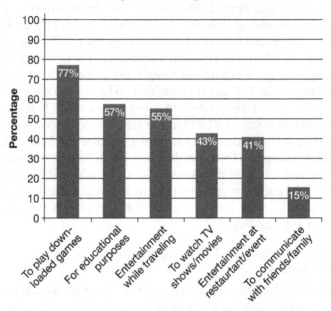

According to Tablet-Owning Adults and Children

Figure 8.1 How do Children Use Tablets?

Reproduced by permission of Nielsen

With the power of the app-driving-merchandise model proven by Rovio, a toy company looking to market its brands would then need to ask whether this is a fluke, or whether there is a broader phenomenon building in terms of digital devices grabbing the attention of its core consumers (i.e., kids). A study by Nielsen in Q4 2011 implies yes: of households with tablets, 77 percent of children under 12 used the tablets to download games, compared to 43 percent that used them to watch TV (Figure 8.1).

These statistics suggest something even more powerful—clever marketing and integration that could take advantage of a tablet's combined power for downloads and watching TV/video suggests that a brand leveraging the power of new digital devices can drive penetration, consumption, and brand awareness on an unprecedented scale. Moreover, because the cost of developing apps is a fraction of producing linear television (suite of top apps in the hundreds of thousands of dollars, versus the cost of a season of animated TV programming in the millions of dollars), access is not controlled by the filter of programming executives (apps can be democratically launched across multiple platforms).

Further, since marketing and advertising costs for apps are lower (though costs are increasing, costs are still significantly lower, as well as capable of being more finely targeted direct-to-consumer rather than direct-to-demographic), toy companies with investments merely focused on controlling a slice of airtime are likely to find themselves playing catch-up with those that can optimize this new ecosystem.

E-Commerce Plus Web-Based and Social Media Extensions

Although discussed in Chapter 9 regarding marketing, it is important to highlight in the context of merchandising the role the Internet plays. Virtually all films and major TV shows have dedicated websites, and within these websites users can often directly link to e-commerce applications to buy related merchandise. When I took over managing www.starwars.com, I was pleasantly surprised to learn (and I guess I really should not have been surprised) that one of the thriving parts of www.starwars.com was the *Star Wars* shop. This store, like many other Internet boutiques, was able to include within its product mix special online exclusives; more targeted marketing, and the ability to offer limited quantities, will sometimes allow a diverse SKU of unique items that may not be viable in the hyper-competitive environment of retail shelf space.

Since my first edition, the concept of dedicated "sites" has expanded such that a website is now not enough; all key brands also have parallel social networking sites, such as a Facebook page. Social networking sites can help cross-promote and link merchandising elements, even if the store may be embedded elsewhere. Additionally, video/TV properties lend themselves particularly well to apps, and a major franchise is apt to drive consumption via a combination of apps, social networking, and websites, all leveraging each other and capturing user data across the spectrum. As discussed in Chapter 9, the challenge today is to create efficient metrics and dashboards to enable brand managers to optimize engagement around key branding events (e.g., launches), capture user data to efficiently update and market to "fans" between events, and push out messaging that is configured for personalized storage and virally spread when touched (be that consumed, viewed, recommended, etc.). The critical element to this new paradigm is the personalized level of communication; in terms of merchandising, it is therefore not surprising that the trend has been pushed down to the personal level as well.

The tangible manifestation of everything being pushed down to the individual level is customization of merchandise, with e-commerce platforms able to create "print-on-demand" solutions for a range of product. Café Press and Zazzle are among the biggest names, with companies enabling fans of shows to customize a range of items, from apparel, to housewares (e.g., coffee mugs), to cell-phone covers. Images and even buzz slogans from characters can be customized with your name, or in a pattern chosen by the consumer. Because (in theory) this business does not require inventory, but rather companies can print or manufacture product on a 1:1 basis based on the particular customer order, a material business can be created with relatively small staff. All order manufacturing, invoicing, marketing, etc. is done via the website, fulfilment can be performed using third-party delivery services (leveraging the Amazon model), and, depending on the product, it is even possible to outsource the actual production. Not surprisingly, there are various companies, such as MashOn, leveraging this new on-demand model to deliver customized products tied to movies, TV series, and even games.

In addition to enabling e-commerce merchandise applications (both for digital and physical product, including items available only via the Web), the Web has enabled the phenomenon of secondary markets. Everyone is familiar with stories of the value of old comic collections, and eBay has enabled a vibrant marketplace for collectors—in essence, giving an entire new life to the collectibles market. While eBay is obviously a broader phenomenon, it is a boon to the world of merchandise.

Licensing Programs

What is a Licensing Program?

A licensing program is based around trademarks affiliated with a movie or TV show, and creates a variety of product categories leveraging the brand and key characters. The categories are as diverse as one can imagine, and the following is just a sample list:

- toys and games (including now app-based and social games)
- apparel and accessories (including backpacks)
- publishing (e.g., books, magazines, activity books)
- interactive (e.g., computer games, platform games)
- mobile (ringtones, wallpaper, etc.)
- domestics (e.g., sheets, towels, bath and bath accessories)
- housewares
- social expression (including greeting cards, stationery, etc.)
- sporting goods

- food (including salty snacks, cereals, packaged goods, frozen, etc.)
- gifts and collectibles.

Top brands can have literally hundreds of licensed properties, and the range of the program and how fine the categories are segmented depends on the property and philosophy of the licensor. The digital and online world is further expanding the possibilities, as movie sounds and music have been adapted for popular ringtones, and it is now possible to license avatars and digital accessories in a variety of environments.

Product merchandising, however, is an area where more is not always better, and the success of a program will depend on the commitment of the licensees and the licensor's ability to exercise controls both with licensees and with retail to ensure quality and a level playing field for product.

Retail Buy-In and Support

A licensing program does not stop with concluding licensing deals, because a successful campaign will also have the licensor working with key retail accounts and licensees to ensure placement and coordination at retail outlets, which today also includes e-tailers. Amazon has a form of retail space and with home page placement, e-mail blasts, alerts, targeted marketing, and cross promotions, a campaign can materially influence the success of tied merchandising. A challenge with online, though, is that it can adjust more quickly and more democratically to index promotions to search and purchase metrics; thus, a successful product may build on its traffic (successful sales lead to a virtuous cycle of more frequent or better-placed search results and cross references), but it is harder to influence an underperforming product as the results, not promise of results, will dictate exposure (i.e., if underperforming, a producer will argue that warrants greater promotion since the title is not being found as expected, and yet the search results and indexing for promotion will actually be reduced since they are often linked to actual results, creating a downward spiral of reduced promotion; the nature of the online metrics linking to actual results tends therefore to accentuate the extremes, adding promotion to what is already successful, and perhaps too early bailing on a title not yet performing). As for large physical retailers such as Walmart, Target, and Toys "R" Us, these key accounts will stock a variety of products related to the brand, but will be dealing with separate and unrelated licensees, with each pushing its product at the level of the department buyer. To the extent an event

457

(e.g., movie launch) or brand warrants it, special standees and sections can be created, pulling product from multiple departments, creating incremental retail placement, and highlighting the brand; moreover, if the retailer buys in and believes aggregating product will drive traffic, then the retailer is also more likely to promote and advertise the selection, either in circulars and/or with hard media using co-op advertising funds. When the last *Star Wars* movie was released, for example, the merchandising program was robust enough that Walmart even participated in special "tent" events at select locations: What could be better than not having to leave the parking lot to fight with a lightsaber?

Any successful licensing program will therefore focus on retail-specific programs. You know you have stepped into a licensing meeting when an executive is talking planograms and live on-shelf dates. Another reason retail engagement is so critical is that the very nature of product merchandising speaks franchises, and if there is oversupply of product or too many licensees, such that the retailers get hurt (as opposed to the product licensees), then a campaign is not only unsuccessful, but the future is undermined. Some will take a "take the money and run" approach, focusing on guarantees, but a successfully managed campaign will spend as much time working retail engagement, placement, and metrics as the deals for the products themselves.

458

Quality Control and Timing

Licensing has a longer development/planning cycle than any of the traditional media categories (e.g., theatrical, video, and TV distribution), which often puts crazy pressure on divisions to lock in plans before the details of a project are even worked out. If cutting a trailer for a film is difficult because the movie is not yet done, then creating product for that movie takes the challenge one step further because decisions often need to be locked before the filming even starts.

Timing

Lead times of two years are not unusual, and anything short of 18 months may make developing product and getting it on-shelf in time impossible. This is simply the nature of product development—the entire supply side, from designs, to materials, to molds, etc., takes time. Virtually everything is outsourced for manufacturing, which means location and subcontractor decisions are involved, plus product samples need to be made and approved. (Note: Product placements (which can sometimes be confused with merchandising), such as a special car being featured in a film, similarly need long lead times, as the integration has to occur before filming. See Chapter 9 for a discussion of product placements.)

Style Guides and Quality Approval

Before any product is made, the licensor will create a detailed style guide. This guide will include the logos and typefaces to be used (including a variety for different types of packaging and sizing), approved artwork for characters, including in different poses and turnarounds (e.g., flat and dimensional), approved trademark and copyright notices, approved color palates, approved phrases, approved peripherals (such as weapons or vehicles from the property), approved size charts (relative scale of one character to another), etc. *KidScreen* magazine, describing how a style guide can differentiate a pitch and is at the heart of any consumer product program, referred to style guides as "doing overtime as a calling card, a presentation piece, a licensee manual and a brand road map all at once. So getting the right style guide is crucial to scoring a [merchandising] hit." It then continued to detail the elements of a guide: "Most guides start off with a general description of the film or TV show and then get into the nitty-gritty graphic components, including icons, logos, color guides (breaking out main, secondary, and accent palettes), character and background art, prints, borders, patterns, phrases and text that can be used, fonts and sample product applications."[16]

459

The goal of the style guide is to create brand consistency. If over 100 products are made in varying media and mediums, the licensor needs to provide a blueprint around which specific items are then designed. In the case of *Barbie*, which has approximately 1,000 licensees working across 45 product categories, there is a template to rein in too-divergent elements, but Mattel claims that while "you do need a few rules, because that's how a brand becomes clear and cohesive," they strive to work with licensees throughout the process and avoid steering the process through too narrow a creative tunnel.[17] The style guide then provides a working anchor for quality control, as sample designs and product must stay within the parameters outlined. To the extent the product is consistent, then the licensor's review for quality approval is infinitely easier.

This is one of those areas where I touch upon it in a paragraph or two, but the execution of the style guide and approval over designs and sample product are the lifeblood of the merchandising campaign. Failure to timely approve items or to properly inspect quality are the surest way to doom a program, and cannot be taken for granted. This becomes an economic consideration, because once deals are signed, there is the temptation to assume "licensees know what they're doing" and relax. In fact, it is tempting to cut budgets around personnel to review product, especially as the numbers and categories grow. Almost all merchandising managers will testify that they have rarely seen cutting corners pay off, because there is nothing more competitive than the retail shelf, and consumers are always savvier than anticipated. This is why companies will invest significant funds up front in the creation of a style guide (most aspects of which can apply to online/digital representations as well), with the bill ranging from tens of thousands to well over one hundred thousand dollars.

Licensing Deals

I have waited until this point to describe key elements of licensing deals to punctuate the point made earlier that while signing up licensees is obviously critical, if a licensor puts full stock in that element at the expense of developing sophisticated plans for approvals, style guides, and retail management, then, at best, license deals will not be optimized and, at worst, undermined.

460

Licensed Products and Property

"Licensed product" is exactly as it sounds: the specific products being authorized, such as action figures, T-shirts, key chains, digital avatars and accessories, or wallpapers. The "Licensed property," in contrast, refers to the underlying rights (e.g., trademarks) upon which the products may be based.

Licensed Rights—Exclusive versus Nonexclusive Rights to Licensed Properties

The license agreement will make it clear (hopefully) whether the licensor conveys either exclusive or nonexclusive rights to use the licensed property in connection with a defined category of licensed products (and to add further legal boundaries, of course during a limited term, and restricted to the defined territory). Because the license rights ultimately derive from the ability to use the licensor's trademarks with products based on the underlying property, to the extent the licensor is allowing multiple products, then conceptually the license is nonexclusive; however, most licenses carve out a measure of category exclusivity, such as the exclusive right to make watches or trading cards. It is this niche level of exclusivity (whether a de facto practice adhered to on a relationship basis, or expressly granted) that allows franchises to spawn hundreds of licensed goods and obtain minimum guarantees against narrowly defined category exclusives.

Although most film-based licenses tend to be category-exclusive, one can also find general market examples of nonexclusive product licenses. A prominent example is found in sports, where individual teams may permit a number of manufacturers to make a product such as multiple companies creating apparel using team logos (in which case, one shirt may bear trademarks of Nike and Team X, and another shirt Team X plus Y).

Not only can the license be bounded by time, territory, product category, and exclusivity, but even by types of distribution outlets (e.g., novelty stores, grocery stores). This is somewhat akin to the video market, which is differentiated into retail categories (such as rental and sell-through), though ultimately much more complex because the segmentation adds the complexity of the character of the outlets rather than resting on the clearer dividing line of price and type of transaction (see Figure 8.2).

Economics: Minimum Guarantees/Advances

Minimum guarantees are important at two levels: first and foremost, they ensure the licensor a revenue floor, and second, they create incentives for the licensee to push the product to meet and hopefully exceed the guarantee. Licensing deals rarely stray from the concept of an advance against royalties, with these two items as the focal point of negotiations. This is not to trivialize other elements of the deal, or argue that when and how advances and royalties are paid is not critical, but it is important to recognize that at the heart of any licensing deal are relatively simple and direct economic terms. Unlike net profits from a film (see Chapter 10), Hollywood has not evolved arcane accounting standards around merchandising: at its guts are how many units are being sold, what the royalties are (and how they are calculated), and what amount, if any, the licensee will front against the royalties.

One wrinkle that can arise around minimum guarantees is that a licensor may want minimum royalty payments over defined periods such as on an annual basis. These thresholds are designed to ensure that licensees are continuing to market and push products; if certain sales targets are not met, this could trigger the right to terminate the license (or, conversely, extend the license if they are met).

Licensors are dealing with brands that have inherent awareness and goodwill (here, someone willing to pay money pursuant to a trademark license to associate a consumer product), and the ability to guarantee

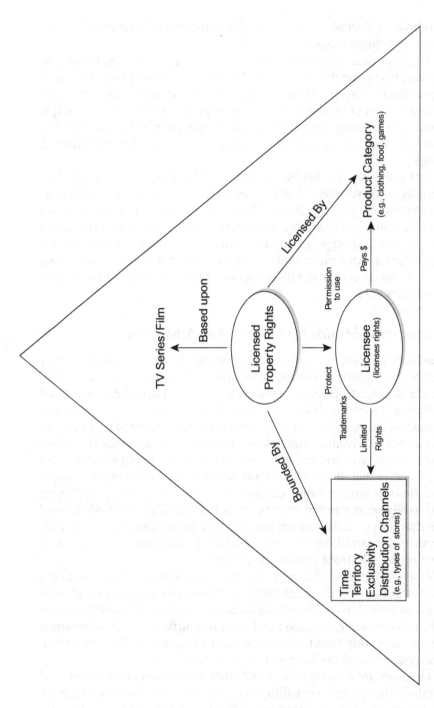

Figure 8.2 Licensing: Product Merchandising Ecosystem

continued levels of sales and exposure can be as critical to brand management as the associated revenues. These types of licensors will not "take the money and run," but rather take the money and make the licensees keep running. This is fundamentally different from deals based on straight license fees (e.g., TV, assuming no ratings bonuses), in which initial marketing commitments may be established, but thereafter the broadcaster has flexibility. In the context of TV, broadcasters typically have the obligation to pay the license fee, but then assuming the fee is paid they do not actually have to broadcast the property. Merchandising deal structures are more like video, where product sales are dependent on shelf space, retail execution, and thousands of points of purchase; similarly, both are consumer products, upsides are generally tied to volume, and with a licensor's participation set as a per-product royalty.

Royalties

Royalty calculations are generally straightforward, and are expressed as a percentage of sales. The challenge is in defining sales, and then specifying what, if any, adjustments or deductions are permitted. First, in terms of sales, the product can be sold at multiple levels, such as wholesale and then retail (with further wrinkles if a product may be purchased from an overseas manufacturing facility where the pricing is pre-shipment and wholesale markup). Much like the context for video sales/royalties, the only pot of money a licensor taps into is at the wholesale level. A licensee makes its product and sells it to a customer (e.g., a retailer), and any corresponding royalty needs to be based on the gross revenue derived at this level. This is nearly an exact parallel to royalties/revenue that are accounted for at the wholesale price with respect to video. The one wrinkle here regards digital goods, for a digital asset—such as a character upgrade or weapon/accessory in a game—does not need to be manufactured, and accordingly royalties will be set off the consumer price.

463

Once the "gross" pot is defined from which the royalty is calculated, the next concern is defining whether there are any adjustments to this gross; a concept that is sometimes made confusing by defining this gross amount as "net sales." There are multiple elements that may come into play to reduce the base from which royalties are calculated (e.g., Can a licensee apply trade and other discounts, such as cash discounts? Can a licensee have an allowance for free or promotion goods?). While it is standard to allow some deductions, as well as apply a cap on total deductions, much of the risk ends up transferred to the licensee. As noted earlier, the concepts of net and gross track common sense expectations and generally do not devolve into arcane accounting schemes.

Finally, it is worth touching on setting royalty rates. Unlike the video context, where there is a relatively clear economic logic to splits (see Chapter 5 for a discussion of setting royalties to approximate cost of the top splits), royalty rates in the merchandising areas tend to be set on straightforward percentages without the parties trying to match a cost of the top split or other structure (likely because of the low cost of goods, the production of which has been outsourced to Asia/lower-cost production centers decades before this became trendy in other businesses, and the opportunity costs of having to deal with this calculation on hundreds of different products). Of course, the notion of splits underlies the setting of any royalty, but the point is that there is less of a conscious mechanism here; rather, the percentages tend to be within customary bands per product category.

It is a trade secret what those bands are, but suffice it to note that certain product categories may be in the very low single digits, while others can be a multiple of this range and command double digits. The *Los Angeles Times*, quoting a toy analyst, noted regarding the range: "The studios license the rights to toy manufacturers and also receive royalties of 7 percent to 15 percent of the sales, said Chris Byrne, an independent toy analyst and contributing editor of *Toy Wishes* magazine."[18] The *Hollywood Reporter*, in its survey article prior to the annual New York Toy Fair (2008), pegged the numbers a bit higher; estimating for top properties that licensors usually receive an advance guarantee in the $1 million range, it references a group publisher from *License Global* magazine in citing that studio licensors receive a 10–15 percent royalty on wholesale (and that wholesale is roughly 50 percent of retail), and that for certain franchises such as Pixar's *Toy Story*, the percentages can be even higher.[19]

A final element worth mentioning in the context of merchandising royalties is the impact of distribution fees, which tend to be much higher than those applied for non-ancillary streams. It is not uncommon for a merchandising agent/distributor to charge fees from 30–50 percent, the high percentage justified by the presumably tougher job of managing (and selling) multiple product SKUS, timelines, and quality control (see also "Role of Agents" below). Accordingly, the net to the licensor is impacted by comparatively low royalty rates (to an extent driven by thin margins) and very high off-the-top fees—a formula that means only a fraction of the wholesale revenues (and remember, this is a fraction of the often-quoted retail sales) ends up paid to the producer/owner of the TV show or film upon which the product is based.

Premiums

Premiums are licensed product that are given away to consumers rather than sold. This may take the form of a figure included with a kids' meal at a fast food restaurant chain, and the issue for the licensor is on what basis is it paid: the consumer has not paid anything for the item of merchandise, and yet the licensor needs to be compensated. Economically, there are two theoretical routes for compensation. The first would be to allocate a portion of the sale, treating the premium as a bundled good and attributing a percentage of the purchase price to the premium. This, however, is not feasible for a variety of reasons: (1) the retailer (e.g., restaurant) is not going to allocate away from its core product; (2) the product is temporary, in that the premiums are offered only during a short promotional window, which means that the same allocation would need to be offered for all product among competitors (e.g., Burger King is not going to give Warner Bros. a better deal in March for the product packed in a kids' meal than they will give Universal the following month); and (3) there may be no wholesale price (as the retailer will sometimes directly commission and manufacture the item).

Given these complications, compensation, to the extent there is direct compensation at all and this is not viewed as marketing, may instead be based on the manufacturing price of the item. A royalty would then be calculated based on the production cost, which amounts to a nominal number per item. The licensor will agree to this small basis because the nature of premiums is promotional (and at some level it is only mutual leverage that keeps them from having to pay for this promotion), the products are very inexpensive (almost disposable), and, at essence, royalties on the product are an incremental upside and not the driver of the deal.

465

Role of Agents

Licensing at an elemental level is about sales, and every company has to make economic decisions balancing the cost/benefit of an in-house licensing department versus outsourcing the function. Even with a large in-house staff, however, some elements will still be outsourced to ensure global coverage (there is simply not enough consistent throughput for most companies to have dedicated staff in all major markets worldwide).

Most companies will therefore utilize either a master agent or a network of agents, managing this sales staff via commission structures. The agent will be responsible for sourcing deals, helping negotiate contracts, monitoring quality and performance levels of the licenses, and in some cases even overseeing collections. The licensor then has the decision of what level of autonomy to authorize, and to what degree it will delegate management functions either up front (deal terms/selecting licensees) or during management and maintenance (e.g., product approvals). The degree of work will dictate whether the agent receives only a commission tied to royalties, or has an additional retainer/higher fees for performing overhead functions.

In addition to agents scouring the market to set up product licenses, the business is now so big that Hollywood agencies separately represent toy companies and individual properties to try to set up tie-in movie and TV deals (e.g., WME represented Hasbro to turn games such as *Trivial Pursuit* and *Candy Land* into film and TV products tapping its talent roster).[20]

Toys as a Driver

Toys are the sweet spot of most merchandising programs, and a licensor leveraging a film property will usually first attempt to sign a master toy license. Such a toy license will cover a range of potential products, such as toy vehicles, action figures, and themed props (e.g., swords, guns, apparel). For perspective, it is important to understand the breadth of the market, not simply in overall licensing program terms, but also in terms of diversity of toy revenue. For example, while action figures are undoubtedly a key driver, creating stimulus for kids' role-playing and buying ancillary accessories and props, action figures make up only a part of the puzzle. Action figure sales have hovered around the same percentage of the overall market in the last several years—$1.25 billion of the $22.6 billion overall toy market in 2006, and $1.3 billion of the $21.18 billion market in 2011 (both estimates by NPD group).[21]

In terms of how big merchandising tied to an individual film can be, it is possible to earn in the hundreds of millions of dollars. *Business Week*, in an article describing how Marvel and the whole industry underestimated the extent to which *The Avengers* (summer 2012) would be a hit, noted that Hasbro would make around $150 million in sales from *Avengers* product. While that may seem like a great success, in quoting an analyst from BMO Capital Markets, it noted: "Normally, a movie that makes more than $1 billion at the box office would produce $250 million to $300 million in toy sales . . ."[22]

Mega Deals: Star Wars and Spider-Man

The amount of money that can be made from toys can reach extraordinary heights, as evidenced by Hasbro's success with *Transformers* and its deal with Lucasfilm for Star Wars merchandise (pre Disney's acquisition of Lucasfilm). Discussing an extension of its initial $590 million agreement with Lucas Licensing (Lucasfilm's merchandising arm), Hasbro advised that, in addition to a term extension, the new agreement lowered "the minimum payment guaranteed to the film producer George Lucas because of less-than-expected sales. The minimum payment was reduced by $85 million, to $505 million."[23]

Another example is Marvel (also pre its acquisition by Disney), where Hasbro put up a $200 million-plus guarantee for toy and game rights across Marvel's properties, including *Spider-Man, Fantastic Four*, and *X-Men* for five years; *Spider-Man* was clearly the driver in the deal, as the *New York Times* reported the "license guarantees Marvel $205 million in royalty and service fee payments, of which $70 million and $35 million would be payable on the theatrical release of *Spider-Man 3* and *Spider-Man 4*, respectively."[24]

These types of guarantees and deals are clearly high stakes. In the case of Hasbro and *Star Wars*, to some degree the toy manufacturer bet the company, as in addition to paying huge guarantees, Lucasfilm was granted $200 million in warrants for Hasbro common stock, which Hasbro had the right to repurchase.[25]

In recouping guarantees in this order of magnitude, one also has to keep in perspective that the dollars available are based on the wholesale amounts. As discussed previously, just like box office and film rentals, the relevant sums here to recoup advances are based on the net wholesale revenues, which extrapolate up to staggering sums needed at retail to break even. In analyzing the risks Hasbro was taking on its Marvel licensing deal covering *Spider-Man* sequels, one analyst that ultimately believed the deal would be profitable, despite its cost, was quoted by the *Los Angeles Times* as saying: "The company needs $1 billion in Marvel-related sales over the next five years to make a profit on the license . . ."[26]

Perhaps with this much at stake, it is not surprising that studios, and in particular Disney, have tried to leverage their consumer products infrastructure to optimize merchandising sales tied to key film properties. Disney, which in the last few years has bought both Marvel and Lucasfilm for the franchise value of their key brands (e.g., *Iron Man, Star Wars*), clearly looked to merchandising upsides as part of its rationale for the deals. When acquiring Lucasfilm, the *Hollywood Reporter* referred to Disney's CFO Jay Rusulo's statements in paraphrasing: "in 2012, Lucasfilm revenue from licensing and merchandising will be around $215 million, which is roughly equal to what Marvel was doing when they acquired that brand in 2009. Since then, Marvel has seen big

467

Table 8.1 Top Licensors

Rank	Company	2011 sales (in $ million)	Brands
1	Disney Consumer Brands	37,500	Mickey Mouse, Disney Princesses, Disney Fairies, *Toy Story, Cars,* Marvel Brands (Note: Marvel, which in 2007 was #5 overall, in 2011 contributed $6 billion of Disney's $37 billion-plus.)
5	Warner Bros. Consumer Brands	6,000	DC Comics superheroes, new characters for film and TV
6	Nickelodeon and Viacom Consumer Products	5,550	*Dora, Diego, SpongeBob SquarePants, South Park, Neopets,* miscellaneous TV properties
14	DreamWorks Animation	3,000	Miscellaneous animated properties/films
15	Lucas Licensing (pre acquisition by Disney)	3,000	*Star Wars, Indiana Jones*

increases in consumer product sales and Disney expects the same to happen with *Star Wars*.[27]

With this level of sales, it is not surprising that studios, networks, and producers controlling franchise rights are among the largest sellers of licensed merchandise, along with sports leagues and other major consumer brands (e.g., clothing, electronics, autos). *License Global* magazine, which performs an annual survey of the industry, listed several media companies in its top rankings (see Table 8.1).[28]

Coming Full Circle: Toys Spawn Films Spawn Toys

In the ultimate example of coming full circle, the Hasbro toy brand *Transformers* spawned a movie, with the movie then serving as the catalyst for a diversified product licensing program. The *Los Angeles Times* noted that Hasbro, confident of boosting its *Transformers* brand, had "signed deals with 230 licensees worldwide for T-shirts, bedding, cell phones and shoes."[29] This *Transformers* campaign turned into a huge success, with the initial film garnering more than $300 million at the

U.S. box office (and more than $700 million worldwide) and increasing Hasbro's sales of *Transformers* toys fivefold from $100 million to $500 million, proving synergy between merchandising and toys.[30] The franchise has since gone on to include three sequels, with *Transformers 4* set for summer 2014, and *Transformers: Dark of the Moon* itself grossing over $1 billion at the worldwide box office in 2011.

This *Transformers* synergy was so successful that the company aggressively moved to repeat this type of success. In 2009, Hasbro and Paramount partnered on *G.I. Joe: The Rise of Cobra*, which garnered more than $300 million at the global box office and led to a sequel, *G.I. Joe: Retaliation*. With its proof of concept, Hasbro struck a multi-picture deal with Universal to develop films related to its other key brands, including *Monopoly*, *Candy Land*, and *Battleship*.[31] Despite significant media hype over this partnership, the companies parted ways at the beginning of 2012. Their biggest film project, *Battleship*, starring Liam Neeson, reputedly cost $209 million[32] to make, but grossed only $65 million from the U.S. box office, debuting in May 2012 leading off the summer season.[33] Hasbro and Universal continued to partner on *Ouija*, but on an entirely different investment scale, with the film originally in the $100 million range and then later reputedly targeted in a low budget range of $5 million for a 2013 release.[34]

The thirst for tie-ins and the perceived virtuous cycle of toys spawning films spawing toys, however, continues, as Sony quickly jumped in to work with Hasbro, partnering with Adam Sandler and his Happy Madison Productions to develop a movie based on the hit game Candy Land.[35] Accordingly, if *Candy Land* comes to fruition, Hasbro will have launched major feature films based upon its toy lines with three different studios, generating global box office well over $1 billion, and making it one of the leading independent production companies in the world.

Toys and the Internet—Growing Crossover with Avatars and Virtual Worlds

One would think, conceptually, that toys, dolls, and stuffed animals would be one category somewhat isolated from the impact of the Web. This is not the case, as toy companies and studios are finding ways to cross over categories, creating new interactive elements to established franchises and growing entirely new brands and worlds.

Mattel, which previously took Barbie from a doll to TV movies and direct-to-videos, launched www.barbiegirls.com, where kids can play with avatars and unlock "VIP" content (by paying for them, or plugging in a Barbie MP3 player bought at retail that unlocks characters when connected). Rival toy company Hasbro built a virtual world to complement its *Littlest Pet Shop*, where each pet has a code in its collar that allows users to enter the site. Not to be outdone by the toy companies, Disney experimented with a couple of Web-related toy lines, including "Clickables," based on Disney fairies, which enables kids to interact with a linked virtual world. Summarizing the trend at the 2008 annual toy conference, Toy Fair, the *Hollywood Reporter* noted: "The biggest trend industrywide at Toy Fair . . . is the increasing number of toys being sold that connect to Internet play and, with the inputting of special codes found on the toys, unlock virtual worlds."[36] And when there is new value, everyone starts to jump on the bandwagon: one of the original success stories, Webkinz, had a value in 2008 estimated by some in the $2 billion range. Their website is kid-friendly and simply states: "Webkinz pets are lovable plush pets that each come with a unique secret code. With it, you enter Webkinz World where you care for your virtual pet, answer trivia, earn KinzCash, and play the best kids games on the net!"[37]

As noted above in the context of Rovio's *Angry Birds*, apps are becoming a leading outlet for creating virtual worlds and playing with avatars. This is apparent by looking at the paid app section of Apple's iTunes store, where apps tied to leading kids brands are often among the top sellers. In fact, the *Wall Street Journal* noted how three of the top five apps in summer 2012, and in fact the top three slots at one point (including *Temple Run: Brave*, tied to the Pixar film *Brave*, and top app *Where's My Perry?* linked to a character from Disney television cartoon *Phineas and Ferb*) were from Disney. The *Wall Street Journal*, focusing on the trend of kids playing apps on smartphones, noted: "Now, with kids spending more and more time playing games on their iPhones, big companies like Walt Disney Co. . . . are increasingly using apps as a distribution channel for their own brands while hunting for hits they can exploit in their broader operations."[38]

Whether or not an avatar, used in a virtual world, on a mobile phone (e.g., tied to instant-messaging services), in a tablet app, or in social networking sites (where the lines are being blurred for kids, as in communities such as Club Penguin), is a type of virtual ragdoll is up for debate. What is clear is that toy companies and entertainment brands are striving to find ways to expand their characters and worlds into the virtual space. Moreover, once this transition is made, the entire merchandising food chain starts anew in the virtual world, with opportunities for e-commerce (pay to dress up your character or buy him or her accessories), linked games, apps, etc.

In my prior edition, I asked Howard Roffman, then president of Lucasfilm Licensing, who had overseen *Star Wars*-branded merchandise for over 20 years, what he thought about the online world's impact and whether virtual merchandise would become as big as toys. He stated:

The online world is definitely beginning to impact the world of merchandise licensing, and that impact is rapidly evolving; we are just seeing the beginning today. Online retailers can offer higher-end collectibles that would be challenging to sell through traditional retail, such as the very large and expensive building sets that are offered exclusively through Lego's online "Shop at Home" outlet. Online also offers opportunities for customization and targeting discrete market segments that would not be practical through brick-and-mortar outlets. While it is hard to imagine purely "virtual" goods such as avatars and ringtones becoming as large a market as traditional toys and many other popular mass-market categories, the day is clearly coming when content-driven items such as video games and DVDs will be consumed primarily via the Internet, all but eclipsing traditional retail.

471

Extending the Franchise: Video Games, Books, etc.

Video games and books are somewhat unique within the merchandising realm, because as opposed to toys or T-shirts, video games and books are derivative properties that often branch a story in a different direction. While still grounded in a movie, or the core iconography or characters of a franchise, games and books allow the creative freedom to explore different tangents and backstories, extending the core franchise (see also prior transmedia discussion). Of course, certain games and books are merely direct translations of a property into another medium, such as a novelization of a film, but the bigger a franchise and the deeper the fan base, the more options the rights holder has for creating new intellectual property grounded in, but not directly parroting, the underlying franchise (see also companion website for discussion of console games).

To an extent paralleling the move of toy companies to control more of their destinies—create channels and content to control more of the pie, rather than simply licensing their properties—book publishers have even set up their own film and TV divisions. Motivated by diverse factors, including watching the erosion of their traditional business, fearing pending additional disruption via e-book companies such as Amazon launching their own publishing arms, and seeing the lion's share of profits from film adaptations of book series go to the studios, publishers such as Random House and Macmillan have launched in-house film and TV arms.[39] Although there is logic in retaining more control, that control comes with a cost and associated high risk—it remains to be seen whether these traditional publishers will have the stomach or cash reserves for the roller-coaster process of financing films, and it is more likely that the experiments will first play out in TV, where there is lower risk and a natural fit for serialized stories. Given the overall challenges of the publishing business and the demise of major bookstore chains and specialists alike, the cycle of "ancillary markets" overtly feuling films that then fuel more ancillaries is unlikely to be commonplace and therefore disruptive to the traditional ancillary cycle. Publishers have done quite well historically with the symbiotic relationships of launching properties (from books) and creating properties (novelizations) tied to Hollywood, and the associated risks and costs in the name of hypothetically increasing profits is probably too big a bet outside the companies' core expertise. Moreover, there is an unspoken snobbery in the book world, where the written word, so engrained for millennia in culture, is perceived either as a higher art form or a more learned form of intellectual property; accordingly, licensing rights to a hit novel is seen as opportunistic capitalism, while consciously targeting film has a whiff of debasement to the purists—meaning development of films within venerable publishing houses is apt to face cultural hurdles.

472

Growth of Social Games and Importance of Data Analytics

Zynga, which went public with a market capitalization more than $7 billion in 2011 (before its stock fell severely back down to earth in 2012), in many ways defined the social games space. Moving beyond its success with traditional games (e.g., poker) and themes (e.g., *Mafia Wars*), Zynga created original properties such as *Farmville, CityVille,* and *Empires & Allies,* leveraging a model utilizing database/customer mining, a freemium economic model, viral growth (as an almost positive parasite feeding off of social network traffic and interactions), and virtual goods. The power of the model not surprisingly spawned other social games companies, with Playdom gobbled up by Disney, Electronic Arts acquiring Playfish (which went on to launch the hugely successful *The Sims Social*, extending *The Sims* brand into this realm), and core-gamer focused independents (Kabam) raising venture capital in amounts exceeding what many IPOs generate. I do not plan to present a case study of or otherwise analyze Zynga or other social game companies; what I do want to highlight are some of the underlying metrics that make it and other social games companies tick.

The Zynga model, grounded in data analytics, has the potential to upend traditional metrics because these companies have tapped into the Holy Grail of customer engagement: networks and Hollywood do not know who their end customer is and rely on statistical samples such as from Nielsen to approximate consumer adoption and engagement, while social games develop a direct personal relationship with their consumers. Social games companies know who you are, can market new games directly to their user base, and can segment their marketing and offerings to users' specific behavioural patterns. A good example is the release of *Empires & Allies*: because of Zynga's customer database, it was able to report an astonishing 21 million-plus MAUs 20 days after launch in June 2011 (see below for a discussion of MAUs and metrics).[40] What would Warner Bros. have paid with a film series such as *Harry Potter* to be able to directly market and engage with potential viewers based upon whether it knew that you had seen the first movie, the prior two, all priors in the series, had bought X items of merchandise . . .? Think about the discussion in Chapter 9 regarding trailering, which is trying to match demographics to target awareness, in an attempt to break down the barriers inherent in experience goods—how valuable would it be for a studio launching a new film in genre X, starring actor Y, to be able to directly market to the specific individuals who had watched/rented/bought a similar film that the studio is using to identify its target market? This is the power of Google and ad targeting brought to bear on the experience good quandary at the microscopic level of the individual.

Social Games Metrics

The metrics behind social game monetization are relatively straight-forward. In simple terms, social games focus on segmenting populations, much like traditional loyalty rewards programs, to create a funnel optimizing revenues (see Figure 8.3). Imagine a tornado, and at the top where the cylinder is the widest is the total population of users who have ever tried a game. How to measure this total population is a function

473

of how a service or site captures registered users. For traditional games, this tends to be counting client downloads of associated software; for social games, the measuring stick is similar, but because they are browser or app-based, it is usually expressed in application installations. From this base, the key metric is then defining from whom this population of "registered users" can then be defined as active users. There is no precise definition of active users; however, because companies (and the industry, in terms of leaderboards) track users on a daily and monthly basis, an active user is usually quantified as an individual that has taken some action to be meaningfully engaged with the game (product) within a one-month period (hence the often-quoted category of monthly active users, or its acronym "MAUs"). What that user has to do within a 30-day period to be labelled "active" is somewhat murky; ideally, he or she should have logged into the game and spent some de minimis time playing. By defining active users, a company automatically also defines inactive users, and in theory the registered users can be segmented into MAUs, those who are active but not on a monthly basis (have not lost them entirely), and truly inactive users (remember, the inactive can still be an important basket to track, as companies have a 1:1 relationship with them, and it may be that they do not like one game, but are participants in another).

474

Daily active users ("DAUs") are then a subset of the MAU base, with the calculation not exact (based on averages), but still precise in that it is simply a tracking/database management issue to identify those participants who are engaging daily. Akin to theatrical box office, these top-line numbers of MAUs and DAUs are publically reported by the bigger companies, and available on sites such as www.appdata.com. These numbers are then used to create leaderboards, and report relative positions on a daily and weekly basis, enabling rankings on both a per-game and per-developer (publisher) basis. Although tracking very different elements, the net result looks a lot like box office rankings, comparing films (what is up/down) and studios; rather than weekend box office, the reports are simply aggregating weekly performance. I have not looked into data in terms of what days are most important, but one can surmise that it is the inverse of box office; whereas box office is dominated by the weekend when people have free time to attend movies, social games are (to the disdain of employers) are often played at work with quick check-ins, and generate heavy weekday traffic.

All of the above is interesting, but falls short of the key metric, which is: Who is paying? Social games employ a freemium model, meaning participation is free, but once hooked in order to accelerate performance, move on, or enjoy the key features, it may be necessary to purchase something (e.g., a weapon, a character, a building); the trade-off is often time, but can also be a substitution for playing with a multitude of friends (as the games incentivize social behavior, to gain a level or complete some equivalent task to move on you may need to have three people join you; if you do not, then the equivalent of paying for a virtual friend to join you will suffice). Accordingly, the most critical metric is average revenue per user (ARPU). Again, how ARPU is calculated may vary. It can be calculated as total monthly revenue divided by the total number of monthly active users; for social games, the calculation, though, is often tied to DAUs (daily revenue divided by DAUs).

From this segmentation, companies then can delve deeper and look at the lifetime value of a user (LTV) and the average revenue per paying user (ARPPU). Lifetime value is simply an extrapolation of how long a user is expected to engage at a certain frequency and monetization rate, and can be calculated in accounting terms much like traditional forecasting. ARPPU is critical as it is capturing the amount of money generated per user from those users that actually pay (real dollars) during a defined period (can again, in theory, be tied either to daily or monthly use, but is almost always viewed as a monthly calculation, as focusing on people that pay everyday is slicing the pie to thin). Once again turning to our tornado, the paying user is the point at the bottom of the funnel. It is this bottom point that is the most important number, and that developers then segment into finer slices, trying to identify the most valuable of the valuable (again, think of traditional customer loyalty programs). The term of art that has developed for the most valuable of these paying customers is "whales"—whales are individuals that can spend thousands of dollars per month paying for virtual items. Different companies then attach varying thresholds, but, for example, whales may represent a small (but critical) fraction of paying users, often in a 10 percent or less range (e.g., could be 2–3 percent). The other 90 percent can then be segmented as well; if half of the paying users pay $2 or less per month ("minnows"), then the other 40 percent (given that 10 percent are whales) are in the mid range. This categorization can then be translated into ARPPU thresholds, such as whales may be those with a value of more than $X (e.g., $50 per month), etc.

475

How to manage the analytics then becomes as important as the measuring sticks themselves, as all numbers and averages can become misleading. A decline in ARPU, for example, may not be a bad thing if it is correlated with a significant increase in total active users (namely, less on average from an expanded base may generate more revenue).

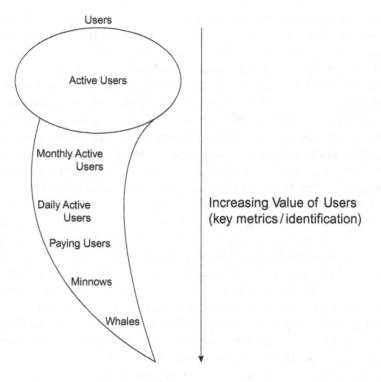

Figure 8.3

In the end, more users and more payers is everyone's endgame at a macro level, with a focus then on monetizing the most valuable users (the whales). Because the business mode, though, is heavily dependent on mining the whales, it will be interesting to see if this remains sustainable, which in turn depends on the strength of product offerings. The natural comparison is gambling, but the "addiction" motivating players there is true money, while the payoff in social games remains virtual and status (leaderboard) oriented. Logic would argue that a business built on maintaining cash flow from a couple of percent of users is subject to upheaval, and the success to date of the leaders has been because of early entry and building remarkably large funnels.

On top of these numbers, companies then layer on traditional market segmentation such as age and gender, and can run reports that will show X percent of revenue comes from women between 25 and 40 who are DAUs. These trends can then be correlated with specific actions taken (types of virtual goods bought, areas visited). It is not difficult to see the possible permutations, and the value in managing the database both for monetization and for marketing. It is also an advertiser's dream to have this level of data on customers interested in their brand (see below regarding implications for other media).

Films as Social Games

Not surprisingly, with the explosive growth of the social games market, creating a social game based on a film is a new ancillary exploitation. While these have been limited to date, this is a growing trend, as evidenced by social game-maker Kabam's licensing deal with Warner Bros. to produce games tied to the new *The Hobbit* films. Venture Beat noted: "Kabam will make two multiplayer strategy games that will be free to play, where users play for free and pay real money for virtual goods. *The Hobbit: Kingdoms of Middle-Earth* will debut on mobile devices. *The Hobbit: Armies of the Third Age* will debut on Web browsers."[41]

Sony, leveraging its animation and interactive units, sees similar synergies, and in fall 2012 announced the launch of a Facebook game *The Hotel Transylvania Social Game* (www.facebook.com/hoteltgame) tied to its animated theatrical film *Hotel Transylvania*.[42] For the films, these efforts provide, at minimum, a marketing boost and viral reach through social media—in the best case scenario, the studios gain marketing breadth, guaranteed licensing revenue (if a brand license, such as in the case of *The Hobbit*), and an upside linked to the success of virtual goods sales.

477

I asked Chris Carvalho, chief operating officer of Kabam and former head of business development at Lucasfilm, whether he saw projects such as *The Hobbit* as exceptions, or going forward we would see movies, and especially franchise-type movies, launch social games with the type of regularity that films tie into traditional console games. He noted:

Absolutely, the market for social games based on licensed film properties will expand. The traditional console world is really struggling—people, and especially families with kids, are no longer as willing to spend $50-plus for a game, especially when there are now such engaging free alternatives. The free-to-play model proven by social games first on Facebook and now on smartphones and tablets is disrupting traditional gaming. At the end of 2012, Kabam had several games that grossed over $1 million per month, including two games where we licensed rights from Hollywood studios. We're already working with Warner Bros. on our *The Hobbit* games, with Paramount on *The Godfather: Five Families*, and with NBC Universal for *The Fast and the Furious*. All these companies entrust their jewels with us because we have consistently delivered extremely high-quality experiences that engage fans with new story arcs, create a touch point to reach new fans, and deliver material financial returns to the studios. And unlike console titles, these games can be developed in 9–12 months—in order to release day-and-date with theatrical releases—and are updated every two weeks like a TV series. Not only do these games make money, but they help extend the franchise and build a community that can create an annuity, rather than just a one-time spike around a release. Our original franchise, *Kingdoms of Camelot*, has been played by over 25 million people, and is now the seventh-largest strategy game of all time in the history of gaming. It is still going strong three and a half years after release. People vested with finding licensing opportunities will, at one simple level, follow the money, the engagement, and the ease of taking games to market, and that means more free-to-play-based social games.

The companion website includes a short discussion of film-based games in the context of the historical games market; further, to set the context, this section addresses basic video game economics (again historical only, focused on the console market), including game development costs, platform history/dynamics (i.e., history of consoles), revenue splits, and pricing.

Additional Ancillary Revenue Streams: Books, Film Clips, Music, Live Stage, etc.

It is beyond the scope of this book to delve into the niche economics of each of these categories. What I want to point out is that depending on the property, any one of a number of categories could be fundamental either to the initial planning for a property, or the ultimate revenues downstream. There are countless films where music is an inherent element (e.g., *8 Mile*, starring Eminem, *Mama Mia*, *Les Misérables*), and expectations of music-related sales can be as important an element in the overall forecasting as the video expectations. In contrast, a musical is a classic ancillary capable of out-earning a related film, but would rarely (if ever) be conceived of at the time of a movie. Mel Brooks'

Broadway musical *The Producers* (originally starring Matthew Broderick and Nathan Lane) almost assuredly earned a multiple of the return on the original film (starring Gene Wilder and Zero Mostel), yet it is highly unlikely these potential monies were factored into the calculus of whether the movie, made decades earlier, was to be made in the first place.

Surely, there was similarly no thought as to *Spamalot*, the 2005 Tony award-winner for best Broadway musical, when *Monty Python* released *Life of Brian* in 1979. The endurance of the *Monty Python* franchise almost reads as a testament to the power of ancillary rights, as well as evidence of the Internet as the next great sandbox. The *International Herald Tribune* elaborated: "For decades, Eric Idle has made sure that the *Monty Python* name continued to grace books, DVDs, concert tours, a Broadway show, even ringtones and video games. And now, he is helping bring *Monty Python* to the Internet. www.pythonline.com, a social network and digital playground, offers clips of old material so that people can make mash-ups, perhaps inserting their own pet in the killer rabbit scene from Monty Python and the Holy Grail."[43]

Ancillaries regarding books are much more common than musicals. Most major films have "novelizations" of the movie that bring in material revenues, and are planned to hit shelves within the marketing window of the related theatrical release. Of course, a movie based on a book or series of books (e.g., *The Lord of the Rings/The Hobbit, Harry Potter, Pride and Prejudice, The Hunger Games*) has a built-in audience, and if successful will cause an uplift in existing book sales. If a franchise is big enough, it may spawn spin-off books (as distinct from novelizations of a particular film) that are an extension of the film's universe or characters, exploring different tangents or time periods (such as the young adult series of *Young James Bond* novels). *Star Wars* is, again, a prime example, with countless *New York Times* best-selling books branded with *Star Wars* and grounded in the films' iconography, but not directly related to a particular movie. In all cases, the producer or copyright owner may secure an advance for a license to the book based on its brand, and then earn negotiated royalties after the publisher has recouped any initial advance/minimum guarantee.

When speaking of ancillary revenues, the line becomes blurred between what may be referred to as an "ancillary" revenue stream and what is classic merchandising. The previous discussion regarding books is generally considered a merchandising exploitation, as are video game sales, whereas live stage productions and licensing of film clips tend to fall into the ancillary basket. This simply punctuates the importance of clearly defining rights and distribution channels, because deals for books, video games, and live stage rights have little in common other than the root ability to license the exploitation right to each category based on the underlying intellectual property rights in the originating film or TV production. Managed carefully, each of these rights can yield in the millions of dollars and are anything but "ancillary" to the entities tailoring the exploitation of these rights within their discrete markets.

And, if there is a distribution/revenue opportunity and it has not been exploited (e.g., a *Batman* musical?), you can be assured that it has been discussed, analyzed, and someone has made an offer for the rights. The danger with ancillary exploitation is that it crosses over into brand management, and it can sometimes be just as important to a franchise what opportunities it turns down as what to license/exploit. For every *Disney on Ice*, there is a disaster on ice looming.

Hotel and Motel

The hotel and motel window is just as it sounds: this is the service you see when in a hotel room, and typically have a choice of several first-run movies that can be ordered (with payment simply added to your hotel bill). All studios offer their first-run movies to the various providers, and the window is typically triggered by notifying the provider of a film's availability. This notification will usually be several weeks prior to availability, as the services need to program available "slots."

As an interesting and not unexpected anecdote, this is a distribution window where "adult entertainment" paces the field. Although statistics are not readily available, the buy rate for adult programming is a significant multiple of the average buy rate for a top Hollywood title (e.g., more than five times). Hotels wised up several years back, changing the billing to simply "film" or "movie" regardless of the program purchased, easing corporate expense accounts (and significant others) of the burden of questioning the details of the charge on the $300 per night hotel bill.

Size of Market and Window

This is a market (US) of a few million hotel rooms that are serviced by various providers, although given the relatively small scale a few providers have historically dominated the market (e.g., LodgeNet, which a few years ago purchased rival On-Command).[44]

As with other distribution windows, the hotel/motel window is jockeying for its exclusive bite of the entertainment pie. Traditionally, this window has been slotted between the theatrical release and the video release. Regarding theatrical, the concern is to capitalize on the exposure in theaters and the awareness generated by the theatrical marketing campaign, while not taking any business away from the theaters. Accordingly, the window generally started in the range of 8–12 weeks from the theatrical release. Very few movies today remain in theaters for this long, however, and to the extent the films are playing out that far, the locations and screen counts have diminished to a marginal number. The issue, then, is: What is "marginal," and would the availability of the film in a hotel detract from potential box office? Most theatrical executives would argue no, and the window from theatrical has been growing shorter over time.

A key factor influencing the timing is also seasonality, as hotels have peaks around holiday times, especially in the summer. Accordingly, July and especially August tend to be peak months. While the rhythm of the market used to be monthly, even the hotel/motel market is impacted by changing technology and the switch to digital media. With the ability to deliver and program digitally (versus physical tapes), hotels can now switch out programs with ease. This means that hotels are able to rotate in new programming more frequently, and in the last few years it has become possible for movies to have variable start dates (as opposed to the historical pattern of first of the month rotation tied to physical elements). Additionally, as availability dates can now be programmed flexibly, it is fair to hypothesize that a form of pay-per-view (PPV) will fully cannibalize the hotel window, and this revenue cycle will be absorbed and consolidated into a VOD/pay-per-view revenue pattern.

Finally, the length of the window is variable, but in some cases can run several months. Intuitively, this is longer than one would expect, because it cuts into the video window. To permit a longer window, it is therefore fair to posit that the distributor: (1) will assume the impact on video will be nominal (reasonable if viewed as an impulse buy, and non-substitutional if assuming you would not rent a video out of town, though a weakened argument as all access moves to VOD-based); and/or (2) has a compelling economic justification, such as receiving an advance guarantee (which, if high enough, needs time to be earned out). It will be interesting to watch whether this flexibility remains as video windows transition to on-demand viewing, and whether hotel/motel remains separate or becomes consolidated into VOD generally; because there is little incentive to upgrade systems and hotels earn margin on higher pricing from captive audiences (see below), any transition may apt to be slower than the pace of what technology enables.

481

Economics

Hotel/motel revenues are obviously dependent on guests paying to view a movie, and the frequency of ordering a program in the hotel is labeled the "buy rate."

In terms of pricing for buys, the average consumer price is at a slight premium to a theatrical ticket price and can be even higher for a hot new title (e.g., $11.95). Pricing in this window, unlike theatrical pricing, has a fair measure of elasticity; the cost may be less for an average title or discounted when a title plays later in the availability cycle. In summary, the overall pricing range is on the high side both because the audience is relatively captive (stuck in a hotel room) and because the availability generally is early; namely, in advance of any other in-home/in-room availability such as on DVD. The resulting revenues are then split between the distributor and the service provider in a negotiated formula (e.g., sliding scale), which no doubt takes into account anticipated buy rates, the speculative nature of buys, and the limited peak window.

The total amount of money generated in this window is small when compared to the major revenue streams of theatrical, video, and television; hence, this is a classic "ancillary" revenue source. The order of magnitude for gross revenues (buy rate multiplied by amount charged) on a major title should, in theory, be capped in the few million dollars range, given the relatively limited points of access.

Let us assume that one room is available for 90 days (e.g., six months, with an occupancy or turnover frequency of every other day), which means five buys equates to 5.5 percent. Compared to redemption rates, which tend, as a general rule, to be in the low single digits for most coupon-type offers, this buy rate appears high, and this in turn supports the argument of a capped range on the revenue stream. Continuing a simple example, a five percent buy rate against 2 million rooms with an average price per transaction of $10 would yield $1 million of gross revenues (100,000 transactions × $10). And remember, this is gross revenue; net revenue to the distributor will be based on a split, which may be low if a guarantee is applied. If, for example, a film has grossed $3 million (triple the previous example) and the weighted average take from the distributor was 40 percent, then the net revenues would be $1.2 million. This is a fair example in terms of how the revenue stream should be viewed: if a successful film can earn a million dollars or more, and a lesser title a few hundred thousand, that is enough revenue to be worth the effort, yet not enough to be a driver of windows or a major source. Hence, we circle back again to the classic ancillary stream.

482

International

The international market is not as mature as the U.S. market. The issue here really is scale, for with the U.S. market being marginal in scale versus other revenue streams, the issue of resources versus return becomes a material concern internationally. The international market is fragmented, and turning a profit within a particular territory with a smaller population (and modern hotel infrastructure generally less sophisticated than the U.S.) becomes a challenge. While the international theatrical, television, and video markets have become major revenue streams, and in some cases surpassed the U.S. market, the same cannot be said of hotel/motel windows. In fact, this revenue stream/window is insignificant (and often nonexistent) for most theatrical fare. As for the future, I would argue that rather than seeing a maturation, it is likely that PPV and VOD opportunities are more likely to flourish and supplant what would have otherwise been a hotel window.

PPV (Cable) and Transactional VOD Roots

With the advent of digital downloads and streaming services online and via apps, the notion of "What is VOD?" is blurring. The changes enabled by download devices/stores (iTunes), together with VOD streaming services (e.g., Amazon Video-on-Demand, Lovefilm in the UK, and Netflix, now frequently labelled as iVOD) are discussed in Chapters 5–7, while this chapter outlines the roots of PPV; there is also premium VOD, offering VOD access to theatrical films close to the theatrical release, as discussed in Chapter 1, and associated evolution of the timing of its distinct window. In my first edition, I included transactional VOD within this chapter on ancillary revenues; however, with the realization of the virtual video store, and competing cable VOD services and iVOD streaming services gaining momentum as the new face of video rental (and depending on one's classifications, pay TV), I debated whether to move the discussion of transactional VOD out of the "ancillary basket." Given the shifting landscape, it is difficult to pigeonhole any VOD discussion, for VOD today cuts across video, TV, online, etc. Although I could accordingly argue that all VOD should be discussed in other chapters, because there still (for the moment) remains a separate VOD window, and because there are still applications of pure PPV, I have elected to include the discussion here within the context of its historical window placement.

PPV and VOD Roots

While PPV has been around for years, until recently being enabled by digital cable set-top boxes, it never matured beyond a relatively small ancillary market. Whether this was due to clunky technology, limited offerings, or simply a market that was not ready for the model, it was clear that the new pay-for-sampling-or-viewing world is changing the historical pattern of consumption.

In the early phases of growth, the limited ability of servers to hold and download programming (both the number of programs and the speed of delivery) created hybrids that were clearly intermediate technologies. What grew up were variations of PPV such as near video-on-demand (NVOD), which were euphemisms for technical delivery. Historically, PPV was an event platform, perhaps most notably associated with sports such as boxing (and fights and out-of-market sports league packages are still a driver of classic PPV). If you want to watch the fight, pay $X and you will have access—no other way to see it. It then evolved into also showing movies that cycled: every time the movie started again you could tap in and watch/buy it. The more servers, the more times a movie could cycle through, which allowed the chance to opt in more frequently.

This gradation of when a viewer could access programming, which was inherently a technical limitation, defined the window or right. If a viewer could gain access only periodically (e.g., live-event basis), then it was PPV. If a viewer could gain access frequently (e.g., every five minutes), but not immediately, then it was defined as NVOD (imagine a back room of 100 VCRs all playing a tape of the same film so that the movie could start anew every few minutes). Anything accessed with nominal waiting time came to be classified as VOD, which clearly, over time, would come to simply mean instant access.

Residential VOD: The Virtual Video Store

Residential VOD had long been hyped as the ultimate consumer service: the technology promised the potential of a virtual video store environment unburdened by inventory costs, stocked with a catalog of limitless titles that were always on the shelf (wide and long tail), and accessible with the click of your remote. This ease of access to non-scheduled programming was a clear threat to the traditional broadcast television landscape, and added another challenge to a model that was already struggling to address consumers skipping the advertising that funded their production—as discussed in Chapter 5, not only is VOD a threat

484

to TV, but residential VOD is in the process of fully cannibalizing the video rental market.

Domestic

In broad concept, there is little material difference between PPV and VOD (here, only talking about à la carte transactional VOD, and not subscription-based). In both cases, a consumer is able to pay to watch a program through his or her television at home. A flat fee is charged, and the program is available for viewing for a limited time. Historically, the movie, once ordered, would run like a live TV broadcast; however, with the advent of TiVo, and similar digital virtual VCR devices, the programming can be accessed and played over an allotted period such as 24 hours from purchase.

As previously described, the principal difference between PPV and true VOD is that PPV services have specific start times. In contrast, VOD allows the customer to select a film and start it whenever they want. These video store via television remote control services enable the ultimate couch potato: not only are you watching on the sofa, but you have not even risen to visit the video store.

Historically, back-end technology limited the selection of content accessible, making the range of movies available via PPV/VOD a fraction of the inventory a customer could find at his or her local video rental store. With technology improvements, such limitations have essentially disappeared, and today PPV and VOD services fulfill the digital consumption mantra of consumers being able to access what they want, when they want. With VOD having subsumed PPV, the only remaining delineating factor is the window. The window limits access overall, defined by when content is made available to the VOD service.

Providers

Like the hotel market, this similarly limited revenue stream has been dominated in the United States by a few players (e.g., InDemand, owned by a consortium of the leading cable providers, including Time Warner, Cox, and Comcast). (Note: The direct-to-home-satellite market, which is dominated by Direct TV, largely parallels the cable VOD market, and accordingly macro-numbers should capture both platforms.) Around 2005–2006, this market started to take off, as digital cable boxes enabled simple access to content. Gross revenues continue to increase, justifying aggressive marketing via cable systems such as Comcast's branding of its Xfinity service. The new level of marketing was a clear signal that the market, which had been relatively flat for years, was entering a phase of potentially explosive growth—by 2009, InDemand reported it delivered

485

200 million paid transactions, and by 2012 it had increased its content offering to what it described as 70,000 hours yearly.[45]

Window

The window for residential PPV/VOD has historically been post video release, in part because in-home viewing of a film in a manner characterized as via a virtual video store is threatening to video sales. Because the PPV/VOD providers want to capitalize on awareness, which has waned significantly since the theatrical release and then received a jolt of life from the video marketing campaign, they naturally want the window to be as early as possible. If they had their druthers, the window would replace the hotel/motel window. Protecting the more lucrative video window has been the key priority, so the next best time is as close to the video release date as possible.

The window used to be several months after video, but as video has matured from a rental to sell-through business, and as the preponderance of DVD sales have become front-loaded, the residential PPV/VOD window kept accelerating. Originally slotted a distant six months, improved cable system offerings pushed the window to three months and then only one month post video. By 2012, studios viewing transactional pay VOD as providing higher margins than the other predominant rental options (e.g., Netflix, Redbox; see the discussion of Redbox pricing in Chapter 5) took the final step, and Warner Home Video offered its new release titles via transactional VOD day-and-date with physical discs;[46] moreover, cable VOD now markets its offerings as being in advance of rental services such as Netflix and Redbox. There were experiments with day-and-date VOD/DVD several years ago—when Disney tested the concept via its MovieBeam service (before it divested the company), and fully collapsed the window and also experimented with different pricing for new versus library films (see also Chapter 1)—but it was not until the recent maturation of VOD, in combination with seismic shifts in the DVD market, that the economics justified a permanent and broad movement of the window. (Note: A premium VOD window has been set before DVD and closer to theatrical release, stirring boycotts from theaters that are wary of any further encroachment on their window, as discussed in Chapter 1.)

Again, lurking behind this window is a fear factor that VOD will fully cannibalize DVD sales. This fear seems to be going away, with studios working harder to harmonize these streams (leveraging one off the other) than they are to fight off cannibalization. (Note: Although there is an incentive to preserve higher-margin DVD sales versus generally lower-margin VOD rentals (see Chapter 5), so long as physical disc sales

486

are material, this tension and balancing is likely to continue.) To some degree, what synergies are best realized may turn on which division the rights are coupled with: some studios place VOD under the video group, while others bundle these rights with the TV group, and more specifically pay TV. The pay TV grouping occurs because on the flip side of the window is pay television, coming several months following VOD. As the pay TV window tries to similarly accelerate to come closer to the video window, VOD has to fight to keep its positioning: close enough to video to capitalize on the marketing spend and corresponding awareness, and short enough with enough space to allow the larger pay TV provider to appear as fresh and early as possible. Because the consumer is only vaguely aware of all this timing, the segmentation works and the revenues are maximized. This is another illustration of the interplay of Ulin's Rule factors.

Finally, coming back to the traditional/historical window, it is worth noting that because of this squeezed timing, the advertising of PPV/VOD availability to customers is in close proximity to the actual availability date. While improved marketing efforts (such as by the key cable operators) and the maturing market are changing awareness levels, historically relatively few people are aware that a title will be coming to VOD, as opposed to awareness of video availability. This historical lack of marketing (which is changing the more that VOD becomes the face of video rental), combined with VOD lending itself to a browsing pattern, means that VOD purchases tend to be impulse buys.

I have not seen specific market research on this issue, but I would speculate that most consumers traditionally ranked VOD as a default choice, scanning VOD availability when they were dissatisfied with the other choices on TV. Perhaps the VOD/PPV operators should be paying Bruce Springsteen for his lyrics "57 channels and nothing's on," for it is the dissatisfied channel surfer already tuned to his or her TV who is most likely to divert to the VOD tangent and be swayed to plunk down a few dollars for instant gratification (if not literal salvation from the negative experience of not finding something on TV that excites him or her). As the market matures, and as VOD becomes more of the norm, then it is fair to expect the consumer pattern to shift and VOD to become the first menu scanned—a change thar is already happening, with "what's new" hosted programming appearing as users move to browse VOD offers (produced by MSOs such as Comcast) already supplanting the static "upcoming titles" signs at video rental stores. Arguably, this will be the tipping point for window changes, but as described in Chapter 7, the competition from OTT services requires sea changes in strategy, not minor window tinkering.

As the consumption pattern shift was accelerating, I asked Jamie McCabe, Fox's executive vice president, worldwide VOD, PPV, EST, how he saw the market's maturation, and he advised:

The fastest-growing segment of VOD is that of the OTT services of all business model: SVOD, free on-demand, and transactional rental and sale. Once dismissed as an inferior video pipeline that would be reserved for short-form content, now Internet video services have grown exponentially as consumers continue to connect not only their big screens, but increasingly engage in smaller-screen personalized viewing.

The breadth of content offerings, sophisticated search engines, visually compelling merchandising, and the seamless integration with multiple devices have fostered a trend toward OTT long-form video growth. The efficiencies, scale, and global device relationships have allowed these services to broaden their availability outside the U.S., in some cases ahead of entrenched video incumbents. MVPD providers are responding to this trend by introducing their own multi-screen offerings, extending their reach well beyond the set-top box.

In my prior edition, when VOD was on the rise but the over-the-top market was still in its infancy, Jamie had presciently noted about the inherent pull of VOD generally: "Once given the benefits of choice, control, and instantaneity, users are very satisfied and the VOD habit is formed." Today, I would argue VOD is the new habit and the landscape change is no longer about the rise of VOD, but rather the access points, as over-the-top and Internet-enabled devices have changed the matrix from "get everything you want now" to also "get it at home or on the go" (see Chapter 7). I recognize that I have digressed a bit from the promise of only describing VOD roots, but given the degree of convergence, it would be misrepresentative to only describe PPV as if VOD and OTT access were in no measure related.

Economics

The PPV and VOD markets tend to work on straight buys, which makes sense given the general impulse purchase. This construct then lends itself to a revenue sharing, or sliding scale model (akin to hotel/motel), with the content provider in position for a larger share absent minimum guarantees. Without an advance, the VOD service can be viewed as

488

simply a pipe or a location for access, such as a movie theater, with a form of sharing matching relative risks taken and the unpredictability of direct consumer consumption.

In terms of macro values/revenues, this window used to be a truly ancillary stream when compared with video, TV, and theatrical revenues. In my first edition, though, I posited that the revenues would become more valuable than hotel/motel and, as an order of magnitude, a strong title properly positioned should theoretically be able to earn a multiple of the money earned from hotels. This bump versus hotel makes sense, for the universe of customers is larger, and the larger base directly corresponds to greater consumption. The tempering factor to the relative market size (base) is timing, as the further out exposure is from the video marketing campaign, the less "fresh" a title seems and the buy rates tend to diminish. In 2012, though, the evidence was finally in, and the promised upside from VOD rentals was demonstrated by the film *Bridesmaids*. *Bridesmaids* was rented 4.8 million times, and grossed more than $24 million through VOD services, making it in 2012 the then top VOD title ever; moreover, if traditional VOD (e.g., Comcast-type cable VOD services) is combined with Internet VOD (iVOD, such as available via Amazon on Demand), hotel and motel, and electronic sell-through, the title generated more than $40 million.[47] The same title crossed the $100 million threshold in DVD sales, but what was most interesting is that when looking at traditional VOD and iVOD rental transactions, the gross revenue was in the order of magnitude of 25 percent-plus of DVD revenues—it is not difficult to see that as DVD revenues continue to decline (or, at best, flatten) and VOD and iVOD continues to grow, that this market will mature from a smaller ancillary market to a major life-cycle market. In fact, as discussed, VOD is already the new rental, and it is only a matter of time before it surpasses traditional video revenues.

While it is relatively easy to posit that VOD will continue to gain in influence, a trickier question is: What form of transactional VOD will be the most common? Namely, will the cable and satellites services, such as Comcast's Xfinity, become the next Blockbuster, or will OTT services and digital technologies come to dominate? Traditional VOD services have had a head start, and are not suprisingly in the lead: by the end of 2011, the market for paid movie rentals by pay/transactional VOD services was $1.3 billion while the iVOD market was a fraction of the size, at $204 million.[48] Although the growth rate of iVOD continues to be robust, cable's stonghold in homes has so far allowed it to stay dominant. (Note: Netflix type SVOD is excluded here, as just focusing on transactional VOD.) In 2012, the NPD Group reported: "Led by Comcast in the first half of 2012, 48 percent of all paid video-on-demand (VOD) movie rentals were generated from cable VOD. With a 24 percent rental-order growth rate year-over-year, telco VOD is the fasting growing segment of the VOD market, outpacing the IVOD growth rate of 15 percent."[49]

Despite OTT VOD being the smaller piece of the transactional VOD pie, it is clearly growing quickly, and is viewed by many studio executives as the fastest-growing new segment. When (and, in fact, whether) it will surpass cable/satellite paid VOD is an interesting question, and but for the installed base of cable, coupled with deep marketing pockets, I would say iVOD leading the market is a good bet—part of a sorting out of the new equilibrium will depend on price, and part demographics, but the cable companies need to be wary of the generational shift where viewers do not need to "cord-cut" because they have had easy access for years with no cord at all (so-called "cord nevers").

Finally, as forms of VOD come to supplant video rental, then it also makes sense to see a harmonizing of the VOD charge and video rental fee—a convergence that is already happening. Also, not surprisingly, VOD pricing is less expensive than renting a movie in the hotel/motel window, arguably because: (1) it is not a captive environment like a hotel room; and (2) the PPV/VOD window is significantly later in the life cycle than the hotel/motel window. The resulting charge to the consumer for viewing the same film at home via VOD/iVOD may be less than half of what it would have cost to see the same film a few months earlier in a hotel room.

International

Unlike the hotel market, with the larger residential VOD consumer base available to be tapped, the international VOD market is growing faster and is generally exploited on most major studio product.

Similar to the United States, the maturation of this window had been held back both by waiting for available technology to execute efficiently and the overriding paranoia of negatively impacting the immensely valuable (and, until recently, stable) video market. Also, paralleling U.S. trends, with the maturation of the sell-through video market, VOD availability has been perceived as less of a threat. As a result, the standard window for VOD in most major international markets has also been creeping forward toward the video availability date, and like the U.S. is apt to become simultaneous with video and become the face of rental.

One interesting difference that may differentiate economics is that while non-Internet VOD in the United States has been dominated by cable, in many global markets where satellite delivery (rather than cable) is the norm, the set-top boxes tend to be part of/distributed by the pay TV services. Accordingly, content suppliers diversifying their deals with

490

pay TV channels to also license VOD rights will naturally look to pay TV structures. Pay TV licenses, however, are premised on minimum guarantees (tied to subscriber bases), whereas VOD deals tend to be structured as revenue shares because of the uncertain buy rates from customers. One can expect that as these markets mature, business models will shift with them; if deals start with guarantees to acquire content (mimicking pay TV structures), then over time they will adjust to reflect the value of buy rates, or change to a revenue-share basis dovetailing with the à la carte nature of impulse buys.

Complicating the picture is the fact that in some territories, broadband and phone company providers are aggressively entering the market; leveraging online delivery/access systems, these companies are trying to co-opt the VOD market by converting their subscriber base and directly competing with the pay services. Accordingly, in some markets, phone company affiliates are battling the pay services; in others, it is broadband services versus pay TV providers; and, in some markets, cable, broadband, phone, and pay services are all competing for VOD. The one common thread is that everyone seems to acknowledge that VOD, grounded in the new on-demand, more open-access-to-content psyche, is the next great frontier.   **491**

Airlines

Market

The airline market, often referred to in the trade as in-flight entertainment (IFE), has been relatively static compared to the explosive growth of video and recent activity in the VOD/PPV sector. While there have been improvements in presentation quality and diversification of delivery systems to allow personalized choice, the economics of growth are somewhat capped. There are simply so many flights and a fixed capacity of premium-priced seats that can generate additional revenue. An airline is a bit like a theater chain. There is a fixed inventory of seating, and while investment can be made to upgrade the experience while in-seat, beyond the key driver of filling capacity the elasticity for revenue increases: (1) has been limited by the ability to increase ticket prices; and (2) remains dependent on the ability to add variable charges (or bundle in charges in premium-priced tickets) for ancillary items (e.g., concessions at a theater, drinks/food or personal VCR with business/first class on airlines).

The most significant change in the market over the last decade or more has been the addition of personal screens, as well as personal video systems to complement the overhead projected main screen. While the main economy cabin on a number of airlines will still exhibit a film in a manner very similar to what was utilized 20 years ago, virtually all airlines offer a premium movie service in business and first class. These premium services include distributed, on-demand, and personalized video systems: these systems all afford passengers greater choice and, in cases, flexibility in viewing.

A distributed system offers a series of programs (e.g., eight choices) that are cycled through, repeating at fixed intervals. A true on-demand system will offer a menu of films, akin to a virtual video store, and the passengers can select from a wide variety of films to play on their individual screens; such a system may offer both additional choice, as well as flexibility, incorporating DVD player functionality (e.g., ability to pause/fast-forward). Finally, as an intermediate option some airlines literally offered a personalized player—mini-digital video players, where a stand-alone machine and a tape or DVD are brought to the seat (meaning that formats and materials are similarly diverse). This is the equivalent of the "old days" at rental stores, when you could rent the hardware and software together.

492

It should be noted that as a corollary to the expansion of "channels," more titles can be accommodated; further, this breadth allows for catalog product, making the menu of options parallel that from on-demand carriers. This is a boon to studios that are dependent on catalog churn, and as technology continues to grow the capacity for more product, the ability to license hits/classics as evergreens will expand in parallel fashion.

Finally, although picture quality on personal screens is sharper than tape projected onto a big screen, and headphones have been improved, the viewing experience on airplanes still remains inferior to other traditional viewing platforms. Moreover, as some form of entertainment has become standard on longer flights, certain carriers such as Virgin have installed systems also capable of playing games, and services such as In Motion Video offer in-terminal DVD rentals for viewing on laptops. Access to programming is therefore becoming more of an expectation than an optional item—why should consumers' expectations and options be less in the air, especially when it is an environment where travellers are accustomed to watching or listening to entertainment?

While the audience is uniquely captive and it should therefore be theoretically possible to charge disproportionate fees, there are both competitive and practical boundaries that have kept pricing to consumers relatively flat. In essence, the improvements in quality, choice, and flexibility have become necessary simply to keep pace with consumer demand and expectations, and there is little premium that trickles down to producers from these platform enhancements. The major changes will come as airlines couple on-demand systems with the ability to pay on an à la carte basis—a complicated way to say offering VOD in-seat. Virgin America, for example, introduced just that, and as more airlines follow suit, revenue will correspondingly grow.

Window

Most airlines want films before the video release, and to some degree match a hotel window: far enough from initial theatrical release that viewing does not materially cannibalize the theatrical run, and before the video release to maintain some measure of quasi-exclusivity. The window is usually short, and can be as short as a couple of months. The squeezing of this window parallels the discussion regarding the historical VOD window. As a true ancillary, the window will be dependent upon the proportion of revenue driven relative to the revenue from juxtaposed windows.

493

Economics

Even today, license fees can still be structured in what seems a bit of an archaic manner: flat fees per film per flight. While general pricing has been relatively flat for years, differential pricing has evolved where there may be a charge for the main screen plus an incremental amount per flight for the on-demand systems. Fees overall can reach a reasonable number because licenses are usually nonexclusive; accordingly, while the price per film/flight may be relatively low, there is a significant multiplier effect (multiplied by number of flights, and then multiplied by number of airlines). Nevertheless, the ultimate revenues are not likely to approach the multimillion-dollar levels of other revenue streams.

For a studio that is regularly licensing a few films per month to an airline, the relatively small per-film revenues can add up over time. Airlines are thus another classic "ancillary," for even though the revenue is small and incremental, it is still significant enough to maintain and exploit the niche. What is slowly changing, and will ultimately make the traditional pricing extinct, is broadly implementing in-seat VOD offerings. When you can select a film and pay by credit card, such as on Virgin America, then the model should naturally shift to a revenue-share scheme akin to models utilized historically in hotel/motel PPV. Even with this major shift in pricing and access, the inherent capacity barrier remains, and airlines will still only be a piece of the overall ancillary basket of revenues.

Non-Theatrical

Non-theatrical rights refer generally to the projecting of a movie on-screen to an audience in a venue other than a movie theater. The easiest frame of reference for most people is a college film night: remember the film club or society that would show movies in a hall on Saturday night using an old 16 mm projector? Although it is no longer common to project a 16 mm print, exhibiting prints at universities remains a source of revenue for non-theatrical business. Other common outlets are ships at sea, libraries, and prisons.

Window

Non-theatrical rights have historically been exploited in the period just before home video, trying to take advantage of the hiatus between theatrical and home video exploitation. This is especially true in the fall when summer movies have had their run, the films are being readied for the big fourth-quarter video push, and colleges are back in session. To some, this is the ultimate time for film clubs to show the hot movies from the past summer.

Beyond this narrow window, non-theatrical rights are often exploited ad hoc, such as when a specific institution requests a one-off screening of a picture. There are niche distributors who specialize in booking movies in this market (sometimes offering classics, which can often involve the body of work of individual directors), and work with a network/circuit of outlets such as bicycling to various universities. The tail of the window is therefore somewhat indefinite: non-theatrical exhibitions/licenses can arise 10 or 20-plus years after a release, and the availability is only limited by whether the picture continues to be in demand.

Economics

Non-theatrical exploitation does not yield much revenue relative to other exploitation outlets. Perhaps more than the money, this distribution outlet recognizes that films are an art form that are in demand, and this avenue helps ensure that films can reach the widest possible audience. In essence, this fulfills a niche satisfying additional demand,

494

almost for the sake of satisfying demand as an end, over and above pure economic concerns.

To the extent revenues are generated, the model is usually for the niche distributor to charge a distribution fee based on the revenues generated. In the university circuit, the splits are a bit like theatrical, with the caveat that there is usually a single tier rather than a sliding scale. Accordingly, a non-theatrical split is likely to be straightforward (e.g., 50/50); of course, in some cases there can be different deals cut and guarantees paid, but the market is small enough and the distribution specialized/ targeted enough that negotiations at the margins take a backseat to securing quality distribution in the channel. Outside of universities (e.g., to prisons), I admit to having no idea how revenues are truly calculated, nor do I probably want to know! (Although my assumption is that the deal is a similar simple split.) Most licensors are simply happy to know that they are exploiting this additional channel, focus on the breadth of distribution to universities (and perhaps ships at sea), and have an overall number they target based on comparable films and rentals.

Online Impact

495

- The online world is not so much changing the notion of product merchandising, but rather the range of merchandise offered and the outlets available to acquire product.
- Avatars, which are now popular surrogates for your own persona (e.g., for instant messaging, on social networking sites, in apps on tablets), and their accessories are an example of digital merchandise (e.g., users can buy digital merchandise, such as weapons or clothes, for their digital character).
- Toys come with codes to unlock Web-based virtual worlds.
- Apps are enabling a new launch platform, where popular content/games (e.g. *Angry Birds*) can spawn merchandising programs (and reach) rivalling TV/film branded content.
- Video games are frequently being created in downloadable form and networked such as via Xbox Live; moreover, social games have shown the power of data analytics in marketing, and taken monetizing virtual goods to a whole new level.
- Film and TV websites and social media pages often combine or link to e-commerce applications, with on-demand manufacturing, coupled with online access, enabling personalization of product merchandise.

- Secondary markets, such as for collectibles, have grown exponentially with online marketplaces, such as eBay.
- Successful franchises can support transmedia-like story extensions, with books, games, and apps taking characters and worlds in different directions, all grounded in the property's core themes/iconography.
- Ringtones (e.g., theme music) are just one example of translating film and video elements into digital merchandising bits.
- PPV has now given way to VOD, which, beyond becoming the new face of video rental, is now expanding access points (e.g., tablets) and altering the dynamics of multiple ancillary markets (e.g., hotel/motel, airlines); additionally, VOD itself is diversifying, with both cable VOD and OTT VOD experiencing some of the most significant growth rates of any media sector.

496

CHAPTER 9

Marketing

Marketing and distribution work hand in hand (or at least they should), **497** with the line often fuzzy. Technically, distribution involves the sales, physical manufacture (or access, if online), and delivery of goods for sale, such as a film print, DVD/Blu-ray disc, television master, or electronic copy. For each category of media that a piece of intellectual property is licensed, distribution addresses how it is consumed and monetized: what the price is, where and how the product is sold (or leased), when the title is available, how many units are being made, how inventory is managed, and what the costs of goods are. Marketing, in contrast, focuses on awareness and interest. Marketing is, to some measure, the business and art of driving a consumer to consumption by making him or her aware that the good is available and creating the impulse to watch, buy, or borrow it. In summary, as noted in Chapter 1, marketing focuses on awareness and driving consumption, whereas distribution focuses on maximizing and making that consumption profitable.

Back to Experience Goods

In Chapter 3, I discussed the problem of predicting the success of a film or TV show (i.e., experience goods), given the factors of imperfect information, cascades, and infinite variety. While it may not be possible to predict the outcome, marketing, by its nature, is an attempt to influence the outcome. Accordingly, marketing comes to the rescue of the experience good quandary and tries to put some experience into that good; the viewer, without having actually consumed the end product (which, per an experience good, is the only way to know whether you really like/want it), is helped to make up his or her own mind.

Marketing through trailers, posters, press, reviews, websites, social networking posts, seeded blogs, advertising, etc. is bombarding the consumer with inputs to influence the selection of a film, TV show, or video in an environment stacked with an infinite variety of creative product. And the most effective marketing may be that which makes you feel you have already (to a degree) experienced the film/show. If a trailer is a microcosm of the experience, and the trailer is well directed to a consumer demographic, then it may seduce that target consumer to see the film, explaining, in part, the unique frustration of having felt hood-winked if the movie did not fulfil the expectations engendered by the trailer signal.

Accordingly, beyond marketing helping to build a brand for distribution windows, it is interesting also to view these activities in the economic context of differentiating information inputs; those inputs, heavily influenced by marketing, are uniquely important in selecting a product you cannot know whether you will like until you have "consumed" it.

It is further interesting to speculate how the online world will impact these traditional patterns and the positioning of inputs. Is there a difference in utilizing Rotten Tomatoes (www.rottentomatoes.com), which accumulates all critics' picks into a single scorecard—does "fresh" (greater than 50 percent positive reviews) really mean it is a good picture, or are variations and cascades baked into the equation such that you have no better reference from the overall verdict versus an individual critic where you have sorted out an internal mechanism to map their biases onto your own? Do social networking sites, where you affiliate with friends and recommend "liked" programs, provide a better predictor and negate cascade behavior or do they exacerbate the problem? Do recommendation engines really work to defeat the inherent uncertainty in consuming an experience good, and do references to "others who bought X also bought Y" further work to defeat the risk of unwisely committing one's time? In the media and entertainment industry, the online world is making the whole concept of marketing a lot more entertaining.

Strategy (Film)

Marketing strategy is impacted by several factors, including the budget, target audience (demographics), timing, talent involved, and partners.

Budget Tied to Type and Breadth of Release: Limited Openings, Niche Marketing, and the Web's Viral Power

For a film, the marketing budget is the most significant cost item outside of making the picture. While there is no exact rule, it is common for the marketing budget (inclusive of prints and advertising) to equal a significant percentage of the cost of producing the film. A film that costs $75 million may, for example, have a domestic marketing budget of $35 million or more (see Table 9.5), inclusive of the following line items:

- media/advertising
- PR
- website
- social media site (e.g., Facebook page)
- travel.

As discussed in Chapter 4, the amount spent to open a film is disproportionately large because the theatrical launch of a film is the engine that drives all downstream revenues. Accordingly, the money spent up front marketing a film, creating awareness, develops an overnight brand that is then sustained and managed, in most instances, for more than a decade. In extreme cases, marketing costs can equal or exceed production costs. The *Wall Street Journal* noted of the March 2009 release of *Monsters vs Aliens*, which was trying to expand the market for 3D films: "DreamWorks Animation spent upwards of $175 million to market the film globally, more than the $165 million the studio used to make the movie."[1]

Word-of-Mouth Limited Openings and Niche Marketing

Not all films, of course, can sustain a marketing budget in the tens of millions of dollars, which forces distributors/studios to employ a variety of strategies for launch (see also Chapter 4 and the section on "Press and PR", page 523). One strategy is not to open a film in a wide, big bang fashion. Opening a film in a nationwide and worldwide manner is the most expensive avenue, requiring national media and costs that make the launch an event. As touched on in Chapter 4, if a picture is opened in limited release, targeting critics and key cities and hoping that reviews and word of mouth will create momentum, the costs are dramatically reduced. This is a typical pattern for art-type movies, films trying to attract critical acclaim leading to award consideration (e.g., *Zero Dark Thirty*), and movies that may appeal to an intellectual base (e.g., Woody Allen),

499

where openings in, for example, New York, Los Angeles, and a few other select locales will draw avid moviegoers and start creating buzz. The risk factor with a staged release pattern, as discussed earlier, is that the reviews or performance will not meet expectations and the film could struggle to gain a wide release (that perhaps could have been achieved if the movie opened day-and-date nationwide)—a risk that tends to be exacerbated by online and mobile sources virally spreading reactions.

Another strategy to open a film with limited marketing dollars is to focus on niche marketing. A perfect example of niche marketing is campaigns targeted at colleges. Distributors will try to tie up with local on-campus film groups, etc. to get the message out on a film that they believe will appeal to this demographic. These types of campaigns can include posters, Internet components, sponsored events with film clubs, etc.

Sometimes niche campaigns may be referred to as "underground campaigns" or "guerilla marketing," which by their very nature can be difficult to orchestrate. There is a bit of inherent hypocrisy for a studio to try to stimulate a grass-roots campaign with an expressed goal of creating a hip factor. This is because what the studio is doing is seeding a bit of money to try to create a groundswell while really saving money. (Note: This generalization is a bit unfair, as given the profile of the niche film in question and resources, there probably is little money available for marketing; nevertheless, perception matters, and studios, as the masters of perception, could be accused of an end run even if, under the circumstances, they may be orchestrating the most viable strategy.)

As a component of a lower-budget campaign, viral campaigns are becoming more popular. These are Internet-driven campaigns using websites, blogs, and teasers. The goal of these campaigns is that the film or an element within it will simply "catch on." One of the most frequently cited examples is *The Blair Witch Project*, a low-budget film that leveraged viral marketing to garner $140 million at the U.S. box office.[2] Lots of people like to point to *The Blair Witch Project* as proof of a strategy, but seldom is it mentioned that the odds of success here are no better than in other areas; namely, there are many more wannabes than *Blair Witch* successes.

Is Viral Messaging on the Web Always a Good Idea?

In the zeal to point out that the Internet's democratization of access affords a platform where anyone can have a shot, it is easy to forget that the Web is the essence of clutter. Gaining impressions and buzz amid the infinite choices online may actually be a longer shot statistically than a low-budget grass-roots campaign. The intersection of execution and luck is not magically better online. Additionally, while there are certain tricks of the trade and optimization strategies that can be employed, any viral campaign ultimately relies on sharing and peer-to-peer excitement. Moreover, in this context, "messaging" is no longer captive, and online users, unabashed in giving opinions and feedback, can be brutal. It is hard to control spin once material is unleashed into the blogosphere, and any campaign needs to be careful about opinion potentially turning negative. There is no guarantee that positive comments, downloads, and buzz will materialize, and as people continue to learn and experiment, this avenue could be a risky awareness strategy (even if compelling) when compared to a traditional media blitz.

Shift of Dollars to Online Tempered by Market Still Evolving

Despite these risks, the Web is no doubt a boon to marketers, and money spent to stimulate viral buzz is both tempting and often productive; moreover, the Web allows unique targeted marketing, and as technology and advertisers become more sophisticated, more dollars will shift online, given the inherent efficiencies of better-matching expenditures and messaging to narrowly defined consumers. As the shift in marketing dollars suggests, this is already happening. However, until Internet spending grows exponentially from its current levels, it will still be dwarfed by traditional media spends.

Further, the world of online is still evolving (with new formats available, and video advertising strategies continually being tested), and creative breakthrough ads are challenging; generally speaking, as of today, online (including social media and mobile) marketing alone still cannot create mass awareness.

Timing, Seasonality, and Influencing External and Internal Factors

Timing of a campaign is critical, and again it depends on several moving parts. Sometimes, it can be an effective strategy to say very little, allowing symbolism and mystery to create interest. One of the best examples of this was the 1989 release of the first *Batman* movie, starring Michael Keaton and Jack Nicholson. Months before the release, the *Batman* logo/symbol was simply plastered around the world: consumers could see it on posters, on buses, and on phone booths in London.

I asked Michael Uslan, who launched the *Batman* film franchise and has served as executive producer of all of the *Batman* films (including, most recently, *The Dark Knight Rises*), how he had seen marketing evolve

501

in almost 25 years between the first *Batman* and the summer 2012 *The Dark Knight Rises*, and in particular how the Internet was influencing campaigns. He noted:

When our first, revolutionary *Batman* film was released in the summer of 1989 by Warner Bros., I considered it the best-marketed film in history. In New York City, you could not walk one block without running into someone wearing a *Batman* T-shirt or hat. That iconic black-and-gold bat symbol was everywhere. Movie posters were being stolen from bus shelters and theater lobby displays. People were paying to walk into movies showing the *Batman* trailer, then leaving before whatever feature was playing came on. Pirates were selling that brief trailer at comic book conventions for $25 a pop. When the Berlin Wall came down, kids were coming through to freedom already wearing *Batman* caps. But marketing via an Internet strategy didn't exist. Today, it's completely different. You cannot successfully and fully market any comic book or similar genre movie in this day and age without a viral campaign on the Net starting 10 months to a year prior to release if your intention is to build a franchise and market a brand. *The Dark Knight* had, perhaps, the best viral campaign ever. Fans of comics, movies, science fiction and fantasy, manga and anime, animation, horror, etc. must be engaged early on and "courted," for they have the capability to make or break a movie by their support or the lack thereof. Studios now bring their filmmakers and stars to the bigger comic book conventions to pay homage to the fans they know they must ultimately win over. There are currently so many dozens of key fan sites on the Internet, with millions of people trolling them all day and late night. It is a bonded community where word spreads like lightning. The Internet is not only important to market a genre film domestically and internationally today, it is essential.

I will come back to websites, social media, and online generally later, but I want first to continue my focus on timing; the matrix of elements associated with timing can profoundly impact a marketing campaign. When it may be best to launch a film is driven by both "internal" factors related to the inherent/specific elements of the property, as well as

502

"external" events that impact consumers' consumption patterns but are otherwise unrelated to the film at hand.

Internal Factors

The most important element of timing is that external events are as influential, and arguably much more influential, than direct elements ("internal") driven by the film/property. By internal, I mean particular relevance of the property that dictates specific optimal release timing. Perhaps the best example of this is films with holiday themes. A Christmas-themed movie, such as *Christmas with the Kranks, Four Christmases, Polar Express,* or even *The Chronicles of Narnia* series, should be released during the year-end holiday period to optimize interest. Similarly, movies with beach themes (e.g., surfing-related) are clearly a more natural fit in the summer. Occasionally, there are movies with literal direct tie-ins to dates, such as *Home for the Holidays* (starring Holly Hunter), which involves family coming home over Thanksgiving; *Independence Day* (about science fiction and not about the Fourth of July), which had a clear marketing hook on July 4th; *Halloween* (and other thrillers) around Halloween, *New Year's Eve* (released in the holiday season 2011), and sports movies that revolve around the sport currently "in season" (such as *The Rookie* or *The Natural* during baseball season, or *Remember the Titans, Leatherheads,* or *Friday Night Lights* during football season). When listing just a few of these tie-in categories, there becomes a larger overlap with theme and timing than one would likely identify without reflection.

503

Because people are looking for films with "the Christmas spirit" in December, about love on Valentine's Day, about the beach during the summer, and about baseball during baseball season, it is obvious to find films with these themes releasing in these time frames. Simply, the themes of these types of films are top of mind; importantly for marketing, they also create an alternative reference (versus key word genre categories such as action, romance, thriller, drama, chick flick, etc.) that subliminally, or probably overtly, drives interest. (Note: It will be interesting to see if such themed movies continue to be as prevalent with the international marketplace becoming dominant; most sports and holiday themes tend to be local, making it challenging to market properties into an increasingly culturally diverse and dispersed global marketplace. Because the U.S. market is so large in itself, these films will not doubt continue to be made, but I would suspect there may be increasing scrutiny at budget levels as studios segment their portfolios.)

External Factors

By external events, I mean outside factors wholly unrelated to the film that have a material impact on people paying money to go to the theater. The four principal elements are: (1) events of national or international importance; (2) holidays; (3) competition; and (4) economic events.

Events of national importance, while obviously a broad category, generally means major events known about significantly in advance, such as political elections or major sporting events. Not only do these events draw attention away, making it harder to compete for viewing, but these events drive up the price of media. On the sports side, distributors take into account dates for the Olympics, the World Cup, and major sports playoffs and championships (whether Formula One events in Europe or the Super Bowl in the United States). For politics, the concerns may be more limited, but periodic major events such as presidential elections will dictate timing. Again, this is driven as much by having to compete with an external event perceived to be monopolizing (or at least drawing) target consumers' attention as with the corollary impact of the cost of media. Having to buy media time during a presidential election when key outlets are able to sell spots at a premium (and when inventory may even, in some cases, be sold out) simply drives up budgets, with no fringe benefits.

The second external category, holidays, is important not because holidays can get in the way (as in the case of an election or sporting event), but because they create free time. The entertainment business is at the heart of the leisure industry, and the more people have free time, the more likely they are to consume an entertainment product. Accordingly, the biggest release dates of the year are around U.S. Memorial Day weekend (commencement of summer break), the Fourth of July, Thanksgiving, and Christmas. Movies are a social experience, and film marketing tries to drive a truck through the gates held open by the dual forces of getting together and compulsory free time. Box office is largely driven by weekends, and in terms of marketing opportunities, key holidays are nothing short of weekends on steroids.

For kids, the summer season is the most critical release period of the year; having extended periods of free time while being out of school drives up weekday box office numbers, validating the holiday/vacation relationship (see also Chapter 4).

The third external category is competition, perhaps the most overlooked and yet, at the same time, arguably the most influential factor in terms of attracting an audience. Competition can be subdivided into a couple of categories: direct competition among films for market share, and competition among studios and rivals (which can, at times, add an emotional and even irrational component). Regarding direct competition, distributors will always be looking for the "cleanest" window. Would you want your next film to be opening against the next *Avator*, *Avengers*, or *Star Wars*? Certain event films can suck so much of the box office out of the market that it becomes questionable whether other films can perform simultaneously. Studios perform sophisticated analysis on the market size, and what portion of a demographic they want to attract, but whether the market can expand to handle certain capacity is always a tricky calculation.

Studios therefore jockey for release dates and try to put a stake in the ground early to ward off would-be competitors. Sony and Marvel, for example, in early 2009 announced it would release *Spider-Man 4* on May 6, 2011, securing the pole position in the summer box office race, a position Marvel covets and similarly secured in 2010 with the slotting (more than a year in advance) of *Iron Man 2* on May 7, 2010.[3] Continuing this trend, in October 2010, Walt Disney Pictures (following its acquisition of Marvel and obtaining distribution rights to future *Iron Man* sequels) announced its release date of May 2, 2013 for *Iron Man 3*. With summer weeks and holiday weekends at a premium, it has become commonplace to map out release date schedules years in advance (see Chapter 4 for a further discussion of release dates).

505

One of the most time-consuming and important parts of the art of theatrical distribution is trying to track the matrix of competitive titles, and both schedule and protect release dates. As a result, dates are either universally known and touted (to ward off others) or guarded with strict secrecy to keep competitors guessing. As dates get close, the cat is, of course, let out of the bag and lots of last-minute jockeying takes place. The most intense poker game is played in the summer (the busiest time of year), since a new tentpole film is releasing virtually every week.

In terms of efficiency, it would be simpler and better for all involved to work through a trade association and schedule dates, eliminating the secrecy and politics, and allocate slots in a fashion that would optimize the pie. This practice, however, is deemed collusive and violates antitrust and international competition laws. I was once involved with a case in Europe alleging collusion among studios in setting release dates, a case that was ultimately dismissed but still sent a chill through the spines of the parties involved.

I would argue that while collusion is possible, and would create more efficient economics, the fact remains that the film business is cutthroat: the desire to best a rival dwarfs the forces of collusion and ensures true and vibrant competition. And remember, this can be a business driven by irrational competition—people's jobs and star can rise and fall by rankings and even perception. There is more than an ego element to where a studio falls in terms of box office rank (e.g., top distributor of the year). With so much riding on a film's performance and its opening, paranoia comes into play. No matter what a film's marketing budget is, there is always fear that the budget of a competitor's title is higher. Add to this equation the fact that when the marketing budget and decisions are being mapped out the film may not be finished (or the people doing the planning may not have even had a chance to see it), and that no matter what the questions may be about your picture you are going purely on hearsay regarding the competition. This is not like marketing one brand of soap against another. This can be a last-minute chess game involving the blind leading the blind. Driven by emotion, imperfect information, extremely high stakes, and fierce competition, passions can run high.

Moreover, given this hyper-competitive environment, a studio may try to maximize results by counter-programming (a strategy that may draft off of increased in-theater foot traffic, target a different demographic than is drawn to a new blockbuster picture, or simply address the too much product, too few weekends challenge). An extreme instance of counter-programming is to spend with the intent of crushing a competitor's film. In the context of battling brands, it can be as much of a success to undermine a key competitor's film as to launch one yourself. Of course, no one will admit to this, but it can be gleaned in the marketplace when there are obvious rivals or niches to protect.

I will label the final key external category as economic events. While this can sound a bit amorphous, marketing at its most base level is trying to encourage people to spend money. Just like periods of holiday that create free time, there are periods that stimulate "free money." Paydays and bonus periods can become catalysts for planning product releases (and conversely, tax day, April 15, is probably a time to avoid). In certain countries, there are traditional bonus periods, and in some countries bonuses are either legally or culturally built into salary structures, such as a "13th month" of pay. This factor is much less influential in terms of planning a theatrical release, because the relative cost of a movie ticket is low. If the price of admission is not a barrier to entry on a weekend, then it is hard to argue that a release should be planned around a bonus period. This timing tends to be much more pivotal at retail (e.g., for DVD release), and is something likely tracked by the Walmarts of the world; a study of product releases to paydays (1st and 15th of the month) would probably yield a closely mapped curve. Perhaps this is overanalyzing, for the likelihood is that in most cases, this factor happens to dovetail with other elements, such as year-end bonuses overlapping holiday periods.

Day-and-Date Release

It used to be the pattern that a film would open in the United States and then be released subsequently in international territories. This had multiple advantages, including: (1) saving money on prints by being able to reuse prints and send them to a different territory when one territory wound down ("bicycling of prints," which is, of course, limited to common-language territories); (2) allowing talent to travel to staggered premieres; (3) enabling the heat from the U.S. release (e.g., box office, reviews) to spread to the rest of the world; (4) allowing the marketing department to learn from the U.S. release; and (5) simply allowing time to complete international versions (e.g., subtitles, dubs). As discussed in greater detail in other chapters (see Chapters 2 and 4), however, piracy and other pressures have led to studios now favoring day-and-date releases (especially in the context of event films, even if this means increased print costs), which simply means near-simultaneous release of the picture in all territories. Moreover, with the size of the international markets now eclipsing any domestic market (whether viewed from a perspective of the U.S., or any other country), if a release is not day-and-date, it is no longer unusual to release overseas first, as was the case with *The Avengers* and *Battleship* in 2012 (see the discussion in Chapters 1 and 4).

507

Given the ever-increasing importance of international markets results, reducing the impact of piracy has grown in importance; moreover, the combined forces of a global economy and easy Web access force distributors to assess the risk of a picture illegally showing up in a territory before its scheduled opening—and this risk is not only very real, but its impact is exacerbated as the size of the international markets' growth as a percentage of overall box office/revenue (see Figure 1.7 and Table 4.1 in Chapters 1 and 4). Day-and-date releases have accordingly come to be perceived as the best prevention against piracy; the pattern also yields the biggest worldwide box office number the quickest. In terms of economics, the calculation is whether the accelerated international release will bring in more money (than would otherwise be lost to piracy) than the incremental costs associated with simultaneous release (e.g., extra prints, overtime to rush international versions). (Note: This is an even more difficult equation in practice because inevitably a simultaneous release means that in some territories, given cultural patterns, seasonality, outside events, etc., the timing will not be optimal.) The elimination of the chance to learn from and tinker with earlier marketing strategies is an intangible that will not lead the decision, especially since global marketing is usually driven off the U.S. campaign.

Third-Party Help: Talent and Promotional Partners' Role in Creating Demand

Talent Involved

Nothing sells a property like a star, and the magnitude of the star and their willingness to promote the film can be a significant factor in the overall strategy. This is a double-edged sword, however, for talent can be unpredictable—both in terms of dedication to the project and timing—and very expensive (think entourages, first-class travel, and accommodations). Much needs to be put in motion in advance of the release, and the mechanics of production are such that most big stars are well into other projects by the time the prior film has completed post production and entered its marketing and release phase. Accordingly, while personal commitment, emotion, relationships, and ego are gossiped about, the fact is that time management can be the paramount concern. Even if a star is committed to promoting a film and willing to travel for publicity, they could be tied up with another project (worse if on location) and simply have limited availability.

The advantage to using talent/stars to promote a film is the enormous amount of free publicity that can be generated. The talk show circuit, ranging from morning shows (e.g., *The Today Show*) to afternoon talk shows (e.g., *Ellen, Oprah*), to late-night programs (e.g., *The Tonight Show*), generates significant exposure and tends to foster other appearances and press opportunities. The downside to using stars (beyond costs) is lack of control.

Unlike a trailer or advertisement, a star as a spokesperson may or may not put on the appropriate spin. Given, however, that the pre-eminent concern at this phase is awareness, the risk is usually worth taking. Stars are paid enormous sums, and that premium is largely for awareness: people want to see them, know about them, go to their films. They are a presumed built-in draw, the "sure-fire" way to entice the consumer to pay money to go see the product (though statistically, this has been proven a fallacy). Famously divorced from Nicole Kidman, engaged to Katie Holmes, and often front-page news for his promotion of Scientology, Tom Cruise had achieved as many headlines for jumping on a couch during *The Oprah Winfrey Show* and behaving erratically as anything else during the promotional window for *Mission: Impossible III*—the public perception was starting to turn from golden boy to eccentric. Shortly following *Mission: Impossible III*'s failure to meet certain expectations, Paramount ended its long-term deal with Cruise's production company, with Sumner Redstone (chairman of Paramount's parent, Viacom) publicly mentioning Cruise's personal behavior among the reasons for its decision (sending some shockwaves through the industry). At this point, many were questioning whether the star's appearance would help the picture, or whether the risk of negative publicity may hurt it.

Stripping away the artistic element, and whatever life and magic they breathe into the end product, at its most base level stars are a vehicle for instantly branding a film. An unknown product, for which hundreds of people have spent months of their lives, becomes a such-and-such film. Given this inherent branding, whether fair or not, it is economically wasteful not to use that branding in turn to create branding and awareness by association for the film. If a movie has lots of talent involved, such as a famous director, then there are simply multiple hooks to exploit.

509

Promotional Partners

Promotional partners can, on occasion, influence timing and positioning. A cereal company or fast food company may be willing to create product tie-ins, and even pay for advertising. An advertisement by a cereal company, Burger King, or McDonald's can create huge demographic-specific awareness.

It is important here to distinguish between merchandising and promotional partners. A merchandising deal (see Chapter 8) is generally a licensing arrangement where a third-party company pays a fee to the property owner for the right to create certain goods featuring elements of the property. The end product is therefore a *Batman* action figure, a *Spider-Man* costume, or a *Toy Story* backpack. In contrast, a promotional partner already has its own product, usually a very well-known branded product. What it is offering is a chance to tie-in its brand in a fun way, utilizing elements of the film brand. Accordingly, a kids' meal at a restaurant may be themed for the week using characters from the movie, or a character from the movie may appear on a box of a well-known cereal. These are instances of cross-promoting brands as opposed to creating a unique new product SKU designed solely around the elements from the film.

If a distributor is fortunate enough to have a property that lends itself to this type of tie-in (these opportunities are limited to big films), then lead time must be built in and limits on content may be imposed. The promotional partner, no matter how much it may like a film idea or property, is still self-interested: it is simply trying to attract more consumers to its product by associating itself with another property (brand) on the assumption that the tie-in will lead to a lift in sales. It is not willing to risk its own brand on a tie-in that could undermine its brand. Accordingly, violence and other content tied to age ratings is critically important. A tie-in partner such as a toy company, for example, targeting a kids demographic is likely going to be extremely concerned about content not being too violent or sexually explicit.

Assuming the content hurdle is cleared, then the next key issue is timing. Product development timelines are years out, and it is not uncommon for promotional partners to be locked in up to a couple of years in advance of a release, and for the partners to demand locked release dates. Given this time frame, promotional partners tend to align with known film brands. This creates a mutual comfort factor—both the product brand and film brand know what they are dealing with—and is also a practical necessity. At the time the partner tie-in needs to be locked, the film may not have even been started. How can a major corporation with a household brand commit to a tie-in and spending up to millions of dollars on blind faith? Only by associating with a known brand, and feeling as if there is only an upside.

One of the best-known partnerships was a deal struck between Disney and McDonald's. Both companies agreed to a 10-year exclusive arrangement. It was a brilliant move by Disney, for in one stroke they gained exposure at the largest fast food retailer in the country and also excluded competition. At the time for McDonald's, Disney was considered the only "studio brand," and as a consistent family-friendly brand, it meant a high-quality, safe association.

Whenever there is a group of sequels coming out in the same period, as now routinely happens in the summer, key brands are courted by rival studios, often leading to intense competition: there are only so many large packaged food companies, soft drink companies, fast food outlets, candy companies, etc., and everyone wants to affiliate with the market leader. Moreover, not only do they want the market leader to associate with their film, but they want that market leader to help brand the film by spending their own advertising money and creating unique in-store displays. A successful campaign spreads the message over the airwaves and at retail, creating millions of impressions and potentially exponentially increasing the media weight behind a campaign. Table 9.1 lists a

510

Table 9.1 Promotional Partners

Film	Promotional Partners	Details and/or $
Spider-Man 3	Burger King, General Mills, Kraft, Comcast, 7-Eleven, Walmart, Target, Toys "R" Us	• Approximately $100 million in media, mainly on commercials • General Mills promo involved 20 brands in 12 categories, putting the film on approximately 100 million packages • Kraft—10 product brands
The Bourne Ultimatum	Volkswagen, MasterCard, Symantec, American Airlines, banks (ABN-AMRO, HSBC, Barclays)	• $40 million value across partners; Volkswagen alone committed to approximately $25 million (Touareg2 featured in film action sequences) • Symantec's Norton Antivirus "Protect Your Identity with Norton" tie-in campaign
The Avengers	Acura, Dr. Pepper, Visa, Wyndham Hotels, Harley-Davidson, Farmer's Insurance, Hershey's Oracle, Red Barron Pizza	• Marvel/Disney secured estimated $100 million in marketing support • Red Barron spent $5 million on *Avengers*-themed packaging on 13 million pizzas and in-store marketing as multiple supermarkets/grocers

few high-profile films, illustrating how major brands can garner tens of millions of dollars worth of promotional partners, and in extreme cases upwards of $100 million in value.[4]

Animated and family-oriented movies often lend themselves to a broad swath of promotional partners. In 2012, DreamWorks Animation's *Madagascar 3: Europe's Most Wanted* had more than 10 partners ranging across food, cards, games, hardware, and apparel. Table 9.2 is a partial sampling of the types of products and categories that were involved.[5]

Table 9.2 *Madagascar 3*—Select Promotional Partners

Product Category	Brand	Tie-In Support
Snacks	General Mills	Film-themed packaging featuring snacks in the shape of the penguin characters
Fast Food	McDonald's	Custom TV commercial, in-restaurant integration, and tie-in with six circus-themed toys in global Happy Meal program
Candy	Airheads	Dedicated TV commercial and in-store displays
Party Goods and Cards	Hallmark	Various retailers and Hallmark Gold Crown stores
Credit Cards	Citibank	Private card member screenings in New York and Los Angeles
Social Games	Zynga	*Draw Something* game tie-in with four themed words players can draw; also video trailers
Toys	Toys "R" Us	Dedicated in-store boutiques
Fruit	Dole	"Go Bananas Every Day" campaign with 100 million specially branded stickers, tied to QR code mobile game; also linked to promotion in Walmart's produce department
Cosmetics and Beauty	L'Oreal	Four *Madagascar 3*-inspired kids' shampoos and conditioners
Hardware	Lowe's	In-store POS, themed clinics, and movie-themed racecar driven by Jimmie Johnson at Dover race weekend

512

Product Placements—Finance-Driven, Not Marketing-Driven

Product placements are similar to promotional partner tie-ins, but are generally distinguishable in that the third-party promotional partner will also advertise outside of the film/property; hence, such third-party will leverage its brand in retail together with the tie-in film. In contrast, a pure product placement will only involve integrating a consumer brand into a film, television, or online property, where there is an indirect association. Examples of a product placement are the judges on *American Idol* drinking a Coke (with the Coca-Cola bottle and logo prominent), or the financing of certain online originals having a character wear a particular fashion accessory (e.g., brand of shoes). In both of these cases, the viewer is drawn to the product, with the character (or in the case of the reality program or contest, the judge or host) using the product as the marketing hook. There is no direct tie-in between the brands. The lines here can be quite fine, as a car used in a film (e.g., a special sports car in a *James Bond* or *Bourne* film) is a kind of product placement; however, because in these types of cases there may also be off-film marketing ("see . . . in the *James Bond* film . . ."), the deal may be better characterized as a promotional partner tie-in.

Another way to distinguish between these types of arrangements is that promotional partner deals are generally designed to add marketing weight and promotion to a show or movie. In contrast, product placements do little to promote the show, but create a separate revenue stream (basically in-show advertising) that can be viewed as defraying production costs (i.e., a method of financing) or a revenue stream helping to recoup production costs. It is for this latter reason that several online original programs, unable to secure enough revenue from new advertising markets, have utilized product placement opportunities to help finance production (see Chapter 3). The challenge with product placements is that creators often bristle that they undermine the integrity   **513** of the show, and the brands that are usually prominently featured (to justify the fees paid) may date the shows in the long tail.

One way to defeat these problems is to create a product placement that has functional relevancy. This, however, is difficult to execute creatively, for the product needs to be built into the show and integrated at an early stage. A few years ago, I saw an example in the online context that may be an ideal model for utilizing product placements. The online social network Gaia Online, which allows people to build environments and socialize via avatars in a virtual world, innovated a clever way to integrate product placements that went beyond simply seeing the visual. As has fast become a trend, users can buy virtual goods to dress up their characters, and in this instance, could buy Nike shoes. What is different is that when the character wears those shoes they go faster, creating a relevancy and functionality that creates more value for the brand and does not detract from or compromise the underlying content. In this example, the Internet has taken product placement to another level. To a degree functional relevancy of products underlies the economic models in social games where the business goal is to seduce players to ante up and pay for additional elements helping them/their characters succeed and progress to a new level; it is accordingly not surprising to see companies searching for tie-ins where products offered contain brand appeal (and benefits) over generic accessories.

Theatrical Marketing Budget

The marketing budget is the largest cost outside of physical production impacting the P&L of a film. Given the increasingly competitive nature of the marketplace, and the compressed periods of theatrical release (see Chapter 4), the costs of marketing have spiraled to almost unimaginable highs. As already referenced, the average domestic cost for an MPAA member studio to market a film in 2007 was $35.9 million, a sum that has continued to hover at roughly this level (see Figure 9.1).[6]

Direct Costs

By far, media is the largest cost category. Media costs and strategy involve mapping placement to demographic targets and achieving a certain reach and frequency. This is often expressed in terms of percentage of target reached, such as 70 percent, and how many times that grouping is hit with impressions (such as one, two, or three times). Media buys are then made on the basis of impressions. The end goal is to achieve a certain awareness level, which then hopefully translates into consumption.

Media buys are aggregated in four principal areas: television and radio, print, outdoor, and online. These categories are exactly what they sound like. TV and radio are simply commercial spots of varying lengths. Outdoor ranges from billboards to sides of buildings to buses and phone kiosks. Newspaper/print involves advertisements that can differ by size, prominence, color, etc., and like TV can be executed locally, nationally, and to finely tuned demographics (e.g., women's magazines). Online is a catch-all encompassing everything digital: Web, mobile, social. There is no magic formula, and different marketing gurus will allocate different weights depending on their experience and, to some degree, gut feeling. Some believe that with increasing media diversity and competition that the middle is disappearing; namely, either spend modestly and targeted, or spend big enough to rise above the clutter.

Allocation of Media Costs

TV advertising alone can often account for more than half of the total media marketing costs. The allocation of costs is a picture-by-picture decision, but historically the largest costs have been first TV advertising, next newspaper advertising, and then the balance of the pie divided among Internet, outdoor (e.g., billboards, buses), and radio advertising. The biggest shifts in recent years have been the decline in newspaper advertising, and the increase in "digital" spending (which is now

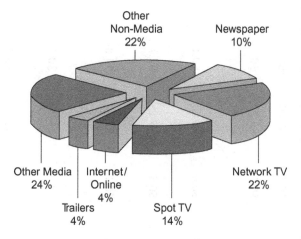

Figure 9.1 MPAA Theatrical Marketing Statistics: MPAA Member Company Average Distribution of U.S. Advertising Costs 2007

Note: Other media includes cable/other TV.

515

not only Web/online, but also encompasses social media and mobile advertising). These are difficult costs to track in the aggregate, but Figure 9.1 gives a snapshot as to the prominence of TV spending in 2007 and the then relatively small amounts of advertising committed online. It is also useful to look at the breakdown on a per-film basis. Table 9.3 provides select examples across key titles from a variety of studios, as referenced in the *Hollywood Reporter*.

Because media costs are front-loaded to open a film, pursuant to the compressed theatrical box office curve, if a film underperforms it is too late to adjust. Accordingly, for films that do not achieve box office numbers greater than $100 million, the percentage of marketing costs relative to box office can be a frightening number. This was the case with *Music & Lyrics*, starring Hugh Grant, where the marketing costs were more than 70 percent of the total box office (and remember, rentals are roughly half the box office, meaning that the marketing costs significantly exceeded the revenues taken in by the distributor at this stage). In the most extreme case, the numbers can exceed the box office, which directly translates into media feeding frenzies about the film bombing, and in the worst of scenarios finding a place among the all-time clunkers.

Table 9.3 Marketing Cost Breakdowns for Selected Films

Studio and Distributor	Domestic Box Office	Total Media Marketing Costs	Network TV	Cable TV	News-paper	Radio	Magazines	Spot TV	Internet
Enchanted (Disney)	$127.8	$44.6	$11.7	$11.6	$6.2	$0.1	$0.1	$13.0	$0.2
Shrek the Third (DreamWorks/Paramount)	$322.7	$45.1	$20.6	$11.6	$4.7	$0.1	$0.1	$5.2	$0.4
I am Legend (Warner Bros.)	$256.3	$39.8	$21.7	$6.8	$4.4	$0.0	$0.0	$4.0	$0.1
Spider-Man 3 (Sony)	$336.5	$41.7	$17.7	$9.5	$4.9	$0.6	$0.3	$5.1	$2.1
The Bourne Ultimatum (Universal)	$227.5	$36.9	$10.2	$10.0	$5.5	$0.5	$0.1	$2.8	$4.8
Live Free or Die Hard (Fox)	$134.5	$33.6	$14.0	$9.0	$3.9	$0.5	$0.0	$4.0	$0.1
Music & Lyrics (Warner Bros.)	$50.6	$35.7	$15.5	$6.5	$5.2	$0.0	$2.1	$5.3	$0.4

Note: all figures in $ millions.

Internet Impact

The power of the Web to target messages to specific demographics is a marketer's dream, and the budgets for online advertising continue to grow. The 4.4 percent that the MPA estimated was spend for online/digital advertising grew to more than 10 percent by 2010, essentially flipping the importance of newspaper advertising, which fell from 10 percent to 4 percent.[8] Although television continues to dominate marketing expenditures for film releases, with *Variety* estimating (early 2010) that TV accounted for 60–70 percent of a studio's promotional budget,[9] it is likely that online/digital marketing budgets will continue to grow and cannibalize part of the TV spends for the next several years. This shift is not specific to the movies, but essentially tracks the broader marketplace. *Forbes*, quoting a forecast by Forrester Research, predicted that online advertising would, in fact, overtake TV by 2016 (see Figure 9.2).

While increased advertising online may seem an obvious trend in terms of promotional campaigns for films, I have heard some argue to the contrary, noting that a trailer that is released virally can be accessed from thousands of points and need not require advertising. As a studio, if your best message is the visual, and online distribution of a trailer is free, then why additionally pay for advertisements? This theory is buttressed by the nature of experience goods. As earlier discussed, advertising helps the consumer feel as if they have experienced the film; the consumer then creates signals that may lead to cascade behaviour, which may be further accelerated by viral sharing among users frequenting social networking sites. Of course, this information flow and result can also turn negative, which is a complicated way of saying that whether a trailer is compelling is now even more important in the online world. I would argue, however, that this line of reasoning is purely theoretical, and that to create viral sharing of a trailer it is necessary to invest in promoting it. More sums will be allocated to online outlets, and especially social network sites, where clever advertising can be a catalyst for sharing. The promise of direct marketing, inherent efficiencies of reaching an exact demographic, the ability to report precise 1:1 metrics, and the inevitable maturation of the space mean that allocations will continue growing. Moreover, they are likely to grow both in sub-markets, such as social medial and mobile, as well across the entire wireless and online/digital spectrum.

Despite my belief in the growth of online (which is clearly happening), a macro shift in allocation from TV to online has not yet happened —largely because TV advertising has proven remarkably robust. In fact, over the last five years, total ad spending on television has increased,

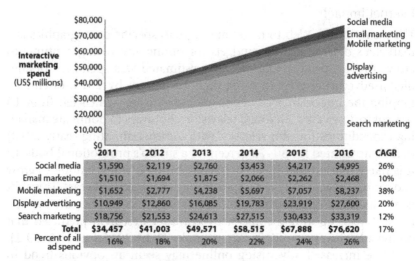

	2011	2012	2013	2014	2015	2016	CAGR
Social media	$1,590	$2,119	$2,760	$3,453	$4,217	$4,995	26%
Email marketing	$1,510	$1,694	$1,875	$2,066	$2,262	$2,468	10%
Mobile marketing	$1,652	$2,777	$4,238	$5,697	$7,057	$8,237	38%
Display advertising	$10,949	$12,860	$16,085	$19,783	$23,919	$27,600	20%
Search marketing	$18,756	$21,553	$24,613	$27,515	$30,433	$33,319	12%
Total	**$34,457**	**$41,003**	**$49,571**	**$58,515**	**$67,888**	**$76,620**	17%
Percent of all ad spend	16%	18%	20%	22%	24%	26%	

Source: Forrester Research Interactive Marketing Forecasts, 2011 To 2016 (US)

Figure 9.2 Projected Online Advertising Expenditure

Reproduced by permission of Forrester Research.

518

with Nielsen reporting that total ad spending in 2011 increased 4.5 percent to a total of $72 billion, and that since 2007 cable advertising spending has increased a whopping 42 percent, with cable and network spending now virtually equal.[10] Figure 9.3 provides evidence of the upward trend in overall spending on television, as well as how virtually all segments (e.g., cable, network, syndication) have either held relatively steady or shown a material increase.

What these trends evidence is that certain traditional promotional areas, such as newspapers, will continue to wane, and that online, television, and outdoor advertising (e.g., billboards) will continue to be a staple for advertising releases. There is already a push to leverage social media in a more proactive way (see discussion below), and it is inevitable that the allocation of marketing budgets will continue to shift as metrics continue to prove the efficiencies that well-orchestrated and well-tuned online advertising can deliver.

Correlation of Marketing Spend to Success

While William Goldman is correct that "nobody knows anything," and most statistical correlations of top box office stars to movie performance evidence that stars, in fact, do not guarantee a project's success, at least one popular benchmark seems true: bigger-budget movies tend to yield

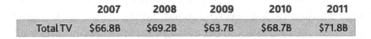

	2007	2008	2009	2010	2011
Total TV	$66.8B	$69.2B	$63.7B	$68.7B	$71.8B

2011 SPEND BY MEDIA TYPE (USD)

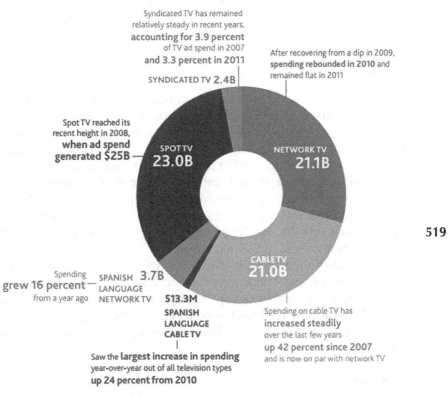

Syndicated TV has remained relatively steady in recent years, **accounting for 3.9 percent** of TV ad spend in 2007 **and 3.3 percent in 2011**

SYNDICATED TV 2.4B

After recovering from a dip in 2009, **spending rebounded in 2010 and** remained flat in 2011

Spot TV reached its recent height in 2008, **when ad spend generated $25B**

SPOT TV 23.0B

NETWORK TV 21.1B

CABLE TV 21.0B

Spending **grew 16 percent** from a year ago

SPANISH LANGUAGE NETWORK TV 3.7B

SPANISH LANGUAGE CABLE TV 513.3M

Saw the **largest increase in spending** year-over-year out of all television types **up 24 percent from 2010**

Spending on cable TV has **increased steadily** over the last few years **up 42 percent since 2007** and is now on par with network TV

519

SOURCES:

1. Nielsen, Ad*Views (2011). Ad*Views Online only reports on estimated Online Display Spend
2. Nielsen, Cross-Platform Report (Q4 2011)
3. Nielsen, Ad*Views (2011)
4. Nielsen, Ad*Views (2009-2011)
5. Nielsen, Ad*Views (2007-2011)

Figure 9.3 Television Advertising Expenditure

Source: Nielsen, State of the Media (Spring 2012), Advertising & Audiences, Part 3: By Media Type. Reproduced by permission of Nielsen.

the best return on investment. Despite the seemingly bigger risks (if we assume higher marketing costs go somewhat hand in hand with higher budgets), the most costly films are, on average, the most profitable, with an SNL Kagan study finding that of all films with wide releases (i.e., more than 1,000 locations) between 2003 and 2007, "the two priciest segments surveyed showed the best profitability . . . 80 films costing more than $100 million to produce showed average profitability of $282.3 million."[11]

Trailers

The goal of the trailer is obviously to entice interest in viewership, and hopefully to create awareness through both direct viewing and word of mouth. The problem with the creative is that the trailers often have to be cut before the film is completed, and this is almost always the case with teaser trailers (which further means there are instances where scenes in the trailer may not make it into the final cut of the movie). This problem is exacerbated by effects-laden films, where shots may be filmed in front of blue or green screens and effects shots then created and integrated into the frame. The job of cutting/creating a trailer is simply to do the best with what you have available.

520

For the distribution budget, the cost is in creating the negative and then printing the physical trailers for distribution. Although the trailer itself is short, the number of copies can be in the several thousands, as the goal is to achieve the broadest possible market coverage. Trailer costs can therefore be significant when adding up the several line-item categories:

- creative and mastering
- focus group testing
- physical prints
- cans for shipment
- freight and transport.

There are accordingly economic decisions regarding trailering, as the distributor needs to judge how many versions of a trailer to make (if the film warrants targeting to different demographics, such as a love angle geared toward women and action sequences skewing toward men) and how many copies to print (although, as discussed in Chapter 4, the growth of D-cinema is eliminating the costs of physical prints, which will in tandem ultimately eliminate the costs of distributing trailers and change this calculus). Complicating these decisions is the fact that there is no guarantee as to how many of those copies will actually be shown—it is up to the discretion of the local theater what trailers will be played. In some cases, a certain number of limited trailers will be attached to the front of the film print, thereby somewhat guaranteeing placement. These attached trailers are precious real estate, and the decisions of what is trailered with what, and what is attached, will even go up to the head of the studio.

The placement of trailers, and direct linking where possible, is critical because everyone wants to have their trailer attached to the film(s) with the best demographic overlay to the target market for the future film. One can imagine the politics of this choice, with different investments in different films, lobbying by directors and producers, key relationships with clout . . . Everyone wants to be on the front of the next blockbuster, and competition will be fierce to piggyback on event films.

The studios will receive reports of trailer coverage after the weekend, which is the ultimate gauge of whether the right range of copies was produced and shipped. Of course, all of the previous discussion addresses physical trailering, but as earlier noted, trailers will also be posted online and can potentially achieve greater reach and frequency via the Web and viral sharing. Trailers, in summary, receive so much attention because, by their nature (including their ability to solve the experience-good problem), these visual teasers continue to be among the most efficient of marketing tools both online and offline. Interestingly, they are an example of a practice as old as films that has found a way not only to survive, but even grow in importance in the Internet age.

Teaser and Launch Trailers

Tentpole-level films typically have a teaser trailer six months or so in advance of release, and then a launch trailer a couple of months in advance of the release date.

Because of the limited material available for teasers, they tend, by their nature, to be short at around a minute in length. Taking into account lead times, for a summer movie teasers will often release in the fourth quarter of the prior year, taking advantage of the holiday box office season and the large audiences that will be attending theaters. Similarly, teasers for holiday films will often accompany summer releases. This is a relatively efficient way for a distributor to start spreading the word about an upcoming blockbuster.

A launch trailer, by comparison, is a very different animal. The launch trailer, released much closer to the theatrical release, will usually be much longer (e.g., two-minute range as opposed to one minute), and rather than "teasing" will give the audience a better sense of the story/what to

521

expect in the movie. Many people often complain that "the best scene was in the trailer or commercial," but it is hard for a marketing executive not to cull from their best assets to entice people into the theater.

Posters

Posters, or in film parlance "one-sheets," have been around as long as movies, and to some are even considered a distinct form of art. The poster is simply a single static image used for the same purposes as the trailer. Knowing that the poster may have more visibility than any other piece of artwork in promoting the film, it needs to convey a succinct and compelling message. This will be the piece most likely picked up by the press for initial coverage, and the enduring image at the box office. Additionally, one-sheets (unless replaced by digital video box art) become the artwork for thumbnails, indexing the image in search engines, websites and virtually all online/digital outlets.

The economics of the poster is similar to trailers, just less expensive (usually). Posters are less costly to manufacture and distribute (with the cost of thumbnails as regards online marketing virtually zero), but interestingly the creative can be much higher. Because movie posters are often deemed works of art, and the commissioning of artwork, simply put, can be as expensive or inexpensive as the budget can bear, this is an area of both real and niche celebrities. The subjective nature of posters also lends itself to focus group testing, as messages can range from direct to mysterious. Additionally, as sometimes happens with high-profile films, posters may mimic trailers, such as when a unique teaser poster accompanies the teaser trailer, and a release poster dovetails with the launch trailer messaging. It is all about what will draw in the audience, and the answer may not be the most clever or creative. This is an area that can be lots of fun, and truly lets creative marketers have a significant impact on the film.

One final item to mention about posters is that they can be sold, thereby creating an ancillary revenue stream not available with trailers. In general, however, these sales are incremental to other merchandise, and it would be rare to factor this revenue into the equation. In fact, the marketing department will have the task of delivering posters within a budget range, and will likely never know anything about the revenues, if any, earned from later sales.

In-Theater

A related element to posters is in-theater advertising. At the simplest level, in-lobby posters provide direct marketing to those making their decision of what to see once at the theater. This element has grown in importance with the expansion of multiplexes, and is critical in enticing would-be customers making an impulse decision once already at the theater. In-theater advertising may also involve more elaborate marketing, such as standees, additional signage, branded concession items (e.g., cups), and even billboard-type advertising outside.

Commercials (Creating) and Creative Execution

Creating advertisements for a property is similar to the process of cutting trailers, in that for bigger films there may be multiple versions generated. Commercials can be tailored to targeted demographics (e.g., playing up action scenes to a hardcore male audience) and then the media bought accordingly. Hence, there can be a very significant range, from very targeted ads to workhorse broad demographic spots.

In addition to the multiple versions, each version may be edited for different lengths. Commercials can range from a tag of a few seconds, up to a minute, with most spots cut to 15 or 30 seconds. Again, what will work best is a gut creative call based on overall budget (although, budgets permitting, distributors will test the spots on focus groups to optimize the outcome).

523

Finally, there is an economic call regarding the extent to which the process is managed in-house versus outsourced. Given the volume of product and challenges it is common for studios to work both with advertising agencies as well as trailer specialists. Only in Hollywood, though, could a trailer specialist become a main character, such as Cameron Diaz's role in the 2006 Christmas release *The Holiday*.

Creative Execution

Although it may sound like a truism, the quality of the creative is a critical factor in the success of a commercial, as well as all the other marketing elements discussed. The same problems that lead to challenges with creative goods underlie the creation of marketing materials, though smaller in scale and tempered by the fact that the creative is derivative of another property (i.e., the film). Commercials win awards too, and whether commercials or other marketing materials achieve their goal of creating awareness and stimulating consumer interest may be subject to the intangible of creative execution.

Press and PR

Press and PR can form a major part of the overall marketing campaign, and few realize both how complicated and time-consuming orchestrating all the elements of PR can be. Areas that PR has to manage include: (1) press kits; (2) press junkets (both long and short lead); (3) reviews; (4) talent interviews and management; (5) tie-ins/placements on other media such as TV shows; and (6) screenings (in coordination with distribution).

Press kits historically included fact sheets, press releases, slides, and some glossy photos. Today, if still used, they can still include these elements, and are supplemented with online elements; however, online press kits (i.e., electronic press kits; EPKs) have been the norm for a few years, and I would suspect that by another edition of this book physical press kits will we seen as a quaint anecdote from the past. Regardless of form, press kits are vital in terms of key messaging, and making available images to be used in print, television, and online coverage. A good press kit is engaging and informative, and also has direct messaging—the film, if not already a brand, will hopefully become one, and staying true to a brand requires concise and bounded messaging. Everyone wants to write the review and article, and the press kit gives the journalist hold of the driving wheel and a guided map. How and where they then drive and chronicle the journey is out of PR's control, but a good press kit guides the less adventurous driver along the scripted route.

Handouts are limited in a business of glitz and images, and studios therefore choreograph press junkets. These interactive sessions will allow invited journalists to talk with key talent, learn about unique production elements, and taste a bit of the film. The cost of junkets can be high, involving renting and decorating venues, catering parties, creating custom reels, flying in and putting up talent/celebrities, and creating takeaways/goodies. Against this budget, the marketing department needs to place a value on the level of awareness and hype that the journalists and bloggers will ultimately create. What is the value of a good piece on *Entertainment Tonight* or a story in *The Huffington Post* versus the cost of a 30-second commercial? Press is, at some level, just another angle and tactic to create interest that will spike awareness and attract consumers.

Beyond the tried-and-true press kits and junkets/press conferences, good PR will take the film into another media space and create tie-ins. Convincing *Saturday Night Live* to have the star of the film host is a good example of this strategy. (Do you think it is a coincidence that Zach Galifianakis happens to host just before his next *Hangover* movie is opening?). Similarly, a star of an upcoming film may make a special guest appearance on a scripted TV show, creating buzz and interest; not so surprisingly, vertical integration between network groups and studios allow this. Everyone loves seeing a character out of context in a cameo appearance, and on occasion, such as when a *Desperate Housewife*

524

shows up in a locker room for a sports promo, the media attention can reach a frenzy. Can there be better publicity than being written into an episode of *The Simpsons*, even if the character or person may be the subject of a witty slander?

Finally, PR is the group that manages talent interviews. Every outlet wants time with the director, producer, or star, and PR orchestrates the maze of interviews. It is PR that has to manage who has an exclusive, whether there is a press embargo (granting information in advance for stories under the pledge that a story will not run before a specified date), and when and where talent will be available. Although talent will have agents and managers, it is the studio machine that will set in motion the blitz of appearances on talk shows. Basically, PR often functions as the gatekeeper to talent, and manages access to talent in a way that at once is hopefully respectful to people's time (and, for talent, time is money) and maximizes positive exposure for a film/property.

For all of the above, take this task and then expand it to a global scale. One day, TF1 in France wants to interview on location, the next ProSieben from Germany, and the following NHK from Japan. To handle the world, there will often be regional press junkets, which may mean at least one in Europe and one in Asia in addition to those in the United States. Requests will be coming in from thousands of newspapers and television stations. And worse, if they are not coming in, it is the job of PR to drum up interest and make them come in, whether that means seeding stories, pitching angles to publications and journalists, or creating special tie-ins. All of this activity needs to happen on a massive scale in a compressed time frame. The incremental budget costs are labor and travel.

In the end, with the global reach of the Internet, and so many new applications in the digital age such as EPKs, it is fair to ask the question whether overall the Internet is a friend or foe to PR. It is a valid concern, given the danger of leaks that can lead to ubiquitous access and news versus the ability to disseminate a message almost instantly to everyone simultaneously around the globe. I asked Lynn Hale, George Lucas's head of PR at Lucasfilm since the 1980s, what she felt about the Internet on balance:

It cuts both ways, although overall I would say that the Internet is a friend. On the one hand, the Internet makes it impossible to keep secrets. I doubt that George could have ever pulled off the surprise of Darth Vader's revelation if *The Empire Strikes Back* were released today, or if the Internet had been around in 1980. But on the other hand, the Internet has given us an instant worldwide platform to immediately disseminate news. Lucasfilm learned early on the power of the Web, and we embraced it. As early as 1998, we were reaching out directly to our fans, providing information that wasn't necessarily of interest for conventional news outlets. Back when we were releasing *Episode I*, www.starwars.com listed theater locations that would be showing the teaser trailer. Fans flooded into theaters in such huge numbers that it became news. Local stations reported on it, and even the late-night shows—like Letterman and Leno—included comments in their opening monologues. It was unprecedented at the time, but now movie studios rely heavily on the Internet to create excitement around a film's opening. It's another piece of the puzzle, and another tool at our disposal.

Screenings

526

To make sure that influential people can be impressed by the film and help spread the word, PR will work closely with distribution regarding screenings. Screenings have a wide range (charity, partners, press, critics, word of mouth, theater chains), and PR has the direct responsibility for ensuring that press screenings are effective. These screenings tend not to involve additional expense beyond the screening costs, but it is important to make the best possible impression on the critics/audience who will be reviewing (and potentially writing about) the film. Accordingly, efforts may be made to ensure high-quality venues, with good sound, picture, and ambiance. PR can only do so much to influence reviews, but at its core one of the jobs of PR is to try to positively influence the outcome and put the film in the best possible light.

Media Promotions

Another category driving awareness is media promotions. This can involve a variety of stunts or giveaways, with radio station contests (and film-based prizes) a common vehicle. The key with these types of promotions is to secure additional media weight, and thereby impressions, by creating a contest, quiz, or similar interactive event engaging consumers with the property.

Exhibitor Meetings

The distribution and exhibition communities have two major U.S. conventions per year, Show East (Florida, moving between Orlando and

Miami) in the fall and Show West (Las Vegas) toward the end of March. (Note: There is also CineExpo in Europe, formerly in Amsterdam, and more recently held in Barcelona.) Distributors use this opportunity for a dog and pony show for theater owners, getting them excited about their upcoming releases. If a producer or studio has already released its trailer, it may use this opportunity to create a separate short piece to show the theater owners.

These markets provide a significant marketing opportunity for the distributor, and depending on the film either the director, producer, or key stars will attend to introduce the movie. This can be "showbiz" at its best: packed audiences waiting for a first look at a film, with press clicking photos of the stars present just to create chatter and excitement.

In the spring of 2005, the atmosphere was electric at Fox's presentation between the photographers' feeding frenzy clicking pictures of Brad Pitt and Angelina Jolie walking out together to promote *Mr. & Mrs. Smith*, and the entrance of Stormtroopers together with George Lucas to highlight the release of what was then believed to be the final *Star Wars* movie. (Note: Influenced by the severe economic downturn starting in 2008, these annual events have been toned down by many studios.)

527

Film Markets and Festivals

There are a variety of major international festivals, which serve as outlets to debut films, gain publicity, and screen films for potential distribution pickup/acquisition.

There are literally markets all the time, but those shown in Table 9.4 are examples that have risen to "major" status (timing is approximate, as dates tend to shift over time).

The impact of independent festivals is significant, as they provide an outlet beyond the studio gatekeepers, and have proven their ability to launch directors, stars, and hits. It is now roughly 25 years since Steven Soderbergh debuted *Sex, Lies and, Videotape* at Sundance (winning

Table 9.4 Festival Locations and Timing

Festival	Location	Timing
Sundance	Utah	Winter
AFM	Los Angeles	Fall
Cannes	France	May
Venice	Italy	Fall
Toronto	Canada	Fall

the dramatic Audience Award), prior to the film going on to win the Palm d'Or in Cannes and catapulting both the director and actress Andie MacDowell into stardom. More recently, *Slumdog Millionaire*'s Best Picture award in Toronto was a precursor to its capturing the Golden Globe for Best Picture and winning the Oscar for Best Picture (2009). Part of the problem with success is that what were once independent festivals intended to provide opportunity and expression for independent filmmakers have become so influential and competitive—with studios trolling to pick up properties for distribution—that the festivals have been swamped with submissions and inadvertently become another kind of gatekeeper.

Websites

In addition to impacting advertising (online expenditures and targeted campaigns), PR, and trailer exposure, the digital and online worlds are profoundly influencing marketing efforts via project-specific websites. Now, not only do producers need to think about reserving titles, but as soon as a project matures it is wise to reserve the related domain name (a common word or title may be translated into a phrase such as www.XYZmovie.com).

Websites need to be built, and the timing of launch, sophistication of site, and budget will all influence the end product. For an event-type movie, there may even be pressure to build the site well in advance as a place for fans to visit during production. This can seed interest and create early buzz. If a director is willing, the website can even be a place for production journals or a regular director blog from the set, as was the case with Peter Jackson during the making of *The Lord of the Rings* films, and more recently with the production of *The Hobbit*, where regular blog updates could be found (www.thehobbitblog.com).

As with a trailer, however, building a website in advance of a release can be challenging, for there may be little or no new material to post initially. When *Indiana Jones and the Kingdom of the Crystal Skull* was announced, there was enthusiasm for updating the older *Indiana Jones* site; however, until new production commenced there were few new key assets that could be posted. Nevertheless, the site became (as are all film sites) a place to post new news, the oldest and simplest function of film/TV sites.

As noted earlier, it is now commonplace to be able to go to a film or TV show's website and see the trailer or other preview of the product. Moreover, the trailer is now "networked" such that it can be found not only on the film's dedicated website, but linked to review sites and theater listings. A few years ago, if you missed a trailer in the theater, you may never see it, but today you can catch it in a variety of locations, replay it, and even link it/e-mail to a friend via a social networking site creating a viral network buzz. For every studio executive complaining about the availability of its programming on video sites without author-ization, there seems a counterbalancing marketing guru eager to take advantage of the platform to widen distribution of trailers, etc. The potential to distribute trailers to target demographics and allow sharing of trailers (or even elements thereof) on social networking sites adds another toolset to the marketing executive (see further discussion below, including "Online Marketing: Expanding the Toolset", page 548).

Beyond News and Trailers: Interactivity

A powerful feature of websites is their ability, beyond posting news and showing trailers, to market a property by more deeply engaging users/fans. Today, with video functionality common online, websites can host a variety of elements, including behind-the-scenes shots, interviews with key cast and crew, Web documentaries (e.g., of a making-of nature), webcam feeds, and live chat video chats. For *Star Wars: Episode III*, Lucasfilm created a series of Web documentaries, such as behind the scenes of creating lightsaber battles and the genesis of creating the villain General Grievous; these included footage of George Lucas approving iterative design elements, interviews with artists at Industrial Light & Magic, and shots of behind-the-scenes green-screen shoots.

529

In addition to video elements, websites may contain mini-games, links to e-commerce sites, links to promotions and promotional partner sites, and downloadable elements for instant gratification. Everyone loves getting things for free, and often sites will allow certain downloads of screensavers, buttons, etc. The cross promotion between online engagement and watching can be very significant for a franchise. Tom van Waveren, former head of Egmont Animation (Denmark), creator and producer of Cartoon Network hit *Skunk Foo*, and producer of hit animated reality show *Total Drama Island*, told me the following regarding the interaction of kids engaging online and watching *Total Drama Island*:

What makes *Total Drama Island* unique is both its teen skew as an "animated reality show" and its online extension on *Total Drama Island: Totally Interactive*. On *Total Drama Island: Totally Interactive*, which was accessible on the Cartoon Network website, each episode's challenge to the contestants is mirrored by a casual game and viewers can create their own avatar to play such games. Two things were remarkable about *Total Drama Island: Totally Interactive*. First of all, we were overwhelmed by the response we got to the site, and had two server crashes in the first week trying to match our capacity to demand of peaks of over 100,000 simultaneous users from the first month. By the time of the season finale, over 3 million unique avatars had been created and being regularly used. And second, we could see a pattern evolving between the viewing figures on air and the activity peaks online. Comparing our data, we could see that 10 percent of the viewers were simultaneously watching a new episode and online playing the games with their avatar. This demonstrated that the world of *Total Drama Island* was, at least to 10 percent of our audience, a multitasking, multiplatform entertainment experience instead of a TV show or an online game. One experience on several platforms simultaneously.

Trying to learn from this experience, we are looking at how we can create equally fluent transitions from one platform to the next with our other properties. This means that all the codes of the on air world need to be respected online and that the nature of the content offered online is closely connected to the on-air experience.

(Note: The finale of *Total Drama Island* broke Cartoon Network records, including, at the time, setting a new record and becoming the top telecast among tweens 9–14 for the network.)

The search to create synergies by crossing over media, whether by interacting with content via the Web or a mobile phone, is now even driving the nature of the programming. When millions of viewers text message a vote on *American Idol*, they are deeply engaged in the content, and producers are ever seeking clever ways to add interactive components (e.g., text message, vote online) to linear programming.

Finally, one great benefit to website marketing is its duration: where most marketing comes and goes (e.g., TV spots), a website is persistent, reaching back in time before a show/film launches to help seed interest, reaching maturity during product launch and offering depth of content, from trailers to interactive features, and remaining available through downstream exploitation allowing complementary marketing to long-tail revenue streams. Depending upon the size of the franchise, there may be periodic updates with key launches, such as with a video release (describing elements of bonus materials, and maybe even some extra

530

features that can only be unlocked with the purchase of a DVD), or re-promotion of titles (e.g., box sets, TV specials).

Social Networking—Sites and Microblogs

While only a few years ago creating a dedicated web site may have been perceived as enough for marketing, today it is deemed imperative to build a social networking page/site, usually at least on Facebook. While a number of assets may be common to the website, the social networking site enables easy viral sharing. For Peter Jackson's first film in *The Hobbit* trilogy (*The Hobbit: An Unexpected Journey*, released December 2012), the film's Facebook page three months prior to launch already had 700,00 "likes" and included sections devoted to photos, trivia, video, and news; additionally, linked on the Facebook page is a "Middle Earth" section that cumulates fans across the franchise, and at the same time boasted over 12 million fans. Also, beyond a dedicated movie page, individuals tied to a project (such as a famous actor or director) are apt to have their own personal social media page, which may have hundreds of thousands (or, in extreme cases, millions) of joined people. Social media has quickly become such an important facet of connecting with fans and potential consumers that when Peter Jackson decided to expand his most recent series from two to three films, he made the announcement not through traditional PR, but via a Facebook post (July 30, 2012):

531

So, without further ado and on behalf of New Line Cinema, Warner Bros. Pictures, Metro-Goldwyn-Mayer, Wingnut Films, and the entire cast and crew of *The Hobbit* films, I'd like to announce that two films will become three.[12]

Facebook is obviously only one example, as a celebrity can further leverage their personal following to promote and tout a project. Twitter is an example where an actor or actress can reach millions of fans. In fact, what was started as personal is now because of its value being turned into business: making certain statements in support of a launch or project, including when they are timed, are now becoming elements negotiated for in contracts. While some may deride whether anything remains sacred, given the nature of PR and media it is hardly surprising for those with a vested interest to want to harness the power of someone that can tangibly influence others—again to the experience-goods quandary, a valuable piece of information that can influence a choice is gold, and what could be better than hearing directly from a favorite star?

When Ashton Kutcher joined the cast of CBS hit *Two and a Half Men*, *Mashable* ran a story entitled "Will Ashton Kutcher's Twitter Following Help *Two and a Half Men*?" and noted:

With 6.7 million Twitter followers and a sizeable following on Facebook, Kutcher is one of the most socially connected celebrities in the entertainment business. The big question now that he has joined the show is, what impact will his social media presence have on the show's ratings?[13]

A Twitter feed, regardless of whether any more real than a prerecorded message from a candidate left on your home answering machine, is the next evolution of 1:1 marketing, targeting an already opted-in base with information crafted just for you (well, and along with maybe a million others). Despite any cynicism, the fact is that this direct link is unquestionably powerful, and as it becomes more measurable, then the value goes up. Celebrity has always been a sort of currency, but now that currency is gaining a new type of quantifiable value—in Chapter 3, I discussed the challenge of comparing advertising values online versus television, and now further complicating the mix is: What is buying a Twitter message from Celebrity X worth and how should it be compensated?

These factors are being increasingly noticed by agencies, and in fact specialized agencies working to exploit the intersection of social media and celebrity are emerging in Hollywood. The *New York Times*, in an article headlined "A-Listers, Meet Your Online Megaphone," describing start-up agency theaudience, noted of the power this new data set vests in agents: "If you cast Ms. Theron in a movie, she comes with an ability to fill seats through her social network, and we can prove it with data. Oh, and she needs to be paid more because of that. The same leverage holds true for sealing endorsement deals, which is where celebrities, and their agency backers, increasingly make their real money."[14] The same article went on to suggest: "If you were wondering how Rihanna was cast in *Battleship*, it was lost on no one at Universal that she came with 26 million Twitter followers."[15]

As a consequence, the major agencies are increasingly forming divisions or backing specialists that can help manage their clients' personas in the digital world—trying to strike a credible balance of making it feel that the celebrity is actually doing the posting while recognizing the time involved often needs some form of proxy. This new form of virtual publicist, managing not an avatar, but the actual client in the blogosphere, extends the role and to some degree the leverage of agencies. William Morris Endeavor and Creative Artists Agency, for example, appear to have embraced this new set of tools, with CAA backing WhoSay, which manages celebrities ranging from Tom Hanks to Shakira, in terms of their messaging and presence in this new arena. As a corollary, producers are now baking into contracts promotional commitments, ranging from best efforts commitments to specific social media commitments to mandate marketing communications to fans and followers.

Being able to cross market to a broader fan base and communicate directly with users who may have liked or touched another part of an ongoing franchise is a powerful tool—mixing fictional timezones and metaphors, one might even say that being able to identify Middle Earth fans on an individual basis is the Holy Grail of internet marketing. The promise of social media is not only to create a richer, more personal, more interactive viral Web of buzz, but also to raise the bar so that there is less drop-off between events (e.g., film releases, TV seasons) while simultaneously expanding the core base by linking to "like-minded" users (such as general fantasy fiction devotees).

I asked Ben Johnson, founder of social media marketing firm Gruvi, that has helped pioneer Facebook marketing for studios such as Sony (e.g., campaign for *The Amazing Spider-Man*) and also recently worked with Warner Bros. on *The Hobbit*, how social media can achieve more retention in fan bases and why this is so valuable to studios:

> This year's release of *The Hunger Games* marketing campaign on social media is an excellent example of what can be achieved. But what happens to those 5 million fans after the campaign has run its course? Like Lionsgate, all major studios across Europe are increasingly investing into social media technologies to help build and maintain communities round their movie products. The dominant platforms are YouTube and Facebook, but Twitter, Pinterest and Google+ are also on the studios' radar.
>
> From our conversations with studios and our own campaign experience we have discovered that marketing on social media like Facebook is complex and outside the normal skill sets and experiences of most of the marketing teams we have worked with. The main challenges are:
>
> ■ Fragmented marketing—many new communities (on Facebook pages) have to be created each year in line with the films that are being released.

- Scattered communities—there is no bridge between communities to retain users between campaigns and market/introduce new films to them.
- Communities erode—communities tend to die off after the product has been released and marketing efforts are directed elsewhere.
- Unclear ROI—no overview possible between the dollars spent on advertising and community management and the resulting returns in sales.
- Silo'd data—regional markets (in larger studios) and internal departments (e.g., home entertainment and theatrical) do not work together or share data so campaigns often flounder between release windows.

Social apps are growing in use among major brands—one only needs to look at the recent successes of the *Independent*, Spotify, the *Guardian* to see the power of the Open Graph and Facebook's hyper-distribution capabilities (ticker, timeline, newsfeed, etc.). However, we feel the real power lies in the fact that once a user has permissioned an application, the application owner has access to their social graph, which contains the connections to their friends, as well as comprehensive overview of their likes and interests. The app owner also has access to Facebook's powerful Open Graph distribution mechanisms that allow the application to publish statements about what the user is doing within the application to his friends (e.g., Johnny Knoxville is going see *The Hunger Games* on Friday 11 at Notting Hill Gate Cinema—who's going with him?)

In the future, we'll see studios starting to take a much more comprehensive view of their social customer relationship management (CRM) strategies. These platforms will allow entertainment brands (film studios, publishing houses) to build and manage their communities through the power of the open graph, so they retain their fans between campaigns, understand their users tastes and connections and deliver targeted recommendations for new content.

The benefits for the studio using a social CRM strategy would be the ability to:

- Retain—fans between campaigns on Facebook and other applications that have been deployed to help market the film.
- Record—fans' tastes, their online activities and connections to their friends.
- Present—new content to the user based on these preferences and potentially links through to some form of point of sale (e.g., cinemas or streaming services).
- Communicate—the right content to each fan via their browsing experience on Facebook or via email.
- Connect—fans' actions through to their friends via Facebook.
- Track—fan behavior relative to campaign KPIs.

Finally, in the context of leveraging microblogging tools and sites, such as Twitter posts, many marketing departments are using the new vehicles in more conventional ways. Rather than simply focusing on Twitter as a way to amplify a celebrity's message, Twitter can be used as a discovery and engagement tool. In an article describing how Lionsgate built up demand for *The Hunger Games*—a film series where marketing was challenged trying to reach teens about a movie (based on a popular book) whose core cinema scenes involved kids killing kids—the *New York Times*, after noting that just following the traditional campaign path of printing posters, running trailers in theaters and blitzing primetime TV with advertising "would get a movie marketer fired," focused on the new use of the Web and social media: "The dark art of movie promotion increasingly lives on the Web where studios are playing a wilier game, using social media and a blizzard of other inexpensive yet effective online techniques to pull off what may be the marketer's ultimate trick: persuading fans to persuade each other."[16]

The *New York Times* article went on to summarize how Lionsgate initially released a trailer including a Twitter prompt via which fans could discover www.thecapitol.pn (website for the film, where The Capitol is where the fictional events occur) and make personal digital ID cards as if they actually lived in the fictional society of Panem; a subsequent Twitter prompt allowed those making IDs to campaign to be elected mayor of various Panem districts, and three months before the film's release a new poster was cut into 100 puzzle pieces and then split up into digital pieces distributed across 100 websites, with instructions for fans to serially post them on Twitter. Whether sophisticated or not, "Fans had to search Twitter to put together the poster, either by printing out the pieces and cutting them out or using a program like Photoshop.

535

The Hunger Games trended worldwide on Twitter within minutes."[17] Add to this a Facebook game, blog postings, and traditional media, and the film, which had by Hollywood standards a small marketing budget of approximately $45 million (perhaps less than half of what is often spent to debut a property tagged with franchise potential for multiple sequels) went on to break records—its opening weekend of $155 million (domestic box office) was the then third-best debut of all time, the best for any film opening outside of the summer, and the best ever for a non-sequel movie.[18] (Note: All at that time, as just a few months later, kicking off the summer 2012 season, *The Avengers* became the first ever film to top $200 million on its opening weekend.)

Market Research

All studios track films, and try to benchmark interest and awareness both in terms of overall levels as well as within specific demographics. There are two primary measuring sticks: awareness (segmented into general awareness and unaided awareness) and interest (comparing definite interest and definitely not interested). General awareness will track the percentage of the sampled population that is aware of an upcoming release, and the person polled will be given a number of upcoming films, including the one the studio is tracking (accordingly, it is a "leading question"). Unaided awareness, which is a barometer of the heat of the film, tracks whether the person will cite the film that is coming up ("What films are you aware of opening soon, or in X week?") without the film's name being mentioned in the question. "Definitely interested"/"definitely not interested," beyond the obvious, is a yardstick as to the effectiveness of the creative messaging. Given that this messaging is designed to influence the input signals (i.e., it is the input), then for "definitely not interested" numbers to rise means that something has gone awry in the crafting of the signal.

The analysis is further broken down into demographics, such as the following:

All kids 7–14:
- Boys 7–14
- Girls 7–14

All under 25:
- Women under 25
- Men under 25

All 25–35:

- Women 25–35
- Men 25–35

All 35+:

- Men 35+
- Women 35+

This segmentation will obviously allow targeting of demographics, and identify where a film is tracking particularly well or poorly. The tracking (which can be expensive) will further correlate to time out from release (e.g., four weeks out), and may additionally segment tracking into levels of interest such as definite or maybe. The further out the tracking, the more the information is driven by long-lead press, expectations from fans that watch for "the next film by *X* or starring *Y*," and the impact of the theatrical trailers and online sources. The studio can then adjust the advertising spend to match where weaknesses occur. If the film is a romantic comedy and is tracking below expected levels among women, advertising may be adjusted to ensure that this key demographic is addressed in an attempt to raise awareness levels to a targeted range (similarly, buying incremental spots on football may be added if the target is males and numbers are low). If overall awareness is low, then it may make sense to buy a spot on a highly rated TV show to jolt the numbers (which is why ads on premium primetime programs, such as *American Idol*, can be so expensive, as a huge number of eyeballs can be reached instantly; this effect is still difficult to achieve online).

Beyond spending to counter tracking numbers that are below targets (or worse, exhibit negative trends), another tactic that can be implemented is to change commercials (i.e., shift the creative messaging). If something is just not working, a new spot can be cut to attract viewers. This can be done to communicate more effectively within the original demographic targeted, to highlight an actor that may be coming off a recent hit, or in cases where there is real fear to switch tactics entirely. These strategies to try to adjust the dial to hoped-for levels are feasible so long as tracking is far enough out to allow time to adjust; however, there are still limits, as marketing budgets are usually relatively fixed in absolute terms, and certain commitments will likely have been made weeks, if not months, in advance. This is, remember, a highly competitive market, and another film is likely chasing the same audience and vying not just for end consumers, but also for space and tie-ins to attract those same consumers.

537

Finally, research will also track the film in question against other films—both past and present. Most importantly, given the competitive environment, is data regarding other films in the marketplace. Further, studios will model potential outcomes by benchmarking results against historical pictures where a comparison is useful. This may take the form of comparing against a genre, a prior film if the movie is a sequel, or a film driven by the same star (e.g., How did the prior Tom Cruise action picture track? How did the prior film directed by Ron Howard open?). The key Hollywood trades (i.e., *Variety*, the *Hollywood Reporter*) will now even regularly print charts comparing Actor *X*'s prior box office openings to targets for an upcoming release.

Indirect/Third-Party Costs

All of the previous categories discussed in conjunction with the theatrical marketing budget, whether hard direct costs or overhead, are costs borne by the distributor. If a property lends itself to becoming a major or even event-level release, then there is the possibility of supplementing this budget with funds of third parties. There is nothing like, and in cases nothing harder than, finding other people's money. The two major categories are from promotional partners and from merchandising licensees.

Promotional Partners

As noted previously, promotional partners who tie into a property need to invest directly for the cross promotion to be realized. The film's budget will not be used to advertise goods in a Happy Meal at McDonald's, or the character on a cereal or candy wrapper. The partners need to invest both in creative and in hard media dollars to make these programs work.

A snack food, beverage, or cereal company will need to create a specific new advertisement incorporating film elements/characters into its own brand. The trick here is to find an appropriate intersection of the brands, where the creative is positive to both brands, leverages one off the other, and creates something fresh and interesting that will attract consumers. In some ways, this is akin to a cameo appearance of an actor in another piece, except in this instance the cameo is into a branded product and the cameo has a theme tying the concepts together.

The economics are therefore the cost of the creative (the spot and related artwork); the cost to roll out the program to affiliates, product distributors, and franchisees; and the media costs for placing related commercial spots. The promotional partner will need to weigh these expenses against the anticipated uplift in sales, and arrive at a budget with a positive net present value weighing the campaign costs against the uplift in contribution margin. As part of this budget, the promotional partner will often offer and/or guarantee a certain amount of media weight/spend on the campaign. Accordingly, the studio knows it will spend $X million with its own ads, and can count on an additional $Y spend from its partners. These numbers can be difficult to quantify precisely, however, because they are frequently pledged in bulk value and may be difficult to track. Nevertheless, the commitments and impact are very real, and can account for a significant amount of the media weight for a campaign.

The distributor benefits from exposure on multiple fronts. First, there is incremental media advertising, thus helping drive awareness and impressions. Second, there are the in-store retail impressions from product on shelves, and, in the best of cases, dedicated displays and standees. Third, there is the impression from consuming the product, whether this is time spent reading details/information on packaging, using packed-in premiums ("find X inside marked boxes of . . ."), and spending time with the property/characters in the physical or online world by consuming/interacting with the tied-in product. If advertising is measured in impressions, and further if effectiveness is measured with time spent (impressions multiplied by time spent with the impression), then a good product tie-in can be worth gold. For the product partner, the same applies—if the tie-in helps improve sales, and if the attractiveness stimulates the consumer to spend more time consuming the product, then it is surely a net win for them as well.

Merchandising and Game Tie-Ins

The second major category is advertising from merchandising partners. It is rare to see hats and T-shirts being advertised, but certain categories can bring valuable media weight. The most important, arguably, is from toys pushed by one of the major toy companies (e.g., Mattel, Hasbro). Kids are fickle customers, but they are malleable targets and voracious consumers. Toy companies are significant spenders, and a new action figure, doll, or toy based on a major franchise will be a major driver of revenues. Accordingly, a leading toy company may create advertising for its product, and then place significant media behind it to stimulate awareness and sales. The formula is exactly the same as from the promotional partner. Every media dollar spent by the merchandising partner is an incremental dollar to the studio's media budget.

Additionally, as discussed in Chapter 8, it is common to launch video games related to the films, and the marketing of the game can also help broaden franchise awareness for the movie (and vice versa, the movie for the game). For this media weight to be effective, however, the game needs to be launched prior to or simultaneously with the film, which is often a difficult challenge, given game development and production lead times.

Net Sum and Rise in Historical Marketing Costs

The true marketing budget for a tentpole-type film may be as follows:

(1)   Distributor Media Budget
+ Promotional Partner Media Budget
+ Merchandising Media Budget
_____
= Total Direct Media Budget

(2) + Imputed Media Value from PR
_____
= Total Media Weight

+ Distributor Direct Costs
(3) + Distributor Incremental Overhead
_____
= Total Marketing Budget/Costs

This is, of course, the ideal scenario. Most films do not benefit from merchandising or promotional partners and are focused on the direct media budgets and PR opportunities.

Over time, the total costs of marketing a movie have risen with the rise in negative costs. Table 9.5 evidences the near-continuous rise of costs over a decade leading to the total costs of making and marketing a major movie being more than $100 million for the U.S. alone.

The trend is not that different when looking at member subsidiaries/affiliates' specialty divisions (e.g., Fox Searchlight, Miramax, New Line, Sony Pictures Classics). The shorter theatrical window and increased competition is forcing higher costs for these "smaller" pictures to compete. These spiking costs perhaps were one of the reasons a number of the studios shuttered specialty divisions (e.g., Paramount Vantage in 2008).

Finally, it is these extreme costs, coupled with inherent risk in the nobody knows/experience goods proposition, that have titans like Steven Spielberg and George Lucas sounding alarms about the future, and lamenting that more niche films may be relegated to TV (noting that even with their clout, they respectively barely got *Lincoln* and *Red Tails* into theatres); this could further lead to variable pricing (as sports teams have implemented, charging more for "premium match-ups"), such as potentially charging $25 for *Iron Man* versus $7 for *Lincoln*.[19]

Table 9.5 Average Annual Major Studios Negative Costs and Domestic P&A Costs

Release Year	No. of Films	Negative Costs ($ million)	Domestic P&A Costs ($ million)	Total Costs ($ million)
2002	141	41.7	24.6	66.3
2003	127	48.8	29.6	78.5
2004	134	48.7	28.0	76.8
2005	135	47.4	26.9	74.3
2006	143	48.2	26.9	75.1
2007	137	49.5	25.8	75.3
2008	114	55.3	31.0	86.3
2009	105	61.5	38.9	100.4
2010	96	72.3	39.6	111.9
2011	93	66.6	40.9	107.5

As of November 12, 2012.

Video Marketing

Even though it is an ancillary market, in many ways video marketing more closely parallels theatrical marketing than television. Virtually every major category of costs comes into play in a video campaign for a major/tentpole film: trailers, posters/box art, commercials, press/PR (and, in rare instances, even promotional partners). Video marketing can be more complex because of the need for direct-to-consumer marketing (like theatrical) and the need to coordinate in-store, retail-specific campaigns (unlike theatrical) requiring significant trade marketing. While theaters may have posters, and an occasional standee, "in-theater" promotion tends not to be on the scale of campaigns run by major retailers such as Best Buy and Walmart.

Macro-Level Spending/Media Plan and Allocation

The same type of media allocation graphs and charts as previously depicted in the theatrical context can be drawn for video. Paralleling theatrical campaigns, television spending is traditionally the dominant direct cost category. Near the peak of the DVD sales curve, this TV

Table 9.6 Video Marketing[20] (%)

Year	Net-work TV	Cable TV	Spot TV	Syndi TV	News-paper	Maga-zine	Out-door	Inter-net	Radio
2003	43.4	25.1	6.5	4.7	1.4	16.2	0.6	0.0	2.2
2005	38.3	32.1	5.7	2.8	1.1	14.0	0.3	2.1	2.3

percentage dwarfed all other categories, with the *Hollywood Reporter* noting: "There is one thing on which most studios agree: Allocating marketing dollars to the small screen makes sense. Nearly 80 percent of video marketing expenditures last year were for television commercials, with broadcast and cable in the lead . . ."[21] Table 9.6 lists allocations for the years 2003–2005 near the peak of the DVD sales curve.

In terms of percentage spend, as a rule of thumb marketing budgets will often be targeted in the range of approximately 10 percent of antici-pated sales, and in cases can approach double that number. Of course, there ends up being an inverse relationship to sales, as big hits with higher-unit volumes drive down the ultimate percentage, paralleling the trend with theatrical. For example, Disney spent $34 million-plus in marketing *Finding Nemo*, including $20 million-plus just for TV spots. While this represented the biggest video marketing campaign for a title that year, the *Hollywood Reporter* noted it was still but "a small fraction (6.4 percent) of the $536.7 million that Adams Media Research estimates the studio grossed from *Nemo* video sales." Similarly, Fox ended up spending only 6 percent of the $200 million video revenues ($12.9 million) on *X2*.[22]

As expected, and as the market has become more cluttered and competitive, expenditures rose and the allocation of media became more diversified. Big titles still need to hit threshold reach and frequency targets, but a variety of titles can be pitched into specialty markets, or in a more targeted manner, increasing the ROI for shifting some weight to the Internet and specialty cable. In 2005, again toward the DVD curve's peak, Fox reputedly spent 5 percent of its video marketing on the Internet, evidencing the new trend. Its SVP of marketing communi-cations, Steve Feldstein, highlighted to the *Hollywood Reporter* that strategy had moved well beyond simply buying TV spots: "There are a lot of elements that go into making a release into an event—from publicity and promotional activities to generating in-store excitement—and with the Internet, it's all becoming much more direct consumer marketing."[23]

This trend continues, with media spending increasingly diversified, and "digital" spending now diversified itself among classic Web targeting, mobile advertising, and social media. Many continue to point to mobile as the next great frontier, but advertising remains challenging given the limited screen size; the challenge faced by Facebook and others to efficiently monetize mobile is no more than the flip side of the challenge faced by studios to more efficiently utilize apps and smartphones to spread their message.

Commercials and Box Artwork; Retail Execution—Point-of-Purchase, Posters, Trailers

Again, like theatrical, significant effort and money is focused on branding the property and creating sales tools. Commercials are critical in a DVD/Blu-ray campaign, and will need to be created just for this market—"buy it today . . ." Although not as common as with a theatrical release (and again limited to bigger titles), a variety of spots may be cut, with different lengths and targeted to different demographics. Trailers and posters do not play as prevalent a role, and tend to be used more for trade and in-store marketing.

The most significant addition to the marketing arsenal is the box artwork, which almost always is a new design/image. Designing the artwork is tricky, because in one shot the image must be true to the property, remind people of why they liked the film (e.g., featuring a character), have a collectible appeal (the goal is to get people to buy it), and also appear fresh (time has passed, and people always want something new). Whereas movies come and go in theaters, this artwork/box will sit on shelves for months or even years as the continuing face of the brand to consumers long after the heat of the release. (Note: This same concept applies to TV box sets as well.)

543

Additionally, today the "box artwork" also becomes the virtual box artwork used for EST and scrolling through VOD options (including rental VOD such as Netflix). The challenge becomes that much greater in communicating a message that is apt to live on in digital thumbnails for the infinite reach of the long tail.

Retail Execution—Point-of-Purchase, Posters, Trailers

Until the Internet's long tail takes over, shelf space is still supreme, and gaining retail support is the lifeblood of any DVD/Blu-ray campaign. This involves specific placement of titles, special merchandising opportunities (e.g., unique displays and standees in the form of specially produced corrugate), in-store events and signage (e.g., posters), and commitment to keeping the title in prominent positions. It also means outside-of-store advertising support, including in circulars and, if the property justifies it, in TV spots. Circulars are more important than most people recognize. Not only do they have very significant reach, but they are obviously directly tied to generating in-store traffic, the ultimate point-of-purchase (POP).

Beyond driving people into the store, campaigns are focused on capturing the attention (impulse buys) of consumers in-store, regardless of what brought them there to shop. In-store programs involve coordinating multiple placement opportunities such as front-of-store POP displays and signage, special in-aisle corrugate, near checkout racks, end-cap placements (e.g., in new release section), and in-line facings. Moreover, as the sales cycle continues, there may be advance planning for subsequent waves, such as special positioning at holiday times and movement to studio-sponsored call-out areas (e.g., the Y Collection, bestsellers).

To help distinguish in-store programs, certain retailer exclusives may be offered. This often takes the form of premiums, such as stickers/buttons/posters, but may also involve unique product SKUs (e.g., special artwork on box, packed-in merchandise). All of these special features may incentivize a particular retailer to support a campaign. This support may be in the form of allocated placement in the retailer's catalog and circulars (which today can be easily searched online), in hard dollar expenditures on TV advertising, or extra in-store efforts and/or commit-
544 ments. Money already exists to execute some of these activities from the co-op advertising and MDF allowances traditionally included within an overall marketing budget; the trick is to effectively spend these sums and earn an appropriate ROI.

Press, PR, and Third-Party Promotions

There is a halo effect from the theatrical release, which obviously benefits video, but as the stakes have grown DVD/Blu-ray marketers have learned a second bite at the PR apple pays dividends. All the studios will hold retail-focused summits, building up their future releases, outlining marketing data, plans, and tie-ins, and even bringing in talent from big pictures to excite the buyers. Further helping generate buzz for the release, studios will sometimes even sponsor "launch parties," inviting key cast members and obtaining press coverage.

As DVD releases have become events, with trade awards for best DVDs (and, like any awards, with multiple subcategories to spread the glory), there are major press opportunities beyond staged parties. To create interest, ideally there needs to be a bit of a new story, which leads many studios to focus on bonus features and navigation. As discussed in Chapter 5, fancy menus, director's commentary, deleted scenes, documentaries, bundled games or demos, and even sneak peeks are examples of value-added material (VAM) typically produced for DVDs/Blu-ray discs.

In terms of economics, it is fair to question the production costs for these elements, as it is a difficult call whether and how much of this material is essential to stimulating sales. Certainly, there is value for collectors and fans, which may be sufficient in cases to justify large expenses; moreover, as discussed elsewhere, it is these "extras" that, in an online/VOD world, may be the differentiating value creating a justification to own physical content as opposed to renting or downloading digital versions that usually exclude VAM. Taking collecting out of the equation, I would argue that among the significant factors for the value-added elements is garnering media and press. These hooks help secure attention and interviews, gaining millions of "free" impressions that are additive to the hard media costs in terms of gaining awareness through targeted reach and frequency goals. Finally, as discussed previously, a critical part of any DVD/Blu-ray campaign is retail buy-in, and if you want the major chains to support a title, including featuring it in their own advertising, then you had better be supporting the title yourself.

Third-Party Promotional Partners

The largest category of third-party media placement is retail spending to execute in-store and to advertise (e.g., circulars). In somewhat rare instances, a promotional partner may tie into a video release, similar to the theatrical context where McDonald's may theme in-store giveaways, or a cereal company will co-brand a popular item. Every studio video marketing head dreams of these opportunities, but also laments that they can count on their fingers the number of times they have been able to execute this type of partnership, which inherently also would come with a third-party marketing commitment for direct consumer advertising. The fact remains that despite the rise of the video market and millions of dollars spent on DVD releases, promotional partners tend to associate this as an "ancillary" and rarely bring the support that is associated with a theatrical release. Nevertheless, select hits, and especially franchise titles, are sometimes able to secure this type of support, such as tie-ins with Papa John's Pizza for the video releases of *Ice Age* (2002) and *Indiana Jones and the Kingdom of the Crystal Skull* (2008).[24]

Net Sum

The same type of analysis could be outlined here as with the theatrical market:

> Distributor Media Budget
> + Aggregate Retailer Media Budget
> _____
> = Total Direct Media Budget

+ Imputed Media Value of PR
+ Imputed Media Value from Retailer Circulars
_____
= Total Media Weight

Television

In contrast to feature films and DVDs, there are several categories previously discussed that generally do not apply in the TV context: trailers, one-sheets, promotional partners, and merchandise on launch. In most cases, commercials and PR/press play a similar, if not more important, role given the more limited promotional vehicles available.

Direct Costs

Many of the direct cost categories from theatrical marketing apply to television: television media, radio, print (newspaper and magazine), outdoor, and online. More and more networks are turning to off-channel media to cross-promote programming. It is not unusual to see advertising on buses for TV shows, and even on billboards for a major launch such as a new season of Series *X* on Fox. Nevertheless, as with movies, the bulk of advertising and media dollars is focused on TV promotion.

Commercials and Opportunity Costs

As a bit of a truism, the most effective advertising for a TV show is on TV, and in particular on the network where the show is airing. The issue for a channel is balancing its commercial inventory—on the one hand, it wants to sell 100 percent of its inventory to garner the largest potential revenue, while on the other hand, it needs to hold back a certain number of spots to cross-promote and advertise its own programming. Accordingly, it becomes an opportunity cost analysis as to how much time to reserve.

As discussed in Chapter 6, the situation is seemingly easier for a cable network, for it has 24/7 inventory to allocate as opposed to a network that is limited to commercial spots within the hours it programs in primetime. A cable station with only a few original series can therefore look to cross-promote shows across its entire schedule, and has enough inventory to carpet bomb a series. In contrast, a network has more limited inventory and has over 20 hours of original primetime programming to promote (e.g., CBS could not afford to devote the amount of cross-promotional time to *CSI* as USA can devote to promoting *Burn Notice*).

Press and PR

Press and PR is very similar to the theatrical realm: press kits are created, talent is made available for interviews and live talk show appearances, and trade pitches are made at festivals and industry trade shows. Reviews and word of mouth are equally important here as in the theatrical market; while weekend box office may be the barometer of films, first and second episode ratings are no less forgiving. Simply, a show that is not pulling its weight will be pulled, and press/PR is a critical tool in helping build awareness and an audience.

There are even screenings. As discussed in Chapter 6, the "LA Screenings" in May have become an annual pilgrimage for foreign broadcasters to screen pilots and episodes of shows various studios/producers are debuting in the fall. Each studio will take a "day," for example, and an acquisitions executive from Spain will spend one day at Fox, the next at Warners, the next at Universal, and so on. During these periods, the studios/networks will wine and dine guests, bring in producers/directors to talk about their new shows, and throw parties and usually screen one of their about-to-be-released summer films. (Note: To be fair, these events are more sales- than marketing-focused.)

Use of Programming Schedules/Lead-Ins

Finally, the inherent nature of a network schedule affords cross-promotional opportunities by leveraging one show against another. Networks are all about lead-ins and lead-outs, tracking what percentage of a show's audience will stick around for the following program. A network takes a hit series and uses its audience to lead into and build awareness for a new show. This staple launch platform guarantees a certain built-in awareness and audience, and it is simply up to the next show to hold or build onto the base. Once a show is established and has taken advantage of piggybacking, it may then be moved to a different time slot on another day, where the process starts anew: Has the show held its prior audience? Is it strong enough to be a platform to help launch another show around it? Is the audience for the following show falling off or building on its base?

Because of this synergistic pull, it is typical to see the same types of shows follow each other. A sitcom following a sitcom will likely hold the prior audience more strongly than a drama following a sitcom (because the audience demographic/expectation will shift). This, in turn, leads to lineups where NBC may be themed around sitcoms/comedies on Thursday evenings, whereas one drama on CBS will lead into another drama. When people criticize television for being formulaic, it is because formulas work (see the discussion in Chapter 1) and like shows will hold similar audiences. It is as if in TV everything is a double feature—staying for the first film just is not good enough. When I once spoke to the CFO of one of the major networks, he likened the process of ratings to receiving a report card every day: in the morning you know how you scored relative to the competition the night before. Leveraging one show against another to create a strong lead-in can, by itself, make the difference.

This is an area where online availability does not mimic the benefits of TV—in a VOD world, while like titles may be packaged together under macro-categories, such as comedy or drama, the absence of scheduling eliminates the benefits of lead-ins; moreover, aggregators tend to bundle titles by genre, not by distributor or network, which further hampers a network's ability to leverage one show against another (and, in fact, a show may be listed in a way where it benefits a competitor).

Online Marketing: Expanding the Toolset

548   As discussed previously in the theatrical context, online marketing today involves a spiderweb of options. First, producers and distributors can market via the TV show's dedicated Web and social media sites. Sites range from relatively simple—where one can watch trailers, learn about the cast and crew, and be updated with PR-related news—to deep and sophisticated. A particularly rich site may include mini-games, e-commerce opportunities, specially produced content exclusives (e.g., talent interviews, behind-the-scenes footage, documentaries), downloadable goodies, chat rooms, blogs, interactive components (quizzes, mash-ups), and avatars, etc.

A second component enabled by the Web is online advertising, where banner and video ads are bought, and the media precisely targeted to narrow demographics. This can be elevated to a partnership level, where key portals may cross-promote properties both generally and within entertainment and appropriate keyword-related links.

TV networks, though, with the ability to promote series episodes week to week, and the need to maintain loyal viewers from season to season, are taking online marketing to new levels. One of the leaders is USA Network, which "gamifys" engagement. The network has created a rewards program, akin to loyalty points, which gives users credits for watching and engaging—such as sharing via a social network site—and then allows them to redeem those rewards for both virtual and real-world items (e.g., DVDs, T-shirts). For example, with its hit show *Psych*,

- Rewards users for watching videos, playing games & sharing content in social space
- Players redeem points for virtual and tangible goods as well as partner offerings
- CREATING BRAND AMBASSADORS

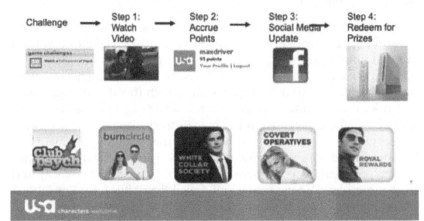

Figure 9.4 The USA Network Rewards Program   **549**

Courtesy of USA Network.

it has created Club Psych. By logging on, members can earn rewards points through completing weekly tasks such as playing games, answering trivia, or watching videos; social media is integrated by granting points for taking digital actions, such as "likes," or sharing content via Facebook or Twitter. USA has even taken the game aspect to the next level, by feeding actions of registered members into a leaderboard. Figure 9.4, courtesty of USA Network, summarizes how the process works across brands.

I asked Jesse Redniss, SVP Digital at USA Network, whether in the context of leveraging gaming elements if he saw direct monetization opportunities or viewed "gamification" as purely a marketing tactic, to which he replied:

The way that we are using gamification now is focused primarily on a user experience strategy rather than simply a marketing strategy. Monetization of the experience comes in many forms; for example, the experiences drive up impressions around the site. Monetization around a subscription model is a different ball of wax. However, digital storytelling is not just an engagement strategy, it is also a new medium for storytelling. We are utilizing all the different platforms now to tell a story. Engaging users onto these different platforms enables the content to flow in two directions.

Social Networking

An emerging component of online marketing is to tap into social networking, seeding blogs, and trying to stimulate a viral effect. Toward this end, more and more people are allowing content to migrate, such that you can embed video trailers, images, and other elements into your own space (e.g., a Facebook page) to share with friends. Not only can a network theme tie into a release, but to a lesser degree so can you—the goal of a viral campaign is for individuals to evangelize on their own.

Few people are aware of just how large the streaming of videos has become linked to social networking sites. I asked Peter Levinsohn, former president of Fox Interactive Media (parent to Myspace) and current president of new media and digital distribution for Fox Filmed Entertainment, about what motivates people to view videos in a social networking environment as opposed to on a pure on-demand video-based portal or site. He noted (back in 2009 when Myspace was still jockeying with Facebook for leadership in the social media space):

550

Social networking sites like Myspace are fundamentally about self-expression, and what someone posts is, to a degree, a reflection of who they are. These sites create an environment for people to discuss a range of topics—a kind of virtual water cooler where friends gather to discuss whether they liked something about a particular TV show like *House*, or if they had seen a funny viral video that had been emailed around recently. Online video content has become a centerpiece of those conversations—in fact, video has become such an important part of that dialogue that Myspace TV is now the number-two site on the Web for consuming video content.

What's more, these interactions benefit consumers, producers, and advertisers, and the best part is that the virtual community can scale and expand beyond what would typically occur in the physical world; for example, an office suite, because the Internet has no geographical boundaries. It becomes a global, real-time conversation and online video is, in many cases, the catalyst that brings all these people together.

Case Study: Marketing a Mega-Film

Marketing a film involves all the elements described earlier in this chapter (e.g., websites, trailers, posters, commercials, social networking pages), but in the case of an event picture, the palette may be expanded and marketing/PR can easily involve countless initiatives carefully choreographed over more than a year. It is therefore interesting to view the different elements in relation to a timeline, which in general terms I will break down as follows in Figure 9.5.

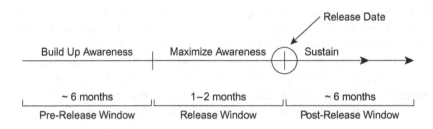

Figure 9.5 Mega-Film Marketing Timeline

The scope of the elements (discussed later) along this timeline presupposes a tentpole-level picture, such as a *Spider-Man, Transformers, Iron Man, James Bond,* or *Star Wars* sequel, or a brand with such assumed expectations (e.g., a new Pixar movie) that this level of activity can be justified.

As with all marketing, the goal of the pre-release and release windows is to start building awareness. Even with sequels, because every movie is unique, the distributor needs to craft a new strategy related to these periods: *Spider-Man* research may predict the base from action themes is solid but other demographics dependent on the love interest may be underperforming and need to be buttressed; *Harry Potter* focus group testing may have revealed concerns about the key characters aging; and *Star Trek* marketers likely struggle how to pitch the latest movies in the franchise to more than the core sci-fi crowd with prequels featuring young, less known actors.

Moreover, there are frequently inherent elements in a project that marketing needs to address, such as preparing its (hopefully) loyal audience for when a character or tone changes and the built-in expectations may therefore not be in sync with the new film in the franchise. This often happens with sequels that strive to enrich a protagonist by adding complexity and emotional character depth (where the character had otherwise risen to household fame as a typical hero). To achieve this shift, the previously family-friendly film takes on a darker tone, as our hero wrestles with a flaw or other torment. Think about the difference between *Batman Begins* and *The Dark Knight* versus certain pictures in the middle of the franchise (e.g., Arnold Schwarzenegger portraying Mr. Freeze), the challenges Harry Potter faces as he matures to adulthood, or the darker James Bond played by Daniel Craig versus the more tongue-in-cheek persona branded by Roger Moore. With *Star Wars: Episode III – Revenge of the Sith*, Lucasfilm had to manage a film where the bad guys win (Anakin Skywalker turns to the dark side and becomes Darth Vader), and most of the good guys die or are at best exiled in bitter defeat (one might even say "hopeless," were these not prequels and we did not already know about *Star Wars: Episode IV – A New Hope*).

A good campaign will recognize, beyond the goal of pure awareness, the challenge of its particular release, what demographics need to be wooed, and what anchor themes will serve as the messaging around which a myriad of independent brand events will be balanced.

552 *Pre-Release Window: Period Leading Up to Time Approximately 30 Days Pre-Release*

The following are some of the events that tend to fall into this window:

- teaser trailer
- teaser poster
- long-lead press (e.g., magazine articles, retrospectives)
- video rereleases
- launch trailers
- launch posters
- press junkets
- special events
- launch of blogs, social media pages, websites (or updates)
- seeded brand placements.

There is no "magic formula," and it is the job of marketing and PR departments to draw up innovative ideas and tie-ins. Trailers, posters, Web/social media sites and press events are somewhat standard fare and, while elements of artwork and messaging are not taken for granted, the system is already geared up to ensure these items effectively communicate a core branding statement. What this long-lead period affords for a mega-picture, however, is an opportunity for out-of-the-box initiatives

—promotions that, while likely requiring extra resources, can still be extremely cost-effective in terms of seeding brand- and/or film-specific awareness.

One of my favorite tie-ins related to *Star Wars* was a unique baseball promotion. Yankees–Red Sox baseball games are among the most fabled sports rivalries of all time, and the teams were heading into another season-ending collision (as it so happens, following a gut-wrenching game 7 playoff loss by the Red Sox the year before, which was to be avenged the next year with a World Series win). Some sportswriters had started calling the Yankees the "Evil Empire," and marketing tapped into this *Star Wars* analogy. During the last regular season series between the teams at the end of September, with the outcome likely to decide the playoff picture, Fox Sports aired an opening montage about the two teams. The montage was interspersed with film clips and, as an example, the long-haired and bearded Red Sox center fielder Johnny Damon appeared followed shortly by the hairy Chewbacca. The Fox Sports headquarters announcers, after introducing the clip, even held up a copy of a newly available DVD, which had an ancillary benefit of helping seed the market for the upcoming new film. A highly rated sports game was thereby leveraged as a tie-in to the film franchise, creating unique marketing exposure (in part because the network liked the idea and had fun with it, and also because of the common Fox ownership).

Sometimes, film franchises with a specific fan base, such as *Star Trek*, may lend themselves to conventions or promotional opportunities at industry conventions such as Comic-Con. Given the phenomenon of "trekkies," it makes sense to rally *Star Trek* fans in advance of the J.J. Abrams-directed prequels. This same strategy may not work on other sequels (e.g., *Bourne* films).

Finally, when a film is one in a series, it may make sense to reinvigorate the brand in the video market by releasing special editions or collector sets. MGM has done this effectively with *James Bond* sets, augmenting anticipation for a new film with new DVDs of the prior features. Similarly, Paramount released prior *Star Trek* films and series on Blu-ray for the first time in advance of its new prequel feature (2009). All of these activities help generate awareness for an upcoming release, and if clever enough will prepare the audience for new themes in the continuing franchise, while not yet tapping the core of the marketing budget reserved for advertising and other promotion closer to a film's launch. (Note: Depending on strategy, such DVDs may be delayed until the release window to tie in with other retail product launches.)

553

Release Window: Approximately 30 Days
Pre-Release Through First Two Weeks Post-Release

The following are elements often found in this window:

- launch of related merchandise
- commercials air/advertising in all media launches
- promotional partners' products hit shelves (with related advertising)
- media promotions (contests, giveaways, which can now also be executed via apps, and linked via social media sites)
- related video games release
- novelizations hit bookstores
- PR media blitz—talk shows, radio, review shows, stimulate blogs
- screenings
- prior films often play on TV
- websites and social media pages ramp up, add features (e.g., sneaks, making-of elements).

554   The most obvious and critical component in this window is advertising, which will saturate the market across all types of media. Beyond direct spending to achieve consumer impressions, this is also a time when marketing/PR will try to leverage other media or events (e.g., talent appearances) to the greatest extent possible. Guest appearances on late-night and morning talk shows are an obvious staple of the trade; special appearances, such as hosting *Saturday Night Live*, can further hype a release. Online efforts will attempt to push positive tidbits, enable sharing via social networking sites, support blogs, help spread favorable reviews from key influencers, and provide Web exclusives.

Also, this release window is when it is most likely that other parties will want to tie in with the movie franchise and devote their resources to cross marketing, leveraging the media awareness for the film to focus on its consumer product. Returning to *Star Wars: Episode III – Revenge of the Sith* for another example, Cingular (phone company) ran one of my favorite third-party advertisements around the movie's release. In the commercial, Chewbacca was doing his signature howl in an isolation booth for a recording producer. The producer asks him to do it this way, then that way ("that was great, now can I have a little . . .") and Chewbacca repeats the only howl sound that we ever hear from him.

Finally, returning to *Star Trek* again, Burger King tied into the release of the first prequel film (2009) and on the merchandising front new toys and games were set to launch in April, the month before the film's release. Given the significance of the franchise, not only was merchandise hitting shelves, but the studio worked to leverage direct retail support: augmenting an array of action figures, comic books, and other products, Walmart was selling a new line of *Star Trek* Barbie dolls.[25]

While on-shelf dates for merchandising can vary significantly, promoting toys and other product linked to a movie during this period has a twofold benefit similar to that found with promotional partners. On one level, there is an uplift in product sales given the surrounding media; further, though, in terms of kindling interest to see the film, kids who play with characters and learn about their background, or immerse themselves in related games, help spread awareness and virtually guarantee a measure of related ticket sales.

Post-Release Window: Approximately 30 Days Post-Release Through DVD and More

By this period, activity has waned and the number of initiatives launched is a fraction of those found in the pre-release and release windows. Nevertheless, there are still a number of elements likely to be launched, such as:

- sustain advertising
- special promotions
- DVD release(s)
- award campaigns (e.g., Oscars).

Once sustain advertising—taking advantage of reviews ("best of . . .") and awards—has run its course, the focus of the post-release window is not converting awareness into box office, but rather converting box office into DVD/Blu-ray sales, and now as importantly, VOD transactions. As noted in the video marketing section, DVDs do not have the same promotional tie-in potential as theatrical releases, but in instances with a big enough film (e.g., Papa John's Pizza and *Ice Age*), it is possible to diversify a campaign beyond traditional DVD retail marketing. Also, because of the size of the DVD market, this affords another opportunity to trot out stars for press junkets, tapping PR one last time (unless Oscar calls) before the activity winds down and marketing hibernates until long-tail re-promotion opportunities arise. It is important to note that the Web uniquely helps keep the long tail alive, as its relatively low cost basis enables dedicated websites and social media pages to post periodic updates and cater to core fans who want to continue touching base with the franchise—key elements are archived and easily accessible, allowing a baseline of information and engagement to be maintained almost indefinitely. When new promotional opportunities later mature, it is often to help launch awareness for the next title in the franchise, starting the described cycle over again; for properties without sequel potential, the sites nevertheless provide stimulus for retrospectives, reunions, anniversaries, and similar events used to stimulate sales and catalog churn.

Online Impact

- Virtually all movies and major TV shows have websites that cross-promote the program/film and provide value-added information and content (e.g., talent interviews, documentaries, mini-games).
- In addition to websites, releases now invariably have dedicated social media pages, often tying in engaging apps, advertising, and seeding content for virtual buzz; additionally microblogging sites such as Twitter are increasingly being used to disseminate information, and leverage celebrities followers.
- Online venues allow consumers to see trailers, which previously were only available in theaters and on TV as commercials/advertisements.
- An increase in online piracy has been an impetus for the global day-and-date releases of content.
- Online sites provide social networking abilities to chat, blog about, or identify with the characters and broader brand-sharing interest, videos, reviews, recommendations, or critiques with friends and virally to wider circles.
- Increasing amounts are being allocated to online campaigns, targeting specific demographics.
- Review sites aggregating critics' opinions, which serve to accelerate and homogenize the "verdict," typify a range of new information that could impact consumption choices.
- Content producers are striving to find ways to add interactive components to linear programming (text messages, online voting) and stimulate crossover online/offline engagement.
- Online sites are creating new opportunities for product placements, which, in addition to serving as sources of financing, may allow new types of functional integration (to the extent an avatar/character is changed by associating with the product).

556

- PR is being turned on its head, with electronic press kits having replaced physical kits and slides, and major announcements now often being released to fans on social media sites (either in place of or in addition to over the newswire).

557

Making Money

Net Profits, Hollywood Accounting, and the Relative Simplicity of Online Revenue Sharing

More content from this chapter is available at
www.focalpress.com/9780240824239

"Hollywood accounting" has become a somewhat infamous phrase, but in practice it simply takes effort to understand the jargon and rules. The greatest single area of confusion is the fact that the term "net profits" has no correlation to the concept of net profits that most companies use in a typical corporate income statement. Rather, the term net profits used in Hollywood contracts is a carefully crafted and defined term of art.

Because most people fail to peel back the onion and learn the nuances (which can be frustrating, and appear unfair devoid of context), an element of prejudice has been affixed to the calculation of profits in Hollywood contracts. There is a pervasive feeling that the studios and networks are "cooking the books": How else can a project earn over $100 million at the box office, sell successfully into large secondary markets such as TV and video, and be in the red? The answer is that under traditional income statements and/or tax accounting, the project may in fact be profitable, but that pursuant to a contractual profit-sharing definition (somewhat unfortunately also labeled net profits), the project still posts a loss.

This gulf creates the common perception that the accounting system is either rigged or unfair. In fact, the system, by many accounts, is very fair, if not generous. From the standpoint of the studio or network that would be paying out net profit participations, it is sharing the upside even though it may have taken all or most of the risk. In what other business proposition would you find the following formula: Party A takes on 100 percent of the financial risk, Party A knows that on the majority of its projects it may lose money, Party A takes no defined or preferred return on its investment before other participants share in the upside, and Party A shares 50 percent of the profits after a defined break-even point with its partner in the project? Nowhere.

This is the context behind why studios and networks have created padded profit-sharing definitions to protect the recoupment of their investment and build in an internal ROI factor before actually paying out profit-sharing; as disruptive online/digital trends put strain on the interplay of value drivers in Ulin's Rule, and by-title profitability comes under attack (as is evidenced from various sources described throughout the book, including the decline in the video market), the desire to protect profits and ensure recoupment becomes heightened. It is simply unfortunate that the resulting payout comes under the heading of net profits, for the use of the phrase is misleading relative to common sense and commonly applied methods of calculating profits in other business contexts. As far as a profit-sharing mechanism that protects the investor first, and shares an upside with the people that helped make the project a success, it makes perfect sense; the only debate, then, is whether the profit-sharing scheme is a good or poor one. The best way to understand "profits" definitions is to acknowledge that any reference to net or gross profits is a misnomer and instead refers to contractually defined schemes of contingent compensation (see Figure 10.1 depicting general structure).

If the system was not already confusing enough, the introduction of online revenues has the potential of creating another level of nuance —simply read the new talent guild agreements (see Chapter 7) where certain residuals are calculated as a percentage of "distributors gross receipts" and are applied, for example, on a sliding-scale basis tied to download volumes (with different tiers tied to different types of content such as TV versus features). Because the online world has evolved a relatively straightforward system of revenue sharing and is not beholden to the arcane Hollywood net profits system, the methods of calculating relative shares are on a collision course. I will discuss some of the implications later, and argue that the root of the problem is trust: net profits has become shackled and institutionalized by feeding on lack of trust between parties, while online revenue sharing has become commonplace and accepted because of the trust engendered by detailed, by-click, electronically tracked metrics. Is Hollywood more likely to challenge the revenues from online clicks by Google, or are the Googles of the new

559

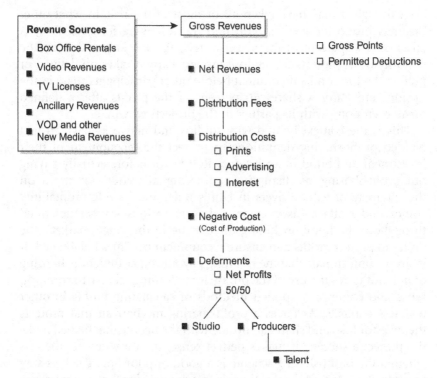

Revenue Sources

■ Box Office Rentals

■ Video Revenues

■ TV Licenses

■ Ancillary Revenues

■ VOD and other New Media Revenues

Gross Revenues

□ Gross Points
□ Permitted Deductions

■ Net Revenues

■ Distribution Fees

■ Distribution Costs
   □ Prints
   □ Advertising
   □ Interest

■ Negative Cost
   (Cost of Production)

■ Deferments
   □ Net Profits
   □ 50/50

■ Studio   ■ Producers
                  ■ Talent

Figure 10.1 Profit Participation Chain

millennium more likely to challenge the perceived revenue-sharing smokescreen thrown up by convoluted net profits definitions?

Finally, given the complexity of profit accounting, the following discussion primarily focuses on the context of film; nevertheless, the same general principles can apply to a network's profit participation accounting to a TV producer or a video on a made-for-video production.

Profit Participation Accounting

Profit participation accounting, which I need to emphasize is not "accounting" in the sense of GAAP or tax books, is simply a contractual revenue-sharing arrangement negotiated between parties; what started out as a rational basis of sharing risk is now usually discussed in pejorative terms (aka Hollywood accounting), and over time has evolved into a bit of an arcane science that I will try to decode.

One threshold point worth mentioning is that all participations are phrased in terms of "X percent of 100 percent of Y" such that 5 percent of net would contractually read "5 percent of 100 percent of the net profits of . . ." This is because net and gross profits are artificial methods of dividing up certain revenue streams and are based on limited pools of receipts and costs. To avoid ambiguity, the definitions are careful to stipulate that the percentage tapped into is 100 percent of the defined pool described—not just of the profits of the contracting party. If Party X were contracting for 10 percent of the profits, and the contract referenced profits as the share of financing entity Party Y (e.g., studio) that had 50 percent of the profits (with the balance going to the talent/production entity), then Party X would find they only had 5 percent of the total pool; whereas, if the contracts of Party X and Party Y both referenced a defined profit pool (100 percent of net profits, out of which they may share differently), then Party X's 10 percent stake is preserved.

Because the pool is shared by multiple people, and the calculations of different individuals are impacted directly by the participations of third parties, it is possible to only share in part of the pool; as described later, and making things even more complicated, it is further possible to share in only part of the revenues in part of the pool.

History of Net Profits

Whether true or not, Hollywood lore attributes the genesis of net profits to a deal made between Jimmy Stewart and Universal Pictures on the film *Winchester '73* in the early 1950s. Jimmy Stewart was already a major star, and his customary fee was deemed too high for the budget that Universal was willing to approve. Stewart's agent, Lew Wasserman, reportedly struck a deal that granted Stewart a share of the film's net profits in lieu of his customary above-the-line guaranteed fixed compensation/fee; in essence, Stewart became a partner with the studio, sharing the profits equally with the studio once the film had earned twice what it cost to make.

The key phrase is "in lieu," for in the original concept the sharing was a parceling of risk where the actor risked his or her salary, and on success reaped a large upside. Today, much, if not all, of that risk has been eliminated and major profit participants get large upfront fees plus share in a big chunk of the upside.

The trend started by Lew Wasserman is a bit ironic vis-à-vis his career. Wasserman, regarded as one of the true Hollywood moguls alongside the likes of Jack Warner and Louis B. Mayer, started the talent agency MCA, becoming an enormously powerful agent and defining the type of clout that is now taken for granted when referring to agencies such as CAA, ICM, and WME. Wasserman's agency later took over Universal, and Wasserman ran Universal as the last of the original Hollywood moguls until the sale of the company to Matsushita (Panasonic) in the early 1990s. (Note: Since then, Universal has changed hands several times, next to Seagrams, then to Vivendi, then to GE to form the combined NBC Universal, and most recently to Comcast). In his capacity as chairman of Universal, he sat on the other side of the table. One can only imagine what he thought about profit participations when Universal struck deals with leading talent, such as Steven Spielberg and Amblin Entertainment for *Jurassic Park*.

Net profits seemed to take a public turn in the 1990s with the cost of talent and budgets growing at an unprecedented pace. Maybe it was the combined growth of the video market, the international free TV market, and the global pay TV markets that gave participants a wake-up call: How could this avalanche of ancillary money be rolling in and pictures seemingly performing well still post losses? Whatever the reason, the concept of net profits, or lack thereof, seemed to start making its way into the headlines, and reached a peak with Art Buchwald's lawsuit against Paramount Pictures over his rights and participation in the film **562** *Coming to America*, starring Eddie Murphy.

Celebrity Lawsuits Spotlight Accounting Practices

Seemingly every few years, a new lawsuit brought by a celebrity alleging mistreatment in his or her profit participation catches media attention. On occasion, some of these suits delve into the nitty-gritty of net profits.

Art Buchwald v. Paramount Pictures in Case Involving the Film *Coming to America*

Probably no case has reached the fervor of *Art Buchwald v. Paramount Pictures*, a case in the 1990s that dragged on in the media and courts for several years. In his suit, Art Buchwald very publicly asked the question: How can this picture have grossed hundreds of millions of dollars and lose money? His claim and the underbelly of Hollywood's net profit accounting system were played out on the front page of *Variety* over the course of the trial. When Eddie Murphy referred to net profits as monkey points during the litigation, it tainted the perception of net profits as never before.

The case involved a treatment called *King for a Day* that Buchwald, a famous columnist and humorist (arguably the most famous humorist/political humorist at the time), wrote and optioned to Paramount (the development of which at the time fell, at least in part, under Jeffrey

Katzenberg). The same studio went on to produce the Eddie Murphy vehicle *Coming to America*, which Buchwald argued was based on his treatment. The court found that *Coming to America* was indeed based upon Buchwald's treatment, and then reviewed in detail the intricacies of net profits in the "accounting phase" of the trial. Among the reasons the case became a cause célèbre is that in the context of this mega-hit film that grossed over $350 million, where Buchwald was initially paid no participation and the studio argued was in the red, the court found "that certain provisions of Paramount's net profit formula were unconscionable."[1]

The book *Fatal Subtraction: How Hollywood Really Does Business*, written by Buchwald's legal team after the case, is a roller coaster ride through the trial, and is about as entertaining a read as one is likely to find concerning the world of net profits.[2]

Sahara Case—*Clive Cussler v. Philip Anschutz Company*

More recently, Clive Cussler, a best-selling author who had 19 consecutive *New York Times* bestsellers (and since, several more), was embroiled in a case over the movie *Sahara*, based on his book of the same name. The case, against Bristol Bay, one of the film companies within the Anschutz Film Group controlled by mogul Philip Anschutz (who also controls Regal Entertainment Group, consisting of Regal Cinemas, United Artists Cinemas, and Edwards Theaters, and *The Chronicles of Narnia* producer Walden Media), was primarily about Cussler's claims regarding his creative rights in the film. However, because of the people involved and the losses reported, the nature of net profits was again put in the limelight. All of the pieces were there for media drama: two high-profile stars in Matthew McConaughey and Penelope Cruz, a famous author in Cussler, a reclusive billionaire financier in Anschutz, an award-winning screenwriter, and even Michael Eisner's (former Disney CEO) son, Breck Eisner, as the director.

The *Los Angeles Times* wrote an exposé, with the headline: "How Do a Bestselling Novel, an Academy Award-Winning Screenwriter, a Pair of Hollywood Hotties, and a No. 1 Opening at the Box Office Add Up to $78 Million of Red Ink?"[3] What it detailed was simply how a movie with revenues of over $200 million was projected to lose approximately $80 million. Table 10.1 is a high-level summary of the net loss based on the numbers highlighted in the article.

The grist for the media was the public listing of star salaries and excesses on the film, but it again thrust the nature of Hollywood profit accounting into the public eye.

563

Table 10.1 Expenses and Net Loss for *Sahara* (Based on Projections for 10 Years, Through 2015)

Negative cost	$160 million
Print and advertising	$ 61 million
Home video costs	$ 21.9 million
Distribution fees	$ 20.1 million
Other	$ 18.2 million
Total expenses	$281 million
Total revenue	$202.9 million
Net loss	$ 78.3 million

Peter Jackson v. New Line in *The Lord of the Rings* Claim

Although it never led to the publishing of figures, as resulted in these cases of Buchwald and *Sahara*, the nature of net profits was thrust onto the front pages when Peter Jackson sued New Line Cinema in 2005. Fresh off his Academy Award wins and having catapulted into the superstar league with his *The Lord of the Rings* films, Jackson alleged that he was underpaid $100 million in net profits from the blockbuster trilogy, which grossed nearly $3 billion collectively. One eye-catching part of the claim was the argument that the studio used "preemptive bidding," allowing divisions within the vertically integrated corporate Warner Bros. group to obtain related rights (e.g., books, DVDs) rather than put them out to the competitive market. The battle, which became a public saga, and held up Jackson's willingness to be involved with the planned *The Hobbit* films, was eventually settled.

In the context of the lawsuit, the New York Times quoted former Carolco Pictures CEO (*Rambo* films), Peter Hoffman, as follows: "Once upon a time, Hollywood studios paid a lot of money to net profit participants, and it was a fair deal ... Then the studios got greedy and stopped paying, and now we have gross players who used to be net players fighting over vertical integration. The studios brought this problem on themselves."[4]

Why So Complicated—Endemic to the Talent System?

At some level, it is possible to argue that the complexity of profit definitions is a necessary outcome of needing to negotiate individual talent agreements. If talent were merely a commodity, akin to an assembly line input, and wage rates could be fixed, then everyone would accept a level of standardization; this is, in fact, what happens with most labor union contracts. However, there is a profound difference when dealing with experience goods of infinite variety with a parallel infinite range of variance in creative input. This is even harder than sports, which in many ways is the most similar market. At least in sports, it is possible to measure an individual's performance via objective metrics such as batting average, points per game, goals, or tackles. With experience good entertainment products, there is such a complex matrix of inputs and variable results that individual contributions are more subjectively measured. Key creative talent is therefore not considered fungible, and cannot easily be homogenized into standard compensation schemes. Even if this was not the case, ego and agents would argue that an individual's value is unique and must be measured on a one-off negotiated basis.

The result of one-to-one varied deals is not efficient for either side. It creates delays for talent, who are usually anxious to close deals rather than postpone them (as virtually all employment is on a per-project basis, and insecurity regarding landing the next project and/or being replaced by the new, younger, hotter X runs high). On the producer/ **565** distributor side, negotiating each deal not only creates an upfront overhead burden (plus the political anxiety of haggling with agents/ lawyers that can point fingers when deals fall through), but in accounting for contingent compensation they frequently have to customize reports and construct a labyrinth of deductions where one person's share is dependent on another's and another's . . .

I asked Jim Mullany, managing director of Salem Partners LLC, a Los Angeles-based investment bank and wealth management/advisory firm primarily involved in media and entertainment M&A advisory transactions and library valuations, if he ever envisioned a more simplified system, especially in light of new, growing revenue streams from new media and technology distribution platforms. He noted the following in confirming the underlying pressures that shape the current system:

While participation accounting is brushed off as a "Hollywood accounting," implying the worst meaning of the phrase, each participation statement that is rendered has to reflect the financial terms of the talent and financial contracts: the revenue and expense definitions, and the order and priorities of cost recoupment are spelled out in the negotiated contracts.

The accounting systems required to create monthly, quarterly, semi-annual, or annual participation statements (the timing of which is also contractually set out) are so massive and complex that many accounting departments have to revert to preparing statements manually using reported data from financial reporting systems from the various divisions (domestic and international) of the distribution company. Sometimes, the participation accounting department will have accumulated the unfiltered financial numbers for revenue and expenses, and must begin the manual customization of reports for each contractual party. They have to take into account:

- the many different definitions of what is reported as revenue, and what is reported as deductible or recoupable expenses;
- the variable distribution fees per source of revenue;
- calculation of contingent compensation paid to other participants are deducted if the contract specifies that priority;
- the addition of studio overhead surcharges to various expense categories, or not;
- surcharges on other costs and fees are to be included or excluded; and
- home video revenue is typically defined as a 20 percent royalty on gross adjusted wholesale video revenues; or an alternative for financial partners is to calculate video revenue as wholesale revenues less an allowance for returns, and then deduct costs of manufacturing, packaging, and shipping video units.

566

It is not uncommon for each member of the creative and financing team of a television or film project to have a different set of definitions for reporting revenue and expenses deducted, before the defined profitability is declared.

In an ideal world, a studio would insist on standard contract terms with uniform definitions for all contracts entered into by the studio. Unfortunately, those fixed, carved-in-stone standard terms would hold only until the studio tries to sign an "indispensable" talent element, and waives policy to craft an individualized contract reflecting more favorable terms negotiated by the talent agent or lawyer representing the indispensable creative talent. The contact terms would be negotiated section by section. The formerly standard template of participation accounting for back-end purposes and payment of contingent compensation would be modified henceforth.

Gross and Net Profits: How are They Defined and Calculated?

All studios and networks have similar gross profits and net profits definitions, but it is critical to remember that these vary by contract and are not fully standardized. The following parameters are industry custom, and have become "terms of art," but nuances exist and any profit participation can only be understood and administered by reference to its defining document.

Included and Excluded Revenues

A key to understanding net profits is to understand the baseline of what revenues are included in the calculation, and which revenues are excluded: *not all revenues are counted*. Film, video, and television revenues are all included in gross and net profits calculations; however, which specific revenues are captured (e.g., film rentals or box office), at what point they are captured (on television sale or broadcast), and what portion of revenues are counted (e.g., video wholesale or video royalty) are issues defined by contract.

Fully Included Revenues (A)

With respect to theatrical revenues, 100 percent of film rentals are included (see Chapter 4); no revenue retained by the exhibitor, even if the theater is an affiliate or directly owned by the studio, is included. Revenues from sales of films to television are similarly accounted for at 100 percent.

Allocations and Timing   A wrinkle on the inclusion of TV sales revenue is that it was (and still can be) common practice for films to be sold in packages. A studio will combine, for example, 15 to 30 films and receive an overall fee for the entire package. What revenue should be attributable to any particular film within the package (see Chapter 6)? This can be a hotly contested area, for allocations can swing revenues on a picture millions of dollars and the interests of the studio and producer may not be aligned.

In addition to allocation issues, television revenues can be subject to timing delays, setting back when revenues are accounted for and shrinking the upfront pool of revenues upon which profits are calculated. Whoever is responsible for paying participations (e.g., studios) may not be apt to adopt the GAAP revenue recognition rules (which accelerate the reporting of revenue over the term of the license in year one, as discussed in the following section). Instead, they will take the logical position of recognizing advances once holdbacks have expired and match the revenues to the term of the contract. Money in hand may not be counted until downstream when the broadcast it has secured takes place.

Partially Included Revenues (B)

Video revenues are included, but only a fraction of the actual video receipts are customarily put into the pot. As discussed in Chapter 5, video revenues are typically accounted for at only 20 percent, equating to a royalty on the gross revenues. Beyond segmenting only a fraction of video revenue for inclusion in profit calculations, the video revenue number is further reduced or delayed by the calculation of return reserves (see also Chapter 5). These reserves set back revenues, and only if and when they are liquidated are the amounts put into gross revenues (off of which the royalty will then be calculated).

Excluded Revenues (C)

Revenues from merchandising and theme parks are generally not included. Also, the following items are usually referenced as simply being excluded: theme park royalties, music and record royalties, books, and royalties derived from derivative works or the underlying material.

A + B + C = Baseline Revenue for Calculating Net Profits

Merchandising and Other Revenues as a "Separate Pot"

Sometimes certain ancillary revenues, such as from merchandising, will be put into a separate pot. In this instance, the participant will receive a separate accounting statement tracking the definition of revenues of that single revenue stream; a distribution fee may or may not be charged, and the timing of payment may be linked directly to the right or may tie into a separate definition (e.g., 5 percent of 100 percent of merchandising receipts, but only after such point as . . .). If there is a separate pot, these revenues need to remain separate, and not be included in the definition of revenues for net profits; otherwise they would be double counted.

Certain Costs Always Deducted

Certain costs are almost always deducted as "off-the-top" expenses for all participants. Even in the context of "gross" or "gross revenues," these terms are actually net of off-the-top expenses; the amount remaining after the off-the-tops are sometimes conceived of as "gross" in terms of the revenue line from which all participants then look to apply deductions or percentages of revenues. The following are standard categories of off-the-top expenses.

Trade Fees and Dues

The studios are members of trade associations that lobby on their behalf and also fight common issues such as piracy. The most well-known group, as referenced in several instances throughout this book, is the Motion Picture Association of America (MPAA). The MPAA maintains affiliated regional offices throughout the world, and plays a key role in lobbying foreign governments on laws impacting piracy and the protection of intellectual property (see Chapter 2) Another association is the Association of Motion Picture and Television Producers, Inc. (AMPTP). This organization, including all the major studios and independents, negotiates union agreements with the various Hollywood guilds (see Chapter 7 for a discussion of new media residuals impacting SAG and WGA negotiations, and leading to strikes). Associations such as the MPAA charge dues and assessments that cover legal and administrative costs, and the studios recoup this money by charging these costs back to pictures as an off-the-top deduction.

Checking

Checking here means costs borne by the studios to send "auditors" out to theaters to ensure that box office receipts (given the predominantly cash nature of the business) are accurately reported. Depending on clout, these costs are often capped. (Note: The cost of collecting money due is also typically an off-the-top.)

Duties, Tariffs, and Licenses: Conversion

These involve costs incurred to permit the exhibition of the picture in foreign territories and the associated costs to convert foreign currency to U.S. dollars, including related costs of converting and transmitting restricted funds (restricted funds are less applicable today given the global economy).

Residuals

These are the payments (see Chapters 2 and 7) required under union collective bargaining agreements (e.g., Screen Actors Guild, Writers Guild of America, Directors Guild of America) for use of the picture in media post its initial release medium (e.g., television following theatrical).

Taxes

This does not refer to income tax, but rather taxes of whatever nature that may be levied on the picture (e.g., relating to the exhibition).

Distribution Fees

Distribution fees are the not-so-hidden charges that compensate the distributor for its work in selling the picture and managing the license (including collections, delivery, and all related back-office functions). Rather than charging a mark-up on a per-product basis, the distributor charges a percentage on the revenues (akin to an agency fee). This percentage, in theory, is designed to: (1) cover the distributor's overhead cost of its sales and distribution infrastructure (including people/salaries and offices, as outlined in Chapter 1); and (2) provide the distributor a profit margin for its work (though many will argue it is only intended to cover costs).

Range of Fees

Distribution fees are charged on theatrical, non-theatrical, television, video, and merchandising receipts. The standard fees, although they will vary by distributor, tend to be in the ranges shown in Table 10.2.

When looking at these fees, it highlights the importance of below-market fees discussed in Chapter 3. If Producer X benefits from a 10 percent fee, then on $100 million of revenues it bears only $10 million,

Table 10.2

Revenue Stream	Distribution Fee
US theatrical	30%
Foreign theatrical	40%
US network TV	25%
US cable and syndication	35–40%
Home video	30–35%
Merchandising	50%

versus a party with a standard fee of 30 percent that would bear $30 million.

Sub-Distributors and Affiliates: Fees as Overrides

With respect to foreign exploitation, studios that do not have captive subsidiaries within a territory will distribute via an independent sub-distributor or an affiliate. The sub-distributor is a full-fledged distribution company, and will charge a distribution fee for its service. The corresponding risk is that the studio may receive a net amount that it reports as its gross receipts, and then charges its own fee on this sum. For example, a sub-distributor in Asia charging Studio X a fee of 20 percent receives $500,000; it would remit $400,000 to Studio X, who in turn would charge 40 percent ($160,000). The net into the pot is $240,000, even though $500,000 was taken in at source. Many contracts will accordingly negotiate either that: (1) the studio fee is inclusive of all sub-distributor fees; or (2) the studio takes a smaller override fee on receipts from the sub-distributor.

The concept of an override needs to be carefully defined. Depending on interpretation, it could mean a fee charged on the net amount remitted (akin to a commission) or a fee in addition to the sub-   **571**

Table 10.3

	($ million)	Assumptions
Box office gross	20.0	
Rentals	10.0	50% of box office
Sub fee	2.5	25% fee
Distribution expenses	4.5	
Revenue remitted	3.0	
Override commission	0.3	10%
Net receipts	2.7	
	($ million)	Assumptions
Box office gross	20.0	
Rentals	10.0	50% of box office
Sub fee	2.5	25% fee
Override	1.0	10%
Distribution expenses	4.5	
Revenue remitted	2.0	Revenue remitted = Net receipts

distributor's fee such that there is a cumulative fee; in the latter instance, the contract would define the total fee to be inclusive of any sub-distributor's fee. Table 10.3 is an example of how this subtle distinction can vary the participation.

At-the-Source Recognition

In the context of revenues that are earned in one locale and then remitted upstream, it is vital to pinpoint where and when revenues are captured. A simple example of how this can vary accounting is to consider how an advance is treated. A participant with clout will want to ensure that they are not disadvantaged by a sub-distributor guaranteeing an amount that ends up higher than the receipts taken in (this can occur when a guarantee is credited but not ultimately earned out), and having the reporting only reflect the actual territory receipts rather than the higher amount received by the studio. (Note: This scenario also raises timing issues. It can be debated whether the guarantee should be recognized when committed, paid, or earned out.)

Second, beyond an advance/guarantee scenario, a participant will want to account for revenue "at the source" simply to ensure it is capturing the greatest amount of revenue. The important rule when capturing items at a certain tier of distribution is to ensure symmetry, such that if costs are applied at the source, so are revenues.

In the case of a third-party foreign distributor (as opposed to a branch of the studio), the studio will report 100 percent of revenues received from the foreign distributor and take a fee on this "gross." In reporting to a participant, however, the cash to the studio is less than at the source gross, because: (1) the foreign distributor may deduct its distribution fee and expenses, with the net amount remitted to the studio being considered the gross receipts; and (2) there may be withholding taxes that further reduce the cash amount tendered. The amounts accounted for become exponentially skewed if there is more than one level of sub-distribution, which can occur absent contractual caps and prohibitions.

To account at the source, the revenues received by the sub-distributor from exploiting the property would be considered gross and then any deductions would be applied from this point. Accordingly, if there were a distribution fee applied, it may be aggregated with any fee of the studio (capped so that the aggregate fee is no greater than X); alternatively, the studio may simply apply an override to sub-distributor remittances.

Expenses should be treated in a similar manner, such that if receipts are captured at the source, then expenses are applied at this level as well.

A corollary to this issue is how costs of affiliates are treated; some may argue that these are not arm's length transactions and the studio can arbitrarily elect to use its own affiliates at rates it establishes. There is, of course, danger for abuse, but checks and balances can be put in place, such as requiring the same (or no worse than) rate card pricing as charged to unaffiliated third parties.

Distribution Costs and Expenses

The "off-the-tops" described previously are simply a subset of the overall category of distribution expenses that are deducted by the distributor. In general, the distributor will be allowed to deduct any and all expenses relating to the distribution and exhibition of the picture. This will be expressed contractually in a catch-all phrase covering monies paid, advanced or incurred by the studio "in connection with the distribution, exhibition, marketing, and exploitation of the picture." The only carveout is that these costs relate to the sale of the picture and are not part of the costs of making the picture. While this sounds straightforward, as mentioned earlier issues can arise such as whether trailers are a production or distribution expense (although the foregoing is routinely accepted as a distribution cost). The principal costs other than off-the-tops are in the following sections.

573

Prints and Physical Materials

The costs of prints, duplicate prints, masters, etc. are obviously a large and legitimate expense (and, as discussed in Chapter 4, part of the impetus for D-cinema, which holds the promise beyond presentation improvements of eliminating the bulk of these costs). The key here is to capture the actual costs, which, when charges go down to the level of tape stock (which may not be easily separable on a per-film basis), can be tricky.

Advertising

This is perhaps the largest single cost relating to distributing a film. "Advertising" is a catch-all for advertising, marketing, and promotional costs, and includes subcategories such as the following:

- publications, including local and national trade and consumer press (e.g., newspapers)
- television, radio, online, mobile advertising
- screenings
- artwork

- promotional materials (e.g., free giveaways)
- trailers
- travel and entertainment costs of marketing executives.

Negative Cost

"Negative cost" means the cost of creating the finished product; namely, the cost of production through to the final delivered film negative. When people are asking the simple question: "What did it end up costing?" the answer will be: "The negative cost was X." As mentioned in a few sections, what costs are included in negative cost can be subject to debate. For example, should advances against gross participations be included in costs, and again where is the line between production costs and distribution costs (e.g., a foreign-language master)?

Other Distribution Costs

Other distribution costs may include the following:

- dubbing and subtitling costs for foreign versions
- shipping and delivery costs (significant in delivering prints to theaters)
- insurance
- copyright registration and protection costs and expenses
- litigation related to the property/picture (e.g., copyright infringement claims).

Gross Participations, Deferments, and Advances as Cost Items

Deferments

A deferment is simply a payment that is agreed to be made in the future, but is tied to the occurrence of a specified event. That event could be something like box office reaching two or three times the negative cost, or when a break-even point with a specified fee (e.g., imputing a reduced distribution fee) occurs. Deferments are a type of contingent compensation since they are not guaranteed, but are usually structured to kick in at a point deemed more certain than the point at which net profits would be due.

Deferments are also a way to skirt budget items, as certain compensation to above-the-line talent may be taken out of the budget to hit a magic mark for green-lighting the project, while promising the dollars at a point that everyone expects to attain. If there is a perceived risk involved, then the deferment will likely be higher than the upfront guaranteed compensation would have been (this also makes sense, since the payment is also delayed).

Gross Participations as a Cost Item

Participations payable before net profits are due, such as gross participations, may sometimes be added into the cost of production and treated as part of the negative cost for the purposes of calculating net profits. As further illustrated, this can obviously have a profound impact on net profits ever being realized.

Advances

Advances are often lumped in with deferments, but are different because a deferment generally refers to the timing of paying a fixed sum, whereas advances are tied to a variable contingent element. The contingent element is the back-end, and by paying a portion of that contingent back-end as a non-refundable advance, the scheme of Hollywood accounting basically turns a contingent payment into a guarantee. A star, for example, may take a budgetary cash fee of $2 million, which is structured as an advance against his or her back-end. While this methodology may have no ultimate impact on the participant (other than accelerating compensation), it can have a profound impact on third parties whose participations are subject to recoupment of production costs; as discussed further, by accelerating the payment, the $2 million goes into the salary/production cost line, thereby increasing the production costs that are then further increased by both overhead and interest, setting back the point of recoupment for all non-gross participants.

Imputed Costs: Production and Advertising Overhead, Interest

Advertising Overhead

Salaries of studio personnel working on advertising and marketing for the picture are not allowable charges. However, it is customary to add an advertising overhead charge (e.g., 10 percent), which is a gross up of the total advertising costs deducted. Some may find this unfair, and argue that the studio's distribution fee is supposed to cover overhead costs, but the advertising overhead fee is generally accepted as a standard provision in net profits definitions.

Interest on Negative Cost

In addition to the negative cost and the administrative fee, the studio will also charge interest on the cost of production from the time the costs were incurred until the production costs are fully recouped. This interest cost is charged whether or not monies are actually borrowed to make the film. Often studios will self-finance, but the argument is there was an opportunity cost and that the studio has, in effect, loaned the money to itself.

Interest costs can add up quickly because costs of production are so high: 7 percent on $50 million is a large number, and interest continues to be recalculated on the unrecouped production costs and then becomes an additional cost to be recouped. Because interest is recouped first (banks are usually at the head of the line), there is a compounding effect of interest delaying recoupment: interest continues to accrue on unrecouped production costs, such that receipts may pay down interest charges but during the same period new interest is accruing on the production costs. This interest treadmill is made more cumbersome from the participant's standpoint to the extent interest is also charged on the overhead added to production costs; further, timing issues can exacerbate interest charges. Does interest accrue from the time expenses are committed or actually paid, and similarly are advances counted into receipts to pay down/stop interest or only recognized when earned?

Overhead Gross Up

In addition to the actual costs, it is customary to add a standard gross up to cover elements of studio overhead, similar to the advertising overhead fee discussed previously. Here, the net profits definition will invariably state that an administrative fee of 15 percent of the cost of production (excluding this fee) will be added to the cost of production. Accordingly, the negative cost is really the cost of production plus 15 percent.

Phantom Revenues: Allocating Taxes and Other Non-Picture-Specific Items

Allocations are always a hotly debated element given the tension between subjective calls inherent in the nature of allocations and what participants want to believe are "exact" costs in accounting. When properties are bundled and fees and/or costs need to be apportioned, what should the formula be (e.g., straight-lined based on relative box office, or another formula)?

Rebates

In the case of rebates, these may be part of a multi-picture deal, where a supplier may grant preferential terms to a customer based on a variety of factors, including length of term and volume of business. Most will consider overall incentive deals as part of the cost of doing business and not allocable on a line-item basis; however, others will dispute this and argue that any rebate incentive must be pro-rated or otherwise allocated back on a by-title basis and passed along.

Taxes/Tax Credits

Many countries impose withholding taxes on remittances of royalties (e.g., Japan), which are triggered because the intellectual property basis of the content means payments are remitted via a license. Moreover, these taxes can be challenging to assess because their application involves both the individual picture and the ultimate tax position of the entity bearing the withholding tax. When withholding taxes have been applied against a specific picture attributable to a specific license, then arguably a corresponding matching tax credit ought to be applied to the picture (the concept being that per tax treaties, a party should not be "double taxed" such that if you bear the tax locally, it should be offset by a tax credit on your corporate taxes). The problem is the utility of such tax credit is tied to the company's overall tax situation, and whether it avails itself of that tax credit is dependent on its corporate tax profile and not the individual transaction.

If, for example, a $1 million license is subject to a 10 percent withholding tax given the tax treaty between the United States and Country X, such that only 90 percent of the license fee is remitted and 10 percent is captured via a tax credit matching the deduction (i.e., a $100,000 tax credit), should the licensee that has 90 percent of the cash reported be grossed up to 100 percent? While the answer may seem a simple yes, issues of "if and when" are significant because at the time of remitting the 90 percent, the distributor/licensor may not know whether it will use the corresponding tax credit. The decision will be determined by unrelated factors, including whether it is even eligible (it needs sufficient overall profits to claim the credit in the first place) and then, if eligible, what strategy is deployed in its overall corporate tax planning. For its part, the content owner bearing the 10 percent with-holding tax is likely to only account for the 90 percent received, arguing it has no control over the withholding (governed by law/tax treaty) and it may or may not use the tax credit (a likely scenario if high production costs/investment and revenues are not matched in timing).

Net Profits: An Artificial Break-Even Point and Moving Target

Net profits are the point at which gross receipts have recouped: (1) distribution fees; (2) distribution expenses; (3) interest on the cost of production; (4) the negative cost, including the studio's overhead fee; and (5) gross participations and deferments payable prior to net profits.

Net profits basically track the definition of initial actual break-even (see later): the point at which gross receipts, from the sources of revenues that are counted toward gross receipts, equals the total costs on the project, including any imputed costs that are included in the definition of costs. The difference between net profits and initial break-even is that with net profits, there is no fixed stopping point; new distribution costs and fees paid or incurred are applied with each accounting period, and continue to "roll" forward. Accordingly, with each accounting period, additional costs, fees, and revenues are thrown into the equation, and the "net profit" line calculated anew. Table 10.4 is an example.

578   Table 10.4 Net Profit Calculation A

Revenues and Costs	Assumptions	Net Profit Calculation ($ million)
Cost of production	$35 million	
Box office	Gross box office	$200 million
Film rentals	Assume 50 percent of box office	$100 million
Distribution fees	Assume 35 percent on average	$35 million
Distribution costs		$45 million
Prints	$10 million	
Advertising	$35 million	
Interest on negative cost	Assume 10 percent	$3.5 million
Total negative cost (cost of production + overhead allocation)	Cost of production + 15 percent studio overhead on costs	$40 million
Profit/loss		($23.5 million)

Gross Participations/Profits

There are multiple types of gross participations, but in general a gross player receives money at a defined point prior to net profits. It could be as early as "first dollar gross," which means participating at the same time that the studio takes money without deductions (although, even in this rare case, individuals are still customarily subject to the "off-the-top" deductions detailed earlier).

The key to gross participations is that distribution fees, print and advertising costs, and costs of production—the major expense categories in making and releasing a film—are not deducted. Individuals participating in true gross profits literally earn a percentage of the defined gross revenues with hardly any deductions at all.

Table 10.5 is an example, comparing the previous net profit participation scenario to one where talent has a 10 percent gross participation.

Table 10.5 Net Profit Calculation B—with Gross Participant

Revenues and Costs	Assumptions ($ million)	Net Profit Calculation
Cost of production	$35 million	
Box office	Gross box office	$200 million
Film rentals	Assume 50 percent of box office	$100 million
Gross participant	Assume 10 percent gross points	$10 million
Distribution fees	Assume 35 percent on average	$35 million
Distribution costs		$45 million
Prints	$10 million	
Advertising	$35 million	
Interest on negative cost	Assume 10 percent	$3.5 million
Total negative cost (cost of production + overhead allocation)	Cost of production + 15 percent studio overhead on costs	$40 million
Profit/loss		($33.5 million)

Impact of Categorizing Costs as Production versus Distribution Costs

Timing

As discussed in the section on advances (page 575), as well as what charges are included within the negative costs, the line between what is a production versus distribution cost may be dependent on timing and contractual definitions; this is because the line is not always clear. Is a trailer a production item? Are certain masters or prints such as foreign language versions properly distribution cost items? If talent delays payment to the back-end, are these fees part of the cost of the picture, and is it fair that advances against a back-end instead are categorized as production costs that then are grossed up by an overhead component and are subject to interest?

In general terms, timing can create a relatively clear line—any costs to get to a finished negative can be construed as a production, and all subsequent costs (foreign masters, dubbing, etc.) for other versions would be distribution expenses.

580

Online Accounting: Simple Revenue Sharing and the Net Profits Divide

Gross is Gross and Net is Net—Sort of

The online world has not yet descended into the complexity of net profits seen in film and TV, and to date employs relatively straightforward definitions of gross and net revenues. In the context of sorting out what sources of advertising maximize the value of their content, this new breed of distributor (whether online ad streaming or downloads) has been first grappling with what is an appropriate revenue split of the resulting advertising mix. To a degree, the corollary question of how a participant (e.g., writer, director) is compensated from this pot has been deferred because the participant in this case is more often than not simply the producer, and the revenue share and participation one and the same.

As far as gross and net are concerned, there are few exclusions from "gross." However, it is possible to segment a website and exclude certain sections or categories (e.g., Yahoo! News could be treated differently from Yahoo! Sports); similarly, certain overall revenues, such as run-of-site advertising, may not be counted on a particular subsection of a website where the revenue sharing/deal is focused on targeted revenues from a discrete area of the site. When thinking about this question, it is easy to postulate how much more complex it could grow, but the dissection has not yet occurred, and generally "gross is gross."

In terms of calculating net profits, there will be various contractual deductions from gross, but again this area has not evolved excruciating complexity. It is more typical to find limited deductions, such as for direct third-party costs incurred (e.g., ad serving fees), but also typical to employ a catch-all percentage deduction from gross to capture the basket of administrative and third-party costs incurred in serving, hosting, tracking, and reporting revenues. Paralleling the treatment of gross revenue recognition, costs are lumped in a rational range and not reallocated back on a line-item basis and subject to allocation scrutiny. Therefore, "net is net" and more generally accepted given parties believe the ability to track by impression results in accuracy and transparency. The question is, however: Is that really the case when baskets of costs are lumped together?

What has happened is that the ability to track costs and revenues at a more detailed level has engendered a culture of trust, even though the ultimate reporting often does not reflect the greater level of detail that the metrics conceptually enable. In the end, actual participant reporting can be just as detailed (if not more so) in film and television even though the information being cumulated is less precise. It will be interesting to watch whether this anomaly continues.

Revenue Sharing

Regarding how to split the revenue, the issues are not dissimilar to the economic analysis in determining what percentage of video revenues should be paid—either as a profit split or royalty—to the content owner/producer (see Chapter 5). What has started to evolve in the online space is a formula of revenue sharing, where parties negotiate a split such as 60/40 or 70/30, with the majority to the producer if the site's share is deemed tantamount to a distribution fee. In the video context, one of the issues in setting formulas is whether true net revenues ("off-the-top" revenue splits) can be tracked and audited, and licensors often default to a royalty basis to approximate what they expect a split to be given the easier monitoring and auditing. The online world, however, is premised on detailed metrics (cost per click, CPM, unique visitors, etc.) and the ability to drill down and share true, actual revenues and costs is assumed.

Again, this underlies one of the fundamental differences the online space is forging: because of the detailed metrics, there is implicit trust in the system, and the accuracy (even, arguably, veracity) of the revenue splits. Simply, people trust and accept revenue sharing. This is in stark contrast to the traditional media world, where skepticism of profit splits and accounting has evolved the byzantine system of net profits discussed throughout this chapter and has provided a subtext to Hollywood guild strikes and stalemates. Actors and writers, in an attempt to provide certainty in the context of where they mistrust accounting, want guarantees of what they will be paid online, as well as assurance that the accounting includes revenues attributable to online usage of their work. Revenue sharing is anathema if some of the revenues to be shared may not be included in the pot in the first place.

Is all this trust properly placed when, in fact, there are a myriad of issues that can arise online, ranging from fraudulent clicks/impressions to allocations of delivery/bandwidth costs? There are only two logical next steps: either online revenue sharing, which to date has been relatively straightforward, becomes more complicated (e.g., "gross revenues" are more finely sliced, and delivery and infrastructure costs allocated) or everything becomes simpler and the "trust in revenue sharing" spreads from Silicon Valley to Hollywood, and everyone accepts simple division of the pie (e.g., 70/30 split of gross revenues, where gross retains its common sense, all in, meaning).

582

What I believe is likely to develop is a hybrid weighted toward the current Internet structure: the Internet world will not stand for a convoluted net profits system, and economic reality is that "gross" and "net" are not as simple as "gross" and "net," and there will be important and legitimate tweaks that need to be made in accounting. I believe this is already taking shape in deals with a Web component, and a simplified system premised on revenue sharing of a straightforward definition of net profits will become the de facto standard.

I turned again to Jim Mullany (from Salem Partners) for his opinion regarding what I am labeling the net profit divide. In terms of whether there would be an element of convergence in accounting given new media delivery systems, he noted that in terms of downloads-to-own, online viewing services such as Hulu, and yet to be invented services, there would be a shift in the revenue versus expense construct; namely, the costs to generate revenues (e.g., advertising, usage fees, subscription fees) would be nominal because only a digital version of the program needs to be provided to the host service, no physical good is delivered to the end consumer, and nothing is manufactured (and therefore not subject to packing, shipping, and inventory logistics). However, he advised that this shift would not so easily lead to a shift in how profit accounting is treated, given the incentives and strong institutional forces at play:

This streamlining of the distribution process should help simplify financial participation reporting for revenue and costs for these sources for a studio or property owner's financing partners and creative talent involved in the project, who have a stake in the "back-end" (contingent compensation) based on the terms of their employment contracts—whether it be a percentage of adjusted gross revenue or adjusted gross proceeds, or a percentage of a defined net profit.

The reality, however, might be different.

- The company providing the delivery service (Netflix, Hulu, Amazon, Comcast, et al.) in the current and announced projects (other than the network websites) will take a fee from gross revenues for providing their delivery service.
- There is no uniform standard digital format requiring the preparation of multiple digital masters.
- Depending on the contractual agreement with the delivery service, there may be a reimbursement or recoupment of the service provider's advertising and promotional costs, along with amounts or percentages for operating overhead.
- There will likely be recoupable costs associated with the sale and collecting of advertising revenues.
- SVOD has inherent tracking and reporting problems in the fair/contractual allocation of subscription revenues to suppliers of product.
- It is also conceivable, and now probable, that the company owning the "pipe" that provides the signals to the home or business will take a slice of gross revenues generated from the consumer and/or the delivery service as a fee for providing the DSL or wireless signal, and allowing the delivery service to provide a high-quality signal or priority streaming access.

However, assuming all the above issues didn't exist—if the revenue streams were very easy to track and collect, the idea of simplifying the profit participation equation is counter to the usual way that studios and/or distributors operate. Typically, the more complicated (causally defined as "creative") the structure of the cash flow waterfall, and opaque the definitions of standard terms, the better.

Accordingly, an industry observer can easily conclude that it is in the studio's best financial interest to keep the contract process and the reporting as complex and opaque as possible. Participation accounting for new streams of revenue and related costs therefore will be interpreted and inserted into templates already established, until a talent guild negotiates different contract terms with the distributors/studios that will define it otherwise. That is why video-on-demand (whether it be from downloading, streaming, or other delivery variations), pay-per-view, and other new media utilized for home viewing of filmed entertainment will be considered as "home video" revenues for participation reporting purposes rather than "television" revenue. These revenue streams will be calculated to the studio/distributor's benefit as a 20 percent royalty based on gross adjusted revenue, rather than a gross revenue subject to deduction of identifiable costs.

But what happens when a company such as Netflix, which started as an aggregator of video to become the leader in video rental, morphs into a kind of pay TV operator, with its subscription aggregation model competing with the likes of HBO and content deals being harmonized with the pay window? Does that mean revenues jump in reporting from 20 percent to 100 percent? Rationally, 100 percent of revenues from Netflix should flow into the gross revenue pot, but as revenues from DVDs overall are declining, there are institutional pressures to try to maximize cash flows at all levels. Conceptually, there are many more battles to be fought as the landscape shifts.

Variations of Profit Participation

Types of Break-Even

Break-even, in theory, is the point of recoupment of all actual costs expended in making and releasing a picture. Depending on the definition, a participant may receive funds with or without additional charges applied. There are at least three types of break-even concepts routinely utilized.

Initial Break-Even (aka Initial Actual Break-Even)

Conceptually, initial break-even is the point at which costs are initially recouped, or in other words, the point when gross receipts equals the aggregate of expenses on the project. The expenses that need to be recouped have all been previously discussed: (1) distribution fees; (2) distribution expenses; (3) negative cost, including the studio's overhead fee and interest on the cost of production; and (4) gross participations and deferments payable before or at initial break-even. Initial break-even is essentially the same point at which net profits are first due.

This creates a trigger point defining which costs are subsequently deducted; for example, a participant that has a right to gross proceeds kicking in once initial break-even is reached will not have additional distribution fees or expenses (save standard off-the-tops) deducted. Essentially, the adding on of additional costs and fees stops at initial break-even for participants that have a gross participation or deferment starting at initial break-even.

Cash Break-Even

Cash break-even differs from initial break-even in that there will often be a reduced negotiated distribution fee; this is, in theory, because the distribution fee includes a profit margin element that is backed out with a reduced fee. Since cash break-even is only granted to players who command a participation in something better than net profits, gross participants and deferments are generally not deducted. Cash break-even is reached when there are gross receipts available to recoup: (1) the distribution fee; (2) distribution expenses; (3) interest; and (4) the negative cost, including the studio's overhead fee. Similar to initial break-even, once this point is reached no further distribution fees and expenses are charged. Although at one level it may seem cash break-even ought to exclude imputed overhead and a distribution fee, some distribution fee and overhead charge needs to be factored in to cover the costs of distribution and production management; the studios are carrying real and significant overhead to bring the product to market (see, again, Chapter 1).

Talent that receives a participation at "cash break-even zero" bears no distribution fee (i.e., the zero fee), and are pushed back only by the film's cost and its distribution expenses (P&A). To the extent they are also not bearing any gross players, and talent has taken a reduced fee betting on their back-end gross points, there may be some juggling. For example, if an A-level star who customarily receives some form of gross participation takes a small cash fee in the budget (e.g., to help get the picture made), then for the purpose of someone else's cash break-even zero deal there may be an amount imputed to the budget on the theory the budget is artificially low; namely, the studio needs to account for the fact that it is paying out significant sums to talent, which need to be deducted at some level before the other participants.

585

Adjusted Gross and Rolling Break-Even

Adjusted gross refers generically to an intermediate type of participation, which has elements worse than first dollar gross and better than net. This can mean there has been a reduced negotiated distribution fee, including a zero fee; typically, however, adjusted gross means that: (1) there is a modified distribution fee; and (2) major distribution expenses, including print and advertising costs, are deducted.

Comparison Website

For additional discussion of adjusted gross, rolling break-even, how net profits may be modified by over-budget penalties, and schemes applying box office bonuses in lieu of profit participation, please refer to the comparison website. This supplementary material also includes a section on how producers' shares may be reduced by bearing participants (applying hard and soft floors), as well as a section on how GAAP and tax accounting (e.g., capitalization rules) differ from profit participation accounting.

586

Online Impact

- Online contracts tend to employ simple revenue-sharing models, rather than complicated net profits.
- Online metrics directly track revenues, by click or impression, without allocations; if allocations are applied, they tend to be off-the-top percentage fees to capture costs of ad serving and related third-party costs.
- The culture of online contracts tends to grant much less audit protection/rights: trust the clicks and metrics. Will this continue? It remains to be seen whether online metrics are quite as trustworthy as they appear.
- Online revenue share splits tend to track distribution fee splits (e.g., distributor retains 30 percent, content owner 70 percent), where content owner's share is treated as gross vis-à-vis sharing percentages with third-party contributors (if there are participants).
- It will be interesting to see how baskets of revenues, which are historically treated differently as regards inclusion in gross revenues (e.g., video versus TV), are impacted by online companies and sources that blur market lines (e.g., should Netflix revenues be treated as video revenues or akin to pay TV?).

References

Chapter 1

1. "Deliverance from Deliverables," *Hollywood Reporter*, May 25, 2010.
2. *Avatar* estimates, "Delivery from Deliverables, *Hollywood Reporter*, May 25, 2010.
3. Motion Picture Association of America Theatrical Market Statistics: Worldwide Box Office Reaches Historic High, www.mpaa.org/researchstatistics.asp; *Motion Picture Theater Industry Statistics 1965–1999*, 5th edition, Cambridge University Press, 2001, by Harold Vogel, Chapter 2, "Movie Macroeconomics, Entertainment Industry Economics."
4. "Around the World in One Movie: Film Financing's Global Future," *New York Times*, December 5, 2011, by Nicholas Kulish and Michael Cieply.
5. Regarding *Life of Pi*, *Box Office Mojo* reports foreign box office representing 80.3 percent as of March 4, 2013, after the picture's Oscar bump and near the end of its run, having debuted in November 2012; see www.boxofficemojo.com.
6. *The Da Vinci Code*'s International box office as a percentage of the worldwide total of 71.3 percent, pursuant to www.boxofficemojo.com/alltime/world.
7. "Summer Movies: End of the World as We Know it?" *Wall Street Journal (Market Watch)*, May 4, 2012, by Russ Britt.
8. "Hollywood Studios Fined for Price Fixing," *Variety*, May 11, 2006.
9. "Studio 3 Networks Announces Epix, the New Brand in Consumer Entertainment," *Reuters*, January 27, 2009.
10. Based on information from MPAA Theatrical Market Statistics, 2012. Rentrak Corporation – Box Office Essentials.
11. "Movies Try to Escape Cultural Irrelevance," *New York Times*, October 28, 2012, by Michael Cieply.
12. "Label-It Is," *Variety*, March 19–25, 2007.
13. "Label-It Is," *Variety*, March 19–25, 2007.
14. www.mpaa.org/researchstatistics; the MPAA has not publicly updated these figures, but SNL Kagan estimates the average negative cost of a major studio motion picture was $72.4 million in 2010 and $66.6 million in 2011—see also Chapter 4 (data provided by SNL Kagan, a division of SNL Financial).
15. "White-Knuckle Summer," *Variety*, January 22–28, 2007.
16. *Hit & Run*, Simon & Schuster, 1996, by Nancy Griffin and Kim Masters.
17. "The Economics of Awful Blockbuster Movies," *The Atlantic*, July 11, 2013, by Derek Thompson. Highlighting the top 25 films by US/Canada Box Office

587

earned in 2012 citing source: Rentrak Corporation, Box office Essentials, CARA (Rating).

18. "Gauls Digital Dilemma," *Variety*, October 13, 2012, by Elsa Kislassey.
19. "Movie Biz on the 'Bubble'—'Bubble' Triple Bow Biz Inconclusive," *Variety*, January 30, 2006.
20. "Window Treatments," *Variety*, March 1, 2006.
21. "Comcast and IFC to Offer On-Demand Day-and-Date Premieres of Independent Theatrical Films," Comcast press release, February 28, 2006.
22. "Sundance 2012: The Day-and-Date Success Story of *Margin Call*," *Hollywood Reporter*, January 18, 2012, by Daniel Miller.
23. "Morgan Freeman Movie Might be Coming to a PC Near You," *USA Today*, February 8, 2006.
24. "European Movie Chains Boycott Major Releases," *Arts Technica*, February 6, 2007; "British Exhibitors Shut *Museum*—Fox Punished for Breaking Window," *Variety*, February 1, 2007.
25. "Universal Aborts *Tower Heist* VOD Plan," *Variety*, October 12, 2011, by Josh L. Dickey and Andrew Stewart.
26. "Universal Drops Early Video-on-Demand Plan for *Tower Heist*," *Los Angeles Times*, October 13, 2011, by Richard Verrier.

588 Chapter 2

1. *Adventures in the Screen Trade*, Warner Books, 1983, by William Goldman.
2. "How Pixar Fosters Collective Creativity," *Harvard Business Review*, September 2008, by Ed Catmull.
3. "NBC Pulls the Plug on *Quarterlife*," *Variety*, February 28, 2008.
4. "ABC Gives Web Moms a Chance at the Tube," *Business Insider, Silicon Valley Insider*, May 19, 2008, by Michael Leamonth.
5. "*Drunk History* Web Series Heads to TV With Presentation Order by Comedy Central; Will Ferrell and Adam McKay to Produce," *Deadline TV*, April 5, 2012, by Nellie Andreeva.
6. "Comedy Central Picks Up *Tiny Apartment* Pilot Based on Web Series," *Deadline*, July 25, 2012, by Nellie Andreeva, www.deadline.com/2012/07/comedy-central-picks-up-tiny-apartment-pilot-based-on-web-series.
7. "Nickelodeon Confirms *Fred* Series, Picks Up Pilot, Sets Premiere for *How to Rock*," *Deadline*, January 14, 2012, by Nellie Andreeva, www.deadline.com/2012/01/nickelodeon-confirms-fred-series-picks-up-pilot-sets-premiere-for-how-to-rock/.
8. U.S. Constitution, Article 1, Section 8.
9. Title 17, U.S. Code, § 102.
10. Title 17, U.S. Code, § 106.
11. Title 17, U.S. Code, § 107.
12. "Judge Again Rules for Youtube in Viacom Suit," *The Hollywood Reporter*, April 19, 2013, by Eric Gardner.
13. Grokster, p. 10, citing *Sony Corp. v. Universal City Studios*, supra, at 442.
14. Grokster, pp. 23–24.

15. *Cartoon Network et al. v. CSC Holdings, Inc. and Cablevision Sys. Corp.*, No. 071480-cv (L) (2d Cir. August 4, 2008), available at www.ca2.uscourts.gov: 8080/isysnative/RDpcT3BpbnNcT1BOXDA3LTE0ODAtY3Zfb3BuLnBkZg==/07-1480-cv_opn.pdf#xml=http://www.ca2.uscourts.gov:8080/isysquery/irl7d48/2/hilite; "Second Circuit Reverses Cablevision Case; Hold Remote DVR Service Not Directly Infringing," Wilson Sonsini Goodrich & Rosati client alert, August 2008.

16. "Fox Appeals Ruling on Dish's AutoHop," *Variety*, December 16, 2012, by Ted Johnson.

17. "Google's Brin, Others Rail Against House Antipiracy Bill," *SNL Financial LC*, December 15, 2011, by Kyle Daly; "Tech Titans Fights Hollywood-Backed Antipiracy Bill," *San Francisco Chronicle*, December 15, 2011.

18. "E.U. Lawmakers Reject Antipiracy Treaty," *International Herald Tribune*, July 5, 2012, by Eric Pfanner.

19. "TV Networks, Aereo Face Off in Court . . .," *Hollywood Reporter*, May 31, 2012, by Eriq Gardner.

20. "Aereo Says People Have a Legal Right to Rabbit Ears and DVRs, Countersues the Big TV Networks," *Venture Beat*, March 13, 2012, by Ben Popper.

21. "News Corp. to Take Fox Off Air if Courts Back Aereo," *Bloomberg News*, April 9, 2013, by Andy Fixmer.

22. "Now CBS is Threatening to Become a Cable Channel if Aereo isn't Shut Down," *Venture Beat*, April 10, 2013, by Tom Cheredar.

23. "What are Patents, Trademarks, Servicemarks, and Copyrights?"—"What is a Trademark of Servicemark?" www.upsto.gov/web/offices/pac/doc/general/whatis.htm.

24. "Anti-Piracy"—"Who are They?" www.mpaa.org.

25. "Piracy Data Summary," 2005, www.mpaa.org/researchstatistics.asp.

26. www.mpaa.org/resources/5a0a212e-c86b-4e9a-abf1-2734a15862cd.pdf.

27. "New Wave of Pirates Plunders Hollywood—Streaming Videos are the Latest Threat," *International Herald Tribune*, February 6, 2009, by Brian Stetler and Brand Stone.

28. "The Nerd Who Burned Hollywood," *Hollywood Reporter*, May 11, 2012, by Daniel Miller and Matthew Belloni.

29. "Some Pirates are More Equal than Others—New 'Piracy Continuum' Splits Offenders into Five Groups," *CommunicAsia*, June 18–July 1 issues, by Janine Stein.

30. "Anti-Piracy"—"Piracy and the Law," www.mpaa.org.

31. EdiMA is an alliance of Internet and new media companies whose members include Amazon EU, Apple, eBay, Expedia, Google, Microsoft, MIH Group, Nokia, Yahoo!, Orange, and others. EdiMA's members provide Internet and new media platforms offering users a wide range of online services, including the provision of audiovisual content, media, e-commerce, communications, and information/search services. EDiMA represents the interests of the Internet and new media sector in Europe in policymaking, standards development, and industry cooperative activities.

32. www.forbes.com/sites/erikkain/2012/05/09/hbo-has-only-itself-to-blame-for-record-game-of-thrones-piracy/.

589

Chapter 3

1. U.S. Theatrical Market Statistics, 2007, www.mpaa.org.
2. "A $500 Million Film Ain't What it Used to Be," *USA Today*, January 13, 2006.
3. "White-Knuckle Summer," *Variety*, January 22–28, 2007.
4. http://en.wikipedia.org/wiki/List_of_most_expensive_films.
5. "Avatar's True Cost—and Consequences," *The Wrap*, December 3, 2009, by Josh Dickey, citing Adams Media Research by request of *The Wrap*.
6. "Bebo's Online Drama Fans in for a Shock," *Guardian*, January 16, 2008, by Mark Sweney.
7. Nielsen: State of the Media—Spring 2012, Advertising and Audiences, Part 2: By Demographic, http://nielsen.com/content/dam/corporate/us/en/reports-downloads/2012-Reports/nielsen-advertising-audiences-report-spring-2012.pdf.
8. "Ratings Service Will Count the Web," *International Herald Tribune*, February 23–24, 2013, by Brian Stelter.
9. *Creative Industries*, Harvard University Press, 2002, by Richard Caves, p. 179.
10. Comparing AP, January 10, 2013, "Box Office Numbers for Oscar Best Picture Nominees," as reported by Yahoo! News versus Box Office Mojo 2012 Yearly Box Office Results, boxofficemojo.com and http://movies.yahoo.com/news/box-office-numbers-oscar-best-picture-nominees-220520933.html.
11. *Creative Industries*, Harvard University Press, 2002, by Richard Caves, pp. 178–179.
12. "Uncertainty in the Movie Industry: Does Star Power Reduce the Terror of the Box Office?" *Journal of Cultural Economics*, 1999, 23: 285–318, by Arthur De Vany and David Walls. © 1999 Kluwer Academics Publishers. Printed in the Netherlands.
13. "Spielberg Predicts 'Implosion' of film Biz," *The Hollywood Reporter*, June 13, 2013, by Paul Bond.
14. "*Ranger* Could Lead to $150 Million Loss For Disney," July 8, 2013, *The Hollywood Reporter*, by Pamela McClintock; see also footnote 22, Chapter 4, regarding *John Carter*.
15. "Slate Debate: Investors Now Get to Pick and Choose," *Variety*, February 24, 2012, by Rachel Abrams.
16. "Heavy Hitters Pick Up Slack as Studios Evolve," *Variety*, February 24, 2012, by Marc Graser; "Slate Debate: Investors Now Get to Pick and Choose," *Variety*, Febraury 24, 2012, by Rachel Abrams; "Fox Extends Film Finance Partnership with Hedge Fund Dune Capital," *Hollywood Reporter*, November 29, 2010; "From IndyMac to One West: Steven Mnuchin's Big Score," *Business Week*, March 22, 2012, by Karl Taro Greenfeld; "Jeff Sagansky-Led Film Fund to Invest in Up to 16 Movies," *Los Angeles Times*, August 2, 2011; "Film Financier Faces a Critical Juncture," *New York Times*, February 3, 2013, by Brooks Barnes and Michael Cieply (article regarding Legendary Entertainment and Thomas Tull); "Universal, Legendary Pair Up in New Five-Year Deal," *Variety*, July 16, 2013, by Marc Graser.
17. "Other People's Money," *International Variety*, January 23–26, 2006.
18. "Other People's Money," *International Variety*, January 23–26, 2006.

19. "Defying the Odds, Hedge Funds Bet Billions on Movies," *Wall Street Journal*, April 29, 2006.
20. "Defying the Odds, Hedge Funds Bet Billions on Movies," *Wall Street Journal*, April 29, 2006.
21. "Defying the Odds, Hedge Funds Bet Billions on Movies," *Wall Street Journal*, April 29, 2006.
22. "Legendary Entertainment Nears Raising $250 Million in Financing," *Los Angeles Times*, March 28, 2012.
23. "Sea Change at Hollywood Newbie: *Poseidon* Capsizes Fund," *Variety*, May 16, 2006.
24. "Sea Change at Hollywood Newbie: *Poseidon* Capsizes Fund," *Variety*, May 16, 2006.
25. "Sea Change at Hollywood Newbie: *Poseidon* Capsizes Fund," *Variety*, May 16, 2006.
26. "Old Studio Moguls Find New Future in Hedge-Funding Financing," *International Herald Tribune*, November 20, 2006.
27. "Slate Debate: Investors Now Get to Pick and Choose," *Variety*, February 24, 2012.
28. *International Herald Tribune*, May 18, 2006.
29. PR Newswire, DreamWorks release, August 26, 2002.
30. "Legendary Seals $700 million in Film Financing," *Financial Times*, June 5, 2011, by Matthew Garrahan.
31. "Studio Nabs Lower Interest Rates to Reduce Debt Load and Costs After Box Office Wins for *The Hunger Games, Twilight*," *Hollywood Reporter*, July 12, 2012.
32. "In Boost for Hollywood, Village Roadshow Secures $1 Billion in Financing," *New York Times*, May 27, 2010, by Brooks Barnes.
33. "Can *Polar Express* Make the Grade?" *Business Week*, October 20, 2004.
34. "As Others Shun Hollywood, FedEx Founder Bets on Movies," *International Herald Tribune*, July 22, 2008, by Brooks Barnes.
35. "How Kickstarter Works," www.kickstarter.com.
36. "Bret Easton Ellis is Using Kickstarter to Finance *The Canyons* Indie," *Hollywood Reporter*, May 4, 2012, by Erin Carlson.
37. "Crowdfunding Sites Launch a Preemptive Strike on Fraud," *Business Week*, April 9, 2012, by Karen Klein; "Obama Signs Bill Easing Securities Laws for Start-Up Firms," *Business Week*, April 5, 2012, by Phil Mattingly and Roger Runningen.
38. "Around the World in One Movie: Film Financing's Global Future," *New York Times*, December 5, 2011, by Nicholas Kulish and Michael Cieply.
39. "As Lucas Goes Digital, Will He Ditch Hollywood?" *Business Week*, April 27, 2001, by Ron Grover; "Fox Feels the Force," *Entertainment Weekly*, April 17, 1998, by Judy Brennan, www.ew.com.
40. "As Lucas Goes Digital, Will He Ditch Hollywood?" *Business Week*, April 27, 2001, by Ron Grover.
41. SEC S-1 Filing: The primary result of giving pro forma effect to the Distribution Agreement as of January 1, 2003 is that we recognize revenue net of (i) DreamWorks Studios' 8.0% distribution fee and (ii) the distribution and marketing costs that DreamWorks Studios incurs for our films, July 21, 2004.

42. "Spielberg Severs Paramount Ties," *International Herald Tribune*, October 7, 2008.
43. "DreamWorks in Deal with Universal," *New York Times*, October 14, 2008.
44. "DreamWorks and Disney Agree to a Distribution Deal," *New York Times*, February 10, 2009, by Brooks Barnes and Michael Cieply.
45. "The *Mad Men* Economic Miracle," *New York Times*, December 4, 2012, by Adam Davdison.
46. www.the-numbers.com/movis/2006; www.abc.net.au/news, November 10, 2006.
47. "International Treaties," Special Section, *Hollywood Reporter*, November 20, 2008.
48. "*The Hobbit*: Should We Have Paid? Majority Back $67 Million in Tax Breaks Given for *The Hobbit*, as Bank Estimates $1.5 Billion in Revenue Retained," *New Zealand Herald*, January 9, 2013, by Issac Davison.
49. "States' Film Production Incentive Cause Jitters," *New York Times*, October 12, 2008.
50. "States' Film Production Incentive Cause Jitters," *New York Times*, October 12, 2008.
51. "States' Film Production Incentive Cause Jitters," *New York Times*, October 12, 2008.

592   Chapter 4

1. www.mpaa.org/statistics.
2. www.boxofficemojo.com.
3. "Movie Theater Deal: When Genius Merged," *Forbes*, June 22, 2005; "Movie Theaters of the Absurd," *Forbes*, March 2, 2001.
4. "The Phantom of the Megaplex," *CFO*, January 1, 2001.
5. "Megaplex Mania," *USA Today*, November 17, 2005
6. "The Phantom of the Megaplex," *CFO*, January 1, 2001; "Movie Theaters of the Absurd," *Forbes*, March 2, 2001; "The Multiplex Under Siege," *Wall Street Journal*, December 24–25, 2005.
7. MPAA Theatrical Marketing Statistics, 2012.
8. "Fox Eyes End to 35 mm Film Distribution in U.S.," *Hollywood Reporter*, April 25, 2012, by Pamela McClintock.
9. MPAA Theatrical Market Statistics, referencing HIS Screen Digest.
10. "Can This Man Save the Movies? (Again?)," *Time*, March 20, 2006.
11. "D-Cinema Grows Under Carmike, Christie Pact," *Hollywood Reporter*, December 20, 2005.
12. "Hollywood Rebounds at the Box Office," *New York Times*, January 23, 2012, by Brooks Barnes; "Box Office Milestone: Daniel Craig's *Skyfall* Crosses $1 Billion Worldwide," *Hollywood Reporter*, December 30, 2012, by Pamela McClintock; MPAA Theatrical Marketing Statistics, 2012.
13. "3D Day—D'Works Ani *Monsters* is Biggest Push into New Realm," *Hollywood Reporter*, March 25, 2009, by Carl DiOrio.
14. "B.O. Mid-Year Report: What's Worrying Hollywood," *Hollywood Reporter*, July 1, 2012, by Pamela McClintock.

15. "Theaters Slow to Warm to 3D, Dispute Over Upgrades Threatens Hollywood's Big New Bet," *Los Angeles Times*, January 13, 2009, by Brooks Barnes.
16. "3D Day—D'Works Ani *Monsters* is Biggest Push into New Realm," *Hollywood Reporter*, March 25, 2009, by Carl DiOrio; "Strong *Monsters* Feeds Hollywood's 3D Hopes," *Wall Street Journal*, March 30, 2009, by Lauren Schulker.
17. Regarding *Avatar*, "Avatar is New King of the World," *Box Office Mojo*, January 26, 2010, by Brandon Gray, noting that, at time of breaking *Titanic*'s all-time worldwide box office record, "*Avatar*'s 3D presentations have accounted for 72 percent or $1.35 billion of its total gross. Breaking that down, 3D's domestic share is 80 percent, and its foreign share is 69 percent."
18. MPAA Theatrical Market Statistics, Worldwide Digital 3D Screens, referencing HIS Screen Digest.
19. "Box Office Milestone: Daniel Craig's *Skyfall* Crosses $1 Billion Worldwide," *Box Office Mojo*, as reported by the *Hollywood Reporter*, December 30, 2012.
20. "*Battleship* Underwhelms with $25.3 Million Stateside," *Variety*, May 20, 2012, by Andrew Stewart.
21. Box Office: *Avengers* Helps Sink *Battleship*," *Los Angeles Times*, May 20, 2012, by John Horn.
22. www.boxofficemojo.com/movies/?id=johncarterofmars.htm, May 28, 2012.
23. "Movie Theaters of the Absurd," *Forbes*, March 2, 2001.
24. "Apple Turns to Indies to Buoy iTunes Film," *International Herald Tribune*, October 24, 2007.
25. "Apple Turns to Indies to Buoy iTunes Film," *International Herald Tribune*, October 24, 2007.
26. "*Madagascar* Downgrades Slow DWA," *Hollywood Reporter*, June 1, 2005; four-day opening box office, www.boxofficeguru.com.
27. "*MIB3* Opens Biggest, but Doubts Remain," *Hollywood Reporter*, May 29, 2012, by Pamela McClintock.
28. www.boxofficeguru.com.
29. "*Sith* Degrees of Separation," *Variety*, May 30, 2005.
30. "Chinese Cinema Firm Bo buy AMC in $2.6 Billion Deal," *Los Angeles Times*, May 20, 2012, by Richard Verrier.
31. "China's Film Market is Proving Tough for Foreign Studios to Crack," *Economist*, April 28, 2012.
32. "China B.O. Revenue Hits $2.7 Billion in 2012," *Hollywood Reporter*, March 22, 2013, by Pamela McClintock.
33. "China's Film Market is Proving Tough for Foreign Studios to Crack," *Economist*, April 28, 2012.
34. "Foreign Box Office: *Titanic 3D* Unsinkable No. 1 Overseas After Sensational China Debut," *Hollywood Reporter*, April 15, 2012.
35. "China Woos Hollywood Studios with Film Fund," *Associated Press*, March 8, 2012, www.cbc.ca/news/arts/story/2012/03/08/china-hollywood-film-fund-co-production.html.
36. "Boost for Hollywood Studios as China Agrees to Ease Quota on U.S. Films," *Guardian*, February 20, 2012, by Mary Hennock.
37. www.mpaa.org/resources/5bec4ac9-a95e-443b-987b-bff6fb5455a9.pdf.
38. www.mpaa.org/resources/5bec4ac9-a95e-443b-987b-bff6fb5455a9.pdf.

593

Chapter 5

1. "Studios' Digital Revenue Will Grow 15 Percent a Year," *Video Business*, May 20, 2008, by Susanne Ault; "Studios Editing Video Strategy," *Los Angeles Times*, June 16, 2008, by Dawn Chmielewski; 2004 home video sales accounted for 51 percent of studios' top-line revenues, Kagan Research estimates.
2. www.museum.tv/archives/etv/h/htmlh/homevideo/homevideo.htm.
3. *Sony Corp. v. Universal City Studios* 464 U.S. 417, 104 S. Ct. 774, 78 L.Ed. 2d 574 (1984).
4. "A History of Home Video and Gaming Retailing," *Entertainment Merchant Association*, www.entmerch.org/industry_history.html.
5. "A History of Home Video and Gaming Retailing," *Entertainment Merchant Association*, www.entmerch.org/industry_history.html.
6. "*Lion King* Rules at Retail," *Billboard*, October 18, 2003.
7. "*Finding Nemo* DVD/Video Sales Reach 20 Million," *USA Today*, November 17, 2003.
8. *Communication Technology Update*, 11th edition, by August E. Grant and Jennifer H. Meadows, Focal Press, 2008, Chapter 14, "Home Video."
9. "2004 Video Wrap," *Hollywood Reporter*, January 19, 2005.
10. http://en.wikipedia.org/wiki/list_of_disney_direct-to-video-films.
11. "*Scorpion 2* Latest Direct-to-Video Prequel," *Reuters*, August 7, 2008.
12. *International Herald Tribune*, December 31, 2007–January 1, 2008.
13. "Sony Prevails in Format War," *International Herald Tribune*, February 20, 2008.
14. "Sony Prevails in Format War," *International Herald Tribune*, February 20, 2008.
15. "Consumer Spending on Home Entertainment Up in First Half of 2012," *Hollywood Reporter*, July 29, 2012, by Thomas Arnold; "Blu-Ray Grows, but DVD Slide Nips Home Video Sales," *USA Today*, January 9, 2012.
16. "For Home Entertainment Releases, a Rare Bright Spot," *New York Times*, October 30, 2011, by Michael Cieply.
17. *Communications Technology Update*, 11th edition, by August E. Grant and Jennifer H. Meadows, Focal Press, 2008, Chapter 14, "Home Video," p. 197, citing K. Gyimesi (December 19, 2006); "Nielsen Study Shows DVD Players Surpass VCRs," *Nielsen Media Research*, retrieved March 12, 2008 from www.nielsenmedia.com.
18. www.entmerch.org/industry_history.html.
19. "Big Green for *Shrek* Vid," *Mania*, November 6, 2001.
20. "Video Slips as DVD Market Matures," *USA Today*, January 4, 2006.
21. "Year End Wrap," *Variety*, December 26, 2005–January 1, 2006.
22. "Studios Editing Video Strategy," *Los Angeles Times*, Business Section, June 16, 2008.
23. "DVD Market Down 5.7 Percent in 2008," *Hollywood Reporter*, January 14, 2009, by Georg Szalai.
24. "Year End Review," *Variety*, December 26, 2005–January 1, 2006.
25. "How DreamWorks Misjudged DVD Sales of its Monster Hit," *Wall Street Journal*, May 31, 2005.
26. www.redbox.com/facts.
27. "Coinstar: Still Money in the Bank," *Barrons*, December 1, 2011, by Andre Bary.

28. "Coinstar: Still Money in the Bank," *Barrons*, December 1, 2011, by Andre Bary.
29. www.redbox.com/facts.
30. "Redbox Agrees to Buy NCR/Blockbuster Kiosks as Revenue Surges," *Los Angeles Times*, February 6, 2012.
31. "Redbox to Acquire NCR's Blockbuster Express for $100 Million, Boast 'More Locations than McDonald's And Starbucks Combined'," *Fast Company*, February 6, 2012, by Austin Carr, quoting Gary Cohen, SVP marketing and customer experience at Redbox.
32. "Universal Keeps Peace with Redbox, spurning Warner Bros.," *Los Angeles Times*, March 1, 2012.
33. "Netflix Delivers 1 Billionth DVD," *Associated Press*, February 25, 2007; www.entmerch.org/industry_history.html.
34. "Is Netflix Good for Hollywood?" *Hollywood Reporter*, January 19, 2011; "Netflix Recovers Subscribers," *Wall Street Journal*, January 26, 2012, by Stu Woo and Ian Sherr.
35. $304.17 on July 13, 2011 and $62.37 on November 30, 2011 www.nasdaq.com/symbol/nflx/historical.
36. "Netflix Messes Up," *Economist*, September 24, 2011.
37. "Under Fire, Netflix Rewinds DVD Plan," *Wall Street Journal*, October 11, 2011, by Stu Woo.
38. "Netflix Recovers Subscribers," *Wall Street Journal*, January 26, 2012, by Stu Woo and Ian Sherr.
39. "Netflix Recovers Subscribers," *Wall Street Journal*, January 26, 2012, by Stu Woo and Ian Sherr.
40. "By the Numbers: Netflix Subscribers," www.news.yahoo.com, July 26, 2013, also referencing The Associated Press, also ir.netflix.com, July 26, 2013.
41. "Is Netflix Good for Hollywood?" *Hollywood Reporter*, January 19, 2011.
42. "Is Netflix Good for Hollywood?" *Hollywood Reporter*, January 19, 2011.
43. "Is Netflix Good for Hollywood?" *Hollywood Reporter*, January 19, 2011.
44. "Netflix Losing Starz Play: Over 1,000 Starz Movies, TV Shows to be Cut," *Huffington Post*, February 27, 2012, as told to *All Things D*.
45. "Is Netflix Good for Hollywood?" *Hollywood Reporter*, January 19, 2011.
46. "Netflix, Disney Sign Deal for Streaming," *Hollywood Reporter*, December 5, 2012, by Paul Bond.
47. "Netflix Signs Streaming Deal with Time Warner," *Wall Street Journal*, January 7, 2013, by John Jannarone and Shalini Ramachandran.
48. "Netflix Messes Up," *Economist*, September 24, 2011.
49. "Netflix—Undoing the Mess," *Economist*, October 10, 2011.
50. "Is Netflix Good for Hollywood?" *Hollywood Reporter*, January 19, 2011.
51. "Netflix Signs Streaming Deal with Time Warner," *Wall Street Journal*, January 7, 2013, by John Jannarone and Shalini Ramachandran.
52. http://jobs.netflix.com/jobs.html, Q2 2012.
53. "What's Driving the Box Office Batty—Hollywood is Pushing Movies to DVD and Video Faster—and Theaters Feels Squeezed," *Business Week*, July 11, 2005.
54. "British Exhibitors Shut *Museum*: Fox Punished for Breaking Window," *Variety*, February 1, 2007.

55. "How DreamWorks Misjudged DVD Sales of its Monster Hit," *Wall Street Journal*, May 31, 2005.
56. *Video Business*, Carl DiOrio, June 2, 2005.
57. "Feds Shred *Shrek* Prove," *Variety*, May 5, 2006.
58. "End of the DVD Party? First DreamWorks' *Shrek 2*, now Pixar's *The Incredibles*. Retailers are Shipping Back Scads of Unsold Copies. A Bad Plot Twist for Tinseltown," *Business Week*, July 2, 2005.

Chapter 6

1. FCC's Review of Broadcast Ownership Rules, as outlined in a Consumer Acts summary on the FCC website, www.fcc.gov/ownership.
2. www.bloomberg.com/news/2012-09-25/nielsen-cuts-u-s-tv-homes-by-500-000-on-census-shift-to-web.html.
3. Comcast Spotlight's West Regional VP of Integrated Media, Chip Meehan, "On-Demand Summit: Comcast Sets Up for 'Hockey Stick' Jump in VOD Advertising," *Multichannel News*, June 20, 2012, by Todd Spangler.
4. "State of the Media: Cross-Platform Report," *Nielsen*, Quarter 3 2012 (US).
5. "Spike's 'Star' Wattage—Cable Net Pays Up to $70 Million for Six Franchise Pics," *Variety*, October 19, 2005, by Denise Martin and John Dempsey.
6. "Nets Share Window on *Worlds*," *Variety*, February 26, 2006.
7. "FX Acquires *Girl with the Dragon Tattoo, Mission Impossible*," *Broadcasting & Cable*, January 5, 2013, by Lindsay Rubino; "FX Acquires *21 Jump Street, The Lorax*," *Broadcasting & Cable*, March 20, 2012, by Andrea Morabito.
8. Pilot Programs, Museum of Broadcast Communications, www.museum.tv/archives/etv/P/htmlP/pilotprogram/pilotprogram/htp.
9. Pilot Programs, Museum of Broadcast Communications, www.museum.tv/archives/etv/P/htmlP/pilotprogram/pilotprogram/htp.
10. "Focus: 2009–2010 Pilot Season—Back on Auto Pilot," *Hollywood Reporter*, March 6, 2009, by Nellie Andreeva.
11. "He Has a Hot TV Series, a New Book—and a Booming Comedy Empire," *Time*, September 28, 1987.
12. www.fundinguniverse.com/company-histories/the-carseywerner-company-llc-company-history.html.
13. "*Sopranos* and *Sex and the City* Estimates," *Broadcast & Cable*, January 11, 2007.
14. "*Office, Earl* Land at TBS," *Variety*, June 21, 2007.
15. "7-Week Itch: USA Nabs *NCIS: LA*," *Hollywood Reporter*, November 6, 2009, by James Hibberd and Nellie Andreeva.
16. "TNT Acquires Off-Network Rights to *Hawaii Five-O*," *Hollywood Reporter*, April 14, 2011, by Kimberly Nordyke, noting "low-to-mid $2 million range."
17. "A+E's Raven Calls Out Rivals in Upfront Speech," *Hollywood Reporter*, May 10, 2012, by Marisa Guthrie.
18. "7-Week Itch: USA Nabs *NCIS: LA*," *Hollywood Reporter*, November 6, 2009, by James Hibberd and Nellie Andreeva.
19. "*The Good Wife* Off-Network Rights Sell to Amazon, Hulu, Hallmark Channel, Broadcast Syndication for Nearly $2 Million an Episode," *Deadline*, March 13, 2013, by Nellie Andreeva.

20. *"The Good Wife* Off-Network Rights Sell to Amazon, Hulu, Hallmark Channel, Broadcast Syndication for Nearly $2 Million an Episode," *Deadline*, March 13, 2013, by Nellie Andreeva.
21. www.museum.tv.archives/etv/f/htmlf/financialint/financialint.htm.
22. www.fundinguniverse.com/company-histories/the-carseywerner-company-llc-company-history.html.
23. "Digital Media Brings Profits (and Tensions) to TV Studios," *New York Times*, May 14, 2006.
24. "Cable Hits the Wall," *Variety*, July 9–15, 2007.
25. "The *Mad Men* Economic Miracle," *New York Times*, December 4, 2012, by Adam Davidson.
26. "The *Mad Men* Economic Miracle," *New York Times*, December 4, 2012, by Adam Davidson.
27. "Sooner Than Expected, CBS Largely Finishes Upfront Sales," *New York Times*, June 7, 2013, by Stuart Elliott.
28. "Turner Wraps Upfront Business—Broadcast Still in Motion," *Adweek*, June 19, 2013, by Anthony Crupi.
29. "Nets Face Muddled Metrics—Upfronts Unsettled by Ad Agony," *Variety*, April 2–8, 2007.
30. "Even With Record Prices, Expect $10 million Super Bowl Ad.," Forbes.com, February 2, 2013, by Alex Konrad.
31. Copyrighted information of the Nielsen Company, licensed for use herein.   **597**
32. www.nielsenmedia.com.
33. www.nielsenmedia.com.
34. www.nielsenmedia.com.
35. "New Rules Roil the Ad Biz," *Variety*, July 9–15, 2007.
36. "Battle Over Dish's Ad-Skipping Begins as Networks Go to Court," *New York Times*, May 24, 2012, by Brian Stelter.
37. "Battle Over Dish's Ad-Skipping Begins as Networks Go to Court," *New York Times*, May 24, 2012, by Brian Stelter.
38. "Fox, CBS, NBC Sue Dish Over Auto Hop," *Hollywood Reporter*, May 25, 2012, by Matthew Belloni.
39. "New Rules Roil the Ad Biz," *Variety*, July 9–15, 2007.
40. "New Rules Roil the Ad Biz," *Variety*, July 9–15, 2007.
41. "A Game-Changing Season," *Ad Age*, August 6, 2007, www.mediakid.adage.com.
42. Neilsen: State of the Media—Spring 2012, Advertising & Audiences, Part 1: Primetime by Genre.
43. "Nets Face Muddled Metrics—Upfronts Unsettled by Ad Agony," *Variety*, April 2–8, 2007.
44. "Ratings Service Will Count the Web," *International Herald Tribune*, February 23, 2012, by Brian Stelter.
45. "As Seen on TV," *Wired*, October 2008.
46. "As Seen on TV," *Wired*, October 2008.
47. "comScore Releases January 2013 U.S. Online Video Rankings," *comScore*, February 21, 2013.

48. "Twitter and Nielsen devise TV ratings," *Financial Times*, December 17, 2012, by Emily Steel and Tim Bradshaw.
49. "HBO GO iPad App Gets Interactive *Game of Thrones* Treatment," *PC Magazine*, March 29, 2012, by Mark Hachman.
50. www.forbes.com/sites/erikkain/2012/05/09/hbo-has-only-itself-to-blame-for-record-game-of-thrones-piracy.
51. "Seeing HBO's *Girls* Without Buying Television," *New York Times*, May 25, 2012, by Brian Stelter.
52. "NBC Launches Olympics Apps," *Hollywood Reporter*, July 13, 2012.
53. Gary Zenkel, president of NBC Olympics, as quoted in "NBC Launches Olympics Apps," *Hollywood Reporter*, July 13, 2012.
54. "The Final Numbers Are in . . . Olympics a Huge Success for NBC," NBC press release, reproduced in *Sports Media Journal*, August 13, 2012.
55. "Fox Feeds HBO's Film Fix," *Variety*, July 9, 2007.
56. "Is Netflix Good for Hollywood?" *Hollywood Reporter*, January 19, 2011.
57. "Netflix, Disney Sign Deal for Streaming," *Hollywood Reporter*, December 5, 2012, by Paul Bond.
58. "Amazon and Epix Strike Movie Deal; Netflix Shares Drop," *Reuters*, September 4, 2012, by Alistair Barr.
59. "Fox Feeds HBO's Film Fix," *Variety*, July 9, 2007.
60. "Scouring the Vaults," *Variety*, October 2–8, 2007.
61. "HBO and the Future of Pay TV: The Winning Streak," *Economist*, August 20, 2011.
62. "HBO and the Future of Pay TV: The Winning Streak," *Economist*, August 20, 2011.
63. "Netflix to offer $11.99 Family Plan, Beats HBO in Subscribers," Forbes.com, April 22, 2013.
64. "Pro7 Inks Deal with WBITTV," *Hollywood Reporter*, February 23, 2007.
65. "Private Equity Firms Win German TV Bid," *International Herald Tribune*, December 15, 2006.
66. "FT-Orange Lures Auds to Pay TV," *Variety*, March 4, 2009.
67. "France's Competition Authority Approves Canal Plus Takeovers with Restrictions," *Hollywood Reporter*, July 23, 2012, by Rebecca Leffler.
68. "Encyclopedia of Company Histories: TaurusHolding GMbH & Co. KG.," www.answers.com/topic/taurusholding-gmbh-co-kg.
69. "Kirch Creditors Line Up for First Payments," *Hollywood Reporter*, January 23, 2007.
70. "How the Mighty Fall," *Time*, April 15, 2002.
71. European Cover Story, "The Fall of Leo Kirch," *Business Week*, March 11, 2002.
72. "How the Mighty Fall," *Time*, April 15, 2002.
73. European Cover Story, "The Cartoon King," *Business Week*, May 10, 1999.
74. International Edition Cover Story, *Business Week*, May 10, 1999.
75. "German Firm to Buy Henson for $680 Million," *Los Angeles Times*, February 22, 2000.
76. "Zounds! EM.TV Slips on Ice (International Edition)," *Business Week*, November 6, 2000.
77. European Cover Story, "The Fall of Leo Kirch," *Business Week*, March 11, 2002.

598

78. "Private Equity Firms Win German TV Bid," *International Herald Tribune*, December 15, 2006.

Chapter 7

1. "At Stake in Viacom vs. Google Lawsuit: Future of Media—Defining Ownership in an Age of Fluid Content," *Ad Age*, March 18, 2007, by Abbey Klaassen.
2. "The Nerd Who Burned Hollywood," *Hollywood Reporter*, May 11, 2012, by David Milles and Matthew Belloni.
3. "Four Guilty in Web Piracy Case," *Wall Street Journal*, April 18, 2009.
4. "Internet to Revolutionize TV in Five Years," *Reuters*, via Yahoo! News, January 27, 2007.
5. "U.K. Commission Confirms BSkyB Has No Material Advantage in Pay TV Movies," *Hollywood Reporter*, August 2, 2012.
6. "Digital Giants Go TV Shopping," *Televisual*, August 2012, by Tim Dams.
7. "Netflix Monthly Viewing Tops 1 Billion Hours," *Hollywood Reporter*, July 5, 2012, by Sophie A. Schillaci.
8. "Netflix's *Arrested Development* to Run Just One Season," *Wall Street Journal*, February 25, 2013, by Greg Bensinger.
9. "Digital Giants," *Televisual*, August 2012, Digital Video-on-Demand section, by Tim Dams; article notes that Netflix was originally committing roughly 5 percent of its overall content budget to original series.
10. "'Arrested Development' A Bust? Netflix Laughs Off the Critics", CNET News May 30, 2013, by Joan E. Solsman.
11. "Netflix Seals Deal for Original Series," *Wall Street Journal*, March 21, 2011, by Nick Wingfield and Sam Schechner.
12. "Emmys 2013: Netflix Scores Big, But HBO remains the Player to Beat," *LA Times*, July 18, 2013, by Susan King and Rene Lynch.
13. *New York Times*, February 5, 2013, by Brian Stelter.
14. "Does the *House of Cards* All-You-Can-Eat Buffet Spoil Social Viewing?" *New York Times*, February 5, 2013, by Brian Stelter.
15. "YouTube Goes Professional," *Wall Street Journal*, October 4, 2011, by Amir Efrati.
16. "A New YouTube, Herding the Funny Cats," *New York Times*, December 13, 2011, by Mike Hale.
17. "YouTube Tees Up Big Talent," *Wall Street Journal*, October 29, 2011, by Amir Efrati and Lauren A.E. Schuker.
18. "YouTube Tees Up Big Talent," *Wall Street Journal*, October 29, 2011, by Amir Efrati and Lauren A.E. Schuker.
19. YouTube/Google press release, May 2, 2012.
20. YouTube/Google press release, May 2, 2012.
21. "YouTube Original Programming: Europe Gets More than 60 New Professional Channels," *Associated Press*, as reposted via the *Huffington Post*, October 8, 2012, by Raphael Satter.
22. "Digital Giants," *Televisual*, August 2012.
23. "Hulu, the Online TV Site, Adds Original Programs," *New York Times*, April 17, 2012.

24. "Digital Giants Go TV Shopping," *Televisual*, 2012.
25. "Hulu Upfronts Present Shows by Morgan Spurlock, Richard Linklater, Seth Myers," *Deadline*, April 19, 2012.
26. "Hulu Debuts Previews of its 2013 Original Programming and Exclusive Series," *Techcrunch*, January 8, 2013, by Sarah Perez.
27. "Canceled Soaps *All My Children* and *One Life to Live* Coming Back from the Dead on Hulu, iTunes," *Techcrunch*, January 25, 2013.
28. "Hulu, the Online TV Site, Adds Original Programs," *New York Times*, April 17, 2012.
29. "Amazon Looks to Produce TV Comedies, Kids' Shows," *Wall Street Journal*, May 3, 2012, by Stu Woo.
30. "Amazon Studios Opens Door to TV: Net Retailer Calls for Submissions of Comedy, Kidvid Pilot Scripts," *Chicago Tribune*, May 2, 2012, by Andrew Wallenstein.
31. "Networks Feel Heat as Unexpected Rivals Pursue Internet TV," *International Herald Tribune*, March 6, 2013, by Brian Stelter.
32. "Amazon to Produce 6 Original Comedy Series Pilots, Viewers Decide Which Shows Survive," *Techcrunch*, January 12, 2012, by Jordan Crook.
33. "Amazon Invests in Original Shows, Taking on Netflix and TV," *USA Today*, January 20, 2012, by Julia Boorstin.
34. "Prime Instant Video to be the Exclusive Subscription Streaming Home for Carnival/Masterpiece Coproduction *Downton Abbey* on PBS," Amazon press release, as confirmed on February 1, 2013, www.amazon.com/pr.
35. "Netflix Shows Take a Hit from Disappointing 'Arresting Development' Reviews," Forbes.com, May 29, 2013, by Abram Brown.
36. "TV Forsees its Future. Netflix is There," *The New York Times*, July 21, 2013, by David Carr; also, "Emmys 2013: Netflix Scores Big, But HBO Remains the Player to Beat," *LA Times*, July 18, 2013, by Susan King and Rene Lynch.
37. "Katie Couric Goes Digital with Weekly ABC News Series for Yahoo," *Deadline*, April 25, 2012.
38. "AOL Launches AOL On Network, Announces Seven New Shows," *Deadline*, April 24, 2012.
39. "AOL Launches AOL On Network, Announces Seven New Shows," *Deadline*, April 24, 2012.
40. "Albie Hecht Keeps an Eye on Web—Spike TV Founder Balances New and Old Media," *Variety*, May 1, 2009, by Dade Hayes; "The Hollywood Treatment," *Wired*, August 2008.
41. Sales reportedly tripled from the prior year, with Anthony Wood claiming sales of upwards of 1.5 million units, and even hinting at a potential public offering; "Apple TV Rival Roku Plans IPO," *C21Media*, March 8, 2012.
42. "Samsung Acquires Boxee for $30 million (confirmed)," Venturebeat.com, July 3, 2013, by Tom Cheredar.
43. www.boxee.tv, 2011.
44. "Boxee to Remove PC Application from its Website," *Venture Beat*, January 31, 2012, http://venturebeat.com/2012/01/31/boxee-pc-app.
45. "Why Chromecast May be Google's Game-changer," CNN.com, July 25, 2013, by Doug Gross.

46. "Microsoft Reveals Xbox 360 Sales to Date—66 Million Sold Worldwide," *IGN*, January 10, 2012, by Andrew Goldfarb, describing CES press conference during which Microsoft revealed more than 40 million subscribers to Xbox Live; "PSN Now Boasts 90 Million Registered Users Worldwide," *Games Thirst*, March 7, 2012, by Ernice Gilbert, quoting Sony's Ted Regulski, manager SCEA developer relations at GDC. (Note: Individuals can have multiple registrations.)

47. "XBox Aims to Bow First Original Series Within the Year," www.adweek.com, February 11, 2013, by Tim Peterson.

48. Ibid.

49. "Nielsen Three-Screen Report," *Nielsen*, May 2008.

50. "Cross-Platform Report: How We Watch from Screen to Screen," *Nielsen*, May 3, 2012.

51. "Tablet PC Market Forecast to Surpass Notebooks in 2013, NPD DisplaySearch Reports," *PRWeb*, January 7, 2013.

52. "Kindle Fire: If Each Amazon Tablet Generates $3 per Month in Digital Sales, that's 20 Percent Profit," *Venture Beat*, January 16, 2013, by Josh Koetsier.

53. "Apple's Revolutionary App Store Downloads Top One Billion in Just Nine Months," Apple press release, April 29, 2009.

54. "App Store Tops 40 Billion Downloads with Almost Half in 2012," Apple press release, January 7, 2013.

55. "As Boom Lures App Creators, Tough Part is Making a Living," *New York Times*, November 17, 2012, by David Streitfeld.

56. "As Boom Lures App Creators, Tough Part is Making a Living," *New York Times*, November 17, 2012, by David Streitfeld.

57. "Nielsen Cuts 500,000 U.S. TV Homes on Census, Web Viewing," *Bloomberg*, September 25, 2012, by Andy Fixmer.

58. "Ownership of TV Sets Falls in U.S.," *New York Times*, May 3, 2011, by Brian Stelter.

59. °On Traditional TV includes live usage plus any playback viewing within the measurement period. Time-shifted TV is playback primarily on a DVR but includes playback from VOD, DVD recorders, server-based DVRs, and services such as Start Over. In response to these services' continued growth, for Q2 2012 forward, this report will no longer feature the "only in homes with DVRs," which was limited to physical DVR presence.

On Traditional TV reach includes those viewing at least one minute within the measurement period. This includes live viewing plus any playback within the measurement period. Q3 2012 television data is based on the following measurement interval: July 2, 2012–September 30, 2012. As of February 2011, DVR Playback has been incorporated into the persons using television (PUT) statistic.

°°In response to client requests for the ability to recreate the quintiles of time spent, from Q2 2011 forward the production of the underlying data for Tables 8a, 8b, and 8c has been fully migrated to the NPOWER system. In addition to allowing clients that subscribe to the Nielsen Cross-Platform Service to generate these and associated reports, it also incorporates production sample weighting (detailed in Chapter 3 of the National Reference Supplement) and universe projections.

Beginning in Q3 2011, average daily minutes statistics are calculated by averaging the total minutes from all persons in the quintile including nonusers. Q1 and Q2 2011 reports averaged the total minutes from users only.

* In July 2011 an improved hybrid methodology was introduced in Nielsen's NetView and VideoCensus product. This methodology combines a census level accounting of page views and video streams where Nielsen measurement tags have been deployed in order to project audience and behavior to the full universe of all Internet users. For VideoCensus, the portion of the total video streams calibrated by census data, previously allocated to Home/Work computers, are now allocated to other devices and locations such as smartphones and viewing outside of home and work. This change affects both "Watching Video on the Internet" and "Using the Internet" figures. Beginning in Q1 2012, Cross-Platform metrics are derived from new hybrid panel. Year over year trends are available beginning in Q3 2012. Data are trendable within this version of the report, but not to previous quarters' published editions.

Hours:minutes for Internet and video use are based on the universe of persons who used the Internet/watched online video. All Internet figures are weekly or monthly averages over the course of the quarter. All "Using the Internet on a Computer" metrics are derived from Nielsen NetView product, while all "Watching Video on the Internet" metrics are derived from Nielsen VideoCensus product. ^ Watching video on the Internet is a subset of Using the Internet on a computer.

^ Mobile video user projection, time spent and composition data are based on survey analysis of past 30 day use during the period. The mobile video audience figures in this report include mobile phone users (aged 13+) who access mobile video through any means (including mobile Web, subscription based, downloads and applications). Beginning in Q1 2012, data reflect enhanced methodology for calculating the Total Minutes spent watching video on a mobile phone. Historically, distributions of key variables (# sessions and # minutes per session) were skewed, warranting the use of the median as the measure of central tendency: Total Minutes = (median # sessions) × (median # minutes). Current analyses of the distributions indicate that the variable # minutes per session fits a more normal distribution and justifies the use of the mean as the measure of central tendency. The current calculation reflects a truer metric of average time spent watching video on a mobile phone: Total Minutes = (median # sessions) × (mean # minutes). All previous quarter/year metrics have been recalculated with new methodology. Data are trendable within this version of the report, but not to previous quarters' published editions.

For Q2 2012, mobile data contained in table 2 are for June 2012 only.

A SPECIAL NOTE ON INTERNET AUDIENCES

+ Due to the release of the Chrome browser v.19 in May 2012, some Nielsen NetView data for a small number of sites that have extensive use of HTTPS are underreported for May and June 2012. A solution has been implemented for July 2012 reporting. This affects the "Using the Internet on a Computer" and "Internet" time spent figures provided in this report for current quarter data.

REFERENCES

Yahoo! Mail and Yahoo! page view and duration data shows an artificial decrease for May–November 2011 and do not reflect the actual activity on these sites. This was corrected with December 2011 forward reporting. This affects the "Using the Internet on a Computer" and "Internet" time spent figures provided in this report for previous year data.

Due to a change in the type of call used behind Facebook's AJAX interface, Nielsen NetView data for Facebook page views and duration were under-reported for June and July 2011. This was corrected with August-forward reporting. This affects the "Using the Internet on a Computer" and "Internet" time spent figures provided in this report for previous year data.

¤ May 2012 volume metrics were affected for two YouTube channel entities. As of June 2012, YouTube Partner reporting became available through Nielsen VideoCensus featuring May 2012 data. YouTube Partner data are reported as individual channels under the YouTube brand in Nielsen VideoCensus. Data for each YouTube partner are aggregated across two entity levels, the broadest as Nielsen VideoCensus channel entity and the more granular being Nielsen VideoCensus client-defined entity. This affects the "Watching Video on the Internet" and "Stream" numbers in this report for current quarter data.

Due to a change in the format of Netflix stream URLs, streaming for the Netflix brand was not reported in the April and May 2011 VideoCensus reports. This was corrected with June-forward reporting. This affects the "Watching Video on the Internet" and "Stream" figures in this report for previous year data.

60. "Netflix Hits 30 Million Members After Q3 Subscriber Growth 'Forecasting Error'," *Techcrunch*, October 25, 2012, by Darrell Etherington, quoting Reed Hastings Facebook posting.
61. "Scripps Networks Interactive's Popular Lifestyle Shows from HGTV, DIY Network, Food Network, Cooking Channel, and Travel Channel Coming to Prime Instant Video and Amazon Instant Video," Amazon press release, February 28, 2013.
62. "Netflix Signs Streaming Deal with Time Warner," *Wall Street Journal*, January 7, 2013, by John Jannarone and Shalini Ramachandran.
63. "One Million Xbox Live Members Download and Activate Netflix on Xbox 360," Joint Microsoft and Netflix press release, February 5, 2009.
64. "Netflix Signs Streaming Deal with Time Warner," *Wall Street Journal*, January 7, 2013, by John Jannarone and Shalini Ramachandran.
65. "Less is More on Video Web Site," *International Herald Tribune*, October 30, 2008; "Hulu's Online Video Explosion," Julia Boorstin's report of her interview with Hulu CEO Jason Kilar, quoting comScore numbers, November 11, 2008, www.cnbc.com.
66. Neilsen Media Research, as referenced in "Video Sites Duke it Out for Content: YouTube, Hulu React to Sign Deals for Movies, Shows that Draw Advertising," *Wall Street Journal*, April 17, 2009.
67. "Number of Hulu Viewers Increases 42 Percent in February, According to comScore Video Metrix," comScore press release, March 24, 2009.
68. "Disney Joins Hulu as Equity Partner," *Hollywood Reporter*, May 1, 2009.
69. "As Seen on TV," *Wired*, August 2010, by Frank Rose.
70. "Hulu CEO Faces Big Changes," *Variety*, August 19, 2012, by Andrew Wallenstein.

71. "Watchever Launches Unique Series and Movie Flat Rate in Germany," Watchever press release, Berlin, January 9, 2013.
72. "Garth Ancier Advises Intel on Virtual-MSO Plan," *Variety*, May 8, 2012, by Andrew Wallenstein.
73. "Garth Ancier Advises Intel on Virtual-MSO Plan," *Variety*, May 8, 2012, by Andrew Wallenstein.
74. "Campaign Trains Viewers for 'TV Everywhere'," *New York Times*, September 11, 2011, by Brian Stelter.
75. "Time Warner Chief Touts TV Everywhere; Disses Netflix Again," *CNET*, December 5, 2011, by Don Reisinger.
76. "Campaign Trains Viewers for 'TV Everywhere'," *New York Times*, September 11, 2011, by Brian Stelter.
77. "Analyst: TV Everywhere Could Create $12 Billion in Annual Revenue for TV Industry," *Hollywood Reporter*, January 20, 2012.
78. "Web Deals Cheer Hollywood, Despite Drop in Moviegoers," *New York Times*, February 24, 2012, by Brooks Barnes.
79. "Netflix Signs Streaming Deal with Time Warner," *Wall Street Journal*, January 7, 2013, by John Jannarone and Shalini Ramachandran.
80. "Web Deals Cheer Hollywood, Despite Drop in Moviegoers," *New York Times*, February 24, 2012, by Brooks Barnes.
81. www.louisck.net.
82. "Louis C.K. Says Internet Experiment Yielded $200,000," *Wall Street Journal*, December 15, 2011; "Louis C.K. Tops $1 Million in Sales of $5 Comedy Special," *CNN MoneyTech*, December 22, 2011, by Julianne Pepitone.
83. "Louis C.K. Says Internet Experiment Yielded $200,000," *Wall Street Journal*, December 15, 2011; "Louis C.K. Tops $1 Million in Sales of $5 Comedy Special," *CNN MoneyTech*, December 22, 2011, by Julianne Pepitone.
84. "Meet Rebecca Black, the Internet's 'Friday' Girl," *USA Today*, April 18, 2011, by Korina Lopez.
85. "Justin Bieber Breaks YouTube Record: 9 Biggest YouTube Stars," *Huffington Post*, October 31, 2011.
86. "Internet-Driven Fame and Fortune for Mideast Comedians," *New York Times*, December 12, 2012, by Sara Hamdan.
87. www.youtube.com, 2012.
88. www.milyoni.com.
89. "Small Screens, New Programs," *International Herald Tribune*, January 29, 2007.
90. "Blockbuster Uploading MovieLink," *Variety*, August 9, 2007.
91. "Wal-Mart Sees Download Upside," *Variety*, November 29, 2006.
92. "In Hollywood, the Picture Blurs for Studio Profits," *Wall Street Journal*, September 5, 2006.
93. "In Hollywood, the Picture Blurs for Studio Profits," *Wall Street Journal*, September 5, 2006.
94. "Wal-Mart's Movie Download Service Passes into Ignominy," *International Herald Tribune*, January 1, 2008.
95. "Wal-Mart Adds its Clout to Movie Streaming," *New York Times*, February 23, 2010, by Brad Stone.

604

96. "Walmart Upgrades Streaming Netflix Competitor Vudu," *Hollywood Reporter*, November 17, 2011.
97. "As Seen on TV," *Wired*, October 2008, by Frank Rose.
98. "Hulu Guru, Kilar Vision," *Future Media*, April 2008; "Less is More on Video Web Site," *International Herald Tribune*, October 30, 2008.
99. "Interview with Andreas Bartl," *Worldscreen*, reprinted from Mipcom 2011 issue of TV Europe, December 12, 2011, by Anna Carugati.
100. "Sneak Preview of PC Film Night," *International Herald Tribune*, February 12, 2007.
101. "Google Channels YouTube," *Hollywood Reporter*, October 10–16, 2006.
102. "Universal Nears Victory in Battle Over Royalties," *International Herald Tribune*, February 13, 2007.
103. "What is Content ID?" www.youtube.com.
104. "Google Wins Battle, but Courts Will Settle the War," *Hollywood Reporter*, June 24, 2010, by Matthew Belloni.
105. "Hollywood Executives Call for End to Residual Payments," *New York Times*, July 11, 2007.
106. "Producers Make Dramatic Call for Residuals Revamp," *Broadcasting & Cable*, July 11, 2007.
107. "WGA Negotiations Set to Start," *Variety*, July 11, 2007.
108. "Contract 2008 TV/Theatrical Negotiations Update," Special Bulletin, www.sag.org/files/documents/sag_contract_2008.pdf.
109. "Contract 2008 TV/Theatrical Negotiations Update," Special Bulletin, www.sag.org/files/documents/sag_contract_2008.pdf.

605

Chapter 8

1. "Toy Makers Bet on Blockbuster Films for Sales," *Reuters*, June 6, 2006.
2. "The Real Force Behind *Star Wars*," *Hollywood Reporter*, February 17, 2012, by Alex Ben Block.
3. The *Wall Street Journal* on the *Star Wars* books: "According to a Random House spokesman, the publisher has more than 160 million copies of *Star Wars* books in print," 1 April, 2005 http://en.wikipedia.org/wiki/list_of_best-selling_books.
4. "The Real Force Behind *Star Wars*," *Hollywood Reporter*, February 17, 2012, by Alex Ben Block.
5. "The Real Force Behind *Star Wars*," *Hollywood Reporter*, February 17, 2012, by Alex Ben Block.
6. "Disney to Purchase Fox Family for $3 Billion," *USA Today*, July 23, 2001, by George Hager; "News Corp and Saban Reach Agreement to Sell Fox Family Worldwide to Disney for $5.3 Billion," Saban Capital Group press release, July 23, 2001.
7. "Remember Squirtle and Jigglypuff? They're Back," *New York Times*, August 7, 2007.
8. "Gotta Catch the *Pokémon* Pirates: Nintendo Goes to Court in Crackdown on Fakes" *New York Daily News*, November 9, 1999.
9. "H'W'D's Musical Mania," *Variety International*, weekly edition, October 6–12, 2008.

10. "Figures in '000s," 2004 Annual Report, discussion of "4Kids TV Broadcast Fee," under Item 7.

11. 4Kids Entertainment 2004 Annual Report, Notes to be Consolidated Financial Statements Years Ended December 21, 2004, 2003, and 2002; "Advertising Media and Broadcast," under Item 1, Description of Business.

12. Item 7, 4Kids TV Broadcast Fee.

13. "*Angry Birds* Developer Rovio is Growing Faster than Zynga," *Forbes*, December 9, 2011, by John Gaudiosi.

14. "*Angry Birds* Soars Past Half a Billion Downloads—Rovio's Physics-Based Game Crosses Massive Milestone; Game-Related Merchandise Efforts Expanding," *GameSpot*, November 2, 2011, by Jonathan Downin, www.game spot.com/news/angry-birds-soars-past-half-a-billion-downloads-6343647.

15. "*Angry Birds* Developer Rovio is Growing Faster than Zynga," *Forbes*, December 9, 2011, by John Gaudiosi.

16. "Elements of Style," *KidScreen*, May 2007.

17. "Elements of Style," *KidScreen*, May 2007.

18. "*Spider-Man, Transformers,* and *Pirates* Toys Battle for Boys' Attention," *Los Angeles Times*, June 12, 2007.

19. "Toy Story," *Hollywood Reporter*, February 13, 2009, by Georg Szalai.

20. "Now Playing: H'w'd's Toy Ploy," *Variety International*, June 11–17, 2007.

21. *Los Angeles Times*, first edition footnote 15 for 2006; re 2011, NPD, as quoted in "Toy Makers Cozy Up To App Gaming With Latest Products," *Wall Street Journal*, February 14, 2012, by Christopher Palmeri and Matt Townsend, www.businessweek.com/news/2012-08-27/hasbro-suffers-missed-gain-as-stores-hold-back-avengers.

22. "Hasbro Suffers Missed Gain as Stores Hold Back Avengers," *Business Week*, August 27, 2012, quoting BMO Capital Markets analyst Gerrick Johnson.

23. "Company News: Hasbro Extends Deal on *Star Wars* Toys by 10 Years," *New York Times*, January 31, 2003.

24. "Hasbro Gets Toy and Game Rights to Marvel Heroes," *New York Times*, January 9, 2006.

25. "Hasbro Profits Fall on Charge," *New York Times*, July 23, 2007; "Hasbro's Net Income Drops 87% on Charge Tied to Warrants," *Wall Street Journal*, July 23, 2007; "Hasbro and Lucas Extend *Star Wars* License through 2018," Hasbro press release, February 30, 2003; www.secinfo.com/d1dzf.2d.d.htm.

26. "*Spider-Man, Transformers,* and *Pirates* Toys Battle for Boys' Attention," *Los Angeles Times*, June 12, 2007.

27. "Robert Iger to Wall Street: Disney Bought Lucasfilm for *Star Wars*," Hollywood Reporter, October 30, 2012, by Alex Ben Block.

28. "Top 125 Global Licensors," *License Global*, May 11, 2012.

29. "*Spider-Man, Transformers,* and *Pirates* Toys Battle for Boys' Attention," *Los Angeles Times*, June 12, 2007.

30. "Toy Story," *Hollywood Reporter*, February 13, 2009, by Georg Szalai; box office from www.boxofficemojo.com.

31. "Toy Story," *Hollywood Reporter*, February 13, 2009, by Georg Szalai.

32. www.boxofficemojo.com.

33. Budget estimate, per "Hasbro Switches Partners in Hollywood Romance," *Hollywood Reporter*, February 10, 2012, by Kim Masters.
34. "Leaner Ouija Pic in Universal's Future," *Hollywood Reporter*, March 6, 2012, by Borys Kit.
35. "Candly Land Movie Lands at Sony with Adam Sandler," *Reuters*, January 31, 2013, by Joshua Weinstein.
36. "Playdate for H'wood Toys," *Hollywood Reporter*, February 15–17, 2008.
37. www.webkinz.com; "$2B Estimate, the Webkinz Effect," *Wired*, November 2008.
38. "Apps Make Leap from Phones to Toys," *Wall Street Journal*, August 2, 2012, by Spencer Ante.
39. "How Publishers Bolster Their Bottom Line by Retaining Film Rights," *Hollywood Reporter*, February 23, 2012, by Andy Lewis.
40. http://company.zynga.com/games/empires-allies.
41. "Kabam to Make Social and Mobile Games Based on *The Hobbit* Film," *Venture Beat*, September 25, 2012, by Dean Takahashi, http://venturebeat.com/2012/09/25/kabam-to-make-social-and-mobile-games-based-on-the-hobbit-film/#dU3cb5Elx3MlEd73.99.
42. "Sony Pictures Interactive Opens a Hotel Game on Facebook," *PR Newswire*, August 15, 2012.
43. "Silly Walking onto the Web," *International Herald Tribune*, September 8, 2008.
44. The service reaches more than 1.5 million hotel rooms according to its website, www.lodgenet.com.
45. "History," www.indemand.com.
46. "NPD: Pay TV Transactional VOD Declines 12%," *Home Media*, February 16, 2012, by Erik Gruenwedel.
47. "Bridesmaids Most Popular VOD Title Ever," *Hollywood Reporter*, February 9, 2012.
48. "The Window for Pay TV Operators to Control the Video-on-Demand Movie Rental Market is Still Open, but for How Long?" NPD Group press release, February 6, 2012.
49. "Nearly Half of All Paid Video-on-Demand Movie Rental Orders Generated by Cable Companies," NPD Group press release, September 24, 2012.

Chapter 9

1. "Strong *Monsters* Feeds Hollywood's 3D Hopes," *Wall Street Journal*, March 30, 2009, by Lauren Schulker.
2. www.boxofficeguru.com.
3. "Marvel's Date Shake Slows Super Releases," *Hollywood Reporter*, March 13, 2009, by Carl DiOrio.
4. "Sequels Spur Spending Spiral," *Variety*, May 14–20, 2007; "Major Brands Get Behind *Bourne*," *Variety*, July 12, 2008; "*Avengers* Wields Big Brand Blitz—Marvel, Disney, Secure Estimated $100 Million in Marketing Spend," *Variety*, March 30, 2012, by Marc Graser.

5. "DreamWorks Animation Announces Show-Stopping Promotional Partners and Licensing Support for *Madagascar 3: Europe's Most Wanted*," DreamWorks Animation press release, June 4, 2012.

6. www.mpaa.org/researchstatistics.asp.

7. "Special Report: Movies & the Media, Slim Pickings," *Hollywood Reporter*, May 30, 2008.

8. "New Focus for Film Marketing," *Variety*, December 30, 2009, by Pamela McClintock.

9. "New Focus for Film Marketing," *Variety*, December 30, 2009, by Pamela McClintock.

10. "AT&T, Verizon Top TV Spenders in 2011—Film Marketing Accounted for $3.5 Bill across All Media," *Variety*, May 8, 2012, by Jill Goldsmith.

11. "Money Buys Happiness," *Hollywood Reporter*, international weekend edition, October 3–5, 2008.

12. Facebook post 2012, as reposted/reported by *Mashable*, by Christina Warren, www.mashable.com/2012/07/30/the-hobbit-trilogy.

13. "Will Ashton Kutcher's Twitter Following Help *Two and a Half Men*?" *Mashable*, May 13, 2011, by Christina Warren.

14. "A-Listers, Meet Your Online Megaphone," *New York Times*, November 10, 2012, by Brooke Barnes.

15. "A-Listers, Meet Your Online Megaphone," *New York Times*, November 10, 2012, by Brooke Barnes.

16. "How *Hunger Games* Built Up Must-See Fever," *New York Times*, March 18, 2012, by Brook Barnes.

17. "How *Hunger Games* Built Up Must-See Fever," *New York Times*, March 18, 2012, by Brook Barnes.

18. "Box Office Shocker: *Hunger Games* Third-Best Opening Weekend of All Time," *Hollywood Reporter*, March 25, 2012, by Pamela McClintock.

19. "Spielberg Predicts 'Implosion of Film Biz'," *The Hollywood Reporter*, June 13, 2013, by Paul Bond.

20. 2003 figures: "Video Marketing—by the Numbers," *Hollywood Reporter*, August 10–16, 2004; 2005 figures: "Video Marketing and the Media—Caught in the Web," *Hollywood Reporter*, July 11–17, 2006.

21. "Video Marketing—by the Numbers," *Hollywood Reporter*, August 10–16, 2004.

22. "Video Marketing—by the Numbers," *Hollywood Reporter*, August 10–16, 2004.

23. "Caught in the Web," Video Marketing and the Media Section of DVD Special Report, *Hollywood Reporter*, July 11–17, 2006.

24. "Papa John's Partners on *Indiana Jones* Promo," *Video Business*, November 7, 2002, by Susanne Ault; "Papa John's Launches First Movie Tie-In with *Ice Age* Promotion," November 7, 2002, www.pizzamarketplace.com.

25. "Enterprise Marketing," *Hollywood Reporter*, February 20, 2009, by Jay A. Fernandez.

Chapter 10

1. Superior Court of the State of California, for the County of Los Angeles, *Art Buchwald, et al., Plaintiffs v. Paramount Pictures Corporation, et al.,* Defendants, Statement of Decision (Third Phase), March 16, 1992.

2. *Fatal Subtraction: How Hollywood Really Does Business*, Doubleday, 1992, by Pierce O'Donnell and Dennis McDougal.
3. "How Do a Bestselling Novel, an Academy Award-Winning Screenwriter, a Pair of Hollywood Hotties, and a No. 1 Opening at the Box Office Add Up to $78 Million of Red Ink?" *Los Angeles Times*, April 15, 2007.
4. "The Lawsuit of the Rings," *New York Times*, June 27, 2005.

609

Index

611

broadcast monopolies 346–348
budgets: films 498–513, 514–540;
marketing 498–544, 546; studios
26–28, 110–112; television 43–45,
546; theatrical productions 514–540;
video marketing 541–544
building costs 264–266
bundled subscriptions 397–400
bundle pricing 433–436
Business Week 240–241, 355

cable bundle pricing 433–436
cable television 272–274, 277–278,
282–286, 302–305; channel range
and quantity 43–53; financing
production 128–129; free television
277–278; licenses 286; original
programming 302–305; revenues
483–491; theatrical feature films
282–285; TV series economics
302–305
Carlos, A. 374, 376
Carvalho, C. 477–478
cash break-even points 585
cash flows 259–264
catch-up services 370
celebrity lawsuits 562–564
changing distribution windows 40–43
channel streaming 406–408
checking: net profits 569
Cinar 141–142
Clive Cussler v. Philip Anschutz Company
563
Cloud Atlas 123–124, 140
cloud services 78–79, 361, 408–422
collapsed distribution windows 39–40,
51–52
Coming to America 562–563
commercials: television distribution
311–315, 546; theatrical marketing
523–540, 554; video marketing 543;
see also advertising
compact discs (CDs) 211
compressed sales cycles 223–226
computers: history 215; video markets
196
concessions 193–194
consent decrees 149
consistent consumer pricing 229–230
content costs 237–240
content interaction tools 416–422
content rights 74–75

content tiers 433–436
coproductions: financing production
103–112, 123–124, 134–143;
international markets 350–356;
Kirch group 351–356; online
considerations 139–143; studio
financing 103–112; television
distribution 350–356
copying and downloads 82–90; *see also*
piracy
copying threats 215–216
copyrights: digital considerations 74,
75–76; intellectual property assets
71–80; law 72–73; nature 74–75;
segmentation 74–75; *see also*
intellectual property assets
cord-cutting 80–82, 361, 383–386,
394–395
costs: development processes 66–68;
DVDs 264–269; intellectual property
assets 66–68; international markets
342–345; net profits 569–570,
573–576, 580; television distribution
342–345; video markets 237–240,
264–269 creating ideas 56, 57–68
creative collaboration 136–139
creative execution 523–540
credit 116–123
critics 100
cross-platform usage 215
crowdsourcing 120–122, 143, 342–345
curve peaking, DVDs 223–226

daily active users 474
data analytics, merchandising revenue
472–478
day-and-date release 166, 507–508
debt financings 104
decay curves 181–189
dedicated hardware boxes 383–386
deferments 574–575
deficit continuum 130–131
demand creation strategies 508–513
demise of joint ventures 19–22
developing intellectual property assets
56, 57–68
digital: access points 53–55; cinema
(D-cinema) 151–160, 195;
considerations, copyright 74, 75–76;
divide 151–160; film rental
158–160; lockers 397–400;
technologies 145, 151–160; upfront

613

614

615

616

intellectual property assets 56–90; limited opening budgets 499–501; mega-films 551–556; merchandising 509–512, 539–540, 554; online distribution 439–441, 499–501, 517–518, 528–536, 548–550, 554–557; piracy 556; product placements 512–513, 552; promotional partnerships 509–512, 538–539; release factors 499–508, 551–556; strategies 498–513; talent involvement 508–509, 525; television distribution 514, 519–520, 546–548, 556; theatrical distribution 145–166, 514–540, 551–556; third-party help 508–513; timing considerations 501–508, 551–556; video marketing 540–546; video markets 199–210; viral messaging 500–501

market leaders, pay television 349–350

market opportunity 1–55

market research 536–538

markets and festivals 343–344

Marvel Entertainment 117–118

mass-market chains 226–230

maturation, DVDs 223–226

media costs 514–520, 526, 541–557

media promotions 526, 551–556

mega-film marketing 551–556

megaupload 84–85

merchandising: licensing program revenues 456–466; marketing 509–512, 539–540, 554; program anchors 82; revenues 446–480, 495–496; toy revenues 447, 452–455, 466–480

metrics: social games 473–477; video-on-demand 279–280

Metro-Goldwyn-Mayer v. Grokster, Ltd 76–78, 79

Meyer, B. 442–443

MGM Worldwide Television 17–18, 22, 110, 149, 273, 553

microblogs 531–536

mini-majors 117–118

minimum guarantees 162–163, 461–466

mock-up costs 67–68

money making strategies 558–586

monopolies 346–348

monthly active users 474

moratorium: video markets 254

motel revenues 446, 480–483

Motion Picture Association of America (MPAA): intellectual property assets 79, 83–84, 86–88; online distribution 365; theatrical distribution 166–167, 515

move-overs 183–184

MPA: intellectual property assets 79

MSOs: streaming online distribution 407–408

Mullany, J. 565–567, 582–584

multiplexes: pay television 319, 320–324, 359; theatrical distribution 150–151

multipurpose boxes 386–388

multi-screen access 361, 389–390

Museum of Broadcast Communications 299–300

music industry 366–367, 478–480

Nalle, N. 300–301, 440–441

national free television networks 276–277

negative control 14–15

negative costs 574, 576

negative pickups 115–116

Netflix: competition 237–240; content costs 237–240; cost considerations 237–240; DVDs 231–232, 234–240; online distribution 365, 369–373, 395–396, 400–402; physical business decline 237; Qwikster debacle 235–236; rights 239; streaming focus 237; subscription rental growth 234–235; video markets 231–232, 234–240

net profits: advances 574–575; advertising 573–574, 575; at-the-source recognition 572–573; break-even points 578–579; calculation 567–580; costs 569–570, 573–576, 580; deferments 574–575; distribution costs 573–574; distribution fees 570–572; excluded revenues 567–568; fees 569, 570–572; gross participations 574–575, 579; history 561–567; imputed costs 575–576; included revenues 567–568; money making strategies 558–586; moving targets 578–579; negative costs 574, 576;

online accounting 558–560, 580–584, 586; phantom revenues 576–577; revenue sharing 558–560, 580–584, 586; taxes 576–577

network hubs 386–392

networks: coverage, television 291–294; diverse roles 1–55; financing production 128; licenses 282–285; online distribution 361, 369–381, 408–422; television channel diversity, quantity and reach 43–45; venture capitalists 91–143

new distribution windows: life-cycle management 40–43

New Millennium 362–369

next-generation DVDs 220–223

next-generation retail environments 230–243

niche marketing 499–501

Nielsen ratings 308–311, 313

non-theatrical market revenues 446, 494–495

off-balance sheet financings 104–106

off-network syndication 296–297

on-demand access 361, 368–369

on-demand catch up 78–79

online distribution 361–444, 548–550, 558–560, 580–584, 586; accounting 558–560, 580–584, 586; advertising 382–383, 426–428, 548–550; Amazon 370, 379–381, 388, 397–400; app markets 383, 389–395, 409–411; break-even points 586; cable bundle pricing 433–436; channel streaming 406–408; cloud services 361, 408–422; content tiers 433–436; convergence considerations 363–365; cord-cutting 361, 383–386, 394–395; dedicated hardware boxes 383–386; developing intellectual property assets 61–66; downloads 366–367, 368–369; DVDs 230–243, 257–258, 270–271, 367; economics 425–437; films 145, 171–172, 194–195, 499–501, 517–518, 528–536, 554–555; financing production 93–98, 131–133, 139–143; Google 437–441; hardware boxes 383–386; history 361–369; hubs 386–392;

Hulu 370, 377–379, 402–405; independent markets 382–383; integrating television distribution 388–392; intellectual property assets 61–66, 75–79, 82–90; international services 405–406, 409–411; legal considerations 437–444; Louis C.K. experiment 413–414; marketing 439–441, 499–501, 517–518, 528–536, 548–550, 554–557; merchandising revenue 453–456; multipurpose boxes 386–388; multi-screen access 361, 389–390; music industry 366–367; Netflix 365, 369–373, 395–396, 400–402; networks 361, 369–381, 408–422; New Millennium 362–369; on-demand markets 368–369; original content 369–381; over-the-top access 383, 391; ownership considerations 423–433; pay-per-download ownership 429–431; personalization 416–422; physical retailers 423–425; pipeline and portfolio 30–31; piracy 76–79, 82–90, 366–367; resistance considerations 437–444; revenues 425–437, 453–456, 469–478, 495–496; revenue sharing accounting 558–560, 580–584, 586; search engines 381–382; smartphones 390–391, 392–395, 417–422; social game revenues 472–478; socialization 416–422; social media 316–317; social networking 550; streaming networks 369–381, 395–408, 426–428; studios 382–383, 422–425, 437–444; subscriptions 397–400, 431–433; tablets 391–395; television 61–66, 131–133, 272–274, 278–280, 297–299, 315–317, 359–360, 383–395, 408–413, 416–422, 426–436, 548–549; theatrical distribution 145, 171–172, 194–195, 499–501, 517–518, 528–536, 554–555; toy revenue 469–471; transactional video-on-demand 428–433; UltraViolet consortium 408–409, 411; user experience influences 363; video content consumption 362–369; video markets 230–243, 257–258,

619

620

622

623

624